PATHS NOT TAKEN

PATHS NOT TAKEN

Fates of Theology from Luther through Leibniz

Paul R. Hinlicky

WILLIAM B. EERDMANS PUBLISHING COMPANY

GRAND RAPIDS, MICHIGAN / CAMBRIDGE, U.K.

Published 2009 by
Wm. B. Eerdmans Publishing Co.
2140 Oak Industrial Drive N.E., Grand Rapids, Michigan 49505 /
P.O. Box 163, Cambridge CB3 9PU U.K.
www.eerdmans.com

Printed in the United States of America

14 13 12 11 10 09   7 6 5 4 3 2 1

Library of Congress Cataloging-in-Publication Data

Hinlicky, Paul R.
  Paths not taken: fates of theology from Luther through Leibniz / Paul R. Hinlicky.
      p.   cm.
  Includes bibliographical references.
  ISBN 978-0-8028-4571-9 (pbk.: alk. paper)
  1. Philosophical theology. 2. Theology — History. 3. Leibniz, Gottfried Wilhelm,
Freiherr von, 1646-1716. 4. Luther, Martin, 1483-1546. 5. Barth, Karl, 1886-1968.
  6. Postmodern theology. 7. Postmodernism — Religious aspects — Christianity.   I. Title.

BT40.H56 2009
230.01 — dc22

                                                    2009010639

The editor and publisher gratefully acknowledge permission to include material from the following sources:

> Karl Barth, *Church Dogmatics*, 13 vols. Edinburgh: T.&T. Clark, 1936-69. Used by kind permission of Continuum International Publishing Group.
> G. W. Leibniz, trans. Langley, *New Essays concerning Human Understanding*. Reprinted by permission of Open Court Publishing Company, a division of Carus Publishing Company, Peru, IL, from *New Essays Concerning Human Understanding* by Gottfried Wilhelm Leibniz, translated by Alfred Gideon Langley, copyright © 1949 by Open Court, La Salle, Il.
> Leroy E. Loemker, *Struggle for Synthesis*. Reprinted by permission of the publisher from STRUGGLE FOR SYNTHESIS: THE SEVENTEENTH CENTURY BACKGROUND OF LEIBNIZ'S SYNTHESIS OF ORDER AND FREEDOM by Leroy E. Loemker, pp. 13, 21, 45-46, 58, 61-64, 82, 87, 177, 198, 212, 250, 280, Cambridge, Mass.: Harvard University Press, Copyright © 1972 by the President and Fellows of Harvard College.
> Review of *The Cosmos in the Light of the Cross*, by George L. Murphy, in *Seminary Ridge Review* 8, no. 1 (Autumn 2005). Used by kind permission of *Seminary Ridge Review*, Lutheran Theological Seminary of Gettysburg.

For Ellen
Thank you

Contents

Acknowledgments

I have accumulated untold debts to teachers, authors, mentors, colleagues, and students in the years of inquiry, research, and teaching that stand behind this book. I have tried to show my gratitude by writing a book for those on theological journeys driven by the same passion that has attended my own. I trust that many, as they read, will hear echoes of their gifts to me over the years. But I also think of the departed in Christ to whom my debts are great: my father, the Reverend William P. Hinlicky, and my seminary professor, the Reverend Dr. Robert W. Bertram. At the risk of overlooking any number of the living, let me try to acknowledge those whose aid most directly bore on this project.

I must mention first and with sincere gratitude my institution, Roanoke College, Salem, Virginia, which has honored me with appointments, most recently as the Tise Professor of Lutheran Studies, which enable the scholarship that stands behind this book. Mr. Jeffery Martin at the Interlibrary Loan Desk has been invaluable in his assistance through the years of research leading to this book. I am blessed in the Department of Religion and Philosophy with excellent colleagues interested in theology; their mutual conversation and consolation have provided both stimulation and encouragement, especially Robert Benne, Ned Wisnefske, Brent Adkins, and Gerald McDermott. I am especially indebted to Ned and Brent for critical comment on earlier drafts or portions thereof of this book. But I am indebted to all I have mentioned for frequent, fulsome, and mind-expanding conversation on themes discussed in this book and beyond. Department chair Dr. Hans Zorn has been solicitous of my special requirements for uninterrupted concentration during the past year. Norman Hjelm provided invaluable aid.

I first presented my ideas on Gottfried Leibniz's relation to Lutheran traditions of theology to a forum at the Tenth International Luther Congress, held in Copenhagen, Denmark, in 2002. Oswald Bayer, whose love for the anti-Kantian Johann Georg Hamann is well known, was personally encouraging and tactfully kept to himself any skepticism about my interest in the seventeenth-century rationalist and "ontotheologian." I received a generous grant and study opportunity in the summer of 2005 for a seminar of the Lutheran Academy of Scholars at Harvard Divinity School under the direction of Ronald Thiemann and DeAne Lagerquist, before whom I presented an initial plan for this book. Subsequently Ron and I shared a trip to my old stomping grounds in Slovakia, during which he debated with me — over ample draughts of beer and *slivovica* — the broad issues that would be taken up in this study. Chapter 4 appeared in first form as a lecture given at Lenoir-Rhyne College's Luther-Aquinas Conference in 2002, and subsequently at the conference of the *Sixteenth Century Journal* in Salt Lake City in November 2006, where I benefited from conversation about it with Prof. Timothy Wengert of the Philadelphia Lutheran Seminary, on whose outstanding Melanchthon studies I have heavily leaned. At the Eleventh International Luther Congress in the summer of 2007 in São Paulo, Brazil, I met and discussed my ideas with the German Melanchthon specialist Dr. Günther Frank, upon whose work I draw heavily in chapter 5.

Erstwhile collaborator on another book project, Prof. Dennis Bielfeldt, also read the draft and provided helpful commentary. Former colleague in pastoral ministry, the Reverend Timothy Anderson, read a penultimate draft and provided important encouragement on the utility of this book for stiffening the theological backbone of faithful working pastors in these challenging times for congregational life. The Reverend Dr. Sarah Hinlicky Wilson, who is the apple of her father's eye, also read the penultimate draft and provided insightful commentary. My son, Will, who is a theology major at Roanoke College, had his studies interrupted for a year of service with the U.S. Army in Kuwait while this book was being written; we helped each other through that stressful time debating by e-mail many of this book's themes as it was being written.

This book is dedicated with gratitude to my life's partner, for things of the good life we share far beyond what concerns the production of a book; but I would also like to acknowledge her support in preparing this text for publication.

I want also to acknowledge the multitude of scholars whose work in the history of ideas is everywhere presupposed and often expressly utilized for purposes that are not, however, narrowly historical according to the academic ideals of today's discipline. I have a story to tell, to be sure, but I make no pretensions to original work in the sense that concerns historians; neither the title of this book nor its ample borrowing of historical scholarship should mislead the reader into thinking that I play ball on that field. Rather, I undertake a kind of tradition-critical interrogation of past thinkers, treating them as contemporary interlocutors in advancing an argument that mutually concerns us about the nature of theology in service to the gospel. As a model, I have in mind the often brilliant forays of this kind that Karl Barth made in the *Church Dogmatics,* which he would set off in smaller print. This is a work then in systematic, more precisely dogmatic, theology, even more precisely, in the prolegomena to dogmatics. In this book the discipline of theology in its nature, functions, and possibilities is under examination by telling the story of the passage of the discipline from the Reformation through early modernity to Karl Barth's great effort at renewal in the twentieth century.

Several pertinent works came to my attention too late to be integrated into this work or were published after I had completed this book. I find that the splendid Ph.D. dissertation of Lea F. Schweitz, "The Difference between the Mirror and One Who Sees: The Theological Anthropology of G. W. Leibniz" (University of Chicago, 2008), corroborates the claim I make about Leibniz's *imago Dei* anthropology, which I locate in the Melanchthonian tradition. Similarly, Maria Rose Antognazza's book, *Leibniz on the Trinity and the Incarnation: Reason and Revelation in the Seventeenth Century,* translated by Gerald Parks (New Haven and London: Yale University Press, 2007), corroborates the claim I make about Leibniz's commitment to classic Christian dogma, while also adding valuable insight into his reserve, which can be explained by the apologetic argumentative strategy he inherited from the jurisprudential tradition in which he was educated. Our apparent disagreement on Leibniz's "Lutheran" Christology (p. 87) proves only apparent in light of a careful reading below on the christological divergence between Luther and Melanchthon (pp. 162ff.). Finally, Olli-Pekka Vainio's *Justification and Participation in Christ: The Development of the Lutheran Doctrine of Justification from Luther to the Formula of Concord (1580)* (Leiden and Boston: Brill, 2008) would have provided greater detail and nuance to my account of the conflicted legacy stemming from sixteenth-century Protestants who claimed for themselves the legacy of Luther. I happily commend these titles to readers of my book.

Finally, I acknowledge the *Lutheran Forum Guidelines* on inclusive language, which I have adopted for *my* language in this book (I have given others' language as it was written, translated, and published), as follows.

> Pronouns create confusion and mistakes in English-language letters nowadays, so we have to set an editorial policy about their use. If we are referring to hypothetical individuals, we find the most felicitous solution to be alternation between "he" and "she," since "s/he" is cumbersome and "one" can be a bit too formal and "they" usually is followed by grammatical errors. (And when we talk about multiple members of the human race, we use terms like "humanity" and "people" rather than "men," since "men" sounds like "many males" rather than "many persons.") When we speak of God and find it necessary to employ a pronoun, we use "He" (also "Him" and "His") with the capital H. This is for two reasons. First, because Scripture authorizes the use of the masculine pronoun while clarifying that God is neither male nor masculine. Secondly, because the lower-case "he" used in the same casual fashion as for human males can in fact be misleading about the non-maleness and non-masculinity of God. The person of Jesus Christ may be referred to with a lower-case "he," however, since he was truly human at the same time He was truly God. . . . We generally do not like endless repetition of the word "God," as in "God Godself saved God's people," as it implies a kind of robotic impersonality alongside the syntactical awkwardness. If, however, as an author you cannot in good conscience see your way to using the "He," you may use the repeated "God," but we ask you to provide a footnote explaining your rationale. "She" as a referent to God has no canonical basis, and to our minds only encourages the erroneous notion that God is sexual or perhaps hermaphroditic, which neither mitigates the problem of the "He" nor finds scriptural warrant. As such we decline to use it in these pages.

PAUL HINLICKY
Advent 2007

Introduction A PROJECT IN
POSTMODERN THEOLOGY

Any theological project requires first and foremost a retrospect. As Christianity is a historical religion arising from the gospel's progress through time and space, every effort theologically to account for its message tells implicitly or explicitly a tale about how those who bear this message have come to the present. I must therefore account for the "post" in "postmodern" theology. In what follows I therefore join with other scholars who in recent years have scrutinized early modernity to find better answers to questions about the sad and perplexing fate of Christian theology in contemporary Euro-American culture: its loss of public and loss of theme.

> Theology since Barth is a sad story. The radical theologies of the 1960s served finally as the *reductio ad absurdum* of the premises with which Bultmann and Tillich tried to save theology from Barth's *Dogmatics*. Those theologians who continue to seek a way between the horns, and thus to remain within the secular academy without abandoning the community of faith, have often been reduced to seemingly endless methodological foreplay. This foreplay, when it leads anywhere, typically leads toward disguised versions of liberalism. But the pathos of liberalism, as Van Harvey has shown . . . , is alienation from both the community of faith and the secular academy — a nearly complete loss of audience being the least painful major consequence. . . . Yet the only alternative to [arguing apologetically for the probability of traditional theistic claims] is either "giving the atheist less and less in which to disbelieve" or a direct (nonapologetic) appeal to the authority of revelation. The problem is that

1

revelation, according to the major Western traditions, is itself a historical event.[1]

I take this description by Jeffery Stout as a starting point.

Particularly impressive in this connection have been two works. From an Anglo-Catholic perspective, John Milbank's *Theology and Social Theory* told the outer story of the loss of theology's public by the social construction of secularism that began in Hobbes. The daunting moral of his story: "a gigantic claim to be able to read, criticize, say what is going on in other human societies, is absolutely integral to the Christian Church. . . . for theology to surrender this claim, to allow that other discourses — 'the social sciences' — carry out yet more fundamental readings, would therefore amount to denial of theological truth."[2] From a Roman Catholic perspective, Michael J. Buckley's *At the Origins of Modern Atheism* told the inner story of the loss of theology's subject matter by analyzing a shift brought about by Cartesianism in the very rationality of the conception of God: "in their search for proof of the divine existence, the theologians had shifted from the god defined by and disclosed in Christ and religious experience to the god disclosed in impersonal nature."[3] Buckley's moral: "if anyone could have reversed this inexorable dialectic, it would have been Nicolas Malebranche . . . [who taught:] 'Let us value nothing save in relation to Jesus Christ; let us not look on ourselves save as in Jesus Christ.'"[4] Hobbes and Malebranche were contemporaries of Gottfried Leibniz, who was foe of the former and friend of the latter.

If the course of modern Protestant theology is conventionally traced from Schleiermacher on through Barth and thence into the present state of endlessly aimless fragmentation, the pivotal role in this telling was played by Kant's dismantling of the cognitive claim of "rational," "natural," or "philosophical" theology — the very thing to which Leibniz, on my reading, dedicated his life. If that is so, then telling the tale of the fate of theology in early modernity from Luther's great endeavor on behalf of the autonomy of revealed theology as a discipline through Melanchthon to Leibniz and on to Barth is the task of this book. The story of early modernity is interesting in its own right. Already in the age of the baroque,[5] all the great issues that continue to challenge Christian theology in Euro-American society had taken shape: the rise of modern science with its breathtaking — and, on some readings, *rival* — cosmology; the schisms of the Western church and the widening breach with the antecedent Great Tradition; the emergence of democratic pluralism in society as a desirable together with the rise of the market economy, attended by a race-based slave market, nation-state imperialism, and colonialism. I do not think, nor do I propose, in studying this epoch, to "return" to some stance of the past, although my devotion to Luther, admiration of Leibniz, and respect for Melanchthon and Spinoza will be evident in the pages that follow (as also my antipathy to Kant). What I do propose is to retrace our path to the present in an unconventional way.

That is possible because, with our current loss of confidence in Kantian epistemology as a foundational discourse, "postmodern" thought represents an argumentative return to the status quo ante. The issues of today are in fact prefigured in the alternatives represented by Hobbes, Leibniz, and Spinoza, whom for ease of understanding we may take roughly as the Epicurean, the Augustinian, and the Stoic respectively. How to orient the discipline of revealed theology in this early modern contention of worldviews is indicative, I am proposing, of *today's* problematic of postmodern Christian theology.[6] That brings into focus another aspect of this book: at every step along the way I conduct an *Auseinandersetzung* with the greatest theologian of the twentieth century, Karl Barth. Fittingly, for it was Barth who in such significant ways pioneered the postcritical criticism of criticism by a resolute stand for theology as a nonapologetic, nonspeculative, autonomous discipline.[7] The arguments made in this book, as will be evident, are in continuous conversation with Barth, and thus also with outstanding contemporaries who followed him: Wolfhart Pannenberg, Eberhard Jüngel, and Robert Jenson in particular. Thus the inquiry in this book is not antiquarian in the sense of a work in the history of ideas remote from us and without bearing on the present. The interrogation of the theological past undertaken in this work is understood as opening a way forward for us today.

What Is at Issue?

A few illustrations of the dubious state of theology today to which Stout referred, particularly in the tradition stemming from Luther, show what is at issue in contemporary theology's loss of public and theme.

As a young scholar at midcentury, Jaroslav Pelikan titled the first book in his illustrious scholarly career *From Luther to Kierkegaard*.[8] The title nicely captured the direction theology in the tradition of Luther had taken, culminating during the postwar years in the historical-critical and existentialist hermeneutics of eminent scholars like Rudolf Bultmann[9] and Gerhard Ebeling.[10] Such thinkers critically asserted a "radical Lutheranism" against the renewal of dogmatic theology by the Reformed theologian Karl Barth.[11] Yet ironically Pelikan's title articulated a trajectory for contemporary theology in the tradition of Luther that Pelikan in the end could not follow. Late in life Pelikan, who had been the first chief editor of the American Edition of *Luther's Works,* quietly turned away from existential Lutheranism to Eastern Orthodoxy.

Drawing upon Kierkegaard, Nygren, and Bultmann, the post-Christian feminist theologian Daphne Hampson argues that existentialist Lutheran and essentialist Catholic anthropologies are irreconcilable, which is tantamount to saying that Christianity collapses from internal incoherence under the conditions of modernity.[12] This would not be, one suspects, a wholly unwelcome result for this author.[13] In any case, her thesis begs several questions. First, it assumes the adequacy of existentialist readings of the Reformation tradition as also of essentialist readings of the Thomist tradition.[14] Second, it ignores Karl Barth's (admittedly complicated) claim to Luther's legacy,[15] i.e., that methodologically a dogmatic approach (which can be traced back to Melanchthon's *Loci Communes*) is required to carry on the Reformation project as the reform, not supersession, of the Catholic tradition. Here, moreover, Luther's paradoxical anthropological claims about "bound will" and "ecstatic faith" or "just people who are at the same time sinners" can be situated to make narrative sense. Isolating a "Lutheran" anthropology of the "breaking of the self," as Hampson tries to do, from the canonical narrative of the resurrection of the Crucified may indeed result in a "profoundly masculinist description" of the human relation to the divine, but the dragon so slain amounts to a worthless caricature.[16]

Instead, I take it to be the case that Luther offered a Cyrillian Christ[17] to Augustinian man.[18] If that is so, what is at issue for theology in his tradition is whether such kerygma can be achieved today. That depends in part on recovering critical perspectives on the good that have some measure of cognitive purchase; this is what I shall intend in the following as the proper task of a "natural theology," or "Christian philosophy,"[19] as a reflective extension of "revealed theology," or dogmatics, *not* as a foundational discourse for it. What the preceding episodes betray, however, is the domination among contemporaries in Luther's tradition of a noncognitive, "anthropological" interpretation of Christian doctrine that, following Kant,[20] offers what can only appear from the perspective of classical dogmatics in Luther's tradition as a "Nestorian Christ for Pelagian man" (C. Gore).[21]

If that is what is at issue, this book then represents a counterproject in contemporary theology that sets out from Luther and leads through Leibniz (more precisely, Leibniz's *failure*) rather than Kant.[22] Accordingly, I share with Luther a certain Augustinian critique of metaphysics, but at the same time I am cognitively interested in scientific-cosmological[23] and even "metaphysical" questions,[24] as were Melanchthon and Leibniz. This approach is deeply rooted in the classical tradition of trinitarian theology, both Eastern and Augustinian, as was classical Lutheranism;[25] it is dedicated to logical clarity and conceptual precision as was the "nominalist" Luther,[26] the Aristotelian pedagogue Melanchthon, and the logician Leibniz; it is engaged as were Melanchthon and Leibniz for the ecumenical reconciliation of Protestantism and Catholicism,[27] yet is willing like a Luther or a Barth to engage prophetically against the self-understanding of the times to assert the Crucified as our reconciliation with God; it is capable along the same lines of providing for the church of the martyrs a theodicy of faith, as in Romans 8– 11, at which, as I will argue, Luther aimed in conclusion of his *De servo arbitrio.*[28] The relation of this complex of Luther's ideas in that volcanic text to cheery Leibniz's *Theodicy* is the tangled knot that this book proposes patiently to untie.

Some Initial Clarifications

I propose then to argue against the current state of affairs in the tradition of Luther across a broad front. A few clarifications are necessary from the outset to deter the criticism I might anticipate of supposedly retreating to a "precritical" mind.

First, I am not attacking historical *method,* modestly conceived as an inquiry that tests interpretation of texts in the light of what they could have meant to an original author and/or audience. I am criticizing a distinctive anticanonical *hermeneutic* "in that it inquires back behind the philologically clear text after something which is hidden, hidden in the first place by a dogmatic and traditional view of the whole into which the text is being fitted. The critical analysis uncovers a fiction which obliterates the true, i.e., historically verifiable, state of affairs."[29] In 1962 the young Carl Braaten urged that this program of deconstructing the canonical text "has its roots deep in Lutheran soil." I will show that this program has rather deeper rootage in the soil of Spinoza's philosophy. Not that that rootage means the problem so denoted can be dismissed. Braaten had in mind a famous passage from Rudolf Bultmann: "Our radical attempt to demythologize the New Testament is in fact a perfect parallel to St. Paul's and Luther's doctrine of justification by faith alone apart from the works of the law. Or rather, it carries this doctrine to its logical conclusion in the field of epistemology. . . . The man who wishes to believe in God as his God must realize that he has nothing in his hand on which to base his faith. He is suspended in mid-air, and cannot demand a proof of the Word which addresses him."[30] We could agree with this antifoundationalist claim of Bultmann if it were carried through consistently so that some other discourse or inquiry than the canonical text would not come to play a foundational role in theological knowledge. Although Bultmann expressly denies it,[31] whether or not this is the case in his theology has been the question.[32]

It is not historical method, but this hermeneutic, that I will be disputing. The canonical hermeneutic, by contrast, represents a historical person, Jesus who was crucified, as risen from the dead and thus *able* to present *as the person who He was* and who *wills* to be so, provided that He is remembered *truly,* as this very person who he was and continues to be. Putting both speaker of *this* Jesus and hearer back down on the earth, Robert Bertram could accordingly provide some historical content to the name Jesus Christ as the bearer to the godless of the merciful promise of God (and giver of His own Spirit so that they believe). He argued that Scripture and tradition are properly understood as one sequential "traditioning" of the same gospel Word of God, the promise in distinction from the divine law, which evokes faith alone in Jesus Christ alone as its proper response. He pointedly commented against the hermeneutic I wish to dispute that the "distorting of the *sola fide* into an aversion against all *Aüsserlichkeit,* aversion even against the publicly transmitted Word and sacraments by the anti-Tradition 'Enthusiasts' and 'sects,' was for Luther perhaps the most grievous miscarriage of the Reformation."[33] Bertram concluded by pointing to the *subordinate* agency of the church that the *sola fide* entails when correlated with a contentful *solus Christus:* "those fallible human agents who transmit the external Word onward, yes, but only as they themselves are holied or hallowed by that Word."[34] Bertram's case for a canonical hermeneutic of the "external Word" in the church manifestly has to identify the trinitarian Word (and Spirit) as real operative agents at work in the time-spanning traditioning of the gospel. It is this that I wish to affirm against a hermeneutical spiritualism (falsely) claiming the name of Luther.

So, *second,* I hardly wish to contest the existential element in faith, but I do wish to reanchor it theologically as what it really was to Luther, *divine* faith, the work of the Holy Spirit, the third person of the Trinity. Bultmann famously wrote,

Paul's teaching of justification is, it could be said, his real christology, for "to know Christ is to know the benefits he confers" (*hoc est Christum cognoscere, beneficia eius cognoscere;* Melanchthon). The teaching of justification demonstrates forcibly that christology does not consist in speculation on the nature of Christ; that christology is the proclamation of the event of Christ's coming, and that an understanding of the event requires not speculation but self-examination, radical consideration of the nature of one's own new existence.[35]

The vacating of what is pejoratively called "speculation" on the nature of Christ comes at a huge cost: it disconnects Christ from the One he called Father and from their Spirit. In fact, this vacating reflects an antitrinitarian motive that isolates the believer in an existential moment of decision; in this way it eclipses Christ's Spirit as the agent of faith, in whose place — in the name, no less, of Paul's "real Christology" — we are pointed to a momentous human decision and act. There is, as we shall see, a real difficulty here; it pulled Melanchthon in two opposing directions. Bultmann to that extent was justified in citing Melanchthon's authority for what I shall describe in chapter 4 as the disappearance of the Holy Spirit in Lutheranism, or perhaps more historically, in chapter 5, as the Holy Spirit's sublimation into a "general pneumatology." By Bultmann's time, general pneumatology itself had undergone further reduction to existential moments of individual authenticity. But if Melanchthon was pulled in opposing directions, Bultmann's cited statement advances outright a false antithesis, one Melanchthon himself could not and did not sustain. Instead, Melanchthon's later theology set upon a historical trajectory that led in the course of time to the *compatibilist* (not in my preferred reading *determinist*) thought of Gottfried Leibniz, the "Lutheran Thomist" of the seventeenth century. And this, we shall suggest, is in arguable continuity with the thought of Protestant theology's twentieth-century giant, Karl Barth.

"Lutheran Thomist"[36] — is that an oxymoron?[37] Fergus Kerr corrects the impression, not only among Protestants, that "Thomas has a doctrine of 'pure nature': human beings who are able, independently of divine grace, to bootstrap their way to God. . . . [But] nature is open to grace by grace — only by grace, as we now have to insist, to rule out any idea of 'pure nature.' . . . But this is to raise the question of co-operation — the problem central in all Western theology: the problem of the co-operation between the graceful God and the graced creature."[38] Kerr acknowledges that this is a "hermeneutic crux" and argues for a version of compatibilism in Thomas that is, as we shall see, similar to (if not in part the inspiration of) what may be found in Leibniz.

> Whether co-operation is necessarily competition is an interesting question. It takes us right to the heart of Thomas's theology. He often quotes Isaiah 26:12: "Lord, thou has wrought all our works in us" — which he takes (e.g. at ST 1.105.5), precisely as *excluding* all competitiveness between divine and human agency. . . . he almost always rules out the picture of two rival agents on a level playing field. . . . God "causes" everything in such a way that the creature "causes" it too. . . . It is always by divine power that the human agent produces his or her own proper effect: that is the doctrine of creation.[39]

Well said, so far as it goes.

Lutherans and Catholics agree with Augustine that God is the cause of all causes, though not the maker of all choices. Today they might well also agree with Kathryn Tanner's fine parsing of how the apparently antagonistic discourses of divine sovereignty and of created grace may be seen as compatible, when taken as rules for living Christianly. Then "unchristian behaviors and attitudes are the results of illicit inferences from claims about divine sovereignty or the integrity of the creature's own capacities,"[40] that is, so far as either rhetoric is taken as an exclusive account. Leibniz, as we shall see, comes to a similar solution. So far as it goes, the rule approach to Christian doctrine, as might be expected, is a "useful" one.

Yet the problem proves more perplexing and troubling than a rule theory of Christian doctrine can satisfy or resolve, particularly insofar as cognitive accounts of the good remain proscribed by Kantian agnosticism. The theological difficulty lies in freedom of choice (*De servo arbitrio* is Luther's title) in distinction from freedom of action. Only pantheism denies freedom of action, namely, that creatures are the owners of their own passions and actions, as the unique patients and agents of their nonsubstitutable, incorrigible experience and effects, with God's concurrence. Thus what makes an action or omission of action my own (and not anyone else's) is that I suffer my own desires and perchance act upon the object of my own desire (or do not act because I critically question the apparent good of the object). Such freedom of action seems theologically clear enough — except to pantheists, who think that the posit of an ego persisting through time to form a biographical narrative of someone's own sufferings and doings already begs the question whether egos genuinely exist as the genuine patients/agents of their own lives, rather than modes of God, the one and only true substance/agent.

But the troubling question for theology concerns freedom of choice, i.e., whether after the fall free choice remains as nothing more than an empty title reminiscent of the paradisaical possibility of pure obedience to God's command that is long since forfeit; furthermore, whether in the time of grace human choices for faith or unbelief resolve into antecedent divine choices for mercy or, evidently, reprobation, as God gives or withholds the Spirit. As Leibniz explained to Locke:

> But the internal grace of the Holy Spirit immediately supplies [a "motive of probability"] in a supernatural way, and this it is which produces what the theologians properly call a divine faith. It is true that God never gives it except when the belief it produces is founded in reason; otherwise he would destroy the means of knowing truth and open the door to enthusiasm; but it is not necessary for all who have this divine faith to know these reasons and still less to have them always before their eyes. Otherwise simple-minded people and idiots, today at least, would never have the true faith, and the most enlightened would not have it when they were most in need of it, for they cannot always remember the reasons for their belief.[41]

If faith were to consist in free, rational, human choice, Leibniz argues, it would exist only in and as a momentary decision according to the good reason thus and so to believe. But the fallen creature cannot recognize the Crucified as a good reason for the investment of trust; this must be supernaturally supplied by the Holy Spirit, not just momentarily but perpetually, if trust is to be a way of life. Apart from this, faith can never rest in those who are able, nor extend to those who are less able; in either case divine faith is robbed of its power as consolation of mercy. By the same token, while such attribution of the decision or choice in divine faith to the Holy Spirit provides the requisite consolation of mercy, it raises the terrible question of why faith is apparently withheld from some. A rule theory tends to cut the Gordian knot here, which I propose patiently to untie.

My point in raising this "horrifying" thought (as Calvin called it) — indeed, it is a central focus in this book's inquiry — is to engage what Kerr calls "the unresolved and perhaps unresolvable difference over the question of grace between Lutheran and pre-Reformation theologies." This "most intractable division,"[42] however, turns out in fact to be a *tension* (not *contra-*

diction, if *compatibilism* succeeds) *internal* to the Lutheran tradition itself (in the relation between Luther and Melanchthon, which may parallel the tension between Augustine and Aquinas in Roman Catholic thought). Kerr pointed to the Finnish School of Luther research, along with Robert Jenson's rereading of Luther in the light of the patristic sources (much as Kerr has re-read Thomas in his study), as opening up a new coordination, not in terms of the traditional conceptuality nature and grace, but in resort to the more biblical and narrative terms of creation and redemption.[43] Here too we may discover in our current ferment *paths not taken* that can liberate us from entrenched partisanships and thus actually advance the cause of the gospel and theology, overcoming "Christian contradictions."

Paths Not Taken

I have intimated that a "Kantian" narrative still holds pride of place in the minds of "modern" theologians. If that is so, the trajectory just sketched that I explore in this book from Luther through Leibniz represents a path *not* taken. It is a path, I will argue, that could yet embrace the modern without succumbing to its imperious pretensions or its disillusioned downward spiral today into constructivism and vulgar relativism. It is a path, I contend, that yet can redeem the achievements of modernity from threatening self-cancellation. Yet I have written in the title "path*s* not taken," and the plural is significant. By the singular, "path," I could, as above, simply refer to Gottfried Leibniz's "theological philosophy" (G. Frank)[44] — one of the last great attempts in early modern Europe to found culture on the Christian dogma of creation as parsed by the classic Lutheran thinkers.[45] In spite of his dislike of polemic, and thus his dislike of the partisan name "Lutheran,"[46] Leibniz drank deeply at the wells of Lutheran school theology. Leibniz set out from this specific tradition of theology. He often assures us of his knowledge of "our" (i.e., Lutheran) theologians, as well as others, especially Augustine, and on occasion Saint Thomas.[47] His stance in philosophy — "determinist, theist, idealist," as one contemporary American interpreter has perhaps a little too neatly summarized[48] — reflects his schooling in the reorganized university curriculum that derives from the *praeceptor Germaniae,* Philip Melanchthon.[49] It is a matter of historical fact that a path exists here.

The plural, "paths," however, indicates that Leibniz's great project — and its failure — may be seen, and certainly must be evaluated, from different angles. I have in mind, in addition to the foregoing, at least the following three. *First,* as already mentioned, Leibniz's is a path that *cannot* be taken after Kant, insofar as Kant still succeeds in recasting Leibniz into a precursor of his own turn to the subject.[50] In other words, so long as we think of Leibniz as a "rationalist" engaged in a precritical attempt to found science on a priori knowledge of essences, we cannot but regard him as outmoded and his entire scheme as fantastic metaphysical poetry. But what if that is not how Leibniz regarded his work, not least his "general pneumatology"? Writing against Locke, Leibniz defined "a proper Pneumatology [as] comprising the knowledge of God, of souls and of simple substances in general" and went to explain: "I believe with the majority of the ancients that all genii, all souls, all simple created substances, are always joined to a body, and that there are never souls entirely separated . . . the difference between one of their states and another, never being and never having been other than that of more sensible to less sensible. . . . [Consequently,] there is no more difficulty in conceiving the conservation of souls . . . than there is in conceiving the change of the caterpillar into the butterfly, and the conservation of thought in sleep, to which Jesus Christ has divinely well compared death."[51] What interests Leibniz in a passage like this is clear: his purpose is not epistemologically to found science but hermeneutically to interpret its discoveries to other minds as works of God — and other minds *as well* as works of God. Thesis 10 of the *Discourse on Metaphysics* denies categorically that the Monadology is intended to ground science, stating "that the belief in Substantial Forms has some basis, but . . . these forms do not change anything in phenomena and must not be used to explain particular effects."[52] After Kant, Leibniz's project of so interpreting scientific discovery turns out to be one of the tasks of revealed theology, not as "natural theology," as we might say today, but as "theology of nature."

So, *second,* Leibniz's is a path that *may* be taken up again by Christian thought in leading us to see ourselves (in Christ!) as embedded in nature under God rather than superior to nature in place of God. Arguably, such a stance today has advantages, given the ecological crisis. That becomes a plausible appropriation of Leibniz insofar as Kant's disingenuous claim to "destroy knowledge to make room for faith" succumbs today to doubt about the pretensions of epistemology. There is a price that must be paid, however, to think this way. My reading of Leibniz as an instructive failure in his self-appointed task of "natural theology" will not break open a path to a priori certainty by means of a foundationalist epistemology nor does it not yield an "ontotheology," in the pejorative sense of the "round square" of a "Christian philosophy"[53] that Heidegger popularized (expressly against Leibniz).[54]

I am retrieving Leibniz for purposes of revealed theology, with its interpretation of being-as-creation, including the human mind as vestige of the Trinity. The question of whether the latter form of thought would any longer count as "philosophy" is utterly secondary, since strong disciplinary distinctions would here collapse along with the Kantian scheme.[55] Philosophy and theology are in any case talking about a shared world. What differentiates them is perspective — what Luther called the lights of nature and of grace. In this reading, Leibniz turns out to be (contrary to his own intention) a theologian interpreting nature in the light of grace.

Third, then, and most complexly and significantly then for the future of Christian thought after Euro-American modernity, Leibniz's project shipwrecked on account of an intrinsic difficulty Heidegger put his finger on. It represents the path that *could not* be taken as Leibniz proposed it, *not* because it transgressed the limits of reason as Kant charged, but because in the final analysis Leibniz's attempt to secure Christian dogma philosophically[56] (as "natural theology") is exposed as a *covert* attempt to refound culture on the Christian dogma of creation. In Leibniz's tradition stretching back to what Günther Frank calls Melanchthon's "epistemological Theo-Rationalism," the initial move was innocent enough: "it is indeed theology — above all the doctrine of Creation and the doctrine of the image of God — which effects the decisive foundational task of philosophy."[57] But by Leibniz's time, this half-forgotten point of departure, trading illicitly on a key notion borrowed from revelation, begged the question to its naturalistic challengers. The borrowing is neither methodologically nor substantively trivial. *It states as an axiom of all thought that the human mind is made in the image of God, who is the free, wise, and loving Creator of all that is not God.* On this basis a "natural theology" that will comport with revealed theology is not only possible but *entailed,* since the human relation to God as image is precisely what is redeemed, restored, and in this way revealed in Jesus Christ. On the other hand, apart from revelation, as it eventually became clear, there are no grounds available to affirm statements about the divine as the free, wise, and loving Creator, namely, as the Father of Jesus Christ with their Spirit. We cannot by nature and natural light alone so definitely declare the infinite. On the contrary, even the notion of a "Creator" becomes suspect as an unwarranted anthropomorphism, potentially even idolatrous. To this extent Spinoza (long before Hume) won the argument for the future (and as such he, not Kant, becomes the true antagonist in our story).

The Plan of Battle

What then is the plan of battle? In *chapter 1,* I set out the case for the relevance of the thought of Leibniz (as an alternative to Kant) for our contemporary intellectual and spiritual situation. I urge that Kantian dualism has defined the epoch of so-called modern theology, but that this epoch is passing away. In this confusing situation, theology has lost both audience and theme. Yet I argue that as the borders erected by Kant and his theological camp collapse, the spiritual and intellectual situation of the contemporary Euro-American mind reverts to the status quo ante. So the Leipzig-born philosopher who flourished at the turn of the eighteenth century claims attention. Most significantly, the question of the compatibility of human freedom and divine determination at the heart of Leibniz's thought reflects quite precisely a deep internal tension in theology, to which I alluded earlier, going back to Luther and Melanchthon (or Augustine and Thomas). This difficulty represents an aporia at the fonts, which, I believe, must be resolved for this tradition of theology to go forward. Whether the solution I propose in chapter 3 — that in his doctrine of election Karl Barth has resolved the question better than contemporary "Lutherans" — succeeds in opening up an alternative to the usual alternatives descended from Kant, the reader must of course decide. But Leibniz, I believe, can point us on an alternate path: not a turn to the subject but a critical grounding of both subject and object in the nature of things, i.e., ultimately in God's *nature* understood as the harmony of power, wisdom, and love. God's nature can be so understood when God as the triune *agent* is understood as redeemer and fulfiller of created nature, *not* an alternative to nature, let alone a cipher for nature.[58] As mentioned, such a shift in orientation offers profound *ecological* advantages for Christian thought today over against the anthropocentric and dualistic tendencies of the Cartesian-Kantian heritage. But it depends on a cognitive interpretation of Christian doctrine.

In *chapter 2,* consequently, I argue that Spinoza emerges from the shadows as the thinker who most radically and therefore most helpfully challenges the received theological tradition. By the same token, the special merit of Gottfried Leibniz in his *Theodicy* is that he grasped Spinoza's challenge and sought to meet it, even if for historically understandable reasons he failed, as we shall explore.

In *chapter 3,* the argument fast-forwards to the middle of the twentieth century to retrace the steps that led Karl Barth to his stunning revision of the doctrine of election. This, I argue, represents a more or less grudging appropriation of the argumentative line that Leibniz had pioneered; it succeeds in the case of Barth because it is presented and argued as revealed, not as natural theology. At the same time, Barth does not succeed in overcoming the classical conundrum of the divine permission of moral evil, and his doctrine of Nothingness is weighed, appreciated, and finally found deficient in this regard. In this deficiency, Barth, in spite of an exaggerated and polemical effort to distance himself from Leibniz, proves to be all too similar. For Barth, as for Leibniz, a "real" devil is unthinkable, and just this separates both great theologians from Luther — who, to be sure, has his own problems with the devil! It is a daunting problem, but something more than the venerable privative theory of evil is required to figure the actual powers of greed and envy that corrupt created being by subverting faith in the Word made flesh.

In *chapter 4,* we journey back in time to the roots of the perplexity that came to paralyze theology in the tradition of Luther on account of the subtle divergences in the thought of the partners in reformation, Luther and Melanchthon. In time this subtle divergence grew into contradictory trajectories, even if still living together under one confessional roof, coming thereby to resemble the contemporary dysfunctional family. A surprising consequence of this analysis, however, is to show the greater continuity of Barth's theology with Melanchthon than with Luther or even Calvin. This further serves to establish a thin line of tradition, stretching from Melanchthon through Leibniz to Barth, even if Barth remains in the final analysis a "critically realistic dialectical theologian" (McCormack), that is, a philosophical Kantian. We can grant that, if at the same time we show that Barth is theologically a Leibnizian.

In *chapter 5,* we return focus upon Melanchthon from a new angle that casts him in a different light: as a Christian philosopher, fending off the encroachments of new Stoics, Skeptics, and Epicureans, and so establishing a school of Christian philosophy in northern German universities. This philosophy was premised upon the application of the leading Lutheran theological distinction of law and gospel to the relation of nature and grace, which in this way specified a delimited provenance for philosophy in a reformed Protestant Christian civilization. This division of culture-forming labor hinged upon a very specific appropriation and revision of the *imago dei* doctrine deriving from Genesis 1:26-28 that in time evolved into a new philosophical discipline that Leibniz inherited: *General Pneumatology,* the forerunner of modern *Geistphilosophie.* Clarity about this allows us to extend our trajectory from Melanchthon through Leibniz and Barth to contemporary W. Pannenberg.

In *chapter 6,* we consider the failure of Leibniz's *Theodicy* to meet the challenge of Spinoza's fatalism in two versions. In Version One, Leibniz the Platonic rationalist, who lives in a world in which nothing happens without a good reason, justifies the way the world is by recourse to evil characters in God's mind that are admitted into existence for the purpose of serving God's accomplishment of greater good. In Version Two, Leibniz the Melanchthonian theologian, who lives in the world Christ redeemed, justifies God as Creator, Redeemer, and Fulfiller on the way to the kingdom, which is the best of all possible worlds. He attempts to do so by recourse to Luther's Augustinian doctrine of the unfreedom of natural desire that by grace can be liberated for true good. The not so rationalistic Augustinian *perspectivalism* involved in Version Two is hauntingly similar to postmodern accounts of the decentered self, or, as Luther would have it, the eccentric self. This eccentric self is the living image of the Trinity, a theological advance for which Leibniz groped, but which he finally could not attain.

In the *conclusion,* I indicate a number of items emerging from this study in need of further work, and then settle upon a path forward for theology in the tradition of Luther through the ruins of contemporary Euro-American Christianity.

A Modern Alternative to Dualism?

Leibniz as Alternative

As a young reader, Leibniz confesses at the beginning of the *Theodicy,* "I flitted from book to book, and since subjects for meditation pleased me as much as histories and fables, I was charmed by the work of Laurentius Valla against Boethius and by that of Luther against Erasmus, although I was well aware that they had need of some mitigation. . . . Nor did I neglect the teachings of our theologians: and the study of their opponents, far from disturbing me, served to strengthen me in the moderate opinions of the Churches of the Augsburg Confession."[1] Yet word that a line across the fascinating epoch that witnessed the end of the Renaissance and the beginnings of the Enlightenment that extends from Luther via Melanchthon to Leibniz comes as a surprise to many. Starting out with Luther hardly requires special justification. Yet a line bypassing the polemical form (though not the dogmatic content) of Lutheran orthodoxy[2] and running on to *Leibniz?* In fact, the suggestion meets with well-established prejudice, not least from the philosophers. In one bitter passage, for example, Lewis White Beck managed to mock both Luther and Leibniz and at the same time to set them fundamentally at odds with each other. Luther's "theodicy" at the conclusion of the *Bondage of the Will,* we are told, "is the source of the strict Lutheran sense of the helplessness of man, the futility of practice, and the indifference or even evil of works." In contrast, the "modern world, with its emphasis on practice, required Arminianism, a polite Protestant name for the Pelagian heresy; hence Luther's denial of man's freedom did not make fruitful contact with humane activism, while Calvin's did." Now that Beck has instructed philosophical readers on the secret affinity of Calvinism and Arminianism, we learn that this modern need for Pelagian activism "is the reason why Lutherans in the Enlightenment acted more like Calvinists than like orthodox Lutherans. And the greatest of these crypto-Calvinistic theodicies is that of Leibniz." Leibniz, we are so instructed, is a secret Pelagian Calvinist, because, unlike an openly helpless Lutheran, he imagined "that a predestinarian system does not entail the denial of freedom." On the basis of compatibilism, Beck generalizes: "the German Enlightenment was secularized Calvinism, not Lutheranism, even though almost every German philosopher from Leibniz to Kant was confessionally Lutheran."[3] Later on, however, we find Beck scolding: "Leibniz' optimism was God-centered and metaphysical; in the Theodicy (but not in most of his other writings) it is a contemplative, not a practical, optimism. Instead of reminding man of how much remains to be done, and how much he can do, it seeks to console him by showing him that things are not so bad as they seem."[4]

If the reader senses a contradiction here between depictions of Leibniz's supposedly crypto-Calvinist activism on the one side and his contemplative, heavenly minded, metaphysical Lutheranism on the other, she is correct. But the contradiction is not in Leibniz. Regrettably Beck's treatment of Leibniz is typical. Going back to Bertrand Russell's influential attempt at an exposé,[5] significant commentators, especially in the Anglo-American sphere,[6] have found in the Hanoverian a tangled mass of insincerity and contradiction. On examination, however, almost every aspersion Russell snidely cast on Leibniz is parasitic upon the parody Voltaire rendered with the figure of Dr. Pangloss in *Candide*. Curiously, as Catherine Wilson has made clear, such attempts to assimilate an insincere Leibniz into the maw of Spinozist necessitarianism goes back to the Pietist theologian of Halle, Joachim Lange, who was actually engaged in battle with Wolff and his followers (whose own appropriation of Leibniz had laundered out the vestiges of trinitarian theology on which my argument turns).[7] As in Voltaire so also in Lange or Russell: hardly a word stands up to scrutiny.

One might, however, refuse Leibniz justly considered. Ned Wisnefske, for example, proposes that the task of "new" natural theology (i.e., after the failure of the kind imputed to Leibniz) is to describe the "predicament in which we live and move and have our being . . . [i.e.] to understand that the blessings of life challenge us beyond what we can achieve, and that the corruption of life threatens us beyond what we can control . . . to understand life and death as powers which control human existence."[8] Wisnefske thus argues that the proper task is not to establish a natural knowledge of God as a foundation for revealed theology, but to uncover the human predicament to which the gospel is addressed. "Religious ideas of God are not worth building Christian theology upon. . . . Jesus' life, his crucifixion and resurrection, and the imparting of his life to the church is the basis of the Christian view of God."[9] In this respect, Wisnefske follows Barth. But he also argues against Barth that theology needs to "prepare" the ground for the address of the gospel by uncovering the natural human predicament. Noting that modern "Christianity may have retreated onto the periphery of the natural world because attempts to find divine causality in natural processes faltered before the explanatory skills of the natural sciences," Wisnefske points out the heavy price theology has paid for this retreat from our common natural existence: "Our supposed religious existence as spiritual individuals subtly disconnects us from our common life where life completely depends on other life and lives, where natural death is a real end to life, and where death is an ever present part of our corporate life. In this way religion does not speak to our life as it is naturally and corporately constituted, but to the existence of spiritual individuals, which is something quite different."[10] Should Leibniz's "natural theology" be understood along these lines as a religiously glossed instance of Cartesian dualism or Gnostic spirituality? I grant that some have read him this way,[11] but I find another interpretation of what Leibniz was doing in so-called natural theology that in much comports with Wisnefske's ethical concerns and appreciation of moral bondage.

We should find Wisnefske's call for a new kind of natural theology largely persuasive, with several qualifications: (1) Leibniz's "general pneumatology" should not be simply equated with the cosmotheological apologetics of deism, for the former has to do with the important theologoumena of humanity's creation in the image of God and hence with the critical capacity (the "passive disposition" — Luther) of the human mind, even in its natural or fallen state, to recognize God as God, should God reveal Himself as God; (2) the task of a systematic theological or Christian philosophical interpretation of natural reality should not be rejected as a false attempt at rationalistic/idealistic foundationalism of the "religious" kind Wisnefske rightly rejects but rather be understood as an antidualist concern for truth; (3) the prophetic critique of sinful idolatry at the root of human bondage to alien powers may not be overlooked, because the God of the gospel is a liberator only as also a reconciler and redeemer. The prophetic indictment that shows human beings to be "without excuse" (Rom. 1:20) in surrendering to false gods is the legitimate function of traditional "natural" theology. As we shall see, the Leibniz who emerges in the pages to follow is one who will have failed in the final analysis to accomplish his own purpose along these lines. But his purpose is simply missed, if not misrepresented, by critics who fail to understand or appreciate its roots in theological "Lutheranism" and philosophical "Melanchthonism" (as indeed Wisnefkse's own proposal is also rooted).

For Beck, on the other hand, all roads led to and from Kant. The still predominant version of our story of theology's passage through modernity turns on his Copernican revolution that justifies noncognitive, "metaphorical" (as if metaphors did not refer!),[12] that is, *constructivist,* versions of theology.[13] But according to the argument in the chapters to follow, Kantianism replaced a dogmatism of the object with a mystification of the subject. Today this subjectivist narrative is losing its grip on account of new awareness of the "decentered self" at the grip of alien or seductive powers (just as Wisnefske implied).[14] Euro-American culture today is thus reverting from Kant's transcendental Ego to the pluralism of accounts of the surrounding world in early modernity, which evolved in turn via the revival in Renaissance humanism of the classical school battles between Epicureans, Stoics, and Skeptics[15] — and Augustinians.[16] The metaphysical wars of those days had been constrained by the boundaries that Kantian philosophy erected and then policed in the past two centuries by means of a strict separation of the realms of natural necessity and human freedom. These were the respective domains of matter and mind, appearances and concepts, fact and value, attended by science and ethics respectively. Patrol of these boundaries was the task assigned by Kant to reason in virtue of its self-critique.[17] At the end of his life, in a polemical writing against the place of the traditional theological faculty alongside those of law and medicine, Kant wrote that as soon as such a faculty presumes "to mix with its teachings something it treats as derived from reason . . . [it] encroaches on the territory of the philosophy faculty, which mercilessly strips from it all the shining plumes that were protected by the government and deals with it on a footing of equality and freedom. . . . [T]ake great care not to enter . . . keep it at a respectful distance."[18] Thus, Richard Rorty writes, we "owe the notion of philosophy as a tribunal of pure reason, upholding or denying the claims of the rest of culture," "to the eighteenth century and especially to Kant, [although] this Kantian notion presupposed both general assent to Lockean notions of mental processes and Cartesian notions of mental substances."[19]

This Kantian truce is breaking down today because of doubts about Cartesian-Lockean dualism and thus corresponding doubts about the capacity of reason to sustain a persuasive self-criticism.[20] Rorty enlists Wittgenstein, Heidegger, and Dewey in his seminal assault on Kantianism "to undermine the reader's confidence in 'the mind' as something about which one should have a 'philosophical' view, in 'knowledge' as something about which there ought to be a 'theory' and which has 'foundations,' and in 'philosophy' as it has been conceived since Kant."[21] In fact, any reader of current literature in the humanities amply experiences doubt about the existence of Kant's Tribunal of Reason, supposedly exalted above self-interest as formed by race, class, gender — to mention only the unholy trinity of today's academic correctness (but why not also in Luther's broad sense — that reason can play the whore, selling itself to the highest bidder?).[22] In this highly diffuse sense, we are all today "Marxists"[23] who pose his early questions, *Cui bono? Quis custodiet custodiem?* All thinking, we now think, is a socially embedded, historically formed, and above all *interested* human practice. That location of thought matters, because it shows that Kant's mystifying elevation of the faculty of reason as a tribunal overseeing all over domains of culture is just as guilty of *hybris* as any traditional form of thought.[24] Significant voices of protest sounded in Nietzsche and the pragmatists, in Rorty's telling, against "the notion of philosophy as a foundational discipline," the conception "of culture as in need of grounding" and "the pretensions of a theory of knowledge to perform this task." Yet philosophy so conceived prevailed until recently, because, as Rorty suggests, it became for the intellectuals in Kantian culture "the substitute for religion. It was the area of culture where one touched bottom, where one found the vocabulary and the convictions which permitted one to explain and justify one's activity as an intellectual, and thus to discover the significance of one's life."[25]

Such activity is incorrigibly religious, even if philosophy, so conceived, was incapable of bearing the burden of meaning thus laid upon it. Now what? Rorty seems to think we should just "get over" our religious needs and take leave of "philosophy" of that kind. More interesting is the observation that with Rorty's true but unsatisfying criticism of criticism, the contemporary mind spins in a vortex of perspectivalist critique in which no one occupies a superior vantage point by virtue of the mere capacity for critical thinking. And so metaphysics — the foredoomed grasping after the truth beyond our reach — return to fill a vacuum that culture no less than nature abhors, now more than ever unsecured as a science. Does that mean that we are doomed to dogmatism and polemic? or retreat for peace of mind to Epicurean gardens? Socratic irony? or perhaps Stoic resignation? Rorty's choice for Socratic irony makes sense in this scenario. What is the alternative?

Christian theology not only needs an alternative to the kinds of alternatives Kant bequeathed, but a place to stand within the vortex created by the
collapse of his systematic separation of freedom and necessity into discrete
realms. I will argue broadly that Leibnizian "metaphysics" are best understood as a *theology* of communication and interpretation, i.e., an account of
what our one single reality must be like, if communication is possible
(namely, it is the creature of a communicating Creator, when the Trinity is
taken as the mystery of the world's *ultima ratio*). The young Leibniz wrote in
his Paris Notebooks on February 11, 1676: "God is not a kind of imaginary
metaphysical being, incapable of thought, will, and action, as some make
Him. This would be the same as to say that God is nature, fate, fortune, necessity, or the world. But God is a definite substance, a person, a mind. . . . It
must be shown that God is a person or substance, intelligence. It must be
demonstrated rigorously that he feels himself to act upon himself. For there
is nothing more admirable than for the same being to feel and to be acted
upon by himself."[26] I will show how this conception of the living, speak-
acting God is trinitarian in structure and how, in turn, Leibniz's revision of
the Thomist metaphysics of substantial form in his *Monadology* mirrors
trinitarianism. Taken together, these ideas constitute a theological interpretation of the world such that the God of the gospel becomes recognizable in
it and for it. It is a matter of semantics whether or not one calls this comprehensive interpretive claim "metaphysics"; it is a matter of considerable perplexity how Leibniz located his thought in or as theology, philosophy, and/or
both. But in any case, the reading of him to follow is one interested in his
thought as a significant, though little recognized, chapter in the gospel's critique and revision of metaphysics.

Staying with Kant, in contrast, may fairly be described as the "Pelagian"
alternative, because Kant in fact regarded freedom as the ability to initiate
causal series, motivated only by rational obedience to the moral law of one's
own being, without regard to, or rather in defiance of, inclination stemming
from the sensual realm, i.e., the causal series to which the self belongs as a
feeling body. This ability to conform to the moral law was named — in a
twist that must have caused Luther to twist in his grave — the "kingdom of
grace," i.e., grace now denoting a domain of nonnatural, moral, or ideal ends
in contrast to the purposeless world of nature. While Leibniz makes a similar
distinction, nature and grace are for him linked theologically by God in the
preestablished harmony, i.e., they are not linked by human agents in the titanic moral act of converting nature to grace but by God who causes all
things to work for good to them that love Him. Thus for Leibniz moral ac-

tion in the world comes about first of all from trust in divine providence in recognition of the human vocation, a stance that is still noticeably "Lutheran" and so "anti-Pelagian." Kant's argument for the "postulate" of freedom as condition for the possibility of moral initiative, on the other hand, recalls verbatim the case Erasmus made against Luther: moral judgments of merit and demerit, reward and punishment, worth and worthlessness depend on the supposition of freedom as physically uncaused initiations in the causal series. Ergo, there must be freedom in the sense Kant specifies. This postulation of freedom in a realm that, by Kant's own account, defies causal explanation, conveniently evades the force of the necessitarianism that Kant's philosophy otherwise assigned to the realm of phenomena. So we have a philosophic *deus ex machina:* noumenal freedom, a mystification of the subject. A new scheme of "grace overcoming nature" (rather than sin) that truly has *nothing* in common with Luther is constructed out of this massive revision of the latter's language.

The early Luther wrote programmatically in his *Commentary on Romans:* "There is not one man who would say that he loves that which is evil and that he hates that which is good . . . [but] everyone calls good what pleases him and evil what displeases him. What Paul means to say, therefore, by his commandment that we test all things and hold fast to that which is good (I Thess. 5:21), is only that we should beware of taking hold of the good through its immediate outward appearance. For here he understands the good to be that of the new man and evil also that of the new man."[27] For Luther as for Augustine before him, the distinction between reality and appearance is *perspectival, not ontological.* That is to say, it is not a dualistic distinction between two realms, phenomenal things-for-us and noumenal things-in-themselves, but between two opposing ways, the carnal and the spiritual, of taking one and the same reality. True good consists in turning by the way of faith to the promised city of God, still invisible but revealed in Christ as Crucified and so grasped *only* in the perspective of the divine gift of repentant faith. More generally, then, for Luther and Augustine human freedom never means the possibility for unmotivated action, a causally indifferent initiation based on pure self-determining preference for X over Y, an objective uncertainty resolved by an act, even of infinite passion. Even God is motivated (as we saw Leibniz thinking above), though in the unique case of the triune Being, self-motivated, unlike created beings whose goods are found outside themselves. Creatures cannot will to will, but only to do (or not do) what already they will, as desire is formed in perception of some good that appears to the finite, embodied, seeking self. In no case can one ever act in a radically unmotivated way. One always acts for some good reason, since the will spontaneously inclines to whatever it perceives as its good, even if that is not really good. Likewise, it involuntarily averts from whatever it perceives as its evil, even if that is not really evil.

The primary issue of spiritual life then is never human sincerity or existential authenticity in an objectively uncertain world, but *what* one perceives to be good and thus *what* one wills, whether these goods are *true* or *false*. Because this is the case, *cognitive* accounts of true and false *goods* are required of revealed theology, and if these are to have purchase in preparing the ground for the preaching of the gospel, a "natural theology" so understood is justified. In the period of the early Enlightenment it was Gottfried Leibniz's singular merit to have taken up this line of argument from Luther and Augustine and advanced it. That is the alternative path to modernity represented by Leibniz: a grounding of both subject and object in critical accounts of the good, even though, as we shall see, this is retroactive reflection of revealed theology, its interpretation of nature in the light of grace.

Imago Dei

A chief burden in what follows is thus to untangle the far-reaching implications of the failure of Leibniz's project, when understood strictly as a pure natural theology. It was a path that should have but could not have been taken on account of the lack of clarity regarding the autonomy of theology as a discipline. What stands between Leibniz and Luther and plays directly into this set of difficulties is the mature thought of Philip Melanchthon and the program he developed from the biblical doctrine of humanity's creation in the image and likeness of God (Gen. 1:26-28). It is worthwhile then to expand our picture here of the crucial theological material borrowed by Leibniz from Melanchthon's tradition. Johann Gerhard's thought (1582-1637) serves as a convenient example.

Writing in the generation before Leibniz's birth, Gerhard was one of the most influential seventeenth-century Lutheran dogmaticians. His teaching on the human being made in the image of God was widely emulated, and it represented, as we shall see, a consensus on theological anthropology extending back to Melanchthon and the Formula of Concord. "Therefore, when Moses says that man was made in the likeness of God, he emphasizes the fact that man not only reflects God in that he has an intellect and will, but that he bears the likeness of God, that is, an intellect and will by which he understands God and wants the things which God wants."[28] The distinction between image as equipment and image as right use of equipment allows Gerhard to explain that the equipment that characterizes the human essence, i.e., the mirror-like mind consisting of intellect and will (and possessing body),[29] cannot be lost in the fall. Rather its relation of love and trust toward God can be lost and in fact is lost (but also restored in Christ).[30] Love and trust in God are thus regarded as *qualities,* i.e., reflections in the finite mirror of the loving being and faithful action of God, while the mind (with its body) is viewed as a created *substance,* i.e., according to this controlling metaphor, the mirror. Thus the mind can lose the reflection of God that it ought to bear without metamorphosis into another kind of being. Instead it becomes filled with false images by turning to others as gods.

To make clear this idea of a mirror-like human nature that, fatefully disoriented, lost its intended reflection of the divine when Adam turned himself with all posterity in the wrong direction, Gerhard speaks about the original state of integrity: "For man was created in such perfect innocence and purity of body and soul that the image of God *would* reflect in him as in a living mirror. . . . As a result of all this man *would* be happy, blessed, and at peace and *would* exult in God his Creator . . . the whole cosmos *should* be truly a school and teacher of the knowledge of God. However, in order that man *should* not be urged to seek the knowledge of God outside of himself and from afar, God set his own image in man himself, so that man, looking at it, *might* know what God was."[31] The subjunctive mood[32] employed by Gerhard here indicates the curious fact that after the fall we know about this paradisaical knowledge of God only by means of a reconstruction based upon the revelation in Scripture. The idea goes back to Luther, who had written in the Smalcald Articles that "inherited sin has caused such a deep, evil corruption of nature that reason does not comprehend it; rather, it must be believed on the basis of the revelation in the Scriptures."[33] Indeed, reflecting, as in fact it now does, all sorts of idols in bewildering array, the human mind cannot even be sure any longer that its nature as mirror is in fact ineradicable. It appears to itself as a confused parade, a kaleidoscope of passing fancies, a house of mirrors.

Thus, while there are partial precedents for the doctrine of the *imago dei* in Platonism's view of the kinship of the soul with the divine and its participation by means of intellection of the eternal ideas, the absence of this Christian doctrine of the image of God among most authors of pagan antiquity was explained by the obscurity brought about by sin subsequent to Adam's fall; creatures no longer know with clarity and certainty that they are intelligent creatures of God, called to live as His representatives on the earth, "happy, blessed, and at peace and exulting in God." Likewise, the seeming self-evidence among Christians of this doctrine of the image of God would be attributed to the light now shed by Christ, in whom we have insight into the human soul renewed in the image of God. Gerhard's Christian culture could have it both ways: for the most part knowledge of human nature is obscured by sin that turns the mirror of created human nature away from its true source to manifold false and confused pictures, even though here and there traces of insight into the underlying mirror emerge, as in the Platonists, since the human essence as mirror is not as such destroyed by sin.

We note here in passing, therefore, a profound ambiguity that, as we shall see, haunted the entire tradition of Protestant Christian philosophy that arose with Melanchthon and came to final flower in Leibniz. As Loemker observed, so long as the Augustinian conviction about the blindness of sin endured, one could hold "to the rationality of the Christian revelation and the incompleteness and unclarity of human reason. . . . Only Christianity, therefore, is the true philosophy, rendering in clear and distinct teachings the rationality of faith."[34] But if now the mirror-mind is to provide first principles of thought, including basic notions of God and soul by which to screen, as it were, contending representations of these first principles, how does it escape from the distortion of sinful egocentrism? If fallenness means that the image of God is turned away from its true source, so that it does not any longer reflect the divine perfections as it ought, then by the same token it would seem to follow that the falsely oriented image of God cannot serve to provide undistorted first principles for human thought. Or, if it can provide them, it must not suffer the radical distortion implied by the doctrine of sin. Beginning with Melanchthon, this difficulty (which had been raised by the notorious doctrine of Flacius that after the fall the human essence itself became evil but was repudiated by the orthodox Lutheran consensus) was simply passed over.[35] What could only be received as a reflection was attributed to the mirror itself; the epistemic dimension of sin (N.B. *not* finitude, which for these authors is capable of the infinite) — so important to Luther's critique of metaphysics — came eventually in this way to be minimized. But, as a modern defender of Flacius protests: "[m]an is not a neutral thinking-machine; his own troubles with God cannot help affecting his judgment."[36]

In any event, Gerhard concluded his discussion of the image of God with one formulation that could have provided Leibniz with a verbatim motto for his entire philosophical vision. The image of God is expressed in the human body, Gerhard writes, "insofar as the body joined with the rational soul bears the image of God and in a sense contains in itself the whole world, and hence man is said to be a microcosm in which the Maker and Archetype of the universe shines."[37] The notion of the whole human being at work on the earth as image of God signals a holistic anthropology (intellect and will together with the desires and perceptions of the mind's own bodily senses); this means that the human *mind,* taken fundamentally as *perceiver* (as mirror *reflecting*), is at once firmly situated in the natural world and only so uniquely, irreplaceably, "personally," related to God, as a knowing perspective on the whole. This is what Leibniz will intend by speaking of the human mind as a substantial, though created, form in his revision of the received doctrine of Saint Thomas.[38] It comes into being contingently, but can never then be destroyed except by a miracle of annihilation. It is immortal, but its blessedness does not consist in immortality as such, nor for that matter can it ever exist without a body of its own. It reflects, but never comprehensively or with utter transparency or with perfect harmony, the divine perfections of power, wisdom, and love. Rays of this divine light shine in the soul and provide the first principles of thought, although for Leibniz knowledge of the world is never acquired without the actual gathering of physical information and experimental discovery of material connections.

Leibniz stands in this tradition of theological anthropology, articulated by Gerhard and descending from Melanchthon. Thus, for example, in the early (1686) *Discourse on Metaphysics,* Leibniz could write that "every substance is like a complete world and like a mirror of God or of the whole universe, which each one expresses in its own way."[39] In the late (1714) *Monadology,* he wrote more precisely "that souls, in general, are living mirrors or images of the universe of creatures, but that minds are also images of the divinity itself, or of the author of nature, capable of knowing the system of the universe, and imitating something of it through their schematic representations, each mind being like a little divinity in its own realm."[40] The affinity is evident,[41] yet what Leibniz *adds* to the inherited theological notions of the created soul as image of God is his trademark "monadology." The "unfortunate metaphor"[42] of "windowless monads"[43] might give the impression that Leibniz pictures the ultimate components of reality as incommunicable atoms in a vacuum of empty space, whose relationships to each other can only be external and coercive.[44] *Nothing could be further from the truth.* It was exactly *against* metaphysical atomism envisioned along such lines by Hobbes ("monads," Leibniz formulates against Hobbes, "are the *true* atoms of nature")[45] that Leibniz came to conceive of monads as organized, goal-directed formations of matter — little systems — ultimately explicable *only* on the level of that which *God* thinks, wills, and enjoys in God's "full and complete notion" of each and every monadic individual constituting the universe. As such fundamental, irreducible complexes, monads are simple in contrast to the collections or aggregates of them that form the phenomenal world,[46] and yet each must "be different from each other."[47] Unlike a medieval realist, for Leibniz there are so many notions in the divine mind as are logically possible, and so many of these individual essences or possibilities that are mutually compossible exist in the best possible world that God actualizes in creation. As mentioned, God has full and complete conceptions of each individual monad, which must each be different in some way from all others, and thus God's foreknowledge is particular, not only general. As such living or at least dynamically organized and unique creatures formed by God, monads "can only begin by creation and end by annihilation."[48] They are "windowless" therefore in that *on this level of immediacy to divine creative action* a monad cannot "be altered or changed internally *by some other creature.*"[49] A "created monad cannot have an internal *physical* influence upon another"; rather "in the ideas of God" each monadic essence or possibility, as it were, *metaphysically* demands "that God take it into account in regulating the others from the beginning of things."[50] Thus God in the metaphysical act of creation thinks-wills each monad to transit from essence to existence in the compossible series of events that composes the universe. God does so in response to the demand of each possibility for existence, yet by a criteria of harmony with all the others, so that the ensuing system of mutual relations is maximally enriched.[51] This mutual "fitness," *metaphysically,* constitutes the best of all worlds.[52] "This interconnection or accommodation of all created things to each other, and each to all the others, brings it about that each simple substance has relations that express all the others, and consequently, that each simple substance is a perpetual, living mirror of the universe."[53] The "windowless" metaphor means only that individuality in this harmony consists in the incorrigible "perspective" of each monad on the universe, as given, or created, by its relation to God,[54] who alone knows any monad's "full and complete concept." No other creature can rob or destroy the soul, though the creature can corrupt itself and yield to moral destruction (on my preferred reading, see chapter 6).

Applied to the soul, monadology teaches that the human mind most fundamentally resembles God by virtue of the simplicity of its act of being, which means for Leibniz as person, not as thing, i.e., as an organized dynamic unity with an integral purpose, not as a mere aggregate of components that can be disassembled and used for other purposes by "brainwashing," technical reason, or social conformism. In the Augustinian triad of memory, cognition, and love on which Leibniz is drawing, "the dignity of every human person is *ontically* founded."[55] A thing is composed of parts and as such is never finally a true unity but only a temporary aggregate, a phenomenon. But a person is person as a genuine, irreducible unity that in the act of remembering its own past knows its own present by the love that integrates the two in view of a projected future. Applied to the soul, metaphysical atomism would not yield a unified personal biography but only a series of states of consciousness, such as a neurologist might map: Macbeth's "tale told by an idiot, full of sound and fury, signifying nothing." Atomism would tell us *that* Julius Caesar crossed the Rubicon but never *why*. Surely, Leibniz reasoned, the human soul or rational mind forms a real unity (= "monad") with its body in its historical journey on the earth, fulfilling its vocation according to the divine plan, analogous to the way an organism or an organized natural system forms a unity (as the proverbial "whole which is greater than the sum of its parts"). Monadology is *systems analysis*.

Monads are the "primary substantial energy" of reality, "substance" understood according to its principle of movement rather than by a list of properties of an underlying, nontemporal thing "I know not what"; monads are the "entelechial" potency out of which, through which, and back to which all movements in the world are foreordained, or, to use the Leibnizian term, "preestablished" by the Trinity Creator, who *tripliciter in se ipso manens innovat omnia*. All systems have this triadic structure, are a "triadically structured circulation" — an onto-logo-ethical wholeness. This *naturally* includes the human mind in its act of memory, knowledge, and love, which is as such not some fantastic imagination out of touch with reality, but *nature* coming to self-awareness. So Erwin Schadel writes in his remarkable meditation on the *Monadology* of Leibniz — an insight into Leibniz's meaning which, he claims, has been obscured by the nihilistic "eclipse of the Trinity" in modern theology.[56] "Leibnizian philosophy is relatively isolated in the midst of the seventeenth century discussion, in which a subjectocentric, rationalistic and anti-trinitarian 'standpoint' was maintained."[57] Nicholas Jolley's research has confirmed in this connection Leibniz's general opposition to Socinianism,[58] but does not as acutely as Schadel bring out the trinitarian basis of the *Monadology*. Schadel rightly brings out the crucial differentiation it entails from Spinoza and even Hegel (to the extent that Hegel followed Spinoza): "Since the divine monad," the Trinity, "*is* actuality in the purest form, it can let other monads be 'beside' itself. That, however, means: The motive for creating is not, as idealism suggests, the all-devouring indigence of hypostasised 'nothing'; it is rather the abundance of the absolute being in itself."[59] Whether God is eternally, or is not, seems indistinguishable: that is the poverty of primary being that motivates God according to post-Kantian idealism. So God creates the world in order Himself to exist, to distinguish God from nothing. This is not the pre-Kantian Trinity who creates the creation from nothing out of the abundance of his eternal act of being as the Father of the Son in the Spirit.

Leibniz's notion of monadological unity cannot make sense then without the thinking-willing and in this way acting Creator God, who is the Trinity of power, wisdom, and love. This is the concept that does the heavy lifting in Leibniz's scheme: without God, he writes, "there would be nothing real in possibles," that is, possibles have the abstract reality they possess as thoughts demanding existence in the eternal mind of God, so that, without God, whose act of creation realizes certain of these possibilities, "not only would nothing exist, but also nothing would be possible."[60] God to whom all things are possible is thus the rational possibility of the creation, in this sense its *ultima ratio*, in that God's mind is the eternal repository of all logical, i.e. noncontradictory notions. But God is also the moral possibility of the creation, since God's antecedent perfection in wisdom and love inclines God to choose not only the best metaphysically, but also something that would be morally better than nothing at all, that is, something that in the end will be worth the terrible cost up to and including the crucifixion of the Son of God. Monadological unity, Leibniz held, is that of a creature being created by God (= conceived, willed, and sustained to its end) in its "series," in its unique place in space and time, and for these reasons of surpassing moral value. God as Creator is actualizing his own full and complete conception of each and every individual on the way to making the best of all possible worlds — just what a loving, just, and wise Creator might be supposed to do, were we thinking ourselves in the image of God.[61]

What Leibniz has to say at *this* juncture about human freedom, divine determination, and the actual evil afflicting the world is of great interest and will occupy us at length later. In the *Monadology,* he seems to think that it suffices "that there will be no good action that is unrewarded, no bad action that goes unpunished, and everything must result in the well-being of the good, that is, of those who are not dissatisfied."[62] Such a rational faith in divine justice manages quite a lot, since it persists in "trust," "duty," and "pure love," laboring to do the will of God — in just this way forming, that is, creating the person worthy of divine felicity, the fulfilled image of God.

For now, the broader point is that the *Monadology* is to be understood in continuity with the theological tradition Leibniz inherited; indeed, it represents an important development of it. It identifies the finite human mind in various arenas of life as genuine partner of the Creator in the progressive unfolding of divine-human governance of the earth; it envisions a grand, human vocation unfolding as the city of God. As Leibniz wrote in a programmatic statement: "only minds are made in his image and are, as it were, of his race or like children of his household, since they alone can serve him freely and act with knowledge in imitation of the divine nature; a single mind is worth a whole world, since it does not merely express the world [as do created things] but also knows it and governs itself after the fashion of God."[63] The *imago dei* doctrine borrowed from theology is axiomatic for Leibniz's philosophy; what is muted but not absent under the form of "natural theology" is the ensuing biblical narrative of humanity's fall into sin, redemption by Christ, and restoration in the Spirit. Patrick Riley has argued that this Lutheran soteriology is in fact exorcised, that only an ethical Christ anticipating Kant remains.[64] I think Leibniz's undoubted reserve can be explained on other grounds, as we shall see.

Why Leibniz Matters

It was Spinoza's thought — "whose aim," writes Matthew Stewart, "was ultimately to destroy the very idea of mind that Leibniz implicitly hoped to defend"[65] — that awoke Leibniz from dogmatic slumbers.[66] Spinoza of course sought to found a new philosophy upon the nature of things as uncovered by the natural light of reason. As influential as was his seminal case for the secularization of philosophy in early modernity, it is deeply complicit in the epoch's foundationalist ambitions[67] in a way that Leibniz's thought arguably is not.[68] Yet to argue the issue on this epistemological level of the authority of faith (theology) versus the authority of reason (philosophy) is sterile; it accomplishes nothing more than the mere exchange of religious fundamentalism for a naturalistic one. If we are right about the leveling effect of postmodern criticisms of epistemology, there is no reason that is not embedded in particular historical traditions and no revelation that is exempt from rational challenge. Concretely, then, Spinoza's critique of biblical revelation[69] did not merely or chiefly call into question for Leibniz what he called the external "motives of credibility" such as the Bible's divine authorship, miracles, and so on, but more searchingly, it challenged the epistemic right long assumed by Christian theology to "take all thoughts captive for

Christ." Spinoza, however, showed the early modern West that one cannot take for granted in philosophy the axial proposition of the human mind as created image of God without smuggling in an unwarranted, anthropomorphic picture of a personal Creator. Thus Spinoza's challenge was radical: he disputed the royal analogy traditionally drawn by the image of God doctrine from Genesis 1:26-28, which, we have noted, formed the very starting point for Leibniz's philosophy. Nobody, Spinoza warned explicitly, "will rightly apprehend what I am trying to say unless he takes great care not to confuse God's power with a king's human power or right"[70] — the chief biblical metaphor of divine action, of course, the very one Leibniz drew upon, indeed *celebrated* at the conclusion of the *Discourse*.[71]

As we shall see in further detail in the next chapter, Spinoza's own, rigorously necessitarian argument from nature as understood by natural light — "things could not have been produced by God in any other way or in any other order than is the case"[72] — not only sounded the death knell over facile doctrines of human capacity. It almost succeeded, as we shall see, in driving Leibniz from Melanchthon's anthropology to Luther's theology. For Luther, if God is free, then we creatures can be freed. But Spinoza's thesis denied not only human freedom but especially divine choice in the act of creation. Stewart cites a letter written right after Leibniz's 1676 encounter with Spinoza, which penetrates to the core issue: "If all possibles were to exist, there would be no need of a reason for existing, and mere possibility would be enough. So there would not be a God, except insofar as he is possible. But a God of the kind in which the pious believe would not be possible, if the opinion of those who believe that all possibles exist were true."[73] Thus Leibniz's famous formulation about God's choice of the best of all worlds originated as an alternative to Spinoza's view about the infinite play of all possibles.[74] In this intention to meet Spinoza's challenge, we cannot today but learn from Leibniz and be instructed by the story of his failure to carry the argument further, that is, all the way to Luther's perspectivalist juxtaposition of the *deus absconditus* and the *deus revelatus,* a strategy in theology that could check, if not defeat, Spinoza at his best. My larger point will be that it is a far more theological Leibniz, indeed a fully trinitarian Leibniz, who, if at all, can survive this final sifting in *Auseinandersetzung* with Spinoza's tradition today.

That will represent an outcome more usable for contemporary theology in sustaining *the narrative paradox of a good though fallen creation — on the way,* if I may so put it, *to the best of all possible worlds.* That *optimism* (more precisely, *meliorism*) would be a desirable outcome, in my view. Here too the young Leibniz set out on his philosophical path on the basis of his theological tradition. The first article of the Formula of Concord — at the cost of a serious conceptual muddle — rightly refused to naturalize sin but instead regarded enslaved nature (Romans 8!) as the very object of redeeming grace. "Therefore, Christ also redeemed human nature as his creation, sanctifies it as his creation, awakens it from the dead, and adorns it in glorious fashion as his creation. But he did not create, assume, redeem, or sanctify original sin. He will also not bring it to life in his elect. He will neither adorn it with glory nor save it. Instead, it will be utterly destroyed in the resurrection."[75] One could therefore say theologically: we are on the way to the best of all worlds of nature redeemed *in Christ, by the Spirit.* And in point of fact, this christological and pneumatological content remains in Leibniz's thought to the end, as we shall see, albeit in reserved form. In what follows, we will have to probe anew the forgotten debates in the background here, as in the Formula. What motivates such an apparently paradoxical affirmation of the goodness of a fallen creation? What kind of distinction is therewith made? How might it be sustained without delusion or cynicism?

There is more recent precedent for this path as well. The young Dietrich Bonhoeffer invoked "Leibniz's *image of the monad*" to explicate the theological paradox of a "net of sociality into which people are woven prior to any will for community." The weaving reflects the "universal person of God [who] does not think of people as isolated individual beings, but in a natural state of communication with other human beings." That divine regard constitutes the goodness of the creation, structured as being-with-and-for-others. Therefore "God does not desire a history of individual human beings, but the history of human *community.* However, God does not want a community that absorbs the individual into itself, but a community of human *beings.*"[76] This latter, two-sided warning reflects the fallenness of creation, warped by the alternating temptations to individual or collective egoism. Yet the warning by its very nature evinces optimism. In the beginning, from the beginning, abiding to the end God wills things otherwise than in fallen egocentrism. Human beings are made for that community in which individuals flourish. Keeping faith in the darkest of times with this theological optimism, Bonhoeffer wrote from his prison cell: "Reason, culture, humanity, tolerance and self-determination, all these concepts which until very recently had served as battle slogans against the Church, against Christianity, against Jesus Christ Himself, had now [under Hitler], suddenly and surprisingly come very near indeed to the Christian standpoint." Referring to Karl Barth, Bonhoeffer noted that this convergence appeared at a time "when the cardinal principles of Christian belief were displayed in their hardest and most uncompromising form, in a form which could give the greatest offence to all reason, culture, humanity and tolerance." Reflecting on his own circle of discussion in the ranks of the resistance, "it was clear that it was not the Church that was seeking the protection and the alliance of those concepts; but on the contrary, it was the concepts that had somehow become homeless and now sought refuge in the Christian sphere, in the shadow of the Christian Church . . . [in] a return to the origin." So Bonhoeffer saw, or perhaps hoped to see, the tale of alienation between modernity and theology resolved: "The children of the Church, who had become independent and gone their own ways, now in the hour of danger returned to their mother."[77] Arguably, it matters immensely whether our story ends in the conciliation at which Bonhoeffer here hints. That is why Leibniz — or rather the instructive story of his failure at conciliation at the outset of our period — matters yet today.

A Counterargument against Leibniz's Relevance

Let us conclude this chapter on the relevance of Leibniz today by considering a counterargument. One of the best critiques of Leibniz's theological entanglements may be found in the German R. W. Meyer's postwar study. Given its historical moment, it contrasts sharply with Bonhoeffer's just-mentioned hope by pronouncing the failure of Leibniz to reconcile faith and science: "mortal man is part of an order of transience; hence he cannot fully survey the beauty of the whole, or the meaning of his fate."[78] Thus Leibniz's attempt by means of the "pre-established harmony" to provide a framework of grace by which to interpret nature is said to fail. What makes Meyer's account interesting, however, is that he charges that it equally fails to be true to the Christian's experience of God. Before reaching this judgment, Meyer provided intriguing historical background in Pietism. His purpose in this was to debunk Leibniz's claim to be "Lutheran"[79] by associating his project with dread at the discoveries of the new science. Meyer used Leibniz's Lutheran Pietist contemporary, August Hermann Francke (1663-1727), to illustrate the cleavage that opens up here: "There is little in common between Francke's and Luther's experience of the religious crisis." Luther sought assurance of grace for the troubled penitent. Francke as an orthodox Lutheran affirmed this doctrine of grace. "But Francke had lost the immediate and personal experience of this love. (Leibniz on the other hand believes that with the aid of 'the light' of science he does possess this experience.)" It was for Francke "a lifeless formula," compensated by "his anxious insistence upon 'the act and reality of faith,'" as if in this way to will faith into existence. It becomes clear that "the religious dilemma becomes identical with an intellectual dilemma unknown to Luther." What was this new dilemma? "When, in his spiritual anguish, Francke turned to the Bible, it occurred to him 'to wonder whether the Scriptures are truly the Word of God. Do not the Turks make this claim on behalf of their Koran, and the Jews on behalf of the Talmud? And who shall say who is right?'"[80] The modern Pietist worries about historical relativism more than a gracious God.

Meyer is certainly right to see Descartes, or according to the present hypothesis, his more brilliant pupil Spinoza, knocking at the door of this "intellectual dilemma": "This combination of rationalist doubt and religious despair is characteristic of 'enlightened' pietism; for it indicates the finality of the effects of the Cartesian revolution. It was not the idea of divine Grace that was now at stake — as it once had been for Luther — but the assurance of man's knowledge of God, the validity of the Bible and of the Christian tradition."[81] The cleavage that Meyer opens up here between *fides qua* and *fides quae* according to the dualism of the spheres is typical of Kantian analysis. While it is difficult to see how assurance of grace can be separated from certain knowledge of God who is gracious, Meyer is in any case undoubtedly correct to point to a shift in context from Luther to Francke, and thus also his contemporary, Leibniz. It is however more than dubious when Meyer concludes this discussion by asserting that this intellectual crisis of enlightened Pietism "was the background to Leibniz's 'proofs of God's existence'; and only his firm conviction that his own 'proofs' were superior to those of any 'enthusiast' preserved him from religious doubt."[82] The evidence here has been forced to fit the hypothesis. We have here suddenly shifted from Meyer's depiction of Francke's nervousness about tottering motives of historical believability to Leibniz's attempt at philosophical theology — a category mistake. In addition, corresponding to his deep debts to the image of God doctrine, for Leibniz pride of place belonged to the ontological proof (to which the cosmological proofs are subordinated in his account). To understand Meyer's misunderstanding of Leibniz on what the so-called proofs of God's existence might accomplish, a brief digression is required here.

Rescher helpfully reconstructed Leibniz's version of the ontological proof as follows: "1) If the Necessary Being is not possible, then no existence is possible. 2) If the Necessary Being is possible, then He exists. 3) Therefore, if the Necessary Being does not exist; then nothing exists. 4) But something exists. 5) Hence the Necessary Being exists."[83] Points 1 and 2 call for brief commentary. Point 1 reflects Leibniz's doctrine that all logically noncontradictory notions exist as eternal possibilities in God's mind. Metaphysically, God's mind is the condition for the possibility of any essence or notion being actualized, so that if God as omniscient mind does not exist, nothing at all is possible. Any worthy notion of God must include this property of omniscience. Socinians who deny divine foreknowledge make God a ridiculous finite artisan, who like creatures depends on data inputs and has not the scope to imagine future contingencies. But existence is possible at all because the omniscient God necessarily knows all possibilities that can be, as well as that series of compossibilities that will take place as the very world that God chooses to enact from among all possible worlds. Point 2 then emerges as the crucial term of the proof. Can we conceive of this necessary God as the free act of perfect power, wisdom, and love in creation, when in fact we who must think are members of this world, as point 4 notes, in which I am writing these words and you are reading them? Is this intelligible *to us?* For this is the same world in which tsunamis drown tens of thousands of the poor already eking out existences on tropical coasts, not to mention killing fields and camps of death. Can we think together power, wisdom, and love as the one Creator God of *this* very world? The difficulty here indicates why *theodicy* emerged for Leibniz as *the* critical question. Maybe God can think God in one act of power, wisdom, and love, but if we with eyes wide open cannot so think God, then God's existence as our Creator is not a possible thought for us. The inconceivability of a God all-good, all-wise, and all-powerful, Leibniz rightly discerned, lies at the root of rising modern atheism.

Günther Frank has devoted an entire monograph under the title *Die Vernunft des Gottesgedankens* to this problem of the "rationality of the thought of God": "The ontological proof according to Leibniz was only strictly demonstrated, if the possibility of God, i.e., the compossibility of the divine predicates could be proved."[84] If the unity of power, wisdom, and love can be thought, Leibniz is suggesting, then this perfection of being would be shown to exist necessarily, as Rescher reconstructed. Recall, however, that the concern here is with the capacity of the finite human mind to recognize God as God, should God reveal Himself, that is to say, should God show Himself as the One who exists in satisfying the requirements of perfect power, wisdom, and love. The basis for this endeavor to articulate the criteria for recognition goes back to Melanchthon's interpretation of the image of God doctrine:[85] God has projected into his creation that which in Himself is the best, wisdom, righteousness, joy, free will, and so forth, in which qualities the human mind naturally participates whenever it thinks at all.[86] The mind can thus ask and answer what kind of thing God is, *qualis sit Deus,* even though who God actually is, the Trinity and savior of human-kind, the *essentia Dei,* is provided only in the gospel revelation. Yet human reason can and should formulate the right question about God, so that rational criticism descended from Plato can expose the folly of idolatry and superstition and require the search for the one, true God. "Natural theology" can tell us what to look for in putative discourse about God. This is what his version of the ontological proof signified to Leibniz. The argument is *modal;* it illuminates how the finite mind is capable of the infinite in asking the right question about the perfect harmony of power, wisdom, and love from its own place and time in this one, real world. The argument is not that existence as a perfection belongs to a necessary being (the straw man Kant demolished when he denied that existence is a predicate). But it is just here that a real difficulty does emerge. The Cartesian version of Anselm's proof (from finitude to the thought of infinity, from imperfection to the thought of perfection) makes acute the problem of the conceivability of God's being as the unity of the perfections.[87] Indeed, as we will momentarily consider, Descartes jettisoned the traditional, trinitarian unity of the perfections of power, wisdom, and love in favor of a unitarian perfection of absolute power. God becomes thinkable for Descartes as the omnipotence that freely (and arbitrarily so far as we can see) determines what shall be rational and what shall be good.

Returning now to Meyer, he is in this light certainly right to argue that Leibniz counts himself among those who "fear . . . to introduce a mechanical cosmology and to do away with final causes" because it "must needs give rise to a belief that the world is not created in accordance with a divine plan, but through blind causes." And he is also correct to point out Leibniz's similarly "scholastic" objections to Cartesianism. He was "unwilling to discard the scholastic notion of substantial forms, refuse[d] to recognize that the nature of bodies lies in extension, because this would be a challenge to the Catholic doctrine of transubstantiation and to the Lutheran doctrine of the Real Presence."[88] There is considerable truth in these statements. Yet it might better have been said that Leibniz's objections to an inanimate world of merely extended things in random motion was theological, rather than the pejorative "scholastic." Nor is the denial of metaphysical mechanism so mindlessly unscientific, as Meyer impugns, in that the *Monadology,* as previously discussed, is thinking of reality organized into unities (not hard bits of irreducible stuff) on a continuum that traverses the cosmos from the smallest subatomic particles to the galaxies. Some of these unities are organized as organisms, and some of these organisms as embodied minds, and these by thinking participate naturally in the deep structures of the universe. Physical mechanism and metaphysical entelechy are, for Leibniz, "different ways of carving up, conceptually, the same facts."[89] In this light, what most indicts Leibniz in Meyer's eyes is how the *imago dei* doctrine, which is the axiom on which monadology turns, challenges Meyer's preferred, Cartesian axiom of the infinite distance of the finite and the infinite. This may be seen in the following account by Meyer of Leibniz's way of relating human minds and the divine Mind: "As the given world of sense experience is infinitely complex, finite man cannot hope ever to conclude his analysis; he cannot, that is, perceive 'facts' as something entirely necessary. But there is no doubt that a full analysis is ideally possible, that God is capable of it, and that there are no fundamental obstacles in man's progress towards it." Because of the *imago dei* relation, human knowledge can progressively approximate the knowledge of the world that God the Creator possesses.[90] As a Kantian, however, Meyer takes the idea of this relation as at best "subjectively" necessary, though objectively uncertain.

In the final analysis, Meyer concludes, Leibniz is relevant as a pre-Kantian failure, i.e., because "the central problem of his philosophical commitment [is] the problem of the validity of the Christian tradition . . . and [that is what] makes it especially relevant to our own way of thinking" — not an idle remark for a German writing in the ashes of Hitlerism. But in what respect is Leibniz's failure instructive? "Looking back we cannot but admit that Leibniz failed," Meyer wrote, "that the new Christian humanism he attempted to establish has been powerless to arrest the gradual decline of traditional Christianity." The loss of theology's audience and subject matter is thus duly noted. "We seem to have arrived at the last stages of a decline which neither theology nor academic philosophies, in spite of renewed efforts and even revolutionary changes, have been able to check." What problem, exactly, has proved insoluble, "so defenseless against the destructive forces of the new ways of thinking, against the new enlightened beliefs? And our answer will be . . . the Christian cosmology."[91] The human mind is a puny ant in the vast and ancient cosmic ocean of matter in motion discovered by the modern natural sciences. "Inherent in the disintegration of the Christian tradition through the new sciences was a new awareness of the limits of human existence,"[92] the Kantian finitude of reason.

So Meyer might have ended, like Kant in the First Critique. But he works out another irony in Leibniz's failure, which is in fact more revealing. By "elevating 'the majesty of Nature,'" Meyer argues, Leibniz actually "advanced in fact the very argument that renders the Christian faith unreal. For to a Christian the limits of man are drawn not by 'the majesty of Nature,' but by God; it is in God that the Christian knows his foundations to lie, and in Him is man's autonomy suspended." Leibniz adopted the new conception of a mechanist universe, even though he wanted to subordinate it to the order of grace. This move permitted the "blind *causae efficientes* [that] intruded itself, as it were, between God and human existence; and God, relegated to a realm distant beyond possible attainment, was no longer experienced as the limit and foundation of all earthly existence. The natural world had lost its sacramental character, because man's science and technology appeared capable of governing it."[93] There is something to this account, but it might more aptly be ascribed to the effects of Kantian dualism than to Leibnizian harmony. In any case, it is at this very point that Meyer's critique of Leibniz takes an important turn.

Meyer argues that Leibniz "placed his 'eternal truths'" into a kind of anonymous realm alongside, or even "prior to God's omnipotence and omniscience." This move, Meyer argues, "actually destroy[s] the condition that makes possible the Christian's experience of God." For "[w]hat agreement is there between the wisdom of man — which perceives the existence of God — and this omnipotence?" he asks. "Between the freedom vouchsafed by the new science and the prayer, 'Thy Will be done'?"[94] In Leibniz God too must do obeisance to Autonomous Reason even though it is attributed to God as His own Mind. Against Leibniz, Meyer pronounces: "Truth, like reality, is a self-determined, that is, arbitrary, creation of God. The Christian nature of Descartes' solution consisted in his making truth depend upon the absolute will of God."[95] Meyer's equation here of a *deus exlex* with true Christian piety as exemplified in Descartes is indeed revealing. Meyer is undoubtedly right to underscore Leibniz's insistence on the divine perfection of wisdom as the precise point at which Leibniz fundamentally diverges from Descartes. "No where in his writings does Leibnitz use such vehement language as in his attack upon the doctrine which makes truth — the quintessence of all common and necessary propositions of reason — depend upon the will of God." The basis for this vehemence, however, is the image of God doctrine deriving from the Melanchthonian tradition: "If we are prepared to do away with the fundamental laws of our thinking, we shall be unable to know any empirical or metaphysical being whatever. For it is absurd to claim the existence of God if we have destroyed all criteria which would enable us to know

Him." Meyer concludes with some semblance of right that for Leibniz "what
is truly absolute is not the will of God, but his reason."[96] Meyer regards this
as a far-reaching change in the traditional conception of God as Creator,
who so "became the hypostatized quintessence of all fundamental principles"; ultimately "an ideal conception of man" that functions regulatively, as
"the aim and result of all our normative reflection, but not its origin and
foundation," the "progressive realization of morality in nature."[97]

In this way Leibniz is none too subtly assimilated to Kant, moving in
the direction of ethical idealism in spite of himself, inevitably so, as his
transcendental illusions are exposed. Meyer's Leibniz is thus converted into
a nineteenth-century progressive: "Leibniz's enlightened view of God is
founded upon an act of human self-assertion in the face of the omnipotence of God. It is a triumph of freedom, and it enables future generations
'to parry the blows of fate.' It issues not in the Christian experience of God,
but in natural philosophy."[98] Precisely so, Meyer concludes, *this* "change
which Leibniz and the subsequent age of Enlightenment have effected is
fundamental; for hereafter the propagation of the Gospel may no longer
rely upon a faith founded in a commonly accepted cosmology."[99] Rather
God too must from now on submit to reason and its scientific discoveries.
"The loss which Christianity has suffered through the establishment of the
scientific cosmology and its 'natural theology' cannot, it seems, be repaired
by anything." The irony of Leibniz's failure is (hints of Nietzsche's
Zarathustra) that this defense of God turned into the funeral of God.
"Once again — and even more urgently than in Leibnitz's time — the question is asked what is to become of the West now that the dream of a Christian humanism is over."[100]

That is to say: Christianity was never a humanism. This was the optimists' dream. Pascal was right religiously as Descartes was right metaphysically, the former to abandon the world for God, the latter to subordinate the
autonomy of reason to the omnipotence of God. Leibniz has confounded
the real issue. In the name of the harmony of nature and grace he presents us
a world where there exists

> nothing alien, unspiritual, meaningless, arbitrary, chaotic or absurd. All is
> governed by the law of sufficient reason; the world is orderly, reasonable,
> spiritual and meaningful. . . . [A]ll differences, all opposition, all limits
> have disappeared — an enchanted world. Nothing in it is strange or arbi-
> trary; there are here no disappointments which would not at the same
> time be ways to reconciliation; there is no possibility of error except

through inertia; there is no sin, only a lack of spirit; nothing absurd or mysterious but is contained and dissolved in something higher — in brief, there is no radical evil which philosophy would have to account for in negative terms. At this highest point of the faith in reason the Theodicy ends.[101]

It is true that radical evil — the evil of a malicious will, the will that knowingly refuses grace — is an indigestible surd in Leibniz's thought, though perhaps (as Barth finally came to think) that is how evil should be represented. In any case, Meyer's critique is highly dialectical. Patently it takes Leibniz's own argumentation in bad faith, since it fails to distinguish between theologies and for that matter between humanisms or rival scientific theories. In fact, Leibniz's theology, descended from Melanchthon, issues in a philosophy of the world according to which the incarnation is not only possible, but from the beginning of creation constitutes the sufficient reason for the plenitude of being as well as the permission of evil. It differs from a theology according to which any world is possible, especially a world without the incarnation, since all other logically possible worlds would prove incompatible with God's being as the perfect harmony of power, wisdom, and love. Meyer's "bad faith" construction in this fashion draws a straight historical line from Leibniz's tacit trinitarianism to the explicit unitarianism of the Wolffians and onto Kantian agnosticism, but the dialectic by which Meyer's tale unfolds denies that ever there was a genuine possibility for Christian humanism as Leibniz represented.

One can now connect both ends of the present critique of Meyer's account: since Meyer cannot fathom the trinitarian God, in whom neither power, nor wisdom, nor love is itself "absolute," but only in harmony with one another, by the same token Meyer cannot fathom the Christian humanism of the incarnation, according to which "one of the Trinity suffered." Meyer was not wrong to suggest that Leibniz's great project failed, nor that it is as a failure that Leibniz is strangely relevant to our times: what is to become of the postmodern West now that it has turned away — not against modernism but with modernism — from Christianity? What is to become of Christianity, now that it no longer may depend on the West? Or, with Bonhoeffer, is reconciliation possible? But Meyer has the reasons leading to these urgent questions exactly backwards. In the end, Leibniz failed because he was unable to proceed explicitly and publicly on the basis of the theses from dogmatic theology he had borrowed; had he done so, the dialectic by which the *meliorism* of his *Theodicy* was transformed into Wolffian opti-

mism, and thence, after Kant, into the nineteenth century's rosy progressivism awaiting deconstruction at the hands of the masters of suspicion, would
have been halted. But there was no church and theology in the seventeenth
century capable of receiving his project, not to mention of sponsoring it: his
vision of a united church, the body of the risen Lord, in a reconciling Europe, fostering Christian humanism on the basis of a generous orthodoxy.
Leibniz wanted this, as Karl Barth grudgingly acknowledged.[102]

"You call yourself an apostolic missionary [of Rome] and we call ourselves evangelicals," Leibniz once wrote in an imaginary dialogue. "Let us return to what is more certain," he pleaded, referring to the common roots in
Augustine. "This is that we must love: God above all things and our neighbor
as ourselves. It is in this that the law consists; it is in this that true active faith
also consists, in conformity to the teaching of Jesus Christ. For he has taught
us this great secret; he has been not only the preceptor but also the redeemer
of mankind. The divinity which dwells in the human nature of Jesus Christ
has established reunion between God and men. There is no salvation at all except in Jesus Christ."[103] Leibniz means: salvation *is* this reunion. Leibniz's was
an exhortation to salvation refused in his own time, and evidently in our time
as well, and it is in this sense also that we can speak of Leibniz's instructive
failure. "I am not, however, of the opinion that we despise antiquity in the
matter of religion; and I also believe that we may say that God has preserved
the truly ecumenical councils hitherto from all error contrary to wholesome
doctrine. For the rest, sectarian prejudice is a strange thing. I have seen people
embrace with ardor an opinion solely because it is contrary to that of a man
of a religion or of a nation which they do not like."[104] This aspiration for ecumenical rapprochement is yet another facet of Leibniz's contemporaneity,[105]
though not one we can further pursue in this study. What we do take up next
builds upon the insight just gained in analyzing Meyer's mistaken account of
Leibniz's pre-Kantian failure, which Meyer would have corrected by Kantian-
izing Leibniz, though at the express cost of Leibniz's abiding concern for the
validity of the Christian tradition. If this is right, what is really at issue is
Spinoza's theological challenge to trinitarianism.

Two AFTER DUALISM

Why Spinoza, Not Kant, Is the True Antagonist of Our Story

Is Christ Necessary? Is God Possible?

Spinoza, not Kant, represents the true antagonist in the story of modern theology's loss of subject matter and of audience. That is to say, the great role apparently played by Kant masks the real story. The knowledge he putatively destroyed to make room for faith was the moral knowledge of God as Judge through the law inscribed upon the human heart (Rom. 2:15) on the basis of which an acknowledgment is due of God as creative Origin worthy of praise and thanksgiving through consideration of His cosmic works (Rom. 1:20; Acts 17). This inchoate "sense of divinity" becomes a historical possibility in the religions, as Wolfhart Pannenberg argued at the beginning of his illustrious theological career. In turn, the philosophical doctrine of the being of perfection inferred from created effects represents a rational critique indigenous to the religions — analogous to the Hebrew prophets' assault on idolatry — which functions ethically to expose the superstitious manipulation and distorting representation that attend the cults.[1] The "natural knowledge" of God thus acquired in philosophical theology ascertains minimal core requirements for any adequate conception of God as origin and norm of what exists. It is this rational/moral knowledge of God as origin and norm of what exists that Kant destroyed; with Kant God becomes a subjectively necessary regulative idea and as such the practical postulate of a transcendent Guarantor of human moral striving. God as origin and humanity as estranged from this origin in guilt and fallen under the powers of sin and death cannot henceforth emerge for theological thought. Christian theology cannot build upon its ruined foundation; it cannot offer a Cyrillian Christ for Augustinian humanity, since neither the need of such a Christ nor the possibility of such a God can any longer appear. So it appears today.

Once the dominant Kantian narrative of the modernization of theology is deconstructed, however, we are able to see what really has transpired. Karl Barth's antifoundationalist[2] doctrine of the advent of God's reign in the act of trinitarian self-revelation accomplished this; it overcame Kant by Kant. John Dillenberger posed the decisive question in this connection in his study of Barth's revisionist "Lutheranism" a generation ago: "Is the transcendence of God to be defined from the side of man's inability to grasp God, or is it grounded upon man's confession of the act of revelation?"[3] Is God's transcendence something we already know when we know that God is ineffable, beyond words, beyond thought? Or is it something we come to know in its own act and event, and so also in words, something available for thought? Is God's transcendence God's inaccessible location, as it were, beyond space and time, or God self-locating into the depths at the cross of Jesus, there in space and time to win back the wayward creation? What if the transcendence we imagine we know about in our state of guilty alienation merely reflects that alienation back outward and projects to infinity the sinful aspiration for escape? What if the unknown God remains, too, just another idol? What if the unknown God is just another strategy for keeping the true God safely away? If transcendence on the other hand is the eternal life of the Trinity into which we are incorporated through faith in Jesus Christ, knowledge of transcendence is "grounded upon man's confession in the act of revelation." The believer comes to ascribe the life that is truly eternal to the love of the Father and the Son in the Spirit. The first possibility of transcendence as professed ignorance or agnosticism but that actually knows how to keep the God of revelation at a safe distance is Kantianism; the second is Kantianism overcome. But, as I have just implied, this latter only awakens us to see what the real problem is.

Barth Overcomes Kant by Kant

"The great gulf that separates the supersensible from appearances completely cuts off the domain of the concept of nature under the one legislation, and the domain of the concept of freedom under the other legislation, from any influence that each (according to its own basic laws) might have had on the other," wrote Kant in the Third Critique. "The concept of freedom determines nothing with regard to our theoretical cognition of nature, just as the concept of nature determines nothing with regard to the practical laws of freedom; and to this extent it is not possible to throw a bridge from one domain to the other" — other than practical endeavor by human beings to make nature become what it ought to be according to moral purpose.[4] Establishing the boundaries for modern culture in this way between the *Naturwissenschaft* and the *Geisteswissenschaften,* Kant's metaphors of the "the great gulf" separating the "domains" of necessity and freedom attained the status of a secular dogma, as it were: one, virtually literal representation of reality by which cultural peace in modernity could be established and enforced. From now on one had to think in terms of these two spheres. Through this scheme all appropriations of the antecedent theology had now to pass.[5] "For if," Kant wrote in a treatise from the same later period of his productivity, "God should really speak to a human being, the latter could still never know that it was God speaking. It is quite impossible for a human being to apprehend the infinite by his senses, distinguish it from sensible beings, and be acquainted with it as such."[6] Theoretical knowledge of God, such as the sciences acquire of nature, is impossible. Natural theology has no cognitive purchase. God is not and cannot be a phenomenon. Even if God should appear in space and time as a phenomenon and speak in an act of revelation, the creature could not recognize this phenomenal voice as God's voice. The claim of revelation is less than the weakest form of argument that can be: transparent appeal to authority in a world full of counterfeit, lacking criteria for discrimination, in service of "priestcraft."

The "great gulf" cannot then be bridged by the human claim to possess revelation, inspiration, vision, or prophecy. All this now succumbs to the fatal charge of "enthusiasm." Whatever a person may privately believe about such things, there is no rational way to ascertain that the claimant in revelation actually speaks on behalf of the infinite God, no way to recognize the signature of the infinite in the realm of finite discourse. Since God is "infinite," any delimitation of God in words and thoughts produces an idol that distorts rather than reflects. Since the infinite cannot for this reason be known by finite minds, it follows that belief in the God who speaks in revelation cannot be justified as a claim to objective knowledge and is thus without rational standing. Any such claim is "enthusiasm" — a pejorative term that originated with the Reformers' rejection of claims to revelation apart from the *verbum externum* of the biblical word.[7]

Leibniz in the *New Essays* could still employ the pejorative in keeping with the Reformers' meaning. This properly, he writes, is "what is meant by

Enthusiasm, which is not adjusted to reason nor to divine revelation, but springs forth only from the imagination of a heated and conceited spirit . . . an immediate revelation, of an illumination without search, of a certainty without proof or investigation. . . . They are sure of these things because they are sure of them, and their opinions are correct because they are firmly fixed in their mind."[8] The problem raises for Leibniz the issue of *criteria* by which to test the spirits. "Thus the issue is that I know how I am to know that God reveals something to me, that this impression in my soul occurs through the Holy Spirit, and that consequently I am bound to follow it. If I do not know this, my confidence, great as it may be, is without the least foundation . . . this must nevertheless before all things be clearly established and proved, that God has revealed this proposition."[9] Leibniz thus thinks that the rational recognition of God as God in revelation is possible because natural theology is capable of providing core criteria for judging putative claims for God. Enthusiasm can thus be defeated. As he wrote in the *New Essays,* "Christian theology, which is the true medicine for souls, is based upon revelation which corresponds to experience; but to make of it a perfect body, we must unite therewith natural theology, which is drawn from the axioms of eternal reason. Is not this principle indeed that veracity is an attribute of God, upon which you acknowledge that the certainty of revelation is based, a maxim taken from natural theology?"[10] Leibniz is reiterating the consensus of his tradition here stemming back to Melanchthon and Luther. Biblical revelation can be received as truth because natural theology already knows that God is truthful, that in God there is and can be no motive to deceive. Biblical revelation can be scrutinized and appropriated, and can stand up to objection on this basis — precisely the critical examination that "enthusiasts" decline.

But in Kant (as in Spinoza before him, as we shall see below) rejection of enthusiasm has turned against the biblical prophecy itself. The traditional criteria do not meet the higher bar that has been raised by epistemology. The theology of the Word of God received in faith through the public tradition of proclamation and confession stemming back to Irenaeus's argumentative differentiation of "Christian theology, true medicine for souls" from claims to new revelations in second-century Gnosticism[11] is now cordoned off into the private ghetto of modern fideism. From now on there can be no rational distinction between orthodoxy and heresy, as a result of which the classical distinction more and more appears to be merely ideological, a pseudo-normative history written by combatants for power from the perspective of the victors.[12] Indeed, Kant penned this shot across the bow in his late brief against the traditional, privileged place of the theological faculty in the university (as had so been organized 250 years earlier by Melanchthon and his followers): even if "God should really speak to a human being, the latter could still never know that it was God speaking." These words were not political hype spoken in the heat of battle. The ideas expressed here were probably first worked out in his late lecture on "ontotheology," where the same argument occurs, although with a different accent.

Kant argued there in fashion more in keeping with the tradition he had inherited: "Even if God were to make an immediate appearance, I would still need rational theology as a presupposition. . . . For how am I to be certain that it is God himself who has appeared to me, or only another powerful being? Thus I have need of a pure idea of the understanding, an idea of a most perfect being, if I am not to be blinded and led astray."[13] Regulated by "transcendental theology's" pure conception of an ideal being that is perfect, reason can and must judge putative revelations. Chiefly this rational judgment excludes, according to Kant, the unworthy picture of "God as a tyrant who makes the punishments of hell eternal or (according to the doctrine of predestination) who unconditionally determines some to blessedness and others to damnation."[14] Here also Kant is in keeping with Leibnizian natural theology, as the neuralgic points of hyper-Augustinianism are identified and repudiated. In Leibniz, as we shall see in detail, this exclusion of second-generation Calvinism or ascetic Jansenism will be made on ontological grounds: because of God's perfection in being, God cannot be conceived of as needy, greedy, or grudging, but rather must be thought of as generous abundance. One really has to *work* at being excluded from the company of God whose metaphysical perfection is manifest in the vast diversity of the creation, whose moral perfection is demonstrated in the loving incarnation of the Word and the wisdom by which God undertakes the creature's own folly and waywardness and makes it His own in order to overcome it and achieve reconciliation.

In Kant's appropriation and reworking of the natural theology tradition in the light of his critical philosophy, however, the impossibility of this tyrannous deity is secured on epistemological, not ontological, grounds. Kant does not deny that God could really speak to a human being with the threat of eternal loss, or for the purpose of hardening the heart; to do so would snare him into making cognitive claims that transgress the limits of reason.[15] The critical philosophy rather patrols boundaries: what beings are in and for themselves transcends the limits of reason whose concepts function only to synthesize the manifold of sensory experience, which yields in turn the only

possible objects of knowledge. What the Tribunal of Reason does know in ad-
ministering this admission test to the republic of minds is the analytical truth
that the infinite cannot be known by finite minds, *finitum non capax infiniti*.
Kant accordingly construes the claim of revelation epistemologically as the
bogus argument from authority appearing in the rigorous field of scientific
inquiry, a question-begging theory of Divine Command in ethics, which
backs itself politically by the play of irrational power, with fearsome but in
truth loathsome claims of eternal punishment for disbelief. This Kant lam-
bastes as "priestcraft," irrational manipulation of the fears and hopes of the
ignorant and unenlightened that must be unmasked as sheer hypocrisy:
"even the clergyman, no matter how highly he commends the happiness of
the world to come, actually perceives nothing of it and hopes fervently that
the doctor can keep him in this vale of tears a while longer."[16] Just so, preachers pounding Bibles and threatening hell fires for those who do not submit
blindly to their cosmic Tyrant are excluded from the republic of minds. So
culture is made safe by and for the free play of reason by the patrolling of a
certain boundary: *finitum non capax infiniti*.

Now we may ask, in all fairness: Is this how the claimants of biblical revelation think of themselves? Is it merely or even chiefly a claim of authority,
a demand to submit that a rational, Kantian mind cannot recognize as divine? To the extent that Karl Barth "everywhere presupposed: 1) the validity
of Kant's epistemology (where it touched upon the knowledge of empirical
reality), and 2) the success of Kant's critique of metaphysics,"[17] it could so
appear from Barth's initial formulations of the doctrine of the Trinity as the
form of revelation: "God reveals Himself as the Lord."[18] Let us look and see.

Barth analyzed this terse statement in its three components: "*God* reveals Himself. He reveals Himself *through Himself*. He reveals *Himself*. If we
really want to understand revelation in terms of its subject, i.e. God, then the
first thing we have to realize is that this subject, God, the Revealer is identical
with His act in revelation, and also with its effect. The question of 'Who God
is in His revelation' governs the questions, 'What is He doing?' and 'What
does he effect?'"[19] Indeed, the latter two questions are rightly understood as
new iterations of the first.[20] The self-same subject "repeats"[21] itself in these
three ways of subject, object, and instrument in the act of self-revelation,
thus remaining subject even as object and instrument; since God is true in
this self-revelation, these three repetitions of God should be understood to
reflect three eternal modes of God's being. "The statement that God is One
in three ways of being, Father, Son and Holy Ghost, means, therefore, that
the one God, i.e. the one Lord, the one personal God, is what He is not just in

one mode but — we appeal in support simply to the result of our analysis of the biblical concept of revelation — in the mode of the Father, in the mode of the Son, and in the mode of the Holy Ghost."[22] God speaks. God is spoken. God is heard. God acts. God is acted upon. God is the effect. When this eternal event is repeated in time, God becomes our Lord and we become God's people. Thus the reign of God dawns on the earth. "It is thus that He is the Lord, i.e., the Thou who meets man's I and unites Himself to this I as the indissoluble Subject and thereby and therein reveals Himself to him as his God."[23]

The rhetoric of "revelation" is epistemic; it could hardly be otherwise in Kantian culture with its preoccupations over the justification of claims to knowledge. But Barth could equally well have made his point by speaking of God's self-presentation or God's self-giving, and he passes over into such ontological rhetoric easily. Even though the form of language is epistemic, the concern is with the royal claim of the biblical God upon His lost and perishing creature, the royal pardon of God spoken to the rebel and deserter, the royal promise of God eliciting and sustaining faith in the dawning Reign. Barth is describing the coming of the reign of God by the Word and the Spirit, in faith and new obedience, as opposed then to the present visible reality of what is in fact a fallen creation, where all appears distorted by the egocentrism of the sinner, who prefers the evidence of her own senses to the gracious promise of God. The epistemic concern in the rhetoric of revelation, then, is to underscore the attendant transformation of human perception and understanding in the very event of meeting the one, true, eternal, indissoluble Subject, who in mercy addresses the human as an I to a Thou. Faith is that response in turn that an I makes to a Thou in committing to their promised future — while unbelief is that response to this I that disregards and distances the claim for their future by regarding the promising I as an It, a thing, a fraud or imposter, not a Thou, i.e., in Kant's words, as "a terrifying picture of fantasy, and a superstitious object of ceremonial adoration and hypocritical high praise."[24] Just so, *faith* in Barth's sense is not dumb and blind; it does not remain the *old* self that might submit to putative revelation on the mere assertion of authority by the demand of a higher power. Faith discerns this divine Thou. Faith is the *new* "I" of trust and obedience called into being by the inclusive generosity of the divine Thou that has spoken and promised a future together — as indeed for Barth in *Church Dogmatics* I/1 faith is *gift*, God *heard*, indeed God Himself in that third iteration of divine being, the *Holy Spirit*. As knower, this *new* human subject of faith *knows* the One in whom it believes and can *give an account* of the hope that

is in it. Thus while the language is epistemic, the concern is not epistemological in the sense of justifying a human knowledge claim by reducing it to
the universal foundations of reason. Indeed, on this account such putative
foundations could only *seem* to be universal in the eyes of the old egocentric
subject who in reality sees and thinks crookedly *most of all* when confidently
laying claim to universals. With this line of argument Barth initiates in theology the postmodern criticism of criticism.

Christian theology is forever in Barth's debt for "putting the doctrine of
the Trinity at the head of all dogmatics,"[25] since this "is the point where the
basic decision is made whether what is in every respect the very important
term 'God' is used in Church proclamation in a manner appropriate to the
object which is also its norm. The doctrine of the Trinity is what basically
distinguishes the Christian doctrine of God as Christian."[26] The salient
point for our investigation, however, is that in refusing to take the word
"God" for granted, Barth has cut the ground out from under the critical,
epistemological assumption that the word "God," having no cognitive content of its own, works as a general appeal to authority or command to be-
have. Instead, Barth has established the fact that the word "God," as rendered
in the biblical tradition, comes on the scene as an event of personal address,
in a meeting of minds, as a merciful claim and promised future, which as
such works to *divide* faith and unbelief. It is then an inherently *controversial*
word. It requires a division of the house. It assembles the church from out of
the world. It generates theology as a new discipline for minds made new. As
the word "God" does not pretend to ground the universal account of common human experience, neither is it subject to criticism along these lines.
Barth's theology sovereignly declines to sit for matriculation exams along
these lines. It will instead administer its own test — of the spirits, by its own
standard, Holy Scripture's narrative testimony to the advent of the promise
of God and its history from faith for faith. It will take account of universal
human experience, of course, yet not as a standard by which to judge the adequacy of its own discourse but rather as material to be judged. In this way,
as mentioned, Barth anticipates the incisive current critiques of Enlightened
Reason's universalistic pretensions, just as he recalls the critiques of reason
in Augustine and Luther before him.

There are, needless to say, difficulties. From theological liberalism the
obvious objection is that Barth has returned theology to barbarism, abandoning the theological version of the epistemological project to ground talk
of God in a universal account of common human experience. That is hardly
the present objection. Classical natural theology developing in Protestant-

ism from Melanchthon up to and including Leibniz, as we shall see, presupposes revealed theology and works to uncover the rational capacity of the human person, made in God's image, to recognize Jesus Christ as the revelation of God. For this tradition, the human mind as image of God means that in appropriately creaturely ways *finitum capax infiniti*. That capacity of the human mind to recognize God as God, should God speak, is something quite different from "grounding" transculturally all peoples in some lowest common denominator and calling *that* "god." Rather, the present unease has to do with the one-sidedly "Western" way[27] Barth executes his move to trinitarianism.[28] His basic and very problematic claim is that "Godhead in the Bible means freedom, ontic and noetic autonomy."[29] Barth in this way virtually eliminates the traditional concept of divine nature as the sum of *all* perfections, the triadic *harmony* of wisdom, love, and power. He rather equates the Lordship of God as the "indissoluble Subject," the self-asserting divine "I," with "what the vocabulary of the early Church calls the essence of God, the *deitas* or *divinitas*, the divine *ousia, essentia, natura* or *substantia*."[30] This move executes, needless to say, a massive revision of the tradition,[31] which scholars denote as Barth's "ontology of act."

Things could have been otherwise for the One who is uniquely free and autonomous. In point of fact, however, God is this one eternal and free Subject *who has decided* in the primal act of grace to grant existence to other, lesser selves in order that He may commune with them. God *eternally passes* from other possibilities to *exist* in this primal act of his being, this free decision to be the God of grace, that is, to be also God *for others*. As such he is the one and only Lord in this singular act of the divine nature, a nature that, as we have heard, repeats itself then among creatures in actions as giver, gift, and reception expressing one, indivisible act of outreaching love. The question Barth is answering in these new formulations of the doctrine of God, in Bruce McCormack's words, runs: "How is it possible for God to become, to enter fully into time as One who is subjected to the limitations of human life in this world, without undergoing any essential (i.e., ontological) change?" The answer Barth gives is that "what God is essentially is itself constituted by an eternal act of Self-determination for becoming incarnate in time."[32] In his probing analysis of Barth's ontology of act, McCormack pushes the logic involved here further than Barth himself did or was willing to do. McCormack calls for a critical correction of any remnants of "free-floating talk of the 'eternal Son' as a mythological abstraction,"[33] as if God is to be imagined as "triune in and for himself, independent of his eternal will to be revealed."[34] To imagine this would be "speculation," according to McCormack, that is, thinking about God that is undetermined by the Word incarnate as a strictly revealed theology ought to think. Rather, we ought to draw the more radical ontological inference: "The decision for the covenant of grace is the ground of God's triunity and, therefore, of the eternal generation of the Son and of the eternal procession of the Holy Spirit from the Father and the Son."[35] McCormack's case for correcting Barth this way is persuasive, *given* Barth's ontology of act, and *given* a Western understanding of the doctrine of the Trinity in which the unity of God's being governs the conception of the triad of persons. In McCormack's endeavor to extend Barth's revolutionary notion of God as event, the unity of God's being in the free decision of grace eternally grounds the generation of the Son and spiration of the Spirit.

Never one to evade a problem, Barth expressly appropriates and articulates the Western way. What "we today call the 'personality' of God belongs to the one unique essence of God which the doctrine of the Trinity does not seek to triple but rather to recognize in its simplicity."[36] God, i.e., the divine nature as freedom, really exists as the one free "Lord," the indissoluble Subject, Person. Correspondingly, Barth expresses horror at the ("Eastern") notion that "there are three personalities in God. This would be the worst and most extreme expression of tritheism."[37] The difficulty, of course, is that this latter (allowing for Barth's polemic exaggeration) is precisely how things appear in the New Testament, which speaks of Jesus, his Father, and their Spirit; it is also how to this day the Eastern church understands the Trinity. Here "the incarnate Logos and the Holy Spirit are first met and experienced as *divine agents of salvation,* and only then are discovered to be essentially one God."[38] In this Eastern approach to the doctrine of the Trinity, moreover, the eternal fellowship in love of the Father and the Son by the Spirit constitutes the freedom of God with respect to creation — an insight Robert Jenson rightly traces to Irenaeus, whom he cites: "For always (i.e., prior to all emanations) there are for [God] the Word and Wisdom, the Son and the Spirit, by whom and in whom he freely and spontaneously does all." The eternal bond of the three as one in love is the immanent ground of the Creator's freedom with respect to any possible creation; as antecedently fulfilled in His own eternal life of love, the Trinity is not coerced into creation to find a beloved. Following this seminal reasoning of Irenaeus, Jenson is a theologian by no means unsympathetic to McCormack's concern. In Jenson's own words, that concern is "to free trinitarian doctrine from captivity to antecedent interpretation of deity as timelessness."[39] Yet Jenson continues to speak of the distinction between the immanent and economic Trinity as a "rule": "it must be that God 'in himself' could have been the same God he is, and so triune, had there been no creation, or no saving of fallen creation, and so also not the trinitarian history there has been."[40] It was on account of this "rule" that Barth too undoubtedly failed to correct himself, as McCormack now urges, even though McCormack's reasoning is more consistent with a protological "ontology of the act." (Jenson's position will be further discussed in the latter chapters of this book.)

Barth's dismay at alleged "tritheism" reflects not only the preference in Western trinitarian doctrine to proceed from the unity of God instead of from the interactions of the three persons whom we meet in the gospel narrative; it is also bound up with the Kantian interpretation of the infinity of God with which Barth cunningly made common cause.[41] To the extent that *religious*, i.e., *idolatrous* claims that objectify God in the effort to put Him at human disposal are debunked by the Tribunal of Reason, *All hail!* Kant is recognized by Barth and even praised for demarcating a philosophy based on reason alone from "the notion of a revealed positive religion . . . , the authority of the Bible when this authority is conceived as a merely historical one, and . . . the merely historically conceived instance of a Word of God made flesh confronting man."[42] Even Christianity as a religion, even Jesus Christ taken and recommended as a brute fact of history, succumbs to this critique of reason if it foolishly plays on this field. Going all the way back to Plato, for Barth God speaks also in this rational-critical shattering of the idols, under the mask of the Tribunal of Reason as well. In distinction from Christianity as religion and Christ as idol, Barth writes of a hitherto untried possibility of theology in response to Kant. He suggests that according to the critique of religion within the limits of reason alone, "only one side of the problem, namely religion as a human function, is seen."[43] Looking at the other side of the problem — namely, of faith as a function of God's revelation — Barth finds in Kant the barest hint at this latter possibility for postcritical theology. It is a possibility given with a "deeply serious segregation of the matters in which the two faculties were to be considered competent." Nonetheless, Kant, Barth says, "finds himself after all, unexpectedly in a position to allocate to a biblical theology its place besides philosophy."[44] That space allocated to biblical theology, citing Kant's own words, "proves that God exists by means of the fact that he has spoken in the Bible."[45] With these sneering words Kant in fact allowed a place at the university's table for official religion and traditional authority,[46] although securely cordoned off from the field of reason. Thus ghettoized, Barth discovered the other possibility for theology after Kant. "Revelation in the Bible means the self-unveiling, imparted to men, of the God who by nature cannot be unveiled to men."[47] What does this paradoxical statement of Barth mean? God will not become the idol of the Ineffable in the hands of the philosophers, the Unknown God at their disposal to slash and attack the prayers of others. It is no less idolatry to be silent when God's Word sounds than to speak when God is silent. Theology arises as obedient *hearing* of faith, in the community of the Spirit, where Christ the Crucified is portrayed before human eyes, a folly to Greeks but the power and wisdom of God at work to save through faith.

Thus Barth immediately tell us: "self-unveiling means that God does what men themselves cannot do in any sense or in any way: He makes Himself present, known and significant to them as God . . . makes Himself the object of human contemplation, human experience, human thought and human speech."[48] The gratuity of grace depends on this paradox of the unknown God condescending to nature: "inscrutability, hiddenness, is of the very essence of Him who is called God in the Bible. As Creator, this God is different from the world, i.e. as the One He is, He does not belong to the sphere of what man as a creature can know directly . . . this God by His grace, i.e., by His self-unveiling says to everyone to whom it is imparted that of himself he could not do what is there done to him and for him."[49] In other words, the paradoxical distinction between the essentially veiled God in sovereign freedom and the unveiled God in the loving act of self-revelation is the basis on which the latter "work is grace, a free divine decision."[50] The gratuity of grace presupposes the freedom of the Giver: "God's presence is always God's decision to be present. The divine Word is the divine speaking. The divine gift is the divine giving. God's self-unveiling remains an act of sovereign divine freedom."[51] Barth expressly affirms in this context what I have termed a "paradox" here: "God is always a mystery."[52] The mystery points to the One who is truly and eternally Subject of His own existence in and for Himself and yet becomes the Subject also of our existence by an unnecessary and so free self-determination of merciful love.

In the light of the foregoing discussion, we may see how right McCormack is to state about Barth: "All of his efforts in theology may be considered, from one point of view, as an attempt to overcome Kant by means of Kant; not retreating behind him or seeking to go around him, but going through him."[53] On the one hand, Kant's stricture against the human possibility of a claim to possess revelation is taken up and affirmed: 'inscrutability, hiddenness, is of the very essence of Him who is called God in the Bible.' Therefore, on the other hand, *revelation* can come only from above, from the paradoxical or mysterious self-unveiling of the veiled. In revelation as this event, God speaks as subject of His own discourse and is heard only as such. God's Word is *God* spoken: it cannot then be taken into possession as an object of human cognition apart from the God who speaks and the God who is heard. There is no Word without the Spirit, no Spirit without the Word, and neither of these without the font of the deity who issues them, the eternal Father. "In a bridging of the gulf (from God's side) between divine and human comprehensibility," Barth writes in terms formally, if not materially, reminiscent of Kant, "it comes to pass that in the sphere and within the limits of human comprehensibility there is a true knowledge of God's essence generally and hence also of the triunity."[54]

It was the great strength of Barth's theology to have taken Kant's criticism of idolatrous claims to speak God more seriously than did Kant himself. The impossibility of human speech about God, for Barth, does not lie in the mere transgression of the limits of reason. Speaking about God is, in general, that idolatrous violation of the freedom of God that Barth denominates as "religion," the pious attempt to be god without God, in defiance of grace. With this move to a strong notion of sin afflicting especially religious claims to knowledge of God, Barth also overcomes in principle the epistemological snare: "Revelation is not made real and true by anything else, whether in itself or for us."[55] That unmediated reality indicates the end of "religion" and the beginning of "faith." We may speak of God only in consequence of the event of God's speech to us, i.e., in faith that cannot and does not justify itself *coram hominibus* since it exists as God heard, as pure gift. We can speak only by keeping faith with this miracle of God spoken and God heard, not by faithlessly seeking somehow to ground it in the universal experience or universal principles of reason we think to possess with all other minds. Only in the state of such faith does human knowledge of God transpire that corresponds to the truth of the unnecessary God, the God who relates to us always, essentially by grace (not law, not need, not necessity). It is the one, free, divine, and sovereign Subject in each of these three modes, therefore also, *especially in the third mode evoking the human response of faith,* which can never understand itself as a natural human possibility, taking into possession the object of its knowledge, for purposes of its own. That exactly is what is *never* possible in true speech of God. That this in fact occurs is precisely the sign of *false* speech about God: religion, idolatry, a merely historical Jesus as our countercultural hero and guru no less than a bourgeois paragon of virtue.

Barth is professedly following Luther throughout *Church Dogmatics* I/1.[56] "As the hearers are gathered into the Spirit's view," Christine Helmer has said of Luther, "they learn to speak about what they have been shown."[57]

From another perspective, Helmer writes: "the Father's speech structures the way in which the other two persons are related to him . . . preaching the Son as his sermon that is heard by the Spirit."[58] The Father speaks, the Son is spoken, the Spirit hears[59] — such is Luther's aural understanding of Barth's more formal and visual "elements of unveiling, veiling and impartation, or form, freedom and historicity, or Easter, Good Friday and Pentecost, or Son, Father and Spirit."[60] Yet herein lies a peculiarity alluded to above. Throughout this section Barth repeatedly takes up not only Luther's theology of the Word and critique of reason but also agreeable elements of his trinitarian theology, which he then, however, sets off in polemical contrast to "the tritheistic weakness of Melanchthon's concept of person."[61] This is exceedingly curious, since in general Luther is responsible, as Helmer has shown, for a dramatic new amplification of the narrative concept of "person" as agent, especially in respect to the Trinity — which Barth here polemically attributes to Melanchthon.

We do not have to search far to find the reason for Barth's one-sided appropriation of Luther's trinitarian teaching. It lies in the aforementioned, one-sided Western approach to the dogma. The reason for Barth's hostility to the tri-personal, as opposed to tri-modal, account of trinitarian personhood has to do with his root idea, taken over from (Fichtean?) idealism,[62] that God as Lord, as indissoluble Subject, exists in the singular act of free decision to be our God, the God of grace. From this perspective, tripersonalism *can only appear* as a recrudescence of paganism: "It would be pagan mythology to present the work of God in the form of a dramatic entry and exit of now one and now another of the divine persons, of the surging up and down of half or totally individualized powers or forms or ideas, of a shifting co-existence and competition of the three hypostases."[63] Yet, and herein lies the genuine problem as already alluded, this "mythology" prima facie is precisely what the gospel narrative confronts us with: the coming of the Son into our world in obedience to His Father, only to be abandoned by His Father at Golgotha, then His vindication in the Spirit on the third day and return to heaven, there to reign in His Father's name until He comes again. In this narrative action, Jesus does not gaze at his navel when He prays. In this narrative, neither the Father nor the Spirit is incarnate. Only one of the Trinity suffers. In short, in the narrative we in fact meet three "persons" over against one another as patients/agents, suffering and working as individuals in harmony, who may or may not then also prove to be three "modes of one being." Barth, of course, can also speak this narrative way, indeed elegantly. But that indicates a problem in general in Barth's theology.

For Barth such is and can only be a *way of speaking,* not a *way of being.* The gospel narrative seems to offer us representations that must after all be conceptually penetrated to be understood, rather than taken as divine ways of personal-social being into which we are incorporated — and in this rather different way "understood."

One must wonder as well about the so-called ontology of act, i.e., that God by nature is the singularly free Subject who in fact exists in the primal, free decision to love us. Barth's motive in this doctrine is clear and something worthy of great appreciation. It renders the notion of God's being as event, as personal, as spiritual, like a life, not like stuff. But a difficulty that arises with it is that this move seems to render the gospel tautological, "a self-enclosed circle,"[64] repeating itself in time. If God is God in eternally deciding to be our God by grace, what else *could* God be in His self-revelation? A protologically conceived act of freedom seems to rob God of temporal freedom. Are there no genuine alternatives in the temporal life of the incarnate Son that God has in fact determined for Himself? Does God decide nothing in time, where and when the Spirit blows as He wills? Is the hardening of wicked Pharaoh's heart a mere appearance that in the end turns out to be grace for Pharaoh too? Can the wrath of God be assimilated to grace as its inverse aspect? Is it not rather annihilating? Along the same lines, we might wonder whether it is right to equate the divine nature exclusively with freedom of self-determination, as Barth does, *without coequal attention to wisdom and love.* Does Barth's equation here reflect a vestige of nominalism's *deus exlex?* If so, can it really overcome the threat of dualism in the depiction of God? Barth famously and rightly inveighed against Luther's sometimes excessive depictions of the *deus absconditus* as the One who is not bound by His Word. But is not any conception of God's Word susceptible to the same objection that does not understand wisdom and love as integral to divine nature but instead thinks of these as freely, albeit eternally, chosen possibilities? These are questions we will pursue further in the next chapter. For now, the point is that Barth's overcoming of Kant by Kant reveals another, deeper problem. Why should we attribute freedom to God at all? Why should "free choice" be divine? This is the problem of Spinoza.

The Problem of "Ontotheology"

Barth's achievement comes down to a simple but drastic move. He takes his point of departure from "the fact that the Christian Church ventures to talk of God, or to regard what it says as talk about God."[65] This remains a fact in the world whether or not it is admitted by the Tribunal of Reason or grounded epistemologically, no matter whether it proves an idol, not an icon. Barth seems to burn all bridges. It is only within this arena that the question arises whether the talk about God is true. Just so, it is not the question whether the talk about God qualifies for admission to the republic of minds, but whether it is true to "a prior Word of God Himself spoken to the Church which speaks about God."[66] This faithfulness of confession to revelation then is the business of theology. Theology is church dogmatics, testing the fidelity of church discourse to revelation. Yet this is not, under Barth's presuppositions, the abandonment of the world to the devil nor the flight into the ghetto that it seemed to Stout, and more broadly, to theological liberalism. "Faith does not stand only, or even in the first and most important sense, in conflict with unbelief. It stands in conflict with itself, i.e., with a form or forms of faith" that express unbelief.[67] *In every Christian, the unbelieving world enters the church.* It is within the church itself that the true line of battle is drawn in the world and on behalf of the world that is only apparently outside it. Here in church dogmatics the real battle for the future of all humanity is being waged, because here the dialectic of the justification of the godless by grace is sustained for the sake of the uncomprehending world.

To sustain this dialectic, the justifying word of revelation is and must ever be understood as an *extrinsic, forensic* word. "The immediate presence of God," McCormack summarizes, "is never the secure possession of the human subject. Human beings do not 'have' God; at best, they are 'had' by Him."[68] In this sense and for this reason, McCormack is right to insist that Barth remained a "dialectical" theologian who "conceived of the relation of God to the world in terms of a fundamental *diastasis* (i.e. a relation in which the two members stand over against each other with no possibility of a synthesis into a higher form of being)."[69] Barth has just so out-Kanted Kant in denying that God is possessed in theological knowledge, in showing how God's reign rather seizes us when we know God as Lord, so that we are new beings in faith, yet new as old beings living new lives on behalf of others. In the process, however, Barth has also disowned Luther and rather drawn closer to Melanchthon (as we shall see in detail in chapter 3).[70]

I differ from Barth on this final point, though stating the difference without falling into a trap is tricky. I hold to Luther's *est*,[71] which Barth finally rejected in favor of Zwingli's *significat,* for fear of an undialectical confusion of divine and human natures.[72] No doubt, in some versions of *Wort Gottes und Luthers Lehre*, it is or has been so poorly understood and triumphalistically claimed. McCormack provides the unsavory example of F. Gogarten in the 1920s identifying faith and history in singing alleluias at the providential sending of *der Fuehrer*. Let me, however, introduce as a counterpoint to the Lutheran Gogarten the Lutheran Bonhoeffer. Bonhoeffer famously described the opposite danger in Kantian culture of "thinking in terms of two spheres":

> The division of the total reality into a sacred and profane sphere, a Christian and a secular sphere, creates the possibility of existence in a single one of these spheres, a spiritual existence which has no part in secular existence, and a secular existence which can claim autonomy for itself and can exercise this right of autonomy in dealings with the spiritual sphere. The monk and the 19th century Protestant secularist typify these two possibilities . . . the modern age is characterized by an ever increasing independence of the secular in its relation with the spiritual . . . [even though] it is quite certain that [thinking in terms of two spheres] is in profound contradiction to the thought of the Bible and to the thought of the Reformation, which think of one world created and redeemed in Jesus Christ.[73]

Karl Barth, dialectical theologian that he is, would hardly disagree. The issue therefore is subtler than Barth's polemic often indicates, given his own ample use of the rhetoric of union (as a way of speaking, though not of being). I will attend to this problem in chapter 3 when we come to parsing out in some measure of real clarity the christological differences between Luther and Melanchthon that belie their official agreement on "forensic" justification.

For the present I can get at the problem by suggesting that (1) it is the fear of that symbol of pantheism, Spinoza (who never makes an appearance in the *Church Dogmatics*!), that finally keeps Barth in philosophical alliance with Kant and so hinders him from seeing any other possibility in Luther's *est* than theopanism; and that (2) Barth proceeds under the tacit Kantian assumption that idolatrous language in the world may be left to fall to the rational critique of anthropomorphism that Kant executes in his "ontotheology." In other words, Barth is thinking that Kantian secularism does the work of suppressing idolatrous claims in the wider culture, while in the church it is Luther's *est* that opens the door to them. I am not so sanguine about such confidence being placed in salutary acids of criticism at work in Euro-American culture, for, as I have argued, these touted criticisms are themselves as guilty of *hybris* as any traditional form of thinking. This is especially clear when the prohibition of images is interpreted by the prohibi-

tion of misusing the name of God, i.e., that idolatry occurs as much in silence when confession is demanded as in false or inadequate representation.
For this reason, as will become evident, I am not persuaded by Barth's critique of Luther's *est* (as a discourse that applies to Christ alone, *Hic est unus
homo, cui nullus est similes*).[74]

Does that *est*, affirming that in the case of this one person *finitum capax
infiniti* holds unrestrictedly, make the present proposal for a way of theology
proceeding from Luther through Leibniz "ontotheological"? I find contemporary discussion of "ontotheology" to be a confused mélange of ideas. As
significant a thinker in this area as Merold Westphal contends that Spinoza,
Leibniz, and Hegel are all of an ontotheological piece; he goes so far as to say
with Heidegger that it "is Leibniz [with his principle of sufficient reason]
who hatches this egg [though] it has been incubating since Plato and Aristotle,"[75] i.e., the ontotheological goal of having the world at our disposal
through metaphysics as a technique for explaining from highest causes, with
God taken ontotheologically as the *ultima ratio* — and, we made add, with
Luther's *est* in mind, Christ the God-man at hand in our doctrinal toolbox.
No doubt such is Heidegger's idea.[76] But the difficulties with this broad
stroke are several. On the one hand, there is no more acute critique of idolatrous anthropomorphism in theology than Spinoza. On the other hand, the
principle of sufficient reason has to do theologically for Leibniz with refusing the voluntarist *deus exlex* of nominalism (though not a Lutheran *deus
supra legem*). Additionally: how anyone gets Heidegger's spin on onto-
theology as covert titanism out of the reticent, if not agnostic, Kant is beyond me. For Kant the notion of ontotheology is rather of a piece with his
own proposal for "transcendental theology," i.e., to dispel the "consequences
of anthropomorphism."[77] I do not know whether the neologism "onto-
theology" originates with Kant, but he uses it already in his *Lectures on Philosophical Theology*, which are dated to 1781 or later.[78] To clear up the confusion created by Heidegger's oracular obiter dictum, repeated ad infinitum by
uncomprehending disciples, let us then briefly lay out what Kant meant by
"ontotheology" and then consider Heidegger's spin on it.

"Human reason has need of an idea of highest perfection, to serve it as a
standard according to which it can make determinations,"[79] and in
"ontotheology we consider God as the highest being, or at least we make this
concept our foundation."[80] This concept is the familiar idea of the necessary
being from the traditional "ontological" proof of God's existence. "Since the
highest being is also the original being from which the essence of all things is
derived, it follows that the order, beauty, harmony and unity which are met

within things are not always contingent, but inhere necessarily in their essence." The Divine Mind, Leibniz's region of the eternal verities, is thus "the substratum of the possibility of things."[81] Kant regards such ontotheology, so far as it goes, as amounting to mere deism, that is, a notion of perfect intelligence, without attributes of power and will that constitute the personal God of theism. Thus he argues that "only what is contingent in things can be derived from the divine will and its arbitrary directives."[82] This differentiation — note the association of divine will with "arbitrary" directives, the *deus exlex* — leads Kant from ontotheology to consideration of "cosmotheology," i.e., to consideration of God's will as manifest in the things God has made. This consideration, he says, "teaches us a theistic concept of God, since in it we come to know God as the supreme intelligence, as a highest being who is author of all things through understanding and freedom. The deist, in his concept of God, understands merely a blindly acting eternal nature as the root of all things, an original being, or a supreme cause of the world. But he does not venture to assert that God is the ground of all things through freedom."[83]

This, then, is how Kant sees the difference between the deist Spinoza and the theist Leibniz. In Kant's presentation, ontotheology serves as the deistic foundation shared by Spinoza and Leibniz on which a theistic cosmotheology might yet be constructed. Yet, before that construction of theism may proceed, the modern complication of atheism arises, i.e., "whether this idea of ours also has objective reality, that is, whether there actually exists a being corresponding to our idea of God."[84] As is well known from the First Critique, Kant denies here as well that existence is a predicate, since being is not a property transcending the categories, but an objective relation between phenomenal appearances in time and space. Consequently, while we can conceive the idea of God as the perfect being in whom all perfections internally cohere without any contradiction, "we cannot grasp or comprehend this internal coherence of perfect being." This comment is made in special, though unspoken, reference to Leibniz. Leibniz believed that if only we could so conceive how God is possible as the perfect being — to wit, the harmony of power, wisdom, and love — then God's existence would be entailed, since this maximal possibility demands existence. If the possibility of God's existence as the "internal coherence of perfect being" can be understood, divine existence would follow[85] and thus the ontological argument would work as a proof. The latter insight into the possible coherence of the perfections in a divine existence, however, is beyond the limits of reason, Kant argues. Consequently, reason can neither establish nor deny the perfect being's existence. Thus it "is true that all we know of God in transcendental theology is the mere concept of a highest original ground."[86] This suffices, however, for the critical purposes of (1) debarring the anthropomorphisms of revealed theology but (2) grounding as rational, practical moral faith in a theistic deity who can serve as guarantor of moral striving.

For Kant, in other words, "ontotheology" is the ideal use the critical philosophy can make of the ontological proof for God's existence, in the light of the failure to demonstrate God's existence from the mere idea of God's perfection. Thinking then *ideally* of the one ground of all perfections, we can indeed scrutinize and judge as nonrational dogmatic claims that appear in the realm of nature just as we can also discover moral duty in the realm of freedom and even query about its ultimate blessedness. Ontotheology is the use Kant can make of Leibniz, once Leibniz's existential claims have been refuted and his idea purified. I have been arguing that Barth really has no problem with this Kantian procedure, indeed that in a dialectical way he presupposes it. Thus I am obliged here to distinguish the story I am telling from that of thinkers like Westphal with whom I would seem to have significant affinities,[87] but, it appears, a fundamental disagreement about just what might be right or wrong about ontotheology that flows, I think, from Westphal's much too uncritical reliance on the Heidegger of the 1920s.

Drawing on Heidegger's 1927 lecture "Phenomenology and Theology," Westphal takes up "Luther's definition of faith as 'letting ourselves be seized by the things we do not see.'" This event of Word and faith demarcates theology from philosophy; theology is not speculative knowledge of God but thematizes "the believing-understanding mode of existing in the history revealed, i.e., occurring, with the Crucified." Lest, however, this understanding of theology take a wholly Bultmannian turn, Westphal hastens to qualify: "This does not mean that faith and theology should be given the noncognitivist interpretations familiar from positivist or Wittgensteinian contexts. Faith . . . stands in relation to something actual [2 Cor. 5:19]." The point then is to untangle biblical faith as existential trust evoked by revelation as "something actual" from "the *pistis* that Plato puts on the lower half of the divided line," i.e., beliefs or opinions based on superficial appearances and formulated as naive representations that must be penetrated in turn by critical reason until the denoted essence is clearly and distinctly comprehended. Westphal endorses "Luther's understanding of faith as opposed to the Platonic reading whose *Wirkungsgeschichte* has distorted so many discussions of faith and reason," especially in Hegel, ontotheologian par excellence. For Hegel "the task of thematizing faith belongs ultimately to philosophy and . . . consists in transforming faith into absolute knowledge by translating *Vorstellungen* into *Begriffe*."[88]

With this analysis, Westphal appears to be telling us that what is wrong with ontotheology is that it misses faith as the passive experience of being seized by God in the very act of aspiring to penetrate the representations that occasion the event of faith, as if seeing through them we could move beyond faith to see as God sees. This, however, is idolatry, "positing God as an excuse for making the claim that we can occupy the divine perspective on the world, or at least peek over God's shoulder."[89] Such a protest against the arrogant transgression of the limits of reason sounds very Kantian. It actually presupposes the validity of the concept of God as *ultima ratio,* at least in the transcendent Kantian sense "as the mere concept of a highest original ground." Yet once again a disavowal immediately qualifies Westphal's apparent endorsement of the theological agnosticism that Kantianism would entail. The "critique of onto-theology . . . is directed not at what we say about God but at how we say it, to what purpose, in the service of what project. . . ."[90] Presumably, then, we may in faith affirm the ontotheological *content* that God is the explanation of the world, its *ultima ratio.* Such an affirmation of faith, as in the creedal representation of "God the Father almighty, creator of heaven and earth," is available to us, but we cannot presume to say what it means. We are disbarred from access to its sense or use. We cannot say anything about what this representation of an ultimate explanation actually explains, lest we claim the divine perspective for ourselves.[91] This is a very odd outcome. What could the affirmation that *X,* i.e, *the unknown Cause,* is the explanation of the world possibly mean, no matter how humbly we say it? What purpose could it *ever* serve?

The Heideggerian retort, of course, would be that to ask for the sense or use of the word "God" or to what end it be rightly employed betrays the representational and calculative thinking of Western humanity's titanic metaphysics, which in fact will deploy the word "God" to mean whatever technological imperative or imperial project requires it to mean. "One can even say that for metaphysics, constituted in this way as onto-theology, 'God exists only insofar as the principle of reason holds' (Heidegger). . . . God's *raison d'etre* has become to make it possible for human reason to give ultimate explanations. . . . God is at the beck and call of human understanding, a means to its end of making the whole of being intelligible in keeping with the principle of reason. In order to place the world at the disposal of human theory (and practice), it becomes necessary to place God at our disposal as well." Leibniz's principle of sufficient reason is thus isolated as articulating the very axiom of ontotheological idolatry because it turns God into a cipher for the metaphysical ambition for a theory of everything. Yet again, however, a qualification quickly comes. Westphal's own objections to ontotheology, he tells us, are "more Kierkegaardian than Kantian," i.e., against the anthropocentric bias of metaphysics where "God is a part of this world that revolves around 'man,'" causing us to lose "touch with the awe, wonder, and even dread we experience before the mystery that metaphysics as onto-theology seeks to demystify. This is every bit as crucial for any theology that would remain religiously significant."[92] Now Westphal's point seems to be that "predication must yield to praise [Pseudo-Dionysius]."[93] This precise criticism seems curiously misdirected when aimed at the ecological and doxological Leibniz, as we shall see.

For what is praise but predicating of God the divine perfections and ascribing them to none other? Least of all for the sake of doxology must one abandon to the devil math and science, calculation and representation, science and technology, in a word, the human vocation in the image of God to subdue the earth and have dominion over it (Gen. 1:26-28). Faith does not displace reason, nor praise supplant predication, nor freedom defy necessity. God's being the ground of the principle of sufficient reason does not exhaust our relation to God but necessitates it (N.B. necessitates us, not God!). Westphal too quickly resorts to false antitheses that he cannot or will not sustain and must then qualify. This leads then to no clear position on the actual relation of faith and reason, but only a kind of critique wavering between Heidegger's worked-over Kant and Westphal's preferred Kierkegaard. Surely the point of a theological critique of metaphysics in Luther's tradition is neither of these. It is rather to show how, at the disposal of egocentrism, the mind's powers of calculation and representation "make a happy science out of a sad creation," by taking as "real" the essences of things as they presently appear (to the self-interested sinner), although the essences themselves mourn and groan over their deformed reality in this fallen age at the exploitative hands of the egocentric sinner and yearn instead for what they will become when God sets the creation free from futility.[94] Reformed by a proper eschatology,[95] however, these same powers of reason would be put to better use. As Leibniz conceives it, progress in coming to know the world by calculation and representation is truly progressive science as it learns to know the creation in and with the triune God, i.e., redeemed in Christ and destined to fulfillment in the Spirit. The point of representation, including theological representation of the *ultima ratio* as "God the Father, creator of heaven and earth," is not to master God and put Him in the service of diverse, arbitrary, and insatiable human appetites, but that we participate knowingly in the life of the Trinity, fulfilling the human vocation (Gen. 1:26-28) as royal stewards of the earth, in union with Christ, the *imago dei* and head of the new humanity.

It is true, as Benjamin Crowe has shown in detail, that Heidegger draws inspiration from the early Luther. But on examination we have here about as good a reading of Luther as we just witnessed Heidegger perform on Kant. "'Destructio' is Luther's name for God's dismantling of the idols of human egoism. . . . All of Luther's polemics against scholasticism, Aristotle, reason, and philosophy amount to his own attempt, as a custodian of the Word of God, to participate in the *destructio* of the 'old man.' . . . Learning from Luther, Heidegger called this philosophy, *'Destruktion.'*"[96] Heidegger saw in Luther's critique of metaphysics a precedent of his own: "'Onto-theology' does not refer to theism as such, but to a very specific version of it. Here, 'God' serves as a justification for human pride and presumption, a kind of clandestine self-congratulation. 'God' serves, in an onto-theological scheme, to ground an all-embracing explanation of reality, a project which has little to do with proclaiming an experience of salvation."[97] This is an interesting antithesis, in that it dissolves the unity of humanity and cosmos in Romans 8 from which Luther derived his critique of metaphysics, even if it is a familiar antithesis by virtue of countless reiterations from the pens of existentialist Lutherans in the twentieth century. There is another significant distortion involved, however, in Heidegger's appropriation of Luther. For Luther, God kills *in order to* make alive; God's salvation aims at the redemption of the fallen creation (not the quasi-Gnostic escape of a handful of true believers into the ethically contentless states of personal authenticity). For these cosmic-soteriological themes of Romans 8 to be warranted, the God in question must indeed be understood as having universal right and almighty power and thus truly be both alpha and omega, the all-embracing explanation.

Luther himself in any case never denied the philosophical acknowledgment of God in majesty, acquired mediately by contemplation of the splendor of created works, according to Romans 1:20. What he denies is that the egocentric self uses this (true) knowledge rightly, in accord with the Creator's intention, that she repent and return thanks by ascribing to God the glory that is God's due, instead of predicating it of creatures. The natural man gets the fact but not the sense of God's existence and so puts the information to work falsely in what prove to be sublimated acts of self-worship. In this connection, there is another aspect to Heidegger's critique that may be more telling. "What Heidegger maintains is that something went somehow awry during the period between Luther and the German idealists. It is not too difficult to see what this is: the reassertion of Greek metaphysics, particularly the category of the subject, culminates in the reflective philosophy of the idealists . . . the traditional concept of humanity . . . 1) a human being as a rational animal, and 2) a human being as a person." The later notion of the human person Heidegger rightly derived from Genesis 1, the doctrine of the *imago dei*. But "Heidegger's worry is that through being mixed with the Greek idea of the 'rational animal,' the original Christian concept of person became universalized and thereby watered down to the point that what is valuable about persons is not that they are unique creations of God, but that they have the capacity for knowledge."[98] The human mind understood and valued as abstract intelligence then displaced the biographical self acquired through a unique history by personal decisions.

But consider: the highest primates do not have biographies nor do they acquire through memory and anticipation a personal identity, a narrative of one's decisions. These are functions of intelligence; persons are minds, embodied minds, to be sure. Should we follow Heidegger in thinking this reflection to denote some fatal, false turn between Luther and the German idealists under the influence of Greek intellectualism? The Leibnizian interpretation of the image of God in the *Monadology* as the reflecting mirror, we may here recall, was a synthesis of biblical and Platonic traditions. As we have seen, it derives from the Lutheran tradition of theology, as we noted in Gerhard. Westphal is thus right to see the continuation of this Leibnizian synthesis of the traditions in Hegel, who considered his philosophical thought a kind of fulfillment of Lutheranism. Thus we may take the opportunity here briefly to discuss the intriguing case of Hegel before returning to the status quo ante of "ontotheology" in Spinoza.

Theological sympathy with Hegel rests upon the perception of his continuity with the *fides quarens intellectum* of Western theology with roots in Augustine and Anselm, such that even the notorious final translation of religious representation into intellectual concepts is not in and of itself objectionable. Westphal's Kierkegaardian reservations notwithstanding, Hegel's firm rejection of the noncognitive interpretation of theology represented by his Berlin rival Schleiermacher is far more impressive, as it in fact recalls Leibniz's brief for the ultimate unity of true faith and true reason. Hegel writes: "Philosophy has been reproached for placing itself above religion. But as a matter of fact this is surely false because philosophy has only this and no other content, although it gives it the form of thinking; it places itself only above the *form* of faith, while the *content* is the same in both cases. . . .

Philosophy *thinks* what the subject as such *feels*."[99] This thinking of faith —
whether we call it theology or philosophy — is as necessary as it is inevitable:

> Just as soon as religion is no longer simply the reading and repetition of
> passages, as soon as what is called explanation or interpretation begins, as
> soon as an attempt is made by inference and exegesis to find out the
> meaning of the words in the Bible, then we embark upon the process of
> reasoning, reflection, thinking; and the question then becomes how we
> should exercise this process of thinking, and whether our thinking is cor-
> rect or not. It helps not at all to say that one's thoughts are based on the
> Bible. As soon as these thoughts are no longer simply the words of the Bi-
> ble, their content is given a form, more specifically a logical form.[100]

In conflict with that pietist of a higher order in Berlin, Hegel says that in his
own day "investigation of these forms of thought falls to philosophy alone.
Thus theology itself does not know what it wants when it turns against philosophy."[101] Or worse, such theology involves itself in a self-deception.
Thinking on the basis of pure feeling, naive reading of the Bible (or equally
naive historical reconstruction of the 'real' history behind the biblical text)
in fact "reserves for itself the option to think as it chooses, in contingent
fashion."[102] Even if elicited from the depths of absolute dependence, this
emoting can only produce arbitrary opinionating, not all remotely close to
Luther's "letting ourselves be seized by the things we do not see" yet promised in the Word. Genuine thinking (again, regardless of whether we call it
theology or philosophy) proceeds by "immersing ourselves in the subject-
matter." That means self-forgetfulness on the part of the exegete, "freed from
all particularity of features, states, etc., . . . giving up our particular opinions
and beliefs and allowing the subject matter to hold sway over us." And it is
with this hermeneutical understanding of reason in service of faith that
Hegel makes his cognitive claim: "the fundamental doctrines of Christianity
[= the Trinity] have for the most part disappeared from dogmatics [=
Schleiermacher]. Philosophy is preeminently, though not exclusively, what is
at present essentially orthodox; the propositions that have always been valid,
the basic truths of Christianity, are maintained and preserved by it."[103]

Sympathetic as I am to Hegel under the conditions of modernity, that is,
in Kantian culture, he is not so simply "orthodox" as he claims. Cyril
O'Regan has unraveled the influence on Hegel of Jacob Boehme, the semi-
Gnostic mystic of later Lutheranism. Hegel consequently made a complex
innovation in orthodoxy, even if we grant his good intention to preserve

"the fundamental doctrines of Christianity" under the conditions of modernity, i.e., under the Kantian proscription of recognition of the infinite by the finite in revelation. This was Hegel's thesis of the temporality of God. He argues that grasping God in the traditional way by means of eternal predicates or attributes is in any case incomplete and misleading because it cannot and does not grasp God as living. The traditional way only produces a ghostly being, the abstract negation of the creation, a false infinite. Thus Kant's proscription of revelation is interpreted by Hegel as his unwitting protest against the false infinite. This line of thought is of course entirely in keeping with Luther's criticism of the theology of glory in favor of a theology of the cross with its teaching that the true God is capable of revealing Himself *sub contrario* in order to mediate a "negation of the negation." Yet the "life, the deed, the activity of God"[104] are grasped, Hegel now innovates vis-à-vis Luther, by thinking after God's positing of His own being in contradiction and then resolution of this contradiction *as the very story of the cosmos* rather than the particular story of Jesus Christ, Savior. The problem of grasping the living God in human thought now lies, not basically in human finitude's incapacity for the infinite à la Kant, but in God's own temporality — grasping God in thought waits in time upon the event of God's self-unfolding. Theology (or true philosophy) is *Nachdenken*. This creative innovation by Hegel entails a daunting revision of the tradition. "But God is the creator of the world; it belongs to his being, his essence, to be the creator; insofar as he is not the creator, he is grasped inadequately. His creative role is not an *actus* that 'happened' once; [rather,] what takes place in the idea is an eternal moment, an eternal determination of the idea."[105]

O'Regan compares Hegel's innovation here to Luther's trinitarianism, for whom the notion of the passibility of God is motivated and conceived by virtue of the superabundance of *Barmherzigkeit*[106] as mediated by the unique act of the incarnation. While "the Patristic and medieval elaboration of God as the Supreme Good struck Luther as unnecessary, nevertheless, Luther does not materially diverge from these traditions in taking for granted the ontological foundations of kenosis in the divine goodness as consummate love, power and fullness."[107] God, in other words, is antecedently in all eternity the blessed life of the Trinity, the one true possessor of the predicates of perfection. The divine *kenosis* in creation is consequently a wonder of the voluntary passion of generosity, an unnecessary and so free self-giving arising out of the fullness of the triune life of love, motivated by no inner neediness. Accordingly one must speak of a *free* divine decision to create a world that befits such a creator, a world so loved that in it the Son would perish on the cross at its hands yet be raised for its life and reconciliation. With Boehme's Valentinian mysticism working "at once a local mutation of Lutheranism and a mutation of the theological consensus," however, a "new ontological foundation" for the divine *kenosis* is suggested: "lack." "When German idealism in general, Hegel in particular, attempt theological or ontotheological construction in modernity," O'Regan concludes, this revision is made.[108] God *needs* a world to become God. God is not *essentially* Father of His own Son in the Spirit who becomes a creator; God is *essentially* creator who becomes a trinity. (This line of thought should be compared to McCormack's proposal, discussed above.)

Leibniz, by contrast, does not make any such move.[109] Nor does Barth: the election of grace "is the demonstration, the overflowing of the love which is the being of God, that He who is entirely self-sufficient, who even within Himself cannot know isolation, willed even in all His divine glory to share His life with another."[110] Barth explicates this self-sufficiency of God as trinitarian: "From all eternity God is within Himself the living God. The fact that God is means that from all eternity God is active in His inner relationships as Father, Son and Holy Ghost. . . . God does not, therefore, become the living God when He works or decides to work ad extra. . . . His being and activity ad extra is merely an overflowing of His inward activity and being. . . . It is a proclamation of the decision in which in Himself He is who He is. The origin of this proclamation within God Himself is predestination . . . transition . . . from God's being in and for Himself to His being as Lord of creation."[111] With Augustine the divine decision to create *is* the initiation of time-space, since God is not eternally or essentially creator. The Nicene rejection of Arius means most fundamentally that God *is* eternally the Father of His own Son in the Spirit; that as such God *becomes* the creator of the world other than God in the initiation of time-space, in the decision to make this world in and for Christ rather than any other. "Thus the incarnation and creation together, the latter interpreted in the light of the former, have quite breathtaking implications for our understanding of the nature of God. They tell us that he is free to do what he had never done before, and free to be other than he was eternally: to be the Almighty Creator, and even to become incarnate as a creature within his creation, while remaining eternally the God that he is."[112] The infinite can include the finite, the eternal is capable of time.

The crux of the matter between Hegel and the orthodox trinitarian tradition is whether this trinitarian counsel and decision can be made intelligible, without surreptitiously positing an incoherent "time before time";[113] if not, the worry is that the being of God and the becoming of the world sim-

ply converge, as in Spinoza. Hegel senses the problem. He acknowledges the
import of Spinoza. "Specifically," he writes, "the eternal idea is expressed in
terms of the holy Trinity: it is God himself, eternally triune." But this is mere
"idea," i.e., God "as he is in and for himself, prior to or apart from the creation,"[114] that is, an abstraction considered apart from the eternal act of creation. The complicated question whether Hegel's innovation is a proper development in the ongoing revision of metaphysics by the gospel or a
deviation, as we have witnessed in McCormack's and will witness in Jenson's
attempts to develop Barth's trinitarianism, is deferred to the conclusion of
this book. For present purposes Leibniz's more traditional trinitarianism
serves better to make clear the stakes for theology and modernity once Kantianism is overcome and Spinozist monism and determinism emerge from
the shadows as the true antagonist in the story of the fates of theology from
Luther through Leibniz.

Kant Saves Leibniz from Himself

We have one more obstacle to remove. At the center of the First Critique,
Kant did succeed in imposing the epistemological scheme on Leibniz for
coming generations.[115] Although he praised Leibniz as "one of the most
acute philosophers of ancient or modern times," Kant took time to lay out in
detail the case that he "has been misled into the construction of a baseless
system of intellectual cognition, which professes to determine its objects
without the intervention of the senses."[116] As prosecuting attorney on behalf
of the Tribunal of Reason, Kant thus charges Leibniz with construction of a
method of scientific cognition; i.e., the epistemological project is superim-
posed on Leibniz. Kant is capable, to be sure, of stating Leibniz's purpose on
the latter's own terms: "the celebrated Leibniz constructed an intellectual
system of the world" — Leibniz's "universal pneumatology" derived, as we
noted, from Lutheranism's doctrine of the *imago dei*. Yet he can hardly contain himself from immediately rephrasing the matter: ". . . or rather, [he] believed himself competent to cognize the internal nature of things, by comparing all objects merely with the understanding and the abstract formal
conceptions of thought."[117] One gets the impression from this account in
the First Critique that Kant has simply hauled up under the figure of Leibniz
the deductive/geometric model of Cartesianism with its apparent lack of
concern for the evidence of the senses. This would be a fundamental mis-
reading of Leibniz's purpose,[118] and Kant, as we shall see, knows better. Nev-

ertheless, here the history of "modern" philosophy is being written for future generations: Leibniz is one of the "rationalists" who "*intellectualized* phenomena";[119] he is pitted dialectically against the "empiricist" Locke, who "*sensualized* the conceptions of the understanding." The golden path between the two errors is found in "transcendental reflection" on these discrete faculties of sense and understanding, which brings the insight that they "present us with objective judgments of things only in *conjunction*" — although never insight into the things themselves.[120]

In reality, Kant is trying to exorcise the ghost of the Divine Mind, a key notion going back to Augustine's discovery of the creative divine intuition of the "eternal now" (but also anticipating theistic readings of Hegel's *Geist*). The Divine Mind haunts Kant's entire discussion of Leibniz in this pivotal section. We may "wish that we possessed a faculty of cognition perfectly different from the human faculty, not merely in degree, but even as regards intuition and the mode thereof, so that thus we should not be men, but belong to a class of beings, the possibility of whose existence, much less their nature and constitution, we have no means of cognizing."[121] But "the intelligible requires an altogether peculiar intuition, which we do not possess, and in the absence of which it is for us nothing."[122] The noumenal or intelligible cannot be an *object* for our thought, "for the representation thereof is but the problematical conception of an object for a perfectly different intuition and a perfectly different understanding from ours, both of which are consequently themselves problematical."[123] Thus the notion of a Divine Mind, Kant urges, is beyond us and should not concern us. Our hankering after it should pass away in favor of another "mystery": "the origin and source of our faculty of sensibility." But here too we come up against a mystery. "Its application to an object, and the transcendental ground of the unity of subjective and objective, lies too deeply concealed for us . . . [this] non-sensuous cause of which we at the same time earnestly desire to penetrate to." Yet that desire to understand why our objective reasoning works so well in comprehending the apparent world fosters the transcendental illusion that we can treat concepts of the understanding as if they were objects of knowledge. They cannot be. All we can have here at this borderline is Locke's posit of underlying substance as a 'thing I know not what.' The mysterious noumenal, the hidden "substance" of things, is a representation for us "quite void," Kant writes, only an "indication of the limits of our sensuous intuition," an "empty space." The critique of pure reason finds a limit concept here, which does not permit us to follow Leibniz in creating "for ourselves a new field of objects beyond those which are presented to us as phenomena, and to stray into intelligible worlds; nay, it does not even allow us to endeavor to form so much as a conception of them."[124] We cannot see how God sees, nor can we imagine what God sees.

From this much alone, it is apparent what is askew in Kant's account of Leibniz's purpose: the theological motive has disappeared. What is systematically exorcised in Kant's account of Leibniz is the notion of Divine Mind that does all the hard work in Leibniz's metaphysics.[125] This is Leibniz's conception of God the Creator, the divine intelligence willing into being the things of this world in a consequent system and series chosen from among all possibles. Removing it permits Kant in turn to construe Leibniz as making an epistemological proposal regarding the justification of human knowledge claims that can now be weighed and found wanting. But for Leibniz the divine act of creation rather identifies the human thinker as one who reflects on the whence and wither of things, and asks after the radical origination of all things — the famous question, Why is there something rather than nothing? And, "since something rather than nothing exists," the human mind is authorized by this factuality to make inferences from the logical possibilities of things (essences) to the actuality of the world as revealed in phenomena.[126] *This* is Leibniz's so-called intellectual system of the world. According to it, the human mind attains some insight into the essences, i.e., the logical possibilities of things, on the basis of its affinity with the divine mind in whose image it was created and so can imagine, as one mind can imagine another, God's exercise of choice in the ultimate origination of things. As one Kant scholar puts it: "The human mind is not for Kant, as it is for Leibniz, a finite God, capable of grasping, albeit obscurely, what the divine intellect apprehends clearly and distinctly. Against this, Kant affirms the *sui generis* nature of the specifically human forms of knowing,"[127] as we saw in the above citations from the First Critique. Kant laid down that for the human mind objects of intellectual intuition are "impossible. . . . And even if we should suppose a different kind of intuition from our own [i.e., God's], still our functions of thought would have no use or signification in respect thereof."[128] The unbridgeable gulf of the transcendental philosophy opens wide: "our mode of intuition is not applicable to all things, but only to objects of our sense, that consequently its objective validity is limited, and that room is therefore left for another kind of intuition, and thus also for things that may be objects of it."[129] God, in other words, may creatively intuit the creation, but we mortals cannot conceive this, neither can we know like this, nor even by grace participate in it. Locke's *nescio quid* trumps the *Monadology*. Zwingli's *finitum non capax* prevails over Luther's *est*.

Be that as it may, the burning issue here for Leibniz on his own terms (not Kant's) is not the justification of our knowledge claims, but the justification of God as Creator of this world. "But, you ask, don't we experience quite the opposite in the world? For the worst often happens to the best, and not only innocent beasts but also humans are injured and killed, even tortured. In the end, the world appears to be a confused chaos rather than a thing ordered by supreme wisdom, especially if one takes note of the conduct of the human race."[130] In face of this objection — Leibniz concedes, "it appears this way" — the question is whether one can draw that chief inference of natural theology: that from among all possibles God wills *this actual world* (i.e., the world of cause and effect being discovered by experimental science in which the abysmal conduct of the human race appears chaotic) *as the best* — not, as Kant's treatment misleadingly impugns, whether human minds might dispense with experimental science altogether and extend knowledge by analysis alone. But in the First Critique, Kant redescribed Leibniz as an epistemologist and proceeded to refute his own caricature. Kant knows better. Or, at least, the later controversy with the Wolffian Eberhard forced Kant to come (somewhat) clean(er) on the rather violent act of appropriation that we just witnessed in the First Critique.

The occasion of the controversy was the first soundings of the criticism of Kantian dualism: positing a *nescio quid* adds up to illicit and arbitrary metaphysics on Kant's own critical terms, since Kant does not and cannot use this merely as a limit concept but treats the noumenal thing in itself as the hidden foundation or substrate of the phenomenal appearance.[131] How then does the human mind know that it does not know the noumenal, which in reality it discovers in experience and cognizes at least minimally as its own limit? We can detect the beginnings of idealism in this probing objection — but that is not the trajectory we wish to pursue here. For the present, the issue is liberating Leibniz from the Kantian interpretation (which is not to vindicate the Wolffian criticism of Kant, insofar as the Wolffians, in distinction from Leibniz, have been snared into the trap of proffering a foundationalist epistemology that Kant can justly rejoin as inadequate). In reply to Eberhard, Kant postures as if to save the "great Leibniz" from his Wolffian followers: "Is it really credible that Leibniz wished to have his principle of sufficient reason construed objectively (as a natural law) . . . ?"[132] "Is it really believable that Leibniz, the great mathematician, held that bodies are composed of monads (and hence space composed of simple parts)? He did not mean the physical world, but its substrate, the intelligible world, which is unknown to us."[133] "Is it possible to believe that, by his pre-

established harmony between soul and body, Leibniz should have understood an adaptation of two beings which are by their nature completely independent of one another . . . ?"[134] With all three of these great themes of
Leibnizian thought, Kant wants to open wide the great gulf of transcendental philosophy by suggesting that the Wolffian interpretation of Leibniz reduces his great themes to absurdity. "The Critique of Pure Reason can thus
be seen as the genuine apology for Leibniz,"[135] who misunderstood his concepts as if objects, while the Wolffians egregiously take objects as if concepts.

The aspect of this controversy that proves most relevant for our inquiry surrounds the analytic-synthetic distinction. For Kant, that is, from
the standpoint of the finite mind separated by an unbridgeable gulf from
an infinite Divine Mind, the distinction is relative to the knower's relation
to the phenomenal world. Analytic statements explicate ideas the knower
already possesses a priori, but a synthetic statement adds by a predicate
something new, not implicit in the subject. By contrast, for Leibniz, the finite mind as image of the Divine Mind participates to some degree in the
region of eternal truths where all logically possible, noncontradictory notions exist, and so recognizes that all truths are ultimately analytic, that is,
analytic to God who has full and complete notions of all individuals, possible and real. Given this world, which the finite human mind thinks is filled
with truths that God chose to instantiate out of all those logically possible,
the distinction between analytic and synthetic knowledge is not relative to
the knower's relation to the phenomenal world as in Kant, but to the human knower's relation to the Divine Mind. Leibniz's doctrine of analytic
truth holds that "all predicates are ultimately contained in the subject" because God has a "full and complete notion" of every monad he actualizes.
To the finite mind, analytic truths are reached a priori by the logical law of
noncontradiction. But synthetic facts are reached only by experiment, since
finite minds lack a priori those full and complete conceptions of things that
only God has, since only God sees the final harmony of things with one another. Understanding synthetic facts philosophically, moreover, depends
upon the logical principle of sufficient reason[136] — which is to say that the
contingent events of the world, which human minds can discover only by
experience, never by analysis, are *understood* truly when understood as
willed by God for good reasons.

Or does God? That is the real issue between Kant and Leibniz. As Patrick
Riley concludes (in face of his own, outspoken Kantian-Pelagian prefer-
ences): "A Leibniz-Kant synthesis, then, is not possible — at least as something that either of them would acknowledge. As usual, God is the problem;

and his knowable presence or absence is decisive in shaping what Leibniz and Kant say about 'substance,' freedom, and morality."[137]

More broadly, however, if we no longer anachronistically divide up the thinkers of early modernity into "empiricists" and "rationalists" obsessing over the methods by which claims to knowledge can be justified with the same force and certitude as found in Newtonian physics, we may quickly discern that the thinkers of early modernity did not so align themselves. Locke in his moral philosophy tried, perhaps against himself, to oppose Hobbes,[138] while Leibniz at first sought on the basis of Locke's opposition to Hobbes to make common cause with him. Leibniz accounted for his disagreement with Locke this way:

> our systems are very different. His has more relation to Aristotle, mine to Plato, although we both differ in many things from the doctrine of these two ancient philosophers. . . . The question is to know whether the soul in itself is entirely empty as the tablets upon which as yet nothing has been written (tabula rasa) according to Aristotle, and the author of the Essay, and whether all that is traced thereon comes solely from the senses and from experience; or whether the soul contains originally the principles of many ideas and doctrines which external objects merely call up on occasion, as I believe with Plato, and even with the schoolmen, and with all those who interpret in this way the passage of St. Paul (Rom. 2:15) where he states that the law of God is written in the heart.[139]

Yet Leibniz criticized Descartes — champion of innate ideas — on a variety of grounds, as we shall see, but above all opposed his greater progeny, Spinoza.[140] Indeed, the early Spinoza's *Principles of Cartesian Philosophy* is a clearer statement of "rationalist" method than anything ever produced by Descartes himself and far from Leibniz's spirit. Considering this rather messier picture than Kant paints, Matthew Stewart (from a normative viewpoint distant from my own) has rightly urged: "Once we set aside suspect narratives of the history, however, it becomes clear that, far from being left behind by their modern successors, Leibniz and Spinoza remain unsurpassed today as representatives of humankind's radically divided response to the set of experiences we call modernity."[141] In Jonathan Israel's formulation of the "pivotal point": "for Spinoza, the philosopher who grasps the reality of things knows that what exists exists necessarily and that what does not exist cannot exist, whereas for Leibniz what happens could have happened differently, and whatever exists could be otherwise, had God so willed."[142] Admittedly this thesis provokes a sense of dissonance in those accustomed to grouping together Leibniz and Spinoza as "rationalists," if not further misled by the textbooks' freakish accounts of "windowless monads," not to mention the imbecile pontifications of Dr. Pangloss.

Domesticating the Sublime[143]

John Milbank, in his insightful and not influential enough study, *Theology and Social Theory*, gave pride of place to Hobbes in telling our tale (as well an Englishman might).[144] Yet in tracing the trajectory of theology from Luther to Leibniz, we do better to focus on the thought of Spinoza, in which "God" becomes the name of the eternal cosmic dialectic of activity and passivity on "the plane of immanence" (DeLeuze), *natura naturans* and *natura naturata*,[145] the infinite and its endless modulations:[146] "the eternal and infinite being, whom we call God, or Nature, acts by the same necessity whereby it exists . . . just as he does not exist for an end, so he does not act for an end; just as there is no beginning or end to his existing, so there is no beginning or end to his acting."[147] Thus demystified, the final causes traditionally understood as inhering the world's structure and reflecting the divine decree are now understood as human, all-too-human projections of purpose onto God/Nature. "What is termed a 'final cause' is nothing but human appetite in so far as it is considered as the starting point or primary cause of some thing."[148] Final causes are unfounded in the nature of things, except as expressions of individual appetites for objects. The liberating result, for Spinoza, is that human beings alone bear responsibility for the desires they admit and the purposes they undertake. Nothing in the nature of things structures them into organized purposes. There is no longer any recourse to the authority of faith, or of reason according to the anthropomorphic metaphysics of the tradition, to assess and prioritize the divine purposes encoded in cosmic structures into which individual appetites are to be ordered.

With this demystification, however, comes as well the characteristic sense of predicament of the modern mind. It is a state of consciousness formed by the new awareness — inescapable thanks to the progress of natural science[149] — of the relative insignificance of *homo sapiens* in the vast and ancient, indeed for Spinoza, eternal, system of things. The well-known sentiment of Pascal expresses it perfectly: "When I consider the brief span of my life absorbed into the eternity which comes before and after — as the remembrance of a guest that tarrieth but a day (Wisdom 5:15) — the small space I occupy and which I see swallowed up in the infinite immensity of spaces of which I know nothing and which know nothing of me, I take fright and am amazed to see myself here rather than there, now rather than then. Who put me here? By whose command and act were this time and place allotted to me?"[150] The demeaning contradiction surfaces here of *knowing* — unlike rocks and stars, DNA or higher primates — *glorious* knowing unlike all the rest of *inglorious* creation, the inglorious fact that one matters little, that one's intentional consciousness with its immanent purposes and unfounded projections are nothing but arbitrary expressions of idiosyncratic "appetites." "God," or Nature, without purpose other than sheer eternal being endlessly playing out the plentitude of all possibles, appears to modern consciousness as the empty screen of the Ineffable. Onto this screen various expressions of faith in human dignity as a purposeful agent are projected, i.e., lifted up, honored in this way[151] but also perhaps reified, absolutized, imposed ideologically on others — as if founded in objective structures of purpose.[152] In either case, final purposes are unfounded in the nature of things — they are our own brief flicker of flame in cosmic night, burst of sound then silence in *die Ewigkeit, die tiefe, tiefe Ewigkeit* (Nietzsche).

To live in this new predicament (the paradoxical "condemnation to freedom" that eventually Sartre would speak of), the *language* of God must be philosophically reconstructed as well. To begin with, Spinoza argues, the "truths" of the Bible, such as they are, are not scientific, but moral; not otherworldly at all, but decoded and demystified, quite worldly, even pedestrian. That being established, the language of God must be "of universal application"; it may not "demand belief in historical narratives of any kind whatsoever"; it "does not enjoin ceremonial rites"; and its supreme reward is wholly intrinsic, "namely, to know God and to love him in true freedom," just as the "penalty it imposes is the deprivation of these things and bondage to the flesh, that is, an inconstant and irresolute spirit."[153] Interestingly, in continuity with the antecedent theological traditions, the language of God is still supposed to work "blessedness": "This, then, is the sum of our supreme good and blessedness, to wit, the knowledge and love of God," since "firstly, without God nothing can be or be conceived, and, secondly, everything can be called into doubt as long as we have no clear and distinct idea of God."[154] The reason for this claim about blessedness in God is that the Cartesian motive remains central: the blessedness of God is deliverance from the doubt the early modern ego experiences.[155] This doubt is not, as in the tradition, sinful doubt of despair about God's love for the sinner, but that Pascalian need of reassurance concerning the dignity of the human mind in the maw of the vast, unknowing, uncaring realm of extended things. The new theology helps. "As everything in Nature involves and expresses the conception of God in proportion to its essence and perfection . . . therefore we acquire a greater and more perfect knowledge of God as we gain more knowledge of natural phenomena."[156] Citing Romans 1:20, Spinoza in turn concludes this discussion with the corollary claim that "by the light of natural reason, all can clearly understand the power and eternal divinity of God, from which they can know and infer what they should seek and what avoid."[157] Ontotheology, indeed.

It is from within this dialectic of the whole of which we are part that we must now speak of God: both to resource human agency in the scientific and political transformation of the world so far as it is possible and, where it is not, to proffer the peace of blessed resignation. In the *Ethics,* Spinoza puts the point expressly: "human power is very limited and is infinitely surpassed by the power of external causes, and so we do not have absolute power to adapt to our purposes things external to us. However, we shall patiently bear whatever happens to us that is contrary to what is required by consideration of our own advantage, if we are conscious that we have done our duty and that our power was not extensive enough for us to have avoided the said things, and that we are a part of the whole of Nature whose order we follow."[158] Thus in the embrace of the emerging new cosmology, reconstructed religious language is to function *existentially* and thus *morally* (not *literally* and thus *superstitiously*), allowing diverse expression to faith in human significance in face of sovereign and indifferent Nature's order: "faith requires not so much true dogmas as pious dogmas, that is, such as move the heart to obedience; and this is so even if many of those beliefs contain not a shadow of truth. . . . Each man's faith, then, is to be regarded as pious or impious not in respect of its truth or falsity, but as it is conducive to obedience or obstinacy."[159] Yet Spinoza cannot quite allow this thoroughgoing cognitive relativism with respect to theological truth. "If one knew that [one's beliefs] were false, he would necessarily be a rebel . . . [who worships] as divine what he knows to be alien to the divine nature." *Dogmatics,* then, cannot be wholly avoided. Indeed, it turns out that a revised language of God, the "dogmas of the universal faith" in the "Supreme Being who loves justice and charity, whom all must obey in order to be saved, and must worship by practicing justice and charity to their neighbors,"[160] matters immensely for discerning the difference between human misery and blessedness. For "the wicked, not knowing God, are but an instrument in the hands of the Master, serving unconsciously and being used up in that service, whereas the good serve consciously, and in serving become more perfect."[161]

In parallel fashion to Spinoza, "God" becomes this "domesticated Sublime" in tandem with a reduction of theological language to the regulative ideas of moralistic anthropology in Kant too. The aesthetic perception of beauty in instances of purposiveness *in* nature (*not* the final purpose *of* nature) plays the important role for Kant of mediating the gap between nature's indifference as known in science and Humanity's Ends as presupposed in free moral action: it suggests the analogy of nature as an artist (think: Plato's Demiurge) and thus provides a model human beings can appropriate as natural beings transforming themselves along with their environment in pursuit of moral purpose. To accomplish this domestication, however, Kant had to wrestle down the anxiety caused by "the feeling of the sublime" as that which appears "contrapurposive for our power of judgment, and as it were violent to our imagination." Consider, he writes, "threatening rocks, thunderclouds piling up in the sky and moving about accompanied by lightning and thunderclaps, volcanoes with all their destructive power, hurricanes with all the devastation they leave behind, the boundless ocean heaved up, the high waterfall of a mighty river, and so. Compared to the might of any of these, our ability to resist becomes an insignificant trifle."[162] Spinoza's Stoic resignation to that which we cannot control does not seem quite adequate to Pascal's doubt in the face of the sublimity of nature. But it is this experience of mighty chaos in nature, the "wildest and most ruleless disarray and devastation, provided it displays magnitude and might," Kant writes, which "most arouses our ideas of the sublime."[163] Indeed, "in tempests, storms, earthquakes, and so on, we usually present God as showing himself in his wrath but also in his sublimity."[164] That remnant of superstition about divine wrath can go, but the threat to human dignity of the sublime in nature remains.

Eschewing Leibnizian theodicy,[165] Kant at first seems simply to dismiss the aforementioned experience on the odd grounds that "this concept indicates nothing purposive whatever in nature so that we can feel a purposiveness within ourselves entirely independent of nature." The topic of the sublime consequently can be treated as a "mere appendix" to the critique of judgment. Nevertheless, Kant cannot leave the matter here, for there are no grounds to judge the beautiful in nature as analogous to the artist, and at the same time to ignore the chaos in nature, analogous to a capricious destroyer — not a model Kant cares to commend. Yet, on Kant's own grounds, or Spinoza's for that matter, why should this latter face of nature in earthquake and tsunami and extinction of the dinosaurs not also provide a mediating concept or model for humanity's relation to itself and nature, as the Nazi ni-

hilism would conclude little more than a century later?[166] Sensing the difficulty, Kant returns again to the topic in a few pages in order to argue that the
experience of the sublime cannot at all be equated with any kind of sensual
experience of nature's immensity. This is a mistake, an anthropomorphism.
Nature has no "face." In fact, the feeling of the sublime arises from our own
"supersensible power," the "use that judgment makes"[167] of such experiences
of disorder in nature. "We like to call these objects sublime because they raise
the soul's fortitude above its usual middle range and allow us to discover in
ourselves an ability to resist which is of a quite different kind."[168] The argument reminds of Spinoza's blessed resignation, cited above, but takes the domestication of the sublime a long step further: "though the irresistibility of
nature's might makes us, considered as natural beings, recognize our physical
impotence, it reveals in us at the same time an ability to judge ourselves independent of nature, and reveals in us a superiority over nature that is the basis
of a self-preservation quite different from the one that can be assailed and en-
dangered by nature outside us. This keeps the humanity in our person from
being degraded." The sublime "is not contained in any thing of nature, but
only in our mind, insofar as we can become conscious of our superiority to
nature within us, and thereby also to nature outside of us."[169] If I may be permitted a parody: "You only thought that the AIDS outbreak was awful; what
is truly awesome is that you think this very thought."[170]

Kant's discussion of the sublime concluded with a decisive theological
move: following Spinoza,[171] the biblical and prophetic language of *the wrath
of God* is to be stricken from theological vocabulary as inimical to rational
human self-respect: "the mental attunement that befits the manifestation of
such an object is not a feeling of the sublimity of our own nature, but rather
submission, prostration, and feeling of our utter impotence . . . worship with
bowed head and accompanied by contrite and timorous gestures and
voice."[172] The sublime thus tamed in nature and history alike, the language
of God becomes the rhetoric of grace overcoming nature (rather than overcoming wrath by the forgiving of sin), which informs "modern" theology
from the beginning of the nineteenth century onward. The antecedent biblical narrative of creation and fall, redemption and fulfillment has been sub-
verted, its language co-opted. The human predicament is now understood as
that of "rising beasts" building the Kingdom of Ends on the earth;[173] they
are no longer mortals exiled from paradise, at war with God, others, self, and
nature, in need of the new and true son of David. Indifferent nature, not the
holy wrath of the Trinity of love, is the enemy of the human spirit.[174]

For the ensuing theology of the nineteenth century, "the religious view of the world, in all its species, rests on the fact that man in some degree distinguishes himself in worth from the phenomena which surround him and from the influences of nature which press in upon him. All religion . . . conserve[s] and confirms to the personal spirit its claims and its independence over-against the restrictions of nature and the natural effects of human society."[175] As Kant was the first, Ritschl writes in the same discussion, "to perceive the supreme importance for ethics of the 'Kingdom of God' as an association of men bound together by the laws of virtue," and Schleiermacher employed this decisive notion "teleologically . . . to determine the idea of Christianity,"[176] religion is now to be conceived as "the freedom of the children of God[; it] involves the impulse to conduct from the motive of love, aims at the moral organization of mankind, and grounds blessedness on the relation of Sonship to God, as well as on the Kingdom of God."[177] Ritschl tells us that such a conception of Christianity is "indispensable for systematic theology," in that "scientific understanding of the truths of Christianity depends on their correct definition" along these lines. Thus "the first task of systematic theology is correctly and completely to outline and clearly to settle the religious ideas or facts which are included in the conception of Christianity."[178] As the work of sorting, assessing, and systematizing models of the God-human communion in moral purpose over against brute nature in this fashion, Ritschl follows Schleiermacher in taking up a logical or philosophical space "above Christianity," i.e., "in the general concept of a religious community or fellowship of faith."

So from this metadogmatic space provided by epistemological foundationalism, "modern" or "philosophical" or "constructive" or "systematic" theology (no longer *dogmatics*) undertakes in the first place a purely historical account of the phenomena of human language about God: "every particular mode of faith can be rightly understood only by means of its relations of coexistence and sequence with others."[179] This inquiry splits off into a discipline of its own, providing material for reflection on the God-human communion, now clearly and distinctly resolved into historically particular modalities, unique expressions of Being that are *never* to be seen in larger linkages or systems that might efface that stubborn historical specificity so carefully uncovered and reconstructed. *Ipso facto*, Being, or "the nature of things, is not understood through the Bible, but the Bible itself is to be understood as a portion of this being, and therefore as subject to its general laws. . . . The Bible is not the key to nature but part of it; it must therefore be considered according to the same rules as hold for any kind of empirical knowledge."[180] The systematic separation of biblical studies from theology is thus established. On the other hand, "modern" theology also tries to determine the distinctive nature or "essence" of religion *as communion with God or union with the All.* This determination can never rest with particular, historically given materials. Instead it takes up the aforementioned dialectic of the phenomenal and the noumenal, immanence and transcendence, human and divine, *natura naturans* and *natura naturata.* Tillich expressly invoked this dialectic in his doctrine of God as at once creative and abysmal,[181] and he is right to suggest that overtly or covertly it drives all modern theology. The value of the dialectic does not lie in any cognitive insight historical discourses about God might lend, who, as beyond existence, is also beyond knowledge.[182] This is the one cognitive claim of modern theology, and it is held axiomatically, a priori; it is purely negative in content, really a kind of rule or stipulation. *God is inexpressible;* any claim to identify the noumenal God with a phenomenal reality that would declare God is "idolatrous." So much the worse, of course, for the antecedent theological tradition over against which "modern" theology views itself. We have here, it would seem, an impasse. In the trinitarianism of the antecedent tradition, the fundamental perception is of God who speaks, is spoken and heard. *The trinitarian God is essentially expressible.* God declares God for God — that is God's eternal mystery of being and the ground for His temporal self-presentation. Is there nothing here but a leap in one direction or another?

The Present Impasse

Jeffery Stout's insightful account of this impasse stems from Alasdair MacIntyre's observation of the "unpleasant" dilemma of traditional theology in modernity: "Any presentation of theism which is able to secure a hearing from a secular audience has undergone a transformation that has evacuated it entirely of its theistic content. Conversely, any presentation which retains such theistic content will be unable to secure the place in contemporary culture which those theologians desire for it."[183] Barth alone in modern theology grasped this situation and resolutely embraced it. In his categorical rejection of apologetics, Barth's theology maintained that "the irreducible language of Christian communal existence must maintain control over *what* is said in Christian theology and *how* the theologian says it." As a result, Stout writes, Barth

> carried the dialectical isolation of theological discourse from the rest of culture to an extreme. This is not to say, of course, that Barth in any sense

withdrew, as a citizen or a churchman, from the political and economic controversies of his time. But Barth's unwillingness to argue, his acceptance of paradox, and his insistence on the irreducibility of God's word undermined the preconditions for genuine debate with secular thought. . . . [T]he only alternative to [arguing apologetically for the probability of traditional theistic claims] is either "giving the atheist less and less in which to disbelieve" or a direct (nonapologetic) appeal to the authority of revelation. The problem is that revelation, according to the major Western traditions, is itself a historical event.[184]

Is this indeed a problem? Certainly, we have seen how it is for Kant, and behind him, Spinoza. But what if, instead, as Barth actually intends and followers like Jenson have seen, this historical event of the gospel is permitted to execute a critique of the antecedent metaphysics of classical paganism — which are, *redivivus* since Spinoza, the current metaphysics?[185]

For the Christian theological tradition, all theological discourse is grounded in the Nicene *homoousios* — the fundamental revision of the antecedent metaphysics by the gospel: "No one has ever seen God, but the only Son, who is in the bosom of the Father, has made him known" (John 1:18). "Traditional" Christian theology, that is to say, makes a cognitive claim in the region of theology that sounds "out of this world" to the ears of modern theology. God is the heavenly Father who is determined to redeem and fulfill the creation through His Son Jesus Christ in the Holy Spirit. There is a "dialectic" at work here as well, as there must be in any theology that does not substantially identify the Creator and the creature but rather relates them in unions, covenants, or communions. But the dialectic of this "traditional" theology is not Kantian and epistemological. It comes as no surprise that according to the Kantian dialectic of the two spheres one finally "has" God in not having God; that in godlessness one acknowledges one's incapacity for God; that God does not "exist"; that God is "nothing" in the world;[186] and so on. But the dialectic in traditional theology is trinitarian and ontological. That is to say, the concern is *not* to fend off concrete cognitive identifications of God in human discourse as such on the grounds of the incapacity of human reason or language to achieve scientific knowledge or adequate representation of the "transcendent." The concern is rather to fend off false identifications of God in human discourse that contradict the heavenly Father's determination to redeem and fulfill His creation through Jesus Christ in the Holy Spirit. That is the cognitive concern of dogmatics.

There is a weighty material consideration at work here as well. While historical-critical and existentialist perspectives continue to have illustrative and reformatory power, the individualistic, reductive, and positivist tendencies of these perspectives have inflicted a gaping wound across the heart of the tradition of Reformation theology: the notion that Christ in His person and work provides the good reason for justifying faith, so that we are justified before God not only *per* or *in* but also *propter Christum,* i.e., not arbitrarily or by divine fiat. Justification is not a word of pardon that just happens to be communicated through Christ as an instrument, but a word of pardon subsisting in His personal fulfillment or satisfaction of divine justice out of boundless love. *Pace* Spinoza, then, justification on account of Christ (as well as through Christ and in Christ) demands that a historical-narrative content be assigned to the term "Christ" that renders intelligible the faith placed personally in Him, and so in turn critically exposes as illicit alternative dogmatics, including Spinoza's own revisionist credo. As Christopher Morse has argued from the Barthian perspective: even as existentially authentic risk, a content-less faith incapable of discernment does not put us in the right relation to God.[187] Indeed, such "decisionism" can and has landed believers in the service of the devil.[188] To speak of Christ as the good reason of God's justifying the sinner, on the other hand, will require theology to make cognitive claims in the region of theology.

The epistemic basis of this traditional conception of theology as dogmatics has not primarily to do with human capacity or incapacity to speak of God, but with the *reality* in faith of the *Deus dixit,* as Barth understood the occasion of Christian theology, particularly in its Reformation iteration. "It is God who speaks from himself, an assertion from Hilary's *De Trinitate* that Luther often cites. 'Sic Hilarius: quis potest, inquit, melius de se loqui quam deus ipse?'"[189] God *is* the One who speaks Himself in Jesus Christ through the Holy Spirit, providing in this faith that comes by hearing the basis of human discourse about God. Epistemology does not map ontology. Ontology in act provides access.[190] Thus "knowing, they are affected by the object known. They no longer exist without it, but with it. In so far as they think of it, with the same confidence with which they dare to think in general they must think of it as a true reality, as true in its existence and nature. Whatever else and however else they may think of it, they must begin by thinking of the truth of its reality."[191] This is stated in distinction from the "Modernist view from which we must demarcate ourselves," Barth writes, going "back to the Renaissance and especially to the Renaissance philosopher Descartes with his proof of God from human self-certainty."[192] "The procedure in theology, then, is to establish self-certainty on the certainty of

God . . . the fact of the knowledge of God's Word that does not presuppose its possibility in man, but coming to man, brings the possibility with it."[193] That God is *heard* in the person of the Holy Spirit from the *speaking* of God's Word in the person of the Son is integral to the trinitarian dialectic, the traditional narrative of trinitarian advent. In theology this reality-creating-access is confessed in the cognitive claim: the heavenly Father is the One determined to redeem the creation through His Son and bring it to fulfillment in His Spirit. This cognitive proposition *represents* the one, true God in the region of theological discourse.

But *is* such an object of theological discourse *there* to lend the asserted *access* to such a "region of theology," the Kantian might hastily object? How could you ever know? If we do not know first that God *exists,* we can hardly appeal to the reality of God speaking in faith. That fact that people certainly think so (and worse, act so) is not to the point of the objection. They may be deluded. Thinking and acting as if one knew the mind of God, the Kantian charges, is the "idolatrous" source of enthusiasm with all the terrorism, fanaticism, and obscurantism that attend "traditional" theology. The point of the Kantian counterquestion then is to preclude access to that "region of theology" where the Christian proposition (among others) can make sense, if not as such be verified. There may be such a region, just as there may be unicorns in a distant galaxy, but we have no access to it and thus we have no rational right to make any claims nor have we any rational way to adjudicate claims. But, the "traditional" theologian responds: we are granted this access in Jesus Christ, understood as the One who sought and found the way to us in our lost and godless state in the same faith of the Holy Spirit who led Him to our place at the cross. In union of repentance and faith with Jesus by that same Spirit, we now share his relationship to the heavenly Father *and so in reality* we have come to know and confess here on the earth in the fullness of time the theological truth that the heavenly Father is the One determined to redeem and fulfill through Christ and the Spirit — this is the one true God and not some other. That is question begging, the Kantian rejoins: you are arguing in a circle, merely asserting conditions of reality without any critical epistemological account of what to all the world must appear as the privileged claims of "enthusiasm." Yes, of course, we are "privileged," the reply comes. That is what is so amazing about "grace" — just so, by the way, theology is not philosophy. It occupies the same space and time as philosophy, and speaks about objects in the shared world, but theology operates by its own rules, proceeding from the particular to the general. Then theology is fideism, comes the rejoinder. It belongs in the private space of interiority; it is the language of a sect, properly sealed off in a ghetto where it can do no harm to the public. And so on and on in the theological stalemate that has emerged in Kantian culture since Barth's attempted insurrection: the stalemated "conflict between the two phenomenologies" of the idol and the icon.[194]

How Barth Appropriated Leibniz's
Teaching on the Divine Decree

A Few Perplexities

Paul Lehmann in his day was a peerless champion of Karl Barth's theology.[1]
When I was a graduate student at Union Theological Seminary in New York
during the late 1970s, he once suggested to me that Kant's was the philoso-
phy most congenial to Lutheran sensibilities. Even then I recoiled at the
thought, for reasons that have become evident in the preceding chapter. But
I admit its plausibility. Why *do* so many modern Lutherans gravitate to
Kantianism? And why do they, unlike Barth, see no need to "overcome"
Kant, as I have just argued? Another perplexity arises in this connection.
George Hunsinger has asked with justified astonishment, "How could
Barth's massive accord with Luther come to be so roundly overlooked?"[2] I
could ask with equal justification, Has any Lutheran ever been able to pro-
vide real theological insight into how the two great theologians differ? That
is, without the tacit revisionism of the Ritschl-Bultmann-Ebeling type?[3]
Anyone could list any number of issues on which the two appear to diverge
without ever reckoning with the "massive accord" of Luther and Barth on
the fundamental autonomy of theology as a nonspeculative discipline arising from the contingent event of the Word of God spoken in Jesus Christ.
This convergence provides the grid through which all issues are recognized,
assessed, and resolved. Without an account of this accord, however, no one
can properly assess the apparent differences; one will rather confuse differences in idiom and audience, not to mention place in history, with substantial disagreement. I will argue in this chapter against several such wrong-

headed Lutheranisms in favor of Barth's doctrine of election in *Church Dogmatics* II/2.

As long as we are inventorying perplexities, however, let me add a few more. I have never known a disciple of Barth's willing to acknowledge, as Barth was (at least on some days), his affinity with Leibniz's "optimism," if not sympathy for Leibniz's theodicy. On the contrary, most that I am aware of have seized upon a single late, brief, and uncharacteristically shallow discussion of Leibniz in connection with the doctrine of evil in Schleiermacher, Heidegger, and Sartre and used it to distance Barth from his comrade in optimism. Nor, however, have I met many Lutherans who could recognize in Leibniz's optimism the full philosophical flower of the reform of the university curriculum undertaken 150 years previous by Philip Melanchthon. In chapter 4 I will lay out Melanchthon's vision for philosophy in a reformed Christian civilization, and in chapter 5 I will show how Leibniz tried to sustain that vision in face of Spinoza's challenge, yet failed. But the task before us now is to contend for the thesis that Barth's optimism is but a deeper, more consistent, and more rigorously christological development of the revealed theology of creation that Leibniz pioneered in the ultimately self-defeating form of "natural theology."

The thesis, however, surely must provoke its own perplexity in students of Barth. This is in part because the negative assessment of the *Theodicy* in *Church Dogmatics* III/3[4] (to which I just alluded) has seemed to many Barth's decisive word on the matter. In what follows, however, I will show how little actual exegesis of Leibniz attends Barth's judgment here; the perfunctory account of Leibniz really serves as little more than a foil for Barth's rhetorical need to differentiate his own conceptually difficult talk of evil as nothingness.[5] At the same time, Barth earlier presupposes far more favorable readings of Leibniz, especially in connection with the doctrine of election worked out in *Church Dogmatics* II/2, as we shall see. But the perplexity that arises from this chapter's thesis is not only due to certain conventional readings of Barth. Certainly there is in Barth a general aversion to systematic, philosophical theodicies that work ideologically as justification of the political status quo ante. These legitimate evil as playing a subordinate but useful part in the divine economy of things, and certainly Barth's aversion to such thinking plays the decisive rhetorical role in volume III/3's criticism of thinkers like Leibniz and Hegel. As we shall see, however, the distinction Leibniz makes between natural and moral evil, much like Barth's distinction between the shadow cast by natural finitude and the destructive fury of the Nothing that God does not will, largely escapes such criticism. The problem lies deeper. One of the best renderings of Barth's teaching on evil articulates the heart of his position this way: "For, given the identity of God, 'the simple alternative[—]either the gracious God (and He alone) is for us, or nothingness is the abyss from which we have emerged and to which we shall return' — does not exist ontologically."[6] Yet it exists ontically in the minds of many today. On the surface, this ontologically impossible alternative reproduces exactly the choice between Leibniz and Spinoza, which, as I am arguing, resurfaces today after Kant, after modernism, after dualism. What then could be the status of this ontologically impossible alternative? Are we simply deluded in attending to it ontically? That is a genuine perplexity!

Leibniz on Election: A Preliminary Account

John Hick would not generally be regarded as among the reliable interpreters of the theology of Karl Barth. But in regard to the reputed failure of Leibniz's theodicy, he speaks for received opinion when he cites Barth's sharp statement that "at bottom [Leibniz] had hardly any serious interest (and from the practical standpoint none at all) in the problem of evil."[7] Hick comments: "Having shown to his own satisfaction that we are living in the best possible world, Leibniz was content to enjoy his own comparatively comfortable lot, leaving it to those who were less fortunate to make the best they could of it."[8] The slur is as contemptible as it is conventional. In any case, Hick bases it upon the aforementioned selective reading of the *Church Dogmatics*. In point of historical fact, Leibniz was an inveterate do-gooder,[9] whose politics were as humane as seventeenth-century horizons allowed.[10] Hick is not beneath resort to caricature — a fate to which the wigged bachelor of the Baroque Court seems especially vulnerable (nor was Leibniz unaware of that — witness his self-parody in *Mars Christianissimus*).[11] Let us painfully elaborate.

Hick writes: "Leibniz offers a kind of cybernetic myth in which the divine intellect, like an infinite calculating machine, sets up every possible combination of existents, surveys them exhaustively, and selects the best."[12] Yet again: "Rejecting the Manichaean form of dualism, and at the same time setting up his own form of it, Leibniz says" that the source of evil lies in "the possibility of things, that which alone God did not make, since he is not the author of his own understanding [cf. *Theodicy,* par. 380]. Hence, 'the source of evil lies in the possible forms, anterior to the acts of God's will' [cf. *Theodicy,* par. 381]."[13] The knowing of all compossibles, for Leibniz, *is* the omniscient God in His perfection of wisdom. Ignoring this, Hick's bizarre critique follows: "such a dualism . . . represents a radical departure from the conception of God that has operated in all the main branches of Christendom; and from this point of view we must say that Leibniz's doctrine of a realm of eternal possibilities, which does not permit there to be a world free from evil, is sub-Christian in the restriction that it sets upon the divine sovereignty."[14] Not only is this to exalt the *deus exlex* as the normative Christian conception of divine sovereignty. It is maliciously to ignore the differentiation between moral and metaphysical evil on which Leibniz's entire argument turns, in that metaphysically no conceivable world of creatures could be free of mutual, often painful, limitation. Hick ought to know better. In his own words, he acknowledges what he regards as "certain mistaken presuppositions . . . : Both Aquinas and Leibniz think in terms of the great chain of being consisting of all the modes of existence from the highest to the lowest, with man about mid-way on the scale. And when they speak of the goodness of the universe they are referring to the adequacy of this complex whole considered as an expression of the overflowing creativity of God. The goodness of the universe is not conceived by them in instrumental terms, as its suitability to fulfill some specific divine purpose, but as an intrinsic goodness which is ultimately equivalent simply to existence itself." So Hick is aware of Leibniz's own meaning. But setting this "mistake" aside in favor of taking up the "teaching that world has been created for the sake of mankind"[15] (which is exactly the ecological point of the "great chain of being"), we come to the real source of Hick's critique (of a caricature) on the following page. Here Hick cites Voltaire's *Candide:* "If this is the best possible world, there can be no hope either for its improvement or for an eventual translation to a better, and despair or resignation could well be the appropriate reaction."[16] What an ad hoc mix of criticism! Leibnizian realism about the creaturely condition as well as optimism about human progress becomes wholly incomprehensible in Hick's account.

If anything, Leibniz is vulnerable to exactly the opposite kind of criticism, namely, that "in his relentless pursuit of the good, he perhaps lost sight of the truth" of the tragic, as Matthew Stewart rightly points out.[17] Calling Leibniz a Manichean and sub-Christian for denying the absolute divine omnipotence, Hick has forgotten what he had written only a few pages earlier. In his "reconciliation of human freedom with divine sovereignty Leibniz stands within the broad Augustinian tradition. His argument parallels the reply made by Augustine to the charge that divine predestination takes away man's liberty: namely, that God's foreseeing of our free actions does not ren-

der them any less free."[18] Noting Leibniz's subscription to the article of faith
that the creation is very good, Hick likewise acknowledges: "Leibniz's conclusion is thus an article of faith derived from the prior faith that this world
has been created by an all-powerful and perfectly good deity." Hick's account
amounts then to what the Germans call "inconsequent" interpretation. The
inconsistencies in his portrait of Leibniz, however, betray Hick's not so hidden agenda, which is to put "the Augustinian tradition" on the horns of a dilemma: "If it insists (with Leibniz) that this is indeed the best possible world,
it thereby implies that God was powerless to make a better one, and so denies His omnipotence; but if on the other hand it asserts (with Thomism)
that this is not the best possible world, it calls in question God's goodness
and love, which were not sufficient to induce Him to will a better one."[19]
Missing in this formulation of the dilemma is a consideration that is essential for Leibniz: divine wisdom.

It is furthermore instructive to see how Hick's use of Barth misleads, for
on examination it is not Barth's critique of Leibniz at all that appears in
Hick. The critique of Leibniz that appears in Hick is — if it is anything more
than a popular resort to Dr. Pangloss — parasitic on Kant's important essay,
"On the Miscarriage of All Philosophical Trials in Theodicy." Hick writes:

> The enigma of evil presents so massive and direct a threat to our faith that
> we are bound to seek within the resources of Christian thought for ways,
> if not of resolving it, at least of rendering [it] bearable by the Christian
> conscience. But, on the other hand, in seeking to justify the ways of God
> to man, one is inevitably tempted to extend faith's dim sense of a hidden
> divine purpose and sovereignty into an open map of providence such as
> could be available only to the Creator Himself. It is this almost inevitable
> pretension of theodicy to a cosmic vantage point that provokes the
> thought that any solution to the problem of evil must be worse than the
> problem itself![20]

We may now set aside Hick's fashionable but inconsequent interpretation in
favor of the more serious borrowing from Kant that actually takes place
here. Kant had written: "Every previous theodicy has not performed what it
promised, namely, the vindication of the moral wisdom of the world-
government against the doubts raised against it on the basis of what the experience of this world teaches." "To be sure," Kant adds immediately, ". . . as
objections . . . neither can these doubts prove the contrary." The critique of
philosophical theodicy, like everything in Kant, turns on the unbridgeable

gap between the two spheres: "insight into *the relationship in which any world as we may ever become acquainted with through experience stands with respect to the highest wisdom*" is "too high for us . . . an insight into which no mortal can attain."[21] This is the real issue, as concluded in the previous chapter. Yet I would be remiss if I failed to point out in this connection that Hick thinks himself to have *just such* insights. If we think, he writes, "of God's goodness and love in more personal terms, we cannot so easily reconcile the existence of cholera, or more generally what might be called the anti-human aspects of nature, with infinite love and power in the Creator. For from man's point of view the presence or absence of cholera germs makes a very poignant difference. And as the loving heavenly Father of mankind, He must surely see disease as an enemy to His purpose and as incompatible with his rule."[22] Unlike Kant, then, who rigorously maintained the agnosticism requisite to those who eschew the "pretension of theodicy to a cosmic vantage point," and thus resolutely refused "anthropomorphism," Hick is willing to storm heaven with objections raised on the basis of finite insight into limited human experience. Yet why should we think at all of God in "more personal terms," as the "loving heavenly Father of mankind"? What warrants any such belief in the first place? A little time with Spinoza would squeeze this kind of childish play out of Hick. And why, by the way, does Hick think of this "loving heavenly Father" so differently than, say, the Sermon on the Mount, where the heavenly Father is said to cause his rain to fall on the just and unjust alike?

Let us listen at some length to Leibniz's own words in response to the egregious anthropocentrism that isolates the human from the ecological web of life:

> [It is always] the same sophism; they change and mutilate the fact, they only half record things: God has care for men, he loves the human race, he wishes it well; nothing so true. Yet he allows men to fall, he often allows them to perish, he gives them goods that tend towards their destruction; and when he makes someone happy, it is after many sufferings: where is his affection, where is his goodness or again where is his power? Vain objections, which suppress the main point, which ignore the fact that it is of God one speaks. It is as though one were speaking of a mother, a guardian, a tutor, whose well-nigh only care is concerned with the upbringing, the preservation, the happiness of the person in question, and who neglect their duty. God takes care of the universe, he neglects nothing, he chooses what is best on the whole. . . . If we infer . . . that God only regretfully, and

owing to lack of power, fails to make men happy and to give the good first of all and without admixture of evil, or else that he lacks the good will to give it unreservedly and for good and all, then we are comparing our true God with the God of Herodotus, full of envy, or with the demon . . . who gives good things in order that he may cause more affliction by taking them away. That would be trifling with God in perpetual anthropomorphisms, representing him as a man who must give himself up completely to one particular business, whose goodness must be chiefly exercised upon those objects alone which are known to us, and who lacks either aptitude or good will. God is not lacking therein, he could do the good that we would desire; he even wishes it, taking it separately, but he must not do it in preference to other goods which are opposed to it. Moreover, one has no cause to complain of the fact that usually one attains salvation only through many sufferings, and by bearing the cross of Jesus Christ. These evils serve to make the elect imitators of their master, and to increase their happiness.[23]

The allusion in the final sentence to the notions of election and imitation might be overlooked, but that would be the singular error that leads to all the misreadings of Leibniz. As may be seen from this passage, at the apex of Leibniz's philosophical theodicy comes another crucial borrowing from Christian theology: howsoever reserved in expression, Luther's early theology of the cross recurs here, in that election is interpreted *substantively* as the actualization of Christ's death and resurrection, as the *realization* of the spiritual death of the egocentric self and resurrection of the new person who is "saved" by passing to the ecstatic existence of the love of God above all and all things in and under God. The appearance of this notion of salvation by bearing the cross of Christ in the *Theodicy* is no pious gloss or afterthought. Years earlier we find in Leibniz's notes from around 1690 a revealing little essay, "On the True Theologia Mystica."[24] Already here basic themes of the *Theodicy* emerge: "Sin is not from God, but original sin has arisen in some creatures from their nonbeing and hence out of nothingness." This means that finitude is the possibility, but not the necessity, of sin, which "God has permitted . . . because he knows how to bring a greater good out of evil," namely, salvation in Christ. The reference here to the *wisdom* of God, as we shall see, is critical to Leibniz's eventual account of the divine economy, which is not defined by a binary dialectic of freedom and love, but by a trinitarian dialectic of power (= freedom), wisdom, and love.

Attention in this little essay, however, quickly shifts to the matter of the

authenticity of faith as per Luther's *theologia crucis*. In echoes of the early
Luther's Augustinian defense of the "good of the cross,"[25] Leibniz exposits
the paradoxical good in spiritual life of negating the negation of self-love to
obtain the true good of love of God above all and of all things in God. "The
denial of self is the hatred of the nonbeing which is in us and the love of the
origin of our self-being, or God. 'Crucifying the old Adam,' drawing near to
Christ, dying to Adam and living in Christ — all these consist in this: that we
deny nonbeing and cling to self-being." As human beings are in Leibniz's
thought distinctly and especially human in being minds that reflect the
world in desiring God their true good, the true human being as image of
God is to reflect the true and generous God who is worthy of all desire in
love for the creation. But false being, distorted being, being turned away
from God to nonbeing is oriented to creatures in place of the Creator, rendering them idols, devouring and being devoured by them. It is conformation to Christ's cross and resurrection that executes the transition from false
to true being. For "what is needed is not the annihilation of the self but the
generous expansion of the self to take in others."[26] The subtler issue that
arises here — after Kant's and Nygren's critiques of charity or interested love
as sub-Christian — is what can only appear in Leibniz's account as an element of eudaemonism, if not hedonism. Thus in interpretation of the theology of the cross, Kantians think of the sheer, kenotic annihilation of the egocentric self, rather than its new formation as an eccentric self, what Riley
calls Leibniz's "expansive self."[27] "It is really a matter of whether one thinks
that love (including self-love) is an integral and necessary part of any adequate morality — so that, in Leibniz' words, 'the good man is he who loves
everyone' — or whether such 'feeling' is morally irrelevant (even harmful):
that one simply 'ought' to act well, and that 'oughtness' or moral necessity is
given by practical reason alone."[28]

Love, for Leibniz, integrates eros under agape in the "expanded self"
that comes from faith. Like the early Luther, Leibniz thus speaks of the *person* who does theology, the *theologian*,[29] in the following statements directed
against "secret unbelief":

> He who merely fears God loves himself and his nonbeing more than God.
> Faith without knowledge comes not of the spirit of God but of the dead
> letter or the empty echo. Faith without light awakens no love but only fear
> or hope and it is not living. He who does not act according to his faith has
> no faith, even though he may boast of it. It is deplorable that so few peo-
> ple know what light and faith, love and life, Christ and blessedness, are.

Christ's teaching is spirit and truth, but many make of it flesh and shadow. Most men have no earnestness. They have never tasted truth and are bogged down in a secret unbelief.[30]

From these observations, Leibniz drew a rule: "Let each examine himself whether he has faith and life. If he finds any other joy and pleasure greater than that in the love of God and the glorification of his will, he does not sufficiently know Christ and does not yet feel the promptings of the Holy Spirit. Scripture gives us a beautiful test to determine whether a man loves God, namely, if he loves his brother and strives to serve others as far as he can. Whoever does not do this boasts falsely of his illumination or of Christ and the Holy Spirit."[31] Leibniz follows Augustine as rendered by Luther: "Since Christ lives in us through faith he arouses us to do good works through that living faith in his work. . . . Thus the deeds of mercy are aroused by the works through which he has saved us."[32] It is as if Leibniz were cribbing from Luther's Heidelberg Disputation!

Election in Christ, therefore — and this is the important point as is evident in the criticism of those "who boast" — is not an arbitrary privileging of some without reason and without effect, but substantively the Holy Spirit's conformation to Christ as the Crucified and Risen One for the sake of the whole creation. "God does not have an unconditional will to power [*Machtwille*] but wills everything with a cause and for the best. Election by his grace [*Gnadenwahl*] has its origin in his foreknowledge of the worth of men and therefore not in his foreknowledge of their faith or their works but from much higher causes. For if a man believes, or says, or thinks, or does anything good, this is a result of God's foreseen election of him in Christ." Leibniz thus thinks his way through the Scylla of a despotic *decretum absolutum* and the Charybdis of moralizing Pelagianism *because* he reckons with the higher *wisdom* of God, who knows how to make good out of evil. Worth is not an intrinsic quality of the autonomous moral agent for God passively to recognize as its merit, but the extrinsic value conferred upon individuals in light of God's saving purpose for all. "For one unimportant thing added to another can often produce something more precious than either of the others. It is here that the secret of the election of grace lies hidden and that its knot is to be untied. *Duo irregularia possunt aliquando facere aliquid regulare* [Two irregularities can sometimes make a regularity]. God wills the salvation of all creatures and their best."[33]

The foregoing yields a thesis: for Leibniz the "loving heavenly Father of mankind" is not the Nanny-in-the-Sky Hick imagines, but the One "who spared not His own Son but gave Him up for us all," whose grace in this act delivers from sinful egocentrism for new lives of cross-bearing service. *Grace delivers from sin, not nature.* Nature included the interested self and its "feelings" is the object of redemption, not the object of some cruel, Stoic discipline. Nature, apprehended as the ecological web of finitude, is good, not evil, even though pain is intrinsic to its operation no less than pleasure. This later take on physical evil that is nevertheless "good" in the ecology of things is essential to any sober theological account, not only of the value of the human mind with its body, but also for right understanding of the uniquely human (and angelic) possibility of moral evil by the refusal of suffering.[34] Arthur Peacocke — certainly a theologian who would otherwise be most unsympathetic with this line of argument! — wrote on the basis of contemporary biological science: "The combination of vulnerability and increased sensitivity to signals from the environment has, as its concomitant, a heightened ability to suffer pain and it is not at all easy to conceive how one could have the former without the latter. . . . We cannot avoid concluding that the pain and suffering consequent upon vulnerability are the inherently necessary price that has to be paid for consciousness to emerge with its associated cognitive powers."[35] Leibniz, with his doctrine of the metaphysical evil of finitude corresponding to the physical evil of pain, already knew just this. So, as we shall see, did Barth. It is a Leibniz along these lines whom, I shall now argue, Barth appropriates, corrects, and deepens by making explicit the christological basis of election to the love of God above all and all things in and under God.

Barth's Leibniz: Partnership in Optimism

Despite his rhetorical self-distancing from Leibniz in *Church Dogmatics* III/3, Barth sees things in much the same way.[36] Unlike Kant or Hick but with the Pauline theodicy stemming from Romans 8, Barth believes that the theology of revelation has no choice but to appear foolish in the eyes of philosophy and in faith assume, as it were, "a cosmic vantage point" that vindicates the creation along with its finitude and pain as good. "The meaning and truth of Christian optimism consist in [Christ's] lowliness and exaltation, in His death and resurrection as the secret of the divine will in creation and the divine good-pleasure in the created world."[37] There is a nuance here. In theology as Barth understands it, the significance of optimism is as an act of faith in God the good Creator against Gnosticism; the theodicy of faith is not meant to proffer a rational demonstration of the wisdom of the world's engineer, as that might appear to any neutral observer, as if to silence general rational doubt about the benevolence or competence of the cosmic architect. In theology, theodicy is that articulation of faith in God for the world's future that against all contrary evidence from experience giving rise to dualistic tendencies in thought vindicates the goodness of the *suffering* creation, *in spite of* sin and death, when it is taken then as suffering with Jesus. Christian metaphysical optimism is, at bottom, the refusal of Gnostic pessimism; its ground is accordingly not found in uncovering the hidden harmony of experience apart from Christ but rather found in the theology of the cross that stood upon this very earth (Moltmann). It is by the solidarity forged there through God's participation in the person of His Son in the sufferings of the alienated creation that sufferers are in turn validated so that they may endure to the end, knowing in faith "that the sufferings of this present age are not worthy to be compared to the glory which is to be revealed."

Accordingly Barth's criticism of eighteenth-century apologetics[38] was that *this* christological possibility for theodicy was never imagined: "even the natural knowledge of God, the knowledge of God in and from the created world, and therefore the knowledge of its perfection, can clearly, solidly and necessarily be reached only through the medium of Jesus Christ the Crucified." In contrast to this general approach of natural theology aimed at uncovering the hidden harmony of things, Barth writes, "it is to the special credit of Leibniz, however, that at least once to my knowledge he found a place for this one essential thing . . . it is in relation to Christ, to His position as Member and Head of creation, as Lord and Savior and Hope of the world that God chose this world as the best. . . . Leibniz did actually write [this]."[39] Barth cites the Latin from the scholastic conclusion to the *Theodicy* (*Causa Dei*, 49), which I translate as follows: "that in choosing the best series of things, the greatest reason would be Christ, the God-man, who is to hold [it] together, insofar as he is the most advanced creature, the most noble in that series, just as he is part of the created universe, indeed the head, to whom all power is given in heaven and earth, in whom all nations ought to be blessed, through whom all creatures ought to be set free from the servitude of corruption for the glorious liberty of the sons of God."[40] Unmistakably the latter reference is to Romans 8. Christ is the world's *ultima ratio* as head of creation in whom all are being reconciled and integrated into the life of the eschatological kingdom.[41] Barth complains, to be sure, that this "greatest reason" for the world's existence seems somewhat underdeveloped in the overall argument of the *Theodicy*, as if Leibniz let it slip on occasion when he ought rather to have sounded a fanfare. Leibniz's Christology should have been fully acknowledged and centrally utilized, since indeed in his thought it is Christ who causes this world's existence to be the "best possible." Barth's complaint here is justified, and in the chapters to come I shall discuss the factors that lead Leibniz down his path of ambivalence.

The observation in any case gives Barth occasion to conclude his discussion of Leibniz's *Theodicy* with his own insightful critique of "thinking in terms of two spheres." "We have no right to throw stones at Leibniz," he writes, "if we tear asunder nature and grace, creation and covenant, the revelation of creation and the revelation of salvation; and if we finally introduce this whole tension even into the Holy Trinity." Looking beyond Leibniz, Barth writes, "the sun of the Enlightenment ruthlessly exposed what must always come to light sooner or later when this double system is used. When the two books [of nature and grace] are juxtaposed as sources of our knowledge of the Creator and creation, it is quite useless to recommend the book of grace. . . . the book which is actually read and from which the knowledge of the Creator and the creation is actually gained is only the one book, i.e., the book of nature."[42] *Deus absconditus* defeats *deus revelatus* in just this way. Thus Barth acknowledged as a cultural reality of the contemporary Western mind the existence of what is for him the ontologically "impossible" choice between Leibnizian grace and Spinozist nature. In an intriguing essay on this problem, Graham Ward has rightly written that "nihilism" (which we can here take as the doctrine of cosmic pointlessness signified by the myth of eternal recurrence that finds its first modern articulation in Spinoza) "is not at all possible, for Barth, outside of a theological worldview. What he detects in the eighteenth-century programme of the Enlightenment (and its Romantic reaction) is the constant secularization of theologically grounded truths." The procedure actually initiates with Descartes. Ward writes, "The absolutism of individualism — where the self-grounded and autonomous I makes its own sovereign judgments about the world and its experience of it — is a parody of the doctrine of the *imago dei*. Man now makes himself in the image of God."[43] The Cartesian ego exists in the negating of the creator God whose wise choice and loving purpose powerfully establish the human person as the image of God; the result in turn is not a mere reduction in the biblical God to a restricted space of interiority but a real transformation in theology: the positing of an omnipotent being in the biblical God's place. Ward's suggestion, as we shall see, is precisely right; the subtle exchange of gods that occurred in Cartesianism is what so deeply troubled Leibniz. Yet Barth's and Ward's point is that this titanic project is doomed to fail. It has no ground in the nature of things but is a philosophy that is parasitic upon the rotting corpse of the antecedent faith.

The failure of Leibniz's theodicy and its defeat *as philosophy* by Spinozism along these lines, that is, its failure as a covert attempt to secure by reason from natural experience a true metaphysics in support of revealed theology, allows a reversal: reading Leibniz *as theology*, that is, as attempting the interpretation of reason and nature in executing a revision of metaphysics from the perspective of revealed religion. This is what Barth generously and appreciatively does in the earlier discussions of Leibniz in the *Church Dogmatics*. Admittedly, none of this is very clear in Leibniz himself (Riley's manifest desire to interpret Leibniz as a consistent Platonic rationalist notwithstanding).[44] But Barth shows how Leibniz can be read *as theology*, i.e., as *Nachdenken*, as thinking out the sense of a world created with a view to its redemption in Christ, "creation" then as redeemed and fulfilled in the coming of the Reign, and thus issuing in "theological optimism." Barth even expressed affinity with Leibniz when read this way: "We, too, have had to state clearly the principle that the nature as well as the existence of the created world is affirmed by God its Creator, so that to this existence it is justified and perfect . . . not simply bad or good, but the best of all worlds, seeing that the good-pleasure of God created it and rests upon it. Hence we, too, have unquestionably espoused a definite optimism, and we cannot be ashamed of the company in which we find ourselves, whether we like it or not." Barth especially points here to the doxological theme that courses through Leibniz's writing: "a moving gratitude which [is] almost exemplary in comparison with the inattention and ingratitude, resentment and indifference, sheer blindness and ignorance characteristic of so many other periods, e.g., with the sardonic sneering of Voltaire,"[45] or the Gnostic malice, contemporaneous to Leibniz, of Pierre Bayle.

Barth marshaled the evidence for this theological reading. "The interest which Leibniz took in the churches as in so many other matters, and the respect with which he approached the Bible and dogma, deserve attention," he writes. "In his *Theodicy* he tried to come to terms with Paul, Augustine, Calvin and especially Luther's *De servo arbitrio*, i.e. to explain them in his own sense."[46] This theological wrestling of Leibniz with Luther's *De servo arbitrio* will especially concern us in the final chapter of this book. In any event, such textual evidence for Leibniz's theological interest, as Barth reports, is abundant. But materially, Barth's own "Christian thesis that the world was willed and created good by God its Creator bears a close resemblance to that of the well-known writings in which Leibniz . . . crowned his metaphysical, scientific, ethical but also theological work. . . . Leibniz, too, in the question which here concerns us [the justification of creaturely existence], resolutely and with a most emphatic appeal to the name of God made a positive choice and decision."[47] When God is taken cosmically with the Bible, not acosmically with Gnosticism, theodicy is as much about the justification of the creature as of the Creator.

Barth is correct in this claim about Leibniz's theological interest, over against the argument of widespread provenance especially in Anglo-American circles, as previously mentioned, beginning with Bertrand Russell and followed by major interpreters like Arthur Lovejoy in the past century. This is the view that Leibniz is a crypto-Spinozist, whose theological interest is so much insincere window dressing. Substantively put, in Lovejoy's influential generalization: "Though most of the optimistic writers of the eighteenth century were less thorough-going or less frank in their cosmical determinism than Spinoza, such philosophic consolation as they offered was at bottom the same as his. It was an essentially intellectual consolation, the mood that it was usually designed to produce was that of reasoned acquiescence in the inevitable, based upon a conviction that its inevitableness was absolute and due to no arbitrary caprice."[48] We heard Lewis White Beck reiterate exactly the same criticism, though extending it backward to its putative source in Luther's alleged ethical passivity and metaphysical consolation. Stoic? Augustinian? What's the difference? In this way, Luther's theology of the martyrs or Leibniz's express differentiation in Luther's tradition of Christian "fate" from Stoic "fate" is simply dismissed, or rather goes uncomprehended. "It is no small thing to be content with God and the universe, not to fear what destiny has in store for us, nor to complain of what befalls us," Leibniz writes. "Acquaintance with true principles gives us this advantage, quite other than that the Stoics and Epicureans derived from their philosophy. There is as much difference between true morality and theirs as there is between joy and patience: for their tranquility was founded only on necessity, while ours must rest upon the perfection and beauty of things, upon our own happiness."[49] This latter too is a reference to Romans 8:18. As Vailati explains it, Leibniz viewed Spinoza "as a reviver of the ancient Stoic doctrines about the world-soul and the frank recognition of the necessity of all events as a prerequisite for achievement of happiness," while Leibniz himself believed that contingent events "are certain and part of a providential plan" presupposing the intelligence and will of a supramundane Creator.[50] Different theologies, different cosmologies, different consolations, different ethics. It may be conceded that on account of the protological bias implicit in his "preestablished harmony" there is a tricky question here about whether Leibniz succeeds in differentiating physical necessity and moral determination, as manifestly he wishes to do. Yet it is interpretation in bad faith that fails to see how this theologically motivated differentiation issues for Leibniz, as Riley has clearly seen, in the alternative between a resigned ethic of duty and an active ethic of charity, just as the above citation indicates.[51]

In contrast to the bad-faith readings of Leibniz's theological interest, Barth is inclined to call attention to Christian Wolff, who, he says, jettisoned Leibniz's starting point in the supreme monad, God, and replaced it with an "even more intelligible . . . 'coherence of the manifold'" of the world machine, crowned by a last chapter on God, "the perfection of the world . . . guaranteed by [its] clockwork character."[52] In Wolff a long stride is taken toward the autonomy of the secular world with God above and beyond as its Guarantor, and as a result, "it is a long way . . . from the perfection of the world which Leibniz found in the predetermined harmony of antitheses primarily actualized and developed in the original divine monad and secondarily in the plentitude of all other monads, to the machine-like character of creation in Wolff."[53] Organism is replaced by mechanism, and in this transformation, despite all similarity,[54] the difference of Leibniz from Wolff is precisely the role Christian theology continued to play in Leibniz's thought. "The system of Leibniz may be described as theocentric because, constructively considered, it undoubtedly has its origin and center in the idea of God as the central monad and the Guarantor of the predetermined harmony of creation. But when we come to Wolff this lead loses its central position and function."[55] The idealistic collapse of the triune God into the collective Mind of evolving humanity is under way. The first step in Wolff is to show that "rational man and the ordered world are an integral whole."[56] In Wolff optimistic man, in a second step, "takes it upon himself to declare the world is good in the light of his own goodness." Barth asks, "Does he need God in this task?"[57]

Thus the focal point of Barth's critique shines on the point where Wolffianism displaced the theological interest in Leibniz. "The judgment of optimism is the judgment of the creature about himself and the world that surrounds him — nothing more," i.e., it is a judgment *qua philosophy* that must eventually fail, as in Voltaire or Kant, in view of the conundrum caused by the actuality of evil. In Barth's view, it is a fatal "presupposition that the goodness which justifies creation must be intrinsic to [the world] and as such amenable to human judgment." But this is "a question which cannot be answered within this circle of ideas — the question of the goodness of this good, or the ultimate meaning and purpose of this harmony or mechanism or useful apparatus."[58] The agnosticism of Kant qua philosopher toward philosophical theodicy is in this way dialectically reaffirmed by Barth. In contrast, however, "the Christian way of affirming the Creator's justifying Yes to His creation . . . includes what is palpably missing in [philosophical] optimism — a true and urgent and inescapable awareness of the imperiling of creation by its limits, of sin and death and the devil."[59] Indeed, for Barth sin, death, and devil appear, or perhaps better, are exposed so that they may be seen for the destructive powers that they are when Christ as the righteousness and life of the incarnate God comes on the scene. The theological way of thinking always begins from the Nevertheless of intervening grace provoking all too real manifestations of sin, death, and devil in reply. This affirmation of the creation thus comes from without, just as it costs nothing less than the Son of God's negation by those destructive powers that He might become in turn "the death of death and hell's destruction." The harmony of creation is a negation of the negation; an ever active harmonization of creation from above into the direction of God's kingdom, a permanent revolution driving an onward evolution, the ever-approaching reconciliation of the sinner and holy God, the ever-anticipated vindication of the dying creature that comes upon the world from the outside, from above, resisting the world for the sake of the world, moving things on to the best possible that God intends from the beginning. For Barth this harmonization is in God's mind in the very act of origin; it is the end to which all things are pressed, the ontology of salvation (*Heilsontologie* — a pejorative term created by Barth's existentialist critics).

With respect to the theological perception of this threat of evil, Barth concedes, "Leibniz did not dispute that we are confronted at this point by an objective conundrum grounded in the reality of the creaturely world." What he denied was that evil's "riddle is ultimate and insoluble, that the actual contradiction can persist."[60] (We shall see that Leibniz derives this conviction from the conclusion of Luther's *De servo arbitrio*.) Barth appreciates, indeed, in his own way *appropriates* Leibniz's distinction between "metaphysical evil" and "moral evil" — not to dissolve the intellectual riddle of moral evil's actuality in the best of all possible worlds but rather to clarify what it is and how it is to be endured, opposed, and finally defeated. Thus Barth rightly interprets Leibniz's meaning: "that the real created world is the best does not mean that it is absolutely good and perfect. If this were so, it would not be the created world. From its being as such, the non-divinity of its existence, there follows necessarily its imperfection." This "nondivinity" is what Leibniz means by the term "metaphysical evil," i.e., the ontological vulnerability to nonbeing of *any* conceivable creature who by definition arises "out of nothing." "Earth to earth, ashes to ashes, dust to dust" — any conceivable creature has come into being and will pass again from being. This imperfection of creation in the metaphysical sense of the nondivinity of the creature, on the other hand, "confirms the good will of God to reflect His glory in the best and most perfect way in this other being." The intended reflection of divine glory in the imperfect creature attests to the good and gracious will of God, if only in faith the creature will trust. Consequently, and here we detect the very origins of moral evil, "we dispute both this good will of God and the actual but limited perfection of creation if we try to dispense with metaphysical evil."[61] Refusing to endure our sufferings ecologically, or to act for public rather than private good, we become morally evil disputants whose egocentric unhappiness fueled by envy or greed drives us to rend the web of life in aggressive acts of exappropriation.

In wanting to be God, if one may here recall Luther's dictum from the *Disputation against Scholastic Theology*, and not wanting God to be God, sin comes into the world, i.e., in disputing *coram Deo* rather than receiving with thanksgiving the real but just so imperfect life of the creature, *coram hominibus*, the greedy sinner seeks self in all things. Barth adopts from Luther this account of the origin of sin in anxiety at the ontological vulnerability to which the creature qua creature is exposed. "It is worth noting that in Gen. 3 the failure of the creature consisted in the fact that, succumbing to the insinuations of nothingness, it desired to be like God, judging between good and evil, itself effecting that separation, unwilling to live by the grace of God and on the basis of the judgment already accomplished by Him, or to persist in the covenant with God which is its only safeguard against nothingness."[62] *Such an account of the rise of moral evil thus turns on metaphysical evil as its presupposition.* A perfect creation would be a second deity, i.e., it cannot be; the idea is a contradiction, according to Leibniz. But the best of all creatures is the one that learns in its history to entrust itself to its Creator's power, wisdom, and love. *The hoary enigma of the world is that it does not learn this fundamental lesson of existence in faith.* It succumbs to the anxiety that attends and must attend the contingency of its existence.

Yet, returning now to Barth's Leibniz, "from the beginning" God, who foreknew the fall of Adam who would then be redeemed by Christ in the fullness of time, "has coordinated the existence of evil with that of the created world, and therefore imperfection with perfection, in such a way that the former necessarily contributes to the increase of the latter."[63] This is exactly right as Leibniz interpretation. Proceeding from divine foreknowledge of redemption in Christ to providence in history, Leibniz's theological philosophy seeks to show why, on the presupposition that this world in which I write these words and you read them is the very world God has chosen to actualize, the creature can love and trust God rather than succumb to anxiety, and so be "genuinely content, because as the One who loves us He seeks and finds His own satisfaction in the happiness and perfection of those who are loved by Him."[64] So the capacity to trust God depends on the knowledge of God, and the burning issue is how to acquire a true knowledge of God as the perfect harmony of power, wisdom, and love. In Barth's account, Leibniz's love for and trust in God is justified because God is "the being which unites in Himself all perfections in their highest degree . . . [and as such is] the ontological ground and noetic pledge of the goodness of the world." Understanding God's perfection of being in relation to the creation thus constitutes the "noetic pledge," the "principle that from the inexhaustible possibilities of creation," God, corresponding to his own perfection of power, wisdom, and love, "did not choose just any world but the best, i.e., the most perfect within the limits of its creatureliness. . . . And this best possible world is our own, the real world." Knowing this as befits rational creatures, "we for our part shall do our best to act with all our power according to the presumed will of God, each fulfilling his duty and promoting the general good in his sphere."[65] Philosophy in service of theology thus vindicates optimism for each and for all. Why will Leibniz so charitably read as here by Barth nonetheless fail?

The Conundrum of Evil

Barth's later criticism of Leibniz in *Church Dogmatics* III/3 — "at bottom he hardly had any serious interest (and from the practical standpoint none at all) in the problem of evil,"[66] which Hick inconsequently and unjustly exploited — may now be properly understood. Barth's concern, as should now be clear, will be rather more complex than Hick indicated. On the surface of it, Barth seems to call into question the Augustinian doctrine of metaphysical evil that, as we have just seen, he shares with Leibniz.[67] "Evil in every form really was for [Leibniz] what he called it, namely, a mere *malum privativum*. . . . From the very first it has nothing whatever to do with the clash of God and evil, but is nourished by a view which the problem of evil

cannot affect or shake or even attack."[68] Actual evil presumably would be
something more than the mere privation of being that attends any creature
that is not God. Yet this presumably actual, moral evil, Barth now says of
Leibniz, "can never negate this system . . . [it is] a pure, monistic optimism,
unbroken from the start, incapable of any break, self-contained and *a priori*
transcendental."[69] Correspondingly, Leibniz's version of the doctrine of the
soul's immortality is said to entail the consequence that "nowhere can a real
vacuum arise through death. Death does not, therefore, provide any serious
reason for opposing the perfection of the created world."[70] Barth is surely on
to something in these comments; a biblical "demonology" cannot rest content with a privative theory of evil, though for anti-Gnostic reasons it rightly
presupposes one. But Barth's harsh words are perplexing, since he himself
emphatically affirms: "Light exists as well as shadow; there is a positive as
well as a negative aspect of creation and creaturely occurrence."[71]

It is clear that Barth now worries about a domestication of evil in
Leibniz and insists on a clearer, crucial differentiation, which he explains as
follows. Leibniz took over from Augustine the basic insight: *malum est
privatio boni.* Evil is no thing, no created being or substance, but the lack of
being that is itself always good; evil is a falling, a defection, a corruption of
being into nonbeing. Augustine, Barth tells us, used this notion "quite correctly" to define "the nullity of sin, evil and death." But with his appropriation, "the great Leibniz successfully undertook to domesticate the adversary"
as "the creaturely imperfection which consists in the fact that the creature is
a creature and not God, and does not therefore possess the divine attributes."
Thus evil becomes "so related to good that it is only a particular form of
good, not opposing, disrupting or threatening it, but rendering it an indispensable service." This, says Barth, "cannot be real nothingness,"[72] that radical moral evil that assaults the creation as such. A stronger differentiation
than may be found in Leibniz, Barth claims, results from his own exclusive
Christocentrism: "In the knowledge of Jesus Christ we must abandon the
obvious prejudice against the negative aspect of creation and confess that
God has planned and made all things well, even on the negative side. In the
knowledge of Jesus Christ it is inadmissible to seek [radical] nothingness
here."[73]

This is perplexing. Surely Leibniz's doctrine of metaphysical evil says
the same as Barth here: that shadow side of creation is part and parcel of its
total goodness. Just as surely Leibniz too provides an account of moral evil
arising from faithless anxiety at ontological vulnerability. But Barth wants to
set off his own more radical account of *das Nichtige* from Leibniz. Barth

wants to distinguish sharply between the imperfection of creaturely being and radical evil that assaults *both* the created light *and* the created darkness. Thus sounding like Leibniz against Bayle, Barth can write: "it is difficult to attack a slander on creation which is so old, multiform and tenacious."[74] It is of course true: "in creation there is not only a Yes but also a No; not only a height but also an abyss; not only clarity but also obscurity . . . success and failure, laughter and tears, youth and age, gain and loss, birth and sooner or later its inevitable corollary, death. . . . Yet it is irrefutable that creation and creature are good even in the fact that all that is exists in this contrast and antithesis."[75] This is pure Leibniz. What is new with Barth is his penetrating insight that the slander on creation for existing in this natural series of antitheses *disguises* "true [i.e., radical] nothingness . . . the real adversary which menaces and corrupts us so long as we look in this direction."[76] The confusion is not benign. In this fog, we interpret the shadow that must be cast whenever lights shine as evil and become Manicheans. Or to avoid the company of the Manicheans we become Platonists, forced into positing some "dialectical relationship to the so-called good, and therefore assume that we can see a higher unity of both . . . [even] ascribe to it a certain good . . . [regard it] as ultimately innocuous, and even salutary." In this confusion of the shadow with true nothingness, evil becomes "an element in a philosophical system in which things are not really so dangerous."[77] The result is that "the enemy goes unrecognized."[78]

We may surely grant Barth's concern here that human beings face radical evil as a surd that cannot be justified or synthesized from some superior vantage point, but that actual evil is, and is experienced as, a devastating attack on the creation, corresponding to the scriptural perception of the demonic — a real outbreak of chaos or meaninglessness that defies comprehension. The inattention to the appearance of this devastating surd in Leibniz's intelligible world where everything happens for a good reason is what Barth had in mind when he wrote that "at bottom [Leibniz] had hardly any serious interest (and from the practical standpoint none at all) in the problem of evil."

Even so, there are several curious things about this outburst. However radicalized, Barth's doctrine of evil as *das Nichtige,* nothingness, is of the same Augustinian vintage as is Leibniz's in regard to metaphysical evil; and it is within this basic consensus of the Christian doctrine of creation that Barth urges his stronger differentiation between the shadow that light necessarily casts in the good creation on the one side, and uncanny demonic darkness breaking out to destroy both created light and darkness on the other. Yet this latter notion proves very difficult to talk about without conceptual confusion. "The creature is natural and not unnatural. . . . There is no common ground between it [in its natural imperfection] and [radical] nothingness, the power inimical to the will of the Creator and therefore to the nature of His good creation, the threat to world-occurrence and its corruption."[79] Kroetke explains: radical "[n]othingness withdraws from every ontological dialectic. . . . Herein lies the main reason for the conceptual unclarity in Barth. Because he must describe nothingness not only as an antithesis to being, but also the nonbeing of creation, apparently dialectical remarks about nothingness arise which are not strictly 'dialectical.' Rather, they express an ontological absurdity. Where creaturely being is, nothingness is the negation of this being. Where creaturely nonbeing is, nothingness is the negation of this nonbeing."[80] Take as an illustration of this latter point the case of death. Barth takes the position that natural death belongs to the order of creation, which God affirms as good.[81] It is good that we not live forever, that our time is rather bounded by the Lord of time. Barth's point is that radical evil manifests then as much in refusing to die when one's time ends as in taking another's life before its time: in either case rebellion against the actual Lord of time manifests as greed over against the future generation waiting to take its time and place.

Even so clarified, thanks to Kroetke, the present question is whether Barth actually succeeds in transcending the Leibnizian dilemma represented by recognition of the reality of moral evil under the sovereignty of God, that is, the enigma of divine permission granted to radical assault on the creation God wills. Clearly, while Barth, unlike Leibniz, wants evil to appear *to us* as devastating surd, like Leibniz, Barth cannot and does not claim the same for God. Yet in *Church Dogmatics* III/3 Barth cuts the Gordian knot and resorts to the caricature of Leibniz as simply Spinoza exposed: "a pure, monistic optimism, unbroken from the start, incapable of any break, self-contained and *a priori* transcendental." Leibniz, we here read, is "obviously guilty of confusing nothingness with the intracosmic antithesis or negative side of creation," and thus "the absorption or at least the assimilation of the negative aspect of creation by the positive," anticipating what eventually found "massive expression in the philosophy of Hegel."[82] This assimilation of Leibniz to Hegel via Spinoza abruptly succeeds in trivializing all three. This assimilation is, we shall argue in chapters 5 and 6, profoundly mistaken, though Leibniz himself may be faulted at least for the perception of it.

For the present, we can note another curious feature of Barth's sharp criticism of Leibniz in *Church Dogmatics* III/3. It is striking how perfunctory the discussion is,[83] how little textual evidence is adumbrated in comparison to the earlier treatments in III/1. This absence of exegesis allows Leibniz's doctrine of moral evil to be minimized, yet here too on examination it may be argued that Barth adopts substantively the same position as Leibniz and consequently involves himself in the same conundrum of how moral evil, i.e., sin, which does not will the will of God, nevertheless really comes to afflict the good creation God wills. Barth acknowledges the dilemma: "if we argue that this element of [true] nothingness derives from the positive will and work of God as if it too were a creature," then we ascribe evil to God and exonerate the creature from all responsibility for it. On the other hand, "if we maintain that it derives solely from the activity of the creature," we make of the Creator a passive spectator, i.e., we rob God of his deity.[84] From yet another angle, we go astray if, in acknowledging the reality of true nothingness "in its relation of opposition and resistance to God's world dominion," it "assumes the form of a monster which, vested with demonic qualities, inspires fear and respect instead of awaking the Easter joy that even in all its power as sin and evil it is no more than the nothingness which as such is already judged in Jesus Christ and can therefore injure but no longer kill or destroy."[85] This latter thought explains why Barth, aside from the fear of looking ridiculous, retreats from the actual demonology his doctrine of radical moral evil might otherwise employ.[86] In any case, these classical considerations of Augustinianism indicate that Barth can by no means claim to have transcended the fundamental conundrum of the absurdity of moral evil's actuality in the good creation of God. They lead Barth to the sober reflection: "we have here an extraordinarily clear demonstration of the necessary brokenness of all theological thought and utterance . . . [that] can never form a system, comprehending and as it were 'seizing' the object. That is true of all theological assertions."[87]

True enough. The point, however, is to illumine the obscure nature of moral evil so that it can be named, repented, forgiven, resisted, and overcome — not decreed out of existence by theological fiat. I will now argue that Barth, while admirably deepening the discussion of the nature of evil, in fact substantively follows Leibniz's doctrine in the decisive respect by regarding "nothingness as God's own problem" (Kroetke), i.e., that God's permission of wills other than God's obliges God to suffer them and only in this way also to reconcile them. Barth rightly wanted *both* to avoid a domestication of evil by presuming to explicate the inexplicable existence of that which God does not will *and* at the same time to implicate God Himself in the permission of, suffering of, and victory over it. He wanted with this double ambition to write neither metaphysical monism nor metaphysical dualism but to think theologically of God as the living, free event of meeting and overcoming this obstacle.[88] Thus true "nothingness," discovered or uncovered in the cross, is "the 'reality' which opposes and resists God, which itself is subjected to and overcome by His opposition and resistance, and which in this twofold determination as the reality that negates and is negated by Him, is totally distinct from Him." This is the knowledge of true nothingness gained in Jesus Christ. "True nothingness is that which brought Jesus Christ to the cross, and that which He defeated there." Knowing our true foe this way, Barth says, we will avoid the "temptation . . . to conceive it dialectically and thus render it innocuous";[89] instead we will expose it and defeat it with the "the Friend and Fellow of the sinful creature," who "would rather be unblest with His creature than be the blest God of an unblest creature."[90] From beginning to end of his treatment, this is the gravamen of Barth's case against philosophical idealism: "We have not sought to apprehend the relationship between the Creator and the creature philosophically and therefore from without, but theologically and therefore from within." From "within" — that means we know the enemy in knowing Christ as victim of and victor over it: "Indeed, we may say that if nothingness is not viewed in retrospect of God's finished act of conquest and destruction, it is not seen at all. It is confounded with the negative side of God's creation, and viewed only in its negative and not in its privative character."[91]

Barth's Kantian and anti-Hegelian intentions in this polemic are thus abundantly clear. Having conceded that, the question cannot be begged: What is this true Nothingness that is exposed by the cross of Jesus? "Nothingness," in perhaps the clearest definition Barth offers, "is that from which God separates Himself in the face of which He asserts Himself and exerts His positive will. . . . God elects, and therefore rejects what He does not elect. God wills, and therefore opposes what He does not will."[92] In a logically meticulous discussion, Kroetke interprets this divine not-willing as an "assignation" that does *not* bestow any peculiar kind of reality to Nothingness but actually regards it as what has been eternally passed over and so assigns it to the sphere of all that is left behind by God's Yes to the creation.[93] But what is "it" so regarded? Kroetke ventures an interpretation of Barth's ambiguous language here in order to meet a searching objection. This is the view that the "eschatological reservation" forbids any speculative answer to the question of the origin of evil. Kroetke *receives* this objection, claiming that it actually makes Barth's intentions clearer: "Nothing is essentially inexplicable because God Himself did not explain it"; God rather "endured" it "for the sake of the creation. . . . From the outset, God willed to allow the entirety of the threat and affliction in which nothingness entangles men and women to be his own threat and affliction."[94] With this inexplicable decision at the font of creation, Kroetke claims, the objection that God could have created a world without evil becomes "meaningless." Does it indeed?

It is important to underscore that this discussion concerns an ambiguity in Barth, which Kroetke is trying to resolve in a certain, nonspeculative direction. For Kroetke, the difficulty consists in speaking intelligibly about a surd, how to "describe the 'being' of nothingness with ontological categories in such a way that it cannot be confused with creation"[95] and so without making the question of its "explicability or inexplicability" primary.[96] Theodicy — a genuinely theological theodicy of faith — of course turns on this latter possibility (Rom. 8:18-21!). I would therefore like to suggest a different possibility — not so much for Barth interpretation as for Christian doctrine of evil — that has its roots in Gregory of Nyssa's account of the fall of the devil out of envy.[97] In this approach, that which God does not choose to instantiate in the creation nevertheless *out of envy* presses for existence and so breaks into created being in outbreaks of chaos, in that God permits creatures to will for themselves a destiny other than God has determined. This Nyssan account of evil becomes intelligible when, in distinction from a certain anthropocentric, unecological tendency in Barth, we do not think of the creation merely as the external basis of the covenant — nature as a kind of physical stage or platform on which the drama of human salvation plays out — but rather think with the Cappadocians of "nature" as the economy of God eschatologically directed, the "real world" being from the outset that glorious liberty of the children of God in the renewed cosmos at which all things are and have from the beginning been aimed.

According to Nyssa, it was upon hearing the divine plan of a glorious destiny for the lowly earthling that the ontologically superior angel, Lucifer, resolved to undo God's work, choosing for himself and the world a destiny refused in God's primal decision. If this divine destination of the earthling is the "real world," the inbreaking of chaos in its history under the forms of the powers of sin and death is *motivated* by the malice of envy, whose *parody* of the principle of sufficient reason is to *exist for the sake of destroying*. Such is the uncanny actuality of the *demonic*. This account has the merit, I think, of locating evil as a positive power, not a mere privation, *within* the creation, as personified in the figure of the devil; it makes evil intelligible, not absurd, in the sense that it can be named as the envy for existence stemming from the possibilities God primordially refused. Moral evil is to choose for oneself a destiny other than God's, and in its actualization therefore it spins episodes of sheer, incalculable chaos into the web of life in its series of development.

In turn, one would have to think of a certain temporal freedom of the Spirit who blows where He wills — determined by God's primordial decision to create, redeem, and fulfill the world in Christ and yet free to innovate in response to these essentially unpredictable, intrinsically incalculable incursions of malicious envy.

Now Karl Barth can speak almost identically with the Nyssan-Leibnizian sketch of a demonology just provided. Nothingness has this "ontic peculiarity" that it exists as evil. "This negation of His grace is chaos, the world which He did not choose or will, which He could not and did not create, but which, as He created the actual world, He passed over and set aside, marking and excluding it as the eternal past, the eternal yesterday."[98] Barth can in this way speak eloquently of existential chaos as an ontic antidivine power, then, but not of its motive, its raison d'être in envy;[99] he would perhaps grimace at the too mythological thought that the peculiar actuality of nothingness is that of a rejected possibility nevertheless straining for an existence in the actual world that God wills but that proves incompatible, in Leibniz's vocabulary, "incompossible," with the rest. Barth describes this reality of evil but, as Kroetke rightly sees, he is reticent to explicate it as a "personal devil," motivated by envy, lest it cease to appear as the surd that it is or that theology descend into ridiculous superstition. In any case, and in spite of his anti-speculative commitment, Barth *must* affirm that God is "Lord of nothingness too. It is not a second God, or self-created. It has no power save that which is allowed by God."[100] Just so it "is": it exists under the form of "man . . . the sinner who has submitted and fallen victim to chaos," yet all the more in the ultimate fact that "God Himself is always the One who first takes this threat seriously"[101] in choosing to create the world that would implicate God Himself in battle against it. That is Barth's final word: we should take evil seriously because God does so, from the beginning, in the mere act of creation. That should suffice. Beyond this theology cannot go.

Yet it remains difficult to regard this ultimate affirmation of God's saving sovereignty as more than whistling in the dark, if Barth's account is taken as purely nonspeculative descriptive of an ultimate, primal mystery. The alternative entails finding a *reason* for that which God passes over and a *motive* for the permission of the rejected possibility nevertheless to assert itself. Nyssa's account provides both. In turn, my claim is not that Barth follows Leibniz consciously or literally (1) in locating moral evil in the region of the eternal possibilities as those which God did not elect in creating the world, but which nevertheless strain for existence[102] so that (2) God may be understood to permit the chaotic outbreak of these rejected possibilities — like the waterspouts in the primeval flood (Gen. 7:11) — in order to defeat them, knowing in his wisdom how to produce from evil a greater good (Gen. 50:20), as revealed definitively for faith in the resurrection of the Crucified. My argument is that Barth does not only follow Leibniz in a general kind of way, but that he could have expressed one not insignificant line of his own thought this way and would have been right to do so. For the *to us* devastating surd of evil actually occurs and yet, as Barth concludes the discussion, that can only mean "under the decree of God." This concession, Barth expressly acknowledges, legitimates the old notion in theology of divine "permission." "God still permits His kingdom not to be seen by us, and to that extent He still permits us to be a prey to nothingness." Invoking the ghost of Kant once again, Barth affirms this state of created anxiety at the creature's ontological vulnerability: God "thinks it is good that we should exist 'as if' He had not yet mastered it for us — and at this point we may rightly say, 'as if.'"[103] Indeed, "even nothingness should be one of the things of which it is said that they must work together for good to them that love Him."[104] By invoking Romans 8 here, one has to ask in all justice, given the prior treatment of Leibniz, whether Barth too now becomes guilty of a systematizing and thus domesticating of evil for the role it ultimately plays by divine permission. Or does divine permission of evil not rather require some explication beyond mere description? Baldly put, it seems to be nothing but the assertion of a contradiction: God reigns over a world in which his will is rejected. It is thus evident that Barth has not escaped the conundrum he held to be fatal for Leibniz's "system," even though his probing christological discussion has deepened the theology of evil considerably. For Barth, too, in the end God in the very act of creation permits outbreaks of what He does not will, and not dumbly, but in divine wisdom and foresight, in order that in the fullness of time God in the person of His Son would be defeated by evil but just so also defeat evil on behalf of all. God elects. God rejects. God permits. God engages. God suffers. God triumphs. Barth differs not a lick from Leibniz in sharing this conundrum, for the basic reason that his account of *das Nichtige* is dependent on the logic of Leibnizian metaphysics, if not directly or consciously drawn from it as a source.

The Electing God

If we turn now from the elusive doctrine of *das Nichtige* to the crowning achievement of Barth's mature theology in *Church Dogmatics* II/2's doctrine of election, we uncover the same underlying affinities with Leibniz, indeed more so. Broadly put, Barth's so-called ontology of act points at the same divine freedom of action by which Leibniz formally differentiated God as Creator from Spinoza's *natura naturans.* In Barth's presentation this plays out as the difference between the "living decree" of the God who decides to love humanity and lives in this decision in ever new actions in time on the one side and the timeless providence of abstract omnipotence on the other.[105] This is the difference between "predestination" as God's primal self-determination to love humanity manifest in the act of election of the rejected in Jesus Christ and the Stoic-deist doctrine of "providence," i.e., rational foreknowledge of future events by an omniscient intelligence.[106] It is the difference between theology that moves from this particular act of election of the rejected in Christ[107] to know God as ruler of the world and philosophy that tries to subsume particulars and apparent contingencies in its general knowledge of the laws of world-occurrence.[108] Even the apparently theological doctrine of the "general benevolence" of the Creator, from which certain deductions might be drawn about divine governance, misses the root perception of God existing in His own act of being as the God of grace for us.[109] "For the divine attitude is not a matter of chance. It is not revocable or transitory. God lays upon us the obligation of this attitude because first of all He lays it upon Himself. In dealing with this attitude we have to do with His free but definitive decision. We cannot abstract from it without falling into arbitrary speculation. But we cannot ignore it. Once made, it belongs definitively to God Himself, not His being in and for Himself, but in His being within this relationship. It belongs to the reality of God which is a reality not apart from but in this decision."[110] Predestination has to do "with the eternal self-determination by which God is God and not not God."[111]

In this initial formulation, Barth seems to allow for an unknown and undetermined God in and for Himself, *potentia absoluta,* as opposed to the decided God in relation to us, *potentia ordinata.* The difficulty is caused by the need to safeguard the freedom of God[112] in this primal self-determination to be our God, that is, by grace and gift, not by nature or need. In the course of Barth's discussion, this primal freedom presupposed in the divine decision to create, redeem, and fulfill the world is exposited more carefully as the eternal life of the Father, the Son, and the Holy Spirit.[113] God's eternal existence as the Father of the Son and breather of the Spirit is the presupposition of God's temporal self-determination as the Father who sends the Son in the Spirit to include in His own life the life of the creature other than God. Thus it may be said that God exists for us in this act and decision of His own being projected into the time and space of the creature. Commenting on Pauline appropriation of the divine name, "I will be He that I am," from Exodus 3:14, Barth writes: "According to this revealed name of His, God's nature consists in the fact that He renews, establishes and glorifies Himself by His own future; or materially, that He renews, establishes and glorifies His being by His future being, or even more materially, His mercy by His future mercy, His compassion by His future compassion. . . . God's nature is that the One He now is in freedom He will be again in the same unconditioned, unassailable freedom to posit and affirm Himself by Himself."[114] Not that this free self-positing is in any way "wayward or arbitrary." "His righteousness indeed consists in the fact that He not only is but always becomes again the merciful one."[115] God's "righteousness" is not a quality passively adhering to an impassible substance, something one might "know" but not necessarily entrust oneself to;[116] it is God's faithfulness to his own primal decision again and again to be for us in time who He has determined Himself to be in free grace and bottomless mercy — an ever-coming event of faithfulness that elicits and sustains human faith through time.

To conceive this kind of temporal faithfulness, any kind of strong dualism between God for God and God for us must be precluded. Like the Kantian noumenal taken as a mere limit-concept, God for God in all eternity in distinction from God for us in time serves only to uncover the condition for the possibility of the latter and so underscore the wonder of God's free decision. "Speaking generally, it is the demonstration, the overflowing of the love which is the being of God, that He who is entirely self-sufficient, who even within Himself cannot know isolation [as the Trinity], willed even in all His divine glory to share His life with another, and to have that other as the witness of His glory. The love of God is His grace . . . free, unconstrained, unconditioned."[117] Unlike the Kantian noumenal, however, Barth can maintain that the freedom of God is manifest as the temporal freedom *to love,* to be God's own most free and divine self by taking all joy in another who is not God, in the free act of self-oblation. Such freedom is never any kind of arbitrary and unlimited power. It reflects no *deus exlex.* It is not the freedom of caprice, but the very eternal God who lives as the love of the Father and the Son in the Spirit and as such turns to the creation. It is as this triune God that God turns to creation, and so the creation that comes forth, the creation that corresponds to this God's purpose, the creation created with a view to redemption and fulfillment in Christ by the Spirit, cannot be any cosmic farce or cruel tragedy; it must be the Leibnizian "best possible." Barth as theologian of revelation can make this inference on grounds that Kant on the basis of reason alone cannot, namely, that God does not deceive in revelation and therefore cannot be conceived to deceive in revelation, but instead makes Himself known and thus wills to be known truly, the One He is for Himself now also for us. The inference is not therefore that of a philosophical theodicy that in principle falls to Kant's critique of the presumption of reason seeing from God's perspective. It is the Pauline theodicy of faith from Romans 8, disclosing the divine perspective to repentant faith through sufferings and the cross. This overcoming of the Kantian dualism that permeates the theology of the nineteenth century is decisive for Barth. He closes this door of dualism as to the secret entrance of the *deus exlex, potentia absoluta.*

In this argumentation Barth presses against the binitarian scheme of freedom and love that formally governs his interpretation of the divine perfections. He gropes to include the notion of divine wisdom. "We must resist the temptation to absolutize in some degree the concept choosing or electing," if we are to see that the choice God freely has made is "the existence of the man Jesus and of the people represented in Him." But if "the distinctive and ultimate feature in God is absolute freedom of choice, or an absolutely free choice, then it will be hard to distinguish His freedom from caprice." But the God of the gospel is not "a tyrant living by His whims," let alone "blind fate"; he is "something other than the essential inscrutability of all being."[118] Such Leibnizian polemic against the God of Hobbes or Spinoza recurs throughout Barth's doctrine of election. We do "not exhaustively define or describe God when we identify Him with irresistible omnipotence. . . . Irresistible omnipotence cannot be made the beginning and end of the being of God. . . . God and not a blindly determining and deciding something rules the world . . . the electing God . . . is the Almighty, and not vice versa."[119] The commonplace stratagem of positing a kenotic *potentia ordinata* presupposes the problematic *potentia absoluta* that we have just seen Barth criticize, and so misses the real electing God who "in His love and freedom determined and limited Himself to be God in particular and not in general."[120] This stratagem takes its revenge in all treatments of the doctrine of election that picture "the absolute God in Himself, who is neither conditioned nor self-conditioning" when instead God's freedom to love is truly manifest in the image of the "Son of God who is self-conditioned and therefore conditioned in his union with the Son of David," i.e., the picture of the electing God who is from eternity "God in Jesus Christ."[121] Indeed, "grace alone," the very divine favor, or good pleasure, that God freely takes in another, can only appear as tyrant's whim or as child's play when the power to choose is not understood in harmony with wisdom and love.

Indeed, "the sovereignty of God bears no relation whatever to the sovereignty of whim or chance or caprice. On the contrary, we learn from the revelation of this sovereignty that the power of whim and chance and caprice is not sovereign power. It belongs to the sphere of evil."[122] The nontrinitarian identification of God with sheer power rather than in the conjunction with wisdom and love is not merely a theological mistake, then. It is diabolic confusion about God, the root, radical doubt about God that the serpent insinuated about the trustworthiness of God. But in "this decree" of God who determines to create, redeem, and fulfill a world other than God, "we do not have to assert a God of omnipotence and cower down before Him. In all His incomprehensibility we may know Him and love Him and praise Him as the One who has truly revealed to us His wisdom and mercy and righteousness . . . Himself all these things."[123] For God exists as God to God and God to us in this very decision and act of freedom to love: "God's glory overflows in this supreme act of His freedom. . . . The Son of God determined to give Himself from all eternity. With the Father and the Holy Spirit He chose to unite Himself with the lost Son of Man. . . . This decree is Jesus Christ, and for this very reason it cannot be a *decretum absolutum*."[124] "Above all," Barth writes in another passage, "we have to expunge completely the idolatrous concept of a *decretum absolutum*."[125] By the logic of Barth's argument, theology should rather have been pursued as a *decretum sapientiae*, folly to the unbelieving world but the power of God to those being saved.

The reference here is, of course, to classical Reformed theology's teaching of a double predestination of the elect and reprobate, i.e., "the thought of an individual purpose in predestination." Indeed, the reformer of Reformed theology writes, "we have to expunge completely from our minds the thought of the foreordination of a rigid and balanced system of election and reprobation."[126] Overcoming *that* mad and lamentable doctrinal development is the major accomplishment of Barth's christocentric doctrine of election. Jesus Christ, at once the electing God, as such the savior of all, and the rejected man, as such the representative of all in need, is the exclusive object[127] of God's predestination; he is *God's* eternal and temporal moral *self*-determination. "What we have to consider in the elected man Jesus is, then, the destiny of human nature, its exaltation to fellowship with God, and the manner of its participation in this exaltation by the free grace of God."[128] He is elected to be rejected in humanity's place. "The wrath of God, the judgment and the penalty, fall, then, upon Him, and not upon those whom he loves and elects 'in Him.'"[129] God "elected our rejection. He made it His own."[130] In this God also justifies Himself. "Why this interposition of the just for the unjust . . . ? Because His justice is a merciful and for this reason a perfect justice."[131] In the justification of the sinner faith discovers the justification of God, of God's creation and of the permission of evil, i.e., God's providential ordering of evil in prospect of the glory to be revealed.

In this fashion, *let us clearly see,* Barth underscores the *theodicy of faith.* "[T]he fact that from all eternity God resolved to take to Himself and to bear man's rejection is a prior *justification of God* in respect of the risk to which He resolved to expose man by creation — and in respect of the far greater risk to which He committed him by His permitting of the fall. *We cannot complain. . . . We cannot blame. . . . We cannot hold it against God."* For even when we think of humanity suffering, falling, godless, and rejected, we must at the same time "think of him as the one whom God loved from all eternity in His Son."[132] This is *"His own justification"* — "whether you are a friend of God like Moses or an enemy like Pharaoh, whether your name is Isaac or Ishmael, Jacob or Esau, you are the man on account of whose sin and for whose sin Jesus Christ has died on the cross *for the justification of God,* and for whose salvation and bliss, and for whose justification, He has been raised from the dead."[133]

The apparent universalism of Barth's doctrine of election elicited bitter attacks, not least from uncomprehending Lutherans who failed to see in it the victory of their own tradition's contention on behalf of the general benevolence of God in creation and of the universality of the atonement over against Calvinism's *decretum absolutum* and the teaching of a limited atonement reflecting it. From the standpoint of his own "purified supralapsarianism," however, Barth did argue an evidently *innovative and provocative* claim: in the person of His Son the electing God from the outset writes Himself into the redemptive center of creation's story. In the primal act of God's being for us, God elects the man Jesus Christ as the representative and therefore destiny of the lost and rejected sinner. This eternal decision and consequent act in the fullness of time reveals the justice of God's free grace in the very decision to evoke a world other than God, vulnerable as it would be to moral evil. Against this "supralapsarian Christology," Emil Brunner spoke for many upon publication of Barth's teaching: "Here some entirely new ideas have been introduced." "Karl Barth has combined a number of his own ideas, which, because they are completely new, need to be specially examined." "No special proof is required to show that the Bible contains no such doctrine [of 'Jesus, the eternally elect man'], nor that no theory of this kind has ever been formulated by any theologian."[134] In Kroetke's words: "Many object that Barth wants to 'explain' nothingness. In particular, the *supralapsarian* starting point of his doctrine of election fosters this charge, as it purportedly blocks the way to honoring 'the *decisiveness* of history'" (Berkouwer).[135]

To which Barth might respond: the decisiveness of history is God's. What matters is that God has free choice, and that God has chosen to engage for our true freedom (which is liberation for love) with us, among us, as one of us. This is the very wonder, that God's eternal being is to exist for us in His own free act of self-determination in time, "the One who from all eternity has willed and ordained that He should act in Jesus Christ." This "election of Jesus Christ [as] the eternal choice and decision of God . . . [so that] there is no such thing as a will of God apart from the will of Jesus Christ"[136] is decisive for the autonomy of theology as a discipline. The famous and poorly understood dispute with Brunner about the so-called point of contact touches the disagreement about election at this point. Starting with God's decision liberates theology from dependence upon *any* notion of a self-sufficient secular realm, "nature" or "history" or even "creation" that would or could exist apart from the concrete divine permission to fall into sin yet be delivered in Jesus Christ for a new creation. For this latter notion "makes it appear as if the universe and man might well have been created and sustained without any inner necessity of the continuation and completion of the divine work in reconciliation and redemption." Not only that, but the fall into sin that befalls the creation "acquires the character of an unforeseen incident which suddenly transforms the good creation of God into something problematical" and God Himself "halted and baffled by sin."[137] Then theology, sharing God's perplexity, may well ask other discourses to inform what the real issues are and set upon the needed work of revisionism. But for the electing God who determines to be our God by faith in Jesus Christ there "is no such thing as a created nature which has its purpose, being or continuance apart from grace. . . . Even sin, death, the devil and hell — works of God's permissive will which are negative in their effects — even these . . . enemies of God are the servants of God and the servants of His grace."[138] The history that is decisive is God's. The event of this decision is manifest in the cross and resurrection of Christ. Theology knows that this and this alone is what causes theology as a discipline to exist. Its task is not the revision of the tradition of the gospel, but participation in the tradition of the gospel's revisioning of the world on the way to the best possible.

As we have seen, on account of his rigorous antidualism Barth *must* embrace the conundrum of the existence of actual, positive, ontic evil in the world that God wills in the sense that evil "must take on the character of an event. It must become the content of a history: the history of an obstacle and its removing; the history of a death and resurrection; the history of a judgment and a pardon; the history of a defeat and a victory."[139] In God this act of being is simple and eternal, but in willing to share this victory with a created other, i.e., since "man is to be the witness of the divine glory — this victory must take on historical form, thus becoming an event in time. In willing man, His man, elected man, God wills that this should be the case."[140] It cannot be otherwise. Just as Leibniz describes metaphysical evil as the presupposition but not the necessity of moral evil, Barth too affirms that "the very fact that man was not God but a creature, even though he was a good creature, had meant already a certain jeopardizing of the honor of God." Yet God undertakes this "risk"[141] in "permitting . . . man's liability to temptation and fall" because "God wills evil only because He wills not to keep to Himself the light of His glory but to let it shine outside Himself."[142]

The conundrum acknowledged, the Pauline theodicy sounds: "the sufferings of this present age are not worthy to be compared to the glory to be revealed." "We cannot balance the fact that Adam fell, or David sinned, or Peter denied, or Judas betrayed, against the resurrection of Jesus Christ. The facts are true, but it is also true that they are far outweighed by the resurrection of Jesus Christ and that as a result of this resurrection they belong already to the vanquished past."[143] Leibniz made the same point: "*O felix culpa* . . . ! [w]here sin abounded, grace did much more abound; and we remember that we have gained Jesus Christ Himself by reason of sin."[144] Is this folly? Or is it that evangelical foolishness of God that is wiser than the wisdom of this world? What matters is that God has choice, not only to do something rather than nothing, but the best rather than anything less. Yet just here Barth stumbles.

Nonuniversal Universalism

In his important essay, previously referenced, Graham Ward concluded by asking whether Barth's project was "fundamentally flawed" because of the binary oppositions or dualities that rendered his account of the grace of God "punctiliar and arbitrary." If so, Ward argues, Barth's dialectic does not finally overcome Kant but perpetuates him and commits him "to a nominalism that can, all too easily, ignore the psychological, the social and the political aspects of embodiment," i.e., to the diastasis in theological language, as McCormack mentioned, that posits a God wholly Other over against a natural domain of godlessness. So the Kantian thesis lives on in the Barthian antithesis. Over against this, Ward argues, "to be theologically postmodern requires a strong doctrine of participation in the operations of the triune God, through the Spirit, in creation and the church as the body of Christ. Nominalism bars the doors to such a doctrine and in this way . . . invents the secular." Ward thinks, however, that the later Barth may be moving in the direction of "a greater theological holism."[145] What that is or could be, we shall shortly consider, but I register here the fact that I am not so sure about the later Barth. As the Nestorian tendency toward diastasis subverts the concrete synthesis of the Cyrillian Christ whom Barth, at least in his rhetoric, would offer to Augustinian man, by the same token I worry that in the later Barth a surprisingly emphatic picture of modern, all-too-modern autonomy emerges.

In any case, Barth's antidualistic, universalist doctrine of election brings along its own series of paradoxes. "Not every one who is elected lives as an elect man . . . [but one] lives as one rejected in spite of his election."[146] Barth acknowledges that human beings can "persist" in rejection, even though they cannot "annul the gracious choice of God." "This grace is for him, the enemy of God, in spite of his enmity and in spite of his negative act, rejecting his representation of himself as rejected, forgiving his sins, as the justification of the godless."[147] For "by permitting the life of a rejected man to be the life of His own Son, God has made such a life objectively impossible for all others. The life of the uncalled, the godless, is a grasping back at this objective impossibility."[148] The church in its proclamation of the "free grace of election in the mighty divine determination of man" can only speak of "the kingdom of heaven open and hell closed; God vindicated and Satan overcome; life triumphant and death destroyed; belief in the promise the only possibility and disbelief in it the excluded possibility."[149] Of course, disbelief "persists" in the way that a futile denial of reality can exist. Barth seeks relentlessly to cut off all avenues of escape. To prevail in being rejected by God in truth and final reality — "this is the very goal which the godless cannot reach, because it has already been taken away by the eternally decreed offering of the Son of God to suffer in the place of the godless."[150]

Yet Barth denies that this teaching of divine, all-sufficing, and universal reconciliation by the electing God taking the place of the rejected sinner amounts to *apokatastasis,* i.e., that the godless "must and will" give up the lie and surrender to love, for this ultimate inference abridges divine freedom.[151]

Does it also abridge human freedom? What Barth clearly says here is that the testimony of faith to the godless world "follows a very definite order" and cannot present "divine electing and divine rejecting as two possibilities which are equally open." Instead, in preaching the gospel, and the sum of the gospel[152] in predestination as God's self-determination in Jesus Christ to elect the rejected, it will be impossible to regard any "as if they were not elect . . . , as if the godlessness in which they deny their real status were to be seriously taken as conclusive."[153] Such is the saving solidarity of the elect with the rejected in Jesus Christ that even in the face of the persistent unbelief of the world, each and every event in it of the great "transition," i.e., "whenever an individual is elected and called," gives "every reason and confidence to suppose that the people of God concealed in this world of men, which does not yet recognize the love of God for men, and its Lord Jesus Christ, and therefore its own true self, may be greater than was previously visible."[154] The statement in 1 John, "it does not yet appear what we shall be," applies to all. No believer, considering her lack of merit in coming to faith, could ever exclude a nonbeliever on account of that identical lack of merit.

But if we are all thus destined to life as the children of God, what sense does Barth make theologically of the great "transition," the "event" of conversion to the truth and faith in the promise? "To hear means to be aware that in Jesus Christ this decision has been made concerning him. To believe means to accept the situation which has been created by this decision. The godless man makes that transition as and to the extent that he hears and believes the promise." Barth develops now *his* version of compatibilism (which comes to fullest flower in volume IV/4, Barth's last, late effort in the *Church Dogmatics*), i.e., "the intimate connexion between theonomy and autonomy, between divine sovereignty and human faith."[155] Alongside the paradox of universal and efficacious election of the godless, Barth's teaching now leads to a further paradox of freedom in, not in spite of, divine determination. To be sure, then, "God is the Lord. . . . God decides. . . . This is the unqualified precedence of God's work."[156] But in the "transition" of faith "a simple but comprehensive autonomy of the creature" is manifest.[157] Excluded by this, of course, are any notions of individuality or autonomy incompatible with the stipulated act of self-recognition; it is a matter of coming to one's true self as the sinner for whom Jesus died. By the same token any and all individuality that is compatible with this singular decision and act of divine goodness is granted, *really* granted to the concrete creature in all blessed idiosyncrasy, as one who may now live royally in the world as God's free and adult partner. God's "self-giving sets man up as a subject, awakens him to genuine individuality and autonomy, frees him, makes him a king, so that in his rule the kingly rule of God Himself attains form and revelation."[158] Barth uses the obedience of the man Jesus as the paradigm of this compatibilism in which "man may rule in that he is willing to serve."[159] Subjecthood in servanthood excludes false notions of autonomy. The motto of true autonomy is neither the Epicurean, Maximize Freedom, nor the Stoic, Maximize Duty, but (dare I say, a Leibnizian) Maximize Individuality in Harmony with the Plentitude of Being, liberated from all oppressive expectations of mere fellow creatures. True autonomy is recognized in the joyful embrace of each individual in its own idiosyncrasy: "[E]ach one is directly envisaged and intended by God as such, and cannot, therefore, be confused or exchanged."[160] Here is the reality of concrete individual faith, "which is distinct from God and yet united with Him in joy and peace . . . [in] historical form as a human electing in which man can and should elect and affirm and activate himself."[161] Autonomous man each in her own particularity sharing a *communion of action* with the determining God, as doers, not hearers only of the Word of their liberation — in just this way each becomes the maximally concrete and specific creature that God wills each to be.

The true freedom of the human individual does not consist in "sinful and fatal isolation" or "godlessness." "It can only be man's own godless choice that wills to be this 'individual,' the man who is isolated in relation to God."[162] The setting free from the bondage of egocentrism that occurs in faith consists in recognition of "the election of Jesus Christ as their own election. The election of the community, moreover, reaches its consummation in the authority and operation of the Holy Spirit in their hearts and in their free personal decisions."[163] In affirming maximal individuation this way, Barth is thus very cautious not to fall back again into the errant individualism with which he has charged the doctrine of the absolute decree.[164] The "content of the life of the individual elect cannot possibly be exhausted by the regulation of his personal salvation and blessedness, and everything belonging to it, understood as a private matter."[165] In fact, behind that errant individualism was a religious form of speculative egocentrism from which Barth's maximal individuation by self-recognition at the cross of Jesus sets free. As election is God's self-determination to be the public representative of all who are lost and rejected in Jesus, this election is mediated in time communally, not individualistically, not for private bliss but for public good. Freedom truly to be one's own person is based upon God's forgiving and liberating embrace, since the dignity conferred by grace does not depend on "natural possession, as a right which is inherent in his human existence."[166]

Barth consequently is able to argue astutely that the modern individual — the false individual who bases freedom on the claim of his own natural capacities and possessions rather than on the gift and calling of God in Christ — "is ripe for every kind of authoritarianism and collectivism, as for every other dishonouring, perversion and destruction of his human existence."[167] For she is not really free as this self-claimed, isolated individual with inherent rights, and so she is driven to look for false gods and political saviors — to whom in time she must sell her soul. In contrast, the true individual is the unique biographical event that occurs when the promise is told and heard in the transition to faith in Christ, as one elected and exalted to service, the adventure of joyful life in the kingdom of God.

While Barth's doctrine of autonomy as liberation for genuine individuality in freedom of action is attractive, it is not so clear that it solves any of the traditional conundrums about divine sovereignty and human freedom of choice (not to mention freedom of desire). Barth makes clear that on the level of history, in the self-knowledge that is possible psychologically in human reflection, this transition occurs as a free human decision, "a self-recognition" as the rejected one elected in Christ. But on the theological level, Barth wants to affirm, this same event is the supervening of the Holy Spirit, whose calling is *effective* in anyone who so hears and believes. "This difference is their calling" and "they are different because of their calling."[168] Thus these others "do not possess the Holy Spirit. They do not stand in the area of proclamation and faith. They even refuse this whole offer with hostility." Barth now makes, as it seems to me, an equation that confuses matters. Being without the Spirit, he writes, is that previously discussed possibility of the "futile attempt to live the life of one rejected by God." This, accordingly, is "how the elect and others [unbelievers, not reprobates!] differ from one another: the former by witnessing in their lives to the truth, the latter by lying against the same truth."[169] Be that as it may, in this account it is hard to see how it is the effective calling of the Holy Spirit that makes the difference between truth-tellers and liars. Barth, as we noted, drew back from a doctrine of *apokatastasis* on the grounds that it would vitiate divine freedom, and likewise in the present connection he maintains that "the intention and power of God in relation to the whole world and all men are always His intention and power — an intention and power which we cannot control and the limits of which we cannot arbitrarily restrict or enlarge."[170] Maintaining divine freedom this way, Barth settles: "It is enough for us to know and remember that at all events it is the omnipotent loving-kindness of God which continually decides this . . . in new encounters and transactions." The "Holy

Spirit of the Father and the Son lives and works at this or that place or time, in which *He rouses and finds faith* in this or that man, in which He is recognized and apprehended by this and that man in the promise and in their election. . . . This event in and for the world . . . are all matters of His sovereign control."[171]

The old question about the scandalous Holy Spirit who blows where He wills now recurs: Why, *according to Barth*, is faith withheld from some but granted to others, if indeed it is no less and none other than God who is determined to redeem the lost and fulfill the creation in the missions of His Son and Spirit? Barth bases his theological optimism on the freedom of God to love as known in the sojourn of the Son of God to the place of the lost and fallen creature. In this light, Barth has argued forcefully that the reason why faith is granted to some is *not*, as in hyper-Augustinian tradition, to save the few and so demonstrate mercy, while simultaneously damning the masses to demonstrate justice. Instead, like Leibniz, and following a more careful exegesis of Romans 9–11, Barth suggests that those effectively called to faith are "elected" for service[172] (just as those "hardened" are for providential purposes leading to the inclusion of others). Both of these reformulations in the doctrine of election are great, indeed invaluable advances in theological understanding. Nevertheless, as we have seen, Barth on their account does not and cannot succeed in transcending the traditional conundrums, whether of actual evil in a world under divine sovereignty or of the compatibility of human freedom of choice with the scandals of grace and particularity. Thus the nagging question now recurs in a new form. If the effective calling of the Spirit, if the ensuing Christian *vocatio* for living as witnesses of the saving truth that applies to all in a community of action with Christ, is not only liberation from the lie of godlessness but also empowerment to live the new life of Christ, why indeed does the Spirit blow as He wills?

For the good reason of respecting divine freedom, so it seems, Barth was unwilling to entertain this new form of the old question, but to settle for an eternal offer of grace. Ironically, this reluctance leaves intact the very individualistic worry about personal fate in the afterlife that Barth has labored so hard to overcome. In addition, one has to wonder whether in the end this makes grace ultimately coercive, just as it seems to deprive human beings of the genuine individuality they responsibly assume in refusing grace. Is Spinoza really an ontological impossibility? A fateful illusion rather than a knowing, deliberate choice? At the same time, can we not from the perspective of the Bible ask whether this posture of grace as eternal offer fundamentally obscures the Spirit's active withholding of repentance and faith — classically, the hardening of Pharaoh's wicked heart — so that at least the long-suffering faithful may discern in this figure of the oppressor the vessel of the wrath of the God of love?[173] This was Leibniz's view, although it is seldom noted, as it was Luther's. Their universalism was not universal.

In a very early letter to Magnus Wedderkopf from May 1671, Leibniz observed that "both views are difficult — that a God who does not decide everything, or that a God who does decide everything, should be the absolute author of all." Either the power or the wisdom of God seems lost, depending on which horn of the dilemma strikes home. "For if he does decide everything, and the world dissents from his decree, he will not be omnipotent. But if he does not decide everything, it seems to follow that he is not omniscient." Leibniz opts for the latter horn, as in Luther's *De servo arbitrio*, with a circumspect statement of the Augustinian doctrine of double predestination. "Hence it follows that God can never be purely permissive. It follows also that there is no decree of God which is really not absolute." He speaks consequently of "*fate* [as] the decree of God or the necessity of events. Those events are *fatal* which will necessarily happen." We need recall here the theology in the back of Leibniz's mind stemming from *De servo arbitrio*. Throughout the treatise Luther spoke of the "immutable necessity of divine foreknowledge" as the basis of the martyr's confidence that even though she has fallen into the hands of sinners and been handed over to the powers of darkness, she has not fallen out of the hands of God. Is this Stoicism or Christianity? The impassible passibility of the martyr or the equanimity of the fatalist? Does this conviction make Luther a theopanist? or Leibniz a crypto-Spinozist? "Is this conclusion hard? I admit it. What of it?" Leibniz now recalls the divine necessity invoked in the passion predictions of Jesus: "Pilate is condemned. Why? Because he lacks faith. Why does he lack it? Because he lacks the will to attention. Why this? Because he has not understood the necessity of the matter (the utility of attending to it). Why has he not understood it? Because the causes of understanding were lacking." Who is the cause of these causes? Who has withheld from Pilate true insight into the Judge he presumes to judge? At this juncture the linchpin of Leibnizian argumentation comes into play, the principle of sufficient reason: "For it is necessary to refer everything to some reason, and we cannot stop until we have arrived at a first cause — or it must be admitted that something can exist without a sufficient reason for its existence." The principle of sufficient reason finds its terminus in God, understood as the sum of perfections and so the origin of all things and the ground of their harmonization. "What, therefore, is the ultimate reason for the divine will? The divine intellect. For God wills the things which he understands to be the best and most harmonious and selects them, as it were, from an infinite number of all possibilities. What then is the reason for the divine intellect? The harmony of things. What the reason for the harmony of things? Nothing."[174] The harmony of things is what pleases God. We have reached the ultimate origination of things, beyond which there is nothing.

Is this Origin then indiscernible from a true Nothing? Or is it the eternal reality of triune life, the infinite harmonizing of the Father's love for the Son and the Son's for the Father by the Spirit? At this early stage Leibniz wavered between these two great possibilities; perhaps he never succeeded in working out the difference between them with the clarity I am suggesting. Yet this much is clear. Reflecting back from God as the principle of harmony upon the world, it is not that sin, taken in the abstract, is somehow good. Rather "sins are evil," but "not absolutely, not to the world, not to God — for otherwise he would not permit them — but only to the sinner. God hates sins, not in the sense that he cannot bear the sight of them as we cannot bear the sight of things we detest — otherwise he would eliminate them — but in the sense that he punishes them. Sins are good, that is, harmonious, *taken along with their punishment or expiation.* For there is no harmony except through contraries."[175] In the *wisdom* of God, which may well seem folly to the wisdom of the world that does not want God to be God, there cannot be Moses without Pharaoh, Jesus without Pilate, resurrection without death. Barth has corrected and deepened Leibniz, but in the final analysis we are justified in asking whether he *has said anything different,* indeed, whether Leibnizian wisdom has something to say in aid of Barthian freedom and love (which otherwise founders as do all "binary oppositions").

How the Holy Spirit Disappeared in
Lutheranism and Never Reappeared in Barth

How Barth and Luther Differ

Gerhard Ebeling was formally correct to point to the fact that Luther's Christology was antithetic and Barth's analogical,[1] meaning that for Luther the
narrative basis of theology is the apocalyptic battle of God against the devil[2]
on behalf of sinful humanity in justification *by faith* while for Barth it is the
sovereign claim of God manifest in the person of Jesus Christ who justifies
the godless *by grace*. This highly nuanced differentiation (i.e., the two positions do not exclude each other) reflects the location of Barth's theology after
Kant, whom Barth labored both consciously and unconsciously to overcome.
Barth's problematic is speaking God in a world Kant made godless. The protest then — often made in the name of genuine "Lutheranism"[3] — against
Barth's supposed "objectivism" on behalf of *Lebensbezug,* as we shall see,
misses the target in several ways. In general, Luther's position on theological
knowledge is *perspectivalist,* as in his important contrast between the old
philosophical language and the new theological language of the Spirit that are
nevertheless speaking about the same things.[4] In Ebeling himself, it is not so
clear that it is Luther's divine and justifying faith grasping the sinner by the
Holy Spirit that is being defended rather than Descartes's and Kant's turn to
the subject with Schleiermacher obediently following. As to the supposed
cancellation of the subject, Barth howsoever reluctantly admits that God *permits* the evil He does not will and so cannot foreclose the possibility of eternal
refusal. What greater "freedom" — if such we would call the creature's willful
hardness of heart — can be conceived, or rather conceded to the subject?

According to the present thesis, the real problem of Barth's theology may rather be traced more to its continuity with official Lutheranism than to the subtle difference from Luther that Ebeling detects, namely, the disappearance of the Holy Spirit as a public player in the forum of church and theology and reappearance as a pious cipher for subjective inspiration. Barth, it seems, split the difference between Luther and Melanchthon. He followed Melanchthon in rejecting any suggestion of a double will in God. Does he not follow Luther, however, with a rigorously anti-Pelagian account of justification? In fact he does not. Here too Barth in the end followed Melanchthon in arguing that "man himself is the free subject of this event."[5] In this Barth appropriated the sequenced scheme of "imputative justification — effective sanctification" that, following Melanchthon, became normative also for the Reformed tradition. The difficulty exposed at the conclusion of the previous chapter is that Barth then has to settle for an eternal standoff: an eternal offer of grace that may yet be eternally declined, since God neither fates anyone to damnation nor coerces the creature's response to His love. The offer persists, the response remains open. At the same time, however, if anyone does respond in faith, *Hallelujah,* this free decision of the free human subject is and must be said to be caused by the Holy Spirit, *soli Deo gloria!* This unstable conclusion, however, represents no progress; indeed, it perpetuates the root internal incoherence of Protestant theology. The difficulty here goes back in the tradition we are investigating to Melanchthon's subtle transformations of Luther's theology of the joyful exchange into an exclusively forensic doctrine of justification and concomitantly of Luther's notion of divine faith wrought by the Spirit into the human will's nonresistance to grace. Investigating this transformation of Luther at Melanchthon's hands is the task of this chapter. As in the last chapter, we trace our steps backward through the thought of Karl Barth, whose ambivalent teaching on the Holy Spirit indicates why and how things went as they did, as an effect indicates its cause.

Barth's "Binitarianism"

In general with Barth, one has to ask: Is it a way of speaking, not being? An accommodation to lesser minds rather than the donation of one's very self to them in the language that performs what it says and says what it does? Certainly a *rhetoric,* deriving from Luther's "joyful exchange" and the antecedent tradition of the *commercium admirabile,* runs through Barth's entire *procla-*

mation of election. In Jesus Christ God "takes upon Himself the rejection of man with all its consequences and elects man to participation in His own glory."[6] "What God is, He wills to be for man also. What belongs to Him He wills to communicate to man also."[7] Barth recurrently speaks of the "amazing exchange between God and man as it was realized in time in Jesus Christ because already it was the beginning of all things. . . . He has given away Himself and all the prerogatives of His Godhead. He has given them to the man Jesus, and in Him to the creature."[8] The very "purpose of the election of this one man is God's will to save this lost man and to make him a participant of the glory of eternal life in His kingdom by taking his place in the person of this one man, by taking to Himself man's misery in Him, by making it His own concern, by clothing him in return with His own righteousness, blessedness and power."[9] Thus "the price which God pays for this great love of His is no less than to make Himself a curse."[10] God "chooses for Himself what is not His due, what is not worthy of Him, the frailty of the flesh, suffering, dying, death, in order to take it away from man, in order to clothe man instead with his glory. This is what takes place in the election."[11] Election is the act of God's being eternally anticipated and in the fullness of time realized in the cross and resurrection of His incarnate Son. Far from unfolding as an arbitrary muster of predetermined ranks of the saved and the damned, the event of election in time occurs in the preaching of the gospel of this "amazing exchange" of life for death, the holy One for sinful ones. This temporal preaching *opens up* human history by awakening it (as from the dead) to God's eternal decision about Jesus through the gathering of the *church* in time, where God's determined choice for the *sinful creature* is actualized on the earth by the preaching of the gospel, the Spirit bestowing faith when and where it pleases God. So Barth can *sound* — very much like Luther.

Yet, it seems equally true for Barth that this destiny can be declined, mercy refused, grace resisted, and that, on the other side of the divide, even where it is received in faith, it can never be possessed, appropriated, or otherwise turned into an object at the disposal of the believer. Not all are gathered to the church. Not all come to faith. We cannot foreclose the possibility of eternal refusal of eternally offered grace, if indeed the creature is a substantial, intelligent reality other than God. On the other hand, since the creature *is and remains* a substantial and intelligent reality other than God, even as believer she can never rest securely in faith, but must rather always venture to follow in obedient action the God who as event eludes her grasp. As we have seen for Barth, this subordinate but real human agency positively or negatively determines individual destiny. Consequently, it may be admitted that Barth does not succeed in overcoming the traditional conundrum (if indeed that was ever his purpose) of reconciling divine sovereignty and human freedom.[12] If anything, he affirms a tension-laden compatibilism that presses the limits of intelligibility: God is determined to save the creature who resists God and His salvation with knowing hostility. Barth leaves the topic here.

Emil Brunner influentially objected in the name of the human subject: "How, then, is it possible for Barth to arrive at such a fundamental perversion of the Christian message of Salvation? The answer to this question lies in an element peculiar to his teaching, which has always been characteristic, and permeates his teaching as a whole: namely, its 'objectivism,' that is, the forcible severance of revelation and faith, or rather — since Barth also naturally wishes to make a basis for faith — the view that, in comparison with revelation, with the objective Word of God, the subjective element, faith, is not on the same level, but is on a much lower plane."[13] Does this critique of "objectivism," as alluded to with reference to Ebeling above, strike its target? John Dillenberger's account of this debate from more than fifty years ago is still as good as any.

"The most pressing and baffling problem," Dillenberger wrote, "is the mystery of why particular individuals are believers and others are not."[14] Brunner, he says, argues one side of Augustine's complex legacy on free will (which today we might call the de Lubac[15] side): "Man therefore is not free to choose God but he is free to reject God. God makes his continual offer to man, but he does not compel." Yet, Dillenberger replies in the voice of the other side of Augustine's legacy (which we might today call the Kolakowski side), and so with Luther and Calvin and (apparently) Barth: "if man cannot make the decision to be a believer unless somehow through the grace of God this happens, why does one man have faith and another not?"[16] Where does nonresistance to offered grace in the Word come from, if not from the Spirit's prevenient grace? The problem is not resolved psychologically. Of course, faith comes as a change in human consciousness. "Without the decision faith cannot occur, but the decision will not make faith." No one can will himself to faith or persuade himself to faith, nor even will to will — a new heart of flesh must be made by the Spirit out of the old heart of stone. Thus also on the level of human consciousness, the question recurs to God's electing will. "Why the possibility of faith has been given to one and not to another is still the mystery of God's election," Dillenberger rightly summarized. "It is exactly this problem which is not solved by the emphasis upon man's self-exclusion from mercy. Nor is it solved by positing a double decree in God. . . . Nor, on the other hand, does the view of Barth — that Christ died also for him who is not of faith — solve the problem. . . . To be sure, Christ died also for him without faith. Yet he died also for the purpose of faith." Surveying all these options, Dillenberger concluded in resignation: "It is better to insist upon the mystery of God without establishing a separate niche for it within the Godhead."[17]

Discretion may be the better part of valor, but we want to be clear that the resignation here is to divine mystery, not a theological muddle. The problem lies in the presupposition of the discussion. Barth clearly wanted to pass beyond a framework of thought in which the "most pressing and baffling problem is the mystery of why particular individuals are believers and others are not." From his new perspective, of course, he too had to comment on the stated problem of disbelief. Just this commentary on the burning issue of *Lebensbezug* is what offends the narcissism of the existentialist opponents; these want above all to save the believing subject constructing its object in momentous, no doubt agonizing decisions of faith amid objective uncertainties, driven by infinite passion. The agonized self is preferred to Barth's (or Luther's) one true God in His Word, who can be trusted in life and in death, since from eternity He has decided for us. Thus Barth wants us to think of an amazing and irrevocable decision of God to save the creature though she yield to Nothingness, becoming both its victim and its agent and as such an enemy of God's reign. He wants us to think of this eternal determination of God actualized in the costly journey of the Son of God into the far country, so that those who do find themselves believing in Christ believe in turn on behalf of all other godless folks just like themselves, arising to live freely and responsibly in a community of *action* with the living God whose kingdom comes as this *event* reconciling *enemies*. It is the world, not a handful of authentic decisions, at which God aims, a world God in Christ is determined from eternity to create, redeem, and fulfill for His kingdom. This is the new perspective of "objectivity" beyond existential narcissism[18] at which Barth's theology aims.

So far then as Barth is willing still to address the perplexity about the persistence of unbelief from the perspective of his new orientation, he does not and cannot transcend the traditional conundrum that attends any conceivable world in which God both *sovereignly* and yet *really* wills the existence of other wills. At the same time, the new orientation Barth seeks and is thinking through in the *Church Dogmatics* is arguably one in which the will of God is strictly understood as the will of the Trinity. Barth does not want this will to be seen as encountering the human will like some kind of rival ego competing on the same plane. Barth is well aware of Ward's kind of criticism of the binary oppositions that haunt the discussion, at the root between one true person of God and human selves trying to be persons falsely without or in place of the fellowship of loving action with the Lord in an I-Thou relation. Thus Barth affirms constantly that there is humility in God. In Jesus Christ we meet the humanity of God, in whom the Lord becomes the Servant, by whom the servant is exalted to become a Lord. This is what Barth clearly strives to say in any fair-minded reading. The problem, however, lies in the structure of thought that he has adopted. It lies in Barth's apparently Fichtean account of the act of God's being,[19] the supreme self-positing subject whose absolute personhood in its incomparable divine supremacy seems not to brook any rival, although He nevertheless exists for us in the unfathomable decision of grace. On account of this scheme, as we noted, the eternal Trinity itself is not understood as "being in communion" (Zizioulas) but as the threefold iteration of a single ego. It is historically understandable, even commendable, that Barth adopted this line of thought during the 1920s and 1930s to oppose Nazi camp followers in the church, who confused the Fuehrer's "triumph of the will" with the Christian message. Thus we can and should honor Barth's intentions here, acknowledging that from the beginning Barth tried to mitigate the Fichtean scheme by tying the free act of God's being as tightly as possible to God's primal decision of love to be the God of grace for the lowly and undeserving creature. Yet it is a "tie" that could have been otherwise, not the fitting expression of an antecedent "being in communion." The gratuity of grace indeed comes to depend in this scheme on the inconceivable decision for humility by an Absolute Ego.

Thus we should also honor the problem this reliance on idealism created, not least for Barth himself, and seek the alternative. "Does Barth suppose," Robert Jenson asks, "that an act of the Spirit cannot transcend subjectivity?"[20] That is to ask whether Barth, following the Protestant teaching that goes back to Melanchthon's scheme of "imputative justification and effective sanctification," equates the Spirit with the private, interior, impersonal animation of human response to the public, exterior, person-to-person, and in this sense "objective" address of the Word? The gracious assertion of God's Lordship as Barth understands it requires that human faith be understood as *both* God heard, God acknowledged as Lord by God, i.e., as the work of the Spirit repeating itself in the human subject, *and* simultaneously as human hearing, human deciding, i.e., the work of a free human subject. In this latter respect, it must be a work that genuinely belongs to this one, not that, i.e., to the one and only creature who is its human doer, its agent, its subject. Like many, then, Barth struggles to articulate a doctrine of compatibilism in which these two accounts of the divine and human agency involved in faith can be reconciled. Rhetorically, human faith is the Spirit's gift, Christ's donation of his own Spirit to provide believers with His own faith in the Father; this is the Bible's way of speaking of divine faith. In human consciousness, however, it is one's own decision, just as the man Jesus' faith was his own human decision and obedience. Faith answers in response to the "I" of the Father addressing one as "Thou." This address occurs in the Word concerning the man Jesus and his decision for God and for us.

This is a very unstable harmonization — like the Nestorian Christology it distantly reflects — which can quickly come apart (as it did among Barth's disciples). The event on the earth is the event of human hearing, human deciding; it is not manifestly the work of God, even for those human egos who would invoke the heavenly way of speaking in order to give God alone the glory. It is thus a curious way of speaking, dubious, fraught with ambiguity if not also its own peculiar peril of idolatry, since it is clearly we creatures who are talking this way about ourselves. An accommodationist account of divine action tends to undermine the very causality that for Barth's theology of grace seems crucial: the "Spirit's calling to faith by the Spirit's gathering of the church" becomes a tentative way of talking about what otherwise appears simply to be individual human intentions and action, not then exclusively divine and personal initiative and action of God's third way in being, efficaciously at work on the earth. A slow and steady erosion caused by doubts along these lines leads to suspicions, voiced with fervor if not insight nowadays, among those who want to turn Barth's entire project on its head: if God's Lordship in faith is no more than a melodramatic way of talking about a certain human decision, it is, à la Feuerbach, exposed as a sophisticated projection. Barth is supposedly unveiled as a crypto-fundamentalist, a "Christomonist," even "Christofascist."[21] Theology turns entirely away from the objectivism to which Barth aspired for a disciplined, nonspeculative hearing and understanding of the one Word of God that we are to obey in life and in death. It repudiates Barth's objectivism as a human, all-too-human conceit and dives merrily into the current maelstrom of perspectivalist critique and freewheeling constructivism in theology.

"Any theologian for whom the doctrine of the Trinity is more than a relic," the Jenson continued in diagnosis of this difficulty, "that is, any theologian who *uses* the doctrine of the Trinity outside its own *locus,* is repeatedly led — indeed compelled — to treat the three as *parties* of divine action, and that also 'immanently,'"[22] i.e., as Zizioulas's "being in communion."

One does not speak generically of "the Lord" as a single subject, but rather of the heavenly Father, the Lord Jesus His crucified and risen Son, and their blessed Spirit, holy Giver of life. A more adequately trinitarian recognition of the sovereignty of the Spirit, i.e., as this latter "party" with the Father and the Son, would help solve the difficulty here, because it would not snare us in the idealistic view that the Spirit represents the third assertion of the self-same divine subjectivity in the form of its self-reflective recognition from the interiority of the other. One would rather be thinking of the Spirit who blows as He wills, who therefore may harden hearts as well as open them, not in executing a *decretum absolutum* but rather making decisions in time for time to fulfill the economy of God (e.g., Rom. 9–11). This Spirit, of course, ever works as the Spirit of the Father of the Son and only as such can be recognized as the *Holy* Spirit. But He does not work as reiterating one and the same subjectivity in the form of its recognition from within another. This would reduce the Spirit to a phantom, nothing but a personification of the I and Thou relation (of the Father and the Son), rather than the One who by the resurrection bonds the Father even to His dead and disgraced Son, and the Son to His Father who had abandoned Him to that very disgrace. As phantom, as cipher for the Father's self-recognition in Jesus as His other, we would have not real love, but narcissism extended into relationships pretending to love, in which the other is shattered and reconstructed to conform to the self who reveals Himself as Lord. This is *not* Barth's intention, of course. Far from it. But as he does not achieve a doctrine of the Spirit as the agent of love between the Father and the Son that can actually perform this initiative and action of bonding between true subjects, especially at the crucial juncture of their most extreme estrangement, and so in time incorporating human persons into these trinitarian relationships, Barth's unstable compatibilism is vulnerable to dissolution along the lines of either of its terms. Nor does calling it a "dialectic" help.

Jenson, in the essay cited from 1993, criticized a common understanding of Augustine's teaching of the Spirit as the bond of love between the Father and the Son as the source of Western trinitarian problems. It seemed to him then to depersonalize the Spirit as the agent of their relationship. The Spirit, he wanted to affirm, is not a mere personification of nonpersonal eros, *vinculum amoris*. Rather the Spirit in the life of the Trinity is to be understood as the personal agent of love between the Father and the Son. On examination, however, Jenson later realized that just this is what Augustine *actually* taught, who was seeking to grasp the personal uniqueness of the Spirit over against the Word. "Now love means someone loving and something loved with love. There you are with three, the lover, what is being loved, and love."[23] The actual differentiation is this: love does not consist in the narcissistic discovery of my I in a Thou, but in the giving of my I for a Thou and the receiving of my donated I back from the giving of a Thou in return. The Spirit is this personal agent of the giving of the Father for the Son by whom the Father donates His being as God from God, and the giving of the Son for the Father by whom the Father receives His identity as Father of this Son.[24] To put it boldly, as Jenson eventually did,[25] were there no Spirit, the Father would not have recognized the Crucified as His beloved Son; if there were no Spirit, the Crucified could never have committed His cause to the Father who had called Him only to abandon Him to that Godforsaken death. It is the Spirit who mediated this giving and receiving at the very juncture in time in which the divine life as one eternal community of giving and receiving was in jeopardy on account of the new, temporal inclusion in it of the godless and perishing creature. In this account, accordingly, the human ego in faith is not crushed and refashioned by God's ego (nor, on the other hand, must it refuse in unbelief God's claim as some divinely egoistic smothering of its own inferior self). Rather the human ego in faith is incorporated by the Spirit of love into these trinitarian relations. On the same account, Jenson observes that the Spirit's other is the community of those thus temporally included. The Spirit at Pentecost indefinitely delays the parousia in order to gather the church. It is the Spirit who in just this way gives life to the world. For the Spirit gives Himself to the beloved community of sinners forgiven and renewed, so making them holy, and in this giving receives His own identity, recognized as the Spirit who bonds the Father and the Son in love for us all, both the godless and the pious.

Jenson's mature account in his *Systematic Theology* is thus more sympathetic to Augustine's "audacious" teaching that the Trinity is one God as this *event* of personal bonding of love by the Spirit: there is genuine otherness within the one eternal life whose existence as eternal event is not that of a self-positing Subject but of mutual self-donation. Thus the gift of the Spirit is the Spirit Himself, i.e., the believer's incorporation into the mutual love of the Father and the Son, as object with Jesus of the Father's gracious favor and as subject with Jesus in the glorifying of God.[26] Traditionally, of course, the Eastern Orthodox account grounds the oneness of God in the Father, as font of the deity. "And let not one imagine me either to affirm that there are three original hypostases," Basil the Great wrote, objecting to the charge of tritheism as a misunderstanding. "For the first principle of existing things is the One, creating through the Son and perfecting through the Spirit."[27] This

God and Father is the one who is determined to create, redeem, and fulfill the world through the processions/missions of His Word and Spirit. Jenson's own proposal calls for balancing, as it were, this protological decision of the God and Father as the font of deity with the eschatological Spirit's work of bonding and including. This latter is the Trinity's immanent goal, such that divine being is not understood as persistence in what has been but rather as persistent anticipation of the community to be.[28] The Spirit is correspondingly free in time to innovate on the way to the kingdom. Jenson understands this innovation as the being of the church, the temple of the Spirit (of course, *that* affirmation entails a vigorous critique of the contemporary self-understandings in the divided churches). Jenson's revision involves a difficult notion of the temporality of the eternal God that cannot be properly pursued here, though it may be noted that the traditional protological bias of theology faces the same difficulty whenever it considers how God passes from eternity to the creation of time, since this too involves God in time.

I am in any case largely persuaded by Jenson's diagnosis of the ills of "binitarianism," though I remain perplexed at elements of his prognosis. In brief, there is no locus in his *Systematic Theology* on the divine perfections, and this absence seems quite deliberate. He wants to say radically and consistently that God is the act of His triadic being, not only then in fidelity to what God has been but also by anticipation of what God will be. Any independent account of divine nature as the sum of perfections, he fears, would seek a set of timeless perfections in contrast to temporal imperfection and would betray as such a prejudice for the protological metaphysics of being as persistence (God as origin and principle of what is) rather than the persistent anticipation that is the life of the Trinity (God as goal and principle of what will prevail eternally through the history that as origin He decided to undertake with us). An important albeit terse qualification Jenson makes here is to affirm against Hegel: it "might have been otherwise."[29] On Jenson's account, God cannot be the God that God will be apart from His self-anticipating decision in the intervening history with us. If this notion of persistence in anticipation is to be sustained against the powerful Spinozistic pressures that already impelled Hegel to deny that there can be any conflict between freedom and necessity in God, so that God's lack of differentiation from nothingness impelled God into becoming, it seems that *some* account of divine nature must help us see *what choices* God made in the act of *origin.* That is simply to ask: What were the divine possibilities? Moreover, it seems both biblically and experientially that what God decided upon includes not only history in the sense of humanity's providentially directed movement in time but also nature in the sense of the plentitude of being to which human-ity also belongs as the stewards of God's nonhuman creation. This beautiful world in all its maximal diversity is to be loved with the very joy of God who delights in it as the multirefracted mirror of His own eternal glory. With Leibniz, then, we who understand ourselves as the created images of this God have the right, the access, and the duty to ask this question about divine nature, in order that we know the mind of our God in His original decision and so to cooperate intelligently with His aims for the earth. Jenson's crucial, though very reserved, affirmation of divine freedom antecedent to the his-tory God actually undertakes with us requires some thicker account of the possibilities of divine nature in view of which the Trinity can be intelligibly said both to have freely chosen and chosen well. In a properly trinitarian ac-count this thicker account will appropriate the perfections to the persons, and in this way permit them no independent and so subversive role, as Jenson fears, as the Trojan horse for the metaphysics of mere persistence.

With Leibniz this kind of account is to be argued a posteriori, on the theological ground that this earth on which the cross stood is the world not only that God redeems but also that God initiated and preserves and presses forward in anticipation of final fulfillment. Even if the metaphysical tradition in its ignorance of eschatological destiny makes a happy science out of a sad creation, it is asking about the divine ground and standard of the shared world: *Why is there something, rather than nothing?* Admittedly this inquiry, with its metaphor of the divine as ground, is prejudiced toward an ontology of persistence rather than of anticipation. But surely the theological task here is not to jettison "metaphysics" but to revise. *Why is there something, rather than nothing?* To deny the question altogether as meaningless is to hand the victory to Spinoza with just a whimper. Whence anticipation, if the world just is and whatever is, is just? But the divine nature may be understood as the in-effable conjunction of power, wisdom, and love, the infinitely mysterious seat and coherence of the perfections manifest in the creation of this world (Rom. 1:20), so far as we understand the Father's almighty work of creation from the perspective of the cross of Jesus as all that is redeemed in Him for fulfillment by the Spirit and so on the way to becoming the best of all possible worlds from the very moment of its origin. From any other perspective, natural awareness of divine perfection will be misconstrued, if not idolatrously mis-used. The solution to the problem of divine nature is not to abandon the lo-cus, as Jenson does, but to complete the trinitarian revision of it, which, I am arguing, may be glimpsed in Leibniz and his patristic sources, especially Gregory of Nyssa, as we shall see in the conclusion of this book.

The Problem of the Divine Perfections

Barth's theology, if not his rhetoric or preaching of election, proceeds on the basis of the apparently *binitarian* scheme of the I and Thou relation of the Father and the Son, with the Spirit tacitly understood as the subjective interiorization of this relation in the decision of the believer, Jesus' faith being imitated in the believer's free act of obedience, forming then a union of action. This binitarianism can be correlated with Barth's account of dynamic divine nature as the act of God's being in freedom to love. Here the traditional ontological perfections of omnipotence and the moral perfections of love come to qualify each other. "The divine being must be allowed to transcend both nature and spirit," Barth writes, both matter and mind, becoming and being, earth and heaven and whatever other cosmic dualities or hierarchies exist and in terms of which idols are made of the supposedly superior term.[30] Instead, the living God who exists in His act is "the freedom of the spirit. . . . It is the freedom of a knowing and willing I, an I which itself distinguishes itself from what it is not, and what it is not from itself, an I which controls its nature."[31] As we heard in chapter 2, Barth justifies this interpretation from the fact that revelation in Scripture "consists in the fact that God speaks as an I, and is heard by the thou who is addressed."[32] In this way Barth now establishes the one pole of divine attributes, the ontological perfections pertaining to an omnipotent ego. "It is the I who knows about Himself, who Himself wills, Himself disposes and distinguishes, and in this very act of His omnipotence is wholly self-sufficient."[33] Barth is arguably developing a thought of Luther's here,[34] that properly speaking freedom as the power of self-determination, of freely choosing one's own way, of sovereignly projecting oneself, is to be ascribed to God alone: "No other being exists absolutely in its act. No other being is absolutely its own, conscious, willed and executed decision."[35] But in distinction from Luther's notorious statement that this free God, considered as such, *remains* "unbound by his Word,"[36] Barth strictly ties the free act of God's being to "the being of God in the nature of the Father and the Son and the Holy Spirit."[37] Accordingly, God *declares* God in His act of revelation and *gives* this free self-determination a particular, *self-binding* content, namely, "that God is He who, without having to do so, seeks and creates fellowship between Himself and us . . . impl[ying] so to speak an overflow of His essence that He turns to us."[38] In this way, Barth establishes the second term of the divine attributes, the moral perfections of love. "That He is God — the Godhead of God — consists in the fact that He loves, and it is the expression of His loving that He seeks and creates fellowship with us."[39] God exists in the freedom of love.

Barth's ensuing account of the traditional attributes of God as descriptive of God's freedom to love is among his many elegant revisions in dogmatics. Yet according to the present thesis, something significant is missing here. This omission leads on the one side to a certain "recklessness" of grace in Barth's thinking and a certain "permissiveness" in his ethics. On the other side, it allows the ambiguous but all the same deeply problematic intimation that in the end, as in Origen's *apokatastasis,* divine love prevails fatally, inevitably, coercively. It simply outlasts and exhausts all opposition. Assessing this problem correctly, however, is difficult because, as suggested at the outset of this chapter, Barth's rhetoric and Barth's theory do not always coincide.[40] In any case I will argue in due course that missing in Barth's *theoretical* account, though not in his *homiletical* account, of these divine dynamics is the divine perfection of *wisdom* — a perfection that takes, as we shall see, center stage in the Leibnizian ode to the conjunction of power, *wisdom,* and love in the *triune* God as the seat of all perfections.[41] The divine perfections of wisdom and love appropriated respectively to the almighty Father's Word and Spirit consequently are not collapsed into each other, as is the tendency in Barth. In election, that means there is wisdom in the *hardening* of Pharaoh's wicked heart, a method to the *folly* of the preaching of the cross, that the *wrath* of God is anything but the irrational fury of a pagan war god or a jealous husband, that the mercy of Christ fittingly *satisfies* and *more* the rightful demand of holy justice. To be sure, faith that is not yet sight confesses as still *inscrutable* the *mysterious* conjunction of divine power, wisdom, and love *revealed* in God's judgments in history (Rom. 9–11). But this confession of depths of mystery is precisely that of faith that knows God revealed as One whose almighty power is expressed in wise love and loving wisdom; in faith the human mind opens to *this* mystery of the internal coherence of God's life and lives now in assurance of seeing someday face-to-face, "knowing as we have been known." My argument, then, will resolve the ambiguity in Luther's own theodicy on the side of Melanchthon's and Barth's denial of a double will in God, Lutheranism's doctrine of universal atonement, and Barth's teaching of potential universalism. But the fact that universal salvation can be affirmed only as a possibility requires us in the interim to look and see what the Spirit is doing publicly and visibly by the preaching of the gospel and gathering of the church. Here and now we are summoned to discern — a posteriori — the wisdom of God, just as paradigmatically Paul made good sense of Jewish disbelief (Rom. 9–11), as the notion of a trinitarian providentialism (see below in this chapter) will imply.

Due care is necessary of course. "God is not different in essence than he manifested himself," Dillenberger agrees with Barth, yet restates Luther's objection in a new form: "that manifestation itself is mystery as well as meaning, and comes out of a God who remains unfathomable, but of whom it may be affirmed that he is trustworthy on the basis of faith . . . even in faith, point[ing] to an abyss which man cannot comprehend. Here, with Luther, one can say that the essence of faith is to believe God just who appears so unjust . . . the God who reveals is the totally mysterious God, whom man trusts on the basis of definite disclosure which emerges in a center of mystery . . . it is the mystery made manifest as truly God."[42] The *sub contrario* of divine foolishness that is wiser than the world stamps everything. All the same, faith makes its own affirmation of divine wisdom; thinking faith carefully asks how this affirmation of divine wisdom is possible. That indicates that there is as well an a priori dimension to this reflection. This was the considered opinion of Leibniz, who wrote in the *Theodicy:*

> And it is not to be doubted that this faith and this confidence in God, who gives us insight into his infinite goodness and prepares us for his love, in spite of the appearances of harshness that may repel us, are an admirable exercise for the virtues of Christian theology, when the divine grace in Jesus Christ arouses these motions within us. That is what Luther aptly observed in opposition to Erasmus, saying that it is love in the highest degree to love him who to flesh and look appears so unlovable, so harsh toward the unfortunate and so ready to condemn, and to condemn for evils in which he appears to be the cause or accessory, at least in the eyes of those who allow themselves to be dazzled by false reasons. One may therefore say that that triumph of true reason illuminated by divine grace is at the same time the triumph of faith and love.[43]

True reason, for Leibniz, is entitled to ask why God has decided as God has, and in just this inquiry it struggles against "those who allow themselves to be dazzled by false reasons." Just this struggle against false appearances and false reasons is the critical juncture at which true theology and true philosophy converge to make common cause. For Leibniz this harmony of faith and reason is possible because the distinction between appearance and reality, the very touchstone of critical thinking, is perspectival, not ontological. Indeed, according to the cited text, this is what Leibniz has learned from Luther and is trying to bring to bear philosophically. True perspective philosophically is attained by seeing intellectually, a priori, i.e., on the basis of the human mind made in God's image, certain maxims that apply to the true God's behavior: that metaphysically God delights in maximal self-expression in His created image, that morally God is true to Himself in His outer works and thus chooses the best possible. True perspective theologically is to see a posteriori on the basis of experience the Crucified as risen from the dead for the justification of all. The two perspectives converge for Leibniz and mutually illuminate one another. Attaining to these perspectives when we otherwise appear as anything but the blessed image of God, rather under the just wrath and reprobation of God for our sinful egocentrism that distorts perception, is precisely the battle of faith against despair and of reason against irrationalism, not for one's isolated self, but for the world to which the believer continues to belong.

Thus, while Barth's theology of revelation is the only possible way of rescuing Leibniz's theodicy from Kant's criticism of the illicit presumption of seeing things in God's perspective, it is arguably the case that Leibniz's theodicy, understood as a theology of divine wisdom, is also the only way to save Barth's theology from Stout's criticism of fideist ghettoization. What is at stake in the public articulation of Christian faith in common cause with Leibniz's true philosophy is our hope for the salvation of the world, we pious and godless alike, since also the believer remains *simul iustus et peccator,* since even the disbeliever is embraced in the world God was reconciling to Himself in Christ, not counting trespasses. This new deliverance of theology to its theme and public will not come about in the fashion of the systematic apologetics that Barth rightly spurned, in that it dissolves theology into other discourses; it comes about as the "ad hoc apologetics" undertaken in service of the scriptural "world-absorbing narrative" (Lindbeck) by theology as dogmatic *Nachdenken,* and, most ambitiously, the systematic redescription of all truths of the world in Christ (Marshall). Barth's theological optimism warrants a discourse of solidarity with the suffering creation as nevertheless good and blessed because destined in Christ for the glorious liberty of the children of God — this affirmation aimed, be it carefully noted, against the powerful temptation to internalize oppression or succumb to despair. Yet in some distinction from Barth, such affirmation and articulation entail at every step along the way a *meaningful disputation* with disbelief about the *wisdom* at work in the world, and that meaningful disputation is possible because the Two Cities are mingled, such that only God can finally rightly separate them. In the interim we are all living in and talking about a shared world whose common future is at stake. Thus in a genuinely

public theology all true descriptions of the common world — even, if not especially, those of a Spinoza! — receive a new signification in Christ (Luther).[44] On
this basis, a theological, not epistemological, critique of metaphysics is both
possible and necessary (what else is the disjunction between *theologia crucis*
and *theologia gloriae?*): a critique of the old thinking, which "makes a happy science of a sad creation," closing the mind against and hardening the heart to its
promised transformation, which the theodicy of faith anticipates. In this disputation, theology cannot act in mimicry of Enlightenment science as if a disinterested observer, nor can it permit to its opponents in dispute the conceit of
disinterested rationality standing above the fray. Insofar as it has anything
whatsoever to do with the Crucified, theology precisely as *science* contends as itself an interested participant in the drama of redemption. *Tolle assertiones,*
Christianismum tulisti.

Barth's Tale of Post-Reformation Ironies

We can finish with Karl Barth's neo-Reformation theology for now by re-
counting his tale of the doctrine of election, which conveniently provides us
with a needed overview of the movement in Protestant thought during the
period that extends from Luther through Melanchthon to Leibniz. Barth's is
a story that is filled with sad ironies. Confining himself to the technical debates in the old dogmatics (i.e., *not* taking sufficiently into consideration the
philosophical context signified by the absence of Spinoza in all the *Church*
Dogmatics), Barth argues in a typically detailed survey that all sides in the
post-Reformation controversies held in common a series of highly question-
able assumptions: (1) that the doctrine of election had first of all to do with
the final destiny of individuals; (2) that it represented a fixed system decided
in advance and now in the process of being rigidly executed; (3) that in this
system justice and mercy play off against one another; and that (4) divine
"good pleasure" is absolute in a way that makes God arbitrary, even tyrannical.[45] With such assumptions universally at work, Barth holds that it is impossible simply to endorse one position or another, even if "the greater right
lay then on the side" of theocentric supralapsarianism. "The objections
against [supralapsarian theologians] . . . do not amount finally to anything
more than a demonstration of the specific dangers in their position."[46]

 With these qualifications in mind, Barth's story goes like this. In *De*
servo arbitrio Luther contended valiantly for the sovereignty of God revealed
in the mercy of Christ, the *deus revelatus*, but was stopped in his tracks theo-

logically by the anomaly of God hardening the heart of wicked Pharaoh in apparent contradiction to his revealed will that all should repent and be saved. With this dark thought — *gemina est praedestinatio* — going back to the late Augustine, however, another God willing something other than that revealed in Christ was posited: Luther's *deus absconditus,* which in certain passages surely looks and sounds like the nominalist *deus exlex:* "But God hidden in Majesty neither deplores nor takes away death, but works life, and death, and all in all; nor has He set bounds to Himself by His Word, but has kept Himself free over all things."[47] This posit of a Word-less Deity cannot but mean that revelation as God's *self*-revelation is logically as well as pastorally undermined. Contrary to Luther's own express intention, "what an abyss of uncertainty is opened up! The thought of the election becomes necessarily the thought of the will and decision of God which are hidden somewhere in the heights or depths behind Jesus Christ and behind God's revelation."[48] Barth acknowledges that the later Luther grew increasingly silent about this supposedly secret God behind God, warned against all speculation about it, and all the more exhorted to faith in the revealed God alone.[49] Yet Luther nowhere as such renounced the posit of a God unbounded by His Word. Consequently, all exhortation aside, anxious speculation could hardly be denied. What is the will of the real, true God beyond and behind Christ, in whom "the decisive word for salvation [or perdition] is spoken"?

Calvin's position, in Barth's exposition, is simply Luther made consistent. In spite of Calvin's emphatic pastoral counsel, akin to Luther's, to lay hold of Christ by faith as the *speculum electionis,*[50] and in this way to affirm the christological content of the revealed God as God determined by mercy to save, it is inevitable under this dualistic assumption that Christ will be reduced to the mere instrument of a decree of salvation (and reprobation) that is resolved upon apart from Him: this becomes the "absolute decree" of second-generation Calvinism.[51] Given the dualism in God posited at the heart of the theology of the leading reformers, "the opposition brought against the doctrine of the *decretum absolutum* by 17th century Lutheran theology is far more significant." Here, says Barth, we can again hear a serious, antidualistic contention for the identity of the eternal decree of election with that which is revealed in Christ.[52] Barth is referring to the "elaborate and complicated" (but also, in Robert Preus's view, "most unsatisfactory") approach of John Gerhard. Gerhard brought together under one topic God's foreknowledge, God's decrees, and the trinitarian conjunction of power, wisdom, and goodness in divine governance,[53] since "whatever God did in time He decreed to do in eternity."[54] This assimilation of the traditionally separated topics of election and providence means that, as in Barth, God's decrees are "acts of goodness in Christ," which foresee and so permit evil, yet only will salvation.[55] Barth is critical of Gerhard's attempt insofar as it subsumes election to providence and providence to general benevolence; it thus fails radically to understand God as the self-determining God of grace in Christ. Barth holds that in this way the justified concern and intention of a Lutheran like Gerhard for the universality of the atonement foundered upon the aforementioned common assumptions; he was consequently unable "to do more than make mere assertions along these lines." In fact, under the pressure of those presuppositions, later Lutherans involved themselves more and more dubiously in a notion supposedly borrowed from Thomas, i.e., that God predestines to salvation those whose faith in Christ, as it were, God passively foresees. Barth takes time here to expose the evasion involved: predestination is not in this case a divine act of choosing but only a sophisticated prediction, not the divine act of mercy that creates its beloved but only a proto-deistic calculation, recognition, and reward of the human merit of faith.[56]

In significant distinction from such Lutherans, however, were the rebels on the Calvinist side, to whom Barth awards the title of the first "liberal Protestants," since they contend against the "horrible decree," not for the sake of the honor of Christ as savior of all, but rather to preserve the dignity of man as arbiter of his own destiny. With the Arminians, "the criterion or measure of all things must always be man, i.e. man's conception of that which is right, and rational, and worthy, therefore, of God and man."[57] Abhorrent to the officially anti-Pelagian Lutherans as the Arminian teaching had to appear, in the course of time the Lutherans came to mimic erstwhile Jesuit foes from whom they adopted the *praevisa fides* with its deistic implications, siding in the seventeenth-century controversy with the Molinists[58] against the Jansenists, and thus in reality against Augustine and their own Luther, whose *De servo arbitrio* became more and more a shibboleth. The way to Kant on the soil of nominally Lutheran culture was thus prepared, not by crypto-Calvinism but by its very opposite. "The Lutheran doctrine could very well become the entrance-gate for a new Pelagianism. And it cannot be denied that the heritage of orthodox Lutheranism on this side — a heritage which dates from as early as Melanchthon — did later work itself out in this direction."[59]

Barth appends one last thought to this tale of ironies he tells. If one were to derive the *praevisa fides,* he writes, "from the grace of the Holy Spirit and therefore from the will of God," then this would amount to Augustine's doctrine of prevenient grace and one would have in view "the free electing of God" as "the foundation of the whole process. It will be decided that it was altogether of God that in faith the work of Christ availed for some men and that in faith they allowed it to avail for them."[60] Indeed, as we shall see, Melanchthon finally thinks that the nonresistance of the will to grace (for which he was accused of semi-Pelagianism) is itself the prevenient work of grace (although this raises once again the theodicy problem). Barth's appeal to prevenient grace on the other hand does not get to the heart of the problem, to which Barth in fact alluded when he spoke against an absolute notion of divine "good pleasure" that makes God's choice arbitrary, even tyrannical. But to overcome this, one has to think not only of freedom to love, that is, of the mission of the Son as the elected and rejected One, but also of the mission of His Spirit, effectively calling through the preaching of the "amazing exchange" every particular sinner to a vicarious faith — the very faith of the man Jesus Himself! — on behalf of the unbelieving world, and so the gathering of the church on behalf of the unbelieving world. One has to grasp divine wisdom in this *sub contrario* of the Spirit, if grace is not to be considered as arbitrary, but nonetheless gratuitous: not *deus exlex* but *deus supra legem*.

How else might the "amazing exchange" transpire in creatures apart from the effective calling of the Holy Spirit who grants the faith that appropriates Christ with His blessings just as Christ in the Word appropriates the sinner and so elects the rejected, as it pleases God wherever and whenever the gospel is proclaimed? Such a theology of the calling, enlightening, gathering Spirit through the Word does not resolve the conundrum of the permission of evil. Indeed, it reiterates that conundrum in a new form: the possibility of refusal of proffered mercy. But neither was it meant to resolve the conundrum. It is meant rather to face both believer and unbeliever with it — a confrontation that is evaded when God is too quickly and too nervously defended from authorship of evil, or rather, what appears to be evil to us — as per the early Luther's "theological paradoxes" concerning the "good of the cross."[61] But such a lively doctrine of the sovereign Spirit in love mediating power by wisdom that appears to be folly to the world — this was the path not taken — not even in Barth's unfinished theology (though it might be continued in this direction). Thus "Barth's theology, too, now has to be read eschatologically. His work is not timeless."[62]

Model One: The Joyful Exchange

The question, raised at the beginning of this chapter, to which we now return, is whether Luther's joyful exchange must be regarded as no more than a way

of talking, a *significat*, rather than a way of being, an *est:* "Was Luther's original insight into the inner, transforming righteousness received by faith distorted by Melanchthon's legal metaphor of forensic justification?"[63] The
question is perhaps tendentiously crafted — the question is whether the latter
displaces the former as a theological claim about reality — even if it points in
the right direction. Recent German scholarship concedes that "for a long
time, the fact that for Luther justification involved not merely forgiveness of
sins or acquittal but also renewal has not been sufficiently appreciated."[64] The
historical reason, as we shall shortly see, is the decisive influence in official
Lutheranism of a subtle reinterpretation of early Lutheran theology by the
Formula of Concord. If this is so, the common understanding, "justification
first, then sanctification,"[65] may be seen as a misleading oversimplification
that is as such false to Luther as also to the earlier Melanchthon.[66]

To make the matter vividly clear, consider the following directive from a
letter to George Spenlein dated April 8, 1516. It comes early on in Luther's career before the Reformation controversies break out, yet it articulates the
consistent pattern of thought, or model, of the life of faith that stands behind Luther's development of the Reformation doctrine of justification:

> [L]earn Christ and him crucified. Learn to praise him and, despairing of
> yourself, say, "Lord Jesus, you are my righteousness, just as I am your sin.
> You have taken upon yourself what you were not and have given to me
> what I was not." Beware of aspiring to such purity that you will not wish
> to be looked upon as a sinner, or to be one. For Christ dwells only in sin-
> ners. On this account he descended from heaven, where he dwelt among
> the righteous, to dwell among sinners. Meditate on this love of his and
> you will see his sweet consolation. For why was it necessary for him to die
> if we can obtain a good conscience by our works and afflictions? Accord-
> ingly you will find peace only in him and only when you despair of your-
> self and your own works. Besides, you will learn from him that just as he
> received you, so he has made your sins his own and has made his righ-
> teousness yours.[67]

The *joyful exchange*[68] of our sin and Christ's righteousness provides the operative model in Luther's mind of how the event of justification transpires in
uniting the believer with Christ in His death and resurrection. According to
this model, forgiveness and the new birth are double-sided aspects of the
one saving event of encounter with Christ in divine faith of the Spirit
through the gospel, such that the sinner dies and a new creature is born.

A generation ago the Danish theologian Regin Prenter tried to disentangle this model of justification from the way Lutherans have traditionally thought. He wrote of "a strongly intellectual, forensic idea of justification, in which Christ Himself becomes merely the ideological content of the doctrine of objective satisfaction with its legalistic demand of acceptance in faith, and [alongside of this] a theological formula about the mystical union, which often becomes almost a nonevangelical mysticism of Christ. . . . the real presence of Christ and justification, which in Luther's thinking were a complete unity, become two opposing tendencies which it became a problem to reconcile, that is, the religious interest of the doctrine of justification and the ethical interest of the doctrine of sanctification."[69] How do these two models differ? In a nutshell, the later Melanchthon thinks *from* a transcendental, forensic act of the imputation of Christ's righteousness *to* the renewal of the believer in faith, hope, and love by the Spirit. Thus the strict psychological sequence: repentance, justification, sanctification, or, law (as accusation), gospel, and law again (as guidance). Luther, in contrast, thinks *from* the "joyful exchange" between Christ and the believer *to* the nonimputation of the persisting sin that continues to afflict the renewed person. Here there is no strict sequencing of states of consciousness, because the story Luther is telling is one of "Trinitarian advent" and human incorporation (C. Helmer) that psychologically can and does occur in all sorts of ways. There is no one psychologically mandated *ordo salutis*. The distinction between law and promise is regulative for preaching, not prescriptive for experience. One may affirm that Luther and Melanchthon agree on forensic justification, that is, on the doctrine that the believer never counts on her progress in the new life as the basis for her acceptance by God but rather on Christ whose unconditional mercy is appropriated in self-entrusting faith. But such agreement on extrinsic righteousness as the basis of assured faith obscures rather more instructive, and in the course of time, significant disagreements.

That is clear as well in Luther's doctrine of the Spirit. In his classic account of it, Regin Prenter established that for Luther the office of the Spirit is to present the crucified Jesus in the proclamation of the gospel as risen and exalted and speaking to the auditor in the first-person promise of peace, "I am yours and you are mine." As the Spirit made alive again once and for all the crucified Jesus on the first Easter, so now the same Spirit makes Jesus really present as the risen One in the preaching of the gospel, so that auditors may encounter Him truly, in the first-person pronouncement of His promises. Just so they may die with Him and rise with Him. For Luther the Holy

Spirit's work is "objective," if one must speak this way, not "subjective"; that is, it is public, not private. The Spirit works to remove the historical or ideal distance that exists between contemporary auditors and Jesus, at which distance Jesus can only appear as model, example, demand. Overcoming this distance and becoming really present to speak His own promise in the first person, "I am yours and you are mine," Jesus passes from the "dead" state of distant exemplar or heavenly ideal and becomes alive to the auditor, the present savior who gives as a gift what is otherwise merely a demand upon the auditor that she is powerless to realize. The Spirit is not then some anonymous, impersonal force, an internal, subjective inspiration or motivation, really then a cipher for the main agent or actor that will be the private decision of an essentially autonomous human ego. The Spirit is the divine and personal agent who by public proclamation bonds the present Christ and the auditor in the sphere of the *ecclesia,* bridgehead of God's new humanity. Here the Spirit comes as the resurrection power of God who makes Jesus present *ubi et quando visum est Deo* in the preaching of the gospel about Him. In this way, faith arises from the shattering of the self-positing ego that is Adam, incorporating this corpse as from the dead into a living member of Christ for a new eccentric existence.[70] Presentation of Jesus Christ as the risen and contemporaneous Lord who in this way gives what God demands is the — so to say, *objective* — work of the Spirit in Luther's understanding. The Spirit bonds the believer to Christ in time by faith, just as eternally He bonds the Son to the Father and the Father to the Son in love, just as once for all He bonded the Father anew to His crucified Son and the dying Son to the Father who had forsaken Him.

Model Two: The Legal Transaction

But with the later Melanchthon not only is "the exchange . . . not made at a joyful wedding; it is a legal transaction in which God rewards faith by imputing to it what still remains to fulfill the law — whereby God himself makes full satisfaction to the law."[71] This legal transaction is to all appearances also Spirit-less. Consider for example the mature presentations of the event of justification in the *Loci* of 1555; it reveals in vivid contrast to Luther the model Melanchthon has in mind: "The beginning occurs when the heart, truly terrified before God's wrath against our sin, hears the gospel through which God, for the sake of the Lord Christ and through him, gives forgiveness of sins and also gives the Holy Spirit. Thus the heart knows

God's wrath and also his mercy. Next, along with this faith and solace, the Holy Spirit effects in the heart joy and love to God, and obedience to this command is thus begun in us through the Lord Christ. And although much impurity still remains in our sinful nature, we are justified, that is, pleasing to God, through righteousness imputed to us *for the sake of the Lord Christ*."[72] Or again from another passage: "The gospel is the *divine* proclamation in which men, once they have heard of God's anger against sin and truly tremble before God's wrath, are presented with the most gracious promise that God, *for the sake of Christ,* graciously, *without merit on man's part,* wants to forgive them their sins and to justify them and that the Son of God will bring comfort to those who believe and bestow on them the Holy Spirit and an inheritance of eternal life — all of which is to be received through faith."[73]

What is striking in Melanchthon's model, on a moment's reflection, is the absence of any personal encounter with Christ (one encounters a report *about* Christ) and the omission of any public work of the Holy Spirit to supply justifying faith to the stricken sinner. The movement to faith seems instead to be motivated by the divinely terrorized sinner grasping naturally (!) enough for succor, a drowning sailor "laying hold" of a lifeline. It is as if one stands all alone contemplating whether to apply oneself to the mercy promised in the gospel report, wondering perhaps whether it is really true, having first then to acknowledge it as valid history, then perhaps also God's own revelation, at last doing God the honor of believing it as true. As Melanchthon imagined things, certainly, hearts come to be troubled by their sins through some preceding proclamation of the Law through which the Spirit terrifies. In this way he appropriates Augustine's doctrine of prevenient grace and correlates it with the Reformation's signature distinction between the Word of God as law and as gospel. Insofar as Melanchthon does adhere to Augustine in this way, on the other hand, the hope of saving God from the appearance of injustice for withholding the Spirit in reprobation collapses. Prevenient grace, in other words, still leaves the onus of injustice on God for withholding the Spirit's work of preparation for faith — if not actually passing some over. In any case, those terrified and those alone are the ones who can appreciate the gospel's promises and so come to ask God to apply to them Christ's merit for forgiveness. This model thus allows for the holy work of the Spirit, who convicts of sin through the prior preaching of the law. Nevertheless, in this model it is the human agent (albeit the divinely terrified one) who makes the critical move. That move is diminished to the pathetic plea of a desperate soul (the groveling which later Kant so de-

spised as inimical to the dignity of man), the stricken soul that does not resist but rather receives the outstretched hand of promised mercy. Howsoever
little this human step of nonresistance, this actively passive *Gelassenheit* is
the critically important "cause" that separates the sheep from the goats.[74] In
response to it, God the heavenly judge keeps His promise and credits the terrified sinner with the requested merit of Christ and so pronounces her account balanced. This accreditation is the transaction of forensic justification. Only now and on this basis of the nonimputation of sin on account of
the imputation of Christ's righteousness does the Holy Spirit come from
above to regenerate the justified sinner with faith, hope, and love, understood as new powers or virtues psychologically at work in the heart. Moreover, it all must happen in precisely this order, lest the ground of justification, Christ's extrinsic merit appropriated by nonresisting faith, be confused
with the new life of the regenerate that follows upon it. "Is faith itself not
also a work?" Melanchthon asked, and he answered: "*for the sake of the Lord
Christ, and through him* we have forgiveness of sins and are justified." He
then continued, in the initial statement of the root incoherence of Protestant
theology: "Nevertheless, we must accept Christ, through faith, for God
wants this Savior, his Son, to be known, and he wants to gather to himself an
eternal Church through knowledge of the gospel. . . . He wants a distinction
to be made between the heathen and us. . . . No distinction would be possible between us and the heathen if God saved men without knowledge of
Christ and without faith!"[75]

The "Free Will" Labyrinth

So are we plunged, willing or not, into the convoluted labyrinth of the doctrine of "free will." It is imperative to keep varying notions of freedom of the
will distinct in order to avoid the morass of conceptual confusion that
haunts the traditional discussion of these matters. In general, for "free will,"
at least three distinct capacities are under discussion.[76] Freedom of *choice*
(liberum arbitrium) requires that logically noncontradictory alternative
goods, or courses of actions for achieving a desired good, are available.[77] The
alternative to such freedom is necessity, as when we say, "I have no choice. I
have to do this and only this." Freedom of *desire (voluntas)* might imply that
one can desire whatever good one chooses, as if the will could be willed to
will anything as one's good.[78] But Leibniz, with Luther and Augustine, denies this conception of the freedom of desire. They all regard volition as the

primal *conatus* of being, the creature's spontaneous attraction to good and aversion from evil.[79] One might call this natural bondage of desire to good and aversion to evil "patency"; in any case, it forms the backdrop of whatever agency a creature possesses or exercises. Desire is free, then, not in the sense of a capacity to create one's own good. But it is meaningful to speak of freedom of desire in the sense that desire is one's own rather than another's, so that the desire is willing, not imposed, forced, or pretended. Finally, freedom of *action (libertas)* implies that one has power to act (or not act) upon any particular good that appears desirable.[80] The alternative to this freedom is servitude.

In the tradition stemming from Augustine under discussion here, freedom of choice and freedom of action are affirmed even of the fallen creature, though its postlapsarian freedom of choice is fatally constrained *in relation to God* and its freedom of action *in human society* is fatefully compromised by forms of subjugation in the ordered disorder of a fallen world, i.e., the "curses" pronounced in Genesis 3. Because of the exile of Adam's posterity from Eden, the original, paradisaical choice for obedience to God and love for one another has been forfeited; in its place fateful, fatal egocentrism appears, which is held in check in turn by the man's subjugation to the soil and the woman's subjugation to her husband until the seed of the woman comes to crush the head of the serpent, setting humanity free again. Thus for this tradition, the main thing to be said about freedom is that liberation comes from God. In the interim, choice for God the true good is no longer available to exiled humanity. Before God, fallen beings choose only between lesser and greater evils. Nevertheless, there remain sufficient choice in human society and, given proper moral education and social support, enough freedom over one's own action to sanction criminal behavior and to reinforce civic virtue.

What Augustine and his tradition chiefly deny, however, is that any conceivable creature, pre- *or* postlapsarian, has freedom of desire. This is the "popular" sense of human free-will (which Luther identified and rejected as presuming "a power of freely turning in any direction, yielding to none and subject to none").[81] Creaturely desire instead spontaneously and as such involuntarily seeks the good and averts from evil. Desire that sought its evil would be pathological. The creature cannot help but seek its good and assent to it, or conversely, avert from its evil. The creature is motivated by its loves.[82] It is analytic to the creaturely state that, as Aristotle famously declared at the outset of the *Nichomachean Ethics, all by nature seek the good.* Being creatures, they do not, as Martin Luther put it commenting on the first article of the creed, have life in themselves such that they can ever be free from desire: "Thus we learn from this article that none of us has life — or anything else that has been mentioned or could be mentioned — from ourselves, nor can we by ourselves preserve any of them, however small and unimportant."[83] As long as they live, in order to live, creatures *must* desire what appears good to them and avert the evil; the will spontaneously desires its perceived *good*. If it did not, it would be sick to death. The will is *bound* to desire and is bound to *desire*. This is what is in mind, then, when this tradition speaks of the bound or enslaved will, *voluntas,* not *arbitrium* (though Luther muddles the two terms). As Jan Lindhardt has shown: "St Augustine (d. 431) determined, in extension of the Platonic tradition, that a man was identical with his love. He defined love itself as concupiscentia (desire)." This yielded a view of "man more as a unity than as a creature subdivided into various departments. . . . It was not the distinction between body/soul/ reason, which occupied his attention, but the direction adopted by the soul or will, or drive," and this "was interpreted during the Renaissance as representing a completely different view of man,"[84] "not conceived of as an active subject, but as a receptive object"[85] taking on the form of what is loved. Luther agreed with this understanding of Augustine's anthropology, that "a man is his love."[86] This is the basis for his eccentric anthropology. Any will other than God's is a will bound to desire the good that appears to it from without; this desire becomes one's own will (not another's) by virtue of free choices from among the available goods that one actually, historically, biographically pursues, since a human being is free to act, or to critically refrain from action, in the face of such choices. In just this way she forms the story of her life, as patient of her own passions and agent of her own actions.

In this light, the apparent paradox involved in speaking of wills genuinely other than God's can be exposed as an ambiguity or equivocation. The reference to wills other than God's can be taken in two ways. On the one hand, the reference can be to the genuine existence — itself willed by God — of creatures with wills of their own, i.e., the *voluntas* that ascribes uniquely to each single human organism, soul and body, in its historical life as constituted biographically by its own choices *(libertas)*. As Augustine put the matter at the conclusion of his seminal debate with Cicero's text *On the Nature of the Gods:* "As He is the Creator of all natures, so is He the giver of all powers — though He is not the maker of all choices." It is possible consequently that creatures make choices of their own contrary to God's desires as well as in accord with God's desires. Abstractly considered, human choice then "is a real power." Indeed, "our choices themselves have an important place in the order of causes."[87] Alvin Plantinga has aptly stated the case in recent times: "God desired to love and be loved by other beings. God created human beings with this view. To make us capable of such fellowship, God had to give us freedom to choose, because love, though it does have its elements of 'compulsion,' is meaningful only when it is neither automatic nor coerced. This sort of free will, however, entailed the danger that it would be used not to enjoy God's love and to love God in return, but to go one's own way in defiance of God and one's own best interest. This is what the story of Adam and Eve in the Garden of Eden portrays."[88] A will other than God's can thus refer concretely to choosing and acting upon desires other than God, our true good, "wanting to be God and not wanting God to be God."

In running roughshod over the important differentiation between freedom of choice and freedom of desire, Luther wanted to indicate how making choices contrary to God's will in disobedience reflects the deeper fault of a root usurpation of God's place as Creator. The root of all evil choices is disbelief in God's love, seeking instead by one's own choices and actions creatively to bestow value on something by one's own sovereign good-pleasure. Human works are never what they appear to be on the surface; they are always acts of faith or disbelief. Choices are never merely temporal decisions, but decide whether or not in faith to rest in God's good pleasure that bestows value on oneself, precisely as patient of one's own sufferings, maker of one's own choices, and agent of one's own actions. Disbelief in God's love is the root of all evil. Thus the ontologically impossible possibility of human freedom of desire, that a desire sovereignly creates the object of its desire by the triumphant assertion of its will. This usurpation no theology that upholds the ontological difference between Creator and creature can admit. Even as arrogant pride presumes this freedom, there comes a Day of the Lord to topple it from its throne. One can want to be Hitler or Stalin, one can really make this choice, one can provisionally and disastrously for self, for others, and for the cosmos act on it. But finally one cannot succeed in it. "God's purpose in this [causing failure of the human choice to be one's own god] is that the heavenly City, during its exile on earth, by contrasting itself with the vessels of wrath, should learn not to expect too much from the freedom of the power of choice, but should trust in the 'hope to call upon the name of the Lord God.'"[89] We may recall here as well Barth's well-intended but problematic teaching that a real alternative between God and the abyss of nihilism is ontologically impossible. Unlike Barth, however, for Luther or Augustine the nihilism of human *superbia* is impossible because hell puts the end to evil that will not otherwise die. The wrath of the God of love *forces* away from His company the usurper who wants to be God and not let God be God. That *finally* (not until then! Rev. 20:10) is how the real evil in the world is refuted. Actual evil is the presumption of divine "power of freely turning in any direction, yielding to none and subject to none," that is met and matched, fire met by fire, not by persuasion but with force. If there are possibilities of mercy beyond this ultimate threat, they cannot in any event be conceived apart from it, only somehow through it and beyond it. In the interim, for Augustine, the relation of human freedom to divine sovereignty is not symmetrical: "when the will turns from the good and does evil, it does so by the freedom of its own choice [i.e., a logical alternative is available], but when it turns from evil and does good, it does so only with the help of God."[90]

A Conflicted Legacy

In the light of these clarifications, the fact is that Melanchthon's teaching on the freedom of the divinely terrified will that lays hold of the promise of mercy remains within the Augustinian framework: since God is not the maker of all choices, since even our fallen freedom of choice is a real power that may refuse proffered grace, the choices we make between the *superbia* of disbelief and the *humilitas* of faith in fact mark the separation of the sheep and the goats. This result should indicate that the difficulty involved in this great complex of issues cannot be resolved on the plane of anthropology. Melanchthon's reliance on prevenient grace to prepare the human will for grace, in any event, subverts any hope he may have held that resort to free will could save the sovereign God from the appearance of evil, as we shall see in detail. Accordingly it is not at all the intention in laying bare the difference in what follows to pit Luther and Melanchthon categorically against each other.[91] Given the apocalyptic turn the excommunicated Luther took to position himself as God's prophet doing battle with Satan's minions — a conceit by which too often Luther allowed himself violently to denounce and abuse theological opponents with lethal consequences[92] — Melanchthon's demands for charity, clarity, and coherence over against Luther's self-indulgence at the expense of hard theological work are more than justified.[93] In the course of history, it has too often been Luther's bluster and raving that is mimicked as prophetic discourse while Melanchthon's careful reasoning is denounced as logic-chopping scholasticism. Along the same lines, it is standard game in Lutheranism to make Melanchthon the whipping boy for any and every contradictory interpretation of what has gone wrong. Ralph Quere once humorously catalogued the phenomenon: Melanchthon is to blame (depending on one's perspective)

> as *proto-Calvinist:* Hans Engelland, *Melanchthon, Glauben und Handeln* (1931); as *crypto-Calvinist:* James W. Richard, *The Confessional History of the Lutheran Church* (1909) and *Philip Melanchthon: Protestant Preceptor of Germany* (1898); as father of all *Lutheran heterodoxy:* Friedrich Bente, *Historical Introduction to the Book of Concord* (1921); as father of all *Lutheran orthodoxy:* Jaroslav Pelikan: *From Luther to Kierkegaard* (1963); Ernst Troeltsch, *Vernunft und Offenbarung bei Johann Gerhard und Melanchthon* (1891); as father of *Reformed Orthodoxy:* Heinrich Heppe, *Reformed Dogmatics* (1950); as father of modern theology: Karl Barth, *Protestant Thought from Rousseau to Ritschl* (1959) and Daniel L. Migliore, "The History of Christian Thought: Schleiermacher to Bultmann" (dissertation, 1968).[94]

No real historical person can simultaneously be all these villains. Criticism of Melanchthon is deeply confused, and good criticism of Luther as a result goes wanting. The legacy of Luther for theology today is deeply conflicted.

Following a lengthy exploration of this tangle in another study, Wengert tried, it seems, to cut the Gordian knot. He pointed to a famous letter to Johann Brenz, jointly signed by Luther and Melanchthon, to conclude that both Reformers agreed on "forensic justification."[95] This is a fact of history, true enough; but it is misleading at the same time. To uncover how this assertion of a consensus on forensic justification misleads, consider certain contemporary arguments of Mark Mattes, Oliver Olson, and Gerhard Forde about the nature of theology in Luther's tradition, each of whom in confused ways tries to extract Luther from Melanchthon while mistakenly asserting a radicalized forensicism as the touchstone of genuine Luther-theology.

Mattes, in his book *The Role of Justification in Contemporary Theology,* held that the test of authenticity is a purified forensic model of justification, i.e., as kerygmatic fiat, as sheer pronouncement of an unmediated divine verdict that saves in the sense, it appears, of securing the modern self threatened by the sublimity of nature. Mattes in this way rejects Barth's or Jüngel's understanding of dogmatic theology as *nachdenken,* thinking after God in the act of revelation: "Is such a theory applicable or adequate when only faith will do? Is defining the proper relation of the human to God nearly as important as delivering the words of law and promise that actually establish the right relationship of fear, love and trust? . . . The ontological attempt to map deity by following in the deity's footsteps and inferring thereby the landscape of the deity's interiority is a closeted attempt to walk by sight, and not by faith."[96] To this a counterquestion: Can the proclamation of law and gospel deliver the right relationship without specifying a narrative content, i.e., the *propter Christum*, and the divine subject of it, i.e., the triune God? Mattes is drawing in this on his teacher, Gerhard Forde, who had claimed that "the absolutely forensic character of justification renders it effective — justification actually kills and makes alive . . . the more forensic it is, the more effective it is."[97] It is the performance of preaching, then, that justifies — not the One who performed obedience of love on behalf of the lost and perishing and yet lives to continue to be this Man for Others in the proclamation (Bonhoeffer). We must, Mattes accordingly writes, "discern God as 'preached,' in which these goods are delivered, from God 'not preached,' and must therefore discern God as 'revealed,' even in the darkness of Jesus' death on the cross, from God as 'hidden,' masked in various forms in creation."[98] Bracketing for the moment the background Kantianism of Mattes's formulation (hidden God = sublimity of indifferent Nature) as well as the problem of the Reformers' undoubted and deliberate appropriation (but also critical transformation) of the Anselmian satisfaction theology of the atonement, it is a matter of historical fact that *Melanchthon is the creator of the exclusively forensic doctrine of justification in distinction from Luther's model of the joyful exchange,* where Christ remains the Speaker who communicates Himself with His Spirit to the auditor. Thus it will be the real, historical Martin Luther, who teaches "true faith, that gift of the Holy Spirit,"[99] who falls as the first victim of this supposed test of genuine Luther-theology. Luther, as alluded above, holds no less than Melanchthon to the Anselmian *propter Christum* of justification based on Christ's penal death,[100] such that what grace delivers from is not nature, but sin and God's wrath.[101] There is in this light an unacknowledged, and in my view illicit, modernization involved in such a claim to be waving the flag of the supposedly true, original Luther-theology. It is Kant, not Luther, who speaks thus. "The gospel offers no theodicy. The hidden God is never deciphered. Only faith secures the anxious conscience in dealing with the masks of God's hiddenness."[102]

Never? Has Mattes a Luther who *never* read Romans 8–11 or Ephesians 1 or 1 Corinthians 15? Mattes's argumentation in this book seems to eschew the hard work of critical dogmatic theology for the shortcut of sheer kerygma, even when dogmatics are strictly, soberly, and nonspeculatively understood with Barth and Jüngel as *nachdenken*. Indeed, even such modest, descriptive procedure such that the church can publicly discern the spirits he castigates as a totalizing theology of glory trying to penetrate and comprehend God. This work is to be abandoned in favor of unmediated assertion that allegedly delivers what it says by deconstruction of any and all systematic thinking after God in His Word and Spirit as so many pagan walls of Jericho falling to the ground at the trumpet blast of the Word alone. In its evidently subconscious Kantianism, the argument of this book is such a tangled mix of erudition, penetrating insight, *obiter dicta,* and passionate insistence upon what prove to be false antitheses that it would require a monograph of equal length to dissect and repair. The Kantianism becomes manifest in its final pages: "What does one make of such violence in nature? . . . To see such violence in nature — a truth that should not be denied — is to experience God in hiddenness."[103] Yet it is *the Father* of Jesus Christ, as we have it on good authority, who sends His rains to fall upon the just and the unjust alike. We do not experience His wrath when mosquitoes swarm, or AIDS kills, or tsunamis devastate. What we experience in these natural evils — beyond our own ecological folly delivered back upon us — is our bodily membership in the web of life and our moral obligations of solidarity; we learn the wrath of God, on the other hand, when we see Jesus forsaken by His God and Father because He has not forsaken us.

Oliver K. Olson undertakes a historicist strategy to a similar end, faulting Melanchthon for surrendering Luther's *sola fide* to Rome during the Leipzig Interim, which transpired shortly after Luther's death.[104] This is a half-truth proffered by means of selective narration: in fact, Melanchthon was willing to concede slogans if substance was preserved.[105] Olson's paean to the crude and myopic Flacius gets the real story exactly backwards. It was not Melanchthon's moral turpitude, but his entanglement in the logic of the very forensic model (first created, as we shall shortly see, to distinguish the pure doctrine from the Catholic Augustinianism in which the Reformation theology originated), that led him astray. Ironically, however, the model Melanchthon erected to protect justification from being based on human renewal is unable finally to account for the initial act of faith — the turning of the terrified conscience to the offered grace — except as cooperating will, a natural human "cause" alongside God's, which then separates the Christian from the heathen, even though, *soli Deo gloria,* the merit of this human movement is ascribed to God's prevenient grace. Luther's *sola fide* — that gift of the Holy Spirit — became ambiguous on account of forensicism, just because it was rigorously and intentionally separated by Melanchthon's new model from its christological mediation in the joyful exchange and thus no longer bestowed by Christ in the Word as "true faith, that gift of the Holy Spirit."

Gerhard Forde is the source of this contemporary contention for an exclusively kerygmatic theology in Luther's name against Melanchthon's legacy. "The cross does not merely inform us of something, something that may be 'above' or 'behind' it. It attacks and afflicts us. Knowledge of God comes when God happens to us, when God does himself to us."[106] Theology is not "about" anything; it does not put the theologian in the position of an active constructer of knowledge.[107] "In fact, it is quite impossible to write 'the' or even 'a' theology of the cross. The attempt to do so would no doubt be just another attempt to give a final propositional answer to Jesus' cry from the cross. . . . We can't answer Jesus' question. We can only die with him and await God's answer in him."[108] Forde thus rigorously declined to offer any "theory" of the atonement: "Theologians of glory are thus always driven to seek transcendent meaning, to try to see into the invisible things of God, to get a line on the logic of God. They look at the cross and ask, 'What is it all about?' They wonder what is 'behind' it all. There is a reason for this, of course. If we can see through the cross to what is supposed to be behind it, we don't have to look at it. It is, finally, a matter of self-defense."[109] That which the kerygmatic theology of the proclamation of the cross "seeks to foster is not a compelling set of doctrines but . . . a different way of operating. The goal here is to become a theologian of the cross, not merely to talk or write about it."[110] The goal of theology that is rigorously for proclamation is the auditor's existential transformation to the pathos of faith.

By contrast, it is the "theologian of glory [who] sees through the cross so as to fit it into the scheme of works. The cross 'makes up' for failures along the glory road."[111] Yet "all such theology accomplishes in the end is to pull the rug out from under the proclamation" since, according to Forde's analysis, its impossible pretensions generate the revisionist pressures visible in contemporary constructivism. "'The suffering of God,' or the 'vulnerability of God,' and such platitudes become the stock-in-trade of preachers and theologians who want to stroke the psyche of today's religionists. . . . But in the theology of the cross it is soon apparent that we cannot ignore the fact that suffering comes about because we are at odds with God and are trying to rush headlong into some sort of cozy identification with him."[112] Sentimentalism is the inevitable price. "Sooner or later a disastrous erosion of the [biblical] language sets in. It must constantly be adjusted to be made appealing. Gradually it sinks to the level of maudlin sentimentality."[113] Against this, Forde appeals to Luther's *vita passiva:* "Now we in turn suffer the absolute and unconditional working of God upon us. It is a suffering because as old beings we cannot abide such working. We are rendered passive by the divine activity."[114] For the "only solution is the cross itself," "the preaching of the cross in the living present, not through theological explanations." The solution is not "in the classroom but in church. . . . In spite of grand and high-sounding theologies, they will likely just undercut the church's task. There is a great divide here."[115] Taking a position, then, that is reminiscent of the early Barth, Forde holds that "what is revealed is precisely that we don't know God. Our problem is not that we lay claim to such little knowledge of God but that we think we know so much. So God hides from us."[116]

One has to wonder whether in all this Forde, like the Barth of the Romans commentary, is driven as much by Kant as by Luther, i.e., by the fear of human construction transgressing the limits of reason. Certainly Luther thinks to understand in his preaching and to have his auditors understand the One in whom they believe. In any case, as it happens, Forde does maintain a definite knowledge of God, though it is not the trinitarian and incarnational knowledge of Luther's *deus revelatus,* nor is it Luther's account of what is happening to the Godforsaken Christ when the Deity withdrew.[117] But Forde offers — more precisely insinuates — an Ockhamist version of natural theology. On the one hand, he writes against the Platonic tradition's inclination to save divine goodness by limiting divine omnipotence, as in, e.g., contemporary Whiteheadianism. This, Forde argues, is but the "vain attempt to assure us that God, of course, has nothing to do with suffering and evil. God is 'good,' the rewarder of all our 'good' works, the pot of gold at the end of the rainbow of merit. But is this prettified God the God of the Bible? Is it not quite probable that just these attempts to whitewash God are the cause of unbelief? Meanwhile, suffering goes on unabated. If God has nothing to do with suffering, what is he involved with?"[118] On the other hand, Forde seems to defend his own version of Platonism, criticizing those theologians who worry about divine "timelessness and immutability" that "seem to cancel out the freedom and responsibility of the creature." He criticizes these who go to work "in some way to explain away the problem of objectionable attributes." But, Forde maintains, in human experience of God the uncanny Other, "the attributes of divine majesty keep coming back like a song. . . . even if such attempts were to succeed, theology would only make God ludicrous. For what is God without the attributes of divine majesty?"[119]

In these curiously ambivalent, if not contradictory, insinuations Forde seems to take for granted an omnipotent, immutable, timeless, majestic

Other, an *Alleinwirksamkeit Gottes*. Indeed, Forde presupposes the validity of (his tacitly preferred, unargued version of) the natural knowledge of God, while criticizing all attempts to mitigate this dark force as Pelagianism. It is arguably better here to take counsel from Luther's later theology. The knowledge of God provided by the Holy Spirit in certain *formulas loquendi*, i.e., the old church dogmas of the person of Christ and the Trinity, and Luther's own explorations in the doctrine (not "theory") of the atonement (i.e., the "penal suffering" of Christ), are not to be regarded as lapses back into Catholicism nor failures to be sufficiently Kantian. These are his account to himself and to his auditors before God of the validity of his kerygmatic assertions. Preaching is not *obiter dicta*. Doctrinal preaching does not perform an execution in any case without first reading the sentence. The gospel is an assertion, to be sure, but it does not work by sheer assertion, by mere fiat. It warrants its assertions; it gives an account of the hope that is in us; it mediates Christ the Mediator. The *vita passiva* is not dead clay in the hands of the Unknown Potter; it is knowing participation by grace in the things proclaimed.[120] A kerygmatic theology without doctrine is, in short, as inconceivable for Luther as it is for Melanchthon. This is *not* the right way to parse the difference between them.

Yet all the thunder and smoke surrounding Melanchthon's legacy to this day indicate that a fire somewhere smolders. How to get to it? In the statement concluding the main body of the argument for justification by faith alone in the Apology of the Augsburg Confession, article IV, Melanchthon formulated the summary statement: "Up to this point, in order to make the matter very clear, we have demonstrated fully enough both from the testimonies of Scripture and from arguments derived from the Scripture that by faith alone we obtain the forgiveness of sins on account of Christ and by faith alone we are justified, that is, out of unrighteous people we are made righteous or regenerated."[121] Given the rhetorically decisive place of this statement from Apology IV,[122] anyone wishing to dispute the simultaneity of the declaration of forgiveness of sins with the gift of regeneration in the event of justification by faith prima facie assumes a burden of proof to the contrary. To be certain, almost fifty years later the formulators of the intra-Lutheran concord of 1580 contradicted the clear text of the Apology in arguing that "'to justify' in this article means 'to absolve.' . . . When in place of this the words *regeneratio* and *vivificatio*, that is 'new birth' and 'making alive,' are used as synonyms of justification, as happens in the Apology, then they are to be understood in this same sense. Otherwise, they should be understood as the renewal of the human being and should be differentiated from 'justification by faith.'"[123] The claim of the formulators here overrules the plain sense of the text of the Apology, which under *regeneratio* and *vivificatio* is thinking of the personal trust, *fiducia,* elicited by the promise, which appropriates forgiveness. Just this appropriation of mercy by faith *is* new birth and vivification, as Melanchthon had learned from Luther in 1519 and taught up until the time of the Apology. Whether his words from 1531 are understood in an "erroneous way," then, depends rather upon the question whether a new model of justification has intervened and is now silently at work.

Not that the formulators themselves understood that. The Formula's reasoning is incoherent even on its own terms, and the inner contradiction involved persisted ever after to haunt orthodox Lutheranism. The Formula knows that justifying faith is divinely given. In the preceding thesis, the formulators have just affirmed that this *justifying* faith, by which we "lay hold" of Christ, "is not a mere knowledge of the stories about Christ. It is a gift of God, through which in the Word of the gospel we recognize Christ truly as our redeemer and trust in him."[124] What is this *gift* of justifying faith laying hold of Christ but the effective call of the Spirit, *vivificatio, regeneratio?* Of course the Spirit calls by means of the declaration of forgiveness; of course the nonimputation of sin and in its place the imputation of Christ's own, to us alien, righteousness come from without as a declaration according, reckoning, imputing, assigning, attributing, predicating it to the sinner as sovereign gift. In the model of the joyful exchange, this declaration is exactly what the Bridegroom of the soul says: "All that is yours is mine and all that is mine is yours." No one criticizing the forensic *model* denies *ipso facto* the forensic *aspect* or its importance. Rather they affirm that the mediation involved is *linguistic,* not magical or mystical, as when a judge pronounces innocence or guilt (but also as when a king pronounces pardon or confers knighthood, or when a lover pronounces troth, or when a priest speaks absolution). One does not need the *model* of the heavenly law court to affirm this *aspect* of justification, least of all by making it the exclusive *theory* of justification. To deny the forensic aspect as a sovereign declaration would be as much as to deny the character of grace as gift for the undeserving that is given personally in the saying of it. The problem arises when the law-court model is made the exclusive theory of justification — a step that proves self-defeating, since then the presence and work of the Spirit in speaking the gift of Christ to effect its reception by faith is unwittingly eclipsed. The gift forever remains outside, reckoned but never reaching, touching, transforming. How *ever* did Melanchthon come to this?

From Anthropological to Christological Divergence

It happened like this. In the course of his extended controversy from the middle of the 1520s with John Agricola over the nature of repentance, i.e., the truthfulness requisite to justifying faith, Melanchthon came more and more to insist upon "the order and form of our justification": first law as accusation, then gospel as forensic imputation of Christ's alien righteousness, and then law again as guidance, all this understood as passage from one state of consciousness to another. "Melanchthon first defined righteousness as properly and truly *fides qua,* the faith by which we believe that we are received in grace by the Father on account of Christ. This was crucial for his argument."[125] As with Luther, true justifying faith pertains to the subject, not the object of faith, the *fides quae.* It is not believing that the stories about Christ are true thus and so, but the personal appropriation of trust that takes to heart the *pro me* of Christ's address found in those stories. At the same time, this *fides qua* "by which we believe that we are received in grace" presupposes something indispensable: "'. . . *poenitentia,* so to acknowledge sins that we truly sense the wrath and judgment of God against sin and are truly terrified.'"[126] Coming into a state of truthfulness about God's judgment on sin in personal repentance is the indispensable presupposition in consciousness of justifying faith and true consolation. "Confession occurs when the conscience, terrified before God, acknowledges its sin and admits that it is justly condemned. It does not accuse God's judgment but only asks for grace and mercy and praises the God who justifies sinners,"[127] that is, it does not contest its sins in untruth, but in truth confesses them. Now the soil of the soul is prepared for the seed of the gospel.

Melanchthon, of course, is not thinking that these "true terrors" before God are the *product* of "human exertion"; working oneself up that way would be only simulation and hypocrisy. It is rather God who brings this state of consciousness about "when he shows us our sin."[128] Wengert tells how Melanchthon's scheme — clearly sequenced and existentially compelling — carried the day against Agricola, not least because of renewed concern for truthful repentance, public morality, and individual responsibility following the tumult of the Peasants' War and the outbreak of sectarianism among erstwhile followers of Luther. In this shift, Melanchthon was also motivated by the search for theological clarity and possible consensus with moderate Catholics by means of scholarly method in which, as he hoped, "theological definitions offered doctrinal certainty for faith."[129] With these precipitating factors in mind, Wengert points to the 1532 commentary on

Romans that spells out for the first time the exclusively forensic doctrine of justification: "'To be justified' properly signifies to be reputed righteous, that is, to be reputed accepted. Thus it should be understood relatively, just as in a law court, according to Hebrew custom . . . it should be understood relatively concerning the will of God: to be approved or accepted by God."[130] This new, clarified definition of justification as external regard "explicitly eliminated any internal change in the person. Virtue was now completely excluded from the definition."[131] It is important in passing to note the tacit equation of the Holy Spirit's work with the *inner* (and now *subsequent*) renewal of human powers, and so its necessary separation consequently from the *outer* (and now primary) announcement of justification. Melanchthon's earlier thought, Wengert comments, had not yet attained this clear distinction "between intrinsic and extrinsic righteousness."

In fact, however, Melanchthon has developed a new position. Melanchthon has come to think that Christ is alien and outside the self in a way that the Holy Spirit is not, exterior in contrast to the subsequent interiority of the Spirit. This exterior covering is alone what protects from God's wrath. "Christian righteousness is what pleases God. God is not pleased with human works, only with Christ. . . . Without Christ as the mediator who satisfies God's wrath, the frightened conscience has no safe haven, must rely on its works, and is driven to despair."[132] Wengert's analysis of this development and its motives is incisive: "To eliminate absolutely every notion of merit from the definition of justification, even that of Augustine, Melanchthon narrowed his metaphors to one, the forensic declaration of forgiveness by God '*gratis propter Christum*. . . .'"[133] Wengert is now in position to expose for us the extraordinary irony in this story. Logically the forensic declaration "demands obedience[; just so,] it also demands that the human being play an increased role in salvation. Because justification is an external declaration to be received in faith, the message itself no longer moves the individual to faith. Instead, the individual must hear and not reject it. Faith is much more the action of the individual over against both the promise of grace and the command to obey. Thus Melanchthon could speak about the individual's active participation in the process before and after justification." He more and more sought "a middle ground between a theology of merit . . . and a theological determinism," culminating in the 1536 *Loci,* where he first came to the conclusion that "the Word, the Holy Spirit, and the human will are the three causes of salvation."[134]

Mitigating factors aside, however, the scheme does not work. Tiny step — rather a mere standing still to let grace overtake — that it is, it is the human act of the will's nonresistance that triggers the divine nonimputation of sin and imputation of Christ's alien merit. Justification no longer happens *ubi et quando visum est Deo* as the joyful exchange, but works like a machine when levers are pulled in correct order (just *this* reliability in clear, precise instruction must be stressed for the sake of pastoral assurance and spiritual certainty!). No matter how much the Spirit has cleared the way, the causality of justifying faith must be shared. Intellectually honest, Melanchthon could not finally conceal his emerging conviction about the role of the human will in justification. "We should not think that a man is a piece of wood or a stone, but as we hear the word of God, in which punishment and comfort are put forth, we should neither despise nor resist it. We should immediately rouse ourselves to earnest prayer. . . . [God] draws the one who is willing, not the one who resists. . . . Whoever even faintly thinks that he would like to be in the grace of God again has made a beginning and God will strengthen him."[135] Saul on the road to Damascus ceases to be the exemplar of justification as the event of God's befriending of an enemy. Just so, justification suffers domestication at Melanchthon's hands in service of the construction of new Protestant Christian culture.

To be sure, Melanchthon is psychologically more right than wrong. It is no one else but the believing person who feels, meditates, resolves, prays, pleads, receives, accepts, welcomes, rejoices. This is unique, incorrigible, precious; it *is* the soul for which Christ died coming to own that unfathomable love. The theological point is that this human consciousness with its states is nevertheless before God always product, never cause, creature, and patient, nor creator and agent, even in its own acts and passions, since indeed it is from conception day to resurrection day the creature being created by God, an agent and doer in the world as the very "passive disposition" being fashioned by God for true life in His eternal kingdom. Without totally abandoning such views (which he had learned from Luther), Melanchthon was right, moreover, to want to protect faith as gift from being confused with a false notion of grace as nonpersonal, coercive, or irresistible. In the next chapter, when we look at Melanchthon from the angle of the revived currents of Stoicism and Epicureanism in Renaissance letters that agitated him, his concern to distinguish divine determination in theology from natural fatalism in philosophy puts these things in another light. As previously mentioned, Melanchthon never ceased to credit God's prevenient grace for the little act of the human will's nonresistance: "they should know that God both made the beginning in them and will further strengthen them."[136]

With his appeal to Augustine's prevenient grace preparing the nonresistance of the human will, it is interesting to observe that Melanchthon satisfies Barth's requirement that all glory be given to God, just as Barth, as we have seen, does not avoid the paradoxes involved when speaking, as does Melanchthon, of both God's grace and the human decision of faith. Is it evident, then, that on this anthropological level there is substantial convergence between Melanchthon and Barth? They are both explicating the same doctrine of a divine embrace that liberates to faith's true freedom for love of God and others, but also allows false freedom its own self-determination to live godlessly. Like Barth, Melanchthon found it a great relief to be delivered from the terrible implication in *De servo arbitrio* of double predestination that made speculation regarding the *deus absconditus* almost inevitable; in Luther's chilling words: "Here, God Incarnate says, 'I would, and thou wouldst not.' . . . He offends many who, being abandoned or hardened by God's secret will of Majesty, do not receive Him thus. . . . It belongs to the same God Incarnate to weep, lament and groan over the perdition of the ungodly, though the will of Majesty purposely leaves and reprobates some to perish. Nor is it for us to ask why He does so, but to stand in awe of God, Who can do and will do such things."[137] In Barth and in Melanchthon, unlike Luther, God is spared from this appearance as author of evil.

Or is He? Does the commonplace theodicy of human free-will solve the fundamental problem? To the extent that prevenient grace is invoked, the question is begged, since the injustice of God's choice in preparing one and not another simply recurs on this prior level. The real problem is a framework in which the question about the asymmetry between divine sovereignty and human freedom is incorrectly imagined as implying a confrontation between competing egos, divine and human, which can be resolved only by concession or capitulation of the inferior to the superior. What we lack is the framework of tri-personal theology in which the divine confrontation with human egocentrism is not resolved by capitulation or concession over against the absolute, self-positing divine Ego of "the Lord," but rather incorporation into the holy life of the Trinity. What we lack is thus the framework for a Christology, in which the loving obedience of the man Jesus Christ *is* (not *signifies*) the loving movement in self-receiving and self-giving *for us* of one of the Trinity, such that his faith can becomes ours, and our minds become incorporated into his, as Philippians 2 teaches. What we gain from that is an anthropological understanding in which the human person by call of Jesus gives away self in the very act of receiving self. This shift accords with Leibniz's criticism of the supposed ideal of a selfless and indifferent love in favor of an expanded self, or again, with Luther's view of the eccentric self.

Bo Kristian Holm has recently insisted that for Melanchthon "freedom is only possible in the divine embrace — that is, only as a consequence of divine saturation of surplus."[138] Holm, building upon the work of Olli-Pekka Vainio,[139] moves the analysis from the plane of anthropology to uncover a *christological divergence* that was papered over by the official agreement in early Lutheranism on forensic justification. Holm accomplishes this by setting the evolution in Melanchthon's thought not only against Agricola and moderate Catholicism, as we learned from Wengert, but also against the background of the controversy with Osiander. Melanchthon opposed what he took to be Osiander's idea that the justifying righteousness that comes from Christ is the divine attribute of God's essential righteousness, which as such comes to inhabit believers by the indwelling of Christ and in this way transforms them into godly people. "The difficulty was that [Osiander described Christ as the righteousness] of faith" in a way that he "separated Christ's historical work of redemption from the Christ who is present and working in the hearts of believers at any given time."[140] Melanchthon in response not only wanted to avoid basing the assurance of faith on the psychological feeling of renewal, as we have already heard, but also to insist christologically upon (1) the unity of divine and human natures in Christ and thus (2) of Christ's saving righteousness as the "merit" gained by his incarnate life of obedience, culminating in his sacrificial death on the cross. It is this latter that provides the basis for justification of people who remain in this life weak and sinful, whose renewal is never sufficient to assure faith of its standing before God. Luther would hardly disagree. For him too justification is in this sense *propter Christum*. Holm rightly notes that the christological divergence between Luther and Melanchthon does *not* lie in the apparent utilization of Anselmian atonement theology,[141] and that to this extent both are trying to move from the plane of anthropology to Christology.

Melanchthon realized after 1531 how inadequate to the New Testament sources, as also for Christian living, a thin, rigorously extrinsic, and polemically exclusive doctrine of justification would be. Thus citing Vainio, Holm argues that "the period of pure forensic justification in Melanchthon's theology is rather short . . . ending before the Loci 1535."[142] The evolution we have described above with Wengert's help is thus not the end of the story. Rather, Melanchthon sought from 1535 on to account for the indwelling of God in the believer — no longer with Luther's joyful exchange, which seemed now to him to open the path to Osiander, but rather with the doctrine of the Spirit, now conceived as the inner inspiration and motivation of new life. As Holm puts it, citing from the 1535 *Loci:* "imputative justification and effective sanctification are connected the following way: *Cumque Deus remittat peccat, simul donat nobis spiritum sanctum, qui novas virtutes in piis effecit* (Cr 21, 421 -cf. 742)."[143] According to Holm, the presence of Christ to the believer (just as we have also described this model above) is a purely external Word and report about Christ, informing of the benefits won on the cross and offered to faith. This stands in contrast with the inner-working Spirit. Christ here is the Giver, to be sure, but not Himself the Gift, which is His merit. This is what really represents a significant divergence from Luther, not on the anthropological plane, but on the plane of Christology itself. It is fascinating, moreover, to observe that this divergence corresponds to the way in which Barth too refused Luther's *est.*

In his study Holm exposits a long-neglected German language edition of Melanchthon's *Loci*, first published in 1553, the *Heubtartikel Christlicher Lere*, which, he argues, constitutes Melanchthon's own last will and testament in theology. This claim becomes intelligible when we recall that the Latin *Loci* were primarily textbooks meant for the training of future pastors, but this German edition of his dogmatics was intended for the educated public. Replete with expansions, illustrations, prayers, and popularizations, it was more catechetical in purpose and thus in accord with the idea of Luther that "true doctrine shows its truth by its ability to communicate what it describes."[144] In this edition, Holm discovers that Melanchthon's use of and explanation of Luther's *communicatio idiomatum* is limited to an explanation of ecclesiastical terminology and is thus not presented as "a structure to be used theologically and rhetorically." In Melanchthon's German, the topic is *dise redden,* this way of speaking, implying a divine accommodation to human limitations.[145] It is for him a permissible way of speaking *in concreto,* regarding Christ, but certainly not *in abstracto.* Strictly speaking, this is in accord with Luther's view, for whom this way of speaking applies only to the unique being of the God-man Christ, that is, concretely, not abstractly, specifically, not in general.[146] Even so, for Luther it is the right way of speaking about the true being of the concrete God-man Jesus Christ. For Melanchthon, however, "the use of the doctrine of *communicatio idiomatum* should not be an occasion to blur the indispensable distinction between divine and human nature." Holm concludes, "Melanchthon's focus seems to lie on the necessity of both natures, where Luther seems to focus on the unification of what is absolutely different" in the unique person of the one, concrete Christ. In other words, for Luther this way of speaking derives from Christ's unique way of being as the incarnate Son, the hypostatic union of classical neo-Chalcedonianism. From this a rule for speaking concretely about Christ is given to us in the *communicatio idiomatum*. In time and under pressure, these two different understandings of the preaching of the great exchange cannot but diverge. In Holm's concluding words: "Luther's model of incarnation identifies Christ as Giver and Christ as Gift, which means that it is easier for Luther to make a 'thicker' understanding of the unification than for Melanchthon, who is more likely to understand Christ as one who gives something else than Himself — that is, his benefits."[147]

We have before us now the subtle question of Luther's synthetic *est* as opposed to the dialectical *significat* to which the later Melanchthon tends, anticipating Calvin and Barth. Ralph Quere's careful and thorough study of a generation ago provides further evidence validating Holm's suggestion. He traces the christological divergence between Melanchthon and Luther to the eucharistic controversies of the 1520s. There is no question about Melanchthon's early and consistent opposition to Karlstadt's, Zwingli's, and Oecolampadius's eucharistic teaching.[148] He opposes any Nestorian tendency "tearing Christ apart,"[149] and distances himself from Bucer in the 1530s: "We, however, require not only the presence of the power but of the body. This Bucer purposefully disguises."[150] Indeed, Melanchthon "had stoutly refused to allow Christ's presence to be reduced to efficacy (whether in terms of a virtual presence or the presence of the Holy Spirit alone)."[151] In all this Luther and Melanchthon christologically agreed. Yet, Quere shows that seeds of doubt were expressed by Melanchthon as early as a letter of May 21, 1526, which states that the "bread is a figure of the body of Christ." The meaning is not very clear,[152] but in this connection "Neuser has ably demonstrated that a crisis occurred in Melanchthon's understanding of the Lord's Supper in the period during and after the first Saxon visitation of 1527."[153] The doubt concerned the location of the body: *cum pane* or *ym brot*. "As Neuser rightly points out the issue was not the real presence but the mode of that presence. Luther had been forced to give an answer to the how-question which he had once stoutly refused to do. . . . The troublesome part of the answer for Melanchthon at this point was not the ubiquity of Christ's body, but 'the making of a dogma of the mixture of the bread and Christ's body.'" This seemed to him, in other words, no longer *communicatio idiomatum* as a way of speaking, but Eutychian synthesis as an ontological assertion.[154]

In the visitation documents of 1527, Melanchthon can distinguish between God-in-Christ "and a more Nestorian understanding of God-with-Christ. . . . Melanchthon's struggle in 1527 seems to be whether this equation can be applied to the Sacrament. Is Christ, the Giver in the Sacrament, also the Sacramental Gift?" — i.e., is the person giving the gift of Himself, in his own body? That question is reflected in the question about the local mode: In bread or with bread? In the latter case, "the focus can be simultaneity rather than identity."[155] The "tension" here appears to lie in Luther: "on the one hand, Luther says the gift is mediated by the Word; on the other, it is given 'in and through the blood of Christ.'"[156] For Luther, "the sign *is* and *gives* the gift . . . for Luther the body and blood of Christ as the sign is the gift in and through which forgiveness is given by means of the Word."[157] So the tension between the models of joyful exchange and forensic imputation recurs here on the level of Christology: "Since Melanchthon does not identify or incorporate grace in the eucharistic body of Christ, it remains something transcendent and external which impinges on man in forgiveness but is in no sense infused into him."[158] In this way a fault line emerged. But the line is not anthropological. It is christological. When the Christ who takes on our flesh to give us His Spirit is absent, so the Holy Spirit will disappear as well.

In correction of one-sided extrinsicism in the doctrine of justification, Eberhard Jüngel has sharply argued for the inner unity of declaration and renewal in justification: "Thus, from a biblical point of view, to talk of the grace of God being in us is not basically wrong. But at the same time in the context of biblical language, the fact of the Spirit, the love and the grace of God being in us means that we are, we live and have our being 'in the Spirit,' that is, outside ourselves."[159] Or again, "grace in the strict sense [is] divine behavior which — at least according to Luther — not only *pronounces* us righteous, but also *makes* us righteous. God's grace justifies us by touching us at the center of our existence as external grace *(gratia externa)*. That is, it comes closer to us than we are able to do ourselves; and it does this in such a way that it places us *outside* ourselves, even as it touches our inmost being. . . . it is so efficacious in the way it works in human beings that it turns us inside out."[160] The self that grace reaches and touches becomes, just so, this new self that lives eccentrically in God's grace by faith and so also in the neighbor by love and, as we should add today, in hope for the best of all worlds on the way to the glorious liberty of the children of God. This is the self whose sin has become Christ's, whose righteousness has become that self's in turn. These appropriations *being* so, this event *having* transpired — "*being* justified by faith we *have* peace with God" — the renewed self is righted, rectified, straightened up to God in thanks and straightened out to the neighbor in love, stretched out to the future of the world in hope, effectively made righteous: not on its own, perhaps even regularly reverting to the sick old self *incurvatus in se,* yet *being* in the Spirit, *united* by faith with Christ, *becoming* just as regularly what it will finally forever *be.*

In this light, the real mystery to untangle is why later Lutherans distanced themselves from Luther's joyful exchange — why it morphed into the so-called mystical union, Prenter's "almost nonevangelical mysticism." The model of Christ speaking through the gospel, bestowing His Spirit to give what He commands and believe what He promises, disappeared in favor of a more and more intellectualized report of the objective teaching of the Bible, rendered into clear and distinct propositions,[161] with the Holy Spirit inwardly inspiring subjects to accept and trust them.[162] Anti-Catholic polemic played a huge role, conscripting the Spirit chiefly to provide an inerrant Bible as counterweight to the inerrant papacy. This strengthened the tendency to conceive of the Spirit as impersonal, inward causality. We have already noted the later Melanchthon's reluctant drift toward apparent synergism, given the subtle transformation of Luther's theology into the anthropological transition through states of consciousness sequenced as law, gospel, and law again.[163] In this scheme faith appropriates the benefits. As Martin Chemnitz, Melanchthon's student, explained: "With firm persuasion it concludes from God's Word that God gives, communicates, and applies to you the benefits of the promise of grace and that you in this way lay hold on and receive unto righteousness, salvation, and eternal life those things which the free promise of the Gospel offers."[164] At the same time, however, this act of appropriation is not and cannot be understood as one's own achievement, but as something elicited or effected in one. As Chemnitz exposits the preceding step of prevenient grace that terrifies the sinner in the *ordo salutis:* "Then from this knowledge and assent in the mind, by the working of the Holy Spirit, the heart or will conceives a groaning or desire so that, because it feels very earnestly that it is burdened down with sins and the wrath of God, it wills, prays, and seeks that these benefits be given to it which are set forth in the promise of the gospel."[165] The idea then is that a special work of terrifying grace by the inward-working Spirit miraculously *causes* personal appropriation of the benefits of Christ, both the desire and the persuasion and the laying hold. Thus appropriating faith — *which otherwise seems to be a quite ordinary decision motivated by desperate need to avail oneself of help* — is credited to the special work in us of God the Holy Spirit.

The Spirit Disappears

Melanchthon had once thought quite differently. Soon after he arrived to teach classical languages at the young university in Wittenberg in 1519, he came under the spell of Luther's new grammatical method in theology, which rescued the New Testament kerygma from its captivity in alien thought forms and unleashed it in its primal force as saving address from God to lost and perishing humanity. As early as his baccalaureate thesis of 1519, Melanchthon succinctly stated the Augustinian anthropology that he had learned from Luther (and that will appear again powerfully in Leibniz): "The intellect can give assent to no proposition without reason or experience. Nor can the will by itself force the intellect to give assent. The will, drawn away by love to an object of faith, orders the intellect to give assent."[166] Already under the influence of the revival of Augustinian studies[167] in the Renaissance,[168] the young Melanchthon had determined upon a scholarly project of reintegrating dialectic (logical studies) with rhetoric (language studies)[169] in correspondence with the Augustinian teaching that "the heart" is the seat of the soul, and the soul as socially formed is moved by language. "Over against a pervasive and tenacious view of emotion as at best sub-rational, Augustine's ability to distinguish reason from volition and argument from pathos, resulted in a point of view that could closely interweave feeling, willing, knowing, and loving. This meant that emotion, instead of undermining the will, was key to how it worked, was, in fact, synonymous with the subjective experience of volition. The important point is that affectivity 'instead of being an irrational perturbation, thus moves into the center of spiritual experience.'"[170] What emerges in view here is not the Cartesian ego dualized over against its own extended body with feelings, as contemporary readers almost inevitable presuppose.[171] Rather, in Melanchthon's words from the 1555 edition of the *Loci Communes:* "when free will is mentioned we mean understanding and will, heart and will, and they belong together, without hypocrisy." Deprived of its original integrity by the fall into sin, the "miserable human heart stands like a desolate, deserted, old and decaying house, God no longer dwelling within and winds blowing through. That is, all sorts of conflicting tendencies and lusts drive the heart to the manifold sins of uncontrolled love, hate, envy, and pride"[172] — the point being that the human person is less the centered agent of its own free intentions than an object at the mercy of its own fickle desires, adrift and drowning in a tide of contending goods, none of them truly good because of our race's exile from Paradise.[173]

The tides are *speech*. This is what keeps even the decentered will *human*. With this thought in mind, the 1521 *Loci Communes* is arguing (as summarized by Wengert) that "as the early church had been misled by Plato and his insistence on the power of the *ratio* (reason), the medieval, scholastic theologians had mistakenly followed Aristotle and his notion of the *liberum arbitrium* (free choice). After presenting a simplified anthropology, in which he differentiated the intellect ('the power of knowing') from the will or *affectus* ('the power by which what is known is either pursued or fled'), Melanchthon attacked attempts to limit the affections to bodily appetites, to divide the soul further, or to define a *liberum arbitrium* or *ratio* between these two powers."[174] He rejected any neutral, intermediate faculty of free choice on grounds of divine predestination and human experience that demonstrated again and again how "the will, drawn away by love to an object of faith, orders the intellect to give assent." "Far from being a mere infirmity of nature, the lack of control human beings exercised over the highest affections lay at the heart of the human predicament."[175] The early Melanchthon thus holds firm to the unfreedom of desire.

If this was Melanchthon's earliest anthropology learned from Paul, Augustine, and Luther, what accounts for the manifest adjustments that take place by the time of the 1536 *Loci?* Wengert rightly criticizes psychologizing explanations of a Melanchthon torn between two heroes, Erasmus and Luther. "To explain Melanchthon's behavior [Maurer] constructs a psychological picture that paints the Wittenberg professor as (almost pathologically) searching for a middle position. . . . he defines Melanchthon's life as if it were lived between the irreconcilable differences of humanism and Reformation, represented by the looming figures of Erasmus and Luther."[176] Wengert demonstrates in this connection that Melanchthon's initial reserve at the publication of Luther's *De servo arbitrio* had to do with its violent style.[177] In Melanchthon's own words: "I have never loved Luther to such an extent that I approve of his acerbity in dispute. The last thing I would want to do to help him would be, if I may say so, to add fuel to his fire. And of this decision of mine Luther himself is my best witness."[178] In any case, what actually gave Melanchthon pause in the course of the controversies of the 1520s was the criticism by papist opponents of the *hedonism* of Luther's teaching on the will: "by equating the will (which directed reason) with the affections and by insisting that the highest affections were in bondage, [Melanchthon following Luther following Augustine had] made human beings no better than beasts."[179]

Wengert comes to Melanchthon's defense: he "was not asking whether it is in a human being's power to eat, drink, come, go, hear, and other natural matters. . . . The question was 'whether without the Holy Spirit we can fear God and believe in God and love the cross, etc.'"[180] This defense then is that Luther's hedonism was that of a higher order. Yet the commonplace distinction here between things above us and things below rings hollow, in that apart from the Word and Spirit of God the self *incurvatus in se* fails to make this very distinction; it exchanges the glory of the immortal Creator for degrading images of creatures; it cannot find its way back unless someone comes and finds it. According to the "hedonist" psychology, the self is bound to do so in our race's state of exile, where the creaturely will is spontaneously bound to love whatever object appears good to it, yet has little, if any, disposal over what appears to it as good. All such appearances are outside us, if not above us, and in any case not within our control. This is what is meant by *servitude* of the will. Thinking this way, the early Melanchthon had grasped Luther's essential theological point: "why [is] the Holy Spirit necessary, if the human will by its powers could fear God, trust God, overcome concupiscence, and love the cross (in one's own life),"[181] i.e., if the human will could apprehend as good the God who spared not His own Son and displayed love for us in the repulsive form of the Crucified? It is the apprehension of God on a cross as our true good that is barred to fallen humanity, which naturally averts its eyes from the shame. It is the coming of the Spirit that makes the cross of Jesus appear as the supreme good it actually is by presenting the same Jesus alive and victorious. In this "objective" way the Holy Spirit alters perception of a sight that otherwise revolts the natural will by giving the same thing a new signification. This is "the work of the Holy Spirit, who *moved the hearts* of true hearers of the Word and helped them effect true virtues."[182] Note well: in the earlier Melanchthon the heart is moved from without, by the Word giving the Spirit and the Spirit illuminating the Word, not, as later in the scheme "imputative justification–effective sanctification," from within, independently of the Word, as human feelings.

The shift that occurs in the later Melanchthon's theological anthropology indicates in part attention to the pressing need for a new construction of culture in Reformation lands. It is "clear that a major shift had taken place in the way Melanchthon expressed the doctrine of justification," Wengert writes. "The church needed to know about human nature and whether it could perfectly fulfill the law, not about 'the arcane counsel of the God who governs all things,' predestination and contingency. Melanchthon wanted to put aside such contentious matters and focus on the nature of human weakness and Christ's benefits." With this shift in focus, the tripartite, hierarchical anthropology of the Greeks returned to displace the more unified, Augustinian view of the human as lover of goods. "He then partitioned human powers according to the philosophical categories of *ratio*, which judged, and *voluntas*, which accepted or rejected the judgment of *ratio*. He stated that 'they' (presumably philosophers) call *liberum arbitrium* the *voluntas* and *ratio* combined."[183] This evolution in Melanchthon's thought, Wengert rightly comments, "has less to do with some internal predilection for synergism than with increasing desire to answer the objections of and build bridges to the so-called reform Catholic party, on the one hand, and with his fear of theological statements that could be used to support antinomianism, on the other."[184] And, we may add, Melanchthon needed to differentiate the Reformation theology from philosophical determinism newly appearing in currents of Renaissance Stoicism and Epicureanism. Among those theological statements that could support antinomianism, and thus subvert the newly assumed task of reconstructing Christian civilization, Melanchthon had to count the apparently necessitarian implications of some passages of Luther's *De servo arbitrio*. It is speculation, Melanchthon tweaked Luther, to ask "if God's concurring activity is present in sinful works, as the horribly lewd blasphemies of the Stoics, and afterwards the Manicheans, suggested; they said that God is bound by natural necessity; *ad causas secundas,* etc."[185] It is hard to imagine that this rebuke is not pointed at Luther, whose teaching of divine concurrence in the hardening of Pharaoh's wicked heart in *De servo arbitrio* seemed to Melanchthon to have just such libertine implications.[186]

Does the Holy Spirit harden wicked Pharaoh's heart? As we have seen, in Orthodoxy the Holy Spirit is no longer needed, as in Luther, "objectively" to present the Crucified as the risen One but only subjectively to gloss the human decision of faith as its divine and supernatural cause. Psychologically speaking, according to the model retained from Melanchthon, in personal faith one does what one is capable of *(facere quod in se!)* as a human being, who is not a block of wood or stone, and so applies oneself to, or at least does not resist, the offered grace. Yet at the same time this willingness is held to be the wholly miraculous product of the Spirit who secretly works to bestir faith in some, though perhaps not in others. By a miracle some such autonomous wills believe, though others do not. What a muddle! Yet the problem of the scandal of grace's particularity cannot but once again reemerge: if God works faith, if God gets the credit for the human act of will in justification, God is *not* spared from blame for the unbeliever's persistence in unbelief. Is God Himself not guilty of a sin of omission here?

Since the problem of theodicy is *not* solved with the Spirit's help, it would prove simpler in the course of time just to drop the pretense that the decision of faith is due to a miracle. Since one is thinking anyway of a genuinely autonomous human will, with the passing of anti-Pelagian passions and the rise of naturalism, this kind of claim for the Holy Spirit became more and more nugatory. The advantage for theodicy was that now at least the damned are at fault for their refusal of grace. The gospel states a proposition: Christ died to take away your sins — *if,* that is, you do your part and believe that Christ died to take away your sins! On the other hand, who wouldn't believe it? What a good deal! Candy offered from the palm of God's hand; all you have to do is reach out and *take* it.

> Cheap grace means grace as a doctrine, a principle, a system. It means the forgiveness of sins proclaimed as a general truth, the love of God taught as the Christian "conception" of God. An intellectual assent to that idea is held to be itself sufficient to secure remission of sins. The Church which upholds the correct doctrine of grace has, it is supposed, ipso facto a part in that grace. In such a Church the world finds a cheap covering for its sins; no contrition is required, still less any real desire to be delivered from sin. Cheap grace therefore amounts to a denial of the living Word of God, in fact, a denial of the Incarnation of the Word of God.[187]

The incarnate One — the One who takes on our flesh to give us his *Spirit* — *His* Spirit, the Lord and Giver of *true* life, who leads through the cross to the crown. So this *Holy* Spirit — fifth wheel — disappeared in Lutheranism, replaced by the idea of "a Church civilization, the absolute certainty of the revelation which formed its basis, or again, the claim which the Church always deduced from this to Christianize, more or less forcibly, life as a whole,"[188] i.e., philosophically to construct a general pneumatology.

We have come to a surprising conclusion in respect to the complex of problems concerning divine sovereignty and human freedom with which we are concerned: Karl Barth's theology finds its best precedent neither in Luther nor in Calvin but in Melanchthon. It is Melanchthon who (1) resolutely denies that there are two wills in God, (2) upholds the honor of Christ as the one Mediator between God and all humanity and thus the potential universality of the atonement, (3) carves out a compatibilist niche for the human act of decision in faith by resort to the prevenient grace of God, and finally (4) guards against a direct, nondialectical identification of God and human speech by leaving Luther's joyful exchange behind as mere kerygma, rhetoric, a way of speaking, not the new language of the Spirit, *cognitive* doctrine that *denotes* the divine-human way of *being* in Christ. According to our hypothesis, this similarity of Melanchthon and Barth is no accident. For Melanchthon these theological moves were driven by apprehension at the rise in Renaissance circles of new appropriations of Stoic fatalism, academic skepticism, and Epicurean atomism;[189] in Barth, similar moves are likewise driven by the crisis of the Christian civilization of Europe: "The God who is truly God cannot vacillate in His dealings with [the fallen] world. The God who indifferently swings to and fro between good and evil, between sin and grace, is the No-God of this world. God must reject such a world but in rejecting it, He can also elect it. What He cannot do is to 'change His mind,' now electing and now rejecting, back and forth with no real progress. God rejects once and for all that He may elect once and for all. He kills in order to make alive."[190] In both theologians, theology in this way takes on a *philosophical* function; it *argues* an alternative to rival views of reality that seem to undermine human freedom, knowledge, or dignity. Barth's nonapologetic, nonfoundationalist approach to authority in theology and his careful construction of a dialectical method to reflect the inherent dynamism of knowledge of the living Lord should no more conceal this function in his work than it should in Melanchthon's. Theology thus comes, however, to be measured by its cogency vis-à-vis philosophic alternatives for the purpose of forming culture. This is quite explicit, for example, in Barth's critiques of Heidegger and Sartre.[191] The difference between Melanchthon and Barth is also intelligible on this basis. After the bloodbath of the Great War, Barth contracts from the general pneumatology of a reformed, Christian civilization to a particularist pneumatology mediated exclusively in Christ, who is alone the *imago dei*. In either case, the Holy Spirit as divine person and public agent in the world has disappeared.

Five GENERAL PNEUMATOLOGY

The Sublimation of the Spirit
into Progressive Christian Culture

Notions Common to Divine and Human Minds

What took the Spirit's place in Lutheranism? A general "pneumatology"
(*Pneumatica seu Pneumatologia*), i.e., "the knowledge of God, of souls and
of simple substances in general," as Leibniz on occasion gave name to the revisionist metaphysics of his Christian philosophy of creation.[1] In such formulations Leibniz was drawing upon a tradition in Protestant German
school metaphysics of the seventeenth century descending from Melanchthon, which formed "the philosophical environment in which Leibniz grew
up."[2] Melanchthon had laid it down in the first chapter of the *Loci communes:* "By nature all men know that there is an eternal omnipotent being
[*Wesen*], full of wisdom, goodness, and righteousness, that created and preserves all creatures, and also, by natural understanding [*Verstand*], that this
same omnipotent, wise, good and just Lord is called God. Many wise people,
therefore, such as Socrates, Xenophon, Plato, Aristotle and Cicero, have said
that there is such an almighty, wise, good, just God, and that we must serve
this one Lord in obedience to the light that he has built into our nature concerning the distinction between vice and virtue."[3] Several things are notable
in this programmatic text beyond Melanchthon's highly selective invocation
of the Greek-Latin philosophical tradition.

First, the divinity of late medieval nominalism does not appear here,
with its sole perfection of divine omnipotence. Instead the trinity of divine
perfections of omnipotence in harmony with wisdom and love is enunciated
as the *Wesen* of natural theology. Second, obedience to this *Wesen* is said to

be possible by obedience to the natural knowledge of virtue in the heart. The law of God is the law of one's own being. In Melanchthon's theonomous world, the law written on the heart is not heteronomous. Not that this *Gesetzverstand* of God suffices, however, for no one finds "peace in this natural understanding." Instead the human mind is afflicted with "grave doubts whether God wants to help men." To meet this need revealed theology is required, "that God for the sake of his Son, out of grace, wishes to forgive our sins and give us righteousness and eternal blessedness." About this Socrates and the rest "know nothing at all." The distinction between natural and revealed knowledge of God corresponds then to "the distinction between law and gospel."[4] Along the same lines, the relation of human and divine minds is articulated in a doctrine of the two kingdoms of nature and grace, corresponding roughly to knowledge of efficient and final causes, mechanism and purpose, respectively.[5] Evoked and properly coordinated by revealed theology, these two domains of inquiry form the basic division of labor for the construction of a reformed Christian civilization. "The kingdom of grace thus became a metaphysically warranted ideal of human order and relations, including science as well as government and religion, criminals as well as saints, the controls of society as well as the grounds for its values," as Loemker notes. A special burden that will fall upon such "Platonism" is that it "must also provide an explanation, through its doctrine of degrees, of privation in the existing order, for both disbelief and immorality."[6] Thus the problem of evil emerges as *the* special difficulty of general pneumatology, as we shall consider in the next and final chapter of this book. For how can a knowing and purposeful spirit, which by nature seeks the good, ever go wrong? That created spirits do go wrong is painfully evident. But how can this be? If obedience to God is possible by obedience to the natural knowledge of virtue in the heart, how can disobedience ever happen? How can evil arise? Or be actual?

This perplexity aside, Melanchthon sympathized with Plato's rational critique of conventional mores by appeal to the nature of things, insight into which was the divine vocation of human reason.[7] He was reserved on the dogmatic Platonic doctrine of the eternal forms,[8] but appropriated Platonic idealism to speak of "true philosophy" as knowledge of divine law that comes by insight into the nature of things and persons and the laws that govern them: "All good sciences are gifts of God, but they should remain in their proper place. The true philosophy, that is, a philosophy that does not stray from method and procedures for proof . . . is knowledge of the divine law. It acknowledges God's existence and judges civil behavior; it sees that the capacity to distinguish between good and evil is established in us by divine arrangement; it proceeds on the supposition that hideous crimes will be punished by God and possesses certain indications of immortality."[9] This typical statement from Melanchthon's pen indicates how misleading it is to describe him either as eclectic in philosophy or even more woodenly as an "Aristotelian."[10] Ever the pedant, Melanchthon preferred Aristotle's prosaic, methodical clarity to Socratic irony and Platonic whimsy. He took from Aristotle the grand, encyclopedic ambition for a coherent and comprehensive system of knowledge.[11] He thought that in this way the two great Greek philosophers corrected each other's deficiencies. Substantively, however, Melanchthon holds to a Platonic position on innate knowledge (although his thinking about this is primarily warranted by Genesis 1:26-28 and Romans 2:15). He admires the program of moral education of the passions in Aristotle's *Nichomachean Ethics,* but shares Luther's (and presumably Plato's) criticism: habituation to the good presupposes the disposition toward the good that supposedly it inculcates.

A reformed version of Christian Platonism was thus integral to Melanchthon's vision of cultural renewal and the intellectual vocation. He held that the natural law is written in the human heart, as Paul attests in Romans 2:15, on the basis of the divine command that humanity have dominion over the earth in Genesis 1:28.[12]

> God has implanted in all individuals certain "inborn elements of knowledge" *(notitia nobiscum nascentes).* These he called variously a "light from above," a "natural light," "rays of divine wisdom poured into us," "a light of the human faculty," without which we could not find our way in the earthly kingdom. These *notitiae* included various "theoretical principles" of logic, dialectics, geometry, arithmetic, physics, and other sciences, such as "two plus two equals four." These *notitiae* also include certain "practical principles" *(principia practica)* of ethics, politics, and law such as the communitarian principle that "men were born for civil society." "All these natural elements of knowledge," Melanchthon believed, "are congruent with the eternal and unchanging norm of the divine mind that God has implanted in us."[13]

The divine mind is characterized by perfections of "justice, truth, kindness, clemency and chastity. God planted seeds of these best things in human minds, when He made us after His own image. And He wished the life and behavior of men to correspond to the standard of His own mind."[14] Accordingly God and humans share common notions of justice (among other things), so that human beings have not only a duty to obey but also a cognitive right to ask about the justice of God and a capacity to recognize it when they see it.

We shall see in this chapter how these basic affirmations developed into the program of "general pneumatology" in the years between Melanchthon and Leibniz, for the very important reason of cultural formation following the trauma of the breakup of Christendom. Such "knowledge, divinely taught both by the light that is born in us and by the true divine voice, is the beginning of the laws and of the political order [of the earthly kingdom]. God wishes us to obey them not only for the sake of our needs, but more, so that we may acknowledge our creator and learn from this same order that this world did not arise by chance, but that there is a creator who is wise, just, kind, truthful, and chaste and who demands similar virtues in us."[15] Noteworthy in this text is the political-cultural task undertaken by Protestant theology as well as the rival dogma that is named and opposed: "this world did not arise by chance." Indeed, the new Epicureanism associated with the rising natural sciences represents the root political-philosophical "heresy" against which general pneumatology did battle. Hardly better was the classic Stoic alternative to Epicureanism. Libertinism or fatalism? Must there not be a third way for a reformed, Protestant Christian civilization, which would foster a responsible faith in a divine destiny? Can Protestantism, on the other hand, undertake such a culture-forming, not to say "political-philosophical," task without losing its soul? Will any victory on this field prove Pyrrhic? Does the move to general pneumatology in the final analysis beg decisive questions that will be posed and pressed hard by emergent, thoroughgoing naturalism? These are the questions that concern us in this chapter.

With such questions in mind, we may also better appreciate the divergence of Melanchthon from Luther laid out in the previous chapter, along lines that Carl E. Maxcey has argued. Melanchthon in fact distanced himself from (at least some of the more unsavory cultural-political implications of) Luther's apocalyptic convictions about the imminent end and instead "attempted to envision that new system of value and unity,"[16] which would provide for a postmedieval synthesis. Crucially, that involved Melanchthon in a subtle but far-reaching theological change in relation to Luther, again, in words from Maxcey's careful investigation: "the natural moral law becomes increasingly important for Melanchthon as a reason for doing good works. Perception of that law is not limited to the reborn, but all men can perceive

God's signs in themselves and in nature. . . . Just as the ability to judge morally is impressed on the mind, so is the eternal and immutable rule of law of the divine mind. This . . . becomes the primary reason for doing good works."[17] Indeed, for Melanchthon and his tradition, as Berman and Witte have shown in great detail[18] (in Loemker's words): "God's creation and providence were conceived as jurisprudential acts. The ideas are given to the natural and moral reason as laws."[19] The macrocosm-microcosm relation, the common ontological order including a common conception of justice based upon the eternal divine law impressed upon the mirror-mind of the human creature — these are variant expressions of a "theological philosophy" or "theology as jurisprudence" grounded in the doctrine of creation. It is the special merit of Günther Frank's *Die Theologische Philosophie* to have shown this in considerable detail.[20]

Melanchthon's theologically determined philosophy opposes as basic philosophical errors naturalism, fatalism, and works righteousness,[21] that is, Epicureanism, Stoicism, and Aristotelian ethics,[22] while the criticism of Platonism is the rather more muted one concerning its uncertainty about God and consequent tendency to skepticism. Theological philosophy by contrast is grounded in the fundamental relation of the human mind to God as its created image,[23] which relation remains in spite of sin.[24] This grounding of reason and its philosophizing does not anticipate, let alone establish, autonomy and limits as in Kant, but rather tightly binds reason as *Abbild* to God as *Urbild,* hence theonomously.[25] Because God wants to be known in creating a world and calling humanity to partnership in care of the creation,[26] even after the fall the human mind is capable of recognizing God,[27] though on account of sin's corruption of the will it will not truly seek God as God and so cannot succeed in finding God religiously. But metaphysically the mind has in its fundamental notions a prolepsis of God.[28] These fundamental notions apply both to physical and moral relationships, i.e., to the natural and social world beyond the individual creature's mind on account of an "original coherence" (cf. Leibniz's "preestablished harmony") of language and world in the mind of the Creator.[29] This original coherence is the reason why the Creator has chosen freely to actualize this particular world, fallen under sin, but redeemed in Christ and destined in the Spirit for fulfillment.[30] On the other hand, such creation-faith optimism generates the perplexing problem of evil,[31] entailing the difficult thought of divine permission.[32] This problem elicits the work of theological-philosophical theodicy in order to warrant human agency and moral responsibility[33] against the Gnostic temptations of cynicism and despair or Platonic skepticism.

Melanchthon's theologically grounded philosophy stands then in some tension with Luther's exclusive Christology, eschatological critique of metaphysics, and regard for the gospel surpassing the law, even if divergence along this front at the same time represents a well-justified break with Luther's obscurantist resort to apocalyptic invective in place of patient reason in theology.[34]

It is all *too* easy, however, to see *only* divergence from Luther in this tradition stemming from Melanchthon's labors for cultural reconstruction running on to Leibniz. The basic question at stake seems to be whether a theology of a reformed, progressive Christian civilization is at all possible or whether Christian theology in the West has no option but retreat to the fideist ghetto to which Stout assigned Barth. I will suggest in conclusion how a robustly public and ecclesial theology might take its place in the pluralistic future of postmodern Euro-America and beyond. But to achieve that, a second look at the mature Melanchthon and the general pneumatology that derives from him is surely in order, tracing its progress to, and denouement in, Leibniz. In this perspective, Melanchthon emerges as a prescient Christian philosopher, who wrote against the proto-Hobbesean political theologians, "the new type of wise men who, since they are without God, do not want any struggles at all to be waged about religion." On the contrary, Melanchthon continued (in prophetic mode more reminiscent of Luther than not): the first commandment, as all the prophets and apostles attest, constrains us "to refute wicked practices and depraved opinion" of the political and ecclesiastical status quo, so that "there must be strifes about the worship of God" in the public forum. "Wherefore" — a Melanchthon quite unlike the cowardly compromiser painted in Gnesio-Lutheran mythology concluded his 1539 treatise *The Church and the Authority of the Word* — "since the pious must refute and abolish irreverent worship, they cannot but be the authors of change . . . although political wisdom recoils from the very name of change." The worship of God forms the nourishing root of a culture, and so whatever hardships conflict over religion and the attendant radical social change bring, Melanchthon concluded in a profession of faith (again not unlike Luther's): "they are all controlled by Christ, to whom all things have been subjected."[35]

Thus the Melanchthon we are now to study was not the weak politician of unprincipled theological compromise his detractors portray — any more than Leibniz was the unprincipled theological diplomat that his detractors portray. Indeed, as we will see in the next chapter, a quite similar motive against the rival political theologies of Hobbeseanism on the right and Spinozism on the left is at work in Leibniz. If Christian theology today cannot quite follow Melanchthon or Leibniz in struggling for, or aspiring to, the restoration of a purified Christendom on the model stemming from Charlemagne and the Holy Roman Empire,[36] it must nonetheless engage in public theology, "strife" and all.[37] Sorting this out presents a tangled knot not hastily to be cut, but patiently untied.

Learning from Failure

As I have indicated throughout this book, the pneumatological path from Melanchthon to Leibniz came to a dead end, though it took several centuries for all to see. As we approach that denouement, it may be helpful to raise again the questions about the reasons the Melanchthon-Leibniz project of general pneumatology ultimately failed. In his great study, Loemker thought broadly of the Western mind as formed by the classic debate between Stoic, Epicurean, and Skeptic that we may find already, for example, in Cicero's *On the Nature of the Gods,* a debate Augustine joined some centuries later in *De civitate Dei.* It is a debate that crystallized, according to Loemker, with particular force in the seventeenth century, when the rise of the natural sciences lent new plausibility to the (long ill-reputed) Epicurean depiction of reality as atoms in motion, with their random fluctuation providing the metaphysical ground for libertine freedom on the level of spiritual life. Acknowledging this new impetus in support of what Leibniz opposed as the chimera of sovereign preference, a "freedom of indifference," i.e., an unmotivated "will to will" that would be undetermined by sufficient reason, Loemker described the struggle of the seventeenth century for a new synthesis of Epicurean *libertas,* the freedom of the freedman who escapes from bondage to arbitrary authority and Stoic *honestas,* the freedom of the enlightened who conforms to the superior order discovered by reason to be the law of one's own being. It is important to recognize that both philosophical versions of freedom claim reformatory power and both claim the mantle of enlightenment. The latter issues no less than the former in a critique of conventional political morality when it asserts rational discovery of a superior order naturally claiming human allegiance.

In either case then, Loemker asked, "could the new sciences, as they developed their own literature, also relate this literature constructively to the larger purposes — educational, social and cultural — which were demanded by European order?"[38] Or would they work instead as a "universal acid" over against that legacy of Augustinian synthesis? Picking up a Kantian term,

Loemker continued, "also needed were regulative ideas which should give direction to thought and action," and thus he went on to identify the century's convergence on "the ideal of harmony." This was the synthetic notion that set thinkers like Leibniz in search of a "single harmony which makes possible the agreement of experience, understanding and faith," providing a standard to judge between progress and regress. Digression "from the ideal which this harmony imposes" is "in danger of error";[39] meliorism depends on it.

At the end of his magnum opus Loemker posed what is for us in the light of the foregoing an incisive question about Leibniz's "synthesis": Does the "microcosm-macrocosm idea as involving a plurality of individual minds capable of self-awareness and therefore of reason, bound together by love, because they participated in one common ideal order, which each expressed from his own point of view, powerful and wise enough to actualize the best common values . . . [contain] the seeds of its own failure in its confusion of the real with the ideal"?[40] Does Leibniz's synthesis represent, as we say in theology, realized eschatology? As if creation had already arrived at fulfillment, as if it were not in dire need of redemption? Should we regard humanity created in the image of God as the presupposition or rather as the prospect of our race?

By now we recognize the rootage of Leibniz's "macrocosm-microcosm idea" in Melanchthon's Protestant revision of the image of God doctrine. John Schneider has written an elegant and precise tribute to that Protestant re-visioning and philosophical generalizing of biblical humanism deriving from Genesis 1:26-28: "Melanchthon's kind of Protestantism was, thus, one which stressed the order of the world and the integrity and goodness of the mind and its best moral intuitions; it was thereby strongly motivated to foster learning of the liberal arts in Christian universities, a spirit of ecumenical peaceableness while holding the full set of one's Protestant convictions and the hope that political and social consensus might one day evolve, if only people would persevere in using the best gifts of both nature and grace." Schneider continued by acknowledging doubts, beginning with the more ardent and suspicious followers of Luther, about Melanchthon's vision on account of the doctrine of sin and the ensuing need of the Holy Spirit to enlighten the mind darkened with false images of God as projected by the proud desire to be God, and not let God be God: "Melanchthon no doubt underestimated the power of sin over human processes of thought, and that will be obvious to 'post-modern' people, who discard these impulses and adopt one or another form of epistemic relativism. Not everyone, however, believes that this option is necessary or that the life of the mind has come to an end in Western theology."[41]

Whether a robust doctrine of sin entails epistemic relativism is an interesting question, which may miss an alternative epistemic possibility in a world on the way to the reign of God. For sin — which in distinction from "error" and "vice" or "passion" is a meaningful concept only in a world taken as creation — implies that true things can be known falsely, that right order can be misappropriated and misapplied. This is what Luther grasped in the twenty-fourth thesis of the Heidelberg Disputation, which asserted that the wisdom of natural theology, as mentioned in Romans 1:20, "is not of itself evil," nor is the law written in the human heart as in Romans 2:15 "to be evaded." But, he continued, "without the theology of the cross man misuses the best in the worst manner."[42] Without the canonical theology of the creation's fall, redemption, and restoration in Christ Crucified, sin can be understood only as intellectual error attended by the vices springing from disordered and undisciplined passions. The notion of sin consequently reduces from that of a seductive and corrosive power to getting things wrong, habitually, correctable in turn by better science and education or moral discipline. But this reduced account of sin gets both nature and grace wrong. In fact, the creature errs in this account insofar as it is measured by an ideal of knowledge as adequation to reality. In fact, however, the creature knows finitely from its own unique perspective; it knows as one swimming in the mighty river of becoming, from here to there for its tiny slice in cosmic time, and so by means of beliefs pragmatically warranted but inadequate to reflect the whole of interlaced reality that itself is yet in motion, in which the mind is immersed as a member. So the real, embodied perspective of finite human mind is in cognitive need of animal faith in an outcome by means of beliefs that can never be secured until the river reaches its ocean. Our knowledge is so situated, according to a perspectivalist account, where it matters for survival, for prosperity, for community that we get things *right in our time and place,* just so believing in the progress of our beliefs inherited from the past and projected into the future, in the process also enabling us to know and resist regress. True things and right order in the world are temporal, that is to say, not eternal, a creation that is eschatological (Rom. 8), known truly when known as God the Creator knows it at last in the resurrection of the dead, the redemption of our bodies, the glorious liberty of the children of God.

But "without the theology of the cross" the fundamental *diastasis* of finite knowledge between appearance and reality is misunderstood. It is taken to imply some timeless noumenal realm behind or beneath phenomena, the true, abiding, way things are as Being, not becoming, the Ground of temporal and spatial appearances. Epistemic relativism in the sense of *skepticism* in fact parasitically plays off just this noumenal faith of the dualist. Since such certain knowledge of the timeless condition for the possibility of phenomena cannot be secured, the skeptic concludes that all our puny representations are equally bad and equally good. Whistling in the dark, the skeptic celebrates our diversity, calls indifference freedom and apathy tolerance, making postmodern heretics out of those who dare still pretend to noumenal knowledge. And so we today use knowledge of our lack of knowledge "in the worst way": to justify our lovelessness and sanctify despair. But the Apostle, from whom Luther learned, had it otherwise: "Hate what is evil; cling to what is good" (Rom. 12:9b), as those no longer conformed to this world but transformed by the renewing of minds (Rom. 12:2). The early Melanchthon too thought otherwise than to underestimate the power of sin over conformist human thought or the corresponding transformation of the mind by the Spirit of the resurrection. In his 1520 essay, "Paul and the Scholastics," he held with Augustine and Luther that "there is need for some other teacher of souls [than philosophy], obviously the heavenly Spirit, to seize the innermost hearts of men, to renew, inspire, take possession, enkindle and transform them." The "living Spirit" is the "creator of every virtue." So the law, which philosophers somehow grasp, teaches what is right, but "Christ bestows his Spirit" who both pardons and renews in Christ, therewith providing the sense of the letter of the law. This is needful because in contrast to the confidence placed in reason by the philosophers, "reason is conquered by the passions . . . the passions shake off reason. . . . That mind is servile which is forced by fear to do its duty. . . . This power of sin is conquered by the grace of Christ alone."[43] Neither Augustine nor Luther could have said it better. Finite reason is embodied, animated by passions liable to seize upon whatever chance goods and evils appear, shaped by the *conatus* of an organism's root desire to live well — a definite and interested perspective in a world of perspectives, no free-floating spectator considering its options like a consumer on payday at Wal-Mart (on analysis as *manipulated* a being as any that these authors expose!).

Noteworthy is the peculiar circle at work in this complex of ideas: the mirror-mind made to know God but fallen from God cannot find God but rather fills God's place with idols and demons. Yet it remains the mirror that can reflect God, should God come to it, since God fills the mirror in ways that idols and demons cannot. Is this the vicious circle of "epistemic relativism"? It is so, only if God does not really appear to fill the mirror. In that case the circle is broken into *from the outside*. The content that fills the mirror even so is *relative* to the perspective. It is not, then, that such are unreal, but that they are taken the wrong way, "confused," as Leibniz would say, falsely related to the rest of reality and so liable to misuse, to misrepresent when taken as the whole. In the far background here is Luther's perspectivalist dictum that faith makes God or an idol in the heart. It does not make God for God, who is antecedently God for God, the Holy Trinity, but faith makes God rather for us just as in faith the Holy Spirit makes us the children of God. The re-turning of the repentant mind to God in faith is incorporation into the God who is God for God, that is, as described on another level, the calling of God the Holy Spirit identifying the believer with Jesus as object of the Father's love and just so as new subject in Jesus' love for the Father. If that is epistemic relativism, so be it. But it is not skepticism. It makes a cognitive claim for Christian doctrine in articulating these tri-personal relations of divine being.

Schneider went on to pose essentially the same question concerning Melanchthon's legacy as Loemker had about Leibniz's: "The question of whether or not the deeper level of ontologically common nature — this native passion for the world and for life in the world, this basic affirmation of *oratio humana* — was itself somehow wrong, may never be settled among Protestants."[44] We may agree with the importance of the question. Since Sartre, the very notion of a common nature has become suspect as the artificial refuge of bad faith. Yet Schneider is right to endorse the philosophical search for what we share on the basis of which we can communicate and perhaps even achieve communion. This quest is surely not wrongheaded or an act of bad faith. General pneumatology deserves attention for this very reason, as it was a rigorous historical attempt to make Genesis 1:26-28 fruitful for the worthy goal of this progressive human vocation. Much depends for us today on understanding why this project failed. In this respect, however, both Loemker and Schneider seem still too much under Kant's sway in posing their questions about the basic, common human values in terms of transcendent ideals or underlying grounds rather than the eschatological creation envisioned in Romans 8.

The counterproposal is to conceive of creation as eschatological, not as the given, solid stage under our feet of "nature" on which history plays out like a drama, comedy, or farce, but as itself historical, just as contemporary physics and biology suggest: nature has a history, and history in turn is natural. With such cosmology, were the notion of common nature sufficiently historicized, and so our access to it accordingly perspectivalized, we could in principle overcome the Protestant theological paralysis in Kantian skepticism. Skepticism is always secretly based upon what is in reality a fantastic ideal of knowledge, an ideal of indubitability, moreover, not particularly well suited to express faith's knowledge of creation redeemed in Christ and fulfilled in the Spirit. Even God's knowledge in its eternal self-determination, as I am suggesting, permits incalculable incursions of rejected possibilities into time and so requires temporal innovations by the Spirit of Jesus and His Father in order that God remain faithful to the anticipated future for all. Luther's "immutable necessity of divine foreknowledge" then pertains to God's knowledge of His own faithfulness to us; it is not necessitarian metaphysics for which nothing new under the sun can ever emerge. At the same time, it pertains to physical events, mechanical explanations and all, up to and including the broadaxe in the hands of the persecutor. The real source of the failure of general pneumatology then lies, as Jenson has suggested, in its protological bias. Its revision in a sense is as simple as saying that *strictly* speaking by *faith's* reasoning we are *on the way* to the best of all possible worlds.

Natural Philosophy Transformed

Such knowing confidence in God's faithfulness to God's purpose in Christ in fact sponsored the rise of the natural sciences and with it modernity's great achievement of the historicizing of nature. General pneumatology arose in tandem with the transformation of natural philosophy into science that in our own day apprehends that nature has a history and that history is natural. In 1528 Melanchthon published a commentary on Philippians, in which he focused on the verse "Do not be deceived by vain philosophy." His purpose was now to augment the Augustinian-Lutheran critique of reason with its vindication in a new key. Thus he distinguished *vain* from *fruitful* "philosophy" and vindicated the latter against the obscurantism and biblicism of emergent Reformation radicals with their "unlearned theology: . . . they are not accustomed to method and . . . do not understand the sources of things sufficiently. Moreover, because they were not educated in philosophy, they understand neither what theology should teach, nor how far it agrees with philosophy."[45] In an oration titled "On the Distinction between the Gospel and Philosophy," Melanchthon expanded on the rhetorical distinction between the gospel as the gracious promise of God and the law as a form of divine speech that demands. "The Gospel is not philosophy or a law, but it is the forgiveness of sins and the promise of reconciliation and eternal life for the sake of Christ, and human reason by itself cannot apprehend any of these things." To use the works demanded by the law to achieve forgiveness, reconciliation, and life is to make Christ nugatory and transform what is offered as an undeserved gift into merited reward. Instead, the one forgiven and destined for life through Christ by faith in the promise of the gospel now uses the divine demands of the law, not for reward and self-justification, but to direct love to the here-and-now needs of the neighbor in society. In the same way, Melanchthon writes, "just as the Christian makes pious use of the law of God, so he can make pious use of philosophy, too," i.e., not to ascend speculatively into the unknowable ground of phenomena but to descend in understanding and love to the world as God's creation, fallen into sin, but redeemed and destined for fulfillment. Christian philosophy thus adopts God's perspective on the world, seeing it and ourselves fallen apart from Christ, but now in Christ reconciled and in the Spirit on the way to fulfillment. Melanchthon adds here a significant qualification: "we call philosophy not all the beliefs of everyone, but only that teaching which has demonstrations . . . only one philosophy is true, that is, the one that strays least from demonstration."[46] Mere opinionating, especially about the metaphysical ground of the (tacitly "eternal") cosmos, he regards as confused emoting, shedding heat but no light.

True philosophy is modest, sober, self-disciplined, limited to the demonstrative method that persuades rationally according to the rules of logic, on the basis of evidence and in keeping with revealed theology. Such philosophy is what can be used by theology to orient love in the world and inform ethical action. It demonstrates what the case is, establishes facts of the matter, grounds us on the earth, fixes us in time, constrains us by knowledge of natural limits. Melanchthon systematizes the insight theologically.[47] The law of nature was scripted by God into the nature of things as well as in souls in the act of origin and sustained ever since; it is both physical and moral. The one tells what must pertain in regard to physical objects, the other what should obtain among moral agents. Reason is the intellectual power that sees the lawful reasons for things. "We shall rightly call happy the man who has comprehended all of philosophy in his mind, and understands the hidden causes of most changes in nature and in the lives of men, the sources of virtue and of honorable duties — as Virgil too said most wisely, 'Happy is he who could know the causes of things.'"[48]

For Melanchthon, that involves both what we understand today as the natural explanations of science and the accounts of human patiency/agency

in the humanities and social sciences, and both of these in relation to the
"cause of causes," God the Creator. Melanchthon distinguishes natural action, both physical and moral, from divine action in this way, but he does
not separate them. Science, as Melanchthon laid it down in a critical axiom
for the new Reformation theology, "does not disagree with Christian doctrine which, although it teaches us that all things are governed by divine
providence, nevertheless does not remove the natural actions and import of
things. . . . It is prudence worthy of a Christian to distinguish which are the
actions of God together with nature and which those of God alone and
placed above nature."[49] As Kusukawa has shown, knowledge of the "natural
actions and import of things," which God works in concurrence with nature,
thus became theologically important in its own right. There is in Melanchthon a theologically motivated turn toward the causal understanding of nature understood as a realm distinct in being from God, as a relatively autonomous *creation*. There is a real "letting be" (Gen. 1), which delights in the
plenitude of being not rigorously designed for a single purpose, yet which
exists as such within its Creator's sovereign, overruling, and final purpose as
made known to other minds. In this way heavenly knowledge comes both to
evoke nature as field of inquiry and to undergird scientific progress in understanding within a transcendent framework of meaning.

In a philosophically precise study, G. Frank has illuminated the transformation of Aristotelian natural philosophy at Melanchthon's hands. He
speaks of a transition from teleology of nature to theology of nature.[50] Likewise, Kusukawa has shown in his detailed study how displacement of Aristotelian final causality from inquiry into the material and efficient causalities
at work in phenomena occurred in Melanchthon and thus contributed to
the rise of modern natural science. Kusukawa shows that this displacement
of final causality was motivated by Melanchthon's new appreciation of the
Creator's *provident* care — in nature as in human history — especially represented by the designation of humanity as the image of God.[51] Final causality, in other words, does not inhere natural things without minds; it is in
minds, beginning with God's, that let things be what they are and then also
adapt these things to purposes of grace.

Melanchthon speaks this way, as we have seen. "Thus, and not in any
other way, the path is open to that companionship with God if first, in this
mortal life, we begin with the first principles of knowledge which He has
handed on to us — and how much in it has He set before us that is incomprehensible, which He nevertheless wants us to consider in our foolishness?"[52] Indeed, God "placed in the minds of men the desire of considering

things and the pleasure which accompanies this knowledge. These reasons invite healthy minds to the consideration of nature, even if no use followed . . . *to consider nature is to follow one's own nature,* and consideration per se leads to the most pleasant joy, even if other uses did not follow."[53] Natural scientific inquiry into the immanent causes of things is an intrinsic good, even if it is not immediately useful as technology; this curiosity is placed providentially in the mind by God as the world's creator, so that to "consider nature is to follow one's own nature." Acquisition of knowledge of nature belongs to human nature as *imago dei,* called in partnership to exercise dominion as a faithful steward of the earth.

What is decisive for Melanchthon then is not simply the conviction of humanity's dignity by virtue of its rational capacity, which he shares with the antecedent tradition. Rather there is a change in the understanding of the image's orientation and with it of the ideal of knowledge: to be the image of God no longer connotes, as it does in more ascetical versions of the tradition, knowing God as opposed to the world, as an almost Gnostic alternative to the dark world of change and matter here below. For Melanchthon, *imago dei* means knowing God in accord with the cosmos on the way to the best of all possible worlds, thus as Creator of this very creation in which the human minds consider things, the world that was called good from the beginning and is moreover the object of divine redemption and fulfillment. This shift from a static-vertical ascent by way of individual intellection of essences to a dynamic-horizontal orientation by the social way of induction from experience may be seen then as a shift in theology from teleology to providence, from deism to theism, from nature to history. It brings with it a new ideal of knowledge: to know the creation as God knows it, the grand object of God's almighty act of wisdom and love approaching in the final harmonization of nature and grace, the resurrection of the dead, the eternal "sabbath," when "we will fully know the great goodness of God and eternal justification of creatures," when "the entire creation shall be renewed"[54] so that "we in this flesh, and in this body, which we now have, will be resurrected," and "our body and entire nature will be renewed . . . [in] knowledge, bright and clear, of God and all creatures."[55]

Thus when Loemker described the early modern reorientation of the traditional vertical hierarchies into dynamic horizontal polarities to situate the thought of Leibniz, he described the shift in theology that has already taken place in Melanchthon under the impact of the Reformation's new appropriation of biblical eschatology: "The effect of the eschatology of the seventeenth century, however, was to eliminate the idea of perfection as a metaphysical force within history but to stimulate Utopianism as an ideal to be aimed at as an end; the result was, therefore, that it was transformed into the modern conception of progress, with its own complex mixture of inevitability and moral responsibility."[56] We can see this shift clearly, complete and hard at work at the end of Leibniz's essay on the origination of all things, where he speaks of "a certain constant and unbounded progress in the whole universe," which indeed "never comes to an end."[57] This shift from vertical and individualistic ascent to horizontal and social progress turned on Melanchthon's theological revision of Aristotle's legacy: the removal of final purpose from the immanent causal explanation of physical things and its re-assignment to supervening divine providence, inclusive of the natural curiosity of human minds and the wonder at things that are the root of doxology. Final causality becomes the redemptive use God makes of things (from the beginning!), which also have their own natural integrity according to the principle of plentitude, for purposes of grace that also judges the abuse of things in human egocentrism.

To bring this complex of ideas up to date, let me suggest that the kinds of revisions of the Aristotelian legacy at work in Melanchthon anticipate the pragmatic account of knowledge to be found, for example, in John Dewey.[58] The kind of Protestant progressivism that he (and Melanchthon and Leibniz) represents has become today virtually an object of scorn, though the objections are a confused blend of two very different complaints. One complaint is that in thinking progress to be natural, human responsibility for choices is obscured. This critique reflects a normative concern that de-nies that any and all change is for the good. Another complaint is that pro-gressivism universalizes what at best is still only a provisional, partial per-spective on the common good of cosmos and humanity, what as such may then turn out to be a terrible distortion of reality when we come to a fuller picture. These are two very different critiques. The first assumes knowledge of the good and responsibility for it. The second denies any workable knowl-edge of the good and rather wishes to debunk pretensions to it. This criti-cism resolves everything into mere relations of power. Melanchthon and Leibniz belong in the first arena of a critical progressivism. For them knowl-edge of God's providential purpose serves not to remove human responsibil-ity, but to specify it, since God's purposes cannot simply be read off a nature taken teleologically but must be understood in stances of reasoned faith. For Christians, God's purpose is known in the resurrection of the Crucified, and it is this knowledge of faith that interprets nature as it is discovered scientifi-cally. In reply to the second kind of critique, critical progressives would or could say that we can rely in faith on God's provident guidance made known a posteriori in revelation, since a priori God is good and wills good for the world He has made. Together our maxims and beliefs in this, as in all other regards, are tested both by their efficacy in dealing with the world and by their coherence with all the other maxims and beliefs we hold. Thus, we may conclude, this Protestant theological progressivism is *in nuce* a version of pragmatism, eschewing fantastic demands for epistemological justification that presuppose absolute ideals of knowledge.

Of course, this move from traditional Aristotelianism entailed the risk for theology, as Loemker notes, that the "modern dynamic theory of history [meant] freedom from . . . theological absolutes."[59] If by theological absolutes one means dogmatic definitions of natures by an a priori essentialism, Loemker is correct. Given the relative autonomy of the world "machine" (as both Melanchthon and Leibniz could speak), and the sufficiency of physical science to account for its evolving states by immanent mechanisms of causality, the modern mind, as Jüngel has stressed, would have no need of the cosmological hypothesis of God as prime mover and final cause, the necessary being from which all imperfect beings by nature derive and to which by nature they strive.[60] The more significant issue in a world in which God is not necessary becomes, according to Jüngel (just as Leibniz intuited), the *thinkability* of God,[61] i.e., as the coherence or unity of the perfections in a single, divine life. By the same token, however, the notion of intellectual progress inclusive of natural-scientific explanation undergirded by providence entailed the possibility of an enormous theological gain: *optimism* that in Christ and by the Spirit we are *on the way* to the best of all possible worlds and just so a cognitive standard by which to measure and aid progress and to identify and resist regress.[62] In place of absolutes, the orientation of thought is found in the eschatology of Romans 8, not of course as a substitute for science but as the framework of grace embracing groaning, yearning nature, sponsoring study of it and interpreting it step-by-step along the way by means of the supervening goals of God whose kingdom comes from above to redeem our bodies with all that goes with them.

Heaven itself for Melanchthon does not leave creation behind. He looked forward, as it were, to the divine library, reading all those books in all the other disciplines that one short human life in time did not allow: "seeing this wonderful variety of work and these arrangements of God looking from without and through a thick darkness, we are dumbfounded, and grieve that we cannot examine nature deeply and see the causes. But then, at least, when we see the 'Idea' of nature in the divine mind, we shall look at this whole machine as from within, and understand the plans of the Creator and the causes of all the divine works."[63] A favored image of heaven was the *school* of God. "And there is an eternal [school], where God will be all for all, and will impart His wisdom and justice to us, where we shall see Him in person, and in the Son, the Word (logos), we shall behold not only the ideas and causes of the workings of the world, but also the wonderful joining of divine and human nature, and the plan for the restoration of mankind. There we shall have complete insight into nature."[64] Holding before the scholar the eschatological prospect of immediate participation in God's creative knowledge of the creation bears in turn upon the approach taken to knowledge of the world here and now. This prospect is more than a Kantian regulative idea: there is an eschatological *terminus ad quem* of knowledge by which its progress can be marked and its momentum sustained amid the confusions and discouragements of the life of the mind — which "trials and tribulations" also belong to the Christian intellectual's pilgrim journey. There is a doxological place in which the final harmony resides, a destination of praise and enjoyment that protests here and now against ecological abuse by the instrumentalization of reason into mere technical wizardry severed from ethical and aesthetic values. There is the overarching goal for making this world a paradise for all beings as announced in Genesis 1:26-28, engineering with, and not against, the grain of things. There is a Sabbath Day for rest along the way in wonder at the grace that begins, accompanies, and ends all things.

It is important to dwell a moment longer on this ultimately *doxological* nature of science for Melanchthon, and it is interesting to observe in this connection how he recorded one of the first versions of the Faust legend — a cautionary tale about knowledge sought instrumentally, only for power's sake, as pure technology fulfilling infantile fantasies for magical power severed from God's final purpose of doxology.[65] Delight and praise in contemplation of the works of God are thus not decoration, so to say, but mark a deep rift between philosophical pragmatism and theological pragmatics: as the final cause of knowledge in the created human mind, the praise of God lends both ethical direction for and aesthetic motivation to reason's patient inquiry into the efficient and material causes of the world. The mandate is progressively to know the world *as God the Creator knows it,* who is not mere power but always power together with wisdom and love, who rests therefore and rejoices in all His works on the seventh day of creation, a type of the eternal sabbath. True knowledge is not merely power but power qualified by wisdom and love. The eschatological doxology of the redeemed and fulfilled creation now anticipated in turn forms a barrier wall against the purely in-strumental, Faustian equation of knowledge with power.

On the other hand, we would also misread Melanchthon's theologically motivated interest in the new natural science if we thought this contempla-tive and doxological goal of knowledge as such sanctioned any kind of intel-lectual passivity. Kusukawa's study shows on the contrary how Melanchthon reconceived *education* as the mainstream Reformation's *social* gospel; i.e., the new paradigm of learning constituted a constructive and reformatory *social* alternative to radicals who despised learning, burned books, and smashed art to pieces as idols (Karlstadt), rose up in arms to "destroy the godless who have no right to live" (Müntzer), or urged the fatalism of the *Alleinwirksamkeit Gottes,* obliterating genuine, individuated creatures in distinction from God in support of theocratic politics (Zwingli). Over against these burning alter-natives of the day, Melanchthon's new model of education in its double-sided turn to the "books" of nature and Scripture aimed to nurture a new form of human society in *analogy* to the reign of God in glory, i.e., as progressive *growth* into the living *image* on the earth of God the Creator.

All this quite clearly represents a different program than the attempt to read divine intentions off from natural arrangements taken in a fixed and static way, reverting in this fashion to the primacy of cosmological ar-guments for God's existence based upon an immanent teleology, as the emerging deistic discipline of natural theology (set free from its previous Thomistic mooring in sacred theology) would largely maintain. It is a "mis-reading," Kusukawa rightly states, to "regard this natural philosophy of Melanchthon's as natural theology simply because of his preoccupation with the Providence of God."[66] It is precisely the opposite. It is a Christian philos-ophy of creation. "Natural theology, in fact, emerged as a discipline later on in the sixteenth century, from metaphysics."[67] The term "natural theology," in other words, ought generally to refer to the philosophical dogma, arising from Socinianism and maturing into deism, which uncouples divine power and wisdom, whether as watchmaker or repairman, from love. But Me-lanchthon's project is *theological* philosophy, as Günther Frank rightly em-phasizes; what Leibniz at length puts forward as natural theology stems from this latter tradition's distinction of law and gospel, even though this latter in the course of time becomes vulnerable to assimilation into deism proper.[68] Melanchthon's tradition, however, presupposes trinitarianism, and it devel-ops general pneumatology, as argued below, based on the idea that the hu-man who acknowledges God with the mind and conforms to God by the will forms the image of God on the earth.[69] Melanchthon is clear that while the capacity of the mind to recognize God as God is innate, it is in the light of the revelation of the supervening purpose of God in Christ that nature is to be interpreted. Similarly Leibniz; although he often calls his endeavor natural theology, that is because, like Anselm, he wants to argue *solo ratione* on a level field with his opponents Hobbes and Spinoza. Also, like Anselm, he so argues on behalf of a deeper understanding of the things that are believed, unlike the obscurantist who thinks theology consists in repeating the words of the Bible verbatim. In Leibniz's version of natural theology, it is the Melanchthonian program of general pneumatology with its meliorism that continues.

It would thus be a mistake to read back into Melanchthon's interest in God's wisdom a nervous apologetic concern to prove the existence of a cosmic Architect from natural purpose, as came to predominate generally in the natural theology of following centuries, based as it was on the return of Aristotelian final causality in nature.[70] But with Luther, and as a trinitarian, Melanchthon theologically rejected as deism the God Aristotle thought on the basis of a teleology immanent in nature. For the same reason, however, Melanchthon also finds himself urging the new natural science upon self-satisfied theologians who think they already know it all. In an oration promoting study of Galen's classical but long-neglected anatomy, Melanchthon asked his young charges to see that

> they are called to the consideration and contemplation of nature by divine providence. What is more appropriate for man than to remember that only our species has been placed in the world in order to contemplate this wonderful world? Furthermore, observing the separate things, what is sweeter than to see the order and harmony of bodies and motions? Or to consider the variety of things springing forth, and to see them made for certain uses, so that we can conclude that all these things are distributed by an eternal mind by marvelous counsel and economy? And indeed, nature has implanted in the minds of all sharp goads towards that consideration, and this knowledge brings by far the richest pleasures.[71]

Desire for harmony, insight by parsimony, contemplation of intricate beauty in nature provide motive powers in natural science — a genuinely aesthetic hunger is innate to the mind and the basis of its hunger for the supernatural. In the cited passage this hunger for parsimony is primary. A lazy reading of it could assimilate it to Aristotelian teleological conventions, but the delight taken in observation and discovery here is explained providentially, not teleologically. Purposiveness, not purposefulness, in nature is observed and then interpreted providentially. The praise of God arises as an inductive conclusion to observation, premised on the human mind's placement in the world as *imago dei*. Certainly rhetorical traces of teleology survive, but they are reworked in accord with the entire approach of theological philosophy: providence here interprets teleology, not teleology providence. In this vein, the exhortation that theologians consider nature is not idle; it is prescient.

What Melanchthon *is* nervous about is the contemporaneous reappearance of Epicurean and Stoic philosophies in Renaissance letters,[72] tendencies that with the rise of natural science would mature into the early modern systems of Hobbes and Spinoza respectively. These would present real but, in Melanchthon's view, false and dangerous alternatives to biblical providence. In place of the philanthropic divine determination to redeem and fulfill the creation in Christ, Melanchthon foresaw with apprehension new forms of "naturalistic" fatalism on the right and on the left that would lead to totalizing aspiration and frightful dehumanization. In this apprehension he was arguably correct.[73] Reading the philosophical schools historically, Melanchthon understood that the philosophical tradition is not a seamless garment woven by pure reason advancing to truth uninterrupted, but proceeds by a dogmatic clash and conflict, since the contingent world is amenable to many plausible interpretations and so to progressive as well as regressive praxis. In this regard, Melanchthon stands in the great tradition of Christian Platonism from which perspective Stoicism, Epicureanism, and Skepticism appear as virtually theological deviations, i.e., as heresies.

An Objection: Melanchthon's Aristotelianism

An objection to the foregoing interpretation is the commonplace complaint that "Melanchthon restored Aristotle" to the university.[74] Kusukawa indeed says at one point in his study on which I have drawn so heavily that the "teleological arguments of Greek philosophy furnished Melanchthon with the philosophical proof for the Providential design of God the Creator." This may be so on first glance. But it seems to me in some tension with Kusukawa's own insight that "knowledge of God's Providence was the single aim of Melanchthon's whole philosophy," correlative as it is with the trust in God denoted by the doctrine of justification by faith.[75] The question is: Which of these is in the driver's seat? Sharing the Renaissance revival of the Augustinian critique of reason, and Luther's renewal of Pauline soteriology, Melanchthon's reformed conception of philosophy as strictly determined by the new law-gospel theology limited philosophy, as previously noted, to natural things and civil morals, the so-called sphere of creation in distinction from the eschatological realm of grace and eternal life. The former is thus the realm subject to reason, *ratio*.[76]

But let us consider the objection to this interpretation by retracing the steps involved in the theological substitution of providence for teleology that we have just argued. The question was how to take Aristotle, whose intellectual power could hardly be denied. "It is very doubtful whether the Latins comprehended the correct meaning of Aristotle."[77] With this thesis, the early Luther (before his relation with Melanchthon) had in mind the scholastic reading of the *Metaphysics* as Christian theology. In this appropriation, Aristotle provided medieval theology the framework of thought into which Christians, as it were, inserted their own specific dogmas from Scripture and tradition for rational processing.[78] In his famous attack on scholastic education in the epochal *Address to the Christian Nobility of the German Nation on the Reform of the Christian Estate* (1520),[79] Luther had asserted in this connection that "the universities, too, need a good, thorough reformation." In it Luther claimed, "I know my Aristotle as well" as anyone, even better, having "lectured on him and been lectured on him, and I understand him better than St. Thomas or Duns Scotus." He would gladly keep Aristotle's *Logic, Rhetoric,* and *Poetics* "as useful in training young people to speak and preach properly." But Luther "completely discarded" Aristotle's best-reputed books *(Physics, Metaphysics, Concerning the Soul,* and the *Ethics),* which "boast about nature, although nothing can be learned from them either about nature or the Spirit." Luther huffs, "any potter has more knowledge of nature than is written in these books[!]" Indeed, "nobody has yet understood [Aristotle on nature]" despite much "fruitless labor and study, at the cost of much precious time" in the reading and writing of commentaries. *Ad fontes!* Luther called for the direct study of nature, not the vacuous study of Aristotle's outmoded books about nature in commentaries upon commentaries. The reformatory exhortation runs in parallel to the summons to a new theology drawn from its own true source in the Bible — not the tradition's commentaries upon commentaries upon it.

"[I]t was this Melanchthon who took to heart the necessity for a more positive programme of arts and [natural] philosophy education."[80] The task suited Melanchthon perhaps better than Luther knew, since Melanchthon had long since broken with the medieval Latin reading of Aristotle.[81] As a student in Tübingen, he was part of the rediscovery of Aristotle in the Greek original, not the Latin translation, and so also Aristotle without Christian Thomist or nominalist commentary. This study had led him to the conviction that the "direction of [Aristotle's] thought was in fact not at all toward otherworldly truth, but rather toward this world. The true essence of Aristotle's system, the [Tübingen humanists] believed, was its scope and teleological function as rhetoric."[82] This yielded "a fresh vision of dialectic in service of rhetoric and thus public life."[83] Melanchthon's Tübingen dissertation on the reunification in scholarship of rhetoric and dialectic, affect and intellect, was aimed at the re-formation of educational curricula by return to original sources in classical antiquity. Melanchthon's criticism of scholasticism's use of Aristotle as substantively mistaken, ahistorical, and irrelevant to urgent worldly tasks preceded his conversion to Luther's theology. This independent assessment also allowed Melanchthon to make more nuanced use of Aristotle and the medieval legacy in general in the course of developing the new relation of nature and grace on the basis of the Pauline-Augustinian-Lutheran theology he adopted after coming to Wittenberg.

The debt to Aristotle is real, but precise: "it is not that there are no causes but that [some] are indeterminable or unknown to us. . . . [As] all fortuitous events are reducible to causes *per se,* Melanchthon eliminated the possibility of accidental events, a conclusion that Aristotle also reaches in his *Physica* II, vi."[84] The world is *lawful,* things cannot happen by chance, and so understanding any event is to explain the causes of things. In this conviction we may detect the antecedents of Leibniz's cherished principle of sufficient reason. For Aristotle the principle of lawfulness had implied divine mind, the final cause, and the prime mover, a notion of divinity as the world soul that was compatible with the eternity of the cosmos and the coeternity of implacable, recalcitrant matter. But for Melanchthon and the tradition of Christian Platonism, God as Creator is the cause of causes, and so God's choice of the regnant system of causes in the cosmos must be conceived as a mysterious primal event of an all-wise and all-benevolent will. With this, Aristotle is transformed, as previously noted. Final purposes do not inhere in things that exist contingently and so may within limits admit of various uses and interpretations, lawful or unlawful, proper or improper by intelligent minds. On the other hand, nominalism also had its influence in this regard and moved thought in the direction of monadology. Real things are individuals, and so substantial forms, not in the sense of medieval realism as instantiations of general form, but in the sense that any and every organized or organic unity exists in its powers of perception and appetite, seeks its own integral good in a surrounding world environment. God has as many thoughts as monads that exist, indeed infinitely more when we consider all the essences to which existence is denied. The goods sought consequently are vast, manifold, diverse as the individuals populating the creation. Just so any such contingent thing can be misused or itself go astray in the confusions that beset finite faculties of perception. It appears then that both the plentitude of forms and the accompanying confusion in purpose are divinely willed, or at least permitted, and that God in turn providentially draws things from chaos to order, confusion to clarity, ultimately from nature to grace by His own purposeful involvement in the world, in this way reconciling wayward wills to His will and making a place for many other minds at His table.

In this we can see how the function of the cosmological arguments as Aristotelian metaphysical theology was transformed in the process of appropriation by Melanchthon's Christian philosophy of nature. As Kusukawa rightly says, "Trust in Providence leads to trust in the Redeemer God: the knowledge that God has made absolutely everything and sustains everything leads to the assurance that God is able to achieve the eternal purposes of his love as they are revealed in his promises."[85] This is basically creation theology, not the cosmological argument as Aristotle intended it, as Luther had already seen when he denied that Aristotle knew or understood the "absolute power of God."[86] The theological argument here is in fact the same as Luther's in *De servo arbitrio:* the immutable necessity of God's will undergirds the martyr's trust in God's power to keep His promise. Even though fallen into the hands of persecutors, the martyr has not fallen out of the hands of God. The immutable God is able to keep His word. Kusukawa calls this a "distinctively Lutheran" doctrine of providence, with the accent falling on the *Alleswirksamkeit Gottes.* God works in all, God is cause of all causes, even causing the persecutor into whose hands the martyr has fallen, though God is not the maker of all choices, especially not the evil choice of that persecutor. But God grants existence to other purposes and so God permits evil purposes for a season, just as God purposes to overcome this opposition by the self-involvement in history of His Word and Spirit, not then by fiat, force, and coercion but precisely through the defenseless witness of the martyrs and the suasion of Word and Spirit. Kusukawa thus sharply distinguishes this Lutheran doctrine of providence from a rival theory of the *Alleinwirksamkeit Gottes* concurrently advanced by Zwingli, i.e., that God alone works all in all the actions of creatures — possibly the antecedent of Spinoza's teaching via the Reformed tradition in the Netherlands and perhaps also of Hobbes in England.[87]

Howsoever he employs the conventional cosmological and teleological language, for Melanchthon, decisively, nature *is not divine* or eternal as the teleological principle inevitably suggests, or conversely, God is not a dimension of the cosmos, the perfection of being in contrast to imperfection in the being of that which becomes. In general, it is not the sources one employs but the substance of the stance taken in the present that should count in schooling thinkers as Platonist, Aristotelian, or whatever. In denying the immanence of final purpose in the contingent world, we rightly detect the nominalist accent on the ultimate nonnecessity of any being other than God, which particularly attends being as physical reality.[88] Yet this contingent nature *is creation,* God's created replica, in which humanity especially is called to correspond as the image of God in dominion over a habitable earth that is yet to become a paradise.[89] This aspect particularly attends being as mind. That is the realist legacy concerning the moral and aesthetic necessity in God purposefully to intend a world that comports not only with infinite power but also with infinite resources of wisdom and love: the human creature made in God's image. Melanchthon unites both accents as aspects of one and the same reality. God's free relation to the creation is not one of a willful *deus exlex* (as Luther's rhetoric of the *deus absconditus* can sometimes sound), but one of intelligible address, which connects with the human mind in the very act of enlightening it. In this way, by the "preaching of the gospel" and calling humanity in Christ to become the image of God, nature and grace, reason and revelation, learning and faith are at once distinguished and at the same time coordinated in a scheme axiomatic for the new scholarship. *Grace interprets nature as creation* to be redeemed from corruption and set free for fulfillment. The distinction and coordination of philosophy and the gospel locate the laws of nature as discovered in science and moral philosophy in the larger interpretive context of canonical Scripture, taken as the "world-absorbing narrative" (Lindbeck) of the reign of God and thus as divine governance, providence.

Such theological convictions *sponsored* the new scientific vocation of exploration into the contingent mechanisms of the cosmos and discovery of its principles, as opposed to lazy belief from a naively anthropocentric perspective that the world was simply a self-interpreting system of contrivances aimed at human convenience. Even Luther, according to Brian Gerrish, already "greeted the new science with enthusiasm . . . [and saw] in the advance of scientific knowledge . . . the gradual recovery of Adam's dominion over the world of nature,"[90] for this is real, material praxis, not the armchair *theoria* of leisured elites. All the more was this the case for Melanchthon. Rigorous knowledge of nature in its own right was now demanded by the

new theology since it would provide the very material of theological interpretation; theological interpretation in turn gave form to the material insights of science in constructing knowledge of the world as envisioned by
the mandate of Genesis 1:26-28. Melanchthon "promoted the academic enterprise as one important tool of God's providence."[91] Divine governance of
history progressing through *studia humanitatis* as its leading instrument —
this was the innovation that Melanchthon as educator made and it gave new
content to the academic calling. Regarding "those who teach or study in the
schools," he more than once decreed, "we are put in our position by divine
providence in order to preserve and spread knowledge useful for humankind. . . . If anyone comes to the school only in order to take away from there
some particular discipline that he could direct to gain and idle show, he
should know that he defiles the most holy temple of knowledge."[92] If we today have difficulty grasping this ideal of education, it is because Melanchthon's scheme depends, like Leibniz's, not on natural teleology but on axial
propositions, i.e., "dogmas" borrowed from biblical faith (but not only from
the Christian canon; both Homer[93] and the Muslim Arab thinker Avicenna[94]
can be invoked as supplying precedents). "Melanchthon transformed traditional natural philosophy into a natural philosophy new and different from
its predecessors because he believed in a faith that was also new and different,"[95] arising from the call of God in Genesis 1:26-28 to join together in labor under His purpose for the redeemed creation revealed in Christ.

The Program of General Pneumatology

From these beginnings there entered upon the stage of European thought
the distinctive program that Leibniz brought to full flower a century and a
half later. The lines of connection here are virtually direct. Berman and
Witte have laid particular emphasis on the transformation of jurisprudence
under the impact of Melanchthonian reform, with its chief doctrine of
"pneumatology" that "God is a wise and righteous being, who out of his
great and proper goodness created rational creatures to be like him."[96]
Through this venue, "generations of students thereafter studied [Melanch-
thon's] legal, political, and moral writings, many of which were still being
published in the late seventeenth century and being used as textbooks in
universities. His basic jurisprudential insights dominated German legal
scholarship until the early Enlightenment."[97] Leibniz's doctorate from Leipzig was in the field of jurisprudence and thus this intellectual heritage came

to stamp his approach as he branched out into other fields of inquiry. The "pneumatology" mediated through jurisprudence was a discipline undertaken in recognition of the continuing primacy of revealed theology, even after the turn of the seventeenth century, when post-Reformation German philosophy witnessed a "return of metaphysics" as the first science of being as such in its principles, modes, and affections.

In continuity with the perspective of Melanchthon, however, philosophical pneumatology recognized (over against the traditional claim of metaphysics as first science) that it is God as Creator and things as creatures that come first: if there were no such pneumatology, neither would the question of being ever arise. Thus propositions borrowed from revealed theology resituate metaphysics as the inquiry of thinking creatures that stand in some special relation to their Creator as His image on the earth. As first premises, these pneumatological notions delimit the scope of the question of being to a this-worldly inquiry, rather than conversely when metaphysical notions of being render the very possibility of rational speech about perfect and imperfect being, God and creature respectively. Given this delimitation, philosophical pneumatology articulates the innate capacity of the rational human mind to recognize God as God and the self as a persisting, indeed eternal patiency/agency in relation to God. It is just this capacity of the finite for the infinite, let us recall, that at length Kant denied in *Conflict of the Faculties* (as elsewhere he disowned pneumatology as a pseudoscience).[98]

Max Wundt in his major study from midcentury described the development of pneumatology in the course of the seventeenth century on the soil of the post-Reformation German universities that had been reorganized by Melanchthon, where metaphysics were thus restricted by pneumatology to the work of a this-worldly ontology. Various new classifications and reorganizations of metaphysics were consequently proposed and debated; in some a separate section devoted to the pneumatological account of God, angels, and souls developed.[99] For philosophical inquiry into nature had to presuppose *some* account of God, angels, and souls, even if no longer in the traditional, Aristotelian way of an acquired knowledge of perfect being through analysis of the world's imperfect ways of becoming and thence by inference to its necessary ground. By the same token, Wundt continued, ontology came more and more in the process of this shift to be conceived as an independent discipline, concerned with the most general account of worldly experience in distinction from the sacrosanct realm God, angels, and the soul. In time, two blocks of unintegrated knowledge began to stand side by side: ontology and pneumatology, with ontology gaining increasing prominence due to the new discoveries of the natural sciences. In this unstable situation, if ontology were to reassert itself against pneumatology as an unrestricted science of first principles, or if pneumatology were to fail in its task of providing a satisfying account of the mind's capacity to recognize God and self (and just so capable of delimiting the scope of ontology to the nonpneumatological world), the entire project of a theologically reformed philosophy would collapse and with it the prospects of the new Protestant-Christian culture.

Melanchthon had envisioned such a philosophical program for cultural reform already in his 1519 baccalaureate theses in theology; there he appended a few "philosophical theses" to the foregoing ones enthusiastically endorsing Luther's Pauline-Augustinian theology; they read as follows: "The laws of nature are the qualities with which the soul is created; Human nature strives for well being *(bene esse)* more than it strives simply to exist *(esse)*. There is one God in the divine categories, and he is the sum of all things."[100] According to these terse statements, a certain kind of knowledge of God, nature, and self can be worked out by Christian philosophy through analysis of human consciousness, premised as this procedure is upon the doctrine of the human soul made in God's image. The procedure here actually goes back to Augustine, who famously told in the *Confessions* how he had turned away from the search for God in the external world where, he says, "I imagined you as some splendid being, but entirely physical."[101] Instead he now examined his own mind to find the trace of God. The books of the Platonists and the Bible's criticisms of idolatry thus turned him from the false images of God he sought among created things and caused him "to return to my own self," the mirror-mind. "Under your guidance," Augustine confessed to his Creator, "I entered into the depths of my soul . . . and with the eye of my soul, such as it was, I saw the Light that never changes casting its rays over the same eye of my soul, over my mind."[102] Not that Augustine found God this way but rather his mind thus became prepared to recognize the truth of God's "severe mercy" in the incarnate Christ, when the time was ripe.

Melanchthon manifestly renews this procedure, which had become current in the revival of Augustinianism among Renaissance humanists, as an alternative to what seemed increasingly dubious cosmological accounts of the Christian God's existence (not in the sense that divine existence was doubted but rather doubt that such existence as cosmology provided was truly divine).[103] According to Frank, Melanchthon, in developing this counter-tradition from Augustine, was the first ever to offer a proof of God's existence from the experience of conscience.[104] Similarly, while not disowning the cosmological proofs, Leibniz would subordinate them to the ontological proof that Anselm[105] had developed out of certain statements of Augustine; as Southern has very rightly written, "this proof was not intended to be a proof of the existence of God, but a proof of the essences of Goodness, Truth, Justice, etc., which [Anselm] had shown in the *Monologion* to be the necessary attributes of God, must cohere in a single Being, and that this single Being, properly understood, cannot be thought of as non-existent."[106] Leibniz recurs to this Anselmian intention against Descartes's revisionist deployment of the argument in the *Meditations,* where Descartes had conceived the ontological argument as a proof of an omnipotent being's perfect existence, existence being taken then as a necessary attribute. Leibniz found this Cartesian version of the ontological argument deeply troubling on account of anti-trinitarian and deistic implications, "Socinianism" as it was called in this time. Thus he devoted his greatest effort to the restoration by modal logic of the Anselmian form of the argument: *if* a coherent idea of God as the trinitarian "sum of all things" is possible, *then* God's existence is necessary.[107]

That is the real issue in the region of theology. Is any such idea of God's life as the harmony of power, wisdom, and love "coherent"? This is what Anselm was arguing in the latter half of the *Monologion,* which becomes articulately trinitarian in conception as well as formulation. Is *this* idea of God *possible?*[108] Or, as ascendant Islam was challenging: Is God to be thought of as "God who neither begets nor is begotten"?[109] Kant not only demolished the later Cartesian proof of divine *existence;* far more profoundly he questioned whether we can ever attain the needed insight into divine *coherence,* i.e., the very *possibility* of the triune God's existence as Melanchthon's "sum of perfections."[110]

We see from the foregoing how the young Melanchthon can be centrally located in a millennium-stretching debate about the soul and its God, extending from Augustine to Kant. If we may reconstruct the terse 1519 theses in the light of Melanchthon's characteristic ideas, the argument is that the rational soul by nature reflects divine light or law as in a mirror; properly enlightened, it strives for the true good that is greater than the physical existence it presupposes; this supreme, spiritual good is God as the real quintessence of all created being, which the rational soul in sundry ways experiences and knows in the world. For in fact, whatever it understands it understands in the eternal light and law of the mind; these rays of wisdom can be formulated in definite common notions that constitute the indemonstrable premises of all possible knowledge, theoretical, practical, and aesthetic. With abandonment of the epistemic realism (*adaequatio intellectus cum re)* of the medieval tradition, however, it is not the case that the external world is abandoned to the subjectivism that actually does become regnant with Descartes. Rather, as argued above, it is the very notion of knowledge of reality that changes. As Frank puts it, knowledge is now the creative conceptualization of things from the perspective of the human mind on the basis of principles of knowledge inscribed on the soul by divine light.[111] The question that does arise now is how this can ever work to enlighten the world, if minds creatively conceptualize. How are mind and world coordinated, if not by a naive *adaequatio intellectus cum re,* nor least of all by subjectivism on the way to relativism and skepticism? How can proximate, progressive, perspectival knowledge acquire validity, even though never full adequacy?

These two, mind and world, are coordinated, Leibniz would eventually answer, as the "preestablished harmony" in God's decision to create, redeem, and fulfill the world. There are, Leibniz wrote, "two kingdoms even in corporeal nature, which interpenetrate without confusing or interfering with each other — the realm of power, according to which everything can be explained *mechanically* by efficient causes when we have sufficiently penetrated into its interior, and the realm of wisdom, according to which everything can be explained *architectonically,* so to speak, or by final causes when we understand its ways sufficiently."[112] Power and wisdom constitute two ways of looking upon one and the same temporal-spatial event of the cosmos, which ways coexist in the embodied mind of the rational soul, as it perceives and expresses. Knowledge is acquired as the passion and action of this monadological relationship in varying degrees across the vast continuum of existents, as the fundamental relation of perception to the cosmos is extended dramatically downward in Leibnizian panpsychism: "In the end my system comes down to this: each monad is the universe in concentrated form, and each mind is an imitation of the divinity. In God the universe is not only concentrated but perfectly expressed; but in each created monad there is distinctly expressed only one part, which is larger or smaller as the soul is more or less excellent, and all the infinite remainder is expressed only confusedly."[113] Monadology provides from top to bottom the interface of the two kingdoms. If it answers the question of how knowledge is possible by making such information exchange the passion and action of *all* organized systems in which anything real consists, the next question to arise is why things are so harmonized. The capacity of the human mind to grasp the world rightly albeit finitely from its particular perspective is based on the "preestablished harmony" of these two kingdoms. The preestablished harmony reflects in turn the divine decision for this world as metaphysically and morally best of all, an insight that only minds can attain and express in their corresponding act of being by which they fulfill their own destinies. Just like the theological doctrine of election, which scandalizes and hardens the unbelieving heart but strengthens the believer in trial and storm, Leibniz's preestablished harmony is a scandal to false reason but supreme insight to true.

Leibniz immediately added to the foregoing account of the preestablished harmony the further Christian dogma of God's freedom of choice, in order sharply to distinguish the Creator *ex nihilo* from the Demiurge or the Cosmic Architect of recurrent Cartesian deism. "But in God there is not only this concentration of the universe, but also its source. He is the originating center from which all else emanates."[114] God is not the soul of the cosmos, *natura naturans*, the dimension of its abiding being in distinction from that of its temporal becoming, *natura naturata*. The Creator *ex nihilo* is the source both of being and of becoming, the cosmos as dynamic interaction of form and matter, cause and effect, and all the other polarities of finite existence. As God is source of both being and becoming, Leibniz frequently differentiates his theology from the Stoic theology he sees in all his deistic opponents, both the watchmaker Spinoza and the repairman Clarke: "I admit that there is no Platonic *soul of the world,* for God is beyond the world, *extra-mundana intelligentia,* or rather *supramundana.*"[115] As such, what is *general* about pneumatology is its all-embracing *scope* as *theological* philosophy accounting for all reality. General pneumatology does not then carve out for itself a special mental or spiritual domain safe from physics as characterized the post-Kantian nineteenth century. Rather the kingdom of nature is preceded by, accompanied by (as monadology), and fulfilled in the kingdom of grace. This "preestablished harmony" reflects the divine *good reason* for the creation of just this nature by just this grace on the way to just this destiny. Buoyed by this rational faith, the republic of human minds progresses toward God's knowledge of the world in conceptualizing things ever more adequately, avoiding the Scylla of a naive *adaequatio intellectus cum re* and the Charybdis of subjectivism declining into relativism and then skepticism.

Returning now to Melanchthon, there are, as indicated, more immediate precedents for his pneumatology, especially in Pico's Renaissance Platonism[116] from whom the student Melanchthon evidently first drew the themes of the image of God and human dignity as well as the notion of how being, one, truth, goodness are united in God, "the sum of all things," reflected in turn in creation. Especially important in this connection is how

Melanchthon evidently learned from Pico the important idea of the image of God as an "indeterminate form," i.e., not scheduled by instinct to develop in such and such determinate ways, like an acorn fated to become an oak tree, but rather uniquely free among the creatures, as the mirror that can reflect lights other than it ought. "Who does not wonder at this chameleon which we are?"[117] As a contingent creature with powers of self-orientation, the created mirror that ought morally to be the image of God in its own concrete destiny may reflect in fact something other and in this way miss its true destiny. This capacity is in distinction from the general principle of plenitude, which envisions the panoply of forms where each by nature reflects God in some particular fashion in a maximal show of diversity. There is according to the principle of plenitude a divinely willed diversity of individuals, each in its own unique time, place, and destiny filling the world and contributing like a grand mosaic of mirrors to the total reflection of God in the creation. In contrast to this, however, the intelligent human form is one also capable of missing its destiny by moral failure and consequent deformation. So Pico had warned, "'Ye are all gods, and sons of the most high,' unless by abusing the very indulgent liberality of the Father, we make the free choice, which he gave to us, harmful to ourselves instead of helpful for salvation . . . for if we will to, we can."[118]

The metaphysical dignity of the human creature above all the other creatures lies knotted together with this indelible and at the same time fateful moral capacity for free choice and action; precisely in its act of choice, the human being really exists as some definite, finite resemblance of God (or dissemblance, as the case may be), not a mode or iteration of God, like a puppet, but the real maker of its own choices. Under the influence of Luther, as we have seen, the young professor Melanchthon sharply qualified Pico's "indefinite form" with the biblical account of the unhappy possibilities available to fallen humanity, as also with the Augustinian doctrine of the unfreedom of human desire; but in the end Melanchthon preserved Pico's freedom of action in order to avoid philosophical fatalism, even though the cost of this move, as noted above, was to make the problem of moral evil in real but wayward images of God the acute difficulty of general pneumatology.

Similarly, it was from Pico's revival of Platonism that Melanchthon evidently learned to conceive of "one God in the divine categories . . . the sum of all things." Pico had argued that the so-called transcendental categories, "being, one, true, and good, include all things" in space and time. These ideas provide no direct access to God's mysterious reality, since these "four are other in God than what they are in things that are after God, because God has them from Himself, and other things have them from Him." The line between Creator and creature is respected in this way. A naive analogy of being is thus denied, but not an analogy of mind. For the transcendentals exist in created things as God's "efficient, exemplary, and final causes," being effected as the concepts of existence, essence, and good respectively in the finite mind.[119] Just this presence of divine effects of existence, essence, and good inscribes upon the human mind the corresponding key notions for metaphysics in a new key, anticipating pneumatology. According to this, God as an *intelligentia extra mundam* may be conceived as the perfect harmony of power, wisdom, and goodness, thus as the Creator effecting the existence of essences that prove good, as we can recognize, though God is this harmony in a self-derived way that is beyond our comprehension.

Pico's humanism is hardly then a simple rejection of metaphysics; it is a form of Platonism from which Melanchthon takes the task of elaborating a satisfying phenomenology and ethically elevating hermeneutics of mind that in turn can progressively integrate scientific knowledge of the world in fulfillment of the human vocation spoken in Genesis 1:26-28. This reading of Melanchthon's debt to (but also transformation of) Pico may be confirmed by a fictional response Melanchthon wrote late in his life to (the long dead) Pico, on behalf of rhetoric and practical life, i.e., the new Reformation ideal the human image of God, not as "contemplator but as orator." Oration here does not designate pleasant decoration in speech, but refers to the skill of one "who teaches men accurately, clearly, and with a certain dignity concerning good and necessary things," as Melanchthon expressed it. "I call a philosopher one who when he has learned and knows things good and useful for mankind, takes a theory *(doctrina)* out of academic obscurity and makes it practically useful in public affairs."[120] This is Pico "protestantized," Plato "horizontalized," doctrine "pragmatized." All these reformatory turns of thought crystallize in general pneumatology.

The general pneumatology that emerged from Melanchthon's appropriations of Pico and of Luther, as we saw, left efficient and material causes to the empirical investigations of the emerging natural sciences; it abandoned medieval science as an a priori essentialism that would grasp the essential form of physical things by sheer intellection, naively unaware of the interest expressed in human attentiveness that constructs objects from the flux of becoming for its own use. As argued above, however, that move is not tantamount to relativism in the sense of an individualistic subjectivism. There is a shared world in which living subjects collaborate and communicate by means of language, and this shared world is in turn safeguarded as the creation of an acting and communicating Creator. Wundt argues in this connection that the distinctiveness of the Melanchthonian tradition in Germany (as opposed to Reformed philosophy centered in Holland and the new British science and philosophy) lay in an aversion to mechanism and deep preference for organism.[121] The monadological notion that the organic whole is greater than the sum of its parts, and that such complex systems admit of various accounts corresponding to the level of complexity on which a system is viewed,[122] resists philosophically simple reductions of dynamic life to lowest-level mechanistic explanation. It looks instead for irreducible unities in nature at every level — such "unities" are what "monads" are in Leibniz's mind — even the lowest. Wundt sees in this antidualistic reverence for organism a reflection of the Lutheran theological concern to uphold the capacity of the finite for the infinite as living forms to the Living One, from the lowliest atom's mechanical bonding with others to form compounds to the highest level of the rational soul's pneumatological capacity to recognize God as "the sum of the categories."[123]

Thus in pneumatology *Wesensphilosophie* gave way to *Geistphilosophie*, as G. Frank shows,[124] in a path that runs directly to Leibniz.[125] It is not the case, however, that pneumatology went unchallenged even in its home camp. The German "school philosophy" of the seventeenth century is characterized by a definite "return to metaphysics," as noted. Even though this was never any kind of simple return to the status quo ante, the return represents the fact that general logical questions about first principles, i.e., the modes and affections of being, could not be avoided. Melanchthon had banned these reflections for fear of their attaining control over the theses borrowed from revealed theology,[126] but in face of new challenges stemming from rival schools of thought, Wundt argues, a "return" became inevitable. Loemker explained the motive well when he spoke of the need for "regulative ideas which should give direction to thought and action . . . [like] ideal of harmony — the notion which impelled thinkers to move beyond mere eclecticism and encyclopedism to a 'general science' and a metaphysics."[127] Pneumatology also sought to mediate just this kind of synthesis, yet first philosophy chafed under the Melanchthonian restrictions imposed by revealed theology. Some in this camp began to regard pneumatology as little more than an artificial and ad hoc solution to problems calling for rigorous, independent metaphysics. Surely some general account of being and nonbeing logically precedes all other discourses, pneumatology included! Indeed, Leibniz's own teacher at Leipzig, Jacob Thomas, represented the tendency toward traditional metaphysics as first philosophy, i.e., "without pneumatology."[128] Thus the seventeenth-century school metaphysics could press hard upon the boundaries laid down for it by Melanchthon, leave behind the suspect discipline of pneumatology, and extend into territory previously forbidden by Luther's theological critique of metaphysics. This brought the danger, as Wundt forcefully elaborates, that in time the would-be servant (philosophy) would turn again into the mistress (of theology).[129]

Wundt suggested in this connection that the difference between a Leibniz and a Luther may be found in the fact, as he concluded on the basis of then current interpretation of Luther along the lines of Kierkegaardian subjectivity, that the Baroque philosopher reappropriates the medieval ideal of knowledge in one decisive respect: it is oriented not to the thinker as thinking thing separated from extended things, but to the objective thought, i.e., to the world humans know in and under God.[130] Leibniz's interest in cosmology is no turn with Descartes to the subject, but a turn of the subject with its object to God, as we have been arguing. Against Wundt on this point, however, there is no great difference between Luther, Melanchthon, and Leibniz. It is Descartes who signifies the real breach with his systematic dualism of subject and object, beginning in the human self. Or, to put it in contemporary idiom, Leibnizian pneumatology articulates an *ecological* concern that qualifies the humanocentrism of the Renaissance and similar tendencies appearing in Protestant Pietism, Catholic Jansenism, Baylean Manicheanism, but above all in Cartesian dualism. In this way Melanchthon and the pneumatological tradition tried to maintain a theonomous balance between apparently opposing trajectories of nature and spirit. Correspondingly, as Wundt insists, we should recognize that pneumatology preceded the division between empiricist and rationalist, so decisive if all roads in fact lead to Kant.[131]

According to pneumatology, then, the *universe* spiritually viewed is a great system of entelechies, each individually striving for its true good; as organized or organic bodies, all physical individuals from microbes to galaxies are best understood as spiritual unities in the act of their being — not blind, irreducibly dense bits of matter in aimless, reactive motion as Hobbes imagined, nor passing modalities of the one substance of the cosmos, as Spinoza thought. These are true individuals because each in its way "perceives" the whole, that is, receives data input from the unique perspective of its own desire for the good; in this just way each is informed in turn for its own action of self-expression in relation to the whole of space and time, forming systems of systems. God's full and complete concept in the preestablished harmony demarcates the journey each monad should make in living its life in such syntheses. In nonrational beings, this occurs by mechanical cause and effect, but in rational beings there is also a limited but real element of choice exercising a "top-down causality," as we say today. The suffering and acting of an individual intelligent patient/agent are in microcosm a concrete harmonization of the two kingdoms of nature and grace; here God's goal for nature intelligently choosing for itself its divine destination is realized. Melanchthon had laid it down in his *Loci communes* like an axiom: "As the divine Majesty in his boundless goodness, wanted to reveal himself, he created beautiful works — heaven and earth, air and water, angels and men. That he might be known, he imparted his wisdom and goodness to angels and men. We should earnestly contemplate this origin and purpose of creation."[132] Just this contemplation rightly informs the *imago dei*.

In general pneumatology, God then is to be known and loved in harmony with this ecology of created things, not at its expense for private pleasure in an understanding that amounts to a monstrous act of self-deception. The general pneumatology ethically teaches something akin to the Edwardean "consent to being."[133] The laws of God are engraved in physical nature as its physical ecology and in the soul as its moral economy; these belong together in the two coordinated orders of the great cosmic system, there to be discovered and obeyed by finite minds to the glory of God and for the happiness of each and all. This latter, *doxological* but never *acosmic* motif stemming from Melanchthon runs throughout Leibniz's works as lifting up God's final purpose in the origination of all things. For the praise of God as God, Loemker writes, "is a kind of echo and duplication of harmony. If God had no rational creatures in the world, he would still have the same harmony, but alone and devoid of echo; he would still have the same beauty, but devoid of reflection and refraction and multiplication."[134] Conversely, as Gregory Brown has pointed out, the "pursuit of theoretical science turns out to constitute the most perfect form of worship and to generate the most profound love of God." Citing Leibniz, Brown argues that he, in distinction from Aristotle, united the active and contemplative lives: "'And what more beautiful hymn can we wing to him than one in which the witness of things themselves express his praise? But the more one can give reasons for his love, the more one loves God. To find joy in the perfection of another — this is the essence of love. Thus the highest function of our mind is the knowledge or what is here the same thing, the love of the most perfect being, and it is from this that the maximum or most enduring joy, that is, felicity, must arise.'"[135]

Knowledge of divine perfections articulates the loving act of adoration that in praise attributes these properties to God as their sole, true subject. The one divine Spirit is reflected, refracted, and so multiplied in a vast host of created images singing praise to the Creator in every act of their being. This is in keeping with Melanchthon's account in the *Loci communes:* "God created man as he did because he wishes to reveal himself to man; he wishes to give even himself to man, his goodness, light, wisdom, righteousness, joy, and eternal blessedness. . . . For this reason man is a rational creature, and fashioned in him are some clearer signs of God than in irrational creatures." Melanchthon then notes how the human mind has the power to observe, categorize, and so distinguish things; also to know virtue from vice, and so enlightened, to command the body to obey. "From this we should further know that in the being of man there is first the being of the soul, then thought, then will or choice." And he concludes: "All this is an indication of the Godhead: the Father contemplates himself, and knows his thoughts, and in this contemplation his essential Image is begotten."[136] Leibniz was still careful (unlike the Unitarian Wolffians to follow) to conceive the one divine Spirit in whose image other minds are made in this trinitarian fashion, descended from Melanchthon.

According to Jordan, Leibniz's appropriation of trinitarianism appears in the decisive role it plays in his thought as early as the ill-fated attempt at Lutheran-Catholic reconciliation, the *Systema Theologicum* (ca. 1683): "From the virtue or Power (Father) of the Divine Essence springs ideas of things, or truths; these Wisdom (the Son) embraces; and thus, in the end, they become, according to their several perfections, objects of the Will (the Holy Ghost)."[137] The Trinity provides the structure of coherence of the Divine Mind, a pattern of thinkability for God as the harmony of the perfections of power, wisdom, and love. Years later in the *Theodicy* Leibniz explains God as Origin, or First Reason of things, in the same way: "Power relates to being, wisdom or understanding to truth, and will to good. And this intelligent cause ought to be infinite in all ways, and absolutely perfect in power, in wisdom and in goodness, since it relates to all which is possible. Furthermore, since all is connected together, there is no ground for admitting more than one. Its understanding is the source of essences, and its will is the origin of existences. There in few words is the proof of one only God with his perfections, and through him of the origin of things."[138] Loemker stresses the crucial significance of this trinitarian thought for Leibniz (although he attributes its influence on Leibniz not to Melanchthon's tradition but to Campanella):[139] "Thus God's Trinitarian nature, conceived as power expressing itself in thought (the Logos) and love, operates through the dynamic qualities of the Ideas which strive from possibility to existence, so that every individual creature in its immanent being 'participates' in the reality of the Divine being."[140] Thus, when God is understood in this way as Trinity "all the way down," participation in divine life, *finitum capax infiniti*, does not represent a blurring of the line between Creator and creature but precisely its true interpretation, since it is as the One in Three that God creates to redeem and fulfill His creature. God is God to be praised as God alone who by grace shares with the perishing creatures the eternal life which by nature is the Trinity's alone. This communion is the fulfillment of created nature, not the abrogation of the ontological difference. Yet the gravamen lies otherwise: general pneumatology is far from being any kind of dualistic foe of nature. It distinguishes the two kingdoms of nature and grace in order to harmonize them — eternally. Is some version of that possible for us today?

The State of the Question

It is by now clear that the usual antinomies are crude: Luther the theologian and Melanchthon the humanist, Luther the preacher and Melanchthon the scholar, Luther the prophet and Melanchthon the diplomat. What is at issue for us at the far end of the internally conflicted legacy stemming from the partners in reformation is the precise nature of their *theological* divergence, granted the historical necessity, if not justice, with which Philip and his school channeled the spewing, foul-mouthed, volcanic theology of Luther's new-creating Spirit into the ordered channels of "general pneumatology," only at length for this great endeavor of cultural construction to suffer deconstruction as a transcendental illusion. Only seen in this light can theology today learn what is of value in both thinkers, and set that free from the deformations that led conflicted Lutheranism, *evangelische Durchbruch* and all, to its own *Aufhebung* in Kant. Only in this way will the intriguing but fatally flawed attempt of Leibniz once more to rescue the Melanchthonian tradition from the twin specters of Hobbes on the right and Spinoza on the left by resort to Luther's *De servo arbitrio* appear in its true form (as we will study in the final chapter of this book) seeking a path that should but could not have been taken.

In fact, the best scholarship of recent years has done much to relocate Luther's own theology in the same swirling currents of Renaissance letters in which Melanchthon, or for that matter Erasmus, swam: the *via moderna* of nominalist logic,[141] the Augustinian revival,[142] and the new rhetorical investigations of ancient letters in the *studia humanitatis*.[143] Moreover, we can now in part situate the disjunctive form of Luther's embattled theology — the dangerous resort to a nonnegotiable rhetorical dualism of the Spirit and the devil — in the apocalyptic turn he took upon the trauma of his excommunication. Luther's too ready resort to demonization of opponents, invoking the Spirit as ground of his own prophetic possession of revealed truth, is both a lamentable feature of Luther's historical deposit and in principle separable from his central convictions about trinitarian advent and joyful exchange, which were well formed before his excommunication. Even a certain "demonology" can be rescued from these ruins, as I have argued elsewhere.[144] In any event, Melanchthon was more than justified in breaking with Luther in this connection.

So the question may now be formulated: Does his break with Luther's apocalyptic posturing mean, as received opinion has it, that "Melanchthon has decisively introduced the development to the later Rationalism and to the philosophy of the Enlightenment . . . in that he sought to set out a synthesis between protestant theology with the tradition of philosophy and philosophical theology. Insofar as human nature is born with a natural consciousness of God, natural knowledge expands into a rational theology which progressively rationalizes the theology of revelation, in fact puts into question and consequently abandons the primacy of faith." So asks Günther Frank, the preeminent specialist on our topic.[145] And so it would seem, as the question may imply, if all roads lead to Kant. Frank at once puts the Kantian question to Melanchthon: How can a finite subject know an infinite God? "How must the human mind be constituted that, in spite of its own finitude it is able to press forward to knowledge of reality, above all of the infinite God?"[146] Melanchthon, as we have seen, answered with the doctrine borrowed from revealed theology of human creation in the image of God: "because man is the creature of God he is also in some way capable of knowledge of God."[147] The issue is whether this *theological* vindication of reason can finally be shown to be cut from the same cloth as the Augustinian-Lutheran critique of reason. That is the state of the question for us today.

Presumably it could be. Recall that according to Luther's critique of metaphysical divinity, fallen humanity wants to be God and does not want God to be God. It thinks of God as the good it wants to be (or, in Melanchthon's formulation: it invokes as god "a projection of their own false thoughts").[148] It recasts God according to the varying images corresponding to its own projected desires and then sets its god to war with others. Or conversely, appalled at the confusion and warfare of the gods, it apprehends God in learned ignorance as the Unknowable Beyond, the incalculable Sublime, the inscrutable Refusal of idolatrous appropriation, the apophatic *deus absconditus*. Just so, this unknowable *Deus-an-sich* ("But above God not worshipped and not preached, that is, God as He is in His own nature and Majesty, nothing can be exalted, but all things are under His powerful hand")[149] does not remain at a safe distance. This construction of God as hidden fast becomes the human enemy, confounding the human mind and limiting the human will. It happens with this reflection, as we saw above in Forde: ludicrous gods we control, but the true God is the Other who defies all grasping.[150] Indeed, natural reason reaches this far, according to Luther. Thinking perhaps of his beloved Cicero, Luther had written that "natural reason itself, which finds this [divine] necessity offensive and labors so hard to get rid of it, would be forced by the convictions of its own judgment to concede this much, even if no Scripture existed. For all men find the following convictions written in their hearts, and acknowledge and acquiesce in them (albeit unwillingly) when they hear them propounded: *first,* that God is omnipotent, not only in power but also in action (as I said) and would be a ludicrous God were it not so; *second,* that He knows and foreknows all things, and can neither err nor be deceived."[151] The latter proposition reflects natural knowledge of divine wisdom. It is written on the heart that God, if there is a Creator of this creation, is *omnipotent and omniscient.* What remains doubtful for natural reason, in the light of bitter experience, is divine goodness and love. Melanchthon, as we saw, followed Luther precisely in this line of thought.

Taking up the rhetorical objection placed on the lips of opponents in Romans 9:19, Luther writes against Erasmus: "This is what Reason cannot receive or bear. This is what offended so many men of outstanding ability, men who have won acceptance down so many ages. At this point, they demand that God should act according to man's idea of right, and do what seems proper to themselves — or else that He should cease to be God. 'The secrets of His majesty,' they say, 'shall not profit Him; let Him render a reason why He is God, or why He wills and does that which has no appearance of justice in it." It would seem here that the way to Leibniz's universal jurisprudence through Melanchthon's common notion of justice is totally blocked, that for Luther God is right because God says so, not because what God wills is right. The inference would follow, were Luther a Cartesian or a Kantian. But in fact Luther is perspectivalist. He continues in the cited passage: "flesh does not deign to give God glory to the extent of believing Him to be just and good when He speaks and acts above and beyond the definitions of Justinian's Code, or the fifth book of Aristotle's Ethics."[152] Notice that according to the analysis, God's goodness must be believed, unlike God's power or wisdom, which natural reason acknowledges under pain of rendering its conception of God ludicrous. The critical turning point in Luther's difficult argument, ever hovering on the verge of dualism, is then *perspectivalist:* "Many things seem, and are, very good to God which seem, and are, very bad to us"[153] as alienated sinners. It is the same point Luther had made seven years before in presenting the *theologia crucis* at the disputation in Heidelberg: "Thus, afflictions, sorrows, errors, hell, and all God's best works are in the world's eyes very bad, and damnable. What is better than Christ and the gospel? But what is there that the world abominates more? How things that are bad for us are good in the sight of God is known only to God and *to those who see with God's eyes,* that is, who have the Spirit."[154] *Perspectivalism* can then include both Luther's critique and his vindication of reason: the fallen humanity "thinks crookedly and speaks crookedly even about its own crookedness" (Barth); in renewed humanity the mind enlightened by the Spirit comes to see from God's perspective (as befits those who have become the children of God), namely, that God is both just and good in spiritually crucifying the egocentric mind of Adam by repentance and raising from its ashes a new, eccentric mind in Christ. To see this work as evil is to see it from the perspective of the old Adam. Thinking changes along with seeing.

Is this also Melanchthon's vindication of reason? Frank titles his work *Die* Theologische *Philosophie.* In it he shows that Melanchthon shares in and presupposes Luther's critique of reason. Broadly speaking, this is the widespread revival in humanist circles of *the Augustinian critique* of reason in the light of Pauline soteriology.[155] But Wengert's considered judgment, by contrast, trends against Frank's case for a common Augustinianism.

> [H]ere Melanchthon and Luther differed most markedly. Luther's critique of reason rested finally in a theology of the cross that discovered the scandal of the God who speaks in words, or the scandal of the Word in the manger, playing on Mary's lap, or hanging on the cross. That scandal, asserted to the hilt, became the very thing that drove a person from reason and its claims of freedom to faith. . . . Melanchthon also rejected reason in favor of the Word of God, accommodated to human weakness and therefore accessible to human beings through the use of reasonable tools.

However, he subsumed the scandal of the cross under the Holy Spirit's work of sanctification. The cross was for him the sign of the Christian experiencing the death of the old creature and the birth of faith. But that scandal never became the means to criticize methods of scriptural interpretation themselves. . . . Law and gospel became answers to the question *quid effectus,* after one had already ascertained the answer to *quid sit.*[156]

Wengert has Luther right here, provided that the asserting of the gospel's *rhetorical* paradoxes is not tacitly taken as Tertullian's assertion of absurdity, accompanied by an all-too-modern existential leap of fideism. The *leap* of faith is, for Luther, the Holy Spirit's snatching of mind out of its antecedent self-centeredness to see anew in the light of the divine perspective, as we have just seen. The leap is the transition to an eccentric existence.

Yet Wengert's analysis of Melanchthon's vindication of reason seems strained on two counts. First, the doctrine of the image of God falls strangely out of the picture here, when it provides the fulcrum by which the human mind may think of its Creator as powerful, wise, and good, and so recognize God as God when He comes to speak in revelation. As we have just seen, Luther holds a similar position, *expressly* in the most difficult text, in its most *difficult* argument (i.e., *De servo arbitrio*). Second, the weakness of Luther's performative view of language, if taken apart from, or at the expense of, painstaking logical clarity, methodical elaboration, and cognitive reference (all of which Luther too is capable and to which he recurs when not tempted to demonize), becomes painfully evident in the old man's increasingly frenetic resort to verbal violence, eschewing rational argumentation for apocalyptic utterance. Asserting the paradoxes of the gospel — like the parables of Jesus — is meant in any case to illuminate, not obfuscate (except in the case of hardening Pharaoh's wicked heart; cf. Mark 4:11-12). Wengert's account tends too much to paint Luther as Kierkegaard ("Truth as subjectivity," an "objective uncertainty held with infinite passion," etc.); correspondingly Wengert rebukes Melanchthon, albeit gently, for placing faith's confidence in the clear doctrinal formulations that could be gained by rigorous method, logically patient procedure, and admirable refusal of invective. In another place Wengert describes the difference between the two reformers as one of "worldview": Melanchthon's creation-faith orientation to cosmology in contrast[157] to Luther's life-and-death struggle against the devil.

In point of historical fact, it was the deeply troubling experience of Luther's divisive bombast that drove Melanchthon toward the 1528 vindication of philosophy, all the while presupposing the earlier critique of reason. Indeed, it was the responsibility for rebuilding a tottering Christian civilization that directed Melanchthon less and less to the Holy Spirit's illumination in redemption and more and more to the universal donation of the image of God in creation. In Melanchthon's vindication of reason, philosophy and theology work together for the construction of a reformed Christian civilization. In this symbiosis, theology in turn benefits from philosophy by borrowing "methodology, which seeks and reveals truth in an organized and correct way," i.e., as dogmatics.[158] Luther, in principle, does not differ.[159] Leibniz, a century and a half later, explicitly picks up this approach to theological method.[160]

In any event, as modest as the scope of "useful" philosophy appears, Melanchthon's confidence in a renewed human reason is breathtaking. Where does such confidence in the power of reason to illuminate and direct the world come from? We can in fact trace the preestablished harmony of Leibniz back to Melanchthon. Following Augustine, as already alluded, reason for Melanchthon originates in the creative mind of God. It is originally the Divine Wisdom that knows intuitively what the originated human mind discovers in finite fashion by experience and reflection. The astonishing capacity of human reason to know the world consequently is based upon the supposition of an "original coherence," in Frank's words, of mind and being in God, what Leibniz will later develop into the doctrine of the "preestablished harmony." By their origin in God, speech and thought, letter and spirit, rhetoric and dialectic cohere, reflecting in creation the eternal generation and spiration of the Word and the Spirit respectively. Temporary formations of matter, the passing parade of phenomenal reality, in turn only exists in, i.e., takes form as, and so becomes accessible in language, through this "original coherence." "Thought refers in an original sense not to things but to language. . . . Knowledge occurs in the space of language, and to that extent the capacity of thought for language is the presupposition of arriving at things themselves," Frank writes. We do not have here the Cartesian picture of reason as of a thinking thing ascertaining itself and then mastering extending things by mapping them in space-time coordinates. The world philosophy is assigned to know by its rational method is not dead bits of hard stuff randomly extended in space, waiting to be mapped, but exists in dynamic temporal-spatial sequences as creation spoken by God: "not as a world of things *(res)*, but rather as world understood as things coming to language."[161] In this matrix human being too comes to language by this same Word of God calling to partnership in God's dominion: creation in the image of God, not an *analogia entis* but an *analogia mentis*.[162]

To many contemporaries of empiricist and nominalist cast, Melanch-thon's theonomous confidence in reason's dominion will seem like idealism; historically for Christian Platonism, however, the creative, active God really *thinks-and-wills* things into existence by His Word and Spirit. "Idealism," so-called, is the empty shell that remains in place of the mind of the Creator God, when in the minds of modernity God has ceased to be living and real, Leibniz's *intelligentia extra mundam*. This is the generative Divine Mind that distinguishes things by words in order to relate them in thought as a cosmos or universe that hangs meaningfully together in a narrative sequence stretching from Genesis to Revelation. Or to say the same, idealism emerges after Kant as the vestige of this tradition of Christian Platonism, general pneumatology now reduced to lifeless regulative ideas. On the other hand, the question that became important for the followers of Melanchthon up to Leibniz — given the dysfunction of the warring churches, the authoritarian and obscurantist turn of confessionalized dogmatics in rival assertions of miracles of inspiration authorizing their mutual anathemas, and thus the gradual disillusionment in their own ranks with Protestantism as Reformation[163] — was whether natural reason could also bring God to lan-guage beyond these confessionalistic partisanships in a natural theology of the perfect being in the suitable form of doxology. Given Christendom's meltdown, could God be yet thought as something worthy of infinite adora-tion? That desire for true worship above the warring churches — not proof of the existence of a cosmic architect — is what first motivated the emer-gence of "natural theology" in this Melanchthonian tradition. Leibniz as a child of his age shared in this justified desire of his contemporaries, though he never abandoned his Melanchthonian conviction about the ultimate har-mony of reason and faith, natural and revealed theology. This latter convic-tion motivated him to criticize the Socinian-Unitarian theology of deists, and to seek vestiges of the Trinity in natural theology. But the ambivalence in Leibniz here is evident to all who study him.

In addition to the canard about idealism, there is yet another legend that needs to be put to bed in the tale of general pneumatology here being told. John Hedley Brooke has rightly written: "Debates that have so often been in-terpreted in terms of the 'conflict between science and religion' turn out, on closer inspection, to be debates in which rival claims are made for the 'cor-rect' meaning to be attached to scientific theories."[164] We do not see that what is really in dispute are rival theologies, attached rightly or not to rival scientific theories. We fail to see this because Kantianism has taught us to dismiss as meaningless the antinomies and paralogisms of pure reason.

Thus Brooke notes that to the middle of the nineteenth century, "it was commonly asserted that because the sciences aimed at achieving consensus on an objective description of the world, they had no relevance to the subjective questions of personal and corporate morality."[165] Such Kantian dualism received new life in the Anglo-American world with G. E. Moore's doctrine of the naturalistic fallacy, intending as it did to defang the evident threat of social Darwinism: "that from scientific statements that purport to say what *is* the case, no conclusion can be drawn about what *ought* to be the case, without smuggling in external value judgments."[166] This modern Kantian tradition of dualism between the realms of freedom and necessity brought cultural peace: "it protected the freedom of scientists to pursue their research without fear of external controls. It was also attractive to moralists and theologians in that it gave them a similar professional autonomy."[167] But "had they been more familiar with the history of science, the proponents of that neat division of labor might have found it difficult to sustain. As soon as one asks why science should be pursued at all, questions of value immediately arise."[168] Brooke calls Francis Bacon to the witness stand to testify to his religious motives: "empirical study of nature was to be valued because it promised an increase in the power of the state, the relief of human suffering, and the restoration of the dominion over nature that humanity had lost at the Fall."[169] With Kusukawa, we have seen precisely the same theological motive at work in Melanchthon. Science as vocation presupposes tacit knowledge of the common good, and is in any case a human practice like all the others, subject to historical criticism and answerable morally, aesthetically (and dare we say, theologically?). But we have lived for two hundred years in a culture that has bought some kind of internal peace by refusing critical assessment of the good in the name of, and for the sake of, cultural peace so defined. In fact, we have handed over to mere libertinism an unjustified pursuit of individualistic happiness that, like a metastasizing cancer, despoils the ecology of things.

Brooke's important study shows that science was not so conceived at the beginning of our era. So also Loemker: "a more general question, however, concerns the wider cultural patterns which permitted the new sciences to develop in relative harmony and agreement . . . with the religious interest in reform and reunion, and with the humanistic ideal of freedom and creativity in the arts." Loemker points to Lutheran Andreas Osiander's 1543 introduction to Copernicus, which defused the apparent conflict between religion and science with a deft move in perspectivalism: "It is not necessary that these hypotheses be true, or indeed, that they be even probable; this

alone will suffice, that they show the calculation to be congruent with observations." Loemker astutely comments: "To use more recent terminology, the
phenomenal and functional truth of science, and the existential truth of salvation, far from entering into conflict or nullifying each other, became mutually irrelevant. . . . What remained for ensuing centuries as a satisfactory
adjustment of two orders of knowledge and truth, the phenomenal and either the noumenal or the more inwardly personal, has become in the twentieth century a radical divorce between the intellectual perspectives of two opposing cultural ideals — the scientific-technological and the existential-
personal." And *that* is deeply problematic. In this light, *the path not taken,* in
Loemker's telling, was the broader revival of Christian Platonism of which
Renaissance and Reformation were both part: what we have described in this
chapter as the "general pneumatology" of Melanchthon's tradition. This
provided the conceptual framework for a new cultural unity in the conviction that "revelation, reason, and experience all converge upon the same
truth . . . which closed the old Ockhamist breaches between knowledge and
belief and provided a common bond, wider than each special interest, for
the kingdom of grace, the Republic of Letters, and the sodality of those who
searched out the secrets of nature."[170] Before this aspiration collapsed under
Kant's Critiques, God was not known acosmically, as alternative to the creation, but cosmically: "God, the *opifex mundi,* was once again seen as Plato
saw him, the potter at the wheel. . . . Man, the artist and poet, created in
God's image and reflecting his glory, became less the servant of faith and
more the craftsman, each man a microcosm giving forth its unique reflection of the macrocosm."[171] Equal credit, or more, might be given to Genesis
1:26-28. In any case, this is the path of general pneumatology refused since
Kant.

Six PROTOLOGICAL DILEMMAS

Two Versions of Leibniz's Failure

What's Really Wrong with Leibniz's Theodicy

From the hour of its first publication, Leibniz's *Theodicy* has puzzled readers.[1] In preceding chapters I have built a case for taking *Theodicy* as seriously intended, when set against its background in Melanchthonian theological philosophy; moreover, I take Leibniz's final, furious correspondence with Samuel Clarke as evidence for the sincerity, indeed the passion, with which Leibniz held to the conviction expressed in *Theodicy:* philosophical theology should enable recognition of the living God Christians know in the Trinity and should not in any form incline toward deism's "God as the soul of the world." Thus Leibniz affirms particular providence — always the touchstone separating Augustinians from Stoics. Wanting not to "deny, as the Socinians do, God's foreknowledge of future contingents and his providence which regulates and governs every particular thing," Leibniz argued against Clarke that "when a wise being, as especially God who has supreme wisdom, chooses what is best, he is not the less free on that account; on the contrary it is the most perfect liberty not to be hindered from acting in the best manner. . . . Without this, the choice would be a blind chance."[2] The living God is the God who does not have to create, but, in deciding to create, is morally bound by

---

The title of this chapter, "Protological Dilemmas," comes from Patrick Riley, *Leibniz' Universal Jurisprudence: Justice as the Charity of the Wise* (Cambridge: Harvard University Press, 1996), 87.

His own goodness to create the best possible world, a good that creatures created in His image can anticipate and recognize. Such "bondage" to the good is true liberty, not only for us but also and first for God. It is indeed divine liberty, the liberty intrinsic to God's perfect life, the liberty of love by which the Spirit sets the Father free for the Son and the Son for the Father (Jenson). What this "best" would be is not immediately evident, however, to finite minds; the insight that God chooses the best is rational and a priori, not factual and a posteriori. Expecting this "best" on the grounds of natural theology, the creature in any case would have to learn as a matter of fact what "best" God has in mind for the world. This latter is the domain of revealed theology, sacred theology, theology as *poesis* of the Spirit (Hütter).

Vailati, however, regards as "unclear" Leibniz's defense of the contingency of God's choice as morally apt but not metaphysically necessary: being the good God that God maximally is, Vailati objects, it is hard to see that Leibniz's God could create any other world than the one supposedly best, even if God could logically have created an infinite number of worlds less good. God's own property of goodness *forces* God to choose the best possible. Thus the alleged contingency of the choice for the best evaporates, given that God is good by nature. "It is hard to see how he could maintain this position consistently without giving up the idea that the moral attributes belong to God as necessarily as the metaphysical ones."[3] Vailati's objection, however, overlooks the "radical" origination of all things, that is, the fact for Leibniz that *there could be nothing* rather than something, that is, nothing other than the eternal Trinity. In this chapter I argue *pace* Vailati on this point that the real but insufficiently spoken ground for the substantial *clarity* of Leibniz's position is that the moral self-determination of this God is revealed theology's trinitarian counsel to redeem and fulfill the creation by the costly self-involvements of the Son and Spirit. *This world is morally chosen as the best by God on account of the divine cost of the Son's Godforsaken death and the Spirit's coming to dwell in a temple made of unclean people.* It is to say that this self-involving cost to God is freely undertaken, out of surplus of love and liberty, since the Trinity had no need to gain a world, nor even less to partake in its sufferings, but only a fecund desire to grant existence and to work within created structures to reconcile and include. There *is* something rather than nothing, and *this* something rather than something else, because God at dear cost to Himself freely willed there to be wills other than God's own. That this something — for all evil and pain — is *better* than nothing at all (besides the eternal Trinity) is Leibniz's root conviction. True human freedom can hardly be indifferent to this most radical of facts, but rather arises from knowledge of it. The true freedom of an informed and passionate *Yes!* to lives other than one's own and to one's own only with all these others is at stake here.

In this final chapter we will therefore examine Leibniz's attempt to defeat the rising and soon-to-become dominant alternative account of freedom as sovereign indifference, reflecting in human miniature and in ominous aspiration the willfulness of the *deus exlex*. This attempt was made — of all things — by Leibniz's resorting throughout the *Theodicy* to Luther's *De servo arbitrio*, where Luther, anticipating the turn of Counter-Reformation polemics to philosophical skepticism to necessitate authoritarianism in theology,[4] had affirmed: "the Holy Spirit is no skeptic."[5] *In this way* Luther's difficult text bore an alternative account of the "immutable necessity of divine foreknowledge" than that advanced by the new Epicureans and Stoics, since, in spite of its ambiguity of language and even in concept, it was as forceful a statement on behalf of the revealed God's faithfulness to His own Word by His own Spirit as Christian theology has ever produced. Luther's text bore as well a corresponding doctrine of the decentered human self who can come to new life in the ecstasy of faith and love by the infusion of the Holy Spirit: divine freedom coming upon the creature as passion that then activates, faith that then works, incorporating as object with Jesus of the Father's good pleasure and so new subject with Jesus in loving obedience to the Father's will. Properly "mitigated," Leibniz rightly sensed that Luther's theodicy of faith, stemming from Romans 8, with its concluding distinctions between the lights of nature, grace, and glory, tacitly embraced a salutary version of epistemic perspectivalism. Properly developing Luther's seminal ideas as "natural theology" (the light of nature) working in partnership with revealed theology ("the light of grace") in anticipation of the doxological "light of glory," Leibniz tried to meet the challenge of the new assertions of human autonomy against the redemptive claim of the triune God that in fact reflected, as he thought, an alternative, increasingly monstrous conception of divinity, already visible in Descartes: the supremely powerful one who could as easily deceive us.[6] This forms a perfect contrast with Luther's supremely powerful one who cannot deceive us but with "immutable necessity" remains faithful to His promise, inclusive of future contingents, i.e., in such particular providence that the martyr fallen into the hands of the persecutor knows with full conviction that she has not fallen out of the hands of God: "take they goods, fame, child and spouse, they yet have nothing won. The kingdom ours remaineth."

Roman Catholic scholars have sometimes criticized Luther's views as "theopanism,"[7] meaning that the human agent in his theology evaporates into the mere patient of the all-working God. Yet, as any student of Augustine recalls, to say that God works all in all is not the same as saying that God alone works all things. Overlooking this distinction, actually very clearly drawn in Luther,[8] the charge paints with such a broad brush that it draws a line in the form of a simple inversion from Luther's theopanism to Spinoza's pantheism, when, *ex hypothesi,* the real culprit here may be Zwingli.[9] This kind of analysis assumes in any case the validity of a traditional dialectic between the transcendence and immanence of God in relation to a static cosmos, when surely the point of Luther's attack on the tradition was revision of the metaphysics of mere persistence in being, with respect to both divine and human agency. The finite is capable of the infinite in the form of eccentric anticipation because the reign of God is imminent (not immanent) in the Spirit's works of liberation. In any event, the problem so indicated cannot be solved on the level of anthropology, rule theory, or even compatibilist clarifications as such. I will rather assign Leibniz's real failure in his important attempt to retrieve and develop these insights of Luther just sketched to his failure to achieve *theology.*

Theology is what is decisive. Whether and how we might be freed and free artisans at work in the world depends on whether God is free, and, as it were, self-liberating, self-surpassing, self-overcoming. Thus in Version One below of Leibniz's failure I show that if the level of analysis is restricted to anthropological reflection, Leibniz indeed becomes vulnerable to the venerable charge of crypto-Spinozism. But the cost of this interpretation is to take Leibniz in bad faith, in the teeth of his own express statements of purpose. In Version Two of the failure, in contrast, I show that if Leibniz had been able to argue explicitly on the basis of propositions he borrowed from revealed theology, he could have met the challenge of the new Stoics and Epicureans as he actually intended, though not in the manner he desired. In other words, his *Theodicy* could have succeeded if, but only if, it had been argued expressly as revealed, trinitarian theology.

There is theological payoff for this latter analysis. Luther's notorious notion of a double will in God has blocked the way forward, and on one reading, it certainly seems that Luther simply holds to the entire scheme of absolutist views in *De servo arbitrio:* "God owes us nothing."[10] God alone has "free will"[11] and is as such bound by no law other than His own will.[12] Compatibilism is impossible.[13] Melanchthon's eventual solution of a little bit of "free will" is repudiated.[14] All this being said, yet in the same book Luther writes: "God does not work in us without us."[15] As I have suggested, this indicates how Luther's stance is in fact perspectivalist, in accord with the biblical dictum "as you believe, so you have."[16] In the eyes of hardened Pharaoh the slave master, God the Liberator of Hebrew slaves does indeed appear otherwise than as the merciful friend of the poor in body and in spirit; he appears as the slayer of the firstborn, tossing horse and rider into the sea. The God of love here appears in the form of wrath, as enemy of the enemies of love, at the same time champion of their victims, the holy Liberator of the oppressed.

Leibniz, to be sure, does not trumpet such views. But he holds them. As previously shown, when he justifies the permission of sin as harmonious with God's surpassing purposes of good for the cosmos as a whole, it is in tandem with the consequent punishment of sin. Presumably sin left unpunished would represent for Leibniz the real absurdity of a God neither good nor powerful to govern the creation. What inhibits Leibniz's view is the difficulty that a critical retrieval of Luther's stance would have entailed as robust a doctrine of sin as of the Holy Spirit of Jesus and His Father, author of divine faith forming the church as the city of God in the midst of the city of man. We have seen what difficulty the concept of actual evil, i.e., willing, knowing refusal of true good, causes Leibniz. At the same time, Leibniz knows about divine faith, that gift of the Holy Spirit. He expressly acknowledges it on more than one occasion. Yet, of this *particularity,* the *general* pneumatology proved in the end incapable (granted, the reactionary forms in which the scandal of particularity was asserted in his day only made matters worse). R. M. Adams is certainly correct when — over against reactionary particularism — he calls it a "powerful theological argument" in favor of general pneumatology that "if God is the creator and governor of the whole world and all its peoples, as Christians have always held, then all peoples must stand in various real relations to God, whether they know it or not."[17] True enough, but just so, if by "real relations" we mean God's own relating to His creatures, these may not be *ipso facto* the relations as perceived by the creatures. That indicates *conflict* between the perspectives of Creator and creatures. In the light of nature, the real relation in which God regards His creature — namely, as beloved in Christ — does not correspond with the egocentric creature's perception of God as omnipotent, omniscient power(s) that may deceive.

The Holy Spirit is God heard in the creature altering its perception by incorporation into the real trinitarian relations of God speaking and God spoken. Yet the Holy Spirit finally disappears in Leibniz as in Lutheranism in general, in favor of conventional, human-all-too-human agency. In Version

Two, as we shall see, far from the ballyhooed charge of crypto-Spinozism, Leibniz remained faithful to the Melanchthonian trajectory at the very point at which it most diverged from Luther, so that in the end he might better be charged with crypto-Molinism. To achieve this better criticism of Leibniz, however, we must first sort through the popular, but from the theological perspective confused, perception of what is problematic in the *Theodicy* according to Version One.

Version One: Leibniz as Platonic Rationalist

According to the general pneumatology, as we have seen, the human mind is capable of rational faith, since it cannot but catch reflections of the divine perfection that on reflection lead the mind to the thought of God. Leibniz, for example, took particular interest in the controversial reports coming back to Europe from Jesuit missionaries in China. Some were claiming that the Chinese had no word for "God," and had been "atheists" from time immemorial; Leibniz saw in this "atheistic" interpretation of Chinese traditions the intellectual influence of his rivals in Europe, the new Stoics and Epicureans. What matters is not the name, God, but the concept involved, he argued. The "Chinese axiom says that all things are one."[18] Rightly understood, this "means that God is everything by eminence (eminenter), as the perfections of effects are in their cause, and not formally (formaliter), as if God was the mass of all things . . . all things are one by emanation (emanenter), because they are the immediate effects of Him; that is, He attends to them intimately and fully, and expresses Himself in the perfections which He communicates to them according to their degrees of receptivity."[19] The concept of God is that of the eminent sum of the perfections effected in the creation and so knowable by created minds, the causal harmony of power, wisdom, and love. People apprehend this living divine unity through its effects in many and various ways, erroneously emphasizing one or two of the triad of perfections at the expense of the other(s), but in all there is a definite, if confused, sense of divinity that "corresponds somewhat to the Trinity of the Christians or of the Platonists."[20]

R. M. Adams has identified a number of interesting features of Leibniz's pneumatological theory of the religions, as evidenced in his interest in China. First, it is normative and theological, not a naturalistic attempt to explain religion by reducing it to nonreligious factors. Second, religions aim at salvation in the sense of attaining noninstrumental love for God, the sum of the perfections. Third, the positive doctrines of religions are not strictly or philosophically demonstrable but are at best probable and to be assessed pragmatically for their ability to conduce to such love for God as constitutes salvation in the previously mentioned sense. Fourth, the religions form organized, deliberate communities, natural societies aimed at eternal happiness. Fifth, the future prospect of religions lies in their harmonization through the hermeneutical activity of interpretation, under Leibniz's Christian assumption, previously cited, that "all peoples must stand in various real relations to God, whether they know it or not."[21] Thus, Leibniz is not a vulgar pluralist (Adams mentions Hick) who wants "an abiding plurality of religious traditions representing diverse paths to a more or less common religious goal," but a critical pluralist who aspires to a "single religious community for all humanity," even if the prospect is eschatological. Natural theology (Adams calls this "metaphysical interpretation") takes an approach to the religions, which is thus critical, normative, and theological. Leibniz thinks "of religious essentials as principles that can be abstracted from their original cultural context and shared by all peoples even if the peoples retain a good deal of cultural diversity."[22] Yet, manifestly, the entire exercise is an extension from the "original cultural context" of Christian faith. It is revealed theology that seeks its echo in the world outside. Unsurprisingly, scholars therefore dispute how successful Leibniz in fact was in interpreting the Chinese.

Yet his attention to the controversy is indicative of the special difficulty to which I want now to turn: the existence of actual evil as willful, knowing refusal of true good, which, as we have seen, constitutes a surd for *general* pneumatology or *universal* jurisprudence. According to Leibniz, the created mind is such that, even if it cannot find God on its own, it can nonetheless recognize God as God should God appear to it, and in this sense can look for the coming of God. This expectation is possible because the human mind is not God, yet is somehow like God and thus knows what to expect. The question that then arises is why humans do *not* universally seek after God "and perhaps reach out and find him, though he is not far from each one of us" (Acts 17:27). Or, why does the search for God, even when "claiming to be wise," so often instead exchange "the glory of the immortal God for images made to look like mortal man and birds and animals and reptiles" (Rom. 1:23)? Why do some deny the putatively universal search altogether, and most others, as it appears, misapprehend its object and goal? In such a world as the general pneumatology conceives, these failures are *surds* that must somehow be refuted as mistakes or illusions or reconciled in theodicy as necessary evils permitted for the sake of greater good. The one thing, it seems, that these failures cannot be in any strong sense is *actual*.

What is this peculiar human nature such that it can recognize — or, as appears in actual evil, withhold recognition of — God as God? How does Leibniz account for the evidence contradictory to his most basic intuitions represented by actual evil? Is actual evil passing appearance that turns out to be something different in reality? If it is what it seems to be, what pathology can human nature be on the grounds of general pneumatology that it refuses its true Good and instead willfully and knowingly seeks what is evil?

In the first place, let it be unmistakably clear: for Leibniz the human mind is something real, a "substance" or "substantial form" in classical terms. Like Pico and Melanchthon, Leibniz too argued for the finite substantiality of each individual rational soul as patient of its own pains and agent of its own biographical acts of choice constituting its own personal identity in time. It is not surprising, given the tradition in which we are locating him, to find him articulating this doctrine of the human person expressly on the basis of Genesis 1:26-28. He argues against all versions of Cartesianism, "which maintains the inertness and deadness of things," that dualism deprives "God's commands of all lasting effect and efficiency in the future" issuing in genuine agents. At the same time, they "regard it as nothing to demand of him always new arrangements," as occasionalists or Newtonians in varying ways imagined God constantly intervening ad hoc to coordinate spectator minds with dead matter. But the biblical *fiat* of Genesis 1, Leibniz pleads, "leaves behind something permanent, namely, the persisting thing itself, so the word *benedictio* leaves behind it something in things no less wonderful — a fruitfulness or an impulse to produce their actions and to operate, from which activity follows if nothing interferes."[23] If it were not so that God creates substantial, though finite, images of Himself consisting in each one's own perception and appetite and so existing as patients/agents in the abiding capacity for choice in action, "it would follow that no created substance, no identical soul, would be permanent, and hence that nothing would be conserved by God, but everything would reduce to certain evanescent and flowing modifications or phantasms, so to speak, of the one divine permanent substance."[24] Spinoza is the end result, since Cartesian dualism is for many reasons unstable and not sustainable.

Whether against Descartes's dualism, Malebranche's occasionalism, Newtonian interventionism, or Spinoza's monism, general pneumatology draws upon the *imago dei* theology to argue the enduring reality of finite human patiency-agency. All other beings concur with God's will physically or mechanically as phenomena that come and go. *Qua* body, so does the human being. Yet *qua* rational soul united with its own body, the human mind concurs with God freely by its own choice in its own action (in tandem with its own body and sense perceptions according to the preestablished harmony). Contingent in its origin, the mind is immortal in its destiny; the created image of God can be disgraced by sinful choices and justly punished but never destroyed, unless by the miracle of an act of annihilation undoing the act of its creation. That is how "real" the human patient/agent is in Leibniz's pneumatological thought. The baffling thing consequently is how the substantial rational soul comes to choose what is in fact evil, and thus acts in a fashion that leads, not to its absolute destruction, but to spiritual death to God, the true Good. How is such actual evil possible, when all by nature seek the good?

Before Leibniz can answer that question for us (according to Version One), we must see, in the second place, that the special nature that by nature can recognize God is intended by God for the vocation of rational worship (cf. Rom. 12:1-2). God as "cause of causes" is the true good of the human mind. Among the cosmic multitudes of monads, the intelligent human mind, purposive and organized like the rest of nature in union with its own body, is the one that uniquely inquires into the reason for things, all things and things as a whole. To be human is to understand the causes of things. After natural science has spoken on the level of physical inquiry, Leibniz argues, "we must move up to the *metaphysical*, by making use of the *great principle*, not very widely used, which says . . . *nothing comes about without a sufficient reason.* . . . Given that principle, the first question we are entitled to ask will be *why is there something rather than nothing?*" And, "*why [do] they have to exist as they are, and not otherwise*[?]"[25] In the grip of this special, uniquely human wonderment, the mind instantiates intelligently the universal desire for the good that motivates all acts of being. The human form of the good is to understand, and to understand maximally is to know God as cause of causes in the doxological act of rational worship. This is to adore God as the mind's own Creator and so attain a fitting kind of communion with God.

Thus in its own self-reflection the mind recognizes the universal passion in all creatures, the desire for completion in beings that are not complete in themselves. The deer pants for the water brooks and the unquiet heart of the human person finds rest only in God. Leibniz holds that all acts of being are motivated by such desire, appetite, i.e., the root pathos of ontological imperfection longing in all things for the union of charity with the fullness of being, the desire for life abundant.[26] The human mind *understands* this desire, and this self-understanding in turn leads the human mind to *think the reality*[27] of the divine completeness as the truth of its fragmentary encounters in creaturely experience with power, wisdom, and love. Thus the mind, which is itself a "trinity" of *posse, scire, velle*,[28] arrives at a rational faith in the sufficient reason for its experienced intimations of wholeness. It conceives the sum, source, and harmony of those perfections that the human mind really, though indistinctly and fragmentarily, experiences in the world and for which it yearns in and beyond all finite satisfactions.

In the third place, however, this very desire for God carries one astray if — in the destructive possibility unique to rational beings — one wants to be as God rather than to know and love God as God. Confused by the welter of finite representations, and unwilling to trust divine goodness as wise and able to accomplish what is fitting, the mind comes to acknowledge only wisdom and/or power as God to be imitated, in fact seized, appropriated for itself. The desire for God converts to an idolatrous self-appropriation of God that manifests as greed *(concupiscientia)* wreaking havoc on the ecology of things and dooming all in its sway to the spiritual death of endless frustration (Rom. 8:20). This is how Augustine thinks, and Luther and Melanchthon after him. Leibniz does not deny this train of thought as an account of what makes sin sinful — recall his account of false self-love; yet, at least in Version One of what's wrong with the *Theodicy*, he does not actually find the *origin* of moral evil in this primordial act of Adam's (or the devil's) *superbia*. On this reading, willfully to refuse true Good as Adam purportedly did seems so fundamentally irrational a choice that it must be ascribed to error, not malice, to confused perception rather than to knowing mistrust. In a creation where nothing can happen without a reason, Leibniz writes, "sins arise from the aboriginal limitation of things," i.e., sins are an intrinsic possibility (not necessity) for any conceivable finite mind. Even angels have fallen. Yet Leibnizian sins seem more like errors than sins. Willfully choosing oneself as God in place of God seems so monstrous a self-deception that, for this more rationalist Leibniz, humans do not so much choose sin and "God does not so much decree sins as he does the admission to existence of certain possible substances whose complete concept already involves the possibility of their freely sinning, and even connotes the whole series of events in which they figure as links . . . sin is permitted only because it cannot be absolutely rejected if certain positive decrees are maintained."[29] God then foresees the possibility of such sinful substances in actuality as the cost of creation, taken as the whole series from Genesis to Revelation. God proceeds like the king in

Jesus' parable, one who has first wisely counted the cost before going to war and is determined to pay the price. "Nothing else would be congruent with wisdom than to compensate sin by a greater good that could not otherwise be obtained."[30]

In this best of all possible worlds, such foreseen, permitted, and yet freely willed "sins are evil, not absolutely, not to the world, not to God — for otherwise he would not permit them — but only to the sinner." In a world populated with wills that are *both* really other than God *and* where at least some of these are also in moral conflict with God's will, "God hates sins . . . in the sense that he punishes them."[31] The good God, the God of love who wills the best, is the God who is against what is against love, against what is actually evil, even though it is the evil He has permitted into the best of all possible worlds. Even for this more rationalistic Leibniz, the divine wrath of love in judgment on sin involves God by penal satisfaction in the person of the incarnate Son by whose death and resurrection the greatest good for the greatest number is gained, since pardon is thereby obtained for all who come to the repentance of true love of God for God's sake, while by the same tree of the cross condemnation is sealed for those who persist in actual evil. Overall, even in Version One, the divine permission of actual moral evil is costly and its remedy self-involving, if the rich, complex, consequent good of the redeemed and fulfilled creation, better than empty nonbeing "beyond good and evil," is to be gained. In this comprehensive sense, "sins are good, that is, harmonious, *taken along with their punishment or expiation*."[32]

What is problematic about the solution to the problem of evil in the best of worlds by this more rationalist Leibniz of Version One is *not* the notion of atonement as achieving the greater good by divine and holy suffering on behalf of the sinful and perishing creature. In his own day and age, Leibniz was virtually alone among those thinking they were orthodox to be willing vastly to extend the scope of Christ's atonement "so that the number of those wicked enough to be damned would be very small";[33] as in the case of the Chinese mentioned above, he employed the then commonplace distinction between the invisible and visible church to think of future glory populated with the righteous of every nation, kindred, and tribe, thus far beyond the walls of Europe's disgraced, warring churches. In this basic intention, as we argued in chapter 2, Leibniz, with Barth, who followed him in this regard, is correct. The divinity of Christ entails universal atonement; limited atonement demotes Christ to the status of the tribal deity of Christians.

What *is* problematic in this account and yet *critical* to it, according to Version One, is rather the intentional sacrifice of certain fore-doomed individuals (howsoever small in number) that seems to be entailed: from eternity God must reprobate Judas and Pilate, or more precisely, release these reprobates into existence in order thereby to gain Christ's victory for the rest. The famous early (1683) account from the *Discourse on Metaphysics* discussed the less volatile secular example of Julius Caesar, arguing that the evil of his "future dictatorship is grounded in his notion or nature, that there is a reason why he crossed the Rubicon rather than stopped at it and . . . that it was reasonable, and consequently certain, that this should happen."[34] It is morally certain, but not a strict physical necessity, that the agent Caesar should act in accordance with his essence or notion (which is God's full and complete thought of this possible character) as the one whose personal ambition could overthrow the rule of law under the conceit of saving the Republic in crisis. Yet in the actual series of temporal events, Caesar's fated and fateful act is free because halting his armies at the Rubicon was a noncontradictory or logical possibility for Caesar. He had a choice to pursue his ambition in lawful ways or not to act at all on the apparent good of saving the Republic by seizing power. Yet, as his choices exist in the thick web of sequences that God has first decreed, it is morally certain that Caesar, like all moral agents, "will always do (although freely) that which appears to be best,"[35] given his own essence and the possibilities providence offers. In this way, the appearance of the good to a moral agent "inclines without necessitating" — a phrase that takes on the status of a mantra in Leibniz. It allows Leibniz to claim that the evil good of overthrowing the Republic and establishing military dictatorship in Rome will infallibly but not necessarily motivate Caesar. Not surprisingly, many have found this fine distinction between physical necessity and moral inclination strained. The question is how.

In the foregoing account, I have described Caesar's "notion" as an original intention that can be foreseen to act in certain ways, while Leibniz himself tends rather to speak of the notion as God's "full and complete concept," i.e., the possibility with its destiny as determined by its compossibility with all others in the series. I may be forgiven this liberty in the light of what follows. As mentioned, the general difficulty in the background here is that the origin of moral evil can only emerge as a singular, enormous perplexity: In a world in which all spirits by nature seek the good, how can any rational being go astray, as manifestly many do? In Version One, the particular difficulty of Leibniz's theodicy is assuredly *not* the idiot pontificating of Dr. Pangloss about the hidden good of being boiled alive and eaten for stew by cannibals. The problem is that Leibniz's solution to the conundrum of actual evil may be worse for God's reputation than leaving evil to appear as a moral surd, which is a huge problem for a philosophy that purports to save God's reputation. It is a horrifying thought: God admits into existence characters like Judas or Pilate, who, to be sure, *freely, indeed eagerly will* — indeed, *from all eternity eagerly strain* — to play their part in the judicial murder of the Son of God. To do so is the perverse good these essences by nature seek. It is perverse relative to the world of compossibilities that God has in fact chosen — yet not perverse in the abstract. In another possible world we can imagine that betraying Jesus or sentencing Him for blasphemy might have been an excellent work contributing to the common good, though not in this world that actually exists. Here God allows the freely willing essences of such evildoers (relative to our world, the best possible that God has in fact chosen) into existence, only because it is strictly required for achieving God's greater purpose. God does not desire that Judas and Pilate exist; it is they — or their abstract essences — that strain for existence like all the other possibilities residing in God's mind. God merely releases these into being, for overriding reasons of His providence.

We have to imagine then in the region of the eternal verities, which is God's own mind knowing all possible characters, essential Judas clamoring to exist in order to betray Jesus, essential Pilate lobbying to be in order that he may wash his hands as he hands Jesus over for execution. And we have to imagine God leaving Judas and Pilate to do as they will. For God these characters exist only in order to play their part in the drama of redemption and then to suffer exclusion from the company of the blessed, for all eternity a public display of the justice of God. Having done their bit, they are ordered off stage, forever to be forgotten.

All this, of course, is quite fantastic, yet even as a fantasy it is disturbing. For although the predetermined essences of these evildoers willingly go to their crimes, and had logically noncontradictory choices in acting out their intentions, as the abstract essences that they are, they have neither freedom of choice nor freedom of action, and so infallibly choose their own best, which in fact becomes evil when released into this actual series of events that constitutes this world. In Version One, we may say, Leibniz the Platonic rationalist prevails,[36] for whom the necessary harmony of things finally trumps both divine and human spontaneity and individuality. This Leibniz *is* the crypto-Spinozist, since the freedom he strains to identify in finite moral agents is strained beyond recognition. In the perspective of thoroughgoing and consistent naturalism (that may not be the worst thing), Leroy T. Howe, for example, has defended this Leibniz and chastised John Hick for his morally extravagant anthropocentrism: "The fundamental issue here is

whether plentitude is at the expense of personhood, whether it can be affirmed that good for the cosmos is better than the good merely for man."
Howe argues then that there are natural limits to "personhood," that a world
"altogether pleasing to man cannot be a relevant consideration." Instead,
"God's nature as unlimited compossibility requires that he create a world
structured not for the sake of any one species or its members, but for the
sake of the unity of the whole."[37] The same considerations would apply to
individuals for the sake of the human whole. Consequently, it is in Christian
theological perspective that we would have to judge that a twofold error has
occurred here that is far more serious than that of a thought-experiment
taken too literally. The twofold error here reflects the protological bias with
its rationalist prejudice that things are decided in advance by intellects —
also God's — and then simply played out like an algorithm. This error appears as error in perspective of the eschatological promise of life together. If
in this light the emergence of others is essential to life, also in God's triune
life, then this protological picture with its intellectualist bias is misleading:
return to Origin, to the One from the Many, implies a final silence, not eternal doxology.

If we balanced the protological with the eschatological, the alpha with
the omega, however, we could and should certainly think theologically of
initial intention, and so also of persistent faithfulness to original intention in
face of challenge and threat. But we would also understand that decision is
retrospective, supremely when the Father in the Spirit recognized the Crucified Jesus as indeed His beloved Son and, vindicating Him, reversed what
had been done to Him, including His own forsaking of Him as the worst of
sinners.[38] If this is God's way of being (not just our way of representing or
talking), judgment comes last, not first. Decision decides an outcome; it is
not the announcement of a mere intention, since decision executes a concrete harmonization of power and wisdom by love as it includes genuine
others with their in-part incalculable outcomes. Decision is thus something
that cannot be wholly known in advance, even in God's life, though God's
original intention of love can be known, and its power and wisdom trusted
to prevail. In the same way, we might think of the human choices that form
the biographical identity of every precious soul for whom Christ died, not
only from their origins in desire through genuine choices amid present possibilities faithfully sustained (or not), but also in terms of the unanticipated,
for incalculable, outcomes of these actions. For good or ill I become eternally the outcome of my story. That can be heaven and that can be hell. On
the one hand, then, as the proverb has it, the path to hell is paved with good

intentions, authenticity doesn't finally count for much, and what is decisive — the retrospective decision about one's human life — is not at last in one's own hands. It is a matter of fate or destiny — of the decision of others about us. Just so, it will matter immensely whether the outcome of my own story belongs to Another who might with justice be called savior and lord. This is what Christians have always meant, though not frequently understood well, by the eschatological Day of the Lord, the ultimate retrospective decision that finally settles all outstanding accounts and reconciles them eternally.

The problem then, according to Version One, lies in Leibniz's curious mutation of the Augustinian doctrine of eternal reprobation — not the traditional *massa damnata* but his comparatively minimal cast of full and complete villain-characters in God the Dramatist's intellect whom God in the executive role of Playwright-Director admits onto the stage of existence to perform crucial roles for greater purposes of poetic justice and aesthetic satisfaction. Riley interprets Leibniz's concluding parable in the *Theodicy*, of Sextus Tarquin's cruel fate as a rapist and destroyer, in this way. The "strong notion (from the 'Discourse on Metaphysics') that every action of a substance is 'certain' and 'determined' turns out to be decisive; for Tarquin was wicked 'from all eternity.'"[39] Despite this apparent determinism, Riley acknowledges the ambiguity or "tension" in Leibniz between varying emphases on "rational substances as rational and autonomous" and "the world as a harmonious whole." He rightly sees that the wall Leibniz tried to build against Spinoza's monism comes tumbling down, if in fact rational substances, howsoever willingly internally, simply play out predetermined parts externally admitted into existence by God. Even more probing is Riley's moral objection (against a position like Howe's above) to the theodicy according to Version One: the "sacrifice of the individual to universal," a philosophy of history in which "the general (and generally good) outcome justifies the ruin of individuals"[40] — the Caesars, Judases, and Pilates. In Version One, the rationalist Leibniz's theodicy self-destructs in justifying a God who must fore-doom characters for the sake of actual good. Adriaan Peperzak has from his Christian philosophical perspective rightly judged this rationalist cosmology in which all apparent evils dissolve when shown to "be an integral part with a positive function within the totality":[41] "the non-utility of the human subject, which is infinite, makes it incapable of functioning in a framework of economic calculation. If such a framework is essential to all generalized teleology, this does not help us in any way to elucidate the meaning of human good or evil."[42] This Leibniz fails to be "prophetic."[43]

Why? Leibniz does not, indeed cannot, allow his own important distinction between physical necessity and moral inclination to play out in temporal series, because he fears this would introduce incalculable events threatening the lawfulness of physical events unfolding in preestablished harmony with the one, full, and complete protological divine determination of all monads in the entire series from Genesis to Revelation. But surely the infallibility of moral inclination (that we shall always seek our own good) cannot be rigorously tied to the empirically given, if freedom of action entails a critical capacity to question the appearance of good and thus also indicates the power of imagination to construct for oneself alternative goods. We have been arguing in correction of the protological bias that, according to God's infallible moral determination to create, redeem, and fulfill the world by Christ and the Spirit, intrinsically unpredictable intrusions of rejected possibles are allowed by God to the genuine creaturely agents He positively wills into existence (not in the sense of God admitting incompossible essences into existence for providential purposes). Rather, as in Genesis 2, God withdraws, and so lets existences fall into doubt about their essential destiny in Christ to become the children of God. Thus these doubting existences in anxiety imagine, and out of envy demand to be, and to some degree then act as essences other than God wills. This acting out of false identities in turn wreaks havoc upon the web of life that God wills, indeed affecting others in widening spirals of chaos, "visiting the iniquity of the fathers upon the children to the third and fourth generation of them who hate God." This outbreak of sin as an overtaking, lethal power is not merely evil as privation, metaphysical evil, which, with Leibniz, is rather its presupposition. But moral evil is the actualization of divinely rejected possibilities in acts of rational choice by existing patients/agents when overtaken by envy in unbelief about their divine destination.

There is actually some textual basis for such an account of actual evil in Leibniz. Taking up David Blumenfeld's observation of a "few places where Leibniz sketches an account of freedom and contingency in terms of our relation to non-actual individuals who are like us in important respects — our counterparts in other worlds,"[44] Thomas E. Baril attempts a "fresh defense" of Leibnizian freedom by calling into question the regnant assumption that God's complete, individual concepts are totally deterministic, "only capable of acting out the pre-established concept"; he argues that this "traditional view erroneously interprets foreknowledge as a completed product and ignores the dynamic, existential and free process."[45] Baril argues that Leibniz's complete, individual concept can only apply to the actual products of God in this actual world so far as God has conceived and willed them to exist as what they are in His foreknowledge, and so in harmony with material and efficient causal processes. Yet what God sees in surveying all possible essences in all possible worlds is essences freely deciding their own individual concepts, not as complet*ed* products but as complet*ing* processes. Baril pictures an actual world coming to be, then, decision by decision in ongoing relation to all possible worlds. Thus, he argues, Adam as complet*ing* process could have freely refused to eat the forbidden fruit — it is not scripted on account of his being a complet*ed* product in God's actual world. Rather, refusing the *sicut deus eritis* was as possible in itself as alternative completions of Adam in other possible worlds. Whether or not this defense of Leibnizian freedom works philosophically, or comports with Leibniz's actual intentions, the reader may decide. Theologically, it virtually makes God a passive spectator, when, for Leibniz the Augustinian, God's knowledge of the actual world is intuitive and creative, and eternally contains this and all other temporal events. I wish accordingly to push the ideas here in another direction and put them to work for a different purpose.

Just because God chooses to produce a voluntary chooser of God, God to that degree makes available to that intelligent albeit finite chooser the alternatives that God passed over in creating it. And this knowledge of good and evil empowers the creature to choose evilly for the completion of its existence other than the way compossible with God's purpose of good for all. As Holy Scripture observes very early on, "The LORD saw that the wickedness of humankind was great in the earth, and that every inclination of the thoughts of their hearts was only evil continually. And the LORD was sorry that he had made humankind on the earth, and it grieved him to his heart" (Gen. 6:5-6 NRSV).

This way then indicates a more "positive" (as opposed to privative) account of moral evil as something actual than in the tradition that runs from Augustine to Barth's *das Nichtige*. It makes intelligible how creatures that by nature seek the good, seek false goods, goods other than the good God wills for one and for all and thus become actually evil, contradicting the actual good that is God and His kingdom. It exposes the actual evil raging against the world God wills as such relatively incalculable free choices of rational minds for possibilities of good other than the Good the Trinity is and wills for us all, i.e., of eschatological inclusion in its own eternal life. These evil choices are incalculable in a relative, not absolute, sense, for absolutely God foresaw in Adam the fall of humanity into sin and so also the eternal Son's temporal suffering for humanity's restoration and the Spirit's temporal mission to gather the nations into the church. But relatively, in the time of trial when God withdraws, the human patient/agent may critically reserve judgment on apparent goods or willfully indulge them, may suffer apparent evils in faith or flee them in mistrust, may resolve never to suffer and so become the enemy of creation, and enemy of God, may be matched by the resolve of the suffering God to gain the persecutor and surrender to redeeming mercy. What happens here, as paradigmatically in Gethsemane, is the hidden drama of every human life, each one's own Gethsemane of the soul, the incalculable moment that decides the outcomes of life as one assents with Jesus, or does not, to the uncanny will of God.

Karl Barth, criticizing the semi-Spinozism of Schleiermacher later on in the *Church Dogmatics,* casually remarked, "This is a real return to Leibniz. Sin is now understood positively. Without sin grace could not exist."[46] I am willing to concede the possibility that according to Version One the critics of Leibniz have rightly understood him, or perhaps better, have made his line of thought consistent from a certain (nontrinitarian) perspective.[47] Having registered my own intended revision of this rationalist Leibniz along the foregoing lines by admitting a relatively incalculable freedom of choice and action (though not of desire) in the creature (even after the fall), there is, as we shall presently explore, yet another version of what went wrong in the *Theodicy.* In this regard, Barth's criticism may hit the mark with Schleiermacher, but even according to what we have witnessed in Version One, it is a careless and unfortunate misrepresentation of Leibniz. It darkens understanding of the problem according to Version Two, and so we must clear it away now before undertaking that alternative account. As we noted in the preceding discussion, for Leibniz crime is harmonized by punishment, not pardon, and if pardon is to be attained, it will be by a fitting propitiation, not a capricious fiat. There may be possibilities of mercy beyond punishment in Melanchthon's tradition of thought, in other words, but certainly not apart from the public satisfaction of divine justice by the judgment on sin.[48] Melanchthon once wrote, "the natural light in wise people may become completely infatuated," supposing "that God is neither a judge nor a helper." Repeating the same old "fantasy," such theologians become "either Epicureans or Stoics."[49] "Precisely!" Leibniz would concur. Particularly for what follows in Version Two of the problem with the *Theodicy,* it is crucial to understand that if sin is understood and recognized as *actual* evil, not mere error, as public and social assault on the kingdom, not private offenses against an oversensitive ego, then any God who would not judge and damn evil as real evil, i.e., acts of choice that ruin the earth and *so* dishonor its Creator, Redeemer, and Fulfiller, disqualifies as God, as lacking the true and powerful goodness that hates what is evil (Rom. 12:9). Schleiermacher's post-Kantian God "without wrath who brings men without sin into a kingdom without judgment through the ministrations of a Christ without a cross" (H. R. Niebuhr) is not the God of Melanchthon (or Luther, Anselm, Augustine, or Paul), and not also of Leibniz, according to Version Two. This must be clearly grasped.

Version Two: Leibniz as Augustinian in Denial

"I start as a philosopher but I finish as a theologian,"[50] Leibniz once said of himself. The present argument has urged the opposite: Leibniz philosophized consciously or not on the basis of theses borrowed from revealed theology. In Version Two, we shall see that for Leibniz (as we saw for Barth), this present world on the way to the kingdom is the creation of *the Trinity;* from the beginning then it is a world according to the divine wisdom and plan in which "one of the Trinity would suffer"[51] so that in Him the image of God would be fulfilled on behalf of a humanity that by sin has missed its destiny but is now being recapitulated. At the center of the *Theodicy* stands the statement (howsoever softly spoken): "we remember that we have gained Jesus Christ himself by reason of sin."[52] While Leibniz would protest, as Riley correctly insists, on behalf of the independent validity of his "natural theology" as philosophy,[53] Jolley is surely right to question whether the notions just mentioned, borrowed from revealed theology, so profoundly form Leibniz's mind as to render his rationalist claim nugatory. Jolley in any case rightly points out that Leibniz not infrequently "claims that his metaphysics is the unique guarantee of Christian orthodoxy against heterodox systems like Spinozism."[54] Likewise, Michael Latzer, who has been particularly concerned to anchor the reading of Leibniz in the Augustinian tradition, argues that the *Theodicy*'s "exoneration of God" points to Christian eschatology: "not because any world [God] might have created would have been more or less evil but because, having brought into existence the best of all possible worlds in spite of the evil which this world does contain, he knows how to bring good out of evil,"[55] as supremely and paradigmatically in the resurrection of the Crucified. From another angle, Diogenes Allen has written on the theological reading of Leibniz's *Theodicy:* "A Christian today may adopt Leibniz' approach. He need not approach a theodicy as though it were an hypothesis which best covers the data of good and evil within our experience. He may hold, as does Leibniz, to the mysteries of Creation, Trinity, and Incarnation by faith."[56] The point of theodicy then would not be rationalistic apologetics in the fashion of the natural theology of the deists, which Leibniz in fact opposed all his life, up to and including the last great polemic with Samuel Clarke.[57] As Allen explains, "When [the Leibnizian] reflects on good and evil, he already has the conviction that God is wise and good; he is not seeking to arrive at that conviction from such data. He is instead reflecting in order to retain his conviction in view of contrary appearances."[58] Such reflection would be the standard operating procedure of revealed theology in its systematic task of interpreting all things in Christ.[59] This is so for Leibniz as well, even though he claims to secure a priori and *solo ratione* the conviction about God's perfections of power, wisdom, and goodness. And that, in this version, is the point at which his project fails.

Historically and psychologically, of course, it remains an open and perhaps unanswerable question whether Leibniz himself actually attained clarity on the many motives at work in his oeuvre. The relevant ambiguity for our study, however, precedes him. It lies in the root conviction of the Melanchthonian tradition itself that, the law being written on the human heart, natural reason could in principle recognize that the powerful "God is wise and good" apart from the revelation of grace in Jesus Christ, and that Leibniz undertook the further step of developing this pneumatology generally — on the independent basis of reason alone — to secure, as it were, the metaphysical condition for the possibility of the gospel. This is an important work of reflection, yet it is and only can be, according to Version Two, warranted as an extension of revealed theology. According to this, the rationalist posture of Leibniz amounts to a shell game. The construction of the antecedent natural reason of the pre-Christian mind is precisely a construction from the definite perspective of the new mind acquired in Christian faith, beginning with the self-interpretation of the justified sinner but extending to the justification of God in his judgment (Rom. 3:22-26). According to Karl Barth's celebrated argument deriving from Romans 5, what Adam was as the sinner only comes into clear focus in Christ, the New Adam.[60] Michael Latzer, accordingly, speaks of the "unmistakable Christocentrism" of Leibniz's theodicy: "the fundamental reason Leibniz gives for God's permission of evil is that the world which witnesses evil's ultimate vanquishing through the incarnation of Christ is superior to any world containing no evil in the first place."[61] *This* is the sense of the theodicy according to Version Two; in it, God's determination is fundamentally a trinitarian self-determination, as Barth so correctly appropriated the lines of the thought first explored in Leibniz and accordingly interpreted election as the election of Jesus Christ to be rejected in humanity's place so that in Him all might become the children of God. This then is the theodicy *of faith* stemming from Romans 8 that anticipates a renewed creation.

Although Leibniz boldly postures that he will justify even the West's "established doctrine that the number of men damned eternally will be incomparably greater than the saved,"[62] he cannot restrain himself from hints of universalism, recalling Origen's teaching of *apokatastasis*.[63] In any case, Leibniz does not shrink from the difficulty. The problem of *massa damnata* is created by the disappearance of the Spirit, whose absence represents on the face of it "a terrible judgment of God, giving his only Son for the whole human race and being the sole author and master of the salvation of men, yet saves so few of them and abandons all others to the devil his enemy, who torments them eternally and makes them curse their Creator, though they have all been created to diffuse and show forth his goodness, his justice and his other perfections."[64] To lessen this tension, Leibniz sometimes argues for a hidden work of the Spirit beyond what is visible to us, and sometimes he argues for the Thomistic *facere quod in se,* i.e., for the natural capacity of human beings as image of God to seek God.[65] The former arguments are ready to hand in his own Lutheran tradition. Thus he argues for the salvation of unbaptized children: "Evangelical theologians are accustomed to speak with fair moderation on this question, and to surrender these souls to the judgment and clemency of their Creator. Nor do we know all the wonderful ways God may choose to employ for the illumination of souls."[66] In the *New Essays* this early champion of generous orthodoxy commented, "It is well for us that God is more philanthropic than men," and went on to deny that optimism about salvation entails a Pelagian lessening of the power and depth of sin but points instead to the hidden power of the Spirit. It "does not follow that those who justify the heathen, or others who lack ordinary aid, must attribute it to the forces of nature only. . . . And since we teach against the Pelagians a supernatural grace in all those who possess faith . . . and as [all] allow also either faith or at least similar movements to infants who receive baptism, it is not very extraordinary to allow as much at least in the article of death to persons of good will who have not had the good fortune to be instructed as usual in Christianity."[67] At the same time, he adopts the Thomistic (or Melanchthonian, not nominalist) version of *facere quod in se,* as in the *New Essays,* when he discusses the "famous question" whether any who "died in the opinions of a natural piety, could have been saved by this means and obtained the remissions of their sins." He lifts up, without committing himself to it, the view of "many fathers [and] a number of excellent doctors of the Roman church . . . [who] maintain that the persons of whom I have just spoken could have been saved by an act of contrition, i.e. penitence grounded in the love of benevolence, in virtue of which we love God above everything, because His perfections render Him supremely lovable. This brings it about that afterwards we are led with all our hearts to conform to His will and to imitate His perfection in order the better to unite ourselves with Him, since it appears right for God not to refuse His grace to those who hold such view."[68]

The difficulty is by now familiar, and in either case, Leibniz's concern is with the reputation of God. From this perspective, moreover, the interpretation of the antecedent mind of the sinner is not idle or devious, when methodologically it is clear that this is the reflection of revealed theology, on the basis of faith's epistemic access to the image of God in Christ, whose eccentric existence in faith, hope, and love exposes as dead and sinful the egocentric existence of the first and fallen Adam. Then this reflective procedure is the hermeneutical matter of interpreting in Christ the mind apart from Christ, not an exercise in epistemological foundationalism. But from that moment when revealed theology secularized itself into philosophical "natural theology" putatively arguing on the basis of reason alone, recognition of God as the transcendent causality, the original coherence, the harmony of power, wisdom, and love devolved into the desperate effort to justify some Cosmic Architect as "wise and good" (but no longer all-powerful, as per Plato, whom Aristotle in this regard follows). What else in this connection could a philosophical demonstration be? Aristotelian teleology and cosmotheology became the only option, until Darwin arrived and dethroned these too (although Hume had already shown that cosmological arguments can demonstrate only that a Cosmic Architect, if one exists, does not tenderly care about you and me, just as Luther's "light of nature" had already suggested on grounds of revealed theology).

Leibniz, however, was well aware of Hume's kind of objection and *embraced* it. He puts it in the mouth of Polidore, in an early *Dialogue between Polidore and Theophile.* Polidore laments the vanity of things: even "the most refined pleasures of the mind are only pleasing deceptions which disappear when closely examined. Is there anything on earth to which great spirits are more sensitive than glory and the immortality of name which we like to imagine? And yet what good will they do me when I am reduced to dust? . . . I shall no longer exert myself to acquire so chimerical an immortality."[69] Theophile tries to console him with deist teleology: "But tell me how it happens that there is a sun, ether, and planets. Could not the world have been made in an entirely different way? And who made things this particular way?" To this, Polidore replies: "A wretched sheep is torn apart by the wolf, a pigeon falls prey to some vulture, the poor flies are exposed to the malice of spiders, and men themselves — what a tyranny they exercise over the other animals, and even among themselves they are more than wolves and more than vultures. What appearance of order is there in all this?"[70] And he concludes in words that anticipate Hume almost verbatim: "we must say that [God] cares not at all for what we call justice and that he takes pleasure in destruction as we take pleasure in hunting the beasts which prey on each other. Individuals must give way; there is room only for the species, some of which subsist through the misfortune of others. And we in our folly are presumptuous enough to imagine that he will exempt us from these universal cycles by means of an immortality which is without example in nature and is all the more incredible, since a beginning must be followed by an end."[71]

Leibniz's counter to this on the lips of Theophile is pure Augustinian Christianity:

> [But] there is some community between God and men. For since both are reasonable and have some commerce with each other, they compose a City which must be governed in the most perfect manner. . . . It is true that our bodies are subject to the impact of other bodies and hence to dissolution. But the soul is a substance entirely different from matter . . . and hence cannot be destroyed. And, since this is so, it is capable of subsisting and of being happy in spite of the destruction in the world. Provided that God leaves it memory and thoughts, the soul can be happy and unhappy, punished and rewarded, according to the laws of this City of which God is the monarch. . . . we must try to perfect ourselves as much as we can, and especially the mind, which is properly what we call ourself.[72]

Finally, lest we take this as world-denying disembodiment: "nothing is neglected in nature; nothing is lost with God; all our hairs are numbered, and not a glass of water will be forgotten; *qui ad iustitiam eruderunt multos fulgebunt quasi stellae* [those who lead many to righteousness shall shine as the stars]; no good action without reward, no evil one without some punishment; no perfection without a series of others unto infinity."[73] Perhaps the only modification the mature Leibniz makes to the Augustinian line of thought adopted here — expressly against skepticism — will be his more Lutheran affirmation of the body's, *pars pro toto* the material world's, redemption.

Yet, according to Version Two, which locates Leibniz in the post-Reformation construction of a theological philosophy to guide a reformed

Christian culture on the basis of the creation of humanity in the image of
God, this very endeavor was from the beginning threatened by fateful ambiguities. Aside from the just-mentioned eclipse of the Reformation's question
about the justification of the sinner by the deist question about the justification of the Cosmic Architect, we can specify several others. First, what could
it ever mean to be the image of the Trinity? The decisive scriptural passage,
Genesis 1:26-28, taken intratextually with the New Testament's total Christ of
Head and Body (as in the letters to the Ephesians and the Colossians), is *social* in its intention, a fact that rationalist interpretation minimizes, if not
obscures, with its focus on calculating rationality as such or in isolation as
essentially human.[74] Religiously the temptation in this connection would be
to think individualistically in terms of a handful of converted minds piously
radiating heavenly thoughts rather than minds together forming a society
on earth thinking together in anticipation of the kingdom of God. Second,
what image would then fill the human mirror-mind if in consequence of
this drift toward rationalism it came to reflect some other, nontrinitarian
deity?[75] Historically this ambiguity surfaced with the resurgent *deus exlex* of
nominalism (which may have mutated from Zwingli's *De providentia*)[76] into
the characteristic modern antitheologies via Descartes of Hobbes on the
right and Spinoza on the left.

   This latter ambiguity became explicit in Descartes's version of the so-
called ontological argument.[77] If we take Anselm's *Monologian* as the argument that situates[78] the so-called Ontological Proof of the *Proslogian,* it is
clear that the possibility of the necessary divine existence under discussion is
the Trinity's,[79] just as the human mind that inquires here after divine existence is the vestige of the Trinity that seeks in faith to understand what it affirms by faith.[80] But Descartes's demonstration proceeds on the basis of a
hearsay notion of the "supreme power of God," who in principle could be a
deceiver: "were he to wish it, it would be easy for him to cause me to err even
in those matters that I think I intuit as clearly as possible with the eyes of my
mind."[81] If Descartes's proof succeeds, it demonstrates an Omnipotence that
could, but would not, deceive — hardly the eternal harmony of power and
wisdom in love. The assurance seems arbitrary; Gillespie has performed the
crucial analysis of the requisite posit of human freedom as sovereign indifference that defense against such an Absolute elicits: "Man is able to reform
the world by virtue of his will. The will in this sense, as Descartes argues in
the Passions, is the human perfection and the sole basis for human self-
esteem. . . . Indeed nothing truly affects man except the free dispositions of
his will or desire, which is so free by nature that it can never be con-

strained. . . . The will is the source of human freedom and also the ground of human power. It is therefore the source of man's freedom from the omnipotent God and his deceptions, as well as the basis for humanity's conquest of nature."[82] The divine Absolute and the freedom of indifference are correlative concepts.

Leibniz from early on sensed the vulnerability of his tradition (with its dual tendencies of deep skepticism about Promethean claims for human freedom deriving from Luther and its confidence in enlightened human reason descending from Melanchthon) on account of these latent ambiguities. His *Theodicy* correspondingly reflected more than one agenda. He was writing against the new Manicheans represented by the apostate Huguenot Pierre Bayle;[83] he undertook the task of classical apologetics in defending the mysteries of the faith against the proto-deist Socinians;[84] he is — to the consternation of the merely conservative confessionalistic-pietistic dogmaticians — speculatively modernizing and liberalizing the Augustinian tradition by taking it more seriously than do its apologists, i.e., in bold interpretation of the real issues of a new age.[85] The *Theodicy* can be therefore read as a sophisticated defense of the Augustinian doctrine against the new fatalisms, "God is cause of all causes but not maker of all choices." According to Version Two, the *Theodicy* is unintelligible apart from the tradition of revealed theology.

This latter point bears some emphasis. "Concerning grace and predestination, I justify the most debatable assertions," Leibniz wrote, thinking of the Augustinian tradition, "as for instance: that we are converted only through the prevenient grace of God and that we cannot do good except with his aid; that God wills the salvation of all men and that he condemns only those whose will is evil; that he gives to all a sufficient grace provided they wish to use it; that, Jesus Christ being the source and center of election, God destined the elect for salvation, because he foresaw that they would cling with a lively faith to the doctrine of Jesus Christ." As God is the cause of all causes, divine foresight is not passive; it is not simply the insight of superior powers of calculation. Divine foresight is causative of all causes, including the free choices of the creatures God creates as those with wills of their own, other than God. Thus Leibniz clarified: "Yet it is true that this reason for election is not the final reason, and that this very provision is still a consequence of God's anterior decree. Faith likewise is a gift of God, who has predestinated the faith of the elect for reasons lying in a superior decree which dispenses grace and circumstance in accordance with God's supreme wisdom."[86] Resort to creaturely free will for the purpose of saving God from the authorship of evil — the Pelagian solution the rationalist Leibniz should have taken according to the criticism of him in Version One — is thus ruled out, not however on rationalist grounds, but rather on Augustinian-Lutheran grounds of the all-sufficiency of grace. Saving faith too is dispensed by God as pure gift (and so, seemingly, withheld as a judgment on sin) in the particular work of the Holy Spirit. Commonplace as the "free will" theodicy of Pelagianism became in deism, it is simply *not* among the "most debatable assertions" that Leibniz undertook to defend.

Leibniz does not make his task easy then by the facile doctrine that gaining heaven and averting hell are within the natural human power of free choice. Instead, he deliberately, as it appears, takes up Luther's pained acknowledgment of the *scandal* of grace, that since saving "faith likewise is a gift of God," it is *not* in human power. This "most debatable" assertion is what must be justified in theodicy. "But the difficulty is great, above all, in relation to God's dispositions for the salvation of men," Leibniz expressly writes of the traditional doctrine of the *massa damnata.* "There are few saved or chosen; therefore the choice of many is not God's decreed will. And since it is admitted that those whom he has chosen deserve it no more than the rest, and are not even fundamentally less evil, the goodness which they have coming only from the gift of God, the difficulty is increased. . . . It is true that those who are not chosen are lost by their own fault: they lack good will or living faith; but it rested with God alone to grant it them . . . [so] there remains the question why God does not deliver all — why he delivers the lesser number and why some in preference to others."[87] Pressing these questions, of course, puts pressure on certain Augustinian truisms, especially of the *massa damnata,* which might be challenged by more universalist statements in the *Grundtext* of Romans, such as Romans 11:32. But that leads in the direction, as we have already considered in Karl Barth's revision of the Reformed tradition's doctrine of the double decree, of modernizing and liberalizing Augustine and Luther, not going over to Pelagius with the deists. Barth's move was prefigured in Leibniz.

Thus justification of *this* scandal of the *particularity* of *grace* in *revealed* theology is the challenge Leibniz undertakes in his *Theodicy;* the task springs directly from Luther's conclusion of *De servo arbitrio.* God, Leibniz avers programmatically, "is a good and just master; his power is absolute, but his wisdom permits not that he exercise that power in an arbitrary and despotic way, which would be tyrannous indeed."[88] Luther, we recall, had affirmed this conviction about the wisdom and justice of God to be revealed in the light of glory on the basis of faith in the revelation of Christ in the scandalous light of grace. This is a stance Leibniz lifts up and praises because Luther's faith trusts contrary to appearances, just as true reason sees beyond appearances, or perhaps better, thinks beyond appearances by means of the principle of sufficient reason. According to Version Two, however, this rational procedure too is theological. It is in actuality *Nachdenken,* thinking after that fact for the reason in what God has wrought in mere creation, in the existence of something rather than nothing. Theology is not the blind and dumb acceptance and repetition on authority of any superior claim, but coming to understand the mind of God revealed to faith in His scandalously particular acts of grace with the rational tools bequeathed the mind as such.

This Leibniz, along with Luther and Anselm and Augustine and all his other models, stands in a line of tradition stretching back to Irenaeus's formative battle with Gnosticism. Theological understanding comes by connecting these acts of God together to discern the unified purpose of the one God of this one world. Understanding connects these by means of the question, Why? The why question in theology is thus the motor force of trinitarian monotheism; it is the act of understanding that fends off dualism in every fashion. As Irenaeus classically explained, "nearly all the heretical sects, many as they are, speak of one God" even though "they alter Him," thereby showing themselves to be "ungrateful to Him who made them, just as the pagans [do] by idolatry."[89] Simplistic appeal to "one God" therefore resolves nothing, since it often makes the cognitively idle appeal to some unknown beyond words, thoughts, concepts. But revealed theology that has God in His Word by His Spirit has to probe, test, question, reflect, and understand the "why" of God's ways. It has to demonstrate the unity of God's works. The question *Why?* seeks and discovers the oneness of God in his agency as Creator, Redeemer, and Fulfiller of this world. Under the press of the Gnostic assault, Irenaeus thought of a total economy or plan of salvation for humankind, centered on Jesus Christ, who recapitulated humankind's history and so restored it to God. With Christ as the key to the Scriptures, greater knowledge of God does not come about by supplanting the scriptural narrative of the creation and redemption of this one world by the one God with new myths. It comes about by putting systematically the question *Why?* to the Scriptures.

> [Greater knowledge of God] does come about, however, by bringing out more fully the meaning of whatever was said in parables and adapting it exactly to the doctrine of the Truth; and by explaining God's dealings and Economy, which He made for the sake of the human race; by making clear that God was long-suffering . . . by announcing *why* one and the same God made some things temporal, others eternal . . . by understanding *why*

God, who is invisible, appeared to the prophets, not under one form, but differently to different prophets; and by indicating *why* several covenants were made with the human race; by teaching what the real nature of each of the covenants was; and by searching out *why* God consigned all things to disobedience that He may have mercy on all; by acknowledging gratefully *why* the Word of God became flesh and suffered . . . by unfolding as much as is contained in the Scriptures about the end and the things that are to come . . . *why* God made the Gentiles, who were despaired of, joint heirs . . . by proclaiming how this mortal body will put on immortality.[90]

In this light we may ask: Does the real problem with Leibniz's *Theodicy* according to Version Two lie in his claim to harmonize true faith and true reason? Does his hope of rational insight by asking the question of sufficient reason to the articles of faith somehow go beyond faith and become "theology of glory"? Or does it properly exercise faith? To be precise, theology of glory in the pejorative sense would mean preferring knowledge of God in majesty on the basis of His visible cosmic works acquired by natural human powers of inquiry (i.e., cosmotheology) to the knowledge of God hidden in sufferings given by the Spirit in the form of repentance and faith. Luther's contrast is between the natural awareness of the Creator in Romans 1:20 acquired through general experience of the world and that given in the gospel by the Spirit in Romans 3:21-26. If we add to this Luther's appropriation of Romans 8, the true theology of glory is the eschatological vision of God in contrast to the false theology of glory, i.e., that metaphysics of being as persistence that makes "a happy science out of a sad creation." How does this account match with Leibniz? "Our end," writes Leibniz, speaking of his own purpose in the *Theodicy*, "is to banish from men the false ideas that represent God to them as an absolute prince employing a despotic power, unfitted to be loved and unworthy of being loved. These notions are all the more evil in relation to God inasmuch as the essence of piety is not only to fear him but also to love him above all things: and that cannot come about unless there be knowledge of his perfections capable of arousing the love which he deserves, and which makes the felicity of those that love him."[91]

What perfections are those? The mere power on display in Romans 1:20? Or the revealed wisdom and righteousness of God of Romans 3:21-26? Parsed this way, Leibniz's theological intention is arguably congruent with Luther's theology of the cross, not to mention Irenaeus's trinitarian and antidualist monotheism. The question then turns on how knowledge of the divine perfections arousing love of God for God's sake is acquired: by the

Spirit's justification of the sinner or by the philosopher's justification of the Cosmic Architect? The former includes, with significant revision (Rom. 8!), the latter; but the latter does not include the former and may even exclude it.

Robert Jenson has performed an essential analysis here that I want to appropriate on behalf of Version Two, according to which Leibniz tried to meet Spinoza's pantheism by resort to Luther. First, Jenson argues, for Luther's argument in *De servo arbitrio* actually to cohere, God's divine way of being must be strictly conceived as trinitarian: "God is freedom antecedently to himself as determinate free will. He can intelligibly be said to be this as the Father is the source of the Son and both are freed in the Spirit. God is rapt by another without dependence on another than God. He can intelligibly be said to be this as the Spirit, as the lively future of God, is himself the very same God."[92] All this is said, be it noted, of God's *antecedent* freedom, i.e., of the eternal Trinity as the Father's love for the Son and the Son for the Father in the Spirit. This being of freedom in love forms the basis for God's determinate free will, i.e., the act of creation with all that it entails. This accounts for the *living* God who can within the overarching purpose of the divine and eternal counsel temporally interact with the creation, hearing prayer, responding to contingencies, changing course strategically, innovating. Jenson accomplishes this biblical understanding of God as event *also in time* in far less Fichtean fashion than Barth, who conceives of God's interaction with us in time as a self-repetition. Jenson, however, is not picturing a single self-positing ego eternally passing through three modes of being, repeated itself in time in the once and for all Christ event. Primordially, as we saw above, Jenson thinks of the three egos of God in their mutually involving acts of being in and for one another as constitutive of the one, eternal God, whose temporal interactions accordingly aim at inclusion by participation of the creature in just these relations. Because the eternal Father cannot be the Father that He is except as the Father of this Son, as the eternal Son cannot be the Son He is except as the Son of this Father, as the eternal Spirit cannot be the Holy Spirit except as bringing about this love of the Father for the Son and the Son for the Father — so the event just described, taken as eternal, is the one being of the one God into which relations creatures are rapt by this God's own involvement as just these three in the space-time of creatures. So creatures may interact with the Creator *just as* Jesus and His Father and their Spirit interact in the gospel narrative. Like Luther, then, Jenson takes the gospel narrative's depiction of Jesus, His Father, and their Spirit theologically as an *est*, not a *significat*; accordingly and with justice, Jenson presses Luther's latent trinitarian theology to become explicit.

Second, this explicated trinitarian theology sustains an alternative account of human freedom — not the usual abstract capacity for individualistic free choices arbitrarily taken, but rather a freedom of ecstasy or rapture,[93] as in Luther's attractive and well-known dictum that "the believer lives outside the self by faith in God and love for the neighbor." This, obviously, is a social image of freedom, with important ecclesial and political implications, that Jenson has been eager to develop. In any event, according to the interpretation Jenson is making of Luther, it was thus within the horizon of historical possibility for Leibniz to have developed Luther's insights in this direction, making Luther's *De servo arbitrio* the "coherent system it urgently seems to be."[94] It will be enough to see how Leibniz groped in this direction, and to understand historically why he failed fully to realize this possibility.

Jenson would in any event share with Leibniz the conviction that the appearance of a *deus exlex* (= some versions of the *deus absconditus* in *De servo arbitrio*) can be admitted, but not finally its reality. Jenson holds this interpretation of Luther's language on grounds enunciated by Barth, that the posit of ontological dualism here subverts the very consolation of assured faith at which Luther pastorally aims. For Leibniz, like Irenaeus, dualism would entail calling into an abyss of doubt the reality of the knowing self with its known world, this present visible world as true creature of God. Cartesian doubt, for Leibniz, is a reckless exercise, on the skeptical cusp of Gnostic alienation. If we think at all, he maintained, we are entitled to take ourselves and our world as granted in an act of primal faith, however inadequate and confused our ensuing knowledge is. That hardly means, however, that Leibniz is uncritical. Rather, on this basis, Leibniz is urging that *our real problem of contending, unreconciled, confused, and conflicting perspectives comes into focus.* The real place of philosophy as a vocation — even a "Christian" calling, *pace* Heidegger — lies here, in what Josiah Royce (the American philosopher who most reflects the Leibnizian heritage) called "interpretation" of minds to minds.[95] Our maelstrom of the real thinker with her real world as one among many apparently contingent perspectives struggling to communicate and perchance to commune but too often lapsing into force repelling force is acknowledged by Leibnizian *perspectivalism*. With perspectivalism, as we have seen, the classic cleavage that philosophy attends between appearance and reality is not taken in dualistic fashion as between phenomenal and noumenal spheres, but holistically as reflecting an infinity of perspectives that can be harmonized only (if at all) by the divine Mind in a final judgment. Believing in that possibility by rational faith, human thinking takes its stand ethically on this earth by the principle of sufficient reason: if knowing minds with a known world exist *at all, if there is some-thing rather than nothing,* indeed if there is *this* something rather than other-wise, there must be good reason, physical and moral. Human curiosity about this is not in principle wild imagination, but is rather rooted in the nature of things. It is natural to inquire about nature, as Melanchthon said. Otherwise, any further pursuit and improvement of knowledge would be pointless and we should more honestly resign from letters than valorize our objective un-certainties with narcissistic displays of infinite passion.

What is the alternative to such rational faith? One might honestly draw the ascetic conclusion about the vanity of the world and human knowledge of it, as did Pascal. "God owes us nothing," said the Jansenists in their hyper-nominalist retrieval of hyper-Augustinianism. For Pascal (whom more ad-mire than follow) the point accordingly is not to know God as Creator of the world or the world as creature of God, but to refuse the world and love God in place of it.[96] It is as if the entire domain of extended things constitutes one enormous withdrawal of God, putting humans to the excruciating test: Whom will they love more? Pascal represents one religiously influential way in which the Cartesian *deus exlex* plays out, to whom we shall return mo-mentarily. But for the present, a few more words on Leibniz's theological criticism of Cartesian voluntarism are needed. As mentioned above, when God is first and primarily thought as able willfully to flit from this world to any other at any moment as it pleases God, thus omnipotently able to de-ceive, Descartes's assurance that God would not do so seems arbitrary, and the pursuit of knowledge by human minds in turn becomes radically point-less (other than for purely instrumental purposes of power). "On Descartes' view of God's indifference, there can be no reason favoring the creation of something rather than nothing nor can there be a reason favoring nothing over something," writes Donald L. Perry. That is so because, according to Descartes, the truth that obtains in this world is an arbitrary creation of God. "Descartes will tell us that it is not within our power to understand God's purposes, so we should not ask the question raised above. But on Des-cartes' view, it is not the case that we simply cannot know God's purpose or God's reasons — *he just cannot have any reasons at all.*"[97] Neither then would there be any need of a theodicy. The point religiously then is not to under-stand the world, but to escape it. Hence, Pascal's wager.

There is text[98] from years before Leibniz undertook the *Theodicy* that shows in detail how Leibniz linked his opponents, Hobbes and Spinoza, to Cartesian voluntarism in theology: "For if matter takes on, successively, all possible forms, it follows that nothing can be imagined so absurd, so bizarre, so contrary to what we call justice, that it would not have happened and will not some day happen." The metaphysical objection is clearly a *moral* one, yet it has traction, since for Leibniz power is truly exercised only in harmony with wisdom and love. In his formulation of the Golden Rule, he defined justice as the "charity of the wise" effectively applied. This formula means that justice is essentially the social form of love, and love is that which takes pleasure in the perfection of another for that other's sake. So justice is wise love, which knows the difference between perfection and deformation. It is finally effective love, which causes things to advance rather than stand idle or regress when justice is empowered to act and change things. On the basis of this common notion of justice, Leibniz can argue back to theology. Our idea of God must conform in some recognizable measure to our idea of justice. Here as elsewhere the division of the house in early modernity becomes apparent. "These are precisely the opinions which Spinoza has expounded more clearly, namely, that justice, beauty and order are things merely relative to us but that the perfection of God consists in that magnitude of his activity by virtue of which nothing is possible or conceivable which he does not actually produce. There are also the opinions of Mr. Hobbes, who asserts that everything that is possible is either past or present or future, and there will be no place for trust in providence if God produces everything and makes no choice among possible beings." Leibniz's argumentation is thus directed against what he takes to be the immoral implications of the new theology, in that it undercuts the Protestant providentialism descended from Melanchthon to which he holds in tandem with the common conception of justice of the general pneumatology.

Leibniz next traces these authors of the new divinity to their contemporary source. "Mr. Descartes was careful not to speak so plainly, but he could not help from revealing his opinions incidentally. . . . In my opinion, this is the 'first falsehood' and the basis of atheistic philosophy, though it always seems to say the most beautiful things about God. The true philosophy, on the contrary, must give us an entirely different concept of God's perfection, one that will be of use in both physics and ethics." The apparent magnification of God as infinite, unknowable power is in fact the seed of atheism, for it separates physics from ethics and aesthetics. "For my part, I hold that far from excluding final causes from physics, as Mr. Descartes tries to do . . . , it is rather by means of them that everything must be determined, since the efficient cause of things is intelligent, having a will and therefore striving for the good." Leibniz does not by this suggest employing final causes in place of efficient causes for the work of physical science, but rather argues for the ethical and aesthetic interpretation of nature by philosophy based on the human mind's privileged place in nature as image of God. Philosophy in this way aspires to form culture. And, in this way, the question reverts again to theology. "But this too differs from Descartes's opinion, since goodness, truth, and justice are such, according to him, only because God has established them by a free act of his will — a most strange thing. For if things are good or evil only as the result of God's will, the good cannot be a motive of his will, being posterior to his will. His will, then, could be a certain absolute decree, without any reason."

In an important essay touching upon our period in this connection, Jean-Luc Marion has dialectically argued Descartes's case for the absolute transcendence of God, signified by the Cartesian doctrine of the creation of the so-called eternal truths. God consequently can be "named" only paradoxically as an "incomprehensible power" by natural reason, i.e., acknowledged in a weak sense as unfathomable omnipotence, not known in a strong sense as the harmony of power, wisdom, and love.[99] Marion wants in this way to clear the ground of metaphysical doctrines of God that can be put at the disposal of imperial human projects, "the identification of human and divine science,"[100] in standard fashion of contemporary critiques of ontotheology stemming from Heidegger. Thus Marion ends, not with Descartes or his followers who inconclusively attempted to "unify the divine names" (above all, presumably, Leibniz), but with Pascal's abandonment of the foredoomed effort to name the infinite.[101] Following Heidegger, Marion takes aim at the "principle of sufficient reason" as the doctrine emblematizing the ontotheological captivation of divinity: this "requirement of comprehensibility opposes the priority of infinity in the divine nature." This demand for comprehensibility or the "determination of the essence of God by univocity" is not merely "failure to perceive God's transcendence," but rather reflects the "growing empire" of the Promethean modern subject. In this vein Marion acutely diagnoses what the success of the principle of sufficient reason would ironically achieve, i.e., the eventual abandonment of deism for atheism, with the passing of the Cosmic Architect in favor of the "algorithmic process" of the Blind Watchmaker. "The ultimate fulfillment of rationalist metaphysics thus ought to make the infinite God a *persona non grata*."[102]

What makes Marion's analysis more complex and interesting than the wrecking ball of Heideggerian *Destruktion,* however, is his willingness to acknowledge the equal threat to revealed theology from the side of Cartesianism: "God creates all finite rationality, and in creating it, He stands above it; such transcendent rationality (if it can be called so) cannot be characterized in terms of representation, logical possibility, or calculation. But if that is the case, can we name God at all?"[103] Marion's treatment of Leibniz in this regard is surprisingly perfunctory,[104] given the importance assigned in this essay to the principle of sufficient reason as grounds for an illicit ontotheological reduction of God to univocity. What is missing in Marion's account is appreciation for the trinitarian theology in which Leibniz's appropriation of the principle is embedded, stretching back as we have seen all the way to the paradigmatic case of Irenaeus against the Gnostics. On the other hand, Marion does not sense, it seems, or recognize any perplexity about how infinity itself is to be taken; he works, as it were, with a univocal notion of infinity. At least in the account under discussion, Marion writes of that which defies finite understanding as if the truism *finitum non capax infiniti* could be taken for granted, when in fact it levels the icon no less than the idol (as he acknowledges above). For Leibniz, on the other hand, the concept of an infinite God as *deus exlex* may be admitted, if it indicates strictly the Creator's freedom of action, i.e., the primordial fact that the Trinity does not *have* to act at all, metaphysically that what is possible does not *have* to become actual, that what is actual exists *contingently*. This consideration of the antecedent perfection of the divine life and thus its freedom in the act of creation is the very one, Leibniz tells us, that brought him back from embracing the metaphysical necessitarianism of Hobbes or Spinoza — thinkers who, *pace* Marion, adamantly criticized imagination, enthusiasm, and anthropomorphism in theology, not least God as *ultima ratio*. Leibniz tells us in the *Theodicy* that he was drawn "very close to the opinion of those who hold everything to be absolutely necessary; believing that when things are not subject to coercion, even though they are to necessity, there is freedom, and not distinguishing between the infallible, or what is known with certainty to be true, and the necessary." But, he continues, "I was pulled back from this precipice by considering those possible things which neither are nor will be nor have been."[105]

What pulls him back to this consideration? With the trinitarian tradition, Leibniz thinks that God is antecedently an eternally fulfilled life of love who cannot be conceived to create out of need but only from surplus.[106] There is not only no motive in God to deceive, but God cannot coherently be conceived to deceive in contradiction to His own eternal being as the perfect harmony of power and wisdom in love. Likewise, this triune God cannot be conceived to desire evil, i.e., to create in ways that willfully and knowingly contradict God's own being as the sum and coherence of the perfections that are expressed in actualizing this best of all possible worlds. The question then reverts to God's antecedent being and counsel, as Barth rightly stressed, and according to the present argument of Version Two following Jenson, it is this trinitarianism that Leibniz presupposed, no matter the reserve with which he expressed himself. By executing the act of creation, as we may reason a posteriori, the infinitely free God in fact has decided on a self-involving history of determined love intelligently directed to a goal, even though that involves God and creature alike in reckoning with determinate incalculables. So God powerfully acts with creatures in conjunction with divine perfections of wisdom and love, which appropriate to the Son or Logos and the Holy Spirit respectively, just as the creed also calls the Father *pantokrator,* the "Almighty." Regarding these three primordial perfections of God, Leibniz accordingly wrote in the *Theodicy* of a "secret connection with the Holy Trinity: that power relates to the Father, that is, to the source of the Divinity, wisdom to the Eternal Word, which is called Logos by the most sublime of the Evangelists, and will or Love to the Holy Spirit."[107] Our wills meet and are converted to God's will according to the beloved Augustinian text of Romans 5:5 when we are incorporated by the Spirit into the love of the Father for the Son and the Son for the Father,

According to Version Two, we should understand Leibniz's difficult distinction between physical and metaphysical necessity and moral inclination or spiritual self-determination this way. Then it corresponds precisely to the (perhaps interpolated) text of the Jena edition of *De servo arbitrio,* where Luther conceded, "I could wish, indeed, that a better term were available for our discussion than the accepted one, necessity, which cannot accurately be used either of man's will or God's. Its meaning is too harsh, and foreign to the subject; for it suggests some sort of compulsion, and something that is against one's will." Luther's "intended signification" is rather the asymmetry between "the immutable will" of God to save, on the one hand, and the "impotence" of the corrupt creature on the other,[108] such that natural powers of the egocentric Adam do not suffice to move him to God as God because Adam does not want God to be God. Thus the new powers of eccentric existence to want God to be God are nothing less than the self-donation of the Spirit of the Father and Son. It is this infusion of God's love by the Spirit that "inclines without necessitating."

What is really wrong then with Leibniz's *Theodicy,* according to Version Two, is the failure to pursue the insight just named, for this would have grounded conceptually the notion of a substantial but malleable human mind in a transformative metaphysics of eccentric anticipation rather than of self-identical persistence in what one has always been. The way forward for Leibniz would have been to apply the same pioneering forays into modal logic and epistemic perspectivalism to Luther's *deus absconditus* from the vantage of the *deus revelatus,* God declared in Christ, the Trinity. That would have eliminated the dualistic *deus exlex* from consideration, but not at all the very real human experience of the wrath of God — not God's hiddenness as "absence" of the Nanny in the sky, but God's love present and actual *sub contrario* in experiences of contradiction, frustration, oppression. This *deus absconditus* would be understood as the form (Luther: *larva,* mask) that the love of God actually takes on and as such appears in opposition to sinful egocentrism, yet for the sake of blessed eccentrism. God kills *in order* to make alive, since the triune God is able to give God without giving God away (Jüngel). But failing to draw fully on his tacit trinitarianism, as would have been necessary to meet the challenges of Hobbes and Spinoza by anchoring the human *Abbild* to the trinitarian *Urbild,* Leibniz in the end retreated to the semi-Pelagianism of the later Melanchthonian tradition, defending half-heartedly free will on purely a priori grounds, in order to maintain his posture as an independent, rational, or natural theologian, as a modern "philosopher" along with all the others after Descartes. Descartes's seminal appropriation of the image of God tradition for the new project of deism then prevailed. The modern God becomes infinite, unknowable power who in principle can deceive — the very thing we modern people would like to be (if we could, or, so far as we can).

But we cannot be the Trinity. We cannot even want to be the Trinity, whose life is inimitable, the one, sole, true life that is eternal. We can only participate in its life as its created images. *Pace* Marion, Leibniz's project — principle of sufficient reason and all — is distinguished in just this way from that of the "metaphysical empire," i.e., the very deism he opposed. From above, God is free *in this trinitarian way* to choose the best — metaphysically a world maximally populated with finite but real wills for God to enjoy, morally a world in which God in the person of His Son would undertake that finite freedom as His own project on behalf of creatures who had squandered it, aesthetically a world in which human minds can and may discover and delight in the harmony of vastly diverse things in the ecstasy of the Spirit. Consequently beings in bondage to egocentrism can be freed by the advent of the Word and Spirit of God. They can be set free from guilt by the word of forgiveness in Christ and from the power of sin by the outpouring of the Spirit's love in their hearts, objectively, as publicly formed to live together in and for that best of possible worlds, the biblical kingdom of God, the eternal republic of minds. That is divine charity

— contra Pascal[109] and his modern followers — that does not so much ascend from the world as include it in an achieved transcendence. Achieved transcendence: not an unnamed Infinite forming the static ground of phenomena, but the eternal life of the Father and the Son in the Holy Spirit laying claim to this world in the cross of Jesus.

The Contemporaneity of Theodicy

I admitted in the introduction to this book that I first became interested in Leibniz as I searched for an alternative to the Kantian frame of reference through which modern research sieved its Luther studies. There is, be it now acknowledged, an additional factor at work in my critical retrieval of Leibniz, and in particular my rereading of his *Theodicy* as theology, that by now may be evident: the American philosopher Daniel Dennett's book *Darwin's Dangerous Idea* is a work that awoke me from proverbial "dogmatic slumbers," by showing me in plain print how the Kantian walls of the past two centuries safely fencing off the realms of noumenal freedom and phenomenal necessity have indeed come crashing down like those of old Jericho. Dennett's is a resolutely necessitarian interpretation of biological evolution as an algorithmic process, random so far as intelligent designs are concerned, except that Dennett argues in the end for human exceptionalism, i.e., the emergence of "free will" as a product of blind "boot-strapping."[110] The book commences with, indeed, is emphatically and polemically directed against, theistic illusions about humanity's special creation.[111] Dennett's clichéd argument, which philosophically does not advance a paltry step beyond Spinoza, vanquishes an infantile caricature ("Tell me why the stars do shine"[112] as hymn of the faithful!). His more serious point is the Epicurean one that, disillusioned by Darwin's "universal acid," human beings may be mentally set free to undertake the long-overdue Promethean project of self-salvation, doing for themselves what hitherto they had haplessly left to God (really to evolution): "We need to grow up, in other words,"[113] which, in the context of this book, may be taken to mean that we take evolution into our own hands by our exceptional powers of intelligence and free will. And we won't let them fundamentalists (i.e., theists) get in the way!

While there are scientific truths involved here that contemporary theology would hardly wish to deny (see the discussion below of George Murphy's work), Dennett's philosophical appropriation of Darwin obtusely ignores the truly "dangerous" precedents for his project in versions of social

Darwinism culminating in Nazism.[114] In Leibnizian mode, I would counter-argue that his necessitarianism undergirds absolutist or monistic aspirations for power as in early modern philosophy, dangers Dennett would seem to check with the objectively desperate ploy of an "ain't we lucky" evolution of free will and a parasitic reliance on the "tradition" of humanistic ethics severed from Christian dogma — *if only* we resolutely act on it. That is a *deus ex machina* if ever there was one. Spinoza, at least, understood how unlikely any such claim to freedom must be in a world that aimlessly evolves by an "algorithmic process."

The contemporary theological alternative to Dennett that I will now briefly explore is little known today; the current options in philosophy are between blind necessitarianism and intelligent design, and in theology between versions of deism, including the interventionist deism championed by Isaac Newton and his theological partner Samuel Clarke, sometimes called "theism." *Trinitarian providentialism* is hardly recognized as a possibility. Providentialism, in the Augustinian, not Stoic, sense I wish to use this term, refers to God's wisdom in making good out of evil for God's final purposes of grace, in the pattern of the resurrection of the Crucified in temporal improvisations responding to actual evils. In this light, neither the aforementioned philosophical or theological options current today are acceptable. In a world filled with actual evils, intelligent design actually makes atheism attractive, since the moral purpose of grace for which the Trinity is creating the world according to revealed theology does not essentially inform such a restricted interpretation. From this perspective, intelligent design is refuted for our times with one word: the gas chambers at Auschwitz were "intelligently designed"! In place of this sterile old dispute between Epicureans and Stoics with Christian theological window-dressing, Ezio Vailati states the theological issue precisely: "The Newtonian God intervenes from time to time to mend the machine of the world. But, Leibniz claimed, 'when God makes miracles, it is not in order to supply the wants of nature, but those of grace.'"[115] The miracles of grace in the tradition of Luther and Melanchthon are the mysteries of creation from nothing that mark the line between Creator and creature: the origination of the world, the justification of the ungodly, the resurrection of the dead. These reveal God as the free, wise, and loving Creator in the works appropriated to the Father, the Son, and the Holy Spirit respectively. Thus they provide the turning points in the canonical narrative of grace in which nature begins, advances, and is fulfilled.

George L. Murphy, in *The Cosmos in the Light of the Cross,* accordingly rejects the predominant modern deistic alternatives between watchmaker and repairman views of divine action in favor of systematic theological interpretation of nature (as scientifically discovered) from the perspective of the revelation of God in the cross: God hidden works all in all, but the revelation of God's "theanthropic" purpose is found in the crucified Christ.[116] Such theological cosmology is necessary. The "mistake" of a "narrowly existentialist theology," Murphy writes, "is the idea that we can understand ourselves adequately as individuals isolated from the rest of the universe. We exist only as parts of humanity and of the whole world."[117] The neo-Protestant tack of carving out some special space in human self-consciousness for theology against or above nature as known by science simply makes theology into the ideology of a false and ecologically dangerous anthropocentrism. Opting for the theology of revelation instead, Murphy faces the enormous difficulties forthrightly: Why can the revealed God of the cross be ignored in scientific investigation of the world? How could the good God of revelation be involved in the "competition for resources and breeding, privation, and extinction [that] play a central role in evolution" as disclosed by science?[118] These are the basic theoretical (though not practical) questions of contemporary theodicy.

The first difficulty challenges the apparent teaching of Romans 1:20 about God's glory seeming evident in the things that are made. The methodological atheism of science as such never allows God to be perceptible this way. The plausibility structure of traditional cosmotheology is bracketed away indefinitely. "God of the gaps" apologetics are unconvincing, because methodologically contemporary natural science regards gaps in understanding as prods to further progress in naturalistic explanation. Murphy accepts this: God hides almighty power by His wisdom at work in the created order, God orders divine power in conformity with the functional integrity of the creation[119] according to the physical laws of the universe. Murphy therewith disavows not merely the deistic natural theology of Newton's repairman, but also the classic cosmological demonstrations of God's existence. Theology has to work in a world in which God seems scientifically unnecessary, if not implausible, *etsi deus non datur,* as Bonhoeffer famously wrote from his Nazi prison cell.

The second difficulty challenges God's goodness. It was the specter of "nature red in tooth and claw" that in fact caused Darwin to lose whatever remainder of Christian faith he still possessed, just as it inspired the post-Christian theological visions of Nietzsche and lesser imitators. Murphy contests this challenge to God's goodness; the theodicy he develops in response to it is the basic theological theme of his book. Granted that "the picture of a creator manipulating countless organisms and species through want, suffering and death in order to accomplish his purpose has an unpleasant look to it," Murphy nevertheless affirms that "God is not just a transcendent creator who manipulates terrestrial life, but Himself becomes a participant in evolution and dies as the dinosaurs and Neanderthals died."[120] This participation of God in the sufferings of His creation revealed in the Crucified, taken together with the revelation of God's theanthropic purpose in His resurrection, justifies the goodness of God in the cosmic process. "The God who is revealed to the universe is the crucified";[121] the universe in turn is stamped by the cross. Providence in the manner of the resurrection of the Crucified, not immanent teleology, issues in a theology of nature, not natural theology.

Thus Murphy's constructive proposal for "chiasmic cosmology" is put forward in answer to the great difficulties for a theology of revelation after the rise of scientific understanding of the natural world: (1) the methodological atheism of science reflects the Creator's kenotic self-limitation in granting existence to a relatively autonomous physical creation that can and does stand over against God and may even understand itself without God; (2) the same God in genuine divine goodness participates — and so cosuffers with the cocreating creature — in the same relatively autonomous natural processes. The result is Murphy's version of the Leibnizian theodicy that turns upon the difficult distinction between natural evil and moral evil, i.e., between the ontological vulnerability as such of any conceivable created beings in relation to others and the existential aggression creatures undertake out of needy greed and envy to secure their threatened existence at the expense of others. No genuine creature can be conceived apart from such intrinsic vulnerability — the metaphysical "evil" that is natural to anything that has come into being.[122] Indeed, the uniquely moral freedom of the rational creature lies in its response to just these intrinsic vulnerabilities manifest in the changes and chances of life. Natural evil provides the possibility of, but does not necessitate, moral evil. Natural evil must then be recognized as "the 'dark side' of an aspect of the goodness of creation, its functional integrity,"[123] e.g., Peacocke's pain, which is the price paid for the evolution of the brain, underwriting our higher consciousness.

With this distinction in hand, the goodness of God may be seen in God asking nothing of the creature that God does not also undertake. "If the divine self-limitation is grounded in a theology of the crucified, then we can say that God shares in paying the price that is necessary for the freedom and integrity of creation by going to the cross."[124] If the post-Darwinian objection to faith is revulsion at any deity who acted through "the 'messy, relentless slaughter' [Gould] of evolution"[125] as unworthy of worship, Murphy plays theological trump: "the hiddenness of God in the origin of the universe and the development of life through privation and extinction are seen in this light [of God's participation in suffering] as the work of the God 'who gives life to the dead and calls into existence the things that do no exist' (Rom 4:17)."[126] In evolutionary extinction and origination of new species we may see a type of the resurrection of the Crucified. Gould and Darwin's objection is not directly refuted. It is allowed to wreck the Nanny in the sky theology of naive anthropocentrism, but is then taken up in a higher synthesis that is instructive, at least, for Christian believers (though remaining, probably, implausible for those who do not believe). For believers, Murphy's crucified God demonstrates divine goodness and is worthy of worship in (1) self-limitation of power in creation so that creatures really can flourish, (2) redemptive participation out of love in the creature's inevitable suffering, (3) wisdom making good out of evil on the way to eschatological fulfillment. Power, wisdom, and love in harmony, since true power is manifest in restraint and grace is made perfect in weakness.

Yet "it would go too far to say that theology can make no contribution at all to the scientific enterprise."[127] Ethical and aesthetic motives for scientific work are found in "Judeo-Christian tradition," of course, which in point of historical fact gave birth to the culture in which modern science arose because the *imago dei* doctrine de-divinized the physical world and rendered it subject to human dominion. Murphy further argues that without reference to this God, science cannot cognitively "explain why some patterns rather than others are found." Theology that knows God's decision for the world could presumably give providential direction to scientific inquiry by speaking of God's supervening theanthropic purpose in creation. This is no longer methodologically science; it is metascientific, "metaphysical" in Leibniz's sense. Yet, if we have gotten past Kant, that can no longer be dismissed as simply noncognitive. It is cognitive as interpretation, as hermeneutics, as interpretation of mind to mind, where a meaningful debate about true and false, better and worse readings can take place. Admittedly the unbelieving rejoinder will be to decline such counsel as not a scientific matter at all. But as just conceded, this counsel is not narrowly scientific. Concealed here is a hidden dogma. Murphy makes note of Bertrand Russell's (Spinozan) disclaimer: "'The world as a whole just is, that's all. We start there.'"[128] Of course, this affirmation too is not narrowly scientific. But it is broadly philosophical. "Why does the universe go to all the bother of existing?" physicist Stephen Hawking asks, like Leibniz rising from the physical to the metaphys-

ical. "Is the unified theory so compelling that it brings about its own existence? Or does it need a creator, and if so, does He have any other effect on
the universe? And who created Him?"[129] The Kantian walls have tumbled.
Naturalism will have to take theological responsibility and own up to its
Spinozist metaphysics — or entertain other interpretative possibilities.

In seeking to establish some cognitive import for revealed theology
within this broadly philosophical field, Murphy thus distinguishes his approach from an abjectly kenotic theology that concedes everything to
Spinoza at the decisive point. Properly understood, "[k]enosis does not
mean God's abdication but God working in a way that is not recognizable to
theologians of glory."[130] Thus perspectivalism makes an appearance in distinction from Murphy's usual "critical realism." Murphy does not wish to
"abandon omnipotence" as in process thought,[131] and wants to affirm that
we "cannot thwart God's ultimate plans for creation, but God will not bring
those plans to fulfillment by protecting us from the consequences of our actions."[132] So also a Luther-like version of omnipotence returns. In this way
qualifications seem to pile up on each other. The difficulty is evident.
Murphy wants it both ways. He wants both the *almighty* God who is competent to fulfill the promise of *cosmic* salvation and at the same time he wants
the *wise and loving* God "who lets Himself be pushed out of the world onto a
cross" (Bonhoeffer). Murphy is right to want both — and for that matter
more. His is the one approach today in the growing literature on faith and
science of which I am aware that does not shrink from a genuine, biological
naturalism, but seeks and almost finds the way to integrate it with the revealed theology of grace. What holds Murphy back?

At bottom it is the ghost that haunts Lutheran theology: the accusation
of "theopanism." Murphy's ambivalence at the decisive point reflects an unacknowledged dogmatic decision, namely, that "Laplacian determinism"[133]
is the enemy, which we ought labor to escape since it threatens to undermine
human freedom. With this an opportunity is lost. Determinism is not taken
as an awareness in human consciousness of the efficacious divine decree
(also on the level of physical events) of trinitarian providentialism for which
we have been arguing: God is the One determined to create, redeem, and fulfill the *world* through Christ and the Spirit, and the *world* in question is the
same one on which the cross stood, the same world that natural science today explores. Instead we have to bet on chaos theory or quantum mechanics
riding to the rescue to preserve an element of contingency in the web of
things. Yet as Luther — one of Murphy's favorite sources — wrote to Erasmus: "all we do, however it may appear to us to be done mutably and contin-

gently, is in reality done necessarily and immutably in respect of God's will."[134]

Unless this thought *(Alleswirksamkeit)* of effective divine power working all things (though not making all choices, *Alleinwirksamkeit)* is followed through radically — whether we end up finally in the lap of Spinoza rather than Luther is the burning question — Murphy's justified desire to see the cosmos in the light of the cross collapses into one more theological apology for the "narrowly existentialist" self-transcending subject of the modern period. His attempt to eschew teleology in favor of providence grinds to a halt at the bogey of "determinism." Instead of looking for purpose in nature, he looks for contingency — as if this in the end made any real difference. The thin red thread of indeterminacy in natural systems cannot in any case provide for the freedom of choice in action that theology needs to establish rational minds as created replicas, not modes of God, and to grasp the determined incalculables of actual evil and actual holiness. The kind of freedom that quantum contingency as random fluctuation provides goes back to Epicurus; it would provide in any case only the "freedom of indifference" that, with Leibniz, is antithetical to Christian theological purposes. This is not the place to look for a solution. Melanchthon, Leibniz, and Barth all point us in a better direction: true freedom is the law of our own created being, when our being is the creature being created by God, each one on our own individual pathway, by the journey with Jesus through the cross to the crown as God has determined in eternity and now innovates by the Spirit in time. False freedom, which is nonetheless real choice in action, is to choose on this way the very possibilities for us that God has rejected, to actualize another self out of mistrust and envy and so trigger whirlwinds of havoc into the web of life. Sin, then, in a public, indeed cosmic, theology is not merely an impossible human possibility. It is *demonic* in origin and cosmic in effects. The problem is whether *just this* entails theopanism.

Theopanism?

With the collapse of the Kantian boundaries that have kept cultural peace, and the new appearance of naive aspirations for totality in secular fundamentalists like Dennett, the vexing debates of early modernity return as our own. According to Leibniz's interpretation, his contemporaries, Hobbes and Spinoza, denied contingency and denied as well human freedom of desire. By a law of nature we simply desire what appears good to us and what appears to us as good is locked in by an inexorable, immanent chain of causality. In turn, these early moderns anchored this necessitarianism, inclusive of human perception, desire, and action, in the immutable foreknowledge of the divine mind, understanding this in a pantheistic way, *deus sive natura.* As mentioned, these authors followed Descartes in thinking this new divinity liberating, since by this light the natural will can become godlike by exercising sovereign preference according to the immanent law of their own nature for self-preservation or expansion. Their usual opponents representing traditional views of moral agency asserted against them an increasingly heteronomous divine law, as if to check one ego with another. In thinking this way, early moderns imagined a choice between impersonal deism and personal theism, trinitarianism increasingly eclipsed by the perception of the *deus absconditus,* as God appears in the "light of nature." In so thinking, these early moderns may well have been taking up ideas that had been disseminated afresh by Luther's arguments against Erasmus in *De servo arbitrio.* Were they justified in doing so?

In the *Theodicy,* Leibniz makes a point of telling us that he did not think so. "Mr. Hobbes maintains that even divine foreknowledge alone would be sufficient to establish an absolute necessity of events. This was also the opinion of Wycliff, and even of Luther, when he wrote *De servo arbitrio;* or at least they spoke so."[135] But Luther's language about the immutable necessity of divine foreknowledge, so Leibniz argues, was imprecise (as Luther himself apparently came to recognize).[136] As previously discussed, Luther's "necessity of divine foreknowledge" was intended theologically to affirm that God cannot deny Himself, no matter how faithless the creatures to whom He has pledged Himself (2 Tim. 2:13); it was intended pastorally to assure martyrs suffering persecution. Luther, with characteristic urgency, impatience, and imprecision, failed here sufficiently to mind his own distinction between the old philosophical way of thinking and speaking and the new theological grammar. The "immutable necessity of divine foreknowledge" means one thing in natural perspective, another in supernatural perspective. Leibniz accordingly interpreted Luther's ambiguous language with his own characteristic modal analysis: "it is sufficiently acknowledged today that this kind of necessity which is termed hypothetical, and springs from foreknowledge or from other anterior reasons, has nothing in it to arouse one's alarm; whereas it would be quite otherwise if the thing were necessary of itself, in such a way that the contrary implied contradiction. . . . This kind of necessity is happy and desirable, when one is prompted by good reasons to act as one does; but necessity blind and absolute would subvert piety and morality."[137] The former "good" necessity reflects the divine determination as *necessitas moralis ad optimum;* the latter is an "algorithmic process" elevated to the status of the divine. The One appears as divine resolve to save, the Other as Crushing. The issue reverts to who or what is regarded as God. That *really* depends on perspective.

In this light, as we shall shortly see, Leibniz's *Theodicy* reads as a new appropriation of Luther's twofold belief[138] that the human will is naturally bound to choose whatever appears best to it, just as God's Spirit alone gives by grace the new eyes of faith to see what is truly best — the Man dying on the cross from whom the natural will averts as repugnant — so that love spontaneously arises for the Lamb of God bearing away the sin of the world, also one's own.

Luther is not of course the whole story of the *Theodicy*. Leibniz's overarching argument is that God, as cause of all causes, though not maker of all choices, is justified in His judgments since divine determination is compatible with human freedom, given certain clarifications. The first clarification is that God's moral determination to mercy for all "inclines without necessitating," that is, human beings always have logical possibilities alternative to the best that God antecedently wills for them, and accordingly, can, albeit to their own destruction, fall into error or will the impossible possibility of sin. In Version One above, we saw how this distinction evaporates when God's moral purpose of love collapses into God's intellectual knowledge of essences. In Version Two, we saw that Leibniz may instead be read as a trinitarian theologian, for whom God's knowledge of things just is the value-bestowing love that He powerfully shows in acts of justice by which He providentially rules. The God who justifies the ungodly by the justice of His own Son's innocent death in their place is the God who knows the creature redeemed in Christ and destined for fulfillment in the Spirit. It is this God who inclines all to mercy, yet without necessitating, that is coercing any. Following Saint Thomas (and correcting Luther's hasty dismissal of Thomas's distinction in this connection between antecedent and consequent will in God),[139] Leibniz therefore affirms that God's immutable foreknowledge is not absolute in the sense of an impersonal, blind, and arbitrary algorithm; it is modal or hypothetical, i.e., an omnipotent, omniscient, and benevolent *counsel* to create, redeem, and fulfill the world through Jesus Christ with all that this involves, including the permission of Adam's fall into sin with all the pain and suffering, including God's own, this entails. As hypothetical or consequent will, God's will to mercy inclines all without necessitating any. It is potentially universal.

The second clarification is that in no case may human freedom be understood as an arbitrary capacity for self-determination, what Leibniz named the "freedom of indifference." This must be denied in order to establish perspectivalism, which insists that any possible agent is also at the same time a patient, i.e., an interested, embodied, situated organism or system of desires formed by its own receptivity to its world with all that appears in it and is so perceived, consciously or unconsciously. In this latter case, there will be neither freedom not to will, nor to desire just anything, nor to will to will. One is bound to will something as good, or perversely, even nothing as something good (as in suicide or other behaviors objectively destructive of oneself as the foregoing patient/agent). This is Luther's most profound insight, building upon Augustine and Paul. There is no freedom of desire (except in the sense of desire being owned as my own, not imposed on me by another). But desire as such is bound spontaneously to avert the evil and seek the good. If this is not the case, the agent/patient in question is pathologically afflicted. In egocentric Adam, however, the creaturely *conatus* is deformed into concupiscence; it seeks self in all things as its good, rather than God. In eccentric existence in Christ, the creaturely *conatus* is reformed by the Spirit into charity. It loves God in all things. Between these there is no neutrality; there is no *conatus* as such before God. The "passive disposition" to love some good, which truly is God, is in thrall of idols and demons in the human world exiled from the paradisaical possibility since Adam's fall. True freedom comes about as liberation from these captors and for the true good, the pearl of great price, the life of the kingdom.

Thus the clarification: by the bondage of the will *(voluntas)* an anthropological concept is intended about the kind of will any conceivable creature has. The captivity of choice *(arbitrium)* in distinction refers to a salvation history concept: human wills exiled from Paradise are now without choice in relation to God, though not with respect to things in the world. Adam's fateful act at the head of the race means that his posterity is born in exile, the original choice for pure obedience is forfeit, the choices now available in relation to God are only between lesser (civil righteousness) and greater evils (social injustice). Given that all post-paradisaical choices are defective in relation to God, in other words, real alternatives nonetheless remain among these, which matter greatly for life in the City of Man, but never as greatly as egocentric Adam thinks. I may out of fear of imprisonment or love of public esteem refrain from cheating on my taxes; the fear of trouble or lust for approval makes the choice not to cheat worthless before God, though not to my fellow taxpayers. A definite freedom of action remains as well, if one can refrain from acting on one's desire by critically challenging the appearance of good and indeed seeking other possibilities of good. With these theological ideas from *De servo arbitrio* in the background, Leibniz acknowledges the determination of human perception by its actual experience in the world, and thus also of the formation of human desire uncovered by the rise of modern science's insight into the chains of physical and social causality. "[C]hoice is always determined by perception."[140]

Therein lies an ambiguity. The question is this: Does Leibniz mean that choice is caused by perception as an effect, or does he mean that it is construed in perception as an appearance of good antecedently sought by the creature in its act of being? In the former case, Leibniz is indeed crypto-Spinozist,[141] and Version One triumphs. In the latter case, Leibniz is an Augustinian, and Version Two triumphs, since (1) sufficient freedom of choice and action remains to the nonpathological civil person to question appearances and seek alternatives, which suffices for human civil morality, and (2) the Holy Spirit in providing "divine faith" must act to change perception of the Crucified from One disgraced to Source of grace. As Leibniz wrote in *Theodicy,* "divine faith itself, when it is kindled in the soul, is something more than an opinion, and depends not upon the occasions or the motives that have given it birth; it advances beyond the intellect, and takes possession of the will and of the heart, to make us act with zeal and joyfully as the law of God commands."[142] Thus Leibniz wants to locate these chains of causality, including the mechanisms of perception that form appearances of the good, within the larger canonical narrative where the Spirit can act temporally and innovate actual holiness, just as the mind can imagine incalculable evil.

The real difficulty for Leibniz's account lies, as Version Two suggests, in the impossible possibility of *knowingly* choosing what on Leibniz's pneumatological account must be irrational and unmotivated. Leibniz acknowledged the difficulty. He was criticized for reiterating the shibboleth of anti-Catholic Lutheran polemics, the Thomistic (or Melanchthonian, not nominalist) motto *facere quod in se,* meaning that if the natural person does what she is capable of, she manifests prevenient grace at work in her that God in turn graciously completes and rewards.[143] Leibniz, as we saw above, had casually employed the loaded expression *facere quod in se* in reference to the possible salvation of non-Christians,[144] that "man helps himself in conversion through the succor of grace." But, he now writes in virtually Gnesio-Lutheran self-defense, this can "mean only that he derives advantage from it through the cessation of the resistance overcome, but without any cooperation on his part: just as there is no co-operation in ice when it is broken. For conversion is purely the work of God's grace, wherein man co-operates only by resisting it."[145] The defensive tone — Leibniz was more than once the victim of uncomprehending conservatives who did not recognize the battlefield on which he was engaged or the stakes for which he played — should not belie the truth of his public confession. "I have expounded sufficiently elsewhere that in relation to matters of salvation unregenerate man is to be considered as dead; and I greatly approve the manner wherein the theologians of the Augsburg Confession declare themselves on this subject."[146] Thus Leibniz can agree that apart from the enlightening grace of the Holy Spirit the fallen mind cannot see the good of Jesus' cross and believe it, or lacking these historical dogmas of revealed religion, come substantively to the same love of God for God's sake and of all others in and under God as Christians see in the dying Son of God.

In this light, the real difficulty emerges. Even if enlightened, does it follow then that the mind is simply *coerced* by sight of the true good to see and believe (think of Saul on the road to Damascus) in the same way that physical evidence *forces* the verdict of science that such and such is the case in the natural world? On the other hand, if it is not coerced, as it were, by the Spirit's illumination putting the evidence in true light, if instead the perceiver herself is transformed to "divine faith" by which to see the good of the cross ("advancing beyond the intellect, and taking possession of the will and of the heart, to make us act with zeal and joyfully"), can one thus behold this true good and yet knowingly, willfully refuse it? Is grace, truly imparted, resistible? Can one so transformed fall again from grace (think of Peter, witness of the transfiguration, who denied the Lord)? The latter conception of resistible grace admits a possibility of actual sin for which Leibniz's system hardly allows. Yet the former idea of irresistible grace seems to compel faith under certain conditions.

Leibniz seems to leave this difficulty unresolved. But in fact he treats the difference as a matter of perspective on the same event viewed from above and from below. For example, in one passage of the *Theodicy* these enigmas lead Leibniz to state concerning the "use of terms like 'necessary,' or 'contingent,' 'possible' or 'impossible,'" that "Luther desired, in his book *On the Will in Bondage,* to find a word more fitting for that which he wished to express than the word necessity." Yet Leibniz, thinking of the first possibility of divine faith as "coerced" by revelation of the true God, allowed to Luther use of the strong term "necessity," according the perspective from above. Here there is "a sense wherein it would be permitted to say, in certain conjunctures, that the *power* to do good is often lacking, even in the just; that sins are often *necessary,* even in the regenerate; that it is *impossible* sometimes for one not to sin; that grace is *irresistible;* that freedom is not exempt from *necessity.*" There are, Leibniz acknowledged, "circumstances, which render [these terms] acceptable and even serviceable." It seems to depend on the rhetorical needs. Just so, he immediately commented: "But these expressions are less exact and less pleasing in the circumstances that prevail about us today." Why is that? Because today, for Leibniz, is marked by the rise of the new fatalisms and so, in the perspective from below "generally, it appears more reasonable and more fitting to say the obedience to God's precepts is always *possible,* even for the unregenerate; that the grace of God is always *resistible,* even in those most holy, and the *freedom* is exempt not only from *constraint* but also from *necessity,* although it be never without infallible *certainty* or without inclining *determination.*" With this dual perspective, from above and from below respectively, on one and the same event of coming to faith, Leibniz thought he had squared the circle. He concluded that "there is no more real contradiction [between these two vocabularies] than between St. Paul and St. James [not to mention Luther and Melanchthon!], or any error on either side that might be attributable to the ambiguity of the terms." Is compatibilism thus achieved then by logical analysis and clarification of terminology on the basis of epistemic perspectivalism or a rule theory of doctrine (K. Tanner)?

Klaus Schwarzwäller would think not. He has influentially argued that Luther's tract against Erasmus has been a "shibboleth" precisely because its unmitigated necessitarianism represents paradoxically the end of all metaphysics by which the "natural man" would secure himself against the *Alleinwirksamkeit Gottes.*[147] As such, *De servo arbitrio* is also said to sound the death knell for all theodicy: "Luther is far removed from any theodicy."[148] This claim is manifestly untrue, however. Luther *develops* the Pauline theodicy of Romans 8; in the light of glory, *De servo arbitrio* concludes, believers shall see how God is and has been just. On the other hand, it is precisely the light of grace shining in the present upon the few faithful amid the *massa damnata* that offends human reason and its sense of justice. It is grace itself that provokes for Luther at the climax of his book a new, intensified question of theodicy. Leibniz clearly grasped Luther's meaning here in a way that Schwarzwäller simply sweeps from the stage. Leibniz had written some years prior to the *Theodicy,* in the essay "On Freedom": "One of the oldest doubts of mankind concerns the question of how freedom and contingency are compatible with the chain of causes and with providence. And Christian investigations of the justice of God in accomplishing man's salvation have merely increased the difficulty of the matter."[149] The latter reference is nothing if not to the conclusion of *De servo arbitrio,* where the Reformer underscored the scandal of particularity as really a scandal to the human sense of God's justice.

I take Luther's argument as follows. By the light of nature human beings acknowledge a sovereign power presiding in the world, but are plagued by doubt concerning its intelligence and wisdom on the one side, and its goodness and care on the other. The light of grace demonstrates to those chosen that God cares for the human creature and in this way meets the doubt about God's goodness. But doubt concerning God's wisdom is not silenced; it is rather exacerbated. Grace comes as *folly,* scandal, stumbling block since, as it is procured by Christ alone, it is distributed by the Spirit's preaching to faith alone. As such saving faith is given, so it appears, to one but not another. This apparent passing over of those not given faith calls into question the justice of God, that is, the wisdom of God's charity. It elicits the new temptation that believers now regard themselves as chosen for reasons of superior merit, as worthy of grace, thus subverting the gratuity of grace. For both of these reasons, the theology of the justification of the sinner *demands* a justification for the scandal of grace distributed through the folly of preaching, a *theodicy* that disbars merit as the cause of election and rather justifies God's wisdom for leaving us ignorant of its cause. Luther himself was satisfied with the assured trust that the prophet Habakkuk had preached six centuries before Christ, a motif the apostle Paul had famously appropriated at the head of his epistle to the Romans: *the just will live by their faith* in the fulfillment of God's promises. Trust in the light of grace professes that it cannot yet see the justice of God's historical choices yet believes that in the light of glory the temporal decisions will be seen as just.

Given the biblical background in Habakkuk ("How long, O Lord!") via Paul, and Luther's utilization of it, it is manifestly false then to assert that "Luther is far removed from any theodicy." Yet for good reason, many find Luther's conclusion unsatisfying as theodicy in that it is not clear what actually he is hinting at. Does he mean that in the light of glory the redeemed shall see the good reason for the damnation of the mass of humanity and be rationally reconciled to it? Or does he mean that in the light of glory the redeemed will include infinitely more than is visible now, as the apostle hinted when he concluded in the seminal discussion of our theme in Romans 9–11 that God consigned all to sin in order to have mercy on all? Leibniz developed Luther's theodicy in the second direction and in this way, as previously argued, anticipated Barth. The present point is that Luther's conclusion cannot stand as it is; it must be developed beyond what he was willing to say (if only to clarify the sense of "necessity"), because the alternative is surrendering the field either to the cheap grace of an easy universalism or the triumphalism of grace merited by accidents of history or self-chosen religious works.

Schwarzwäller, however, writes: "It is absurd to submit, by itself and in all its exclusivity to the God-for-us, Jesus Christ, who is nonetheless identical with the hidden God — and that as a risk, without security, without guarantees, only on the mere word of the gospel."[150] "Absurd" is precisely the right word. No one should surrender to any fiats under any circumstances, least of all in critical theology that tests the spirits. If Schwarzwäller is right, not only is the unity of God snuck in here by the backdoor with a passing comment, but also the name Jesus Christ no longer refers to Melanchthon's mediator, not to mention Luther's joyful exchange; it refers to nothing but an act of bald assertion: Christ as contentless kerygma announcing grace. "Beneath this radical question about Jesus Christ, beneath this renunciation of all other questions, metaphysics collapses, and it can immediately be added here: Whatever in this text is found as a metaphysical construction becomes so completely dysfunctional through the entire context, that it serves precisely the destabilization [*Absicherung*] of metaphysics. Precisely because Luther asks only about Jesus Christ and does not also ask about overcoming metaphysics — as if that were a theological theme — it collapses."[151] This melodramatic characterization of Luther's treatise does not stand up to scrutiny.

First, as we have seen, the critique of metaphysics deriving from Romans 8 is an important theme for Luther's theology. Second, *De servo arbitrio* is far more about pneumatology than Christology; the issue is not whether Christ lived and died and rose for all, but why the Spirit grants faith to one and not another, when Christ died for the purpose of faith. Therewith, third, the problem of *the unity* of God in his works and so faith's *own* question about the justice of God *because* of the scandalous particularity of grace is raised in a way that must be expressed and confessed, not simply rejected out of hand as the indicating "return of metaphysics." Schwarzwäller writes: "The unity of God does not let itself be established or ascertained conceptually; much more God transcends all conceptual possibilities."[152] But certainly for Luther the tri-unity of God can be conceptually expressed (*opera dei sunt indivisibila*);[153] if we interpret Luther's rhetorical excesses in *De servo arbitrio* in the light of the *theologia crucis* of the Heidelberg Disputation, or in the light of the second Galatians commentary's formula, "God kills in order to make alive," we are speaking of the *one* God hidden in revelation and revealed in hiddenness, i.e., whose mercy is hidden in anger at sin and whose anger is hidden by the justification of the naked sinner now clothed by faith in the crucified Christ. Otherwise, what is to keep Luther's light of grace from assimilating to the light of nature as in modern pantheism? Or evolving into the benign but impotent god of contemporary neo-Gnosticism? It was with such justification that Leibniz sought to make common cause with *De servo arbitrio* in his *Theodicy*.

The *Theodicy*'s Appeal to *De Servo Arbitrio*

At the beginning of this book, I cited Leibniz's autobiographical remark about how as a young reader, he "flitted from book to book, and since subjects for meditation pleased me as much as histories and fables, I was charmed by the work of Laurentius Valla against Boethius and by that of Luther against Erasmus, although I was well aware that they had need of some mitigation."[154] In the intervening pages, we have learned that the "mitigation" was at hand in his own Melanchthonian tradition. "Nor did I neglect the teachings of our theologians: and the study of their opponents, far from disturbing me, served to strengthen me in the moderate opinions of the Churches of the Augsburg Confession."[155] Thus Leibniz locates both his attraction to necessitarianism and his "mitigated" version of it to countervailing tendencies latent in his own theological tradition going back to Luther's *De servo arbitrio* on the one side and Melanchthon's general pneumatology on the other. Were this theological milieu in late-seventeenth-century Lutheranism not clear enough, Leibniz's scorn in the *Theodicy* is reserved for the supralapsarian doctrine of the double decree of election and reprobation stemming from second-generation Calvinism. He articulates the standard Lutheran position: "As for the destination of the elect to eternal life . . . those who are called Evangelicals, that is, those of the Augsburg Confession, hold . . . that one need not go into the hidden causes of election while one may find a manifest cause of it shown in Holy Scripture, which is faith in Jesus Christ; and it appears to them that the prevision of the cause is also the cause of the prevision of the effect."[156] Presupposing an "unlimited atonement," which implicitly, though not yet (until Barth!) explicitly, made Lutherans potential universalists, Leibniz focused criticism particularly on "the oration made by Theodore de Beze at the Conference of Montbeliard in the year 1586. . . . 'God created the World to his glory: his glory is not known (according to Beze) if his mercy and his justice are not declared; for this cause simply by his grace he decreed for some men life eternal and for others by a just judgment eternal damnation.'" Leibniz laconically comments: "This system is not of the best conceived: it is not well fitted to show forth wisdom, the goodness and the justice of God; and happily," he adds, "it is almost abandoned today."

Why does the doctrine fail? "If there were not other more profound reasons capable of inducing God to permit guilt, the source of misery, there would be neither guilt nor misery in the world," he argues in terms of the principle of sufficient reason, "for the reasons alleged here do not suffice."[157] Leibniz enlists Luther as well as Calvin[158] in support of this critique of the *decretum absolutum,* which runs like a red thread through the *Theodicy.* "If there are people who believe that election and reprobation are accomplished on God's part by a despotic absolute power, not only without any apparent reason but actually without any reason, even a concealed one, they maintain an opinion that destroys alike the nature of things and the divine perfection." Leibniz sarcastically called this a doctrine of an *"absolutely absolute decree,"* and he averred that "Luther and Calvin were far from such a belief: the former hopes that the life to come will make us comprehend the just reasons of God's choice; and the latter protests explicitly that these reasons are just and holy, although they be unknown to us."[159] Leibniz's theological purpose in the *Theodicy* is defined by opposition to Beza's brand of hyper-Calvinism: "Our end is to banish from men the false ideas that represent God to them as an absolute prince."[160]

It was out of this milieu of a tension-laden theological tradition, Leibniz continues, that in "the year 1673 . . . already I laid down that God, having chosen the most perfect of all possible worlds, had been prompted by his wisdom to permit the evil which was bound up with it, but which still did not prevent this world from being, all things considered, the best that could be chosen." Leibniz's autobiographical reflection in the *Theodicy* concludes by coming full circle: "I have endeavored to make progress in the knowledge that seems to me proper for banishing all that could have obscured the idea of supreme perfection which must be acknowledged in God." Accomplishing the justification of God in this way consists in taking up and defeating the most powerful counterarguments, and thus Leibniz seamlessly extended his project from criticism of Beza to Hobbes and Spinoza. "I have not neglected to examine the most rigorous authors, who have extended furthest the doctrine of the necessity of things, as for example Hobbes and Spinoza . . . that all has come from the first cause or from primitive Nature by a blind and geometrical necessity, with complete absence of capacity for choice for goodness and for understanding in the first source of things."[161] What is at stake in theodicy is true blessedness confirmed and false doctrine, which deviates from true blessedness, refuted. "It is no small thing to be content with God and the universe, not to fear what destiny has in store for us, nor to complain of what befalls us," Leibniz writes in an echo of Luther's theology of the martyrs. "Acquaintance with true principles gives us this advantage, quite other than that the Stoics and Epicureans derived from their philosophy. There is as much difference between true morality and theirs as there is between joy and patience: for their tranquility was founded only on necessity, while ours must rest upon the perfection and beauty of things, upon our own happiness."[162]

Theodicy is doctrinal theology; it as much about refuting false doctrine that leads astray from blessedness as it is about the mind justifying God's ways by understanding and rendering thanks in true blessedness. Leibniz can as readily swing back to rival theological positions emerging in his own day. Thinking of God as the arbitrary power at work in nature whose grace is a despotic act indistinguishable from the factual course of events has the two-sided effect, in Leibniz's view, of collapsing the light of grace back into the light of nature on the one side, and of calling forth in protest against the tyranny of the God of this world a revival of Manichean dualism on the other. Pierre Bayle represented that revival of Manicheism, in Leibniz's words, restoring "the lapsed dogma of the two principles, or two gods, the one good, the other evil, as if this dogma were a better solution to the difficulties over the origin of evil."[163] The opposite error belongs to the Socinians, who collapse God back into nature, reduce grace to good fortune, and make happiness depend on a putative human freedom of indifference. These, like Plato, have limited God's power, "have rather chosen to deny to God a knowledge of the detail of things and, above all, of future events, than to admit what they believed repellent to his goodness."[164] At the root of all these philosophical and theological errors of his times, Leibniz identifies the voluntarists, as discussed above, who "have indeed renounced the dogma which recognizes God's justice and goodness. They thought that, being supreme Master of the universe, he could without any detriment to his holiness cause sins to be committed, simply at his pleasure, or in order that he might have the pleasure of punishing." These theologians "liken us to earthworms which men crush without heeding as they walk," and so we can hardly be surprised when people begin to think like earthworms (who would in turn like to become crushers). "For what idea shall we form of such a justice as has only will for its rule, that is to say, where the will is not guided by the rules of good and even tends directly toward evil?"[165] Three errors here are convertible: "All these three dogmas, albeit a little different from one another, namely, (1) that the nature of justice is arbitrary, (2) that it is fixed, but it is not certain that God will observe it, and finally, (3) that the justice we know is not that which he observes, destroy the confidence in God that gives us tranquility, and the love of God that makes our happiness." The reason why is that "there is nothing to prevent such a God from behaving as a tyrant and an enemy of honest folk, and from taking pleasure in that which we call evil. Why should he not, then, just as well be the evil principle of the Manichaeans as the single good principle of the orthodox?"[166] All the erring positions, in other words, miss the trinitarian conjunction of power, wisdom, and love in God in virtue of which God is God worthy of supreme love, the One in whom all created things may be loved truly.

Fundamental to this justification of God that culminates in doxology is Luther's problem: "there remains the question why God does not deliver all — why he delivers the lesser number and why some in preference to others. He is in truth their master, but he is a good and just master; his power is absolute, but his wisdom permits not that he exercises that power in an arbitrary and despotic way, which would be tyrannous indeed."[167] Leibniz argues earnestly in this connection that Luther in fact agrees with him. "The Reformers, and especially Luther, as I have already observed, spoke sometimes as if they rejected philosophy, and deemed it inimical to faith. But, properly speaking, Luther understood by philosophy only that which is in conformity with the ordinary course of Nature, or perhaps even philosophy as it was taught in the schools." The observation is shrewd and may reflect knowledge of the later Luther's "new and theological language," which nevertheless trades upon the "old philosophical or natural language." (This is not so much a "double truth theory"[168] as a double perspective theory, as I have argued elsewhere.)[169] Leibniz is in any event historically right to observe that "Aristotle was the object of [Luther's] anger; and so far back as the year 1516 he contemplated the purging of philosophy." Leibniz, again correctly, observes that "at last [Luther] curbed his vehemence and in the Apology of the Augsburg Confession allowed a favorable mention of Aristotle and his Ethics." Its author, Melanchthon, he immediately added, was "a man of sound and moderate ideas, made little systems from the several parts of philosophy, adapted to the truths of revelation and useful in civic life, which deserve to be read even now."[170]

Leibniz's apparent knowledge of the tensions between Luther and Melanchthon is thus evident. Yet our claim is stronger than to depict for

Leibniz a merely psychological preference for moderate Melanchthon's judi-
cious appreciation of Aristotle over Luther's irrational vehemence. In fact,
Melanchthon is otherwise absent in the *Theodicy* where Leibniz instead takes
up as the very model of rational faith the question Luther framed at the end
of *De servo arbitrio*. "By the light of grace, it is inexplicable how God can
damn him who by his own strength can do nothing but sin and become
guilty. Both the light of nature *and the light of grace* here insist that the fault
lies not in the wretchedness of man, but in the injustice of God; nor can they
judge otherwise of a God who crowns the ungodly freely, without merit, and
does not crown, but damns another, who is perhaps less, and certainly not
more, ungodly. But the light of glory insists otherwise."[171] Thus Luther summons readers to trust in the future revelation of a "God Whose justice is
most righteous and most evident" — a trust of which the good reason in the
interim can only be the *deus revelatus in Christo*.[172] Leibniz *expressly agrees*
with Luther's appeal to such faith in the *Theodicy:* "It is thus that, being
made confident by demonstrations of the goodness and justice of God, we
disregard the appearances of harshness and injustice which we see in this
small portion of his Kingdom that is exposed to our gaze. Hitherto we have
been illumined by the *light of Nature* and by that of *grace,* but not yet by that
of *glory.* Here on earth we see apparent injustice, and we believe and even
know the truth of the hidden justice of God; but we shall see that justice
when at last the Sun of Justice shall show himself as he is."[173]

Leibniz in this way lays claim to the correct interpretation of Luther's
argument as the theodicy of faith, which for him is harmonious with the
theodicy of true reason; and so Leibniz argues against the interpretive possibility of equating Luther with Tertullian's (or Schwarzwäller's) *certum est,
quia impossibilia*.[174] He cites the thought of Luther just quoted from *De servo
arbitrio's* conclusion: "'Si placet tibi Deus indignos coronans, non debet
displicere immeritos damnans.'" Reducing it, Leibniz explains, "to more
temperate phrasing, [this] means: If you approve that God give eternal glory
to those who are not better than the rest, you should not disapprove that he
abandon those who are not worse than the rest." It is justice that God condemns the guilty. If it pleases you to have been singled out from these guilty
to be received into favor, you cannot deny that those left in guilt are nevertheless justly condemned. Having said that, Leibniz continues, "to judge that
[Luther] speaks only of appearances of injustice, one only has to weigh these
words of the same author taken from the same book: 'In all the rest,' he says,
'we recognize . . . that [God] has promised us that the time shall come when
his glory being revealed all men shall see clearly that he has been and that he

is just."[175] Leibniz takes this to mean that what makes faith in God's revealed choices rational is not only that it probes motives of credibility and tests the spirits, but that it expects to see satisfied a common standard of justice when all the evidence becomes available to all. It remains rational faith in divine Reason: "there are reasons for God's choice . . . but it does not seem that this choice can be subjected to a rule such as we are capable of conceiving, and such as may flatter the pride of men . . . that we not have cause to vaunt ourselves, it is necessary that we be ignorant of the reasons for God's choice."[176]

This would amount to an extraordinary concession on the part of the *rationalist* Leibniz, but as Steven Nadler has suggested, for the *theologian* Leibniz, like his Jansenist correspondent Arnauld, "it is all a matter of perspective."[177] With the necessary ignorance of rational faith that cannot yet see all things in their final coherence thus affirmed, Leibniz writes, "it is not to be doubted that this faith and this confidence in God, who gives us insight into his infinite goodness and prepares us for his love, in spite of the appearances of harshness that may repel us, are an admirable exercise for the virtues of Christian theology, when the divine grace in Jesus Christ arouses these motions within us." In this way Leibniz embraces the "theological paradoxes" of the early Luther's *theologia crucis* about what appears to be evil yet in reality is good (though probably Luther's thoughts on this have been mediated to him through *De servo arbitrio*). "That is what Luther aptly observed in opposition to Erasmus, saying that it is love in the highest degree to love him who to flesh and look appears so unlovable, so harsh toward the unfortunate and so ready to condemn, and to condemn for evils in which he appears to be the cause or accessory, at least in the eyes of those who allow themselves to be dazzled by false reasons." It is the *theologia gloriae* that is "dazzled by false reasons," while true faith apprehends the mercy hidden in sufferings and the cross. Thus Leibniz concludes, "one may therefore say that that triumph of true reason illuminated by divine grace is at the same time the triumph of faith and love."[178] *Credo, ut intelligam.* Otherwise (as already Anselm contended against the fideists),[179] faith is dumb submission, a mass of uncomprehended beliefs accepted on mere authority, or, what is worse, a willful leap in the dark. But, Leibniz argued, "We should see, and should not believe only, that what God has done is the best. I call 'seeing' here what one knows a priori by the causes; and 'believing' what one only judges by the effects."[180] Intellectual seeing, in other words, is grasping the reasons for the divine effects, as these paradoxes appearing *sub contrario* are grasped in turn by divine faith, the gift of the Holy Spirit. Thus "triumph of true reason illuminated by divine grace is at the same time the triumph of faith and love."

We should surely see at work in this Melanchthon's correction of Luther: "But since reason is a gift of God, even as faith is, contention between them would cause God to contend against God; and if the objections of reason against any article of faith are insoluble, then it must be said that this alleged article will be false and not revealed: this will be a chimera of the human mind, and the triumph of this faith will be capable of comparison with bonfires lit after a defeat."[181] The deep reason is that God and His creation stand and fall together. Grace can go beyond what God has given in nature but not against it, "lest God contend against God," as the Manicheans have it. Having affirmed this principle, however, Leibniz *never* claims that reason already can see empirically into the good reasons of God for every event. As we have just seen, he expressly denies it. Such criticism of Leibniz is based upon a misreading. His point is the same as Luther's: faith on the basis of the grace revealed in Christ and given to some, but not others, is sufficient for sustaining faith in God's ultimate justice, even in face of contrary experience. "It is true that the counsels of God are inscrutable, but there is no invincible objection which tends to the conclusion that they are unjust. What appears [as] injustice on the part of God, and foolishness in our faith, only appears so."[182]

Thus we see in Leibniz's *Theodicy* an interest in Luther's *De servo arbitrio* that is serious, insofar as Leibniz followed Luther in seeing Erasmus as a proto-deist. He followed as well the theological shift away from anxious inquiry into the hidden cause of an individual's fate in God's absolute decree to the manifest cause of election through faith in Jesus Christ who died for all, as this dogma is in turn probed by the principle of sufficient reason. This justifies as rational the Christian's faith in the universal justice of God, even though the divine choices in history remain inscrutable. At the same time, this shift yields a fundamental reconceptualization of the doctrine of election more in keeping with the actual teaching of Scripture (Rom. 9–11), namely, "that men are chosen and ranged not so much according to their excellence as according to their conformity with God's plan."[183] Leibniz is explicit about the source of his views in this regard.

> The Formula of Concord, building upon some passages of St. Augustine, comprised in the same Decree of Election salvation and the means that conduce to it. . . . God, before decreeing anything, considered among other possible sequences of things that one which he afterwards approved. In the idea of this is represented [fall, redemption through Christ, salvation and damnation, the whole economy]. . . . Thus God's pronouncement concerns the whole sequence at the same time; he simply decrees its

existence. In order to save other men, or in a different way, he must needs choose an altogether different sequence, seeing that all is connected in each sequence . . . there would be only one total decree, which is to create such a world.[184]

With this appeal to trinitarian providentialism, the idea so damaging to God's reputation that this world is all a show to sort out the sheep and the goats is overcome. Any idea that one must choose theologically between protology and eschatology, between creation and fulfillment, between nature and grace represents for Leibniz a collapse of the dynamic and comprehensive claim of Christian theology to interpret all the world as the event of grace on the way to God's reign on the basis of the redemption that is in Christ Jesus, the one Mediator between God and humanity, Alpha and Omega.

Version Two is then vindicated, but that means the foregoing insight of Leibniz is vindicated at the cost of his manner of proceeding in theology. "Thus wisdom is in the understanding, and goodness is in the will, and as a result justice is in both," he once wrote. "Power is another matter. But if power is added, it brings to pass the Right and causes that which should be to exist really as well, insofar as the nature of things permits. And this is what God does in the world."[185] This stands "if power is added," that is, if God speaks-acts and so reveals His reign, if indeed the God under discussion is the Trinity and the justification of God is of the God who justifies the ungodly. Then theodicy issues in prophetic criticism of religious ideology and protological metaphysics of God as Origin and Standard only, making a "happy science out of a sad creation." In tension with this manner of proceeding from gospel and faith that he everywhere, like Melanchthon before him, presupposed, Leibniz argued for a different *manner* of proceeding in "natural theology" in his dialogue with John Locke: "Christian theology, which is the true medicine for souls, is based upon revelation which corresponds to experience; but to make of it a perfect body, we must unite therewith natural theology, which is drawn from the axioms of eternal reason." The reason for this addition is that apart from notions common to divine and human minds we are not able to recognize God as God and so to trust His promise in revelation, in Luther's own words, as "immutably necessary." "Is not this principle indeed that veracity is an attribute of God, upon which you acknowledge that the certainty of revelation is based, a maxim taken from natural theology?"[186] In fact, Leibniz has understood Luther very well at this point, all the more so Melanchthon. Yet Leibniz has forgotten here that just this is what Descartes had *denied* on the basis of a more rigorously "natural" theology than his own, one that thinks of God as omnipotently indifferent to us, as displayed in nature unfiltered by revelation, the rigorously depersonalized *natura naturans* that Spinoza eventually represented as divine. Must we not concede that Spinoza's perspective is the more "natural" one? That Leibniz's natural theology issues in a highly interpreted nature from the perspective of grace and the prospect of glory? It is in any case an injustice against Spinoza as well to call Leibniz his secret disciple.

Conclusion

In the preceding pages, many issues in dogmatics have been raised and discussed only to be left aside as our argument about the passage of theology through modernity pressed forward. I have raised thorny issues, taken controversial positions on them, and then moved along in ways that undoubtedly beggar the reader's patience for further evidence, elucidation, and argument. To this complaint I can only reply: patience is the eschatological virtue. Nor can it be my purpose in this conclusion to tie together all these loose threads. Rather I can only acknowledge certain *mandates for further work,* before settling upon a path now to be taken.

Future Tasks

I must leave for the future *the* problem of theological anthropology, which is to work out the compatibilism indicated in the preceding pages, not only between the divine sovereignty of the Trinity and the responsible freedom of the human being made in God's image, but also between so-called Lutheran existentialism and so-called Catholic essentialism. I hope to have rekindled attention in what precedes to Leibniz's monadology, descended from Melanchthon's trinitarian, providential, and historical-horizontal reading of Genesis 1:26-28, as a forgotten resource for reconciling the breach of the sixteenth century, at least on one level. Yet the solution is not a matter of repristination, whether of the monadology or the general pneumatology or Thomism for that matter; it will come, I think, by resituating discussion of human personhood in the dramatic-narrative categories of "eschatological creation," as in Romans 8. Such a move entails abandoning nature and grace as polar, static, mutually delimiting categories and speaking instead of the frustrated creation oppressed under the alien, usurping powers of sin-and-death as figured in the devil and thus groaning for the glorious liberty of the children of God. Into this state of bondage, true human patiency-and-agency appeared in the public persona, Jesus Christ, and becomes ours too in anticipation of Him in hope, by participation in His faith and through imitation of His love. This patiency-and-agency is, as the Eastern theologian Vladimir Lossky says, an ecstatic personhood,[1] that is, as I have parsed Luther and his followers, incorporation by the Spirit into the love of the Father for the Son and of the Son for the Father. "Man created 'in the image' is the person capable of manifesting God in the extent to which his nature allows itself to be penetrated by deifying grace" in this trinitarian way of theosis,[2] Lossky writes, still using the traditional terminology that he actually overcomes.

This "suffering of divine things" (Hütter), this surrender of repentance to faith, I have urged, comes by the Spirit who blows as He will for God's providential purposes, bringing about the Gethsemane of the soul of surrender to the Father's will, which is the first commandment of Moses and the summons to Islam that Muhammad recited.[3] Christian theology takes such preachments as movements of the Spirit for prophetic reform over against regnant theologies of glory and cheap grace — wherever they may be found. This transition by the Spirit is what matters — "all that matters is new creation" (Gal. 6:15) — not artificial assurances about final glory for all at the cost of grace so cheap it can't be given away. For all its conceptual difficulties, the deep justification of Luther's *De servo arbitrio* lies in contending for the costly grace of a crucified Christ with theological realism that faces up to the actuality of evil since it knows the actuality of holiness in the Spirit.[4] This Spirit-wrought surrender of ecstatic faith reverses the divine permission of sin in the believing person; it constitutes salvation as the substantive exodus by the Holy Spirit from actual evil to the actual love of God above all and all things in and under God, even though the passage is partial, short of the eschaton, and so reckoned totally to faith along the way, never recognized as something achieved on the basis of the merit of an autonomous agent. Thinking this way, therefore, presupposes a theological anthropology in which, as Lossky concluded, "the image, which is inalienable, can become similar or dissimilar, to the extreme limit: that of union with God . . . [or] the gloomy abyss of Hades."[5] That is what human "free choice" as an actual power other than God decides, as it resists or surrenders to the Spirit.

The Christian message is thus one of potential universalism: "These are the two extremes between which the personal destiny of man may veer in the working out of his salvation, which is already realized in hope for everyone in the incarnate Image of the God who willed to create man in His own image."[6] A solution in theological anthropology along these lines, let us recall, is not a resolution of the conundrum described and maintained in this book: we are not free in our election, although we are free in our resistance to it. Rather, potential universalism is an attempt to pass beyond the framework of soteriological individualism, without simply abandoning the existential and pastoral question of the individual's assurance of salvation.

I must also leave for the future the problem of the proper *est* in Christology over against the *significat* that subverts the very affirmation that is intended in the gospel of God's love reaching, grasping hold of, and never letting go of the weak and the enemy, as in Romans 5. Interestingly, the *significat* subverts assured faith for the same reason that a dualistic reading of the *deus absconditus–deus revelatus* distinction subverts it. If this could be clearly grasped, a greater appreciation of Karl Barth's theology of election would be overdue among "Lutherans," as I would hope also a greater appreciation and openness to Luther's *est* might be among "Barthians." In the meantime, I can merely refer to the very few illuminating discussions of such better criticism of Barth on the plane of Christology than the usual huffing and puffing for *Lebensbezug*, e.g., aside from the previously mentioned Risto Saarinen,[7] also Regin Prenter,[8] Dietrich Bonhoeffer,[9] and of course our contemporary Robert Jenson.[10] I have also in this christological connection indicated unpopular ideas nowadays about the actuality of moral evil and thus the theological need of an account of the moral patiency of Christ as propitiation for sin — notions that also beg further argumentation. Connected with this as well are ideas about the withdrawal of God and the aforementioned, nondualistic interpretation of the *deus absconditus* as the self-concealment of the revealed God. In a properly trinitarian theology, I would contend, the hidden God is no alien operator, but precisely and excruciatingly none other than the One whom Jesus addressed as Abba, Father; the cleavage that Luther so profoundly experienced in his own "Gethsemane of the soul" takes place *within* this relationship, *not* as some alternative to it. Neither Marcionism nor realized eschatology nor Platonism successfully negotiates this very real tension of Romans 8 — it is God who for the sake of hope "subjects creation to futility" — but all such options have in common too naively realistic an ontology in a world that as creation is essentially in motion on the way to the kingdom. Thus my frequent but scattered remarks throughout this book on perspectivalism in theology — that reality is affected by perception, fittingly, since the supreme reality lives as a trinity of perception — require nothing less than a fully worked-out doctrine of the Word of God. Only such would make it abundantly clear that I do not advocate anything like a "double truth" theory, but am adopting and developing (after Nietzsche! no longer according to Kant!) Luther's distinction between the old philosophical language and the new language of the Spirit as the basis for a nonspeculative and autonomous theological discipline that extends into what we traditionally (well, since Kant) regard as philosophical territory. "Independence is not enough!" Christoph Schwöbel rightly asserts, and asks, "Could it be that a general theology of revelation — not a theology of general revelation! — is a necessary complement of the theology of God's special revelation in Christ . . . ?"[11]

A troublesome issue connected to Schwöbel's proposal came up at the end of the discussion of George Murphy's cosmological proposal; it surfaces again and again in Leibniz's attempts to make intelligible the interface of his kingdoms of nature and grace — is perception caused by appearances mechanically, or does perception construct appearance in the individual perspective of each monad's *conatus?* The trouble is how to take scientific necessitarianism in a theology that wants, on theological grounds, to correct the Protological Prejudice. God is so exclusively understood in deistic traditions as origin and standard that Stephen Hawking famously claimed that a universal theory of everything in physics would give us the "mind of God." There is in this construal of God as alpha a certain projection, it seems, regarding causality: what comes first in a temporal sequence causes the next. This bias, as it appears, does not readily comport with the baffling insight of contemporary physics that space-time itself originates; this projection of causal sequence from our finite experience seems to support the mechanistic picture in metaphysics of ultimate reality as irreducibly dense atomic units bouncing each other around in confined space through unlimited time, just as it correspondingly frames the question of God in terms of first cause, prime mover, and necessary ground. In a theology for which God is both Alpha and Omega, however, mechanism in physical reality would be, as Leibniz argued, well-founded appearance of things from the finite perspective of an embodied soul. But the embodied soul itself is better understood as organism rather than as mechanism, as *conatus,* as entelechy, as desire. Metaphysically, then, the system of systems that is the cosmos would already "know" where it is going; or better, its destination, God as Omega, already knows and wills where things are going, and thus providentially — or should I say postvidentially? — effects as it were a reverse causality upon immanent causes from out of that future destination, which God already and eternally is. In this perspective the goal of the system causes the causes, though not all the choices.

In such a world, moreover, every event remains ineluctably open to incursions from incompossibles by created causes freely willing, though against the grain of things as morally determined by God, other identities for themselves aimed at other destinations than God's reign as Omega of all things (1 Cor. 15:28). As God's purposes are cosmic, so also the actual evil that opposes it has ripple effects extending from persons to things. How this metaphysics might make sense of contemporary physics, and whether that would be good sense, is beyond my competence to judge. Constrained as it is by the best available scientific thinking of its day and age, revealed theology by the argument of this book nevertheless has to think its own thoughts. These about the nature of actual evil are among my least certain and most adventuresome. But these are theological thoughts, recalling how Gregory of Nyssa figured the devil: out of envy at the election of humanity, the angel of light fell into the violent assertion of his rejected primacy, seeking to bring to naught God's election of the lowly. Correspondingly the Holy Spirit responds temporally, as the entire Bible is record, up until today — perhaps now leaving Euro-American culture behind for better soil,[12] perhaps ready to raise up even here from the "ruins of the church" (R. Reno) the community of Jesus, which believes in Him and with Him on behalf of others.

In any case, on Christian theological reading the cosmos is a morally determined, physically regular system open on the level of personal life to regress and to progress. Innovation in time is possible "from the top down," as it is said, since from the origin God has written Himself into the script by the person of the Spirit, who is free to improvise creative solutions to those incalculable deviations from divine destiny that God permits in willing the existence of wills genuinely other than His own. What is foreseen is thus general, but this general providence includes the Spirit's temporal and spatial attendance to all incalculable particulars along the way, weaving all things together for good to them that love God. What is promised is accompaniment through the particulars and the improvisation of God in time that ushers in the reign. Correspondingly there is limited but real human agency both in sin and in holiness, for even the bound will willingly surrenders to the alien, usurping powers, just as the liberated will willingly cooperates with God.[13] The theological limitation of human freedom is the prior patiency in the Spirit of the Father and the Son, who by the intercessory prayer of the total Christ opens new possibilities in history (but who may also harden Pharaoh's wicked heart). For God is not the sole causal agent/ substance (Spinoza), but God is the free divine counsel of wisdom and love who exists for us in His decision to create, redeem, and fulfill the world (defeating forever the actual evil of other wills that incorrigibly opposes the coming of the reign).

Finally in this laundry list of unfinished business I come to the so-called social doctrine of the Trinity that appears rather decisively in these pages, yet as it may seem, unintegrated alongside an Augustinian doctrine of the Trinity on the analogy of the soul's self-reflectivity. Yet Luther combines vivid tri-agency with the harmony of power, wisdom, and love,[14] and I have found that Origen[15] and Gregory of Nyssa[16] in turn work with the trinity of power, wisdom, and love. No doubt, a common relation to Platonism with a common opposition to Thrasymachus in all his wicked works and ways is in the background here. Needless to say, the point I make about incorporation into a social and public life of God (rather than a confrontation between private egos for superiority), and the corresponding restriction this places on certain popular, sometimes "Lutheran" notions of divine absoluteness, are controversial and in need of much deeper elaboration. Probably I have left many other important questions hanging, but the foregoing are the items that seem to me at the moment most serious.

Prolegomena as Prolepsis

The foregoing list is also indication that discussions in the prolegomena to dogmatics are not some neutral foundational-epistemological consideration of method as such that may abstract from the matter of dogmatics, but rather a kind of preliminary take on the matter itself. In any event, this was certainly so with Melanchthon for whom method in theology was about illuminating a subject matter that is not created or even constructed by an isolated, supposedly autonomous thinker but rather delivered by the church in the tradition of the gospel.[17] This notion of academic theology as at the same time a critical tradition-discourse has been as eclipsed as "biblical narrative" (Frei) under Kantianism, which simply decreed out of existence revelation as a historical event passed on as a historical event. I am perhaps unfair to Kant to isolate him this way; I have treated him in the preceding pages as much as a symbol as the great thinker he was. Certainly the foundationalist impulse was at work already in Descartes, Locke, and Spinoza before Kant consolidated it into the cultural synthesis of modernity. Nicholas Wolterstorff put the matter that is before us here very well in his probing critique of Locke's hope of grounding knowledge in pure empirical experience in order to overthrow the claim of tradition:

> Locke's proposal will not do. Our problems with traditions remain, however. Traditions are still a source of benightedness, chicanery, hostility and oppression. And our moral, religious, and even theoretical traditions are even more fractured today than they were in Locke's day. In this situation, examining our traditions remains for many of us a deep obligation, and for all of us together, a desperate need. But we shall have to acknowledge what the thinkers of the Enlightenment would have found appallingly unpalatable; namely, that examination of tradition can take place only in the context of unexamined tradition, and that in our examination, our convictions as to the facts are schooled by our traditions. The thinkers of the Enlightenment hoped to bring about a rational consensus in place of fractured tradition. That hope has failed. In my judgment it was bound to fail; it could not succeed.[18]

Tradition is a *critical* discourse; that is certain, since any appropriation of the past — as this book demonstrates throughout — if it is to be itself honest and plausible to honest readers must negate in order to affirm, leave behind in order to continue.[19] Yet one wonders whether Wolterstorff's historicist conclusion is so broadly justified. Much of Leibniz's criticisms of Locke's Socinian tendencies in the *New Essays* might be said to anticipate Wolterstorff's,[20] even though Leibniz holds on to the critical function of philosophical theology in Plato's tradition that probes for the general criteria by which credible candidates for the title of divinity might be recognized.

Is Leibnizian natural theology then a path that *cannot* be taken for the same reasons that apply to the Lockean Enlightenment? Or in fact is Leibniz's procedure itself a product of tradition? Indeed, a part of the story of Protestant Reformation theology, as I have tried to demonstrate in this book? Could it be renewed in this latter way? Could "liberalism" recognize itself as a tradition and still remain liberal? Or would that make it "conservative"? In that case, has "liberalism" always been a utopian conceit? Or, are these superficial categories still playing out the antiquated quarrels of Stoics and Epicureans in postmodernity — forcing us to describe an odd duck like Leibniz with such apparent oxymorons as "conservative modernizer" or "progressive conservative"? In a memo forming a perfect foil to Kant's

"What Is Enlightenment?" Leibniz declared at the outset of his own "Memoir for Enlightened Persons of Good Intention": "I find that even enlightened men of good intention usually let themselves be carried away by the torrent of general corruption, and do not think with enough skill about the means to pull themselves out of it and do some good."[21] That sounds very Augustinian. Dare I suggest that being fashionably "liberal," or self-consciously "enlightened," is *the* pretext of lazy thinking in our times as well? Or, that "conservatives" who trace their ancestry to Hobbes are no less radical in their progressivist ambitions and corresponding pretensions to "radical enlightenment"? And that Augustinian tradition as a critical discourse comports *with neither?*[22]

Contemporary Options and the Path Now Taken

In contemporary Christian theology, no one stands closer to the trajectory of theology from Luther through Melanchthon to Leibniz than does Wolfhart Pannenberg. He expressly acknowledges this relation to Melanchthon: "It has rightly been said that the knowledge of Rom. 1:20 is not innate, like that of Rom. 2:15, but acquired. It is linked to experience of the world and gained by this. Melanchthon had agreed to this in 1532. . . . Yet he rightly maintained that an innate knowledge underlay it. Intuition of an indefinite infinite, a mystery of being which transcends and upholds human life, and gives us the courage to trust it, achieves a differentiation from finite things only in the course of experience."[23] Pannenberg thus draws upon the Melanchthonian image of God anthropology. The cited statement in fact follows an important and illuminating discussion about the Reformers' conviction that the first commandment is written on the heart. Shared by Luther and Melanchthon, this theological innatism "was closely bound up with their distrust of reason. . . . According to Luther the turning to idolatry goes hand in hand with the false conclusions reason draws from the inextinguishable *(inobscurabilis)* knowledge of God in the heart. Reason wrongly links the thought of God to something else that it thinks God is like."[24] The actual knowledge of God acquired in experience in the fallen creation at once exchanges the Creator for the creature and so transits from vague awareness of infinite mystery into fixed idolatrous representations at human disposal. Yet in just this confused and sinful way we also know what it means to have a God: we are "referred to some reliable basis of life in which we can put our trust,"[25] even though we in fact latch on to unreliable creatures in God's place.

Pannenberg likewise remains close to Melanchthon in insisting on the "critical function" of "natural theology" of "imposing minimal conditions for talk about God that wants to be taken seriously as such"[26] — to wit, the aforementioned "reliable basis for life." In Pannenberg's own appropriation of the natural theology tradition, however, he draws closer to Descartes than to Leibniz. He expressly invokes the Third Meditation in which Descartes "ascribed priority to the idea of the infinite over apprehension of the finite"; this move, as we have seen, must be sharply distinguished from the thematic conjunction of power, wisdom, and love that Leibniz finds reflected in creaturely experience of the finite world. Pannenberg associates "non-thematic" awareness of infinitude with Melanchthon's innate knowledge of God: "from the very first we are set before a transcendent mystery in the sense that the silent infinity of reality that is beyond our control constantly presents itself to us as a mystery."[27] But historically, as we have seen in preceding pages, Melanchthon and his tradition gave rather different and far more concrete content to the innate knowledge of God. In Gerhard's words, as we may recall: "God has manifested his *power, wisdom and goodness* in the creatures in such a way that the whole cosmos should be truly a school and teacher of the knowledge of God. However, in order that man should not be urged to seek the knowledge of God outside of himself and from afar, God set his own image in man himself so that man, looking at it, might know what God was — righteous, holy, merciful, pure, etc."[28]

The issue is then the *thematic* thinkability of God's *nature*, as Leibniz, to my knowledge, was the first to grasp in his criticism of Descartes: "what Descartes has borrowed from Anselm, Archbishop of Canterbury, is very beautiful and really very ingenious, but that there is still a gap therein to be filled,"[29] since "it is tacitly assumed that this idea of the all-great or all-perfect being is possible, and implies no contradiction."[30] The difficulty is that "what Descartes alleges, that in speaking of God we know what we are saying, and that consequently we have an idea, is a deceptive indication . . . only an apparent idea."[31] This is in reference of course to Descartes's hearsay report of a perfect qua omnipotent being, who is in fact the *deus exlex*, as we saw above in chapter 6.[32] Leibniz strives against this apparently purely apophatic idea of God, a posteriori, on the grounds that this world on which the cross stood is a self-revelation of the Creator, from which it follows that our dim and confused perceptions of the *thematic* coherence of wisdom, power, and love *in, not beyond,* experience of the world (as analyzed philosophically by the principle of sufficient reason) yield *thematic* knowledge of God as the One to be recognized in Christian revelation as the actually existing Trinity. Such *thematic thinkability* is Leibniz's project for natural theology. The modal version of the ontological proof — if God as perfect being is conceivable, then God necessarily exists — situates the proof, Leibniz tacitly thinks, relative to the thinker *as a member of this world* (created for Christ and for which Christ died) and for whom the principle of sufficient reason is the law of her being as a rational soul.

If, in spite of this divergence from Leibniz in favor of a nonthematic Cartesian awareness of infinite mystery, Pannenberg is closest among contemporary theologians to the trajectory of theology that leads through Leibniz, then Jüngel would be closest to a contrasting trajectory that might be drawn from Luther to Barth by virtue of the theological critique of metaphysics. The God of the gospel is the God who becomes thinkable in, not above, the contradiction of being and nonbeing exposed at the cross of Jesus. And this "explodes the entire concept of one who grounds, one who is the reason" for something rather than nothing, for this something rather than something else.[33] What does Jüngel mean by this "explosive" — if not (Luther-like) bombastic — claim denying God as ground and origin and standard of what is? "It is not necessary, when one experiences one's own being and that of the world in view of the possibility of nonbeing, to arrive at talk about God. Here, too, God is not necessary. Against Leibniz and the metaphysical tradition, this is the meaning of our proposition that God is groundless. The fact that something exists at all and not nothing is in and of itself ambivalent and does not exclude that that which exists could be destroyed by nothing."[34] On the one hand, according to this criticism, Leibniz reduces to Spinoza and yet, on the other hand, like Luther, the prophetic criticism of metaphysics for "making a happy science out of a sad creation" nevertheless stops short of utter renunciation: "Thus the question, 'Why is there anything at all and not nothing,' leads to that dimension within which the question of God is raised," Jüngel writes, "but it does not lead to God as the necessary God."[35]

What is this but to say that the ontological argument fails as a "mathematically evident" proof? Has Leibniz ever actually claimed to have succeeded? Did he indeed aspire to or intend anything more than to raise the question of God that must be answered in turn by revealed theology? We have seen that there are (at least) two (basic) ways of reading him (and what Jüngel calls "the metaphysical tradition" — hardly a seamless garment). Just here, Jüngel rightly invokes Luther's *posteriora dei* (and Thomas Aquinas too!) on behalf of revealed theology: "If God is experienced in this sense as the one who distinguishes between being and not being and who decides in favor of being, then this experience for its part cannot be grounded out of the context of the one who exists. God does not come from the context of the world — not even as the result of basic trust [*Urvertrauen*]! — but rather always from God himself . . . on the basis of self-revelation, *God comes from God*."³⁶ So trinitarian advent is the true condition for the possibility of theology. Carefully put, however, for Jüngel the point of *Christian* talk about God in distinction from metaphysical talk about God is a *certain revision* of the latter: "although [God] is the one who decides between being and not being," Jüngel concedes, theology locates God speaking God "not just above" the contradiction of life and death, but "in the midst of it," i.e., in the resurrection of the Crucified.³⁷ This location *revises* how God is to be thought, since in self-revelation God has moved into a new place. It is a passage from an old to a new way of speaking, since with Luther, Christian theology is about the sinful, perishing creature and the coming to her of the redeeming God.

In this dispute between two giants today in the tradition of Luther we may see at work the conflicted legacy that the sixteenth-century Reformer left behind. Have we nothing here but a choice? A choice for audience at the cost of theme or for theme at the cost of audience? Surely the theological critique of reason (i.e., metaphysics) in the tradition of Luther must be and remain prophetically primary; yet it must also lead to a new vindication of reason, just as newly vindicated reason in turn serves to elucidate the God who comes from God in dogmatic *Nachdenken*. Christian theology needs partners in philosophy, even, *pace* Heidegger, "Christian philosophers," understanding by this a vocation much broader than the academic specialty that emerged under Kantianism. Christian theology needs scientists and social theorists and engineers and artists and lovers of letters as well as lovers of the Western mind and other minds, who are in real dialogue with dogmatic *Nachdenken*, as well as each other, in working for that reconciliation in Euro-American culture of Enlightenment and Holy Spirit that in his sufferings Bonhoeffer glimpsed and hoped.³⁸ Such non-Kantian philosophy refuses a wall of separation between facts and values, since truth itself is a value (an increasingly precarious one at that!), just as goods that are not truthful are no good at all. Such Leibniz-like philosophers are engaged in public arguments about the good under the assumption (of Christian faith among others) that good can be *known*, and critically *distinguished* from evil. They will not be seduced by the siren song of a new philosophy "beyond good and evil." On the other hand, theology that tries to do this for philosophy overreaches. Likewise philosophy that does not confess to the dogmas it borrows from theology begs questions for which Spinoza unsparingly demands an accounting.

A path that can yet be taken, then, for Christian philosophy is "Leibniz by way of Luther." This is to say, recognizing the erroneous confusion in realized eschatology of the ideal and the real that occurred with the sublimation of the Holy Spirit into a general pneumatology, one can today reconceive the philosophical project of contemporary Christian thought as a missionary enterprise, as corresponds to the situation of Euro-American Christianity today in the ruins of Constantinianism. With Christian ideas about finite perspective that is capable of the infinite, egocentric distortion, the Nevertheless of grace, and hope that extends to the cosmos, such philosophers contend for the best account of our experience by the truly enlightened light of nature, i.e., nature that knows of further lights of grace and glory — not the otherwise de rigueur reduction of everything to relations of power, parasitic upon the *deus exlex* — as if this of all things were genuinely new and liberating!

As the *new* language of the Spirit, theology in turn requires such accounts of our experience as its *old*.[39] As Bonhoeffer recognized, the glimpses of reconciliation he saw in the resistance to Hitler came paradoxically when the scandal of grace in all its particularity was again being proclaimed in all rigor (but also with new inclusiveness) by Karl Barth. Christian theology in this way has a path before it that may yet be taken in "Luther by way of Leibniz (and Barth)," that is to say, standing on its own two feet of the tradition of the gospel and its scriptural-dogmatic exposition as probed by the why question. The decay of general pneumatology in the culture requires this self-reliant posture today, beginning in the desiccated life of the Euro-American churches themselves: "most of those who need catechesis to prepare for life in the church are already members," another giant of contemporary theology in the tradition of Luther writes, "and suppose themselves already qualified for her life."[40]

> During the time in which the church and the culture are separating but not separated, this ambiguity cannot be avoided or denied. Much of the late modern church has dealt with the ambiguity by capitulating to it, by mitigating the church's liturgy, morality, and theology to accommodate "seekers" and incompetent members. That way lies apostasy from the faith, which in broad stretches of Western Protestantism has already occurred. However it is to be managed in times of uncertain boundaries, the church must not dilute or estrange her sacramental culture but instead train

would-be believers in its forms, not dispense with God's *torah* but instead
reform would-be believers' moral structure, not succumb to theological
relativism but teach would-be believers the doctrine of the Trinity.[41]

This is a remarkable statement from a theologian who had staked his creative theological work on a summons to the *unfinished* business of dogmatic
theology. Thus what sounds defensive in this passage should no doubt be
understood in that light. The church's "liturgy, morality, and theology" are
not only a deposit to be preserved but also one to be developed, not least by
facing the uncanny challenges of this unprecedented time, which may not be
so much "after virtue" as "after Christendom." In that light, I conclude this
book with the following reflection on Jenson's diagnosis of the path by
which theology today regains both its theme and its audience within (not
above) Euro-American culture.

This too is "in the hands of Christ" (Melanchthon), for it is an episode
on the way to that best of all possible worlds, namely, the one that God in
Christ nevertheless loves and has loved from eternity to eternity and has destined for the glorious liberty of the children of God. As Bonhoeffer, in far
more dire straits than we who write and read at leisure a book like this, med-
itated in the chapter that Bethge set at the head of his *Ethics*: "Now anyone
who reads the New Testament even superficially cannot but notice the complete absence of this world of disunion, conflict, and ethical problems. Not
man's falling apart from God, from men, from things and from himself, but
rather the rediscovered unity, reconciliation, is now the basis of the discussion."[42] If, with this well-founded theological optimism (certainly not —
under Hitler — an optimism of reason alone!), we negotiate the painful separation Jenson rightly recognizes by the renewal of *sacred* theology — *nova
lingua Spiritus sancti* — as the dogmatic *Nachdenken* of "revelation in history," itself traditioned through history, it is in hope a surprising and better
future that surpasses the status quo ante of Kantian dualism. "God and the
world are thus at one in Christ in a way which means that although the
Church and the world are different from each other, yet there cannot be a
static, spatial borderline between them."[43]

In facing our necessary separation in this newly interactive way, there
are unexpected possibilities for joy in theology on the way to the best also of
all possible churches. To take naturalism seriously and with ethical respect,
as in Spinoza, and so to see clearly what is given in Christ as well as what it is
that God in Christ redeems; to find common cause with Jewish and also Is-
lamic thought, which too knows about humanity called to live as the image

of God and struggles with us against tyrannous conceptions of God;[44] to understand justifying faith as the very faith of Jesus who believed for all of us unbelieving and so to be gathered by His Spirit into the doxological community interceding in faith on behalf of our unbelieving world (how dare such a community remain sinfully divided in itself?); to know God cosmically in solidarity with the groaning earth in the labor of hope of an ecological ethic anticipating cosmic fulfillment — these, among others, are the special joys of theology in our time and place, venturing forward on the path that has been pioneered before us (Heb. 12:1-2).

Notes

Notes to the Introduction

1. Jeffery Stout, *The Flight from Authority: Religion, Morality, and the Quest for Autonomy* (Notre Dame, Ind., and London: University of Notre Dame Press, 1981), 147.

2. John Milbank, *Theology and Social Theory: Beyond Secular Reason* (Oxford, U.K., and Cambridge, Mass.: Blackwell, 1997), 388.

3. Michael J. Buckley, S.J., *At the Origins of Modern Atheism* (New Haven: Yale University Press, 1987), 350.

4. Buckley, *At the Origins,* 351-52. For Leibniz's affinity with Malebranche, see Patrick Riley, *Leibniz' Universal Jurisprudence: Justice as the Charity of the Wise* (Cambridge: Harvard University Press, 1996), 98-105.

5. G. N. Clark, *The Seventeenth Century,* 2nd ed. (Oxford: Clarendon, 1947), 306-24; Carl J. Friedrich, *The Age of the Baroque, 1610-1660* (New York: Harper and Brothers, 1952), 93-123.

6. John Webster, "Theology after Liberalism?" in *Theology after Liberalism: A Reader,* ed. John Webster and George P. Schner (Oxford, U.K., and Cambridge, Mass.: Blackwell, 2000), 52-61.

7. Christoph Schwöbel, "Theology," in *The Cambridge Companion to Karl Barth,* ed. John Webster (Cambridge: Cambridge University Press, 2000), 17-36.

8. Jaroslav Pelikan, *From Luther to Kierkegaard: A Study in the History of Theology* (St. Louis: Concordia, 1950).

9. Of particular interest for the present study would be Bultmann's position on natural theology, which he denies in the "Catholic" sense since, referring to Kant, "philosophical criticism has shown the impossibility of giving a proof of God." "The Problem of 'Natural Theology,'" chapter 13 in Bultmann, *Faith and Understanding,* ed. Robert W. Funk, trans. Louise Pettibone Smith (Philadelphia: Fortress, 1987), 313. In this essay Bultmann argued for the recovery of the "preunderstanding" of the "lost, meaningless possibility of faith as original obedience, of which philosophy knows" in the light of the Christian revelation, and he

expressly noted that "*this natural theology* does not have the significance of a foundation for dogmatics" (330). Bultmann's antifoundationalism is noted with approval. But we shall see that the line of "natural theology" extending from Luther through Leibniz indeed assumed a natural knowledge of God in the ontotheological sense going back to Augustine, though not in the sense of cosmological metaphysics.

10. The influential argument was made after the Second World War in Germany by Gerhard Ebeling, "The Significance of the Critical Historical Method for Church and Theology in Protestantism," in *Word and Faith*, trans. J. W. Leitch (Philadelphia: Fortress, 1964), 17-61.

11. See below, especially chapter 3.

12. Daphne Hampson, *Christian Contradictions: The Structures of Lutheran and Catholic Thought* (Cambridge: Cambridge University Press, 2001). Hampson's case had been asserted, of course, again and again by modern Lutherans, e.g., Ernst Käsemann. In an early volume treating the Lutheran-Catholic ecumenical relation, he made a statement about the supposed stance of the apostle Paul into a vehicle for his own "radical Lutheranism": "The gospel of the unknown God who justifies the ungodly, always them alone, and who deals with us only in this way, then comes into conflict with the Christian religion which is concerned about the piety of the pious. Then the one Lord, with the demand of this exclusive Lordship, shatters those authorities which claim to be his earthly deputies. The Church becomes the creation of the word, instead of being the mother of the faithful and the possessor of the truth. Worship in the secularity of the world replaces the Christian cult. Faith in him who is always and exclusively the one who awakens the dead replaces the superstitious belief in history and history of salvation as sources of revelation. The universal priesthood of all believers rises up against the sacramentally guaranteed office, which claims authority on the strength of tradition. The freedom of the Christian man and of the Church of Jesus breaks through the ecclesiastical ethic and uniformity. Mission pushes aside pious self-admiration and self-assertion." *Distinctive Protestant and Catholic Themes Reconsidered,* vol. 3 of *Journal for Theology and the Church,* ed. Robert W. Funk, in association with Gerhard Ebeling (New York: Harper and Row, 1967), 26.

13. Hampson wants "the transformation of the self rather than the breaking of the self," i.e., a "much more optimistic" view of "a self being able to be centered-in-relation" (*Christian Contradictions,* 238), thus arguing for a "Catholic" (really Pelagian) anthropology without the Catholic dogma. Untangling the false antitheses involved here would take a volume in itself. Helmut Thielicke already anticipated Hampson's critique: "Against our thesis that the Holy Spirit does not let us begin with the axioms of our own self-understanding but turns our gaze on what has happened historically, this [Cartesian] theology can advance a weighty counter-argument. . . : How *can* I look outwards to let myself be defined by what takes place and to receive my self-understanding therefrom?" Helmut Thielicke, *The Evangelical Faith,* vol. 1, trans. G. W. Bromiley (Grand Rapids: Eerdmans, 1974), 138. Thielicke responded in terms of the "incorporation of the self into the salvation event instead of the reverse" (152-73).

14. Bruce D. Marshall has indicated how misleading this supposed antithesis, among others, can be in "Faith and Reason Reconsidered: Aquinas and Luther on Deciding What Is True," *Thomist* 63 (1999): 1-48.

15. Hampson deals extensively with Eberhard Jüngel's initial objections to the Joint Declaration but fails to grasp the deeper significance, not only of his eventual reconciliation

to the Joint Declaration, but also of his Lutheran adaptation of Barth's dogmatic approach to theology. Jüngel, *The Freedom of a Christian: Luther's Significance for Contemporary Theology*, trans. R. A. Harrisville (Minneapolis: Augsburg, 1988) and *Justification: The Heart of the Christian Faith*, trans. J. F. Cayzer (Edinburgh: T. & T. Clark, 2001).

16. See Hampson's *Auseinandersetzung* with the author in *Christian Contradictions*, 239-40. I argue the alternative in "The Lutheran Dilemma," *Pro Ecclesia* 8, no. 4 (Fall 1999): 391-422.

17. O. Bayer and Benjamin Gleede, eds., *Creator est creatura: Luthers Christologie als Lehre von der Idiomenkommunikation* (Berlin and New York: De Gruyter, 2007).

18. Lubomir Batka, *Peccatum radicale: Eine Studie zu Luthers Erbsuendenverstaendnis in Psalm 51* (Frankfurt am Main: Peter Lang, 2007).

19. A splendid instance of the kind of reflection I have in mind may be found in Adriaan T. Peperzak, *The Quest for Meaning: Friends of Wisdom from Plato to Levinas* (New York: Fordham University Press, 2003), which does not fall into the Heideggerian trap of denying the possibility of Christian philosophizing for the sake of criticizing the metaphysical tradition, although, in my view, it is at the cost of too apophatic a distinction between God and His Word. I will consider Peperzak's excellent discussion of Leibniz below in chapter 6.

20. Immanuel Kant, "The Personified Idea of the Good Principle," in "Religion within the Boundaries of Mere Reason," in *Religion and Rational Theology*, Cambridge Edition of the Works of Immanuel Kant, trans. A. W. Wood and G. Di Giovanni (Cambridge: Cambridge University Press, 2001), 6:60-63. "In this practical faith in this Son of God (so far as he is represented as having taken up human nature) the human being can thus hope to become pleasing to God (and thereby blessed); that is, only a human being conscious of such a moral disposition in himself as enables him to believe and self-assuredly trust that he, under similar temptations and afflictions (so far as these are made the touchstone of that idea), would steadfastly cling to the prototype of humanity and follow the prototype's example in loyal emulation, only such a human being, and he alone, is entitled to consider himself not an unworthy object of divine pleasure" (105).

21. "The Nestorian conception of Christ . . . qualifies Christ for being an example of what man can do, and into what wonderful union with God he can be assumed if he is holy enough; but Christ remains one man among man, shut in within the limits of a single human personality, and influencing man only from outside. He can be a Redeemer of man if man can be saved from outside by bright example, but not otherwise. The Nestorian Christ is logically associated with the Pelagian man . . . the Nestorian Christ is the fitting Saviour of the Pelagian man." Charles Gore, "Our Lord's Human Example," *Church Quarterly Review* 16 (1883): 298, cited in Alister McGrath, ed., *The Christian Theology Reader* (Oxford, U.K., and Cambridge, Mass.: Blackwell, 1999), 196. For Kant's "Nestorianism," see n. 13 above.

22. For an account of the "alternative," see D. Bielfeldt, M. Mattox, and P. Hinlicky, *The Substance of the Faith: Luther's Doctrinal Theology for Today* (Minneapolis: Fortress, 2008).

23. George L. Murphy, *The Cosmos in the Light of the Cross* (Harrisburg, Pa., London, and New York: Trinity, 2003).

24. "Metaphysics," like "ontology," is a controverted term, which I use loosely to designate a logical region of ultimate questions or possible eternities, not narrowly as first science of being. "Ontology" I likewise take semantically as descriptive of a range of possibilities, not insight in the being of something in and for itself.

25. In addition to *The Substance of the Faith*, especially Mattox's contribution, see

Manfred Schulze, "Martin Luther and the Church Fathers," in *The Reception of the Church Fathers in the West* (Leiden and New York: Brill, 1997), 573-626.

26. Graham White, *Luther as Nominalist: A Study of the Logical Methods Used in Martin Luther's Disputations in the Light of Their Medieval Background,* Schriften der Luther-Agricola-Gesellschaft 30 (Helsinki: Luther-Agricola Society, 1994). I regard White's thesis as successful with the clarification that Ockhamism is here taken as precursor of analytic philosophy's concern for semantic analysis and logically valid procedures of inference, i.e., *not* as precursor of the metaphysical *deus exlex* of early modern voluntarism/absolutism. White's thesis is that Luther "was interested in the believer's knowledge of, and talk about, this absolutely unique individual, i.e. God" in distinction from philosophy, which, according to the medieval conception, is concerned with general truths, at the same time retaining an Augustinian "emphasis on the publicly accessible nature of language, including religious language" (White, 16). To this end, Luther introduces a "technical concept, i.e. the idea of a new language, the mastery of which distinguishes believers from nonbelievers, theologians from philosophers" (16).

27. G. J. Jordan, *The Reunion of the Churches: A Study of G. W. Leibnitz and His Great Attempt* (London: Constable and Co., 1927). This is a dated though still useful study; the topic demands fresh investigation.

28. Thomas Reinhuber, *Kaempfender Glaube: Studien zu Luthers Bekenntnis am Ende von* De servo arbitrio (Berlin and New York: De Gruyter, 2000), 181-86.

29. Heinz Liebing, "Historical-Critical Theology," in *Distinctive Protestant and Catholic Themes Reconsidered,* 62.

30. Carl E. Braaten and Roy A. Harrisville, eds. and trans., *Kerygma and History: A Symposium on the Theology of Rudolf Bultmann* (New York and Nashville: Abingdon, 1962), 13-14; the citation is taken from *Kerygma and Myth,* ed. H. W. Bartsch, trans. Reginald H. Fuller (New York: Harper and Row, 1961), 210-11.

31. See above, n. 9.

32. James F. Kay, *Christus Praesens: A Reconsideration of Rudolf Bultmann's Christology* (Grand Rapids: Eerdmans, 1994), 174-75.

33. Robert W. Bertram, "How Scripture Is Traditioned in the Lutheran Confessions," in *The Quadrilog: Tradition and the Future of Ecumenism; Essays in Honor of George H. Tavard,* ed. Kenneth Hagen (Collegeville, Minn.: Liturgical Press, 1994), 90.

34. Bertram, "How Scripture Is Traditioned," 91.

35. Bultmann, *Faith and Understanding,* 279.

36. Broadly speaking. Strictly speaking, Leibniz's meditation upon the divine counsel as morally necessitated is arguably more Scotist than Abelardian or Thomist in its medieval ancestry. See Allan B. Wolter, O.F.M., *Duns Scotus on the Will and Morality,* translation edition (Washington, D.C.: Catholic University of America Press, 1997), 56-67, and John Marenbon, *Medieval Philosophy: An Historical and Philosophical Introduction* (London and New York: Routledge, 2007), 290-93.

37. By the early nineteenth century it seemed to be an "oxymoron." The discovery and publication then of the early Leibniz's *Systema Theologicum* dated around 1683 created the scandalous perception of a pro-Catholic Leibniz. Jordan, *Reunion,* 74, 96. Jordan gives a broad overview of the document that was exploring doctrinal agreement between Lutherans and Catholics; he finds it with the bounds of Calixtus's brand of Lutheranism, rejecting

"points of doctrine and practice which . . . might detract from the merits of Jesus Christ and the sacrifice of the Cross" (56).

38. Fergus Kerr, *After Aquinas: Versions of Thomism* (Malden, Mass.: Blackwell, 2002), 142.

39. Kerr, *After Aquinas,* 143. Thus the "essence of the finite is to be incomplete — to be essentially open, that is, open to the activity of God, who without annulling or withdrawing anything can always give more." Kerr concurs with Milbank's praise of de Lubac for "overcoming of a grace/nature duality" as the theological revolution of our times: "de Lubac 'supernaturalizes the natural': 'our mere desire to see God' is already 'a sign of the actual presence of grace within us' — not of a merely possible gift." Milbank, *Theology and Social Theory,* 148. Theosis constitutes the background theological anthropology against which something like the Reformation's message of justification makes sense.

40. Kathryn Tanner, *God and Creation in Christian Theology: Tyranny or Empowerment?* (Minneapolis: Fortress, 2005), 115.

41. G. W. Leibniz, *New Essays concerning Human Understanding,* trans. Alfred Gideon Langley (La Salle, Ill.: Open Court, 1949), 585.

42. Milbank, *Theology and Social Theory,* 148.

43. Kerr, *After Aquinas,* 153.

44. Günther Frank, *Die Theologische Philosophie Philipp Melanchthons (1497-1560),* Erfurter Theologische Studien 67 (Leipzig: Benno, 1995). I am applying Frank's description of Melanchthon to Leibniz because, as I will show, Leibniz represents the final flower of Melanchthon's tradition. Frank's seminal work will be discussed in detail in chapter 4.

45. "The central problem," writes R. W. Meyer, of Leibniz's "philosophical commitment [is] the problem of the validity of the Christian tradition." R. W. Meyer, *Leibniz and the Seventeenth Century Revolution,* trans. J. P. Stern (Cambridge: Bowes and Bowes, 1952), 141. See the discussion of Meyer at the end of chapter 1.

46. "I cannot, however, refrain from disapproving the term 'Lutheranism' . . . which a bad custom has authorized in Saxony." Leibniz, *New Essays,* 543-44. Or again, "the Evangelicals, as those are named by way of preference in Germany whom many inaptly call Lutherans" (585).

47. See here Michael Latzer, "Leibniz's Reading of Augustine," *Il Cannocciale* (Rome: Carucci), January-April 1999, 17-33, which calls attention to Leibniz's dependence on *Confessions* 12–13, the exposition of the creation story in Genesis.

48. Robert Merrihew Adams, *Leibniz: Determinist, Theist, Idealist* (Oxford: Oxford University Press, 1994). I will lean heavily on Adams's impressive interpretations, though I find important ambiguities in each of the three designators in his title, especially when, according to version 2 in chapter 6 below, we read Leibniz as a Melanchthonian natural theologian.

49. Max Wundt, *Die deutsche Schulmetaphysik des. 17. Jahrhunderts* (Tübingen: J. C. B. Mohr, 1939), 143-44. For Leibniz's location in the Melanchthonian tradition, see also James William Richard, *Philip Melanchthon: The Protestant Preceptor of Germany (1497-1560)* (New York and London: Putnam, 1902), 139-40, and Frank, *Theologische Philosophie,* 5, 11, 339.

50. See below, chapter 2, on Kant's treatment of Leibniz in the first *Critique.*

51. Leibniz, *New Essays,* 52.

52. G. W. Leibniz, *Discourse on Metaphysics and Other Essays,* trans. D. Garber and R. Ariew (Indianapolis: Hackett, 1991), 9.

53. "Anyone for whom the Bible is divine revelation and truth has the answer to the question, 'Why are there essents rather than nothing?' even before it is asked: everything that is, except God himself, has been created by him." Martin Heidegger, "The Fundamental Question of Metaphysics," in *Philosophy in the Twentieth Century,* vol. 3, ed. W. Barrett and H. D. Aiken (New York: Random House, 1962), 223. This is of course correct and it applies against those today who imagine they can adopt Heidegger's critique of ontotheology and remain Christian thinkers. Leibniz borrows a thesis from revealed theology and tries to engage it philosophically against alternatives represented by Hobbes and Spinoza in a way that throttles the task of putatively radical, in fact parasitical, questioning that Heidegger regards as essential to philosophy: a believer "cannot really question without ceasing to be a believer and taking all the consequences of such a step" (223). This critique exposes the ambiguity of Leibniz's posture perfectly — but also of the aforementioned imitators of Heidegger.

54. On "ontotheology" see the discussion below of M. Westphal. On Heidegger's criticism of Leibniz as the metaphysician who thinks of beings as beings, forgetful of Being itself, because he asks the fundamental question of metaphysics causally, see Martin Heidegger, "The Way Back into the Ground of Metaphysics," in *Philosophy in the Twentieth Century,* 3:217-18.

55. See Patrick Riley's discussion of Leibniz's late (1714) treatise, "An Unpublished Lecture by Leibniz on the Greeks as Founders of Rational Theology: Its Relation to His 'Universal Jurisprudence,'" *Journal of the History of Philosophy* 14 (1976): 205-16. The question of Leibniz's personal integrity in matters pertaining to Christian faith has been raised from the beginning. E. J. Aiton, *Leibniz: A Biography* (Bristol and Boston: Adam Hilger, 1985), reports that Eckhart, Leibniz's first biographer (1799), "speculates that this complete neglect by the King and his ministers [to attend the funeral] may have been a result of the widely held opinion that Leibniz was an unbeliever. During the nineteen years of their association, Eckhart had never known him to take communion. On many occasions, he recalled, Leibniz had described himself as a priest of natural justice and remarked that he found nothing other than this in the New Testament. Eckhart testifies further that Leibniz always spoke well of everyone and made the best of everything. A more likely reason for the official indifference would seem to be the fact that he had incurred the King's displeasure [for failing to finish the history of the House of Brunswick]" (349). See Jordan's defense of Leibniz in his *Reunion,* 36-40.

56. See the discussion below of R. J. Meyer on Leibniz's attempt to secure culture on the foundation of Christian dogma.

57. Günther Frank, *Die Vernunft des Gottesgedankens: Religionsphilosophische Studien zur frühen Neuzeit* (Stuttgart: Frommann-Holzboog, 2003), 73.

58. Diogenes Allen, "The Theological Relevance of Leibniz's Theodicy," *Studia Leibnitiana. Supplementa* 14, no. 3 (1972): 83-90, rightly argues that the "values enshrined in the 'best' help liberate a Christian from anthropocentrism, and can help anyone to see what sort of things are of value" (90).

Notes to Chapter 1

1. G. W. Leibniz, *Theodicy: Essays on the Goodness of God, the Freedom of Man, and the Origin of Evil,* trans. E. M. Huggard (Chicago and La Salle, Ill.: Open Court, 1998), 67.

2. Leibniz expressed exasperation at the polemical cast of contemporary Protestant orthodoxy and argued for the irenic, disputational procedures of medieval scholasticism. G. W. Leibniz, *New Essays concerning Human Understanding,* trans. Alfred Gideon Langley (La Salle, Ill.: Open Court, 1949), 477, 494. G. J. Jordan, *The Reunion of the Churches: A Study of G. W. Leibnitz and His Great Attempt* (London: Constable and Co., 1927), associates Leibniz with Calixtus and the so-called syncretist party (48). Fresh research in this area is sorely needed.

3. Lewis White Beck, *Early German Philosophy: Kant and His Predecessors* (Bristol, England: Thoemmes Press, 1996), 99.

4. Beck, *Early German Philosophy,* 235.

5. Bertrand Russell, *A Critical Exposition of the Philosophy of Leibniz* (Cambridge: University of Cambridge Press, 1900; 2nd ed., London: George Allen and Unwin, 1937), stands, it seems to me, *unaware or unacknowledged* in the philosophical tradition of Samuel Clarke's brief on behalf of a Newtonian physics cum theology. Leroy E. Loemker, *Struggle for Synthesis: The Seventeenth Century Background of Leibniz's Synthesis of Order and Freedom* (Cambridge: Harvard University Press, 1972), 212, explains the popularity of Newtonian theology: "God, the perfect Machinist, having created a machine universe, operating with perfect precision, yet leaving room within it for the free man of the libertine." This is Russell's own view of things, sans God. Russell's idiosyncratic, not to say unfair, exposition of Leibniz has in turn suffered a systematic dismantling at the hands of Nicolas Rescher, *The Philosophy of Leibniz* (Englewood Cliffs, N.J.: Prentice-Hall, 1967). Broadly put: "Modern commentators tend to remark disparagingly upon the striking contrast of Leibniz' system between its daringly innovative logic, epistemology, and metaphysics and its extremely conservative ethics and theology. . . . Bertrand Russell has even suggested that Leibniz had two systems: 'the good philosophy which he had kept to himself, and . . . the vulgarized version by which he won the admiration of Princes and (even more) of Princesses.' This view of the matter seems to me wholly unjustified. Quite the reverse seem true: the guiding aim and aspiration of Leibniz' philosophy is to establish a rigorous rational foundation for what he accepted as the fundamental teachings of ethics and theology. To do this in detail and provide the means for a solid demonstration of 'the conformity of faith with reason' took Leibniz into construction of a highly novel philosophy . . . the purpose of this theory was to provide a conceptually solid underpinning for certain essentially orthodox views in ethics and theology" (159). Against the Russell interpretation, and also in support of a cosmic, rather than acosmic theology in Leibniz, see also Gregory Brown, "Leibniz's Theodicy and the Confluence of Worldly Goods," *Journal of the History of Philosophy* 20, no. 4 (October 1988): 588-89.

6. Influential examples include Arthur O. Lovejoy, *The Great Chain of Being: A Study of the History of an Idea* (Cambridge: Harvard University Press, 1964), 173-74, which explicitly follows Russell; and more recently, the otherwise excellent study of Patrick Riley, *Leibniz' Universal Jurisprudence: Justice as the Charity of the Wise* (Cambridge: Harvard University Press, 1996), 75-88, which sometimes tends in the manner of Beck to chastise Leibniz for failing to be the outspoken Pelagian that his system, rightly interpreted, required, even though this would make Leibniz the proto-Kantian that Riley clearly sees Leibniz is not. A nuanced discussion may be found in Robert Merrihew Adams, *Leibniz: Determinist, Theist, Idealist* (Oxford: Oxford University Press, 1994), 34, 50, 52, 80, 89 n. 131, 302. A counterargument is made by Brown, "Confluence," and Rescher, *The Philosophy of Leibniz* (see n. 5 above).

7. Catherine Wilson, "The Reception of Leibniz in the 18th Century," in *The Cambridge*

Companion to Leibniz, ed. N. Jolley (Cambridge, U.K., and New York: Cambridge University Press, 1995), 449-53.

8. Ned Wisnefske, *Preparing to Hear the Gospel: A Proposal for Natural Theology* (Lanham, Md.: University Press of America, 1998), 65.

9. Wisnefske, *Preparing,* 112.

10. Wisnefske, *Preparing,* 23.

11. For example, Gregory Brown: Leibniz "could not tolerate the idea, which we should be inclined to embrace, that the differences in the mental faculties of brutes and humans are due merely to differences in the relative complexity of their organic structures. Dualism, in conspiracy with a religiously based prejudice dictating that a metaphysically exalted position be attributed to humans in the order of creation, continued to cloud Leibniz's thinking in these matters." Gregory Brown, "Miracles in the Best of All Possible Worlds: Leibniz's Dilemma and Leibniz's Razor," *History of Philosophy Quarterly* 12, no. 1 (January 1995): 33.

12. Janet Soskice, *Metaphor and Religious Language* (Oxford: Clarendon, 1987), 119-61; Eberhard Jüngel, "Metaphorical Truth," in *Theological Essays I,* ed. J. B. Webster (Edinburgh: T. & T. Clark, 1989), 16-71.

13. Cf. the critique of *poeisis* in Reinhard Hütter, *Suffering Divine Things: Theology as Church Practice,* trans. D. Stott (Grand Rapids: Eerdmans, 2000). Hütter makes a powerful argument in this book for a public, not privatized, understanding of the Spirit's work.

14. So Wisnefske, but in some tension with his Kantian assumption about noumenal freedom of moral agents.

15. I am relying on the analysis in R. W. Sharples, *Stoics, Epicureans, and Sceptics: An Introduction to Hellenistic Philosophy* (London and New York: Routledge, 1996). These schools of thought were mediated in part to the medieval Latin and early Rennaisance mind through Cicero's *On the Nature of the Gods.*

16. Ake Bergvall, *Augustinian Perspectives in the Renaissance,* Acts Universitatis Upsaliensis Studia Anglistica Upsaliensia 117 (Uppsala: Uppsala University, 2001). This is a rich, multidimensional study that explodes a deeply entrenched stereotype of "the arch-reactionary system-builder standing behind a strictly vertical, logocentric, hierarchical and patriarchal construct." In the author's considered view, "the Augustine of political pessimism, existential angst and the decentered subject" shares with Derrida — our contemporary icon of iconoclasm — more than a strikingly similar personal trajectory: "outsiders born on the margins of empire, indeed the very same periphery (present-day Algeria)"; for Bergvall, "both cross borders as they move toward the political and cultural centers (Paris and Milan) only to radically question the basic assumptions of those centers" (212-13).

17. Richard Rorty, *Philosophy and the Mirror of Nature* (Princeton: Princeton University Press, 1979), 3-7. I will suggest, however, that there are resources in Leibniz for understanding "mind as mirror" in its original theological setting (i.e., the human as image of God), and correspondingly, for reconstruction in philosophy along the hermeneutical lines that Rorty himself wished to pursue. Rorty, 315-56.

18. Kant, *The Conflict of the Faculties,* trans. Mary J. Gregor (New York: Abaris Books, 1979), 251.

19. Rorty, *Philosophy,* 4.

20. There have been significant, though not very influential, theological challenges to this conceit, e.g., Helmut Thielicke, *The Evangelical Faith,* vol. 1, trans. G. W. Bromiley

(Grand Rapids: Eerdmans, 1974), 138-73; Alan Richardson, *Christian Apologetics* (New York: Harper, 1948).

21. Rorty, *Philosophy*, 7.

22. "When Luther said that Reason was the 'devil's Whore,' he meant that Reason may be prostituted for the ends of evil." B. A. Gerrish, *Grace and Reason: A Study in the Theology of Luther* (Oxford: At the Clarendon Press, 1962), 137.

23. Reinhold Niebuhr, *Moral Man and Immoral Society: A Study in Ethics and Politics* (New York: Scribner, 1960).

24. Frederick C. Beiser, *The Fate of Reason: German Philosophy from Kant to Fichte* (Cambridge: Harvard University Press, 1987). See the account of the seminal critiques of Kant's "purism of reason" by Herder, Hamann, and Jacobi on 16-91. For theology, Hamann's linguistic turn is especially important: "There is no special faculty of reason, there are only rational ways of thinking and acting. To identify reason, we must refer to the ways that people think and act; and that means, more specifically, how they act, write, and speak in their language and in their culture" (39). Materially, "Hamann criticizes the assumptions common to much post-Cartesian psychology and epistemology that self-consciousness is self-illuminating, the self-evident starting point of philosophy . . . we have no such privileged access to ourselves. . . . Rather than being self-illuminating, self-awareness is problematic, mysterious, and obscure." We must instead "penetrate into the very bosom of God, who alone can determine the whole mystery of our being." Hence, we should begin "not with self-knowledge but with the knowledge of being" (21). To put the matter in Leibnizian idiom: we should come to know ourselves and the world as God does, whose knowledge is the creative trinitarian conjunction of power, wisdom, and love.

25. Rorty, *Philosophy*, 4.

26. Gottfried Wilhelm Leibniz, *Philosophical Papers and Letters: A Selection*, trans. and ed. Leroy E. Loemker, 2 vols. (Chicago: University of Chicago Press, 1956), 246; hereafter Loemker, *Papers*.

27. *Luther's Works: The American Edition*, ed. J. Pelikan et al. (St. Louis: Concordia; Philadelphia: Fortress, 1960-), 25:342.

28. H. A. Preuss and E. Smits, eds., *The Doctrine of Man in Classical Lutheran Theology* (Minneapolis: Augsburg, 1962), 35.

29. Preuss and Smits, *Doctrine of Man*, 49.

30. Preuss and Smits, *Doctrine of Man*, 61.

31. Preuss and Smits, *Doctrine of Man*, 38, emphasis added.

32. I am relying here on the English translation.

33. Smalcald Articles III.1.3, in *The Book of Concord: The Confessions of the Evangelical Lutheran Church*, ed. Robert Kolb and Timothy J. Wengert (Minneapolis: Fortress, 2000), 311.

34. Loemker, *Struggle for Synthesis*, 64.

35. Günther Frank, *Die Theologische Philosophie Philipp Melanchthons (1497-1560)*, Erfurter Theologische Studien 67 (Leipzig: Benno, 1995), 90, 103.

36. Oliver K. Olson, *Matthias Flacius and the Survival of Luther's Reform* (Wiesbaden: Harrassowitz Verlag, 2002), 326.

37. Olson, *Matthias Flacius*, 50.

38. Adams, *Leibniz*, 352; cf. 291, and in analogy to the incarnation, 298, 305.

39. G. W. Leibniz, *Discourse on Metaphysics and Other Essays*, trans. D. Garber and R. Ariew (Indianapolis: Hackett, 1991), 9.

40. Leibniz, *Discourse*, 80.

41. Adams, *Leibniz*, 187-88, 189, 315, 331, 367.

42. Erwin Schadel, "Monad as a Triadic Structure — Leibniz's Contribution to Post-nihilistic Search for Identity," *Journal of Indian Council of Philosophical Research* 14, no. 1 (1996): 26.

43. *Monadology*, #7, in Leibniz, *Discourse*, 68.

44. Leibniz expressly denies this in *Monadology*, #61, in Leibniz, *Discourse*, 77.

45. *Monadology*, #3, emphasis added, in Leibniz, *Discourse*, 68. See also Adams, *Leibniz*, 340. In another aspect, Adams shows how monadology conceives of wholes, 244, 346, or entelechies, 79-81, 128, 131, endowed with agency of their own and not as mere modes of another agency, 101, 312, 314, so that the rational soul forms a unique biography, 105.

46. *Monadology*, #1-2, in Leibniz, *Discourse*, 68.

47. *Monadology*, #9, in Leibniz, *Discourse*, 69.

48. *Monadology*, #6, in Leibniz, *Discourse*, 68.

49. *Monadology*, #7, emphasis added, in Leibniz, *Discourse*, 68.

50. *Monadology*, #51, emphasis added, in Leibniz, *Discourse*, 75.

51. *Monadology*, #52, in Leibniz, *Discourse*, 75.

52. *Monadology*, #54-55, in Leibniz, *Discourse*, 76.

53. *Monadology*, #56, in Leibniz, *Discourse*, 76.

54. *Monadology*, #57, in Leibniz, *Discourse*, 76.

55. Schadel, "Triadic Structure," 27.

56. Schadel, "Triadic Structure," 17.

57. Schadel, "Triadic Structure," 18.

58. Nicholas Jolley, "Leibniz on Locke and Socinianism," *Journal of the History of Ideas* 39 (1978): 233-50.

59. Schadel, "Triadic Structure," 28.

60. *Monadology*, #43, in Leibniz, *Discourse*, 74.

61. *Monadology*, #85-86, in Leibniz, *Discourse*, 80; *Discourse*, 12-16.

62. *Monadology*, #90, in Leibniz, *Discourse*, 81.

63. Leibniz, *Discourse*, 39.

64. Riley, *Leibniz' Universal Jurisprudence*, 112.

65. Matthew Stewart, *The Courtier and the Heretic: Leibniz, Spinoza, and the Fate of God in the Modern World* (New York and London: Norton, 2006), 197.

66. Stewart, *Courtier*, 203.

67. Baruch Spinoza, *Principles of Cartesian Philosophy with Metaphysical Thoughts*, trans. S. Shirley (Indianapolis: Hackett, 1998), 7.

68. "Of the great early modern philosophers, however, Leibniz was probably the least preoccupied with epistemology. . . . The Leibnizian approach to metaphysics might seem embarrassingly uncritical, and perhaps it would be, if strong constraints on metaphysics could be derived from an epistemology that deserved our full confidence." Adams, *Leibniz*, 3.

69. Baruch Spinoza, *Theological-Political Treatise*, trans. S. Shirley (Indianapolis: Hackett, 1998).

70. Baruch Spinoza, *Ethics, Treatise on the Emendation of the Intellect and Selected Letters*, trans. S. Shirley (Indianapolis: Hackett, 1992), 65.

71. The generosity of God the Creator is a "moral quality," Leibniz writes, "which makes him the lord or monarch of minds. . . . It is because of this that he humanizes himself, that he is willing to allow anthropomorphism, and that he enters into society with us, as a prince with his subjects." *Discourse*, 40.

72. Spinoza, *Ethics*, 54.

73. Stewart, *Courtier*, 207.

74. Adams, *Leibniz*, 20-21, 28, 114, 119, 124.

75. "The Formula of Concord," article I, in *The Book of Concord*, 488.

76. Dietrich Bonhoeffer, *Sanctorum Communio: A Theological Study of the Sociology of the Church*, trans. R. Krauss and N. Lukens, Dietrich Bonhoeffer Works, vol. 1 (Minneapolis: Fortress, 1998), 79-80. In a comment Bonhoeffer edited out of the final version, he referred to "Leibniz's theory of monads" as one "with which the social philosophy being presented is closely connected" (68 n. 22).

77. Dietrich Bonhoeffer, *Ethics*, trans. N. H. Smith (New York: Macmillan, 1978), 55-56.

78. R. W. Meyer, *Leibniz and the Seventeenth Century Revolution*, trans. J. P. Stern (Cambridge: Bowes and Bowes, 1952), 168.

79. Though Leibniz himself disliked the label "Lutheran"; see above, n. 32.

80. Meyer, *Revolution*, 76.

81. Meyer, *Revolution*, 76.

82. Meyer, *Revolution*, 77.

83. Rescher, *The Philosophy of Leibniz*, 67-68.

84. Günther Frank, *Die Vernunft des Gottesgedankens: Religionsphilosophische Studien zur frühen Neuzeit* (Stuttgart: Frommann-Holzboog, 2003), 328.

85. Frank, *Die Vernunft*, 319.

86. Frank, *Die Vernunft*, 65, citing from Melanchthon, *Corpus Reformatorum*, 12:592; 13:124f.

87. See Adams's "deepened" analysis of Leibniz's view of "essence's demand for existence," such that "the existence of a possible being can be prevented only by its incompatibility with something more perfect"; in the unique case of God, then, "if it would exist through itself, its existence can be prevented only by inconsistency in its own essence." Adams, *Leibniz*, 172-73.

88. Meyer, *Revolution*, 113.

89. Adams, *Leibniz*, 386.

90. Meyer, *Revolution*, 114. Meyer claims to note "here a certain change in Leibnitz's religious views; as a Lutheran he accepts that absolute separation of God and man; yet as a mathematician he sees both moving along asymptotic courses. In so far as man thinks in an a priori fashion, he thinks in the same sequences of ideas as God; in other words, he expresses God. And we reach the dangerous point where *mathesis universalis* suddenly turns into *mathesis divina;* where divine reflection is 'comprehended' as infinitely heightened human reflection; and where theocentric reflection merges with anthropocentric reflection" (114). But arguably, the classic Lutheran Christology merges theocentric and anthropocentric reflection. In that case, Leibniz is developing, not deviating from, his tradition.

91. Meyer, *Revolution*, 141. "Leibniz, convinced that he had succeeded in establishing once and for all the wonderful harmony of the realms of Nature and Grace, could, at the very end of his life, believe that a new and truly Christian era of peace was about to begin" (141).

92. Meyer, *Revolution*, 142.

93. Meyer, *Revolution*, 142.

94. Meyer, *Revolution*, 151.

95. Meyer, *Revolution*, 151. "Descartes' circumspect answer had been this, that the foundations of our knowledge are to be sought in the 'veracitas Dei'; and that the truth of our thinking — the 'clare et distincte percipere' as criterion of all being — is a divine gift of our intellect, a gift not absolute in itself, but determined by divine decree."

96. Meyer, *Revolution*, 151. "And God's reason is (and contains) nothing else but a perfect condensation of all eternal truths, and these we are able to grasp from the law of our spirit. God's will too cannot determine itself except in conformity with those transfinite orders which He embodies and realizes."

97. Meyer, *Revolution*, 151. "Ultimately this faith in God became nothing but the most certain knowledge of that invisible order which man, 'that noblest part of the Universe,' was to realize in the natural world in the form of a moral world."

98. Meyer, *Revolution*, 153. "'The inventive and ruling spirit of man' is now free; it is to be given its justification in the Theodicy. But 'at the end of its works and days' the human spirit will once again question the diskaiosyne theou, the justice of God, and plead with Him the predicament of his freedom." Meyer, *Revolution*, 153.

99. Meyer, *Revolution*, 142.

100. Meyer, *Revolution*, 142.

101. Meyer, *Revolution*, 161.

102. See chapter 3, below.

103. Loemker, *Papers*, 331.

104. Leibniz, *New Essays*, 618.

105. Jordan, *Reunion*, 215-16.

Notes to Chapter 2

1. Wolfhart Pannenberg, "The Appropriation of the Philosophical Concept of God as a Dogmatic Problem of Early Christian Theology," in *Basic Questions in Theology*, vol. 2, trans. G. H. Kehm (Philadelphia: Fortress, 1972), 119-83.

2. Karl Barth, *Church Dogmatics* I/1, trans. G. W. Bromiley (Edinburgh: T. & T. Clark, 1975), 36, hereafter cited as *CD* I/1.

3. John Dillenberger, *God Hidden and Revealed: The Interpretation of Luther's Deus Absconditus and Its Significance for Religious Thought* (Philadelphia: Muhlenberg, 1953), 174.

4. Immanuel Kant, *Critique of Judgment*, trans. W. S. Pluhar (Indianapolis: Hackett, 1987), 35-36.

5. Philosophical reason "alone is the source of the *universality, unity,* and *necessity* in the tenets of faith that are the essence of any religion as such, which consists in the morally practical (in what we *ought* to do). On the other hand, what we have cause to believe on historical grounds (where *'ought'* does not hold at all) — that is, revelation as contingent tenets of faith — it regards as nonessential . . . revelation is useful in making up the theoretical deficiency which our pure rational belief admits it has (in the questions, for example, of the origin of evil, the conversion from evil to good, man's assurance that he has become good, etc.) and helps . . . to satisfy a rational need. . . . I have praised [Christianity] as the best and

most adequate means of public instruction available for establishing and maintaining indefinitely a state religion that is truly conducive to the soul's moral improvement. . . . Its best and most lasting eulogy is its harmony . . . with the purest moral belief of religion." Immanuel Kant, *The Conflict of the Faculties,* trans. Mary J. Gregor (New York: Abaris Books, 1979), 17.

6. Immanuel Kant, "The Conflict of the Faculties," 7.63, in *Religion and Rational Theology,* in the Cambridge Edition of the Works of Immanuel Kant, trans. A. W. Wood and G. Di Giovanni (Cambridge: Cambridge University Press, 2001), 283.

7. E.g., Luther in the Smalcald Articles, in *The Book of Concord: The Confessions of the Evangelical Lutheran Church,* ed. Robert Kolb and Timothy J. Wengert (Minneapolis: Fortress, 2000), 322.3-6.

8. G. W. Leibniz, *New Essays concerning Human Understanding,* trans. Alfred Gideon Langley (La Salle, Ill.: Open Court, 1949), 33.

9. Leibniz, *New Essays,* 34.

10. Leibniz, *New Essays,* 474. The editor notes: "revelation presupposes a natural idea of God, philosophically derived and including the attribute of veracity, to which it may appeal and by which its character and claims to authority may be judged."

11. John Lawson, *The Biblical Theology of Saint Irenaeus* (London: Epworth, 1948), 87-114.

12. Walter Bauer, *Orthodoxy and Heresy in Early Christianity,* ed R. Kraft and G. Krodel (Philadelphia: Fortress, 1971; reprint, Mifflintown, Pa.: Sigler, 1996); Martin Werner, *The Formation of Christian Dogma: An Historical Study of Its Problem* (New York: Harper, 1957). Against these: J. N. D. Kelly, *Early Christian Doctrines,* rev. ed. (San Francisco: Harper, 1978). More recently, Arland J. Hultgren, *The Rise of Normative Christianity* (Minneapolis: Fortress, 1994).

13. Immanuel Kant, *Lectures on Philosophical Theology,* trans. A. W. Wood and G. M. Clark (Ithaca, N.Y.: Cornell University Press, 1978), 161.

14. Kant, *Lectures on Philosophical Theology,* 79.

15. Barth incisively captured this point in his discussion of Kant; Karl Barth, *From Rousseau to Ritschl,* trans. B. Cozens (London: SCM, 1959), 188-96.

16. Kant, "Conflict of the Faculties," in *Religion and Rational Theology,* 251.

17. Bruce L. McCormack, *Karl Barth's Critically Realistic Dialectical Theology: Its Genesis and Development, 1909-1936* (Oxford: Clarendon, 1995), 130. Briefly put: McCormack's exhaustive study of the formation of Barth's theology is a dramatic account of Barth "veering towards Lutheranism," to wit, some version of the *finitum capax infiniti,* but finally withstanding that temptation to arrive at a "dialectic" position. The christological communication of idioms is verbal, not real; a manner of speaking, not being. The necessary dialectic of revelation plays out in an ever elusive conjunction of divine and human in the event of Christ, rather than through the trinitarian relations disclosed in that event. In the latter case, we have the incarnate Word in our hands to abuse, even to crucify and bury, though we do not have Him truly except the same raised from death by the Spirit and so in our hands, on our lips, in our mouths as *we* are called to faith by the same Spirit — as *from the dead.*

18. Barth, *CD* I/1:295ff.

19. Barth, *CD* I/1:297.

20. Barth, *CD* I/1:303.

21. Barth, *CD* I/1:350, 366.

22. Barth, *CD* I/1:359.

23. Barth, *CD* I/1:348. Barth will insist that we put aside preconceived ideas of Lordship and learn from God's thrice-repeated self-presentation what it is to have a God: "All else we know as lordship can only be a copy, and is in reality a sad caricature of this lordship. Without revelation man does not know that there is a Lord, that he, man, has a Lord, and that God is this Lord" (306).

24. Kant, *Lectures on Philosophical Theology*, 161.

25. Barth, *CD* I/1:300.

26. Barth, *CD* I/1:301.

27. I am referring to the well-known Regnon thesis: "Latin philosophy considers the nature in itself first and proceeds to the agent; Greek philosophy considers the agent first and passes through it to find the nature. The Latins think of personality as a mode of nature; the Greeks think of nature as the content of the person." Cited in John Meyendorff, *Byzantine Theology: Historical Trends and Doctrinal Themes* (New York: Fordham University Press, 1979), 181. Barth's innovation from within the Latin approach was to understand divine nature as the sovereign freedom of the divine, self-positing Subject who exists in the act of his own decision. Dennis Bielfeldt had argued that Luther's trinitarian theology militates against a strong version of the Regnon thesis; see Bielfeldt, "Semantics, Ontology and the Trinity," in *The Substance of Faith: Luther's Doctrinal Theology for Today,* by Dennis Bielfeldt, Paul R. Hinlicky, and Mickey L. Mattox (Minneapolis: Fortress, 2008), 59-130.

28. As Barth himself with characteristic honesty acknowledges, *CD* I/1:367, with respect to his critique of the notion of "person" and its replacement with the concept of "modes of being."

29. Barth, *CD* I/1:307.

30. Barth, *CD* I/1:349.

31. "Barth's revolution is finally a revolution in the doctrine of God — which means, among other things, that he is working with a very different divine ontology than did his forebearers in the Reformed tradition." Bruce McCormack, "Grace and Being," in *The Cambridge Companion to Karl Barth,* ed. John Webster (Cambridge: Cambridge University Press, 2000), 93.

32. McCormack, "Grace and Being," 96-97.

33. McCormack, "Grace and Being," 103.

34. McCormack, "Grace and Being," 102.

35. McCormack, "Grace and Being," 103.

36. Barth, *CD* I/1:350.

37. Barth, *CD* I/1:351.

38. Meyendorff, *Byzantine Theology,* 180.

39. Robert W. Jenson, *The Triune Identity* (Philadelphia: Fortress, 1982), 138. Recognition of the "rule" involved here is separable from Jenson's important but controversial proposal to view the Son's deity, and so the "immanent" Trinity, eschatologically rather than protologically (140-41).

40. Jenson, *The Triune Identity,* 139.

41. Beginning expressly with the second edition of his *Epistle to the Romans,* trans. E. C. Hoskyns (London: Oxford University Press, 1972), 4.

42. Barth, *From Rousseau to Ritschl,* 188.

43. Barth, *From Rousseau to Ritschl,* 191.

44. Barth, *From Rousseau to Ritschl,* 195.

45. Barth, *From Rousseau to Ritschl,* 196.

46. See above, n. 5.

47. Barth, *CD* I/1:315.

48. Barth, *CD* I/1:315. Again: "This is what self-revelation is. This is what man cannot provide for himself, what only God can give him, what He does give him in His revelation" (316).

49. Barth, *CD* I/1:320.

50. Barth, *CD* I/1:371.

51. Barth, *CD* I/1:321.

52. Barth, *CD* I/1:321.

53. McCormack, *Critically Realistic,* 465.

54. Barth, *CD* I/1:371.

55. Barth, *CD* I/1:305. "As regards the question of the 'historical' certainty of the revelation attested in the Bible we can only say that it is ignored in the Bible itself in a way that one can understand only on the premises that this question is completely alien to it, i.e., obviously and utterly inappropriate to the object of its witness" (325).

56. E.g., Barth, *CD* I/1:70-71.

57. Christine Helmer, *The Trinity and Martin Luther: A Study on the Relationship between Genre, Language, and the Trinity in Luther's Works (1523-1546)* (Mainz: Verlag Philipp von Zabern, 1999), 230.

58. Helmer, *The Trinity,* 242.

59. *Lutherforschung im 20. Jahrhundert: Rueckblick-Bilanz-Ausblick,* ed. R. Vinke (Mainz: Verlag Philipp von Zabern, 2004). See the review by Paul R. Hinlicky in *Sixteenth Century Journal* 38, no. 2 (2007): 616-17.

60. Barth, *CD* I/1:332. "He possesses Himself as Father, i.e., pure Giver, as Son, i.e., Receiver and Giver, and as Spirit, i.e., pure Receiver" (364).

61. Barth, *CD* I/1:365. But see Günther Frank, "Zur Gottes- und Trinitätslehre bei Melanchthon und Calvin," in *Melanchthon und der Calvinismus,* ed. G. Frank and H. J. Selderhuis (Stuttgart-Bad Cannstatt: Frommann-Holzboog, 2005), 159-71, who rightly argues, in dialogue with Pannenberg's critique of the eclipse of trinitarianism that began in Ockhamism, that if the inadequacy of conceptions of God based on divine unity alone can be established philosophically, the ground is laid for an inner differentiation of the divine life, a speculative doctrine of the Trinity. Just this move according to Frank attends Melanchthon's approach, in which he assigns philosophical knowledge of the one God to the doctrine of the law and revealed knowledge of the Trinity to the gospel. If Melanchthon is guilty of "tritheism" as a result, so will also be Luther.

62. I am indebted to my colleague, the philosopher Brent Adkins, for this suggestion and for the following reference. See J. G. Fichte, *The Science of Knowledge,* ed. and trans. P. Heath and J. Lachs (Cambridge: Cambridge University Press, 1993). Here Fichte claims that his philosophy "is nothing other than Kantianism properly understood" (43), which he sharply distinguishes from the Spinozistic dissolution of the ego into a mode of being, noting that "when fully thought out, the system of Leibniz is nothing other than Spinozism" (102). What distinguishes Fichte's properly understood Kantianism is the self-positing subject, "the self as absolute subject *whose being or essence consists simply in the fact that it posits itself as existing*" (98, emphasis in original).

63. Barth, *CD* I/1:374.

64. Barth, *CD* I/1:380.

65. Barth, *CD* I/1:42.

66. Barth, *CD* I/1:43.

67. Barth, *CD* I/1:33.

68. McCormack, *Critically Realistic,* 182.

69. Barth, *CD* I/1:129.

70. That is, if we take Luther's "joyful exchange" as indicating his doctrine of justification *by divine faith,* thicker than a thin version of the forensic justification *by grace.* The early Barth had some sympathy for this, according to McCormack, *Critically Realistic,* 76, but later emphatically and polemically disowned it as "Osiandrian"; cf. *CD* I/1:180-82.

71. Paul R. Hinlicky, "Luther's Anti-Docetism in the Disputatio de divinitate et humanitate Christi (1540)," in *Creator est creatura: Luthers Christologie als Lehre von der Idiomenkommunikation,* ed. O. Bayer and Benjamin Gleede (Berlin and New York: De Gruyter, 2007), 139-85.

72. McCormack stresses this in *Critically Realistic:* 76, 366, 392, 464-65. The old man Barth is unequivocal in *Church Dogmatics* IV/4, trans. G. W. Bromiley (Edinburgh: T. & T. Clark, 1969), 19, in which the charge of Christomonism is laid upon (the unnamed) Luther, and the Holy Spirit is instead assigned the task according to a proper "Christocentrism" of the subjective appropriation of the objective work of Christ so that "the man who with the same organs could once say No thereto, again with the same organs, in so far as they can be used for this purpose, may and can and must say Yes" (27). The Holy Spirit provides the "change in which a man, in virtue of God's faithfulness to him, becomes faithful to God in return, and thus becomes a Christian" (33). This line of thought leads Barth to a systematic disjunction between baptism in the Spirit and baptism by water, as divine and human acts respectively, that latter meaning "the free man who determines himself under this pre-determination by God . . . taken seriously, as the creature which is different from God, which is for all its dependence autonomous before Him, which is of age" (35). As we shall see, Barth's motive here is the same as in Melanchthon over against Luther: to keep God and creature from confusion even at their most intimate union. The tendency is Nestorian, even though within the bounds of Chalcedonian orthodoxy.

73. Dietrich Bonhoeffer, *Ethics,* trans. N. H. Smith (New York: Macmillan, 1978), 196-97.

74. *Dr. Martin Luthers Werke* (Weimar: Böhlau, 1883-1993), 39II:116, A, 2.

75. Merold Westphal, *Overcoming Onto-Theology: Toward a Postmodern Christian Faith* (New York: Fordham University Press, 2001), 12.

76. See above, chapter 1.

77. Kant, *Lectures on Philosophical Theology,* 80.

78. Kant, *Lectures on Philosophical Theology,* 44, according to the editor, the lectures "cannot have predated 1781," i.e., the controversy with Eberhard.

79. Kant, *Lectures on Philosophical Theology,* 21.

80. Kant, *Lectures on Philosophical Theology,* 44.

81. Kant, *Lectures on Philosophical Theology,* 66.

82. Kant, *Lectures on Philosophical Theology,* 67.

83. Kant, *Lectures on Philosophical Theology,* 81.

84. Kant, *Lectures on Philosophical Theology,* 46.

85. Adams regards this "the most solid part of Leibniz's modal version of the ontological argument," in distinction from Anselm and Descartes: "if the existence of a necessary God, the God of what the Germans call 'ontotheology,' is so much as possible, then such a deity actually (and also, of course, necessarily) exists." Robert Merrihew Adams, *Leibniz: Determinist, Theist, Idealist* (Oxford: Oxford University Press, 1994), 137. The difficulty lies in grasping the unity of the perfections as the possibility of divine existence, the thinkability or conceivability of God.

86. Kant, *Lectures on Philosophical Theology*, 80.

87. Westphal writes: "Within Christian history, the critique of onto-theology belongs to a tradition of dehellenizing repristination. Heidegger explicitly links his critique with Luther, and thus by implication, with a tradition that looks back to Augustine and ahead to Pascal, Kierkegaard, and Barth" (Westphal, *Overcoming Onto-Theology*, 18). "My project is to appropriate Heidegger's critique of onto-theology for theistic theology, for religiously significant discourse about the personal Creator, Lawgiver and Merciful Savior of Jewish, or Christian, or Muslim monotheism." His target is not only "such paradigmatically onto-theological systems as those of Spinoza and Hegel but also against what we might call onto-theologies of the right, more popularly known as fundamentalisms" (21). His purpose is to deny theory, the primacy of insight over interpretation, hermeneutics, for the sake of practice, i.e., not the "ascent from that which is inferior (body . . .) to that which is superior (soul . . .)" but "a loving, trusting relation with a God before whom one might sing" (27). My concern here is that necessary differentiations become false, even categorical antitheses. Dehellenizing repristination is not, in any case, a correct grasp of Luther's reformation theology (nor Augustine's nor Paul's nor Barth's).

88. Westphal, *Overcoming Onto-Theology*, 15.

89. Westphal, *Overcoming Onto-Theology*, 6.

90. Westphal, *Overcoming Onto-Theology*, 7. This differentiation almost literally echoes Luther's Heidelberg Disputation: "Since men misused the knowledge of God [His eternal power and deity, Rom. 1:20] through [His created] works, God wished again to be recognized in suffering" (*Luther's Works: The American Edition*, ed. J. Pelikan et al. [St. Louis: Concordia; Philadelphia: Fortress, 1960-], 31:52; hereafter *LW*), i.e., as the victim of the aforementioned abuse.

91. Westphal, *Overcoming Onto-Theology*, 7. "[T]he believer might speak as follows: 'In affirming God the Creator I am affirming that there is an explanation of the whole of being and I am pointing in the direction of that explanation; but I am not giving it, for I do not possess it. . . . My affirmation of God as Creator is not onto-theological because it is not in the service of the philosophical project of rendering the whole of being intelligible to human understanding, a project I have ample religious reasons to repudiate'" (7).

92. Westphal, *Overcoming Onto-Theology*, 7.

93. Westphal, *Overcoming Onto-Theology*, 27.

94. Luther, commentary on Rom. 8, in *LW* 25:360-64.

95. "Luther affirms that faith is 'in the understanding' (in intellectu); that it is a kind of 'knowledge' (notitia); that its object is 'truth' (veritatem); that it is an 'instructor and judge' (doctor et iudex); and so on. Elsewhere, he calls faith 'right thinking about God' (recte cogitare de Deo). And reason, he says, is wrong thinking" (B. A. Gerrish, *Grace and Reason: A Study in the Theology of Luther* [Oxford: At the Clarendon Press, 1962], 82). How to unravel this apparent contradiction? For Luther, *ratio* "has become almost synonymous with a cer-

tain opinion . . . one grave misunderstanding and one false inference" (Gerrish, 84). This is the *opinio legis* of works righteousness, *vult per legem iustificari. Ratio* is thus not a synonym for rationality but denotes a "definite attitude of the natural man" (99 n; cf. 169). "The consequence is that reason has to pretend that the burden of sin is lighter than it really is" (85). The false inferences this *ratio* habitually makes: "only he who obeys will be saved," or conversely, if salvation is by grace, then "the law is nothing and men may as well do evil" (88). Thus the real sacrifice of the intellect is "removal of a particular false understanding about God which makes of Him a harsh Judge . . . reason imagines that Christ's 'office' is to show us what we must do to be saved . . . what reason cannot grasp is, in the final analysis, the sheer miracle of forgiveness" (90).

96. Benjamin D. Crowe, *Heidegger's Religious Origins: Destruction and Authenticity* (Bloomington and Indianapolis: Indiana University Press, 2006), 66. See Paul R. Hinlicky, "Luther and Heidegger," review essay on *Heidegger's Religious Origins,* by Benjamin D. Crowe, *Lutheran Quarterly* 22, no. 1 (Spring 2008).

97. Crowe, *Heidegger's Religious Origins,* 49.

98. Crowe, *Heidegger's Religious Origins,* 153.

99. G. F. Hegel, *Lectures on the Philosophy of Religion,* one-volume edition, the Lecture of 1827, ed. P. C. Hodgson (Berkeley and Los Angeles: University of California Press, 1988), 488 n. 265.

100. Hegel, *Lectures,* 400.

101. Hegel, *Lectures,* 402.

102. Hegel, *Lectures,* 402.

103. Hegel, *Lectures,* 404.

104. Hegel, *Lectures,* 413.

105. Hegel, *Lectures,* 417.

106. "No ultimate explanation is offered, neither for the divine capacity to suffer, nor for the turn towards the Son, other than the inexplicable ground of the divine nature itself. . . . Mercy is the groundless ground of the divine turn towards creation" (Helmer, *The Trinity,* 168). "Not a turn from wrath to love, the inner-trinitarian turn is told as the narrative of the attribute of mercy" (169). I would differentiate here: love turns from wrath to mercy, since love is opposed to what is against love yet finds the way even to reach the unloving. But the gravamen of Helmer's claim is correct over against readings that virtually posit a God at the mercy of conflicting feelings rather than a God of mercy in conflict with unmerciful creatures.

107. Cyril O'Regan, *The Heterodox Hegel* (Albany: State University of New York Press, 1994), 228.

108. O'Regan, *The Heterodox Hegel,* 229.

109. Aiton cites Leibniz's letter of February 6, 1706, to Sophie (K 9, pp. 155-63) "explaining that God is a simple substance standing outside the series, who sees the universe clearly (that is, as it really is), and that each soul is a world apart, representing things outside it confusedly from its point of view." E. J. Aiton, *Leibniz: A Biography* (Bristol and Boston: Adam Hilger, 1985), 280.

110. Karl Barth, *Church Dogmatics* II/2, trans. G. W. Bromiley et al. (Edinburgh: T. & T. Clark, 1957), 9; hereafter cited as *CD* II/2.

111. Barth, *CD* II/2:175.

112. T. F. Torrance, *The Trinitarian Faith: The Evangelical Theology of the Ancient Catholic Church* (Edinburgh: T. & T. Clark, 1993), 89.

113. As Torrance describes it: "Behind the beginning of creation there is an absolute or transcendent beginning by God who is himself eternally without beginning. This is what makes the creation of the world out of nothing so utterly baffling and astonishing. It is not only that something absolutely new has begun to be, new even for God who created it by his Word and gave it a contingent reality and integrity outwith himself, but that in some incomprehensible way, to cite Athanasius again, 'the Word himself *became* the Maker of the things that have a beginning.'" Torrance, *The Trinitarian Faith,* 88. Hegel's point will be: then "eternity" is itself a kind of time. Time and God are not metaphysically repulsive to each other. A false eternity, like a false infinite, is merely an abstract negation that is defined by, and so limited by, its opposition. Eternity is the infinite possibility of the embrace of time.

114. Hegel, *Lectures,* 417-18.

115. Immanuel Kant, *Critique of Pure Reason,* trans. J. M. D. Meiklejohn (Mineola, N.Y.: Dover, 2003; 1st ed., London and New York: Colonial, 1900), First Division, Book Two, Chapter Three, Appendix and Remark on the Amphiboly, 168-86. I prefer the readable English of this translation, even though it lacks the A/B pagination preferred by Kant scholars.

116. Kant, *Critique of Pure Reason,* 179.

117. Kant, *Critique of Pure Reason,* 173.

118. Witness the opening words of *New Essays:* "Mr. Locke . . . had good reasons for opposing himself on this point to ordinary prejudices, for the name of ideas and principles is greatly abused. Common philosophers manufacture for themselves principles according to their fancy; and the Cartesians, who profess greater accuracy, do not cease to entrench themselves behind so-called ideas of extension, of matter and the soul, desiring to avoid thereby the necessity of proving what they advance, on the pretext that those who will meditate on these ideas will discover in them the same thing as they; that is to say, that those who will accustom themselves to their jargon and mode of thought will have the same prepossessions, which is very true. My view, then, is that nothing should be taken as first principles but experiences and the axiom of identity or (what is the same thing) contradiction, which is primitive, since otherwise there would be no difference between truth and falsehood; and all investigation would cease at once, if to say yes and no were a matter of indifference" (13-14).

119. Henry E. Allison rightly points out that Kant tends to interpret monadology "in the metaphysical or idealistic sense" as "'metaphysical points,' purely intelligible substances without any materiality" instead of, correctly, "from the standpoint of the philosophy of nature (realistically), and from this point of view, although the monads are still immaterial, their combination yields the objective material world, and they can be regarded as parts or elements of that world, and thus as located in space." Allison, *The Kant-Eberhard Controversy: An English Translation Together with Supplementary Materials and a Historical-Analytical Introduction of Immanuel Kant's "On a Discovery" according to Which Any New Critique of Pure Reason Has Been Made Superfluous by an Earlier One* (Baltimore and London: Johns Hopkins University Press, 1973), 35. This latter view, which is surely Leibniz's view for whom no monad except God can exist without a body, would obviate the crucial Kantian attack on the principle of indiscernibility (Kant, *Critique of Pure Reason,* 170), i.e., that it is undermined by numerical plurality of phenomenal objects. But God does not create generic ranks of monads that are haphazardly instantiated in space and time. Leibniz is a virtual nominalist on this issue. God has and actualizes full and complete notions of each

and every organic unity in the cosmos. "In opposition to Descartes, he believed: (i) that the laws of mechanics, which are the foundation of the whole system, depend on final causes, that is to say, on God's will determined to make the most perfect; (ii) that matter does not take all possible forms but only the most perfect." Aiton, *Leibniz*, 84. "The doctrine of occasionalism, he thought, had dangerous consequences which its defenders did not intend; namely, the implication of pantheism; for, since that which does not act can in no way be a substance, the doctrine implies created things to be mere modifications of the one divine substance and so, like Spinoza, makes out of God the nature of the world itself." Aiton, 235.

120. Kant, *Critique of Pure Reason*, 174.

121. Kant, *Critique of Pure Reason*, 178.

122. Kant, *Critique of Pure Reason*, 179.

123. Kant, *Critique of Pure Reason*, 183.

124. Kant, *Critique of Pure Reason*, 184.

125. Splendidly stated in the succinct essay of 1697, "On the Ultimate Origination of Things," in G. W. Leibniz, *Discourse on Metaphysics and Other Essays*, trans. D. Garber and R. Ariew (Indianapolis: Hackett, 1991), 41-48.

126. Leibniz, *Discourse*, 43.

127. Allison, *The Kant-Eberhard Controversy*, 9.

128. Kant, *Critique of Pure Reason*, 182.

129. Kant, *Critique of Pure Reason*.

130. Leibniz, *Discourse*, 46.

131. See Frederick C. Beiser, *The Fate of Reason: German Philosophy from Kant to Fichte* (Cambridge: Harvard University Press, 1987), 194-97, for an excellent summary of the Wolffian counterattack.

132. Allison, *The Kant-Eberhard Controversy*, 157.

133. Allison, *The Kant-Eberhard Controversy*, 158.

134. Allison, *The Kant-Eberhard Controversy*, 158.

135. Allison, *The Kant-Eberhard Controversy*, 160.

136. Beiser, *The Fate of Reason*, 195; Allison, from the Kantian perspective, rejects "Leibnizian panlogism": the "crucial question" is "the transcendental or material question whether or not a predicate stands in a real relation to the object. Synthetic judgments assert such relations, while analytic judgments merely assert logical relations between concepts." Allison, *The Kant-Eberhard Controversy*, 54. But surely, as an argument against Leibniz, this is a *petitio principii* that simply asserts anew the unbridgeable gulf of transcendentalism. Conversely, as Allison himself writes: Leibnizian use "of the principle of sufficient reason completely begs the question which concerned Kant" (45). Of course that is so, the point being that the two are engaged in different projects. Kant, having misappropriated Leibniz as an inchoate epistemologist to illustrate the delusions of idealism, must now, despite knowing better, save his revisionist Leibniz from himself.

137. Patrick Riley, *Leibniz' Universal Jurisprudence: Justice as the Charity of the Wise* (Cambridge: Harvard University Press, 1996), 85. The entire section comparing Kant and Leibniz and leading to this conclusion is most illuminating (79-85).

138. "Leibniz therefore rejects Descartes' doctrine that what may be conceived clearly and distinctly in something is true and may be predicated of it. For what may seem clear and distinct in symbolic thinking [with images instead of ideas] is often obscure and confused. Instead, he adopts the position that an idea is true when the concept is possible and false

when it implies a contradiction. In reply to the suggestion of Hobbes that truths are arbitrary because they depend on a free choice of definitions, he distinguished between nominal definitions and real definition. The former contain only symbols for discerning one thing from others. A real definition, on the other hand, is one through which the possibility of the thing is ascertained, and such a definition is not open to free choice, since not all concepts can be combined with each other." Aiton, *Leibniz,* 118. "Locke's relationship to Hobbes, like his relationship to Descartes, is a complicated one which includes elements of overlap as well as opposition. . . . What does seem fair to say is that the Second Treatise of Government is haunted by the ghost of Thomas Hobbes." Nicholas Jolley, *Locke: His Philosophical Thought* (Oxford: Oxford University Press, 1999), 195-96. Put otherwise, Locke's dependence on Hobbes in metaphysics and epistemology conflicts with Locke's inclinations in moral philosophy: to the end of his life, Locke "seeks largely to undo the Hobbsean revolution [i.e., 'the reduction of natural laws to self-interested maxims'] and return to a more conservative tradition . . . 'writ in the hearts of all mankind'" (Jolley, 199). As happens in the interpretation of Leibniz, however, the temptation is to reduce Locke to Hobbes by disregarding the philosophical role played by dogma borrowed from Christian theology. Jolley acknowledges this role: "The idea that we are God's property thus does important work in Locke's political theory" (203). See Paul R. Hinlicky, "Luther and Liberalism," in *A Report from the Front Lines: Conversations on Public Theology; A Festschrift in Honor of Robert Benne,* ed. Michael Shahan (Grand Rapids: Eerdmans, 2009), 89-104.

139. Leibniz, *New Essays,* 42-43. As we shall see, the roots of this disagreement lie in Leibniz's Melanchthonian Lutheranism, which worked out a philosophy of culture on the basis of common principles, prolepses, general notions, *semina aeternitatis* on the basis of Rom. 2:15 and Gen. 1:26-28. So construed, the argument with Locke is about the principles of human knowledge in a world created by God, *not* justification of knowledge by the newly autonomous human mind.

140. On Descartes, see above, n. 135. "From his earliest youth he had believed in a plurality of substances, taking for the subject of his first dissertation the demonstration of the principle of individuation. On this issue Spinoza was easily refuted; his definition of substance was obscure and his reasoning unsound. . . . Spinoza had not really defined a substance. . . . Another of Spinoza's propositions rejected by Leibniz was the assertion that existence necessarily belongs to substance. For not everything that can be conceived, he argued, can be produced, since it may be incompatible with more important things . . . not all possibles can exist but only those which are compossible. . . . [Spinoza] made no attempt to demonstrate that the concept of God is possible. As Leibniz points out, having defined God as a substance which consists of infinite attributes, he should have demonstrated that they are compatible. . . . In opposition to Spinoza's necessitarianism Leibniz thus sets his belief in the determination of existence by God's free choice of the best among the compossibles." Aiton, *Leibniz,* 82-83.

141. Matthew Stewart, *The Courtier and the Heretic: Leibniz, Spinoza, and the Fate of God in the Modern World* (New York and London: Norton, 2006), 310. This study draws on the Anglo-American tradition of interpretation begun by Bertrand Russell and followed by Arthur Lovejoy in his magisterial *The Great Chain of Being,* i.e., that Leibniz was in spite of himself a Spinozist. This interpretation, I argue, has to devalue the theological background, more specifically, the Melanchthonian-Lutheran background on which Leibniz draws.

142. Jonathan I. Israel, *Radical Enlightenment: Philosophy and the Making of Modernity, 1650-1750* (Oxford: Oxford University Press, 2001), 510.

143. With apologies to William Placher, *The Domestication of Transcendence* (Louisville: John Knox, 1996), and John Milbank, "Policing the Sublime," in *Theology and Social Theory: Beyond Secular Reason* (Oxford, U.K., and Cambridge, Mass.: Blackwell, 1997), 101.

144. Milbank, *Theology and Social Theory,* 12. I share with Milbank the Bonhoefferian critique of "thinking in terms of two spheres": "the self-understanding of Christianity . . . which completely privatized, spiritualized and transcendentalized the sacred, and concurrently reimagined nature, human action and society as a sphere of autonomous, sheerly formal power" (9). In choosing to begin my account with Spinoza, and to find an alternative in Leibniz, however, I am diverging from his, as it seems to me, undifferentiated litany on the sources of disaster in "late-medieval nominalism, the protestant reformation and seventeenth-century Augustinianism" (Milbank, 9).

145. Ernst Cassirer, *The Philosophy of the Enlightenment,* trans. F. C. A. Koelln and J. P. Pettegrove (Princeton: Princeton University Press, 1979), 189.

146. The enormous significance of Spinoza for theology as well as culture is increasingly recognized, and not only in relation to the Jacobi controversy during the formative stage of German idealism; see Beiser, *The Fate of Reason,* 45-91.

147. Baruch Spinoza, *Ethics, Treatise on the Emendation of the Intellect and Selected Letters,* trans. S. Shirley (Indianapolis: Hackett, 1992), IV, Preface; 153.

148. Spinoza, *Ethics,* IV, Preface; 153.

149. Not, of course, that the discovery of the vast and ancient cosmos is cognitively disputed in "modern" theology: the creationist tack of fundamentalist theology (equally modern, but reactionary) is emphatically refused.

150. Blaise Pascal, *Pensees,* trans. A. J. Krailsheimer (London and New York: Penguin Books, 1995), #68; 19. In Lezek Kolakowski's interpretation, Pascal's modernity anticipates Kant's divorce of the spheres of faith and reason; see *God Owes Us Nothing: A Brief Remark on Pascal's Religion and on the Spirit of Jansenism* (Chicago: University of Chicago Press, 1995), 170-75.

151. As Feuerbach famously analyzed: "Man — this is the mystery of religion — projects his being into objectivity, and then again makes himself an object to this projected image of himself thus converted into a subject. . . . In the religious systole man propels his own nature from himself, he throws himself outward; in the religious diastole he receives the rejected nature into his heart again." Ludwig Feuerbach, *The Essence of Christianity,* trans. G. Eliot (New York: Harper Torchbooks, 1957), 30-31.

152. Karl Marx, "Theses on Feuerbach," in *Karl Marx on Religion,* ed. and trans. S. K. Padover (New York: McGraw-Hill, 1974), 63-65.

153. Baruch Spinoza, *Theological-Political Treatise,* trans. S. Shirley (Indianapolis: Hackett, 1998), 52-53.

154. Spinoza, *Theological-Political Treatise,* 51.

155. This fundamentally Cartesian motive is acknowledged by Spinoza from the beginning and arguably remains with him throughout his oeuvre: "Finally, to achieve certainty about what he had called into doubt and to remove all doubt, [the Cartesian wise man] proceeds to enquire into the nature of the most perfect Being, and whether such exists. For when he realizes that there exists a most perfect Being by whose power all things are produced and preserved and to whose nature it is contrary that he should be a deceiver, then

this will remove the reason for doubting that resulted from his not knowing the cause of him." Baruch Spinoza, *Principles of Cartesian Philosophy with Metaphysical Thoughts,* trans. S. Shirley (Indianapolis: Hackett, 1998), 11. "[Before proceeding], I have thought it helpful to give a concise account as to why Descartes doubted everything, the way in which he laid the solid foundations of the sciences, and finally the means by which he freed himself from all doubts. . . . Descartes, then, so as to proceed with the greatest caution in his enquiry, attempted: 1) to put aside all prejudice; 2) to discover the foundations on which everything should be built; 3) to uncover the cause of error; 4) to understand everything clearly and distinctly. To achieve his first, second, and third aims, he proceeded to call everything into doubt, not indeed like a Sceptic whose sole aim is to doubt, but to free his mind from all prejudice so that he might discover the firm and unshakable foundations of the sciences. . . . To achieve his fourth and final aim, that of understanding everything clearly and distinctly, his chief rule was to enumerate the simple ideas out of which all others are compounded and to scrutinize each one separately" (7-8).

156. Spinoza, *Principles,* 11.

157. Spinoza, *Principles,* 59.

158. Spinoza, *Ethics,* IV, Appendix, #32; 200.

159. Spinoza, *Theological-Political Treatise,* 166.

160. Spinoza, *Theological-Political Treatise,* 167.

161. Letter, January 1665, in Spinoza, *Theological-Political Treatise,* 275.

162. Kant, *Critique of Judgment,* 120.

163. Kant, *Critique of Judgment,* 99.

164. Kant, *Critique of Judgment,* 122.

165. Kant, "On the Miscarriage of All Philosophical Trials in Theodicy," in *Religion and Rational Theology,* 24-37.

166. "Those who want to live, let them fight, and those who do not want to fight in this world of eternal struggle do not deserve to live. Even if this were hard — that is how it is! Assuredly, however, by far the harder fate is that which strikes the man who thinks he can overcome Nature, but in the last analysis only mocks her. Distress, misfortune, and diseases are her answer." Adolf Hitler, *Mein Kampf,* trans. R. Manheim (Boston: Houghton Mifflin, 1971), 289.

167. Kant, *Critique of Judgment,* 106.

168. Kant, *Critique of Judgment,* 120.

169. Kant, *Critique of Judgment,* 123.

170. Kant, *Critique of Judgment,* 120-21. Kant concedes: "I admit that this principle seems farfetched and the result of some subtle reasoning."

171. Since "God's intellect and his power and will, whereby he has created, understood, and preserves or loves created things, are in no way distinct from one another save only in respect of our thought," God cannot be understood to be "angry with anyone [nor does he] love things in the way that is commonly believed." Spinoza, *Principles,* 124-25. On grounds of divine immutability the inference would hold; the question, as we shall see, is precisely whether God's intellect and will, i.e., God's knowledge of all possibles, and God's decision to instantiate this world and not another, are "in no way distinct from one another save only in respect of our thought."

172. Spinoza, *Principles,* 122.

173. Kant's programmatic discussion of "The Gradual Transition of Ecclesiastical Faith

toward the Exclusive Dominion of Pure Religious Faith in the Coming of the Kingdom of God," "Religion within the Limits of Mere Reason," 6:115ff., in Kant, *Religion and Rational Theology*, 146.

174. David Lotz rightly observed: "It is particularly noteworthy that both Ritschl and Orthodoxy failed to grasp Luther's profound doctrine of God in which the divine love and wrath were held together in dialectical tension. Ritschl simply dismissed the notion of God's wrath as incompatible with the theological procedure which comprehends God from the perspective of eternity, i.e., in the light of God's Kingdom as the final end of the world the idea of God's love alone has validity. . . . Ritschl thus eliminated the idea of God's wrath as a subjective illusion." David Lotz, *Ritschl and Luther: A Fresh Perspective on Albrecht Ritschl's Theology in the Light of His Luther Study* (Nashville: Abingdon, 1974), 185 n. 86.

175. Albrecht Ritschl, *The Christian Doctrine of Justification and Reconciliation: The Positive Development of the Doctrine*, trans. H. R. MacIntosh and A. B. McCaulay (Clifton, N.J.: Reference Books, 1966), 17.

176. Ritschl, *Justification and Reconciliation*, 11.

177. Ritschl, *Justification and Reconciliation*, 13.

178. Ritschl, *Justification and Reconciliation*, 14.

179. Friedrich Schleiermacher, *Brief Outline on the Study of Theology*, trans. T. N. Tice (Atlanta: John Knox, 1977), 29.

180. Cassirer, *Enlightenment*, 186.

181. Paul Tillich, *Systematic Theology*, 3 vols. (Chicago: University of Chicago Press, 1967), 1:237. Tillich carefully qualified his understanding of the dialectic in the introduction to the second volume in a discussion titled "Beyond Naturalism and Supranaturalism." 2:5-10 includes the endorsement: "The phrase *deus sive natura*, used by people like Scotus Erigena and Spinoza, does not say that God is identical with nature but that he is identical with *natura naturans*, the creative nature, the creative ground of all natural objects." 2:6: If the word "God" is not to become "semantically superfluous," as in contemporary "materialism and mechanism," the dialectical understanding of the *naturans/naturata* distinction must be sustained.

182. As Feuerbach acutely observed in his pioneering act of demystification: "A being without qualities is one which cannot become an object to the mind, and such a being is virtually non-existent. Where man deprives God of all qualities, God is no longer anything more to him than a negative being. To the truly religious man, God is not a being without qualities, because to him he is a positive, real being. The theory that God cannot be defined, and consequently cannot be known by man, is therefore the offspring of recent times, a product of modern unbelief." Feuerbach, *The Essence of Christianity*, 14.

183. Jeffery Stout, *The Flight from Authority: Religion, Morality, and the Quest for Autonomy* (Notre Dame, Ind., and London: University of Notre Dame Press, 1981), 146, cited from Alasdair MacIntyre, "The Fate of Theism," in *The Religious Significance of Atheism* (New York: Columbia University Press, 1969), 3-29.

184. Stout, *The Flight from Authority*, 145.

185. Robert Jenson, *God after God: The God of the Past and the God of the Future, Seen in the Work of Karl Barth* (New York: Bobbs-Merrill, 1969).

186. Echoing Spinoza via Schelling, Tillich wrote: "But God is his own fate; he is 'by himself'; he possesses 'aseity.' This can be said of him only if he is the power of being, if he is being-itself. As being itself God is beyond the contrast of essential and existential being. . . . For this reason it is as wrong to speak of God as the universal essence as it is to speak of him

as existing . . . grave difficulties attend the attempt to speak of God as existing. . . . God ceases to be God, the ground of being and meaning." Tillich, *Systematic Theology,* 1:236.

187. Christopher Morse, *Not Every Spirit: A Dogmatics of Christian Disbelief* (Philadelphia: Trinity, 1994).

188. Richard Steigmann-Gall, *The Holy Reich: Nazi Conceptions of Christianity, 1919-1945* (Cambridge: Cambridge University Press, 2003).

189. Helmer, *The Trinity,* 221.

190. "Where epistemology is the first problem, we are always in the situation of the potential threat to the nature of revelation. But where the ontological character of revelation is accepted from the start, one can proceed to a phenomenological description of the reception of this ontological factor . . . epistemology can be said to flow out of ontology . . . [as] analysis of the situation in which he knows." Dillenberger, *God Hidden and Revealed,* 181. "Is the transcendence of God to be defined from the side of man's inability to grasp God, or is it grounded upon man's confession of the act of revelation?" If the former, the result will be Hegel's false infinite whose content is only the negation of the world (Dillenberger, 174). "The church has not and does not start with the question of how God is revealed. It starts with the fact of reception and then begins to ask questions concerning the nature of this reception in relation to all other problems of knowledge. Theology has too often lost itself in the problem of the 'how' of revelation . . . how God can and must operate in the world. . . . In short, theology cannot put itself in the position of having to argue whether there can be or is revelation" (177). "It is rather that revelation defines God as the hidden God. Because one knows God revealed in Christ, one knows that he is a hidden God. . . . Hiddenness is therefore necessarily established through revelation. God can only be known through God" (119).

191. Barth, *CD* I/1:188.

192. Barth, *CD* I/1:195. See also Jean-Luc Marion, "The Idea of God," in *The Cambridge History of Seventeenth Century Philosophy* (Cambridge: Cambridge University Press, 1998), for Pascal's immanent and "most radical critique of any metaphysical conception of God." It is immanent to the extent that Pascal "takes up the Cartesian thesis" of the infinite incomprehensibility of God; but it is radical in that "the concept of infinity does not uniquely pick out God, since numbers, motion, speed, space, and even nature can be infinite as well" and because "this knowledge [of infinity], without Jesus Christ, is useless and sterile." The "real obstacle to acknowledging [God] does not rest in the uncertainty of the understanding, but in the arrogance of the will." Thus the metaphysical "project of proving the existence or determining the essence of God must yield to the recognition of a God to be loved, because He Himself loves first." What is evident, Marion concludes, is that in passing to the question of love "Pascal reaches an entirely different transcendence from that which metaphysics (above all Cartesian metaphysics) can envisage" (292-93). See the fuller discussion of Marion and Pascal below, in chapter 6.

193. Marion, "The Idea of God," 196-97.

194. Jean-Luc Marion, *God without Being,* trans. Thomas A. Carlson (Chicago: University of Chicago Press, 1995), 7.

Notes to Chapter 3

1. Paul Lehmann, *Ethics in a Christian Context* (New York: Harper and Row, 1963).

2. George Hunsinger, *Disruptive Grace: Studies in the Theology of Karl Barth* (Grand Rapids: Eerdmans, 2000), 280.

3. Risto Saarinen has provided as acute an answer to Hunsinger's question as may be found: Barth himself remained captive to Kant, if not to Schleiermacher, and so to the theology of the nineteenth century, which could conceive of the union with Christ by faith only as an effective community in action rather than the community of being indicated by the "joyful exchange." Risto Saarinen, *Gottes Wirken auf Uns: Die transzendentale Deutung des Gegenwart-Christi-Motivs in der Lutherforschung* (Stuttgart: Franz Steiner Verlag; Wiesbaden: GMBH, 1989), 185-208.

4. Karl Barth, *Church Dogmatics* III/3, trans. G. W. Bromiley and R. J. Ehrlich (Edinburgh: T. & T. Clark, 1960), 316-19; hereafter cited as *CD* III/3.

5. Wolf Kroetke, *Sin and Nothingness in the Theology of Karl Barth,* trans. P. G. Ziegler and C.-M. Bammel, Studies in Reformed Theology and History, n.s., no. 10 (Princeton: Princeton Theological Seminary, 2005), 48.

6. Kroetke, *Sin,* 46, cited from Karl Barth, *Church Dogmatics* III/2, trans. Harold Knight et al. (Edinburgh: T. & T. Clark, 1960), 569.

7. Karl Barth, *Church Dogmatics* III/1, trans. J. W. Edwards, O. Bussey, and Harold Knight (Edinburgh: T. & T. Clark, 1958), 392; hereafter cited as *CD* III/1.

8. John Hick, *Evil and the God of Love* (New York: Harper and Row, 1966), 160.

9. Patrick Riley, ed., *Leibniz: Political Writings,* 2nd ed. (Cambridge: Cambridge University Press, 2001), 25-26.

10. Matthew Stewart, *The Courtier and the Heretic: Leibniz, Spinoza, and the Fate of God in the Modern World* (New York and London: Norton, 2006), 76.

11. Riley, *Leibniz,* 136.

12. Hick, *God of Love,* 162.

13. Hick, *God of Love,* 171. The internal references in the quotation are to G. W. Leibniz, *Theodicy: Essays on the Goodness of God, the Freedom of Man, and the Origin of Evil,* trans. E. M. Huggard (Chicago and La Salle, Ill.: Open Court, 1998). On the grain of truth here, see below, chapter 6, Version One.

14. Hick, *God of Love,* 171-72.

15. Hick, *God of Love,* 173.

16. Hick, *God of Love,* 172.

17. Stewart, *Courtier and the Heretic,* 94.

18. Hick, *God of Love,* 164.

19. Hick, *God of Love,* 172.

20. Hick, *God of Love,* ix.

21. Immanuel Kant, *Religion and Rational Theology,* in the Cambridge Edition of the Works of Immanuel Kant, trans. A. W. Wood and G. Di Giovanni (Cambridge: Cambridge University Press, 2001), 30-31.

22. Hick, *God of Love,* 170.

23. Leibniz, *Theodicy,* 196-97.

24. G. W. Leibniz, *Philosophical Papers and Letters: A Selection,* trans. and ed. Leroy E. Loemker, 2 vols. (Chicago: University of Chicago Press, 1956), 609-12; hereafter cited as Loemker, *Papers.*

25. "God can only be found in suffering and the cross, as has already been said. Therefore the friends of the cross say that the cross is good and works are evil, for through the

cross works are dethroned and the old Adam, who is especially edified by works, is crucified." *Luther's Works: The American Edition,* ed. J. Pelikan et al. (St. Louis: Concordia; Philadelphia: Fortress, 1960-), 31:53; hereafter cited as *LW.* For contemporary arguments in this
vein, see Diogenes Allen, *Christian Belief in a Postmodern World: The Full Wealth of Conviction* (Louisville: Westminster/John Knox, 1989), and Amy Carr, "A Hermeneutics of Providence amid Affliction: Contributions by Luther and Weil to a Cruciform Doctrine of Providence," *Pro Ecclesia* 16, no. 3 (2007).

26. Patrick Riley, *Leibniz' Universal Jurisprudence: Justice as the Charity of the Wise*
(Cambridge: Harvard University Press, 1996), 152.

27. Riley, *Leibniz' Universal Jurisprudence,* 144-50.

28. Riley, *Leibniz' Universal Jurisprudence,* 262-63.

29. *LW* 31:52-53.

30. Loemker, *Papers,* 611.

31. Loemker, *Papers,* 612.

32. *LW* 31:57.

33. Loemker, *Papers,* 611.

34. See here the insightful analysis of the Muslim scholar Talal Asad, *Formations of the
Secular: Christianity, Islam, Modernity* (Stanford: Stanford University Press, 2003), 67-99.

35. Arthur Peacocke, *Theology for a Scientific Age: Being and Becoming — Natural, Divine, and Human,* enlarged ed. (London: SCM, 1993), 79.

36. Barth, *CD* III/1:388-414.

37. Barth, *CD* III/1:412.

38. The reference is to a Lutheran pastor Friedrich Christian Lesser, who published an
"Insecto-Theologia": "What sayest thou now, thou hardened atheist, With all thy doubts of
the creator's being and might, When the polity of bees strikes thy sight!" Barth, *CD* III/1:412.

39. Barth, *CD* III/1:413. Riley strains hard to minimize the import of this statement for
Leibniz interpretation, by means of an invidious comparison with the ordained priest
Malebranche's less reserved expressions of the christological faith, *Leibniz' Universal Juris-
prudence,* 38-50.

40. My translation of the Latin text Barth provides at *CD* III/1:413.

41. A statement of Barth's might be read as commentary on Leibniz's claim here: "concealed within the creaturely movement [of prayer in union with Christ], yet not the less
really, there moves the finger and hand and scepter of God who rules the world. And what is
more, there moves the heart of God, and He Himself is there in all the fullness of His love
and wisdom and power. We then find ourselves at the very seat of government, at the very
heart of the mystery and purpose of all occurrence. . . . [Prayer] conceals and contains and
actualizes the most objective of all things, the lordship of the One who as King of Israel and
King of the kingdom of grace holds all things in His own hands, and directs everything that
occurs in this world for the best: *per Jesus Christum, Dominum nostrum.*" *CD* III/3:288.

42. Barth, *CD* III/1:414.

43. Graham Ward, "Barth, Modernity and Postmodernity," in *Cambridge Companion to
Karl Barth,* ed. J. Webster (Cambridge: Cambridge University Press, 2000), 278.

44. Riley's dramatic pronouncement after acknowledging evidence to the contrary:
"Leibniz's 'Platonic rationalism' always outweighs mere Scripture" (*Leibniz' Universal Jurisprudence,* 69). This is true but trivial, since theology, as per Hegel above and Melanchthon
below, is always a rational activity of interpretation when it passes beyond mere repetition

of Scripture. See "An Unpublished Lecture by Leibniz on the Greeks as Founders of Rational Theology: Its Relation to His 'Universal Jurisprudence' (1714)," in *Leibniz: Political Writings,* 225-40. Riley himself again and again acknowledges Leibniz's Augustinianism, that is, his Christian revision of Platonism, not least in vigorous rejection of pure intellection divorced from the body. See Riley, *Leibniz' Universal Jurisprudence,* 65-69, 74, 142-45, 193.

45. Barth, *CD* III/1:404.

46. Barth, *CD* III/1:412.

47. Barth, *CD* III/1:388.

48. Arthur O. Lovejoy, *The Great Chain of Being: A Study of the History of an Idea* (Cambridge: Harvard University Press, 1964), 211.

49. Leibniz, *Theodicy,* 282-83.

50. Ezio Vailati, *Leibniz and Clarke: A Study of Their Correspondence* (Oxford: Oxford University Press, 1997), 89.

51. Riley, *Leibniz' Universal Jurisprudence,* 261-66.

52. Barth, *CD* III/1:393, 396.

53. Barth, *CD* III/1:403.

54. Barth continues the foregoing citation, "Yet for all the obvious differences we are always in the same sphere and on one and the same ground." *CD* III/1:403.

55. Barth, *CD* III/1:408.

56. Barth, *CD* III/1:409. Barth draws out the implication: "Atheism, which knows all that the optimists know but can dispense with the almighty and wise Creator, is lurking somewhere at the doors. The optimists themselves are more immediately sure of the perfection of the world . . . than of the very different Figure who is so frequently referred to as the basis of these things. . . . Who or what is the God of the optimists? Why does He point imperiously in one direction rather than another?" *CD* III/1:409.

57. Barth, *CD* III/1:410. Again, Barth explicates: "as the system of Wolff reveals, [the optimists] made use of Him only as an afterthought and not essentially . . . in spite of all the superlatives there was not to be found in the perfection of God anything basically new or different from that of man. . . . In fact, the Gospel of optimism can be preached . . . only as a system of Law. God will help him only as and to the extent that he helps himself . . . a position of fearful loneliness" (410).

58. Barth, *CD* III/1:408. "The most striking feature of optimism, and at the same time its clearest weakness, is to be found in the way in which it does not so much eliminate as assimilate the shadowy side of human existence. . . . Was it already walking in the kingdom of God where there will be no more pain and tears and crying? Was it still walking or had it relapsed into the heathen fields of the blessed? Who can finally say? . . . Only the great earthquake, the mockery of Voltaire and later the guillotine began to draw the attention of some to the fact that there exists a disharmony and enigma which cannot be ignored" (406).

59. Barth, *CD* III/1:407. Barth continues: "If Leibnizian optimism passes too lightly over the problem of evil, sin and death, the same is true of its treatment of the positive aspect of the world . . . [the relentless 'superlatives,' 'maximal expressions'] . . . it is characteristic of this whole literature continuously to exhort and admonish and implore, constantly to take the reader by the coat button and to challenge him — sometimes with violent scoldings for his hard-heartedness — to such monotonously repetitive reflection in the form of the acknowledgment of the intelligent design, beauty and utility observable in the creation, the inevitable inference from creation to the wise, almighty good and providential Creator, and

the gratitude which this necessarily evokes. These writers are clearly unable to make their insights plausible either to themselves or others without vigorous and constant moralizing. . . . Their Gospel has so strongly legal a tone and colouring" (407).

60. Barth, *CD* III/1:390.

61. Barth, *CD* III/1:390.

62. Barth, *CD* III/1:356.

63. Barth, *CD* III/1:390.

64. Barth, *CD* III/1:389.

65. Barth, *CD* III/1:389.

66. Barth, *CD* III/1:392.

67. Under the heading "The Misconception of Nothingness," Barth devotes himself, in other words, essentially to elaborating the same doctrine as that which Leibniz called "metaphysical evil." Indeed, he begins emphatically: "We must indicate and remove a serious confusion which has been of far reaching effect in the history of theology." *CD* III/3:295.

68. Barth, *CD* III/1:392.

69. Barth, *CD* III/1:393.

70. Barth, *CD* III/1:392.

71. Barth, *CD* III/3:295.

72. Barth, *CD* III/3:318.

73. Barth, *CD* III/3:301.

74. Barth, *CD* III/3:296.

75. Barth, *CD* III/3:297.

76. Barth, *CD* III/3:299.

77. Barth, *CD* III/3:300.

78. Barth, *CD* III/3:301.

79. Barth, *CD* III/3:296.

80. Kroetke, *Sin,* 48.

81. Kroetke, *Sin,* 45.

82. Barth, *CD* III/3:317.

83. Barth, *CD* III/3:316-19, which serves as platform for the ensuing discussions of Schleiermacher, 319-34; Heidegger, 334-38, 347-49; and Sartre, 338-47.

84. Barth, *CD* III/3:292.

85. Barth, *CD* III/3:293.

86. Barth, *CD* III/3:519-31. "Sinister matters may be very real, but they must not be contemplated too long or studied too precisely or adopted too intensively. It has never been good for anyone — including (and particularly) Martin Luther — to look too frequently or lengthily or seriously or systematically at demons (who for Luther were usually compressed into the singular figure of the devil)" (519). In keeping with his doctrine of nothingness, Barth here too makes the decisive point that "it is quite inappropriate to speak of God and the devil or angels and demons in the same breath. They have no common denominator. They do not grow from a common root" (520). This makes sin unintelligible as the evil will that in unbelief chooses for itself out of greed or envy another destiny than that which God wills. Of course, it is Barth's point that sin should appear absurd.

87. Barth, *CD* III/3:293. Apropos of the distinction between philosophy and theology, for Barth theology can only take the form of a *Nachdenken.* Theology as such takes the form

of _dogmatics,_ not _system,_ thinking out from the particularity of the Christ event to the world rather than reducing this particularity to the general laws of the world.

88. Kroetke, _Sin,_ 24-25.

89. Barth, _CD_ III/3:305.

90. Barth, _CD_ III/3:357, 358.

91. Barth, _CD_ III/3:366.

92. Barth, _CD_ III/3:351.

93. Kroetke, _Sin,_ 28.

94. Kroetke, _Sin,_ 28.

95. Kroetke, _Sin,_ 29.

96. Kroetke, _Sin,_ 23.

97. Gregory of Nyssa, _The Great Catechism,_ in _Nicene and Post-Nicene Fathers,_ ed. P. Schaff and H. Wace (Grand Rapids: Eerdmans, 1979), 481.

98. Barth, _CD_ III/3:353. "Nothingness is the past, the ancient menace, danger and destruction, the ancient non-being which obscured and defaced the divine creation of God but which is consigned to the past in Jesus Christ, in whose death it has received its deserts, being destroyed with this consummation of the positive will of God which is as such the end of His non-willing" (363).

99. Barth, _CD_ III/3:352.

100. Barth, _CD_ III/3:351.

101. Barth, _CD_ III/3:352.

102. G. W. Leibniz, "Ultimate Origination," in _Discourse on Metaphysics and Other Essays,_ trans. D. Garber and R. Ariew (Indianapolis: Hackett, 1991), 45-47.

103. Barth, _CD_ III/3:367.

104. Barth, _CD_ III/3:368.

105. Karl Barth, _Church Dogmatics_ II/2, trans. G. W. Bromiley et al. (Edinburgh: T. & T. Clark, 1957), 44; hereafter cited as _CD_ II/2.

106. Barth, _CD_ II/2:48.

107. "[I]t is wholly and utterly in these happenings that we are to know what really is the good-pleasure of His will, what is, therefore, His being, and the purpose and orientation of His work as Creator of the world and Controller of history. There is no greater depth in God's being and work than that revealed in these happenings and under this name." Barth, _CD_ II/2:54 and passim.

108. Barth, _CD_ II/2:53.

109. Barth, _CD_ II/2:69.

110. Barth, _CD_ II/2:6.

111. Barth, _CD_ II/2:143.

112. Even the "man Jesus as such has nothing to bring before the electing God which would make Him worthy of the divine election . . . but God wills and posits another being from Himself, His creature. Be it noted that this determination of the will of God, this content of predestination, is already grace, for God did not stand in need of any particular way or works ad extra. He had no need of a creation. . . . the fact that He wills the creation, and the man Jesus as the first-born of all creation, is grace, sovereign grace, a condescension inconceivably tender . . . in His Son He makes the being of this other His own being." Barth, _CD_ II/2:121. Yet it could have been otherwise. "From all eternity God could have excluded man from this covenant. He could have delivered him up to himself and allowed him to fall.

He could have refused to will him at all. He could have avoided the compromising of His freedom by not willing to create him. He could have remained satisfied with Himself and with the impassible glory and blessedness of His own inner life" (166). Against this background of freedom, the content of the divine self-determination in Christ becomes clear: "to make good this affronting and disturbing of His majesty, this devastating of His work, not by avenging Himself on its author, but by Himself bearing the inevitable wrath and perdition" (166).

113. Barth, *CD* II/2:175.

114. Barth, *CD* II/2:218.

115. Barth, *CD* II/2:219.

116. Barth, *CD* II/2:89, 148.

117. Barth, *CD* II/2:10.

118. Barth, *CD* II/2:25.

119. Barth, *CD* II/2:45.

120. Barth, *CD* II/2:49.

121. Barth, *CD* II/2:134.

122. Barth, *CD* II/2:193.

123. Barth, *CD* II/2:158.

124. Barth, *CD* II/2:158.

125. Barth, *CD* II/2:143.

126. Barth, *CD* II/2:143.

127. Jesus Christ "is not merely one of the elect, but *the* elect of God." Barth, *CD* II/2:116.

128. Barth, *CD* II/2:118.

129. Barth, *CD* II/2:124.

130. Barth, *CD* II/2:164.

131. Barth, *CD* II/2:124.

132. Barth, *CD* II/2:165, emphasis added.

133. Barth, *CD* II/2:223, emphasis added.

134. Emil Brunner, Appendix, "Karl Barth's Doctrine of Election," in *Dogmatics*, vol. 1, *The Christian Doctrine of God*, trans. O. Wyon (Philadelphia: Westminster, 1974), 346-47. The gravamen is Brunner's protest against the "objectivism" of Barth's theology, i.e., that "the real decision only takes place in the objective sphere, and not in the subjective sphere. . . . If the decision of faith is not deadly serious, then salvation through Jesus Christ is not deadly serious either; everything has already been decided beforehand . . . and there remains no room for man to make a real decision" (351).

135. Kroetke, *Sin*, 22.

136. Barth, *CD* II/2:115.

137. Barth, *CD* II/2:90.

138. Barth, *CD* II/2:92.

139. Barth, *CD* II/2:141.

140. Barth, *CD* II/2:141.

141. Barth, *CD* II/2:163.

142. Barth, *CD* II/2:172.

143. Barth, *CD* II/2:174.

144. Leibniz, *Theodicy*, 129-30.

145. Ward, "Barth, Modernity and Postmodernity," 292.
146. Barth, *CD* II/2:321.
147. Barth, *CD* II/2:317.
148. Barth, *CD* II/2:346.
149. Barth, *CD* II/2:326.
150. Barth, *CD* II/2:319.
151. Barth, *CD* II/2:417.
152. Barth, *CD* II/2:13, 18, 76, 77, 91, 107.
153. Barth, *CD* II/2:416.
154. Barth, *CD* II/2:418.
155. Barth, *CD* II/2:184.
156. Barth, *CD* II/2:176.
157. Barth, *CD* II/2:177.
158. Barth, *CD* II/2:179.
159. Barth, *CD* II/2:180.
160. Barth, *CD* II/2:314.
161. Barth, *CD* II/2:180.
162. Barth, *CD* II/2:316.
163. Barth, *CD* II/2:314.
164. Barth, *CD* II/2:306ff.
165. Barth, *CD* II/2:423.
166. Barth, *CD* II/2:315.
167. Barth, *CD* II/2:318.
168. Barth, *CD* II/2:345.
169. Barth, *CD* II/2:346.
170. Barth, *CD* II/2:422.
171. Barth, *CD* II/2:422.

172. Instead of the foregoing "cul-de-sac," Barth says the biblical view "opens at this point another door. For as those who expect and finally receive eternal life, as heirs in faith of eternal glory, the elect are accepted for this employment and placed in this service. They are made witnesses." *CD* II/2:423.

173. Barth can and does, of course, speak with prophetic passion on the wrath of God: "Where the opposition does not break down in faith in the Son given, even the love of God must itself be destructive." But Barth always qualifies this. "Even in such a descent the creature cannot escape God. Even in this abyss it is still in the hands of God, the object of His decision. . . . It is by love that the creature is confounded." *CD* II/2:27. But presumably not coerced.

174. Loemker, *Papers,* 226.

175. Loemker, *Papers,* 228, emphasis added.

Notes to Chapter 4

1. Gerhard Ebeling, "Karl Barths Ringen mit Luther," *Lutherstudien,* vol. 3 (Tübingen: Mohr Siebeck, 1985), 428-574. Summing up his case in *De servo arbitrio,* Luther writes: "Since Scripture everywhere proclaims Christ categorically and antithetically, as I said, and thereby subjects all that is without the Spirit of Christ to Satan, ungodliness, error, darkness, sin,

death and the wrath of God, every statement concerning Christ is a direct testimony against 'free-will.'" *The Bondage of the Will,* trans. J. I. Packer and O. R. Johnston (Grand Rapids: Revell, 2000), 312.

2. "You [Erasmus], who imagine that the human will is something placed in an intermediate position of 'freedom' and left to itself . . . imagine that both God and the devil are far away, mere spectators, as it were, of this mutable free will; you do not believe that they are the prompters and drivers of an *enslaved* will, and each waging relentless war against the other!" Luther, *Bondage,* 262.

3. I have profited from the critique of Ebeling's systematic misunderstanding of Barth in a (to my knowledge) unpublished paper by Christine Poeder, "The Doctrine of Justification according to Karl Barth, Its Lutheran Reception and Its Potentials." Poeder employs Hans Frei's typology of orders of theological discourse to show how Ebeling's existentialist reduction of everything to *Lebensbezug* mangles Barth by failing to appreciate the audience, context, and purpose of the various orders of theological discourse.

4. See Paul R. Hinlicky, "Luther's Anti-Docetism in the Disputatio de divinitate et humanitate Christi (1540)," in *Creator est creatura: Luthers Christologie als Lehre von der Idiomenkommunikation,* ed. O. Bayer and Benjamin Gleede (Berlin and New York: De Gruyter, 2007), 169-80, and Hinlicky, "The New Language of the Spirit: Critical Dogmatics in the Tradition of Luther," in D. Bielfeldt, M. Mattox, and P. Hinlicky, *The Substance of the Faith: Luther's Doctrinal Theology for Today* (Minneapolis: Fortress, 2008), 152-57.

5. Karl Barth, *Church Dogmatics* IV/4, trans. G. W. Bromiley (Edinburgh: T. & T. Clark, 1969), 4-5. On this very page, Barth faults the view of "Melanchthon and the Lutheran Orthodoxy which followed" (after faulting Catholic views of infused grace and neo-Protestant Pelagianism) for "restrict[ing] the possibility to God's power to introduce a man who has been judged afresh and with grace, but who is in himself unaltered." Given the options, Barth will naturally be closest to Melanchthon, but none of these views, he says, "makes it clear how there comes into being the Christian, the man who responds to God's faithfulness with faithfulness, the man who as a free subject is God's true partner in the covenant of grace." But in fact, we shall see, Barth almost verbatim follows Melanchthon's scheme of objective justification in Christ and subjective sanctification in the Spirit. The view on behalf of which I argue Barth dismisses as the unnamed Luther's "christomonist" solution (IV/4:19). But this is because for Barth the Christian's community and correspondence with Christ is strictly one of ethical action, not something that rests in the faith of the church and so is ethically active as the body of Christ at work in the world.

6. Karl Barth, *Church Dogmatics* II/2, trans. G. W. Bromiley et al. (Edinburgh: T. & T. Clark, 1957), 94; hereafter cited as *CD* II/2.

7. Barth, *CD* II/2:238.

8. Barth, *CD* II/2:173.

9. Barth, *CD* II/2:205.

10. Barth, *CD* II/2:207.

11. Barth, *CD* II/2:261.

12. John Dillenberger, *God Hidden and Revealed: The Interpretation of Luther's Deus Absconditus and Its Significance for Religious Thought* (Philadelphia: Muhlenberg, 1953), 169.

13. Emil Brunner, *Dogmatics,* vol. 1, *The Christian Doctrine of God,* trans. O. Wyon (Philadelphia: Westminster, 1974), 349-50.

14. Dillenberger, *God Hidden and Revealed,* 167.

15. Henri de Lubac, *Augustinianism and Modern Theology,* trans. L. Sheppard (New York: Herder and Herder, 2000), 240. De Lubac is as capable as a Luther in criticism of Molinism's graceless, purely natural *facere quod in se,* yet the Jansenist notion that *desire itself,* the fundamental desire of the *cor inquietem* for the good that binds the human mind as such to seek God, could be extinguished practically or denied anthropologically, he rightly argues, "destroyed the whole of ancient anthropology" (261).

16. Dillenberger, *God Hidden and Revealed,* 168.

17. Dillenberger, *God Hidden and Revealed,* 168.

18. On existential narcissim, see Brent Adkins, *Death and Desire in Hegel, Heidegger, and Deleuze* (Edinburgh: University of Edinburgh Press, 2007), 54-71.

19. See chapter 2, n. 59 above.

20. Robert W. Jenson, "You Wonder Where the Spirit Went," *Pro Ecclesia* 2, no. 3 (Summer 1993): 298.

21. More seriously, Jenson again: "It is tempting to speculate that the pressure may work backwards, here from a merely two-sided understanding of human community and so of historical reality, inherited from the 'I-Thou' tradition of 19th century German philosophical anthropology, to a merely two-sided understanding of trinitarian community and history. Were this the case, it would be the symptom of a deep flaw indeed. It would mean that Barth's use of the image-analogy principle had opened a channel in his thinking for the projection of perceived human value onto God, for theological analogy in which a human phenomenon is the primary analogate also in the order of being. I will not pursue this horrid possibility." Jenson, "You Wonder," 302. But that "horrid possibility" is further confirmation that Barth's lineage may be traced to Melanchthon's general pneumatology via German idealism.

22. Jenson, "You Wonder," 299.

23. Saint Augustine, *On the Trinity,* book 8, trans. E. Hill (New York: New City Press, 1991), 255.

24. Robert W. Jenson, *Systematic Theology,* 2 vols. (Oxford: Oxford University Press, 1997), 1:156.

25. "That the Son once slain would rise is, after the fact, an eternal certainty; but it was not beforehand, and also not for God." Jenson, *Systematic Theology,* 1:160.

26. Jenson, *Systematic Theology,* 1:148.

27. Basil, *On the Spirit* 16.38, in *Nicene and Post-Nicene Fathers,* 2nd ser., 8:23.

28. Jenson, *Systematic Theology,* 1:159.

29. Jenson, *Systematic Theology,* 2:175.

30. Karl Barth, *Church Dogmatics* II/1, trans. T. H. L. Parker et al. (Edinburgh: T. & T. Clark, 1957), 266; hereafter cited as *CD* II/1.

31. Barth, *CD* II/1:267.

32. Barth, *CD* II/1:267.

33. Barth, *CD* II/1:268.

34. ". . . 'free-will' is obviously a term applicable only to the Divine Majesty. . . . If 'free-will' is ascribed to men, it is ascribed with no more propriety than divinity would be . . . a power of freely turning in any direction, yielding to none and subject to none." Luther, *Bondage,* 105. It should be borne in mind that the translators are generally rendering *liberum arbitrium* as "free-will," when the Latin means "free choice."

35. Barth, *CD* II/1:271.

36. "But God hidden in Majesty neither deplores nor takes away death, but works life, death, and all in all; nor has He set bounds to Himself by His Word, but has kept Himself free over all things." Luther, *Bondage*, 170.

37. Barth, *CD* II/1:170.

38. Barth, *CD* II/1:273.

39. Barth, *CD* II/1:275.

40. One may ask, not to put too fine a point on it, whether the above-mentioned rhetoric of the "amazing exchange" is for Barth only a Zwinglian-Nestorian way of talking about God in Christ — the *extra Calvinisticum* — or a Lutheran-Cyrillian confession of the being of God in Christ — the *genus maiesticum*.

41. This will find detailed treatment below in chapter 6 and the conclusion.

42. Dillenberger, *God Hidden and Revealed*, 171.

43. G. W. Leibniz, *Theodicy: Essays on the Goodness of God, the Freedom of Man, and the Origin of Evil*, trans. E. M. Huggard (Chicago and La Salle, Ill.: Open Court, 1998), 99.

44. Hinlicky, "New Language," 131-90.

45. Barth, *CD* II/2:306.

46. Barth, *CD* II/2:139.

47. Luther, *Bondage*, 170.

48. Barth, *CD* II/2:64.

49. Barth, *CD* II/2:59-60.

50. Barth, *CD* II/2:62.

51. Barth, *CD* II/2:67. See Donald Sinnema, "God's Eternal Decree and Its Temporal Execution: The Role of This Distinction in Theodore Beza's Theology," in *Adaptations of Calvinism in Reformation Europe: Essays in Honour of Brian C. Armstrong*, ed. Mack P. Holt (Aldershot, England, and Burlington, Vt.: Ashgate, 2008), 55-78.

52. Barth, *CD* II/2:70.

53. Robert D. Preus, *The Theology of Post-Reformation Lutheranism*, vol. 2, *God and His Creation* (St. Louis: Concordia, 1972), 197.

54. Preus, *Post-Reformation Lutheranism*, 198.

55. Preus, *Post-Reformation Lutheranism*, 198. Preus, a traditional Lutheran if ever there was one, objects that in this "Gerhard is closer in a formal sense to Calvinism than to the Lutheranism of the Formula of Concord," which makes "election Gospel and damnation Law and never brought the two concepts together in such a fashion" (198). It becomes clear that Preus's deeper objection derives from the Melanchthonian fear of necessitarianism, which he smells in the notion of providence as the execution in time of an eternal decree. Thus we must link "providence with God's absolute freedom and omnipotence. . . . If necessary God will perform a miracle and break the laws of nature to answer the prayers of His people . . . no matter how much the believer feels caught within the inexorable nexus of secondary causes, God is free" (204). When the antinomy of grace is nature, rather than sin, we have passed with Pascal from the antecedent Augustinian Christianity of Luther to the modern theology after Kant, whether in the liberal form of personalism or in the conservative form of Preus's supernaturalism. Nature is the creature of grace, the object of redemption and fulfillment.

56. Barth, *CD* II/2:70, 74-75.

57. Barth, *CD* II/2:67.

58. "[T]he whole of Lutheran orthodoxy thought it justifiable to appropriate the Jesuit

doctrine of the divine *scientia media*," not only to combat the absolute decree of Calvinism but also to buttress the *fides praevisa*. Barth, *CD* II/2:75.

59. Barth, *CD* II/2:75.

60. Barth, *CD* II/2:74.

61. See Diogenes Allen, *Christian Belief in a Postmodern World: The Full Wealth of Conviction* (Louisville: Westminster/John Knox, 1989), for a contemporary meditation on the "good of the cross."

62. Graham Ward, "Barth, Modernity and Postmodernity," in *Cambridge Companion to Karl Barth*, ed. J. Webster (Cambridge: Cambridge University Press, 2000), 293.

63. Timothy J. Wengert, "Melanchthon and Luther/Luther and Melanchthon," *Lutherjahrbuch* 66 (Göttingen: Vandenhoeck & Ruprecht, 1999), 55.

64. Bernhard Lohse, *Martin Luther's Theology: Its Historical and Systematic Development*, trans. Roy A. Harrisville (Minneapolis: Fortress, 1999), 262. For a contrary view, see Bruce L. McCormack, "What's at Stake in Current Debates over Justification: The Crisis of Protestantism in the West," in *Justification: What's at Stake in the Current Debates*, ed. M. Husbands and D. J. Treier (Downers Grove, Ill.: InterVarsity, 2004), 81-117, which faithfully sustains the view of Barth, which I am tracing back to Melanchthon, that union with Christ consists in "the conformity of my life to his life of obedience," a "union of wills." McCormack, 110.

65. Melanchthon: "By *are justified* [Paul] means this comfort in the midst of true anguish, forgiveness of sins received through faith, and being pleasing to God for the sake of the Lord Christ. But the renewal that follows, which God effects in us, he calls *sanctification* [*Heiligung*] and these two words are clear and distinct." Philip Melanchthon, *On Christian Doctrine: Loci Communes, 1555*, trans. C. L. Manschreck (Grand Rapids: Baker, 1982), 163.

66. Alister E. McGrath, *Iustitia Dei: A History of the Christian Doctrine of Justification*, 2 vols. (Cambridge: Cambridge University Press, 1986), 2:14.

67. *Luther's Works: The American Edition*, ed. J. Pelikan et al., 55 vols. (St. Louis: Concordia; Philadelphia: Fortress, 1960-), 48:12-13; cf. 35:49; hereafter cited as *LW*.

68. See the classic articulation of it in *The Freedom of a Christian* (*LW* 31:343). See also Robert W. Bertram, "The Human Subject as the Object of Theology: Luther by Way of Barth" (Ph.D. diss., University of Chicago, 1964). I am speaking of *models*, not *doctrines*, of justification, since on the level of doctrine, taken as second-order rules for conducting the church's first-order discourse, Luther's and Melanchthon's models are compatible. As David Yeago has written to me in personal correspondence (November 4, 2000): "Lindbeck's rule-theory is helpful in accounting for the relationship between Luther and Melanchthon. It has always seemed to me that they agree at the doctrinal or dogmatic level — on justification, for example, they agree on the rule that all discourse and practice in the church should promote trust in Christ alone and not in our own merits. But they seem significantly different on the level of theological execution of the dogmatic rules — for example, I can't see that union with Christ plays any profound role in Melanchthon's thought, very different, in my judgment, from Luther. They also seem to me to agree on a rule that remains more implicit than explicit: that the gratuitous mercy received by faith alone radically transforms the one who receives it. On this, I think Luther is more successful, as his theology of union with Christ accounts for why this should be so more helpfully than Melanchthon's theology does. But they seem to me to agree on the principle."

69. Regin Prenter, *Spiritus Creator*, trans. John M. Jensen (Philadelphia: Muhlenberg,

1953), 62-63. Prenter continues: "The only way out of this very unfruitful question ['between the tendencies of Melanchthon and Osiander'] is found in the rediscovery of Luther's realistic understanding of the Spirit." "Holl and Seeberg are correct in maintaining that justification and sanctification — or as Luther generally stated it, the nonimputation of sin and the expulsion of sin — are woven together in Luther in such a way that Melanchthonian, forensic doctrine of justification cannot anticipate it. But the mistake is that sanctification in Holl's and Seeberg's Luther research is seen in the idealistic perspective . . . not as an existence within the sphere of the Spirit in which Christ himself at the same time is both the alien righteousness, which qualifies all man's righteousness as flesh, and the active subject of all the activity of man. But instead of this the new life is considered as identical with man's gradually increasing empirical piety" (96-97). See also Pekka Karkkainen, *Luthers trinitarische Theologie des Heiligen Geistes* (Mainz: Philipp von Zabern, 2005).

70. Helmut Thielicke, *The Evangelical Faith,* vol. 1, trans. G. W. Bromiley (Grand Rapids: Eerdmans, 1974), 152.

71. Wilhelm Mauer, *Historical Commentary on the Augsburg Confession,* trans. H. George Anderson (Philadelphia: Fortress, 1986), 343. It is equally true according to Mauer, however, that with Melanchthon's help Luther "rejects two misunderstandings and quietly corrects ideas from his own past. The suffering Christ ought not be taken simply as a type of the suffering Christian; he is rather the true purchase price for the forgiveness of sin. And that brings the second idea to light: God's wrath is not a false hypothesis but sober truth. If it were otherwise, his mercy would also be a fiction and our faith would be futile" (317).

72. Melanchthon, *Loci,* 87, emphasis in original.

73. Melanchthon, *Loci,* 142, emphasis in original.

74. Luther too, however, speaks of such passive disposition, even in his hardest texts like *The Bondage of the Will.* "Note, however, that if we meant by 'the power of free-will' the power which makes human beings fit subjects to be caught up by the Spirit and touched by God's grace, as creatures made for eternal life or eternal death, we should have a proper definition. And I certainly acknowledge the existence of this power, this fitness, or 'dispositional quality' and 'passive aptitude' (as the Sophists call it). . . . God did not make heaven for geese!" Luther, *Bondage,* 105.

75. Melanchthon, *Loci,* 167.

76. Leibniz distinguishes at least these two: "Freedom of will is furthermore understood in two different senses. The first is when it is opposed to the imperfection or the slavery of the spirit, which is a coaction or constraint, but internal like that arising from the passions. The other sense has place when freedom is opposed to necessity." G. W. Leibniz, *New Essays concerning Human Understanding,* trans. Alfred Gideon Langley (La Salle, Ill.: Open Court, 1949), 179. The first sense of freedom here denotes what I am calling freedom of action, such that one can deliberate over the appearance of good, and act or refrain from acting upon the desire for it. The second sense denotes what I am calling freedom of choice.

77. Explaining what I am calling freedom of choice, Leibniz continues: "But the freedom of spirit, opposed to necessity, concerns the naked will, and in so far as it is distinguished from the understanding. This is what is called free-will (franc-arbitre) and it consists in this, that we will that the strongest reasons or impressions which the understanding presents to the will do not prevent the act of the will from being contingent, and do not give it an absolute, and, so to speak, metaphysical necessity. And it is in this sense that I am accustomed to say that the understanding can determine the will, according to the prevalence of

perceptions and reasons, in a manner which, even where it is certain and infallible, inclines without compelling." *New Essays,* 179-80. In other words, the mind can deliberate between logically possible alternative goods, or alternative paths to a good.

78. Many "ask for the absurd and the impossible, in desiring a freedom of equilibrium absolutely imaginary and impracticable, and which indeed would not serve them, were it possible for them to have it, i.e., to have the freedom of willing against all the impressions which can come from the understanding, which would destroy true freedom together with reason, and lower us below the beasts." Leibniz, *New Essays,* 184.

79. Ezio Vailati, *Leibniz and Clarke: A Study of Their Correspondence* (Oxford: Oxford University Press, 1997), 96.

80. Regarding freedom of action, Leibniz acknowledges it but tends to assimilate it to freedom of choice. "[T]he Stoics said that the wise man alone is free; and in fact the spirit is not at all free when it is filled with a great passion, for one cannot then will as he should, that is to say, with the deliberation that is requisite. Thus God alone is perfectly free, and created spirits are so, only to the extent that they are superior to their passions. And this freedom concerns properly our understanding." *New Essays,* 179. "[Y]ou can will only what you find to be good, and according as the faculty of understanding is improved the choice of the will is better, as on the other hand, according as man as *vigor of will* he determines his thoughts according to his choice, instead of being determined and carried away by involuntary perceptions" (185). The reason for the lack of clarity at this point is that Leibniz is trying to sustain the infallibility of moral determination, and so also of divine foreknowledge of particulars, under the assumption that clear thinking and calm deliberation incline, without necessitating the will to choose the best. This is, however, in some tension with the statement that the will is *determined* by perception, howsoever properly processed by the understanding. As Gregory Brown has pointed out, Leibniz clearly affirms freedom of action when he observes that the mind "'does not always choose what at present appears better; for it can delay and suspend its judgment until a later deliberation, and turn the mind aside to think of other things.' . . . minds are not mechanical in nature. Thus the fact that their behavior is ultimately beyond our ability adequately to understand in accordance with natural laws seems due not so much to their being minds, as opposed to non-rational souls, but rather more to their being, like all souls, non-mechanical." Brown, "Miracles in the Best of All Possible Worlds: Leibniz's Dilemma and Leibniz's Razor," *History of Philosophy Quarterly* 12, no. 1 (January 1995): 31-32. But this consideration lends an intrinsically incalculable quality to lived experience.

81. Luther, *Bondage,* 105.

82. "It is true you speak incorrectly when you speak as if we willed to will. We do not will to will but we will to do, and if we willed to will, we should will to will to will, and this would go onto infinity. . . . They say that after having known and considered all, it is still within their power to will not only what pleases them the most, but furthermore wholly the contrary, merely to show their freedom. But you must consider that this caprice or obstinacy, or at least this reason which hinders them from following other reasons, also enters into the balance and makes that please them which otherwise not do so, so that choice is always determined by perception." Leibniz, *New Essays,* 185.

83. *The Book of Concord: The Confessions of the Evangelical Lutheran Church,* ed. Robert Kolb and Timothy J. Wengert (Minneapolis: Fortress, 2000), 432-33.

84. Jan Lindhardt, *Martin Luther: Knowledge and Mediation in the Renaissance,* Texts and Studies in Religion, vol. 29 (Lewiston, N.Y.: Edwin Mellen Press, 1986), 25.

85. Lindhardt, *Martin Luther,* 30. Lindhardt states that in fact Augustine's "theology was only a modification of the tripartite view of man . . . [that] created some odd misunderstandings" in the Renaissance appropriation (72). Cf. Augustine, *On the Trinity,* book 12.

86. Lindhardt, *Martin Luther,* 108. Lindhardt continues, "with the difference that for Luther affectus is a receiver-concept, which is to say that affectus is not characterized as a drive or desire (contra Augustine) but as an experience that comes to one." This last differentiation of Luther from Augustine is highly problematic.

87. Augustine, *The City of God,* an abridged version from the translation by G. G. Walsh et al. (New York: Doubleday, 1958), 108.

88. Alvin Plantinga, "The Free Will Defense," in *Philosophy of Religion: Selected Readings,* ed. Michael Peterson et al., 3rd ed. (New York: Oxford University Press, 2000), 71.

89. Augustine, *City of God,* 362.

90. Augustine, *City of God,* 362.

91. Melanchthon is denounced for turning the doctrine of justification into a legal fiction and sneaking in by the back door the Anselmian doctrine of the substitutionary death of Christ — as if precisely these accents are not also found in Luther's teaching. Luther is praised as a religious virtuoso for his determined and prophetic resistance to papal authoritarianism, for his lively and free style (even his doctrinal incoherence is celebrated as subversive of dogmatism!) — as if Luther's sometimes reckless outbursts, lack of rational self-discipline, and literary restraint, historically understandable as these may be, were not sins against the wounded body of Christ. The game of dividing Luther and Melanchthon can be played to the opposite effect as well, lifting up Melanchthon's faithful commitment to unity that involved him in the abortive Wittenberg Concord with the Reformed in 1537, then took him once again into secret negotiations with Rome at Regensburg in 1542. This ecumenical activity can be praised over against the later Luther's fanaticism and obscurantism. No one works for the visible unity of the church who thinks the world is about to end.

92. We are indebted to the scholarship of Mark U. Edwards, Jr., who located Luther's verbal violence against peasant, pope, Turk, and Jew in an apocalyptic interpretation of events following up his excommunication. "Luther's Polemical Controversies," in *The Cambridge Companion to Martin Luther,* ed. D. K. McKim (Cambridge: Cambridge University Press, 2003), 194. "Luther understood his disagreement with [opponents] in the context of this struggle between God and Satan. Behind them all loomed the figure of the devil, the father of lies. Often Luther directed his attacks not at his human opponents but at the devil whom he saw as their master, and, of course, no language was too harsh when attacking the devil" (195). See also Edwards, "Supermus: Luther's Own Fanatics," in *Seven-Headed Luther: Essays in Commemoration of a Quincentenary, 1483-1983,* ed. P. N. Brooks (Oxford: Clarendon, 1983), 123-46, and Edwards, *Luther's Last Battles: Politics and Polemics, 1531-46* (Ithaca, N.Y.: Cornell University Press, 1983). Also instructive is Heiko A. Oberman, *The Roots of Anti-Semitism in the Age of Renaissance and Reformation,* trans. James I. Porter (Philadelphia: Fortress, 1981).

93. Wengert lays emphasis on the differing methods the two Reformers employed: "Luther was the preacher, Melanchthon the preceptor," but acknowledges that the difference in method reflects differing "world views" (Wengert, "Melanchthon and Luther," 84-85). Luther's apocalyptic worldview had him doing battle with Satan; Melanchthon's "conviction"

in the "created order" had him turning to law to master "the disordering effect of nature" (86). "This difference also affected their view of justification by faith alone. Even when the two agreed on the forensic nature of justification, their approach betrayed disparate intentions. For Luther God's decree destroyed evil and comforted the weak. For Melanchthon God educated, made certain and comforted the simple" (87). Wengert's concluding reflection "about the way one's learning can distort the very gospel one learns" is sobering: "Just as Luther did not subject to critical analysis his own apocalyptic association of the devil with disagreements in the gospel, so Melanchthon never fully appreciated the hermeneutical circle created by his use of humanist methods and Aristotelian philosophy in interpreting the gospel" (88).

94. Ralph W. Quere, *Melanchthon's Christum Cognoscere: Christ's Efficacious Presence in the Eucharistic Theology of Melanchthon*, Bibliotheca Humanistica & Reformatorica, vol. 22 (Nieuwkoop: B. De Graaf, 1977), 6 n. 9.

95. Wengert, "Luther and Melanchthon," 87. The conclusion, however, is subtly differentiated: Even as the two agreed, he writes, "their approach betrayed disparate intentions. For Luther God's decree destroyed evil and comforted the weak. For Melanchthon God educated, made certain and comforted the simple" (87). I am not persuaded that this gets to the heart of it, and I am concerned that this way of articulating the difference entails a false antithesis between kerygma and doctrine. Luther's "decree" is no less mediated than Melanchthon's "education" is hortatory.

96. Mark C. Mattes, *The Role of Justification in Contemporary Theology* (Grand Rapids: Eerdmans, 2004), 45. Mattes has acknowledged to me in personal conversation regarding my 2008 book, *The Substance of the Faith*, the need for a "correction" of the Fordean tradition along these lines; I trust that the necessary critique expressed here will be received as a friendly one.

97. Gerhard Forde, *Justification by Faith: A Matter of Life and Death* (Philadelphia: Fortress, 1982; reprint, Mifflintown, Pa.: Sigler, 1991), 36.

98. Mattes, *Justification in Contemporary Theology*, 16.

99. Thesis 1, "Theses concerning Faith and Law," 1535, *LW* 34:109.

100. This claim could be massively substantiated. Let this suffice: citing *Dr. Martin Luthers Werke* (Weimar: Böhlau, 1883-1993), 47:205.27 (hereafter cited as WA), Ian Siggins writes: "His flesh and blood, born of the Virgin Mary, was given because He had to bear the cost of death and endure hell in our stead, on account of sins He never committed, as if they were His own; which He willingly did and received us as brothers and sisters." Ian D. Kingston Siggins, *Martin Luther's Doctrine of Christ* (New Haven and London: Yale University Press, 1970), 202.

101. Burnell F. Eckhardt, Jr., *Anselm and Luther on the Atonement: Was It 'Necessary'?* (San Francisco: Mellen Research University Press, 1992).

102. Mattes, *Justification in Contemporary Theology*, 188.

103. Mattes, *Justification in Contemporary Theology*, 188.

104. Oliver K. Olson, *Matthias Flacius and the Survival of Luther's Reform* (Wiesbaden: Harrassowitz Verlag, 2002), 90-101.

105. David A. Lumpp, "Promise, Liberty, and Persecution: Exploring Philip Melanchthon's Contextual Theology" (paper delivered at the 11th International Congress of Luther Research, Porto Allegre, Brazil, July 2007).

106. Gerhard O. Forde, *On Being a Theologian of the Cross: Reflections on Luther's Heidelberg Disputation, 1518* (Grand Rapids: Eerdmans, 1997), 90.

107. "A theology of glory will always leave the will in control. It must therefore seek to make its theology attractive to the supposed 'free will.' A theology of the cross assumes that the will is bound and must be set free. The cross story does that. Either it claims us or it doesn't. If it does, it is the end of the glory story." Forde, *On Being a Theologian*, 9. Or again: "Knowledge of God does not comprise a set of doctrinal truths that may be taken or left at our discretion. . . . As long as we think the matter is at our discretion, we remain the acting subjects. God is ultimately an insignificant cipher" (89).

108. Forde, *On Being a Theologian*, 3. "To claim such an answer would be simply to leave the actual cross behind for the sake of the theology in our books. It would be just another theology about the cross, not a theology of the cross. Basically all theologies about the cross turn out to be theologies of glory. The difficulty here is that the cross is the theo-logy, the logos of God. . . . The cross is an event. Theology is reflection on and explanation of the event. Theology is about the event, is it not?" (3).

109. Forde, *On Being a Theologian*, 76. See Forde's major statement on "actual" atonement in "The Work of Christ," in *Christian Dogmatics*, vol. 2, ed. C. E. Braaten and R. W. Jenson (Philadelphia: Fortress, 1984), 79-99.

110. Forde, *On Being a Theologian*, 4. Theologians of the cross "are led by cross to look at the trials, the sufferings, the pangs of conscience, the troubles — and joys — of daily life as God's doing and do not try to see through them as mere accidental problems to be solved by metaphysical adjustment. . . . the only move left is to the proclamation that issues from the story. The final task is to do the story to the hearers in such a way that they are incorporated into the story itself" (13). "The cross is not transparent but more like a mirror. Our line of sight is bent back upon itself, upon ourselves and our world" (77).

111. Forde, *On Being a Theologian*, 12.

112. Forde, *On Being a Theologian*, viii.

113. Forde, *On Being a Theologian*, 17.

114. Forde, *On Being a Theologian*, ix. On spiritual suffering: "For Luther the sufferings of the spirit, the pangs of conscience, the terrors of temptation *(Anfechtungen)*, were always more agonizing and serious than the physical pain he also knew well. Even physical death, though heartrending enough for loved ones, was a far lesser matter than the kind of death experienced when the wrath of God assaults the sinner" (Forde, 86, citing *Operationes in Psalmos*, WA 5:176m.32 on "being passive under the divine operation." "To feel the very presence of death," i.e., the way it hits the soul and spirit — this is the real death. Forde, 100.

115. Forde, *On Being a Theologian*, 74-75.

116. Forde, *On Being a Theologian*, 80.

117. *LW* 12:124-28.

118. Forde, *On Being a Theologian*, 85, citing — curiously enough — James Turner, *Without God, without Creed: The Origins of Unbelief in America*, regarding the nonmajestic, i.e., nonmetaphysical "patsy not worthy of commanding belief." Forde, 85. "Instead of being brought to the praise of God, we bend our efforts to justify him" — citing Job against theodicy: "in actual suffering all theorizing is over. One enters into contention with God." Forde, 88.

119. Forde, *On Being a Theologian*, 74.

120. With Hütter, who associates *poiesis* with the Spirit and pathos with the human

creature on the basis of Luther's *De servo arbitrio;* Reinhard Hütter, *Suffering Divine Things: Theology as Church Practice,* trans. D. Stott (Grand Rapids: Eerdmans, 2000), 129. "The Holy Spirit is now to be understood as the real subject of these practices. . . . Although the human being is always present in these activities, and is always and especially actively present, listening, receiving, responding, praising, and rendering obedience, still this human activity does not constitute these practices . . . in them the human being is always the *recipient,* that is, always remains in the mode of pathos . . . is qualified and receives a new 'form,' the one who thus is modeled through the Spirit of Christ, the *forma fidei*" (132). Thus collectively, "the church subsists enhypostatically in the Holy Spirit" (133). "The mission of the church must thus be identified with the mission of the Holy Spirit. This constitutes neither a reification of the Spirit nor an incorporation of the church into the deity as the fourth hypostasis. The church remains strictly separate from the Holy Spirit insofar as it perpetually receives . . . this gives the church its own, unique public character. Through the Holy Spirit (Pentecost), Christ becomes 'public' in the world" (145).

121. Apology IV:78 in *The Book of Concord,* 139. This statement in the Apology is in *material* agreement with the claim of the recent Lutheran–Roman Catholic Joint Declaration that forgiveness and renewal are joined together in justification by faith in Christ. *Joint Declaration on the Doctrine of Justification: The Lutheran World Federation and the Catholic Church,* 4.2.22. See Paul R. Hinlicky, "Process, Convergence, Declaration: Reflections on Doctrinal Dialogue," *Cresset* 64, no. 6 (Pentecost 2001): 13-18. To be sure, Apology IV:252, in the context of interpreting the Epistle of James (!), affirms the forensic sense, immediately after affirming that "since faith is a new life, it necessarily produces new impulses and new works." Needless to say, the exclusive alternative of forensic and effective justification that will be set in a psychological sequence is not yet in view here.

122. Charles P. Arand, "Melanchthon's Rhetorical Argument for *Sola Fide* in the Apology," *Lutheran Quarterly* 14, no. 3 (Autumn 2000): 297.

123. *The Book of Concord,* 495-96.

124. *The Book of Concord,* 495.

125. Timothy J. Wengert, *Law and Gospel: Philip Melanchthon's Debate with John Agricola of Eisleben over Poenitentia* (Grand Rapids: Baker, 1997), 158.

126. Wengert, *Law and Gospel,* 159.

127. Wengert, *Law and Gospel,* 160.

128. Wengert, *Law and Gospel,* 161.

129. Wengert, *Law and Gospel,* 178.

130. Cited in Wengert, *Law and Gospel,* 179.

131. Wengert, *Law and Gospel,* 180.

132. Wengert, *Law and Gospel,* 183.

133. Wengert, *Law and Gospel,* 205. Wengert's chief concern in this development is the legalism that attends it: "however, this definition left Melanchthon and the Reformers open to the charge of antinomianism or libertinism. . . . So while eliminating human works from God's declaration of righteousness, Melanchthon asserted that the law continues in terms of obedience. Here suddenly law and gospel merge into one command: obedience to God. For the totally disobedient conscience, there is justification 'gratis propter Christum' that makes the conscience good. For the good conscience, in which still reside the remnants of sin and whose best works are still impure, there is nevertheless divine acceptance of flawed obedi-

ence because the person is in Christ. To inform the good conscience and encourage it to obedience, a third use of the law is necessary" (205).

134. Wengert, *Law and Gospel,* 206.

135. Wengert, *Law and Gospel,* 206.

136. Wengert, *Law and Gospel,* 206.

137. Luther, *Bondage,* 176.

138. Bo Kristian Holm, "Doctrine and Life in Melanchthon's German and Late Latin *Loci*" (paper presented at the 11th International Congress for Luther Research, Porto Allegre, Brazil, July 2007), 26, cited from *Melanchthons Werke* II/1:245.36–246.8.

139. Olli-Pekka Vainio, *Justification and Participation in Christ: The Development of the Lutheran Doctrine of Justification from Luther to the Formula of Concord (1580)* (Leiden and Boston: Brill, 2008).

140. Friedrich Mildenberger, *Theology of the Lutheran Confessions,* trans. E. Lueker (Philadelphia: Fortress, 1986), 163.

141. Holm rightly argues against the thesis of Friederike Nuessel that Melanchthon's fixation on the notion of satisfaction blocks his understanding of Luther's communion with Christ, not least because Luther himself does not "totally quit" on either the Augustinian notion of sacrifice or Anselm's theology of satisfaction. The important point for Holm, following Risto Saarinen, is that for Luther the gift is not separable from the Giver, and consequently, in receiving the gift, the recipient gives herself to the Giver in turn: "in receiving what God gives, the recipient becomes a giver him- or herself." Holm, "Doctrine and Life," 10.

142. Holm, "Doctrine and Life," 7.

143. Holm, "Doctrine and Life," 14.

144. For this claim see Bo Kristian Holm, "Zur Funktion der Lehre bei Luther," *Kerygma und Dogma* 51 (2005): 17-32.

145. Holm, "Doctrine and Life," 17; the reference is to *Heubtartikel Christlicher Lere,* 122.

146. This accords with theses 4-10 of Luther's *Disputatio de divinitate et humanitate Christi.* See Hinlicky, "Luther's Anti-Docetism," 154-66.

147. Holm, "Doctrine and Life," 19.

148. Quere, *Melanchthon's Christum Cognoscere,* 144.

149. Quere, *Melanchthon's Christum Cognoscere,* 174.

150. Quere, *Melanchthon's Christum Cognoscere,* 303.

151. Quere, *Melanchthon's Christum Cognoscere,* 376.

152. Quere, *Melanchthon's Christum Cognoscere,* 145.

153. Quere, *Melanchthon's Christum Cognoscere,* 195.

154. Quere, *Melanchthon's Christum Cognoscere,* 196.

155. Quere, *Melanchthon's Christum Cognoscere,* 251.

156. Quere, *Melanchthon's Christum Cognoscere,* 164.

157. Quere, *Melanchthon's Christum Cognoscere,* 165.

158. Quere, *Melanchthon's Christum Cognoscere,* 167-68.

159. Eberhard Jüngel, *Justification: The Heart of the Christian Faith,* trans. J. F. Cayzer (Edinburgh: T. & T. Clark, 2001), 192.

160. Jüngel, *Justification,* 195.

161. "[T]he knowledge of God is based upon the clear and certain knowledge of a text of Scripture, a knowledge obtained through the entire dialectical method, but especially through the search for sure definitions based upon logic. Such a text reaches its true end, or

purpose, when it consoles and enlightens its hearers. . . . Wittenberg theology and Aristotelian logical categories converge in Melanchthon's thought so that it is not possible to sort them out." Timothy J. Wengert, *Philip Melanchthon's Annotationes in Johannem in Relation to Its Predecessors and Contemporaries* (Geneva: Librairie Droz S.A., 1987), 210.

162. Heinrich Schmid, *The Doctrinal Theology of the Evangelical Lutheran Church,* 3rd ed. (Philadelphia: Lutheran Publication Society, 1899), 407. Especially clear is Quenstedt: "Thus confidence is nothing else than the *acceptance or apprehension* of the merit of the God-man, appropriating it to ourselves individually. . . . *Appropriation* is indicated by the applicative and possessive pronouns *my, me, mine.* . . . This apprehension belongs to the will and is practical; it involves the reclining of the whole heart and will upon the merit of Christ; it denotes desire for and access to Christ, and the application and confident appropriation of His merit; and this is truly confidence." Schmid, 414.

163. Wengert is concerned to uncover the origin here of the doctrine of the third use of the law. In this connection, he speaks of a dramatic shift in Melanchthon's understanding of justification evident in revisions he made to the Colossians Scholia in 1534: "it was in the Scholia of 1534 that Melanchthon argued most clearly for the necessity of good works in the believer's life. And here the forensic nature of justification became the bedrock for his explanation of that doctrine." Wengert, *Law and Gospel,* 178.

164. Martin Chemnitz, *Loci Theologici,* trans. J. A. O. Preus, vol. 2 (St. Louis: Concordia, 1989), 502.

165. Chemnitz, *Loci Theologici,* 502.

166. *Melanchthon: Selected Writings,* trans. C. L. Hill (Westport, Conn.: Greenwood Press, 1962), 17.

167. Ake Bergvall, *Augustinian Perspectives in the Renaissance,* Acts Universitatis Upsaliensis Studia Anglistica Upsaliensia 117 (Uppsala: Uppsala University, 2001).

168. Martin Brecht, *Martin Luther: His Road to Reformation, 1483-1521,* trans. J. L. Schaaf (Minneapolis: Fortress, 1993), 278.

169. Dialectic presupposes rhetoric; without it the scholastics "deviated from the author's intent and taught things foreign to true piety, in large part, 'on account of ignorance of these arts.' . . . [S]ince the Spirit taught 'through the Word,' the nature of speech must be known. Indeed, because without the knowledge of these arts no one can make a judgment about a speech, we apply this instrument to the interpretation of scripture." Timothy J. Wengert, *Human Freedom, Christian Righteousness: Philip Melanchthon's Exegetical Dispute with Erasmus of Rotterdam* (New York and Oxford: Oxford University Press, 1998), 49.

170. Michael B. Aune, *To Move the Heart: Philip Melanchthon's Rhetorical View of Rite and Its Implications for Contemporary Ritual Theory* (San Francisco: Christian Universities Press, 1994), 16-17, cited from Debora K. Shuger, *Sacred Rhetoric: The Christian Grand Style in the English Renaissance* (Princeton: Princeton University Press, 1988), 41-50. "Rhetoric as a way of speaking and ritual as a way of acting are able to explain a social world, to shape and define a community, to generate a certain kind of knowing, to construct a particular kind of person, and to stretch the daily experience of human beings into more grand, noble and delightful meanings." Aune, 5.

171. Aune cites Clifford Geertz's criticism of the Cartesian ego as "a bounded, unique, more or less integrated motivational and cognitive universe, a dynamic center of awareness, emotion, judgment, and action organized into a distinctive whole and set contrastively both

against other such wholes and against its social and natural background." Aune, *To Move the Heart,* 109.

172. Melanchthon, *Loci,* 52.

173. Aune comments, "'The autonomous, transcendent self,' writes theologian Timothy Sedgwick, 'is an illusion.' Such 'de-centering' of the human subject is 'old news' from both Classical and Christian perspectives. . . . The selfhood or 'moved heart' formed in the interaction between the Spirit and human being is an activity, not an autonomous, unique entity. It is a loving response experienced as *fiducia* and *notitia.*" Aune, *To Move the Heart,* 75.

174. Wengert, *Human Freedom, Christian Righteousness,* 68.

175. Wengert, *Human Freedom, Christian Righteousness,* 69.

176. Wengert, *Human Freedom, Christian Righteousness,* 70.

177. "Erasmus was in his eyes the chief culprit. . . . Not a word is spoken here against Luther's theology, only against his bombast." Wengert, *Human Freedom, Christian Righteousness,* 75.

178. Quoted in Wengert, *Human Freedom, Christian Righteousness,* 77. *This* reserve, by the way, is well justified. Luther's "acerbity in dispute" — a euphemism for his apocalyptic turn to demonizing theological opponents — provides relative justification for the revision of Luther's theology suffered at the hands of Melanchthon.

179. Wengert, *Human Freedom, Christian Righteousness,* 81.

180. Wengert, *Human Freedom, Christian Righteousness,* 89.

181. Wengert, *Human Freedom, Christian Righteousness,* 90.

182. Wengert, *Human Freedom, Christian Righteousness,* 142.

183. Wengert, *Human Freedom, Christian Righteousness,* 143.

184. Wengert, *Human Freedom, Christian Righteousness,* 145.

185. "If God could not act except as natural necessity dictated, then invocation and pleas for help would be useless. . . . To this and many more questions of blind reason, and mad Stoicism there is an eternally true and sure answer: God acts voluntarily [freiwilliglich]; he is not imprisoned in nor bound to created nature; on the contrary, he can and often does will to give counsel, volition, movement and strength to angels and men, which they of themselves, in their own natural ability, cannot have." Melanchthon, *Loci,* 41-42.

186. Wengert, *Human Freedom, Christian Righteousness,* 146. Thus Wengert concludes his analysis: "the more justification was understood as God's gracious imputation, the more questions of human participation demanded answers," i.e., if the difference between Pharaoh and Moses were to be known and distinguished. In 1556 the Gnesio-Lutheran Gallus accused Melanchthon of borrowing from Lombard and Erasmus the teaching that "the free will could apply itself to grace." Wengert comments, there is "some truth" in this charge. Wengert, 156. As Clyde Manschreck, editor and translator of *Melanchthon's Loci 1555,* commented: take away the miracle and Melanchthon becomes an Arminian. Melanchthon, *Loci,* xix.

187. Dietrich Bonhoeffer, *The Cost of Discipleship,* trans. R. H. Fuller (New York: Simon and Schuster, Touchstone Edition, 1995), 43.

188. Ernst Troeltsch, *Protestantism and Progress: A Historical Study of the Relation of Protestantism to the Modern World,* trans. W. Montgomery (Boston: Beacon Press, 1966), 49. But one can no more concede the Spirit to "fanatics," "enthusiasts," and "sectarians," as Troeltsch wickedly insinuates, than to claim it for moribund Lutheranism.

189. Theodore K. Raab, *The Last Days of the Renaissance and the March to Modernity*

(New York: Basic Books, 2006), 115-17. Raab describes this as a reaction to the wars of religion: "western Christendom, once united and coherent, was falling into irreparable disarray" (112). "With the antagonists asserting exclusive and incompatible versions of truth, it seemed only appropriate to question the very nature of such claims" (115).

190. Bruce McCormack, *Karl Barth's Critically Realistic Dialectical Theology: Its Genesis and Development, 1909-1936* (Oxford: Clarendon, 1995), 267. The Adam-Christ dialectic that emerges in the second edition of Barth's Romans commentary is in tacit reply to the criticism of Paul Althaus that in the first edition a skeptical dialectic of timelessness and time reduces God to a limit-concept and forbids incarnation and salvation history. McCormack, 262-66.

191. Karl Barth, *Church Dogmatics* III/3, trans. G. W. Bromiley and R. J. Ehrlich (Edinburgh: T. & T. Clark, 1960), 334-49. Barth, of course, does this on the basis of the autonomy of theology: "In theology, at least, we must be more far-sighted than to attempt a deliberate co-ordination with temporarily predominant philosophical trends in which we may be caught up, or to allow them to dictate or correct our conceptions" (334).

Notes to Chapter 5

1. Leibniz presupposed this conception of philosophy in distinction from the emerging natural sciences in his opening remarks against Locke in *New Essays concerning Human Understanding,* trans. Alfred Gideon Langley (La Salle, Ill.: Open Court, 1949): "But it belongs only to the supreme Reason, whom nothing escapes, distinctly to comprehend all the infinite and to see all the reasons and all the consequences. All that we can do in regard to infinites is to know them confusedly, and to know at least distinctly that they are such; otherwise we judge very wrongly of the beauty and grandeur of the universe." Not only shall this deprive us of a sound natural science, but of a "proper Pneumatology comprising the knowledge of God, of souls and of simple substances in general" (51). The scope of pneumatology is vast: "[T]he perfect unity must be reserved to bodies animated, or endowed with primitive entelechies; for these entelechies are analogous to souls and are as individual and imperishable as they are; . . . their organic bodies are practically machines, but which surpass the artificial machines of our invention as much as the inventor of the natural machines surpasses us. For these natural machines are as imperishable as the souls themselves, and the animal with the soul subsists always. . . . All this shows that the philosophers have not been wholly in the wrong in putting so great a distance between artificial things and between natural bodies endowed with a real unity. But it belonged only to our time to develop this mystery and make understood its importance and consequences in order thoroughly to establish natural theology and what is called Pneumatics, in a manner truly natural" (362).

2. Max Wundt, *Die deutsche Schulmetaphysik des. 17. Jahrhunderts* (Tübingen: J. C. B. Mohr, 1939), 143-44. The presupposition about philosophy as general pneumatology derives from Melanchthon and the German school philosophy in which Leibniz was nurtured. Günther Frank speaks of "Die theologische Geistphilosophie als metaphysisches Rueckgrat der humanistischen Philosophie Melanchthons." Frank, *Die Theologische Philosophie Philipp Melanchthons (1497-1560),* Erfurter Theologische Studien 67 (Leipzig: Benno, 1995), 86, all translations are mine. For Leibniz's location in the Melanchthonian tradition, see also James

William Richard, *Philip Melanchthon: The Protestant Preceptor of Germany (1497-1560)* (New York and London: Putnam, 1902), 139-40, and Frank, 5, 11, 339.

3. Philip Melanchthon, *On Christian Doctrine: Loci Communes, 1555,* trans. C. L. Manschreck (Grand Rapids: Baker, 1982), 5.

4. Melanchthon, *Loci,* 6.

5. Frank, *Theologische Philosophie,* 92.

6. Leroy E. Loemker, *Struggle for Synthesis: The Seventeenth Century Background of Leibniz's Synthesis of Order and Freedom* (Cambridge: Harvard University Press, 1972), 58.

7. *Melanchthon deutsch,* vol. 1, *Schule und Universitaet, Philosophie, Geschichte und Politik,* ed. Michael Beyer, Stefan Rhein, and Günther Wartenberg (Leipzig: Evangelische Verlagsanstalt, 1997), 140. All translations are my own.

8. *Melanchthon deutsch,* 1:150.

9. *Melanchthon deutsch,* 1:153.

10. Frank, *Theologische Philosophie,* 4-44.

11. *Melanchthon deutsch,* 1:165. The "failure of the encyclopedists rooted in the tension between the two goals 1) of discovering the gaps in knowledge (the new science) and 2) of arranging material for pedagogical purposes (classical erudition) . . . could the new sciences, as they developed their own literature, also relate this literature constructively to the larger purposes — educational, social and cultural — which were demanded by European order?" Loemker, *Struggle for Synthesis,* 45. "By setting literary standards and by stressing the interrelations and human worth of scientific knowledge, the tradition of learning served to sustain a balanced view of the scientific enterprise, to prevent narrow overspecialization, and to call attention to the complexity of scientific endeavor, to encourage the organization and conservations of its results in a useful form, and thus to assure its place in a realistic world view which may be not only theoretically fruitful but strong enough to prevent the split between scientist and humanist in education and between scientist and layman in life." Loemker, 52.

12. Timothy J. Wengert, *Human Freedom, Christian Righteousness: Philip Melanchthon's Exegetical Dispute with Erasmus of Rotterdam* (New York and Oxford: Oxford University Press, 1998), 119.

13. John Witte, Jr., *Law and Protestantism: The Legal Teachings of the Lutheran Reformation,* with a foreword by Martin E. Marty (Cambridge: Cambridge University Press, 2002), 123-24, cited from *Corpus Reformatorum,* 21:25-27.

14. Witte, *Law and Protestantism,* 123-24. See also Harold J. Berman and John Witte, Jr., "The Transformation of Western Legal Philosophy in Lutheran Germany," *Southern California Law Review* 62, no. 6 (September 1989): 1611-34, and Frank, *Theologische Philosophie,* 110-28, 168.

15. Witte, *Law and Protestantism,* 124, drawn from *Corpus Reformatorum,* 11:918-19.

16. Carl E. Maxcey, *Bona Opera: A Study in the Development of Doctrine in Philip Melanchthon* (Nieuwkoop: B. De Graaf, 1980), 297. This important study clearly demonstrates the linkage of the *imago dei* theology with Melanchthon's new, "protestant" interpretation of "natural law," arguing that it forms a trajectory that will finally lead to the categorical imperative of practical reason.

17. Maxcey, *Bona Opera,* 282-83.

18. Berman and Witte, "Western Legal Philosophy," 1611-60.

19. Loemker, *Struggle for Synthesis,* 121. Riley assigns Leibniz's political philosophy ver-

batim (as his title indicates) to this Melanchthonian notion of theology: Patrick Riley, *Leibniz' Universal Jurisprudence: Justice as the Charity of the Wise* (Cambridge: Harvard University Press, 1996), 11-12, 54-55, 90, 128, 200.

20. Frank, *Theologische Philosophie*, 60, 64-65, 156, 162, 206, 312-13.

21. Frank, *Theologische Philosophie*, 65-66.

22. Frank, *Theologische Philosophie*, 218, 259, 263, 270, 285, 287.

23. Frank, *Theologische Philosophie*, 88-89, 102-3, 109, 335.

24. Frank, *Theologische Philosophie*, 90, 94, 97, 103, 157, 187.

25. Frank, *Theologische Philosophie*, 100, 102, 157, 334.

26. Frank, *Theologische Philosophie*, 185-90, 323.

27. Frank, *Theologische Philosophie*, 213.

28. Frank, *Theologische Philosophie*, 232, 316.

29. Frank, *Theologische Philosophie*, 62, 73-74, 208, 282.

30. Frank, *Theologische Philosophie*, 129, 244, 254-55, 324.

31. Frank, *Theologische Philosophie*, 291.

32. Frank, *Theologische Philosophie*, 295-97.

33. Frank, *Theologische Philosophie*, 135, 158, 294, 308.

34. Such divergence from Luther, on the other hand, has been the source of appreciation for Melanchthon among others. Charles Leander Hill, for instance, wrote at the outset of his doctoral dissertation: "For after the great controversy between Luther and Erasmus on the freedom of the human will, it was Melanchthon who addressed himself to the task of softening the biblicistic-augustinian theology and school at Wittenberg by giving it a humanistic-philological turn. But he went a step farther. He began to freely inject the new theology with reason, science, natural law, and ethics." Hill, "An Exposition and Critical Estimate of the Philosophy of Philip Melanchthon" (Ph.D. diss., Ohio State University, 1938), 2. The implied disjunction between Augustinianism and humanism, as we shall see, does not stand up to scrutiny, although the task of cultural reconstruction Hill imputes to Melanchthon's life-labor is on target. Similarly Frank, *Theologische Philosophie*, 228.

35. *Melanchthon: Selected Writings* (Westport, Conn.: Greenwood Press, 1962), 178-79.

36. Leibniz's politics were very much in defense of Christian Europe against the rise of nation-state imperialism, particularly directed in his own day against French imperial expansion. His *Mars Christianissimus* of 1683 savagely satirizes Louis XIV for hypocrisy in betraying the ideal of Christendom (Patrick Riley, ed., *Leibniz: Political Writings*, 2nd ed. [Cambridge: Cambridge University Press, 2001], 121-45). On the other hand, his resort to crusade against Islam as a solution to European disunity (Riley, 34) reflects all that is wrong about the ideal of Christendom.

37. I say "Christendom" as a political form, not the visible unity of the church. But there is still a perplexity for Westerners about how their culture will fare with the progressive severing from its rootage in Christianity. At the conclusion of his careful study of the Melanchthonian legal tradition, Witte concluded: "a good deal of our modern Western law of marriage, education, and social welfare, for example, still bears the unmistakable marks of Lutheran Reformation theology." Witte, *Law and Protestantism*, 295. He emphasizes that "the state has a role to play not only in fighting wars, punishing crime, and keeping peace, but also in providing education and welfare, fostering charity and morality, facilitating worship and piety. . . . law has not only a basic use of coercing citizens to accept a morality of duty but also a higher use of inducing citizens to pursue a morality of aspiration" (296). On

the negative side, he notes that ever since Reformation times "Germany and other Protestant nations have been locked in a bitter legal struggle to eradicate state establishments of religion and to guarantee religious freedom for all" (303).

38. Loemker, *Struggle for Synthesis*, 45.

39. Loemker, *Struggle for Synthesis*, 46.

40. Loemker, *Struggle for Synthesis*, 250. Loemker, to be sure, qualifies this criticism with a nod to theological agape: "Leibniz was thus justified in criticizing the possessive theory [of Hobbes] . . . as well as the egoism [of Spinoza]. However short Leibniz' definition falls of the active responsiveness of love, it does in intent preserve the idea that even if unresponded to, love enriches both its subject and its object" (249).

41. John R. Schneider, *Philip Melanchthon's Rhetorical Construal of Biblical Authority: Oratio Sacra* (Lewiston, N.Y.: Edwin Mellen Press, 1990), 248.

42. *Luther's Works: The American Edition*, ed. J. Pelikan et al., 55 vols. (St. Louis: Concordia; Philadelphia: Fortress, 1960-), 31:55; hereafter cited as *LW.*

43. *Melanchthon: Selected Writings*, 38-39. Indeed, according to the mature Melanchthon, human reason "is capable neither of proving the existence of certain fundamental inborn moral concepts nor of apprehending and applying them without distortion." Berman and Witte, "Western Legal Philosophy," 1617. For this reason, the revelation of the natural law in the Decalogue, and the narratives of Hebrew Scriptures, play important roles in correcting misapprehension and misuse of natural law. Berman and Witte, 1621.

44. Schneider, *Rhetorical Construal*, 248.

45. Sachiko Kusukawa, *The Transformation of Natural Philosophy: The Case of Philip Melanchthon* (Cambridge: Cambridge University Press, 1995), 82, cited from *Corpus Reformatorum*, 11:282, 280.

46. "On the Distinction between the Gospel and Philosophy," in *Philip Melanchthon: Orations on Philosophy and Education*, ed. Sachiko Kusukawa, trans. Christine F. Salazar (Cambridge: Cambridge University Press, 1999), 24; cf. also 203. Cf. also Frank's discussion of the 1536 Declamation on Philosophy, in *Theologische Philosophie*, 68.

47. "Philosophy is neither gospel nor any part of it; but it is a part of divine law. For it is the law of nature itself divinely written in men's minds, which truly is the law of God concerning those virtues which reason understands and which are necessary for civil life. For philosophy, properly speaking, is nothing other tha[n] the explanation of the law of nature." Kusukawa, *Transformation*, 70.

48. Kusukawa, *Transformation*, 97.

49. Kusukawa, *Transformation*, 109. Melanchthon follows Luther's teaching that the works reserved to the divine majesty alone are *creatio ex nihilo* as expressed in the origin of the world, the justification of the sinner, and the resurrection of the dead. These "wonders" are constitutive of nature, and even if they are revealed within nature, they can have no "natural" explanation.

50. Günther Frank, "Gott und Natur: Zur Transformation der Naturphilosophie in Melanchthons humanistischer Philosophie," in *Melanchthon und die Naturwissenschaften seiner Zeit*, ed. G. Frank and S. Rhein (Sigmaringen, Germany: Jan Thorbecke Verlag, 1998), 52.

51. Kusukawa, *Transformation*, 75-124.

52. *Philip Melanchthon: Orations on Philosophy and Education*, 153.

53. Kusukawa, *Transformation*, 150, cited from *Corpus Reformatorum*, 13:189, emphasis added.

54. Melanchthon, *Loci,* 281.

55. Melanchthon, *Loci,* 283.

56. Loemker, *Struggle for Synthesis,* 82.

57. G. W. Leibniz, *Discourse on Metaphysics and Other Essays,* trans. D. Garber and R. Ariew (Indianapolis: Hackett, 1991), 48.

58. John Dewey, *Experience and Nature* (New York: Dover, 1958), 48-49.

59. Loemker, *Struggle for Synthesis,* 82.

60. Eberhard Jüngel, *God as the Mystery of the World: On the Foundation of the Theology of the Crucified One in the Dispute between Theism and Atheism,* trans. D. L. Guder (Grand Rapids: Eerdmans, 1983), 14-35.

61. Jüngel, *Mystery of the World,* 126-51.

62. On "preestablished" in "preestablished harmony," which has "unfortunately suggested a deistic interpretation which his thought does not support. This 'pre-existent harmony' (preexisting not in time but as an eternal cause) is but an abstract aspect of the harmony of mutual consent and congruence which the sequences of action in the many existing individuals show by virtue of their natures having been (and continuing to be) determined by the Ideas or the perfections of God. The harmony of existence *is never complete, and never will be until* each individual and the whole total of individuals in their various limited perspective and qualities, achieve the greatest perfection of which they are capable — when the total symphony of existence (to use the musical analogy) has been performed and the dissonances have been resolved *in the final sustained chord by many voices* but in the major dominant mode. Then the Composer's design will have been executed and will stand complete for all to grasp." Loemker, *Struggle for Synthesis,* 198, emphasis added. What was needed to achieve this was the distinction, lacking in Descartes and Spinoza, between the power of God as expressed by intellect as omniscience, and power as expressed by moral will as agape.

63. Kusukawa, *Transformation,* 119, cited from *Corpus Reformatorum,* 13:57.

64. *Philip Melanchthon: Orations on Philosophy and Education,* 153.

65. Kusukawa, *Transformation,* 187. See also Clyde Leonard Manschreck, *Melanchthon: The Quiet Reformer* (Westport, Conn.: Greenwood Press, 1975), 106-7.

66. Kusukawa, *Transformation,* 167.

67. Kusukawa, *Transformation,* 167.

68. Frank, *Theologische Philosophie,* 65, 188, 334.

69. Frank, *Theologische Philosophie,* 109.

70. "But the chief weapon of the intellectual defense was a new appropriation of the doctrine of the natural light." So Loemker: it was a double-edged sword: "it was also clear that this reasonable light which lighteth all peoples could not be safely divorced from the more general parts of the Christian revelation without itself reviving the old charge of unbelief" (Loemker, *Struggle for Synthesis,* 63).

71. *Philip Melanchthon: Orations on Philosophy and Education,* 213.

72. Robert Rosin, *Reformers, the Preacher, and Skepticism: Luther, Brenz, Melanchthon, and Ecclesiastes* (Mainz: Von Zabern, 1997), 259; Frank, *Theologische Philosophie,* 67, 209, 218, 259, 263, 272-73, 285, 287, 324.

73. A century and some years later "the young Leibniz grieved at this very shipwreck of atheism around him," "'Hobbes condemned for his extreme nominalism, his materialism, and his political absolutism, Spinoza for his political toleration, his identification of God with nature, and his denial of teleology.'" Loemker, *Struggle for Synthesis,* 61-62.

74. Walter R. Boumann, "Melanchthon's Significance for the Church Today," in *Philip Melanchthon Then and Now (1497-1997)*, ed. S. H. Hendrix and T. J. Wengert (Columbia, S.C.: Lutheran Theological Southern Seminary, 1997), 33-55.

75. Kusukawa, *Transformation*, 160.

76. Frank, *Theologische Philosophie*, 65.

77. This is what the early Luther contends in his 1517 *Disputation against Scholastic Theology*, Thesis 51, *LW* 31:12. To "misunderstand Aristotle is to transfer his philosophical categories into the sphere of theology." B. A. Gerrish, *Grace and Reason: A Study in the Theology of Luther* (Oxford: At the Clarendon Press, 1962), 39. According to Gerrish, Luther's relation to Aristotle is highly differentiated. The philosopher "is valuable in his own proper domain; that we must not evaluate all his works alike; that his champions never really understood him; and that, even if Aristotle is to be condemned, there are other philosophers who are to be preferred" (33). Contradictory statements on Aristotle's ethics pertain to the two kingdoms: he is the best in moral philosophy, yet the worst enemy of grace (34). Luther has an abiding appreciation of *epieikeia* from the *Ethics* (35). Luther calls attention to Aristotle's circle: while practice makes us virtuous, no just act is genuine if he does not come from a just disposition. Luther knows Aristotle well enough to call attention to this against the schoolmen (96 n. 3).

78. Augustine, *Confessions* 7.9 — to wit, that philosophy at its best knows nothing of the incarnation and the cradle and the cross. Reason, under the power of the fallen will, willfully refuses to receive these mysteries of redemption until won by the Spirit's outpouring grace in the heart to a new vision of the child in Mary's arms as the Son of God in humility of love come to regain the proud and arrogant creature.

79. *LW* 44:200-207.

80. Kusukawa, *Transformation*, 49. Cf. Frank, *Theologische Philosophie*, 56.

81. Although Luther was also aware — before his partnership with Melanchthon began — that "it is very doubtful whether the Latins comprehended the correct meaning of Aristotle." *LW* 31:12.

82. Schneider, *Rhetorical Construal*, 29.

83. Schneider, *Rhetorical Construal*, 34.

84. Kusukawa, *Transformation*, 157.

85. Kusukawa, *Transformation*, 167.

86. *LW* 31:41.

87. Kusukawa, *Transformation*, 160-63. Zwingli, "On the Providence of God," in *The Latin Works of Huldreich Zwingli*, trans. S. M. Jackson, vol. 2 (Philadelphia: Heidelberg Press, 1922), 128-234. Originally a series of sermons preached to Elector Philip of Hesse against Luther's *De servo arbitrio* ("all things are not wisely ordered according to the dictum of one man," Zwingli, 129) ahead of the Marburg Colloquy, Zwingli published these as a unified tract in 1530. According to Gäbler, Zwingli's agreement with Luther is confined to the one point of bound choice. "The treatise is otherwise permeated with a refutation of chief statements of Lutheran theology, especially of those developed against Erasmus. . . . The sharpest contrast is revealed in the image of God. Zwingli opposed the statements, essential for Luther, about the 'hidden' God with the 'simplicity' of God whose will can be totally recognized in his revelation." Ulrich Gäbler, *Huldrych Zwingli: His Life and Work*, trans. Ruth C. L. Gritsch (Philadelphia: Fortress, 1986), 147. In the treatise Zwingli argued for a trinity of power, goodness, and truth that of necessity regulates all things. Interestingly, he explicitly

parses the doctrine of the Trinity with *this* triad that omits wisdom and reverses the traditional ascriptions of goodness from the Spirit to the Son, so that truth is ascribed to the Spirit. Then he adds: "Yet all these we know belong to one and the same divine being, just as here I have shown that power, goodness and truth, though distinguished in conception and definition, are yet to be considered as the one and the same supreme good." Zwingli, 134. The tract deserves a more thorough analysis and study of its reception history. The appropriation of the perfections to the persons in this way seemingly assimilated them into the substantially indistinguishable qualities of a single, simple substance. According to G. J. Jordan, *The Reunion of the Churches: A Study of G. W. Leibnitz and His Great Attempt* (London: Constable and Co., 1927), 191, Leibniz saw a line running from Zwingli through Socinianism to deism, whether in Clarke's interventionist or Spinoza's necessitarian versions.

88. On Melanchthon's critical relation to nominalist philosophy, see Frank, *Theologische Philosophie*, 29-36, 184.

89. A Platonic position that Frank terms *exemplarism: Theologische Philosophie*, 136, 315.

90. Brian Gerrish, "The Reformation and the Rise of Modern Science," in *The Reformation Heritage* (Chicago: University of Chicago Press, 1982), 171.

91. Robert Kolb, "Phillip Melanchthon: Reformer and Theologian," *Concordia Journal* 23, no. 4 (October 1997): 315.

92. *Philip Melanchthon: Orations on Philosophy and Education*, 101.

93. "Certainly Homer agrees in this with Plato and some most distinguished men, that there is a God and that He cares for human affairs; therefore he assembles so many counsels of the gods, in order to show that human affairs do not arise fortuitously or by chance, but are arranged and ruled by the immortal gods. . . . If human nature strives by its own powers, what better or more sublime can it imagine about the will of God than that He loves, protects and helps the good, hates the impious and the wicked and afflicts them with punishment, and attends to and rules human affairs?" *Philip Melanchthon: Orations on Philosophy and Education*, 50.

94. *Philip Melanchthon: Orations on Philosophy and Education*, 220.

95. Kusukawa, *Transformation*, 4.

96. Berman and Witte, "Western Legal Philosophy," 1629, cited from *Corpus Reformatorum*, 22:615.

97. Berman and Witte, "Western Legal Philosophy," 1635.

98. According to Catherine Wilson, in his 1765 *Traeume eines Gestersehers*, "Kant was never, at any stage of his career, a Leibnizian." "The Reception of Leibniz in the 18th Century," in *The Cambridge Companion to Leibniz*, ed. N. Jolley (Cambridge, U.K., and New York: Cambridge University Press, 1995), 457-58.

99. Wundt, *Schulmetaphysik*, 116.

100. *Melanchthon: Selected Writings*, 18.

101. Augustine, *Confessions* 4.2, trans. R. S. Pine-Coffin (New York: Dorset, 1961), 72.

102. Augustine, *Confessions* 7.9, in Pine-Coffin, 146.

103. Frank, *Theologische Philosophie*, 200-201, 233-34. See Paul Tillich's idealistically colored but still insightful "The Two Types of Philosophy of Religion," in *Theology of Culture*, ed. R. C. Kimball (London and New York: Oxford University Press, 1959), 10-29.

104. Frank, *Theologische Philosophie*, 333.

105. Jasper Hopkins, *A New Interpretive Translation of St. Anselm's Monologian and Proslogian* (Minneapolis: Arthur J. Banning Press, 1986).

106. R. W. Southern, *Saint Anselm: A Portrait in a Landscape* (Cambridge: Cambridge University Press, 1993), 128.

107. Robert Merrihew Adams, *Leibniz: Determinist, Theist, Idealist* (Oxford: Oxford University Press, 1994), 135-56.

108. Frank clarifies: *rationabilitas,* not *rationalitas; Theologische Philosophie,* 228.

109. "Say: God is One, the Eternal God. He begot none, nor was He begotten. None is equal to him" (Sura 112:1-4). *The Koran,* trans. N. J. Dawood (London: Penguin Books, 1993), 434.

110. Immanuel Kant, *Lectures on Philosophical Theology,* trans. A. W. Wood and G. M. Clark (Ithaca, N.Y.: Cornell University Press, 1978), 55.

111. Frank, *Theologische Philosophie,* 169.

112. G. W. Leibniz, *Philosophical Papers and Letters: A Selection,* trans. and ed. Leroy E. Loemker, 2 vols. (Chicago: University of Chicago Press, 1956), 780; hereafter cited as Loemker, *Papers.*

113. G. W. Leibniz, *Philosophical Texts,* trans. R. S. Woolhouse and R. Francks (Oxford: Oxford University Press, 1998), 239.

114. Leibniz, *Philosophical Texts,* 239.

115. Leibniz, *New Essays,* 383.

116. Frank, *Theologische Philosophie,* 26, 44, 101.

117. Pico della Mirandola, *On the Dignity of Man, On Being and the One, Heptaplus,* trans. C. G. Wallis, P. J. W. Miller, and D. Carmichael (New York: Bobbs-Merrill, 1965), 4-5. Cf. Frank, *Theologische Philosophie,* 102, 104-5, 181.

118. Pico, *Dignity,* 7.

119. Pico, *Dignity,* 55-56.

120. Quirinus Breen, "Melancthon's [*sic*] Reply to G. Pico Della Mirandola," *Journal of the History of Ideas* 13, no. 3 (June 1952): 417-18; cf. Frank, *Theologische Philosophie,* 104-5.

121. Wundt, *Schulmetaphysik,* 18. I do not know whether Wundt in any way connects this German exceptionalism in philosophy with the Third Reich. I see no explicit sign of this in his 1939 book and take these factual points and historical suggestions without prejudice.

122. A contemporary necessity for "the theology of human being in the light of the sciences," according to Arthur Peacocke, *Theology for a Scientific Age: Being and Becoming — Natural, Divine, and Human,* enlarged ed. (London: SCM, 1993), 213-54.

123. Wundt, *Schulmetaphysik,* 17 n. 1.

124. Frank, *Theologische Philosophie,* 86.

125. So Wundt, *Schulmetaphysik,* 15-19, and with especially detailed argumentation, Günther Frank, *Die Vernunft des Gottesgedankens: Religionsphilosophische Studien zur frühen Neuzeit* (Stuttgart: Frommann-Holzboog, 2003), 319.

126. Wundt, *Schulmetaphysik,* 14, 279.

127. Loemker, *Struggle for Synthesis,* 46.

128. Wundt, *Schulmetaphysik,* 143.

129. Wundt, *Schulmetaphysik,* 266-67.

130. Wundt, *Schulmetaphysik,* 276.

131. Wundt, *Schulmetaphysik,* 25.

132. Melanchthon, *Loci,* 39.

133. Stephen H. Daniel likens the *Monadology* to Edwards's "doctrine of excellency" as his "most important contribution to modern philosophy" since, like Leibniz, it refuses "efforts to ground philosophy on doubt, simplicity, and atomistic individualism" but seeks instead "the harmonious unity of nature and experience." Daniel, "Edwards as Philosopher," in *The Cambridge Companion to Jonathan Edwards,* ed. Stephen J. Stein (Cambridge: Cambridge University Press, 2007), 164-65.

134. Loemker, *Struggle for Synthesis,* 177.

135. Gregory Brown, "Leibniz's Theodicy and the Confluence of Worldly Goods," *Journal of the History of Philosophy* 20, no. 4 (October 1988): 571-91. Cited from Loemker, *Papers,* 280.

136. Melanchthon, *Loci,* 13-14. Note already here how truncated is the account of the Holy Spirit; later he will add that "spirit here means something essential and eternal, not created, a movement; it means the love and joy in the Father and the Son" (16). The possibility for the depersonalization of the Spirit into general pneumatology is evident.

137. Jordan, *Reunion,* 78.

138. G. W. Leibniz, *Theodicy: Essays on the Goodness of God, the Freedom of Man, and the Origin of Evil,* trans. E. M. Huggard (Chicago and La Salle, Ill.: Open Court, 1998), 127-28.

139. Thomas Campanella "introduced the century to a new conception of the trinity in his doctrine of the 'primalities' — God must be understood as power manifesting itself in the parallel attributes of wisdom and love, which are therefore basic throughout creation as well . . . how can power be exercised in harmonious and orderly ways, or in the social field, how can it be rendered just." Loemker, *Struggle for Synthesis,* 13.

140. Loemker, *Struggle for Synthesis,* 21.

141. Graham White, *Luther as Nominalist: A Study of the Logical Methods Used in Martin Luther's Disputations in the Light of Their Medieval Background,* Schriften der Luther-Agricola-Gesellschaft 30 (Helsinki: Luther-Agricola Society, 1994).

142. Jan Lindhardt, *Martin Luther: Knowledge and Mediation in the Renaissance,* Texts and Studies in Religion, vol. 29 (Lewiston, N.Y.: Edwin Mellen Press, 1986).

143. Timothy P. Dost, *Renaissance Humanism in Support of the Gospel in Luther's Early Correspondence: Taking All Things Captive* (Aldershot: Ashgate, 2001). Paul R. Hinlicky, review of *Renaissance Humanism in Support of the Gospel in Luther's Early Correspondence: Taking All Things Captive,* by Timothy P. Dost, *Sixteenth Century Journal* 34, no. 3 (Fall 2003): 796-97.

144. Paul R. Hinlicky, "The New Language of the Spirit: Critical Dogmatics in the Tradition of Luther," in D. Bielfeldt, M. Mattox, and P. Hinlicky, *The Substance of the Faith: Luther's Doctrinal Theology for Today* (Minneapolis: Fortress, 2008), 180-90.

145. Frank, *Theologische Philosophie,* 15.

146. Frank, *Theologische Philosophie,* 87.

147. Frank, *Theologische Philosophie,* 88.

148. Melanchthon, *Loci,* 5.

149. Luther, *Bondage,* 170.

150. Robert Jenson made this argument in his interpretation of Barth's *Epistle to the Romans* as the final dialectical outcome of Kantian agnosticism in his early *God after God: The God of the Past and the God of the Future, Seen in the Work of Karl Barth* (New York: Bobbs-Merrill, 1969).

151. Luther, *Bondage,* 218.

152. Luther, *Bondage,* 232-33.

153. Luther, *Bondage,* 203.

154. Luther, *Bondage*, 203, emphasis added.

155. The "principal force of Luther's assault on reason, so far from being explicable in Nominalist terms, is directed precisely against the *via moderna* and its tendency toward Pelagianism" in spite of "some resemblance to Ockham's religious epistemology." "Luther struck out on a line of his own which eventually ranged him, not with, but against the champions of the *via moderna.*" Gerrish, *Grace and Reason,* 6. "For the problem of human reason, according to Luther, is that it cannot comprehend the Gospel's message of free forgiveness by grace alone" (9). Gerrish, citing Karl Holl: "'A God who concerned himself with sinners was, on this proposition, something incomprehensible' . . . it is this aspect of Luther's thought which makes his understanding of the 'unreasonableness' of Christian doctrine utterly different from anything that Occam had to say on the subject. Luther's opposition to reason is as much directed against Scotus and Occam as any others of the Schoolmen" (Gerrish, 97; cf. 120ff.). "[F]or Luther the problem of faith and reason is not so much an epistemological question . . . it is a soteriological question" (135). "Should we call anyone an irrationalist who allows that reason has its place, though it also has its limits? And should we call anyone an antinomian who is as insistent as Luther on the need for good works, albeit *in suo loco?*" (136).

156. Wengert, *Human Freedom, Christian Righteousness*, 108.

157. Wengert, "Melanchthon and Luther/Luther and Melanchthon," *Lutherjahrbuch* 66 (Göttingen: Vandenhoeck & Ruprecht, 1999), 85-86.

158. Wengert, "Melanchthon and Luther," 68.

159. "Everywhere we should stick to just the simple, natural meaning of the words, as yielded by the rules of grammar and the habits of speech that God has created among men; for if anyone may devise 'implications' and 'figures' in Scripture at his own pleasure, what will all Scripture be but a reed shaken with the wind, and a sort of chameleon." Luther, *Bondage*, 192. Confidence in the capacity of reason to read and understand words is based on the creation of God. Given Luther's apocalyptic rhetoric — "the world is the kingdom of Satan, where, over and above the natural blindness engendered from our flesh, we are under the dominion of evil spirits, and are hardened in our very blindness, fast bound in a darkness that is no more human, but devilish!" (*Bondage*, 132) — the decisive concession Luther makes here to Melanchthon and the entire line of thought that emerges from him could easily be, and often is, overlooked.

160. "I commend you strongly, sir, when you wish faith to be grounded in reason: without this why should we prefer the Bible to the Koran or to the ancient books of the Brahmins. Our theologians also and other learned men have clearly recognized it, and it is this which has caused us to have such fine works concerning the truth of the Christian religion, and so many excellent proofs as have been put forward against the heathen and other unbelievers, ancient and modern . . . unless to believe signifies to recite or repeat or to let pass without troubling themselves, as many people do." Leibniz, *New Essays*, 581.

161. Frank, *Theologische Philosophie*, 74.

162. Frank, *Theologische Philosophie*, 155, forerunner of the *Monadology*, 198, 203.

163. Jordan, *Reunion*, 1-20. "In the youth of Leibniz the universities were not so much centers of learning as centers of confessional prejudice, and even the most liberal of them, the University of Helmstedt, had difficulty in securing a free and liberal discussion of any question. . . . 'Not a few Princes were drawn towards Rome by the natural affinity between State absolutism and ecclesiastical concentration, agreeing with the Jesuits that obedience is

the only remedy against dissidency and insubordination to authority in Church and State" (Jordan, 18). Jordan rightly locates the young Leibniz in this "disillusionment with Protestantism" following the Thirty Years' War (6). Likewise Loemker: "Leibniz undertook to write a harmonizing and persuasive Christian apologetic and like Malebranche, he considered his entire philosophy as an argument, addressed to modern man, for the Christian faith." Loemker, *Struggle for Synthesis,* 59. "But the tattered remnants of that 'seamless robe of Christ,' the church, left after the Reformation and Counter-Reformation in the preceding century, evoked bitterness and hatreds far deeper than any controversies in the field of letters" (Loemker, 54). He also mentions the Calixtus connection (83).

164. John Hedley Brooke, *Science and Religion: Some Historical Perspective* (Cambridge: Cambridge University Press, 1993), 275.

165. Brooke, *Science and Religion,* 336.

166. Brooke, *Science and Religion,* 337.

167. Brooke, *Science and Religion,* 336.

168. Brooke, *Science and Religion,* 337.

169. Brooke, *Science and Religion,* 337.

170. Loemker, *Struggle for Synthesis,* 87.

171. Loemker, *Struggle for Synthesis,* 87.

Notes to Chapter 6

1. "By 1737, there was . . . radical uncertainty about how to read the work, which . . . 'divided learned and Christian Europe.' Was the work optimistic or pessimistic? An occasional piece currying favor or a serious contribution? Was the writer a friend of religion or a Spinozist in disguise . . . a sort of relativism? Was not the attribution of perfection to this world a denial of Paradise?" Catherine Wilson, "The Reception of Leibniz in the 18th Century," in *The Cambridge Companion to Leibniz,* ed. N. Jolley (Cambridge, U.K., and New York: Cambridge University Press, 1995), 452.

2. Ezio Vailati, *Leibniz and Clarke: A Study of Their Correspondence* (Oxford: Oxford University Press, 1997), 36-37.

3. Vailati, *Leibniz and Clarke,* 90.

4. Michael Allen Gillespie, *Nihilism before Nietzsche* (Chicago: University of Chicago Press, 1996), 26-27.

5. Martin Luther, *The Bondage of the Will,* trans. J. I. Packer and O. R. Johnston (Grand Rapids: Revell, 2000), 70.

6. Gillespie, *Nihilism before Nietzsche,* 1-63.

7. Edward T. Oakes, for example, calls attention to the impact on Barth of Erich Przywara's criticism of Lutheran "theopanism." *Pattern of Redemption: The Theology of Hans Urs von Balthasar* (New York: Continuum, 2002), 15-44.

8. Also in the state of grace, e.g., the explanation of thesis 27 of the Heidelberg Disputation: *Luther's Works: The American Edition,* ed. J. Pelikan et al., 55 vols. (St. Louis: Concordia; Philadelphia: Fortress, 1960-), 31:56-57; hereafter cited as *LW.* Or the 1519 "Two Kinds of Righteousness": "The second kind of righteousness is our proper righteousness, not because we alone work it, but because we work with that first and alien righteousness." *LW* 31:299.

9. Oakes, *Pattern of Redemption,* 36. See above, chapter 5, n. 87.

10. Luther, *Bondage*, 216.

11. Luther, *Bondage*, 65.

12. Luther, *Bondage*, 209.

13. Luther, *Bondage*, 215.

14. Luther, *Bondage*, 270.

15. Luther, *Bondage*, 268.

16. Luther, *Bondage*, 291-92.

17. R. M. Adams, "Leibniz's Conception of Religion," in *Proceedings of the Twentieth World Congress of Philosophy* (1998), 7:67.

18. Gottfried Wilhelm Leibniz, *Writings on China*, ed. D. J. Cook and H. Rosemont, Jr. (Chicago and La Salle, Ill.: Open Court, 1994), 94.

19. Leibniz, *Writings on China*, 95.

20. Leibniz, *Writings on China*, 72. The passage continues: "The Taike is the power or first principle; the Li is wisdom which contains the ideas or essences of things; the primitive Ether is the will or desire — what we call spirit — from which activity and creation is effected."

21. Adams, "Leibniz's Conception of Religion," 63-67.

22. Adams, "Leibniz's Conception of Religion," 68.

23. G. W. Leibniz, *Philosophical Papers and Letters: A Selection*, trans. and ed. Leroy E. Loemker, 2 vols. (Chicago: University of Chicago Press, 1956), 814-15; hereafter cited as Loemker, *Papers*.

24. Loemker, *Papers*, 814-15. Confirming the target of his polemic, Leibniz continues: "And, what reduces to the same thing, God would be the nature and substance of all things — a doctrine of most evil repute, which a writer who was subtle indeed, but irreligious, in recent years imposed upon the world, or at least revived" (815).

25. Leibniz, "Principles of Nature and Grace, Based on Reason" (1714), in Leibniz, *Philosophical Texts*, trans. R. S. Woolhouse and R. Francks (Oxford: Oxford University Press, 1998), 262.

26. Riley, *Leibniz' Universal Jurisprudence*, acknowledges, without the author's view sufficiently weighing, Leibniz's debts to the Gospel of John, 142-43; Luther, 143-44; and Augustine, 193-95, in his notion of charity that takes its own pleasure at the perfection of another, enjoying for its own sake even if without utility.

27. For "God's perfections are not only 'univocal' with the attributes of his finite creations, but are, with finite limitations, identical with them." Leroy E. Loemker, *Struggle for Synthesis: The Seventeenth Century Background of Leibniz's Synthesis of Order and Freedom* (Cambridge: Harvard University Press, 1972), 21.

28. Riley, *Leibniz' Universal Jurisprudence*, 17.

29. Loemker, *Papers*, 408.

30. Loemker, *Papers*, 408.

31. Loemker, *Papers*, 228.

32. Loemker, *Papers*, 228, emphasis added.

33. G. W. Leibniz, *Theodicy: Essays on the Goodness of God, the Freedom of Man, and the Origin of Evil*, trans. E. M. Huggard (Chicago and La Salle, Ill.: Open Court, 1998), 132.

34. G. W. Leibniz, *Discourse on Metaphysics and Other Essays*, trans. D. Garber and R. Ariew (Indianapolis: Hackett, 1991), 13.

35. Leibniz, *Discourse*, 14.

36. As Riley, *Leibniz' Universal Jurisprudence,* 69, urges, though not to the same end as the author.

37. Leroy T. Howe, "Leibniz on Evil," *Sophia* 10, no. 3 (October 1971): 16-17.

38. Eberhard Jüngel, *God as the Mystery of the World: On the Foundation of the Theology of the Crucified One in the Dispute between Theism and Atheism,* trans. D. L. Guder (Grand Rapids: Eerdmans, 1983), 367.

39. Riley, *Leibniz' Universal Jurisprudence,* 134.

40. Riley, *Leibniz' Universal Jurisprudence,* 135; also 268.

41. Adriaan T. Peperzak, *The Quest for Meaning: Friends of Wisdom from Plato to Levinas* (New York: Fordham University Press, 2003), 184.

42. Peperzak, *The Quest for Meaning,* 186-87.

43. Peperzak, *The Quest for Meaning,* 188.

44. Thomas E. Baril, "A Fresh Defense of Leibniz's Concept of Human Freedom," *Southwest Philosophy Review* 15, no. 1 (1999): 132, cited from David Blumenfeld, "Freedom, Contingency, and Things Possible in Themselves," *Philosophy and Phenomenological Research* 49, no. 1 (September 1988): 100-101. See also Robert Merrihew Adams, "The Metaphysics of Counterfactual Nonidentity," in Adams, *Leibniz: Determinist, Theist, Idealist* (Oxford: Oxford University Press, 1994), 75-110.

45. Baril, "Defense," 127.

46. Karl Barth, *Church Dogmatics* III/2, trans. Harold Knight et al. (Edinburgh: T. & T. Clark, 1960), 333.

47. "If one abstracts God from Leibnizianism one is left with this morally attractive residue . . . charity, benevolence, generosity — [which] may struggle against what he took to be necessarily true. That, indeed, is the problem in Leibniz. For all of Leibniz' most serious problems flow from God. . . . It might at first seem more promising, then, to 'bracket' God. . . . But this is just what one cannot do: for Leibniz there is one necessary being whose essence entails existence. The 'Anselmian' strand in Leibniz cannot be lifted out — except as a provisional thought-experiment." Riley, *Leibniz' Universal Jurisprudence,* 265.

48. "So there are for Anselm some things not even God can do, not because he lacks ability or strength, but because they are inconceivable for God. He cannot do what is not fitting, not because he is impotent in this regard, but because there is no way he would be found doing what is unfitting. It is in this sense that Anselm contends that God cannot do without atonement if he desires to save his people." Burnell F. Eckhardt, Jr., *Anselm and Luther on the Atonement: Was It "Necessary"?* (San Francisco: Mellen Research University Press, 1992), 25. In this light Luther "begins to look very Anselmian. . . . Faith per se is not really sufficient alone; its sufficiency is derived entirely from the sufficiency of Christ in whom it trusts. . . . It is not the believing which in itself constitutes righteousness before God, but rather the Christ in whom one believes" (30). "Luther's placement of so much stress on the fact that this righteousness of Christ is that by which sin is cancelled points to a tacit agreement in principle with Anselm's refusal to skirt the justice of God. . . . Althaus (1966) agrees: 'God cannot simply forget about his wrath and show his mercy to sinners if his righteousness is not satisfied. Luther, like Anselm, views Christ's work in terms of satisfaction' citing Luther: 'Now although God purely out of grace does not impute our sins to us, still he did not want to do this unless his law and his righteousness had received a more than adequate satisfaction. This gracious imputation must first be purchased and won from his righteous-

ness for us' [*Dr. Martin Luthers Werke* (Weimar: Böhlau, 1883-1993), 10I/1:470.18-22; hereafter cited as WA]." Eckhardt, 31.

49. Philip Melanchthon, *On Christian Doctrine: Loci Communes, 1555*, trans. C. L. Manschreck (Grand Rapids: Baker, 1982), 6.

50. Leibniz, cited from E. Bodemann, "Die Leibniz Hanschriften der koeniglichen öffentlichen Bibliothek zu Hannover" (Hanover, 1890), 58, in Nicholas Jolley, "Leibniz on Locke and Socinianism," *Journal of the History of Ideas* 39 (1978): 250.

51. The fifth ecumenical council held at Constantinople in 553 affirmed the "hypostatic," i.e., "personal," union, i.e., that the agent/patient in the incarnation in the second person of the Trinity who unites the human nature to himself and makes it His very own, His alone, this one human organism born of Mary (although all other humans share with this human a common nature). The decisive import then: "If anyone does not confess that our Lord Jesus Christ who was crucified in the flesh is true God and the Lord of Glory and one of the Holy Trinity, let him be anathema." *Nicene and Post-Nicene Fathers*, 2nd ser., 14:314.

52. Leibniz, *Theodicy*, 130.

53. Patrick Riley, "An Unpublished Lecture by Leibniz on the Greeks as Founders of Rational Theology: Its Relation to His 'Universal Jurisprudence,'" *Journal of the History of Philosophy* 14 (1976): 205-16.

54. Jolley, "Socinianism," 250.

55. Michael Latzer, "Leibniz's Conception of Metaphysical Evil," *Journal of the History of Ideas* 26 (1988): 14.

56. Diogenes Allen, "The Theological Relevance of Leibniz's Theodicy," *Studia Leibnitiana. Supplementa* 14, no. 3 (1972): 88.

57. It is true that Clarke was an interventionist deist, and in this respect did not conform to the general views of contemporary deism; he claimed to defend the intelligent providence of God, and this is exactly why he and Leibniz could engage in a meaningful debate over what natural theology could ascertain and why. In Leibniz's view, Clarke's view amounted to a finite God as the "soul of the world" who could, as cosmic need required it, intervene "from the top downward." Leibniz, recall, does not in general adopt such a view. For him soul and body act each on their own principles according to the preestablished harmony, and thus Leibniz on general grounds would have rejected interventionism, while regarding miracles as natural products of providential ordering through angelic mediation, i.e., mechanisms beyond our human comprehension yet essentially natural. The mysteries on the other hand are divine acts, but predetermined for purposes of grace. Vailati lays out the difference between Clarke's "soul of the world" and Leibniz's *intelligentia supramundana*. Vailati, *Leibniz and Clarke*, 8-9.

58. Allen, "Relevance," 88.

59. "A Christian view of the things will be one which orders the whole open field of possible sentences or beliefs so as to achieve at least consistency with a christological and trinitarian center; in this way it will match its epistemic priorities to its truth commitments, and so hope to come up with a plausible interpretation of the whole field." Bruce D. Marshall, *Trinity and Truth* (Cambridge: Cambridge University Press, 2000), 140.

60. Karl Barth, *Christ and Adam: Man and Humanity in Romans 5*, trans. T. A. Smail (New York: Macmillan, 1968).

61. Latzer, "Metaphysical Evil," 15.

62. Leibniz, *Theodicy*, 134.

63. Leibniz, *Theodicy*, 132.

64. Leibniz, *Theodicy*, 126.

65. Adams, "Leibniz's Conception of Religion," 62.

66. Leibniz, *Theodicy*, 175.

67. G. W. Leibniz, *New Essays concerning Human Understanding*, trans. Alfred Gideon Langley (La Salle, Ill.: Open Court, 1949), 595.

68. Leibniz, *New Essays*, 590-91.

69. Loemker, *Papers*, 332.

70. Loemker, *Papers*, 334.

71. Loemker, *Papers*, 336.

72. Loemker, *Papers*, 336.

73. Loemker, *Papers*, 338.

74. This rationalist bias then must either revert to the atomism of an asocial core individuality or the collectivism of a single, social rationality — so Bonhoeffer argued in his survey of modern philosophy, *Sanctorum Communio: A Theological Study of the Sociology of the Church*, trans. R. Krauss and N. Lukens, Dietrich Bonhoeffer Works, vol. 1 (Minneapolis: Fortress, 1998), 24-80, leading up to his appeal to Leibniz's monadology. "The tragedy of all idealist philosophy was that it never ultimately broke through to personal spirit. However, its monumental perception, especially in Hegel, was that the principle of spirit is something objective, extending beyond everything individual — that there is an objective spirit, the spirit of sociality, which is distinct in itself from all individual spirit. Our task is to affirm the latter without denying the former, to retain the perception without committing the error." Bonhoeffer, 74. This task led Bonhoeffer to break with the general pneumatology, even in Hegel's highly dialectical attempt to save this tradition after Kant, and instead to think of the community of the church as a society, a public, of the objective Holy Spirit.

75. Vailati, *Leibniz and Clarke*, 51.

76. See chapter 5, n. 87 above.

77. Rene Descartes, *Meditations on First Philosophy*, trans. D. A. Cress (Indianapolis: Hackett, 1993), 3.51; pp. 34-35.

78. Anselm, *Monologian*, chapters 75–80; see Jasper Hopkins, *A New Interpretive Translation of St. Anselm's Monologian and Proslogian* (Minneapolis: Arthur J. Banning Press, 1986), 205-11.

79. Anselm, *Monologian*, chapters 28–65; see Hopkins, 131-91.

80. Anselm, *Monologian*, chapters 66–74; see Hopkins, 192-204.

81. Descartes, *Meditations on First Philosophy*, 3.36; p. 25.

82. Gillespie, *Nihilism before Nietzsche*, 54.

83. David Norton, "Leibniz and Bayle: Manicheism and Dialectic," *Journal of the History of Philosophy* 2 (1964): 23-36.

84. Gregory Brown, "Miracles in the Best of All Possible Worlds: Leibniz's Dilemma and Leibniz's Razor," *History of Philosophy Quarterly* 12, no. 1 (January 1995): 19-39; Maria Rosa Antognazza, "The Defense of the Mysteries of the Trinity and the Incarnation: An Example of Leibniz's 'Other Reason,'" *British Journal for the History of Philosophy* 9, no. 2 (June 2001): 283-309.

85. Michael Latzer, "Leibniz's Reading of Augustine," *Il Cannocciale* (Rome: Carucci), January-April 1999, 17-33. "It must, however, be admitted that in many instances we cannot

avoid yielding to authority. St. Augustine has produced a quite remarkable book 'De utilitate credendi,' which deserves to be read on this subject. . . . [Regarding received opinions:] although we are not obliged to follow them always without proofs, we are no more authorized to destroy them in the mind of another without having contrary proofs. This it is which does not allow us to change anything without reason." Leibniz, *New Essays*, 616.

86. Leibniz, *Theodicy*, 62.

87. Leibniz, *Theodicy*, 59-60.

88. Leibniz, *Theodicy*, 60.

89. Irenaeus, *Against the Heretics* 1.22.1, in *Ante-Nicene Fathers*, p. 347.

90. Irenaeus, *Against the Heretics* 1.10.3, in *Ante-Nicene Fathers*, p. 331, emphasis mine.

91. Leibniz, *Theodicy*, 127.

92. Robert W. Jenson, "An Ontology of Freedom in the *De Servo Arbitrio* of Luther," *Modern Theology* 10, no. 3 (July 1994): 250.

93. Jenson, "An Ontology," 251.

94. Jenson, "An Ontology," 251.

95. See "The Real World and the Christian Ideas," in Josiah Royce, *The Problem of Christianity* (Washington, D.C.: Catholic University of America Press, 2001), part 2, pp. 229-406.

96. Jean-Luc Marion, whose opposing thesis is shortly to be discussed, concludes his important survey of seventeenth-century metaphysical ideas of God with this. Pascal takes up the Cartesian notion of the divine as infinity, to work out "the most radical critique of Descartes imaginable and, in general, the most radical critique of any metaphysical conception of God." Marion says there are two reasons for this. "First, the concept of infinity does not uniquely pick out God. . . . Second . . . 'this knowledge, without Jesus Christ, is useless and sterile.' What is at stake for Pascal is not to know God, but to love Him; the real obstacle to acknowledging Him does not rest in the uncertainty of the understanding, but in the arrogance of the will. . . . The project of proving the existence or determining the essence of God must yield to the recognition of a God to be loved, because He Himself loved first. . . . Pascal reaches an entirely different transcendence." Marion, "The Idea of God," in *The Cambridge History of Seventeenth Century Philosophy* (Cambridge: Cambridge University Press, 1998), 292. The gravamen of this argument, I shall argue, is correct, but it really misses the theological motive in Leibniz's "metaphysical" notion of God as the world's *ultima ratio* — as if one could love God who first loved us, without knowing that I am His creature together with all created, redeemed and destined by this *Ultima Ratio* for fulfillment.

97. Donald L. Perry, "Leibniz' Answer to Descartes on the Creation of Eternal Truth," *Southwest Philosophy Review* 12, no. 1 (1996): 20 n. 14. This splendid account argues to the conclusion: "there is no dilemma. I have argued that the Cartesian view that God's will is the ground of all truth is internally inconsistent. . . . I have also pointed out that Leibniz does not hold that the eternal truths are entirely independent of God, but in some way depend on his understanding. . . . Thus God's inability to understand or will the impossible is not a limitation of his freedom" (19). Leibniz's view of the eternal truths as originally residing in God's mind, and thus grounding common notions with human minds, may have its pedigree in Anselm, *Monologian*, chapter 34; see Hopkins, 145. Leibniz himself writes: "But it will be asked in reply, where would these ideas be if not mind existed, and what then would become of the real ground of this certainty of the eternal truths? This leads us finally to the ultimate ground of truths, viz.: to that Supreme and Universal Mind, which cannot fail to ex-

ist, whose understanding, to speak truly, is the region of eternal truths, as St. Augustine has recognized and expresses in a sufficiently vivid way . . . these necessary truths contain the determining reason and the regulating principle of existences themselves, and, in a word, the laws of the universe. Thus these necessary truths being anterior to the existence of contingent beings, must be grounded in the existence of a necessary substance." Leibniz, *New Essays*, 516-17. The editor provides *De trinitate* 10.14.14.7.

98. For the next two paragraphs, all citations Loemker, *Papers*, 420-21.

99. Marion, "The Idea of God," 274.

100. Marion, "The Idea of God," 291.

101. See the introduction, n. 24 above.

102. Marion, "The Idea of God," 292.

103. Marion, "The Idea of God," 274.

104. Marion, "The Idea of God," 282-83.

105. Marion, "The Idea of God," 282-83.

106. Interestingly, El Fadl, from the expressly nontrinitarian tradition of mainline Islam, argues in precise parallel against the *deus exlex* of the "puritanical" Muslims. Khaled Abou El Fadl, *The Great Theft: Wrestling Islam from the Extremists* (San Francisco: HarperCollins, 2005), 129-41.

107. Leibniz, *Theodicy*, 216.

108. Luther, *Bondage*, 81.

109. Leibniz commented on Pascal in a letter of 1683: "Pascal had recently died when I lived in Paris, but his sister was there, a learned and clever woman, and also his nephews, the sons of his sister. I had many associations with them. . . . I will say one thing. Pascal paid attention only to moral arguments, such as he excellently presented in his little posthumous book of Thoughts, but he did not put much value on the metaphysical arguments which Plato and St. Thomas, and other philosophers and theologians, have used in proving the divine existence and the immortality of the soul. In this I do not agree with him. I think that God speaks to us, not merely in sacred and civil history, or even in natural history, but also internally, within our mind, through thoughts which abstract from matter and are eternal." Loemker, *Papers*, 423.

110. Daniel C. Dennett, *Darwin's Dangerous Idea: Evolution and the Meanings of Life* (New York: Touchstone, 1996), 48-60.

111. Dennett, *Darwin's Dangerous Idea*, 17-22.

112. Dennett, *Darwin's Dangerous Idea*, 17.

113. Dennett, *Darwin's Dangerous Idea*, 514-15.

114. Richard Weikart, *From Hitler to Darwin: Evolutionary Ethics, Eugenics, and Racism in Germany* (New York: Palgrave Macmillan, 2004), is an impressive documentation of intellectual history that is ignored at peril. More broadly and with greater balance is Michael Burleigh's *The Third Reich: A New History* (New York: Hill and Wang, 2000). In Burleigh's words: "an Aryan-Germanic mission to redeem Graeco-Roman civilization, to affirm a non-Jewish or de-orientalized Christianity and to lead the peoples into a 'new, splendid and light-filled future,' which only the Jews issuing from darkness could thwart. A mutant, racialized Christianity, divested of unGerman 'Jewish' elements, and purged of humanitarian sentimentality, that is sin, guilt, and pity, was a very potent ideal indeed. . . . In this sense, Nazism was neither simply science run riot, however much this definition suits critics of

modern genetics, nor bastardized Christianity, however much this suits those who see Nazism simply as the outgrowth of Christian anti-Semitism" (14).

115. Vailati, *Leibniz and Clarke,* 154.

116. George L. Murphy, *The Cosmos in the Light of the Cross* (Harrisburg, Pa., London, and New York: Trinity, 2003). This following discussion of Murphy is based upon the author's review, which originally appeared in *Seminary Ridge Review* 8, no. 1 (Autumn 2005): 55-58.

117. Murphy, *The Cosmos,* 82. In accord with this, Murphy approvingly cites Thomas's stricture on the play of worldviews in theology: "the opinion is false of those who asserted that it made no difference to the truth of faith what anyone holds about creatures . . . error concerning creatures, by subjecting them to causes other than God, spills over into false opinion about God" (74).

118. Murphy, *The Cosmos,* 2.

119. Murphy, *The Cosmos,* 61, 79.

120. Murphy, *The Cosmos,* 124.

121. Murphy, *The Cosmos,* 22.

122. Thus Murphy is closer to Leibniz than to Thomas, since he does not, like Thomas, think that God could have created a perfect world.

123. Murphy, *The Cosmos,* 87.

124. Murphy, *The Cosmos,* 87.

125. Murphy, *The Cosmos,* 3.

126. Murphy, *The Cosmos,* 200.

127. Murphy, *The Cosmos,* 62.

128. Murphy, *The Cosmos,* 62.

129. Stephen Hawking, with Leonard Mlodinow, *A Briefer History of Time* (New York: Bantam Dell, 2005), 142.

130. Murphy, *The Cosmos,* 81.

131. Murphy, *The Cosmos,* 86.

132. Murphy, *The Cosmos,* 170.

133. Murphy, *The Cosmos,* 49.

134. Luther, *Bondage,* 80.

135. Leibniz, *Theodicy,* 395. "Mr. Hobbes refuses to listen to anything about moral necessity either, on the ground that everything really happens through physical causes . . . blind necessity whereby according to Epicurus, Strato, Spinoza and perhaps Mr. Hobbes, things exist without intelligence and without choice, and consequently without God" (395).

136. Robert Kolb calls attention to the passage, lamenting the terminology of "necessity" inserted by the editor G. Roerer in the year Luther died: Kolb, *Bound Choice, Election, and the Wittenberg Theological Method: From Martin Luther to the Formula of Concord,* Lutheran Quarterly Books (Grand Rapids: Eerdmans, 2005), 27. Kolb argues that Luther's real idea of creative divine foreknowledge as grounds for certainty about divine faithfulness to promises distinguishes itself "very clearly from the determinism of philosophical systems that assign to an impersonal fate the liability for all that happens" (34). See Luther's extended discussion from late in life in his commentary on Gen. 26:9-10 in *LW* 5:42-50.

137. Leibniz, *Theodicy,* 395.

138. Leibniz, *Theodicy,* 298. *Pace* Sven K. Knebel, "Necessitas Moralis ad Optimum: Zum historischen Hintergrund der Wahl der bessten aller möglichen Welten," *Studia*

Leibnitiana 23, no. 1 (1991): 3-24, which argues Leibniz's dependence on Jesuit-Molinist thought. This is a plausible reading on account of the way late Melanchthonianism sided with the Molinists against the Jansenists, but the sources of this move lie in Leibniz's own Lutheran tradition.

139. Luther rejected the antecedent/consequent distinction, *Bondage*, 82, 217-12, as an evasion of divine reprobation.

140. Leibniz, *New Essays*, 187.

141. Riley, *Leibniz' Universal Jurisprudence*, 77.

142. Leibniz, *Theodicy*, 91.

143. Luther had attacked this "scholastic" doctrine of the nominalists when he declared: "The person who believes that he can obtain grace by doing what is in him adds sin to sin so that he becomes doubly guilty." *LW* 31:40.

144. Leibniz, *Theodicy*, 176. Leibniz's early dialogue between Poliander and Theophile presents Poliander as an "apostolic missionary" of Rome who "had grown old in controversy and had not hesitation in starting in on people," and Theophile, "a very honorable man of the Augsburg Confession" who "defended himself with a certain self-effacement and simplicity which gave ample evidence of great resources and an enlightened and tranquil soul." Theophile: "Whoever truly loves God above all things will not fail to do what he knows conform to his commands. That is why it is necessary to begin with this love, since charity and justice are its inescapable results." Poliander: "A pagan philosopher can love God above all things, since his reason can teach him that God is an infinitely perfect and a supremely lovable being. But this will not make him a Christian, for he may not have heard anything about Jesus Christ, without whom there is no salvation. So the love of God is not enough." Theophile: "This question of the salvation of pagans is too much for me. However, I have much liking for the ideas of certain learned and pious theologians who believe that God will illumine all those who sincerely seek him . . . following the incontestable rule that God does not deny his grace to those who do their part." Loemker, *Papers*, 326-27. This latter *facere quod in se* is the shibboleth for which Leibniz was criticized by orthodox Lutherans.

145. Leibniz, *Theodicy*, 69.

146. Leibniz, *Theodicy*, 69-70.

147. The German expression is my attribution of his position, not Schwarzwäller's own language.

148. Klaus Schwarzwäller, "Sibboleth: Die Interpretation von Luthers Schrift De servo arbitrio seit Theodosius Harnack: Ein systematisch-kritischer Überblick," *Theologische Existenz heute*, no. 153 (Munich: Chr. Kaiser Verlag, 1969), 12, my translation.

149. Loemker, *Papers*, 404.

150. Schwarzwäller, "Sibboleth," 12.

151. Schwarzwäller, "Sibboleth," 9.

152. Schwarzwäller, "Sibboleth," 11.

153. See Luther's December 28, 1544, sermon on Titus 3 on the unity of the Trinity in the work of salvation. WA 49:645-51.

154. Leibniz, *Theodicy*, 67. See Chapter 1, n. 1 above.

155. Leibniz, *Theodicy*, 67.

156. Leibniz, *Theodicy*, 167.

157. Leibniz, *Theodicy*, 274.

158. Evidently with some justice. See William J. Bouwsma, *John Calvin: A Sixteenth Century Portrait* (Oxford: Oxford University Press, 1988), 162-76.

159. Leibniz, *Theodicy*, 328.

160. Leibniz, *Theodicy*, 127.

161. Leibniz, *Theodicy*, 67.

162. Leibniz, *Theodicy*, 282-83. In the conclusion of the *Dialogue between Polidore and Theophile*, Leibniz puts it this way: "It can be said that this resignation of our will to that of God, whom we have every reason to trust, follows from the truly divine love, whereas our dissatisfaction and every sore disappointment in mundane matters contain something of hatred toward God, which is the ultimate of misery" and "we ought to give witness of the supreme love which we bear toward God through the charity we owe to our neighbor . . . to contribute something to the public good. For it is God who is the Lord; it is to him that the public good pertains as his own. And all that we do unto the least of these." Loemker, *Papers*, 337.

163. Leibniz, *Theodicy*, 58.

164. Leibniz, *Theodicy*, 58.

165. Leibniz, *Theodicy*, 58-59.

166. Leibniz, *Theodicy*, 237.

167. Leibniz, *Theodicy*, 59-60; cf. 125-26, 62.

168. Leibniz rejected double truth theories. Loemker, *Papers*, 581.

169. Paul R. Hinlicky, "Luther's Anti-Docetism in the *Disputatio de divinitate et humanitate Christi* (1540)," in *Creator est creatura: Luthers Christologie als Lehre von der Idiomenkommunikation*, ed. O. Bayer and Benjamin Gleede (Berlin and New York: De Gruyter, 2007), 169-80.

170. Leibniz, *Theodicy*, 81.

171. Luther, *Bondage*, 317, emphasis added.

172. Luther, *Bondage*, 317.

173. Leibniz, *Theodicy*, 120.

174. In the *New Essays* Leibniz takes direct aim at the *credo quia absurdam est*: "St Paul speaks more justly when he says that the wisdom of God is foolishness with men; because men judge of things only according to their experience, which is extremely limited, and everything not agreeing therewith appears to them an absurdity. But this judgment is very rash, for there is indeed an infinite number of natural things which would pass with us as absurd, if they were told us, as the ice which was said to cover our rivers appeared to the king of Siam. But the order of nature itself not being of any metaphysical necessity, is grounded only in the good pleasure of God, so that he may deviate therefrom by the superior reasons of grace, although he must proceed therein only upon good proofs which can come only from the testimony of God himself, to which we must defer absolutely when it is duly verified" (582).

175. Leibniz, *Theodicy*, 101.

176. Leibniz, *Theodicy*, 180. "[I]t is too great and too beautiful for spirits with our present range to be able to perceive it so soon. To try to see it here is like wishing to take a novel by the tail and to claim to have deciphered the plot from the first book; the beauty of a novel, instead, is great in the degree that order emerges from very great apparent confusion. . . . But what is only suspense [*curiosite*] and beauty in novels, which imitate creation, so to speak, is also utility and wisdom in this great and true poem, this word-by-word creation, the uni-

verse. The beauty and justice of the divine government have hidden in part from our eyes." Loemker, *Papers,* 919. The hiddenness of God's plan is "proper in order that there may be more exercise of free virtue, wisdom, and a love of God which is not mercenary, since the rewards and punishments are still outwardly invisible and appear only to the eyes of our reason or faith. This I find to be a good thing here, since the true faith is based on reason. . . . To recognize this point is to have a natural foundation for faith, hope, and the love of God, since these virtues are based on a knowledge of the divine perfections." Loemker, 920.

177. Steven Nadler, "'Tange montes et fumigabunt': Arnauld on the Theodicies of Malebranche and Leibniz," in *Interpreting Arnauld* (Toronto and Buffalo: University of Toronto Press, 1996), 156.

178. Leibniz, *Theodicy,* 99.

179. R. W. Southern, *Saint Anselm: A Portrait in a Landscape* (Cambridge: Cambridge University Press, 1993), 123-27.

180. Leibniz, *Theodicy,* 98.

181. Leibniz, *Theodicy,* 96-97.

182. Leibniz, *Theodicy,* 101.

183. Leibniz, *Theodicy,* 181.

184. Leibniz, *Theodicy,* 167-68.

185. Leibniz, *Theodicy,* 917.

186. Leibniz, *New Essays,* 474.

Notes to Conclusion

1. Vladimir Lossky, *In the Image and Likeness of God,* ed. J. H. Erickson and T. E. Bird (Crestwood, N.Y.: St. Vladimir's Seminary Press, 1985), 120.

2. For a fuller consideration, see Paul R. Hinlicky, "Theological Anthropology: Towards Integrating Theosis and Justification by Faith," *Journal of Ecumenical Studies* 34, no. 1 (Winter 1997): 38-73.

3. Karen Armstrong, *Muhammad: A Prophet for Our Time* (New York: HarperCollins, 2006), 96-123.

4. Martin Luther, *The Bondage of the Will,* trans. J. I. Packer and O. R. Johnston (Grand Rapids: Revell, 2000), 294.

5. Lossky, *Image,* 139.

6. Lossky, *Image,* 139.

7. See chapter 3, n. 3 above.

8. Regin Prenter, "Karl Barths Umbildung der traditionellen Zweinaturlehre in lutherischer Beleuchtung," in *Theologie und Gottesdienst* (Arhus: Forlaget Aros; Göttingen: Vandenhoeck & Ruprecht, 1977). See also Jorg Baur, "Ubiquität," in *Creator est creatura: Luthers Christologie als Lehre von der Idiomenkommunikation,* ed. O. Bayer and Benjamin Gleede (Berlin and New York: De Gruyter, 2007), 186-301.

9. Dietrich Bonhoeffer, *Christ the Center,* trans. E. H. Robertson (New York: Harper and Row, 1978), 89-98.

10. "[T]he second identity of God is directly the human person of the Gospels, in that he is the one who stands to the Father in the relation of being eternally begotten by him."

Robert W. Jenson, *Systematic Theology,* 2 vols. (New York and Oxford: Oxford University Press, 1997), 1:137.

11. Christoph Schwöbel, "Theology," in *The Cambridge Companion to Karl Barth,* ed. John Webster (Cambridge: Cambridge University Press, 2000), 34.

12. Philip Jenkins, *The Next Christendom: The Coming of Global Christianity,* revised and expanded ed. (Oxford: Oxford University Press, 2007).

13. Luther, *Bondage,* 268.

14. See Luther's "Promotionsdisputation of Petrus Hegemon," in D. Bielfeldt, M. Mattox, and P. Hinlicky, *The Substance of the Faith: Luther's Doctrinal Theology for Today* (Minneapolis: Fortress, 2008), 204-7.

15. Origen, *Against Celsus* 3.70, in *Ante-Nicene Fathers,* 4:492.

16. Anthony Meredith, S.J., *Gregory of Nyssa* (London and New York: Routledge, 1999), 76, 80, 83.

17. Richard A. Muller, *Post-Reformation Reformed Dogmatics: The Rise and Development of Reformed Orthodoxy, ca. 1520 to ca. 1725,* vol. 1, *Prolegomena to Theology,* 2nd ed. (Grand Rapids: Baker, 2003), 178.

18. Nicholas Wolterstorff, *John Locke and the Ethics of Belief,* Cambridge Studies in Religion and Critical Thought (Cambridge: Cambridge University Press, 1996), 246.

19. Richard P. Heitzenrater, "Tradition and History," *Church History* 71, no. 3 (September 2002): 636-38.

20. "I am not, however, of the opinion that we despise antiquity in the matter of religion; and I also believe that we may say that God has preserved the truly ecumenical councils hitherto from all error contrary to wholesome doctrine. For the rest, sectarian prejudice is a strange thing. I have seen people embrace with ardor an opinion solely because it is contrary to that of a man of a religion or of a nation which they do not like." G. W. Leibniz, *New Essays concerning Human Understanding,* trans. Alfred Gideon Langley (La Salle, Ill.: Open Court, 1949), 618.

21. Patrick Riley, ed., *Leibniz: Political Writings,* 2nd ed. (Cambridge: Cambridge University Press, 2001), 103.

22. Alasdair MacIntyre, *Three Rival Versions of Moral Inquiry: Encyclopedia, Genealogy, and Tradition* (Notre Dame, Ind.: University of Notre Dame Press, 1990).

23. Wolfhart Pannenberg, *Systematic Theology,* vol. 1, trans. G. W. Bromiley (Grand Rapids: Eerdmans, 1991), 117.

24. Pannenberg, *Systematic Theology,* 109.

25. Pannenberg, *Systematic Theology,* 113.

26. Pannenberg, *Systematic Theology,* 107.

27. Pannenberg, *Systematic Theology,* 114.

28. H. A. Preuss and E. Smits, eds., *The Doctrine of Man in Classical Lutheran Theology* (Minneapolis: Augsburg, 1962), 39, emphasis mine.

29. Leibniz, *New Essays,* 502-3.

30. Leibniz, *New Essays,* 504.

31. Leibniz, *New Essays,* 504-5.

32. Robert Merrihew Adams, *Leibniz: Determinist, Theist, Idealist* (Oxford: Oxford University Press, 1994), 72.

33. Eberhard Jüngel, *God as the Mystery of the World: On the Foundation of the Theology of the Crucified One in the Dispute between Theism and Atheism,* trans. D. L. Guder (Grand

Rapids: Eerdmans, 1983), 33. The judgment follows a perfunctory discussion of Leibniz's principle of sufficient reason as necessitarian (29-30), although Jüngel limits his criticism by saying that he is "interested only in the proposition about the ground" that, as Jüngel thinks following Barth, domesticates the experience of nothingness.

34. Jüngel, *Mystery,* 34.

35. Jüngel, *Mystery,* 34.

36. Jüngel, *Mystery,* 34.

37. Jüngel, *Mystery,* 35.

38. A splendid example of what I have in mind is Fritz Oehlschlaeger, *Love and Good Reasons: Postliberal Approaches to Christian Ethics and Literature* (Durham, N.C., and London: Duke University Press, 2003).

39. Hinlicky, *Substance of the Faith,* 155.

40. Jenson, *Systematic Theology,* 2:305.

41. Jenson, *Systematic Theology,* 2:305.

42. Dietrich Bonhoeffer, *Ethics,* trans. N. H. Smith (New York: Macmillan, 1978), 26.

43. Bonhoeffer, *Ethics,* 206.

44. See above, chapter 6, n. 106.

Works Cited

Adams, Robert Merrihew. *Leibniz: Determinist, Theist, Idealist.* Oxford: Oxford University Press, 1994.

———. "Leibniz's Conception of Religion." In *Proceedings of the Twentieth World Congress of Philosophy,* 7:57-70. 1998.

Adkins, Brent. *Death and Desire in Hegel, Heidegger, and Deleuze.* Edinburgh: University of Edinburgh Press, 2007.

Aiton, E. J. *Leibniz: A Biography.* Bristol and Boston: Adam Hilger, 1985.

Allen, Diogenes. *Christian Belief in a Postmodern World: The Full Wealth of Conviction.* Louisville: Westminster/John Knox, 1989.

———. "The Theological Relevance of Leibniz's Theodicy." *Studia Leibnitiana. Supplementa* 14, no. 3 (1972).

Allison, Henry E. *The Kant-Eberhard Controversy: An English Translation Together with Supplementary Materials and a Historical-Analytical Introduction of Immanuel Kant's "On a Discovery" according to Which Any New Critique of Pure Reason Has Been Made Superfluous by an Earlier One.* Baltimore and London: Johns Hopkins University Press, 1973.

Antognazza, Maria Rosa. "The Defense of the Mysteries of the Trinity and the Incarnation: An Example of Leibniz's 'Other Reason.'" *British Journal for the History of Philosophy* 9, no. 2 (June 2001): 283-309.

———. *Leibniz on the Trinity and the Incarnation: Reason and Revelation in the Seventeenth Century.* Translated by Gerald Parks. New Haven and London: Yale University Press, 2007.

Arand, Charles P. "Melanchthon's Rhetorical Argument for *Sola Fide* in the Apology." *Lutheran Quarterly* 14, no. 3 (Autumn 2000): 281-308.

Armstrong, Karen. *Muhammad: A Prophet for Our Time.* New York: HarperCollins, 2006.

Asad, Talal. *Formations of the Secular: Christianity, Islam, Modernity.* Stanford: Stanford University Press, 2003.

Augustine. *The City of God.* An abridged version from the translation by G. G. Walsh et al. New York: Doubleday, 1958.

———. *Confessions.* Translated by R. S. Pine-Coffin. New York: Dorset, 1961.

———. *On the Trinity.* Book 8. Translated by E. Hill. New York: New City Press, 1991.

Aune, Michael B. *To Move the Heart: Philip Melanchthon's Rhetorical View of Rite and Its Implications for Contemporary Ritual Theory.* San Francisco: Christian Universities Press, 1994.

Baril, Thomas E. "A Fresh Defense of Leibniz's Concept of Human Freedom." *Southwest Philosophy Review* 15, no. 1 (1999): 125-35.

Barth, Karl. *Christ and Adam: Man and Humanity in Romans 5.* Translated by T. A. Smail with an introduction by W. Pauck. New York: Macmillan, 1968.

———. *Church Dogmatics.* Translated by G. W. Bromiley et al. 13 vols. Edinburgh: T. & T. Clark, 1936-69.

———. *Epistle to the Romans.* Translated by E. C. Hoskyns. London: Oxford University Press, 1972.

———. *From Rousseau to Ritschl.* Translated by B. Cozens. London: SCM, 1959.

Batka, Lubomir. *Peccatum radicale: Eine Studie zu Luthers Erbsuendenverstaendnis in Psalm 51.* Frankfurt am Main: Peter Lang, 2007.

Bauer, Walter. *Orthodoxy and Heresy in Early Christianity.* Edited by R. Kraft and G. Krodel. Philadelphia: Fortress, 1971; reprint, Mifflintown, Pa.: Sigler, 1996.

Bayer, O., and B. Gleede, eds. *Creator est creatura: Luthers Christologie als Lehre von der Idiomenkommunikation.* Berlin and New York: De Gruyter, 2007.

Beck, Lewis White. *Early German Philosophy: Kant and His Predecessors.* Bristol, England: Thoemmes Press, 1996.

Beiser, Frederick C. *The Fate of Reason: German Philosophy from Kant to Fichte.* Cambridge: Harvard University Press, 1987.

Bergvall, Ake. *Augustinian Perspectives in the Renaissance.* Acts Universitatis Upsaliensis Studia Anglistica Upsaliensia 117. Uppsala: Uppsala University, 2001.

Berman, Harold J., and John Witte, Jr. "The Transformation of Western Legal Philosophy in Lutheran Germany." *Southern California Law Review* 62, no. 6 (September 1989): 1575-1660.

Bertram, Robert W. "How Scripture Is Traditioned in the Lutheran Confessions." In *The Quadrilog: Tradition and the Future of Ecumenism; Essays in Honor of George H. Tavard,* edited by Kenneth Hagen. Collegeville, Minn.: Liturgical Press, 1994.

———. "The Human Subject as the Object of Theology: Luther by Way of Barth." Ph.D. diss., University of Chicago, 1964.

Bielfeldt, Dennis. "Semantics, Ontology and the Trinity." In *The Substance of Faith: Luther's Doctrinal Theology for Today,* by Dennis Bielfeldt, Paul R. Hinlicky, and Mickey L. Mattox, 59-130. Minneapolis: Fortress, 2008.

Bonhoeffer, Dietrich. *Christ the Center.* Translated by E. H. Robertson. New York: Harper and Row, 1978.

―――. *The Cost of Discipleship.* Translated by R. H. Fuller. New York: Simon and Schuster, Touchstone Edition, 1995.

―――. *Ethics.* Translated by N. H. Smith. New York: Macmillan, 1978.

―――. *Sanctorum Communio: A Theological Study of the Sociology of the Church.* Translated by R. Krauss and N. Lukens. Dietrich Bonhoeffer Works, vol. 1. Minneapolis: Fortress, 1998.

The Book of Concord: The Confessions of the Evangelical Lutheran Church. Edited by Robert Kolb and Timothy J. Wengert. Minneapolis: Fortress, 2000.

Boumann, Walter R. "Melanchthon's Significance for the Church Today." In *Philip Melanchthon Then and Now (1497-1997)*, edited by S. H. Hendrix and T. J. Wengert, 33-55. Columbia, S.C.: Lutheran Theological Southern Seminary, 1997.

Bouwsma, William J. *John Calvin: A Sixteenth Century Portrait.* Oxford: Oxford University Press, 1988.

Braaten, Carl E., and Roy A. Harrisville, eds. and trans. *Kerygma and History: A Symposium on the Theology of Rudolf Bultmann.* New York and Nashville: Abingdon, 1962.

Brecht, Martin. *Martin Luther: His Road to Reformation, 1483-1521.* Translated by J. L. Schaaf. Minneapolis: Fortress, 1993.

Breen, Quirinus. "Melancthon's [*sic*] Reply to G. Pico Della Mirandola." *Journal of the History of Ideas* 13, no. 3 (June 1952): 417-18.

Brooke, John Hedley. *Science and Religion: Some Historical Perspective.* Cambridge: Cambridge University Press, 1993.

Brown, Gregory. "Miracles in the Best of All Possible Worlds: Leibniz's Dilemma and Leibniz's Razor." *History of Philosophy Quarterly* 12, no. 1 (January 1995): 19-39.

Brunner, Emil. *Dogmatics.* Vol. 1, *The Christian Doctrine of God.* Translated by O. Wyon. Philadelphia: Westminster, 1974.

Buckley, Michael J., S.J. *At the Origins of Modern Atheism.* New Haven: Yale University Press, 1987.

Bultmann, Rudolf. *Faith and Understanding.* Edited by Robert W. Funk. Translated by Louise Pettibone Smith. Philadelphia: Fortress, 1987.

Burleigh, Michael. *The Third Reich: A New History.* New York: Hill and Wang, 2000.

Carr, Amy. "A Hermeneutics of Providence amid Affliction: Contributions by Luther and Weil to a Cruciform Doctrine of Providence." *Pro Ecclesia* 16, no. 3 (2007).

Cassirer, Ernst. *The Philosophy of the Enlightenment.* Translated by F. C. A. Koelln and J. P. Pettegrove. Princeton: Princeton University Press, 1979.

Clark, G. N. *The Seventeenth Century.* 2nd ed. Oxford: Clarendon, 1947.

Crowe, Benjamin D. *Heidegger's Religious Origins: Destruction and Authenticity.* Bloomington and Indianapolis: Indiana University Press, 2006.

Daniel, Stephen H. "Edwards as Philosopher." In *The Cambridge Companion to Jonathan Edwards,* edited by Stephen J. Stein. Cambridge: Cambridge University Press, 2007.

Dennett, Daniel C. *Darwin's Dangerous Idea: Evolution and the Meanings of Life.* New York: Touchstone, 1996.

Descartes, René. *Meditations on First Philosophy.* Translated by D. A. Cress. Indianapolis: Hackett, 1993.

Dewey, John. *Experience and Nature.* New York: Dover, 1958.

Dillenberger, John. *God Hidden and Revealed: The Interpretation of Luther's Deus Absconditus and Its Significance for Religious Thought.* Philadelphia: Muhlenberg, 1953.

Distinctive Protestant and Catholic Themes Reconsidered. Vol. 3 of *Journal for Theology and the Church,* edited by Robert W. Funk, in association with Gerhard Ebeling. New York: Harper and Row, 1967.

Dost, Timothy P. *Renaissance Humanism in Support of the Gospel in Luther's Early Correspondence: Taking All Things Captive.* Aldershot: Ashgate, 2001.

Ebeling, Gerhard. "Karl Barths Ringen mit Luther." *Lutherstudien,* 3:428-574. Tübingen: Mohr Siebeck, 1985.

———. "The Significance of the Critical Historical Method for Church and Theology in Protestantism." In *Word and Faith,* translated by J. W. Leitch, 17-61. Philadelphia: Fortress, 1964.

Eckhardt, Burnell F., Jr. *Anselm and Luther on the Atonement: Was It "Necessary"?* San Francisco: Mellen Research University Press, 1992.

Edwards, Mark U., Jr. *Luther's Last Battles: Politics and Polemics, 1531-46.* Ithaca, N.Y.: Cornell University Press, 1983.

———. "Luther's Polemical Controversies." In *The Cambridge Companion to Martin Luther,* edited by D. K. McKim. Cambridge: Cambridge University Press, 2003.

———. "Supermus: Luther's Own Fanatics." In *Seven-Headed Luther: Essays in Commemoration of a Quincentenary, 1483-1983,* edited by P. N. Brooks, 123-46. Oxford: Clarendon, 1983.

El Fadl, Khaled Abou. *The Great Theft: Wrestling Islam from the Extremists.* San Francisco, HarperCollins, 2005.

Feuerbach, Ludwig. *The Essence of Christianity.* Translated by G. Eliot. New York: Harper Torchbooks, 1957.

Fichte, J. G. *The Science of Knowledge.* Edited and translated by P. Heath and J. Lachs. Cambridge: Cambridge University Press, 1993.

Forde, Gerhard O. *Justification by Faith: A Matter of Life and Death.* Philadelphia: Fortress, 1982; reprint, Mifflintown, Pa.: Sigler, 1991.

———. *On Being a Theologian of the Cross: Reflections on Luther's Heidelberg Disputation, 1518.* Grand Rapids: Eerdmans, 1997.

———. "The Work of Christ." In *Christian Dogmatics,* vol. 2, edited by C. E. Braaten and R. W. Jenson. Philadelphia: Fortress, 1984.

Frank, Günther. "Gott und Natur: Zur Transformation der Naturphilosophie in Melanchthons humanistischer Philosophie." In *Melanchthon und die Naturwissenschaften seiner Zeit,* edited by G. Frank and S. Rhein. Sigmaringen, Germany: Jan Thorbecke Verlag, 1998.

———. *Die Theologische Philosophie Philipp Melanchthons (1497-1560).* Erfurter Theologische Studien 67. Leipzig: Benno, 1995.

————. *Die Vernunft des Gottesgedankens: Religionsphilosophische Studien zur frühen Neuzeit.* Stuttgart: Frommann-Holzboog, 2003.

————. "Zur Gottes- und Trinitätslehre bei Melanchthon und Calvin." In *Melanchthon und der Calvinismus,* edited by G. Frank and H. J. Selderhuis, 159-71. Stuttgart-Bad Cannstatt: Frommann-Holzboog, 2005.

Friedrich, Carl J. *The Age of the Baroque, 1610-1660.* New York: Harper and Brothers, 1952.

Gäbler, Ulrich. *Huldrych Zwingli: His Life and Work.* Translated by Ruth C. L. Gritsch. Philadelphia: Fortress, 1986.

Gerrish, B. A. *Grace and Reason: A Study in the Theology of Luther.* Oxford: At the Clarendon Press, 1962.

————. "The Reformation and the Rise of Modern Science." In *The Reformation Heritage,* 163-78. Chicago: University of Chicago Press, 1982.

Gillespie, Michael Allen. *Nihilism before Nietzsche.* Chicago: University of Chicago Press, 1996.

Gore, Charles. "Our Lord's Human Example." *Church Quarterly Review* 16 (1883): 298. Cited in Alister McGrath, ed., *The Christian Theology Reader* (Oxford, U.K., and Cambridge, Mass.: Blackwell, 1999), 196.

Hampson, Daphne. *Christian Contradictions: The Structures of Lutheran and Catholic Thought.* Cambridge: Cambridge University Press, 2001.

Hawking, Stephen, with Leonard Mlodinow. *A Briefer History of Time.* New York: Bantam Dell, 2005.

Hegel, G. F. *Lectures on the Philosophy of Religion.* One-volume edition, the Lecture of 1827. Edited by P. C. Hodgson. Berkeley and Los Angeles: University of California Press, 1988.

Heidegger, Martin. "The Fundamental Question of Metaphysics." In *Philosophy in the Twentieth Century,* vol. 3, edited by W. Barrett and H. D. Aiken. New York: Random House, 1962.

————. "The Way Back into the Ground of Metaphysics." In *Philosophy in the Twentieth Century,* vol. 3, edited by W. Barrett and H. D. Aiken. New York: Random House, 1962.

Heitzenrater, Richard P. "Tradition and History." *Church History* 71, no. 3 (September 2002): 621-38.

Helmer, Christine. *The Trinity and Martin Luther: A Study on the Relationship between Genre, Language, and the Trinity in Luther's Works (1523-1546).* Mainz: Verlag Philipp von Zabern, 1999.

Heubach, J., ed. *Der Heilige Geist.* Ökumenische und Reformatorische Untersuchungen, vol. 25. Ratzeburg: Luther-Akademie; Erlangen: Martin-Luther Verlag, 1996.

Hick, John. *Evil and the God of Love.* New York: Harper and Row, 1966.

Hill, Charles Leander. "An Exposition and Critical Estimate of the Philosophy of Philip Melanchthon." Ph.D. diss., Ohio State University, 1938.

————. *Melanchthon: Selected Writings.* Westport, Conn.: Greenwood Press, 1962.

Hinlicky, Paul R. "Luther and Heidegger." Review essay on *Heidegger's Religious Origins*, by Benjamin D. Crowe. *Lutheran Quarterly* 22, no. 1 (Spring 2008).

————. "The Lutheran Dilemma." *Pro Ecclesia* 8, no. 4 (Fall 1999): 391-422.

————. "Luther and Liberalism." In *A Report from the Front Lines: Conversations on Public Theology; A Festschrift in Honor of Robert Benne*, edited by Michael Shahan. Grand Rapids: Eerdmans, forthcoming.

————. "Luther's Anti-Docetism in the Disputatio de divinitate et humanitate Christi (1540)." In *Creator est creatura: Luthers Christologie als Lehre von der Idiomenkommunikation*, edited by O. Bayer and Benjamin Gleede, 139-85. Berlin and New York: De Gruyter, 2007.

————. "The New Language of the Spirit: Critical Dogmatics in the Tradition of Luther." In D. Bielfeldt, M. Mattox, and P. Hinlicky, *The Substance of the Faith: Luther's Doctrinal Theology for Today*, 131-90. Minneapolis: Fortress, 2008.

————. "Process, Convergence, Declaration: Reflections on Doctrinal Dialogue." *Cresset* 64, no. 6 (Pentecost 2001): 13-18.

————. Review of *Augustinian Perspectives in the Renaissance*, by Åke Bergvall. *Sixteenth Century Journal* 37, no. 3 (2006): 936-37.

————. Review of *The Cosmos in the Light of the Cross*, by George L. Murphy. *Seminary Ridge Review* 8, no. 1 (Autumn 2005): 55-58.

————. Review of *Law and Protestantism: The Legal Teachings of the Lutheran Reformation*, by John Witte, Jr. *Sixteenth Century Journal* 35, no. 2 (2004): 534-36.

————. Review of *Lutherforschung im 20. Jahrhundert: Rueckblick-Bilanz-Ausblick. Sixteenth Century Journal* 38, no. 2 (2007): 616-17.

————. Review of *Renaissance Humanism in Support of the Gospel in Luther's Early Correspondence: Taking All Things Captive*, by Timothy P. Dost. *Sixteenth Century Journal* 34, no. 3 (Fall 2003): 796-97.

————. "Theological Anthropology: Towards Integrating Theosis and Justification by Faith." *Journal of Ecumenical Studies* 34, no. 1 (Winter 1997): 38-73.

Hitler, Adolf. *Mein Kampf.* Translated by R. Manheim. Boston: Houghton Mifflin, 1971.

Holm, Bo Kristian. "Doctrine and Life in Melanchthon's German and Late Latin *Loci*." Paper presented at the 11th International Congress for Luther Research, Porto Allegre, Brazil, July 2007.

————. "Zur Funktion der Lehre bei Luther." *Kerygma und Dogma* 51 (2005): 17-32.

Hopkins, Jasper. *A New Interpretive Translation of St. Anselm's Monologian and Proslogian.* Minneapolis: Arthur J. Banning Press, 1986.

Howe, Leroy T. "Leibniz on Evil." *Sophia* 10, no. 3 (October 1971): 8-17.

Hütter, Reinhard. *Suffering Divine Things: Theology as Church Practice.* Translated by D. Stott. Grand Rapids: Eerdmans, 2000.

Hunsinger, George. *Disruptive Grace: Studies in the Theology of Karl Barth.* Grand Rapids: Eerdmans, 2000.

Hultgren, Arland J. *The Rise of Normative Christianity.* Minneapolis: Fortress, 1994.

Israel, Jonathan I. *Radical Enlightenment: Philosophy and the Making of Modernity, 1650-1750.* Oxford: Oxford University Press, 2001.

Jackson, S. M., ed. *The Latin Works of Huldreich Zwingli.* 2 vols. Philadelphia: Heidelberg Press, 1922.

Jenkins, Philip. *The Next Christendom: The Coming of Global Christianity.* Revised and expanded ed. Oxford: Oxford University Press, 2007.

Jenson, Robert W. *God after God: The God of the Past and the God of the Future, Seen in the Work of Karl Barth.* New York: Bobbs-Merrill, 1969.

————. "An Ontology of Freedom in the *De Servo Arbitrio* of Luther." *Modern Theology* 10, no. 3 (July 1994): 247-52.

————. *Systematic Theology.* 2 vols. New York and Oxford: Oxford University Press, 1997.

————. *The Triune Identity.* Philadelphia: Fortress, 1982.

————. "You Wonder Where the Spirit Went." *Pro Ecclesia* 2, no. 3 (Summer 1993).

Jolley, Nicholas, ed. *The Cambridge Companion to Leibniz.* Cambridge: Cambridge University Press, 1995.

————. "Leibniz on Locke and Socinianism." *Journal of the History of Ideas* 39 (1978): 233-50.

————. *Locke: His Philosophical Thought.* Oxford: Oxford University Press, 1999.

Jordan, G. J. *The Reunion of the Churches: A Study of G. W. Leibnitz and His Great Attempt.* London: Constable and Co., 1927.

Jüngel, Eberhard. *The Freedom of a Christian: Luther's Significance for Contemporary Theology.* Translated by R. A. Harrisville. Minneapolis: Augsburg, 1988.

————. *God as the Mystery of the World: On the Foundation of the Theology of the Crucified One in the Dispute between Theism and Atheism.* Translated by D. L. Guder. Grand Rapids: Eerdmans, 1983.

————. *Justification: The Heart of the Christian Faith.* Translated by J. F. Cayzer. Edinburgh: T. & T. Clark, 2001.

————. *Theological Essays I.* Edited by J. B. Webster. Edinburgh: T. & T. Clark, 1989.

Kant, Immanuel. *The Conflict of the Faculties.* Translated by Mary J. Gregor. New York: Abaris Books, 1979.

————. *Critique of Judgment.* Translated by W. S. Pluhar. Indianapolis: Hackett, 1987.

————. *Critique of Pure Reason.* Translated by J. M. D. Meiklejohn. Mineola, N.Y.: Dover, 2003.

————. *Lectures on Philosophical Theology.* Translated by A. W. Wood and G. M. Clark. Ithaca, N.Y.: Cornell University Press, 1978.

————. *Religion and Rational Theology.* In the Cambridge Edition of the Works of Immanuel Kant, translated by A. W. Wood and G. Di Giovanni. Cambridge: Cambridge University Press, 2001.

Karkkainen, Pekka. *Luthers trinitarische Theologie des Heiligen Geistes.* Mainz: Philipp von Zabern, 2005.

Kay, James F. *Christus Praesens: A Reconsideration of Rudolf Bultmann's Christology.* Grand Rapids: Eerdmans, 1994.

Kelly, J. N. D. *Early Christian Doctrines.* Rev. ed. San Francisco: Harper, 1978.

Kerr, Fergus. *After Aquinas: Versions of Thomism.* Malden, Mass.: Blackwell, 2002.

Knebel, Sven K. "Necessitas Moralis ad Optimum: Zum historischen Hintergrund der Wahl der bessten aller möglichen Welten." *Studia Leibnitiana* 23, no. 1 (1991): 3-24.

Kolakowski, Lezek. *God Owes Us Nothing: A Brief Remark on Pascal's Religion and on the Spirit of Jansenism.* Chicago: University of Chicago Press, 1995.

Kolb, Robert. *Bound Choice, Election, and the Wittenberg Theological Method: From Martin Luther to the Formula of Concord.* Lutheran Quarterly Books. Grand Rapids: Eerdmans, 2005.

————. "Phillip Melanchthon: Reformer and Theologian." *Concordia Journal* 23, no. 4 (October 1997).

Koran, The. Translated by N. J. Dawood. London: Penguin Books, 1993.

Kroetke, Wolf. *Sin and Nothingness in the Theology of Karl Barth.* Translated by P. G. Ziegler and C.-M. Bammel. Studies in Reformed Theology and History, n.s., no. 10. Princeton: Princeton Theological Seminary, 2005.

Kusukawa, Sachiko. *The Transformation of Natural Philosophy: The Case of Philip Melanchthon.* Cambridge: Cambridge University Press, 1995.

Latzer, Michael. "Leibniz's Conception of Metaphysical Evil." *Journal of the History of Ideas* 26 (1988): 1-15.

————. "Leibniz's Reading of Augustine." *Il Cannocciale* (Rome: Carucci), January-April 1999, 17-33.

Lawson, John. *The Biblical Theology of Saint Irenaeus,* 84-114. London: Epworth, 1948.

Lehmann, Paul. *Ethics in a Christian Context.* New York: Harper and Row, 1963.

Leibniz, G. W. *Discourse on Metaphysics and Other Essays.* Translated by D. Garber and R. Ariew. Indianapolis: Hackett, 1991.

————. *New Essays concerning Human Understanding.* Translated by Alfred Gideon Langley. La Salle, Ill.: Open Court, 1949.

————. *Philosophical Papers and Letters: A Selection.* Translated and edited by Leroy E. Loemker. 2 vols. Chicago: University of Chicago Press, 1956.

————. *Philosophical Texts.* Translated by R. S. Woolhouse and R. Francks. Oxford: Oxford University Press, 1998.

————. *Theodicy: Essays on the Goodness of God, the Freedom of Man, and the Origin of Evil.* Translated by E. M. Huggard. Chicago and La Salle, Ill.: Open Court, 1998.

————. *Writings on China.* Edited by D. J. Cook and H. Rosemont, Jr. Chicago and La Salle, Ill.: Open Court, 1994.

Lindhardt, Jan. *Martin Luther: Knowledge and Mediation in the Renaissance.* Texts and Studies in Religion, vol. 29. Lewiston, N.Y.: Edwin Mellen Press, 1986.

Loemker, Leroy E. *Struggle for Synthesis: The Seventeenth Century Background of Leibniz's Synthesis of Order and Freedom.* Cambridge: Harvard University Press, 1972.

Lohse, Bernhard. *Martin Luther's Theology: Its Historical and Systematic Development.* Translated by Roy A. Harrisville. Minneapolis: Fortress, 1999.

Lossky, Vladimir. *In the Image and Likeness of God.* Edited by J. H. Erickson and T. E. Bird. Crestwood, N.Y.: St. Vladimir's Seminary Press, 1985.

Lotz, David. *Ritschl and Luther: A Fresh Perspective on Albrecht Ritschl's Theology in the Light of His Luther Study.* Nashville: Abingdon, 1974.

Lovejoy, Arthur O. *The Great Chain of Being: A Study of the History of an Idea.* Cambridge: Harvard University Press, 1964.

Lumpp, David A. "Promise, Liberty, and Persecution: Exploring Philip Melanchthon's Contextual Theology." Paper delivered at the 11th International Congress of Luther Research, Porto Allegre, Brazil, July 2007.

Luther, Martin. *The Bondage of the Will.* Translated by J. I. Packer and O. R. Johnston. Grand Rapids: Revell, 2000.

———. *Luther's Works: The American Edition.* Edited by J. Pelikan et al. St. Louis: Concordia; Philadelphia: Fortress, 1960-.

Lutherforschung im 20. Jahrhundert: Rueckblick-Bilanz-Ausblick. Edited by R. Vinke. Mainz: Verlag Philipp von Zabern, 2004.

MacIntyre, Alasdair. *Three Rival Versions of Moral Inquiry: Encyclopedia, Genealogy, and Tradition.* Notre Dame, Ind.: University of Notre Dame Press, 1990.

Manschreck, Clyde Leonard. *Melanchthon: The Quiet Reformer.* Westport, Conn.: Greenwood Press, 1975.

Marenbon, John. *Medieval Philosophy: An Historical and Philosophical Introduction.* London and New York: Routledge, 2007.

Marion, Jean-Luc. *God without Being.* Translated by Thomas A. Carlson. Chicago: University of Chicago Press, 1995.

———. "The Idea of God." In *The Cambridge History of Seventeenth Century Philosophy.* Cambridge: Cambridge University Press, 1998.

Marshall, Bruce D. "Faith and Reason Reconsidered: Aquinas and Luther on Deciding What Is True." *Thomist* 63 (1999): 1-48.

———. *Trinity and Truth.* Cambridge: Cambridge University Press, 2000.

Mattox, Mickey L. "Luther's Interpretation of the Old Testament." In D. Bielfeldt, M. Mattox, and P. Hinlicky, *The Substance of the Faith: Luther's Doctrinal Theology for Today,* 11-57. Minneapolis: Fortress, 2008.

Marx, Karl. "Theses on Feuerbach." In *Karl Marx on Religion,* edited and translated by S. K. Padover, 63-65. New York: McGraw-Hill, 1974.

Mattes, Mark. *The Role of Justification in Contemporary Theology.* Lutheran Quarterly Books. Grand Rapids: Eerdmans, 2004.

Mauer, Wilhelm. *Historical Commentary on the Augsburg Confession.* Translated by H. George Anderson. Philadelphia: Fortress, 1986.

Maxcey, Carl E. *Bona Opera: A Study in the Development of Doctrine in Philip Melanchthon.* Nieuwkoop: B. De Graaf, 1980.

McCormack, Bruce. "Grace and Being." In *The Cambridge Companion to Karl Barth,* edited by John Webster. Cambridge: Cambridge University Press, 2000.

———. *Karl Barth's Critically Realistic Dialectical Theology: Its Genesis and Development, 1909-1936.* Oxford: Clarendon, 1995.

———. "What's at Stake in Current Debates over Justification: The Crisis of Protestantism in the West." In *Justification: What's at Stake in the Current Debates,* edited by M. Husbands and D. J. Treier, 81-117. Downers Grove, Ill.: InterVarsity, 2004.

McGrath, Alister E. *Iustitia Dei: A History of the Christian Doctrine of Justification.* 2 vols. Cambridge: Cambridge University Press, 1986.

Melanchthon, Philip. *On Christian Doctrine: Loci Communes, 1555.* Translated by C. L. Manschreck. Grand Rapids: Baker, 1982.

————. *Philip Melanchthon: Orations on Philosophy and Education.* Edited by Sachiko Kusukawa. Translated by Christine F. Salazar. Cambridge: Cambridge University Press, 1999.

Melanchthon deutsch. Vol. 1, *Schule und Universität, Philosophie, Geschichte und Politik.* Edited by Michael Beyer, Stefan Rhein, and Günther Wartenberg. Leipzig: Evangelische Verlagsanstalt, 1997.

Meredith, Anthony, S.J. *Gregory of Nyssa.* London and New York: Routledge, 1999.

Meyendorff, John. *Byzantine Theology: Historical Trends and Doctrinal Themes.* New York: Fordham University Press, 1979.

Meyer, R. W. *Leibniz and the Seventeenth Century Revolution.* Translated by J. P. Stern. Cambridge: Bowes and Bowes, 1952.

Milbank, John. *Theology and Social Theory: Beyond Secular Reason.* Oxford, U.K., and Cambridge, Mass.: Blackwell, 1997.

Mildenberger, Friedrich. *Theology of the Lutheran Confessions.* Translated by E. Lueker. Philadelphia: Fortress, 1986.

Morse, Christopher. *Not Every Spirit: A Dogmatics of Christian Disbelief.* Philadelphia: Trinity, 1994.

Muller, Richard A. *Post-Reformation Reformed Dogmatics: The Rise and Development of Reformed Orthodoxy, ca. 1520 to ca. 1725.* Vol. 1, *Prolegomena to Theology.* 2nd ed. Grand Rapids: Baker, 2003.

Murphy, George L. *The Cosmos in the Light of the Cross.* Harrisburg, Pa., London, and New York: Trinity, 2003.

Nadler, Steven. "'Tange montes et fumigabunt': Arnauld on the Theodicies of Malebranche and Leibniz." In *Interpreting Arnauld,* 147-63. Toronto and Buffalo: University of Toronto Press, 1996.

Niebuhr, H. R. *The Kingdom of God in America.* New York, Evanston, Ill., and London: Harper Torchbook, 1959.

Niebuhr, Reinhold. *Moral Man and Immoral Society: A Study in Ethics and Politics.* New York: Scribner, 1960.

Oakes, Edward T. *Pattern of Redemption: The Theology of Hans Urs von Balthasar.* New York: Continuum, 2002.

Oberman, Heiko A. *The Roots of Anti-Semitism in the Age of Renaissance and Reformation.* Translated by James I. Porter. Philadelphia: Fortress, 1981.

Oehlschlaeger, Fritz. *Love and Good Reasons: Postliberal Approaches to Christian Ethics and Literature.* Durham, N.C., and London: Duke University Press, 2003.

Olson, Oliver K. *Matthias Flacius and the Survival of Luther's Reform.* Wiesbaden: Harrassowitz Verlag, 2002.

O'Regan, Cyril. *The Heterodox Hegel.* Albany: State University of New York Press, 1994.

Pannenberg, Wolfhart. *Basic Questions in Theology.* Vol. 2. Translated by G. H. Kehm. 2 vols. Philadelphia: Fortress, 1972.

————. *Systematic Theology.* Vol. 1. Translated by G. W. Bromiley. Grand Rapids: Eerdmans, 1991.

Pascal, Blaise. *Pensees*. Translated by A. J. Krailsheimer. London and New York: Penguin Books, 1995.

Peacocke, Arthur. *Theology for a Scientific Age: Being and Becoming — Natural, Divine, and Human*. Enlarged ed. London: SCM, 1993.

Pelikan, Jaroslav. *From Luther to Kierkegaard: A Study in the History of Theology*. St. Louis: Concordia, 1950.

Peperzak, Adriaan T. *The Quest for Meaning: Friends of Wisdom from Plato to Levinas*. New York: Fordham University Press, 2003.

Perry, Donald L. "'Leibniz' Answer to Descartes on the Creation of Eternal Truth." *Southwest Philosophy Review* 12, no. 1 (1996): 13-19.

Pico della Mirandola. *On the Dignity of Man, On Being and the One, Heptaplus*. Translated by C. G. Wallis, P. J. W. Miller, and D. Carmichael. New York: Bobbs-Merrill, 1965.

Placher, William. *The Domestication of Transcendence*. Louisville: John Knox, 1996.

Plantinga, Alvin. "The Free Will Defense." In *Philosophy of Religion: Selected Readings*, edited by Michael Peterson et al. 3rd ed. New York: Oxford University Press, 2000.

Poeder, Christine. "The Doctrine of Justification according to Karl Barth, Its Lutheran Reception and Its Potentials." Unpublished paper.

Prenter, Regin. *Spiritus Creator*. Translated by John M. Jensen. Philadelphia: Muhlenberg, 1953.

———. *Theologie und Gottesdienst*. Arhus: Forlaget Aros; Göttingen: Vandenhoeck & Ruprecht, 1977.

Preus, Robert D. *The Theology of Post-Reformation Lutheranism*. Vol. 2, *God and His Creation*. St. Louis: Concordia, 1972.

Preuss, H. A., and E. Smits, eds. *The Doctrine of Man in Classical Lutheran Theology*. Minneapolis: Augsburg, 1962.

Quere, Ralph W. *Melanchthon's Christum Cognoscere: Christ's Efficacious Presence in the Eucharistic Theology of Melanchthon*. Bibliotheca Humanistica & Reformatorica, vol. 22. Nieuwkoop: B. De Graaf, 1977.

Raab, Theodore K. *The Last Days of the Renaissance and the March to Modernity*. New York: Basic Books, 2006.

Reinhuber, Thomas. *Kämpfender Glaube: Studien zu Luthers Bekenntnis am Ende von De servo arbitrio*. Berlin and New York: De Gruyter, 2000.

Rescher, Nicolas. *The Philosophy of Leibniz*. Englewood Cliffs, N.J.: Prentice-Hall, 1967.

Richard, James William. *Philip Melanchthon: The Protestant Preceptor of Germany (1497-1560)*. New York and London: Putnam, 1902.

Richardson, Alan. *Christian Apologetics*. New York: Harper, 1948.

Riley, Patrick. *Leibniz' Universal Jurisprudence: Justice as the Charity of the Wise*. Cambridge: Harvard University Press, 1996.

———. "An Unpublished Lecture by Leibniz on the Greeks as Founders of Rational Theology: Its Relation to His 'Universal Jurisprudence.'" *Journal of the History of Philosophy* 14 (1976): 205-16.

———, ed. *Leibniz: Political Writings*. 2nd ed. Cambridge: Cambridge University Press, 2001.

Ritschl, Albrecht. *The Christian Doctrine of Justification and Reconciliation: The Positive Development of the Doctrine.* Translated by H. R. MacIntosh and A. B. McCaulay. Clifton, N.J.: Reference Books, 1966.

Roberts, A., and J. Donaldson, eds. *Ante-Nicene Fathers.* Grand Rapids: Eerdmans, 1975.

Rorty, Richard. *Philosophy and the Mirror of Nature.* Princeton: Princeton University Press, 1979.

Rosin, Robert. *Reformers, the Preacher, and Skepticism: Luther, Brenz, Melanchthon, and Ecclesiastes.* Mainz: Von Zabern, 1997.

Royce, Josiah. *The Problem of Christianity.* Washington, D.C.: Catholic University of America Press, 2001.

Russell, Bertrand. *A Critical Exposition of the Philosophy of Leibniz.* Cambridge: University of Cambridge Press, 1900; 2nd ed., London: George Allen and Unwin, 1937.

Saarinen, Risto. *Gottes Wirken auf Uns: Die transzendentale Deutung des Gegenwart-Christi-Motivs in der Lutherforschung.* Stuttgart: Franz Steiner Verlag; Wiesbaden: GMBH, 1989.

Schadel, Erwin. "Monad as a Triadic Structure — Leibniz's Contribution to Post-nihilistic Search for Identity." *Journal of Indian Council of Philosophical Research* 14, no. 1 (1996): 17-33.

Schaff, P., and H. Wace, eds. *Nicene and Post-Nicene Fathers.* Grand Rapids: Eerdmans, 1979.

Schleiermacher, Friedrich. *Brief Outline on the Study of Theology.* Translated by T. N. Tice. Atlanta: John Knox, 1977.

Schmid, Heinrich. *The Doctrinal Theology of the Evangelical Lutheran Church.* 3rd ed. Philadelphia: Lutheran Publication Society, 1899.

Schneider, John R. *Philip Melanchthon's Rhetorical Construal of Biblical Authority: Oratio Sacra.* Lewiston, N.Y.: Edwin Mellen Press, 1990.

Schulze, Manfred. "Martin Luther and the Church Fathers." In *The Reception of the Church Fathers in the West,* 573-626. Leiden and New York: Brill, 1997.

Schwarzwäller, Klaus. "Sibboleth: Die Interpretation von Luthers Schrift De servo arbitrio seit Theodosius Harnack: Ein systematisch-kritischer Ueberblick." *Theologische Existenz heute,* no. 153 (Munich: Chr. Kaiser Verlag, 1969).

Schweitz, Lea F. "The Difference between the Mirror and One Who Sees: The Theological Anthropology of G. W. Leibniz." Ph.D. diss., University of Chicago, 2008.

Schwöbel, Christoph. "Theology." In *The Cambridge Companion to Karl Barth,* edited by John Webster, 17-36. Cambridge: Cambridge University Press, 2000.

Sharples, R. W. *Stoics, Epicureans, and Sceptics: An Introduction to Hellenistic Philosophy.* London and New York: Routledge, 1996.

Siggins, Ian D. Kingston. *Martin Luther's Doctrine of Christ.* New Haven and London: Yale University Press, 1970.

Sinnema, Donald. "God's Eternal Decree and Its Temporal Execution: The Role of This Distinction in Theodore Beza's Theology." In *Adaptations of Calvinism in Reformation Europe: Essays in Honour of Brian C. Armstrong,* edited by Mack P. Holt, 55-78. Aldershot, England, and Burlington, Vt.: Ashgate, 2008.

Soskice, Janet. *Metaphor and Religious Language.* Oxford: Clarendon, 1987.

Southern, R. W. *Saint Anselm: A Portrait in a Landscape.* Cambridge: Cambridge University Press, 1993.

Spinoza, Baruch. *Ethics, Treatise on the Emendation of the Intellect and Selected Letters.* Translated by S. Shirley. Indianapolis: Hackett, 1992.

———. *Principles of Cartesian Philosophy with Metaphysical Thoughts.* Translated by S. Shirley. Indianapolis: Hackett, 1998.

———. *Theological-Political Treatise.* Translated by S. Shirley. Indianapolis: Hackett, 1998.

Steigmann-Gall, Richard. *The Holy Reich: Nazi Conceptions of Christianity, 1919-1945.* Cambridge: Cambridge University Press, 2003.

Stewart, Matthew. *The Courtier and the Heretic: Leibniz, Spinoza, and the Fate of God in the Modern World.* New York and London: Norton, 2006.

Stout, Jeffery. *The Flight from Authority: Religion, Morality, and the Quest for Autonomy.* Notre Dame, Ind., and London: University of Notre Dame Press, 1981.

Tanner, Kathryn. *God and Creation in Christian Theology: Tyranny or Empowerment?* Minneapolis: Fortress, 2005.

Thielicke, Helmut. *The Evangelical Faith.* Vol. 1. Translated by G. W. Bromiley. Grand Rapids: Eerdmans, 1974.

Tillich, Paul. *Systematic Theology.* 3 vols. Chicago: University of Chicago Press, 1967.

———. "The Two Types of Philosophy of Religion." In *Theology of Culture,* edited by R. C. Kimball, 10-29. London and New York: Oxford University Press, 1959.

Torrance, T. F. *The Trinitarian Faith: The Evangelical Theology of the Ancient Catholic Church.* Edinburgh: T. & T. Clark, 1993.

Troeltsch, Ernst. *Protestantism and Progress: A Historical Study of the Relation of Protestantism to the Modern World.* Translated by W. Montgomery. Boston: Beacon Press, 1966.

Vailati, Ezio. *Leibniz and Clarke: A Study of Their Correspondence.* Oxford: Oxford University Press, 1997.

Vainio, Olli-Pekka. *Justification and Participation in Christ: The Development of the Lutheran Doctrine of Justification from Luther to the Formula of Concord (1580).* Leiden and Boston: Brill, 2008.

Ward, Graham. "Barth, Modernity and Postmodernity." In *Cambridge Companion to Karl Barth,* edited by J. Webster, 274-95. Cambridge: Cambridge University Press, 2000.

Webster, John. "Theology after Liberalism?" In *Theology after Liberalism: A Reader,* edited by John Webster and George P. Schner, 52-61. Oxford, U.K., and Cambridge, Mass.: Blackwell, 2000.

Weikart, Richard. *From Hitler to Darwin: Evolutionary Ethics, Eugenics, and Racism in Germany.* New York: Palgrave Macmillan, 2004.

Wengert, Timothy J. *Human Freedom, Christian Righteousness: Philip Melanchthon's Exegetical Dispute with Erasmus of Rotterdam.* New York and Oxford: Oxford University Press, 1998.

———. *Law and Gospel: Philip Melanchthon's Debate with John Agricola of Eisleben over Poenitentia.* Grand Rapids: Baker, 1997.

————. "Melanchthon and Luther/Luther and Melanchthon." *Lutherjahrbuch* 66. Göttingen: Vandenhoeck & Ruprecht, 1999.

————. *Philip Melanchthon's Annotationes in Johannem in Relation to Its Predecessors and Contemporaries.* Geneva: Librairie Droz S.A., 1987.

Werner, Martin. *The Formation of Christian Dogma: An Historical Study of Its Problem.* New York: Harper, 1957.

Westphal, Merold. *Overcoming Onto-Theology: Toward a Postmodern Christian Faith.* New York: Fordham University Press, 2001.

White, Graham. *Luther as Nominalist: A Study of the Logical Methods Used in Martin Luther's Disputations in the Light of Their Medieval Background.* Schriften der Luther-Agricola-Gesellschaft 30. Helsinki: Luther-Agricola Society, 1994.

Wilson, Catherine. "The Reception of Leibniz in the 18th Century." In *The Cambridge Companion to Leibniz,* edited by N. Jolley, 442-74. Cambridge, U.K., and New York: Cambridge University Press, 1995.

Wisnefske, Ned. *Preparing to Hear the Gospel: A Proposal for Natural Theology.* Lanham, Md.: University Press of America, 1998.

Witte, John, Jr. *Law and Protestantism: The Legal Teachings of the Lutheran Reformation.* With a foreword by Martin E. Marty. Cambridge: Cambridge University Press, 2002.

Wolter, Allan B., O.F.M. *Duns Scotus on the Will and Morality.* Translation edition. Washington, D.C.: Catholic University of America Press, 1997.

Wolterstorff, Nicholas. *John Locke and the Ethics of Belief.* Cambridge Studies in Religion and Critical Thought. Cambridge: Cambridge University Press, 1996.

Wundt, Max. *Die deutsche Schulmetaphysik des. 17. Jahrhunderts.* Tübingen: J. C. B. Mohr, 1939.

Index